THE

CHINA

GUIDEBOOK

1989 Edition

World's Best-Selling Guide
to the
People's Republic of China

THE AUTHORS

FREDRIC M. KAPLAN is founder and publisher of Eurasia Press. A specialist on contemporary China, he is co-author of *Encyclopedia of China Today* (M.E. Sharpe/Eurasia Press, 1989) and the *JAL Guide to the People's Republic of China,* and is a member of the National Committee on US-China Relations, the New York-Beijing Friendship City Committee, and former member of the National Board of Directors of US-China Peoples Friendship Association. Mr. Kaplan is director of the China Book Club and president of China Passage, which organizes specialized and "adventure" tours to China. During the past decade, Mr. Kaplan has visited China on over 60 occasions.

JULIAN M. SOBIN is Fellow at the Center for International Affairs, Harvard University. He is retired corporate senior vice president of International Minerals and Chemical Corporation. Mr. Sobin was the first US business-man invited to Beijing (in March 1972). Over the next 12 years, he nego-tiated some of the largest Sino-US trade contracts, including the first US purchase of Chinese crude oil in 1977. Co-author of *Encyclopedia of China Today,* Mr. Sobin was chairman of the International Marketing Institute at Harvard Business School and is a member of the US government Advisory Committee on East-West Trade.

ARNE J. DE KEIJZER is founder of A.J. de Keijzer & Associates, Inc., a consulting firm specializing in the development of trade between the US and the PRC. He is also a director of Asia Business Communications Ltd. He was previously the New York representative for the National Council for US-China Trade and served for seven years on the National Committee on US-China Relations. Since 1973, he has visited China numerous times. He is co-editor of *China: A Resource and Curriculum Guide* (University of Chicago Press, 1976) and author of the *JAL Business Guide to China* (Eurasia Press, 1985) and *The China Business Handbook* (China Books, 1986).

CHINA

GUIDEBOOK

1989 Edition

Fredric M. Kaplan
Julian M. Sobin / Arne J. de Keijzer

HOUGHTON MIFFLIN COMPANY
Boston

EURASIA PRESS
Teaneck, New Jersey

Distributed in the United States of America and Canada by
Houghton Mifflin Company, 2 Park Street, Boston, MA 02108.

The assistance in preparing this book provided by
The China Phone Book Company, Ltd., GPO Box 11581, Hong Kong,
publisher of *The China Phone Book & Business Directory*,
is gratefully acknowledged.

TENTH EDITION (1989), 1989
First Printing
Typography by V & M Computer Graphics, Inc. and Genesis Typography, Inc.
Text set in Goudy Old Style. Chinese typography by TNT/BP Marketing.
Book design by Kathie Brown; cover design by Michaela Sullivan;
cover photograph ©1988 Dallas and John Heaton: Click/Chicago.
Color maps and city maps cartography by Lovell Johns Limited, Oxford, England.
Maps on pp. 168, 259, 432, and 719 prepared by Judy Teener;
maps on pp. 5 and 6 prepared by Jon Livingston.

LIBRARY OF CONGRESS CATALOGING IN PUBLICATION DATA

Kaplan, Fredric M.
  The China Guidebook
    Includes reading list and index
      1. China–Description and travel–1976–Guidebooks.
I. Sobin, Julian M. II. deKeijzer, Arne J.
DS712.D4   1979   915.1'04'5   81–70809
ISBN 0–395–48679–3

THE PEOPLE'S REPUBLIC OF CHINA
Provinces and Autonomous Regions

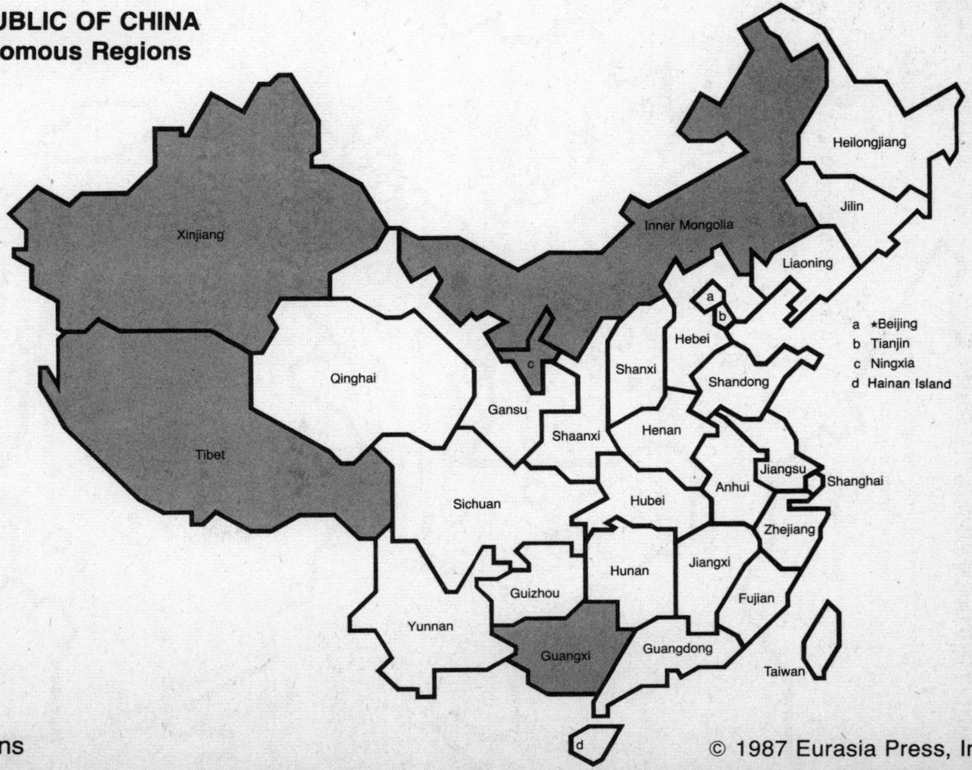

a ★Beijing
b Tianjin
c Ningxia
d Hainan Island

Heilongjiang

Jilin

Liaoning

Inner Mongolia

Shandong

Shanghai

Jiangsu

Zhejiang

Anhui

Fujian

Hebei

Shanxi

Henan

Hubei

Jiangxi

Guangdong

Shaanxi

Hunan

Guangxi

Gansu

Sichuan

Guizhou

Yunnan

Qinghai

Xinjiang

Tibet

Taiwan

© 1987 Eurasia Press, Inc.

■ Autonomous Regions

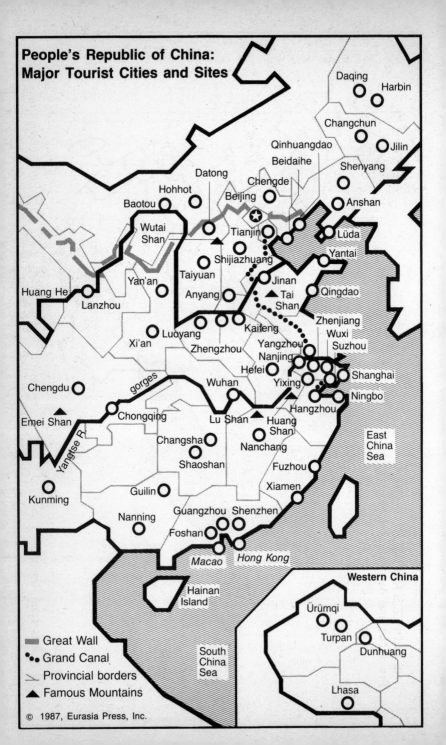

CONTENTS

III ▣ GETTING TO CHINA

IV ◼ TRAVELING IN CHINA

11
CONTENTS

V ■ DOING BUSINESS IN CHINA

VI ▪ FOR TRAVELERS WITH SPECIAL INTERESTS

VII ▪ THE CHINA TOUR: CITIES AND SITES

14

CONTENTS

15
CONTENTS

◀ GATEWAYS TO CHINA ▶

VIII ▣ APPENDIX AND INDEX

MAPS OF CHINA

NOTES AND ACKNOWLEDGMENTS

The tenth anniversary edition of *The China Guidebook* endeavors to provide travelers to China with the most useful and comprehensive information possible in portable format. Detailed coverage has been extended to more than 125 major tourist cities and locales, with descriptions of over 1,000 significant individual sites—historic and contemporary—as well as of hotels, restaurants, shops, and other points of interest for travelers.

The possibilities for independent travel through China have grown dramatically in recent years, mainly due to an official relaxation of travel restrictions on foreigners coming to China. *The China Guidebook* now incorporates a wide new array of detailed information for budget travelers and others seeking to explore China's cities and countryside on their own.

Throughout the text, we have inserted Chinese characters above the English names of all major sites, hotels, and restaurants, enabling readers to "point out" their destinations while in China.

Getting to China is much easier than it was just a few years ago. The range of options for group travel to China has expanded to offer considerable choice in format, time span, itinerary, and cost. To assist travelers in planning their trip, Sections II–VI of the *Guidebook* discuss the variety of choices now available for group and individual travel and explain the special procedures and protocol required by the circumstances of organized travel in China.

Since a large proportion of visitors to China, including many tourists, travel to pursue professional or special interests, the *Guidebook* includes extensive references to organizations and agencies inside China and around the world that can provide advice and assistance for China travel. The book also includes seven sections prepared especially to aid trips that will focus on business, education, health care, art, archeology, religion, or cuisine. In addition, a special section in Chinese offers advice for those visiting relatives in China.

All major cities and sites included in general itineraries available through 1989 are covered in Section VII. Along with its tourist amenities, each city is discussed in terms of its role in traditional China as well as its place in the cultural, political, and economic context of today's China. The emphasis of the *Guidebook* is on life and cultural values in the People's Republic of China today—a bias that attempts to reflect the ways in which China's people have come to view their own country.

For most travelers to China, time for free activity is limited. To enable travelers to make maximum use of the free time available, the *Guidebook* includes several step-by-step "freelance" walking tours for sightseeing and shopping in the larger cities, along with 24 updated city and regional maps. Monthly, climate charts have been added for almost all cities.

The staff at Eurasia Press played an indispensable role in assembling and updating materials, editing, and producing the tenth edition. We are indebted to the core staff for this project: Debra E. Soled, managing editor; Oscar Bernal, editorial coordinator; Adam Price, Peter Freundlicht, Mary

18

Lou Teel, and Joshua Grant, researchers; Jenny Gibbs, copy editor; and Edward Villamaria, editorial assistant. Dr. David Robertson provided a wealth of first-hand research on northwest China, including articles on Kashgar, Turpan, and Jiayuguan. His erudition and perception have clearly enhanced the usefulness of the book. Dr. Nick Middleton prepared an expert's view of the rarely visited Mongolian People's Republic.

Invaluable editorial assistance was also provided by Randy LaPolla, Avron Boretz, Deirdre Chetham, Annie Wang, David Levi, Shimei Pang, Ann Byrd Platt, Xing Guangwen, John Northington, Marlena McGinnis, Ruth Misheloff, and Martha Cameron. Specialists in China travel were extremely helpful in providing up-to-the-minute information: Norval Welch and Diana Nairn of Special Tours for Special People, and Larry Delson and Clarence Lu of China Passage. For the section on "China Travel for Overseas Chinese," our thanks go to Helen Yau of Kuo Feng Travel and to Dolly Ling for the translation into Chinese. Coverage of several cities in this edition was augmented with first-hand information provided by long-term residents or frequent visitors: special thanks are due to Mark Sidel (for help with the sections on Beijing and Shanghai), Timothy Brook and Michael Cooper (Beijing), Krystyna Horko and Jacques Andrieu (Guangzhou, Hong Kong, Macao), Rebecca Weiner (Qufu, Qingdao, and information on budget travel); Carole Rosen and Xing Guangwen (Tianjin); Hugh Deane (Chengdu and Chongqing); Thomas B. Gold (Guiyang, Quanzhou, Wenzhou), and Deirdre Chetham (Xishuangbanna, Yangtse River Gorges). Grateful acknowledgement is extended to artist Chen Chi for the sketches taken from his *Sketchbook*; and to Wingie Chiu and Jerry Chang for the calligraphy for new city sections. The index was prepared by Flex, Inc. Kathie Brown is owed special thanks for the original design of the text.

We are grateful to our friends at China National Publications Import Corporation for selecting *The China Guidebook* as the first Western book to be offered for sale throughout China since 1949. A heartfelt acknowledgment is due the many other friends in China—among them representatives of the Chinese People's Association for Friendship with Foreign Countries (YOUXIE) and the Chinese International Travel Service (LUXINGSHE)—whose gracious hospitality and patient explanations made possible what we hope will be a small contribution to mutual understanding. Many US colleagues shared their insights as well. The National Committee on US-China Relations, the US-China Business Council, and the US-China People's Friendship Association were true pioneers in areas of US-China travel.

Finally, thanks are owed to Helena Benz, Managing Editor at Houghton Mifflin for her infusion of energy and support, and to Stephen Pekich for his generous technical advice.

The authors welcome comments and criticisms of readers, as well as suggestions for additions to future editions.

F.M.K., J.M.S. and A.J.deK.

Teaneck, New Jersey
September 15, 1988

I

CHINA

AT A

GLANCE

CHINA'S PEOPLE

The People's Republic of China (PRC) is far and away the world's most populous nation. China's official census of 1982 listed a total mainland population of 1,008,175,288, making China the home of nearly one out of every four persons in the world. Since 1964, the population has been expanding at an annual rate of 2.1%, or by an average of 17.4 million people per year. China's urban population has remained relatively stable for the past three decades, accounting for about 20% of the total in 1984.

China is a multinational country in which 93% of the population is Han, or ethnic Chinese. The remaining 68 million are distributed among 55 "minority nationalities" (*shaoshu minzu*) ranging in size from the 12 million Zhuang to some groups which number fewer than 1,000. Most of these minorities differ from the Han in language and customs. The Muslim Hui are distinguished by religion alone, and the Manchu are almost completely assimilated. National policy encourages cultural continuity and a limited political autonomy, and representatives are trained for local leadership at nationalities institutes which also promote research in ethnic languages and history. Most of these groups are scattered in the sparsely settled border areas, five of which—Inner Mongolia, Ningxia, Xinjiang, Xizang (Tibet), and Guangxi—have been designated "autonomous regions." Where significant concentrations of a particular minority exist, autonomous prefectures and counties have been created, both within these regions and in western provinces such as Yunnan and Guizhou. Minorities have been exempted from China's stringent birth control program, and their numbers have been increasing at a greater rate than the Han.

URBAN LIFESTYLES

A Chinese person asked to describe urban lifestyles in the People's Republic would no doubt be quick to point out their great diversity across the nation. When northerners or southerners are transferred to work in other parts of the country, they often complain about the difficulty of adjusting to the new environment—climate, local dialects, lifestyle, and, not least of all, cuisine. Most foreign visitors, on the other hand, tend to see urban life as the same throughout China. Above all, travelers from the West are struck by the technological simplicity of China's cities. With the exception of some newly erected high-rise apartment buildings in the major cities, architecture seems to be dominated by a mixture of traditional one-story *pingfang* (literally, "flat-houses") with their three walled-in wings facing into a courtyard, and four- or five-story apartment houses. The latter provide indoor amenities such as toilets, running water, and gas stoves, with many facilities shared among two or more families.

Housing is in relatively short supply in most of China's cities. A typical urban residence for a family of four consists of only one or two rooms. These are generally furnished with huge wooden beds, each covered with

Neighborhood open-air market

---

a half-inch-thick cotton pad mattress and a decorative plastic or cotton bedspread; a dresser or two upon which inevitably sits a large old-style radio and a collection of family photographs; and, in many homes, a sewing machine. Families in the newer apartment buildings have their own small kitchens and bathrooms. In the older, more crowded flats, three or four families commonly share these facilities, while the *pingfang* dwellers have their own cooking and toilet facilities outdoors in their yards.

Transportation is likely to remind the tourist of a bygone era. A small number of cars (fewer than 1 million in all of China) function exclusively either as taxis or vehicles for officials and collective units. These share the road with buses, trucks, animal-drawn carts, and bicycles. Pedestrian congestion, however, rivals that of large cities anywhere in the world. Government policy has stressed the expansion of China's mass transit systems to serve the majority of the people. Automobiles can now be privately owned, although the cost is such that fewer than 1,000 households in the entire country were thought able to afford them. In the cities, even the number of private bicycles is controlled—a policy not immediately apparent to anyone trying to cross a Chinese urban boulevard at rush hour.

Work schedules for virtually everyone—employees of the factories, the service sectors, in white collar jobs, and professionals—consist of eight-hour days and six-day weeks. Most factory workers take Sunday off, but the retail sector has instituted a system of staggered rest days. Virtually everyone takes a nap during the daily hour lunch break, although in a recent move to improve efficiency, government office workers are now permitted just one hour both to eat and take their midday naps. Indeed, daily urban schedules tend to be highly ritualized and uniform, as might be expected in a society where planning and coordination are vital to the successful allocation of limited resources and facilities among such huge numbers of people.

China's goal is to rapidly modernize industry in the coming years. At present, much of the machinery used is still simple by Western standards, hand work is still widespread, and the pace of work is fairly relaxed. China's system of socialism is predicated on the assurance of gainful employment to virtually everyone who seeks to work. In the 1980s especially, much attention has been paid to an unintended by-product of this system: the "iron rice bowl"—a reference to the high degree of job security that has led in some instances to poor work habits, absenteeism, and even indigence on the part of workers whose salaries were in no way tied to performance. A variety of remedies to this problem are now being tried, many utilizing some form of material incentive to spur productivity. Critics have hastened to brand such policies as a drift towards capitalism. Officials have countered that the principle "to each according to his work" is wholly consistent with the fundamentals of Marxism.

Salaries, averaging Y75–100 per month in the cities appear appallingly meager (urban per capita income, nonetheless, is rising rapidly—up 21% in 1986 alone). However, the cost of living in China is commensurately low: the average rent, including utilities, is Y5 per month, and clothing and furnishings are reasonably priced. More than half of an urban household's monthly income, however, must be spent on food (compared to about 18% in the US). Most workers use their surplus cash to buy expensive "luxuries" (bicycles, watches, radios, televisions, cassette-recorders), or deposit it in savings accounts (which earn approximately 3% interest). The provision of free or extremely low-cost health care, pensions, and other social services has been gradually expanded in post-1949 China, and such benefits now extend to most of the population.

Shopping is another side of life which highlights the simplicity of China's urban lifestyles. Long queues are common at the separate stalls for vegetables, fruits, meats, fish, oil, grains, and baked goods in the local shopping centers. Lack of refrigeration makes daily shopping a necessity for families dining at home. In many instances, the retired grandmother assumes most of the marketing chores and also cares for the pre-school-age children, a system that frees both parents to pursue full-time employment. The extended, three-generation family living under one roof is a tradition that still prevails in China. In marked contrast to Western preferences, Chinese newlyweds, looking ahead to the need for babysitters, often vie with their siblings for the privilege of housing their parents. Of course, mother-in-law jokes abound in China as they do everywhere.

On Sundays, the day off for most city workers, the parks fill up with families and couples out relaxing together. Leisure time is also spent attending operatic, theatrical, musical, and dance performances and watching television and films. On summer evenings, neighborhood residents love to mingle on the sidewalks in front of their homes to play cards or Chinese "chess" and, of course, to gossip. The garrulous, outgoing residents of Shanghai, often described as the world's greatest "kibbitzers," pursue these activities with a special passion.

CHINA'S PEOPLE

Copying political poetry at a rally, Beijing

Pollution-conscious Westerners point to the urban smog hovering above many of China's cities. The smoke of coal cooking stoves and emissions from the low-grade fuel burned by mufflerless buses and trucks and from industrial enterprises—compounded in winter by residues from the coal used for indoor heating—all combine to produce an unpleasant, if not noxious, haze. Urban smog is more marked in the industrialized cities of the north than elsewhere. By 1984, antipollution regulations and campaigns were in effect virtually throughout the country, although results were at best mixed.

RURAL LIFESTYLES

The lifestyle of the typical Chinese peasant and the technology on which it is based have improved significantly during the last three decades. Yet, life in China's countryside is arduous by any standard. In the planting and harvesting seasons, the rural population labors from dawn to dusk at backbreaking field work, while during the slack season the days are spent in construction and repair work, as well as some light-industrial activities.

Diet in the rural areas is based primarily on grain, generally rice in the south and wheat in the north, with vegetables and protein-rich meat, poultry, and fish available to virtually all households, albeit in small quantities. Rural housing is spacious compared to city dwellings. Homes are usually family-owned. The simple furnishings consist of a bed or two, a dresser—often custom-made at home—perhaps a sewing machine, and a radio. A speaker can be optionally connected by a wire hooked into each dwelling to tune in to the local broadcast. Cooking and toilet facilities are located outside the house proper.

Families today are encouraged to grow their own vegetables and to raise a few animals both for their own consumption and for sale at rural fairs as a means of earning supplemental income. The farming of small private plots by individual households was being actively encouraged in the mid-1980s as a means of both raising overall productivity as well as augmenting peasants' incomes. Most agricultural production, however, is still carried out on collectively-owned fields and income is distributed according to individual output. A common fund finances social services such as medical care, pensions, and education.

Cultural activities are made available even in remote areas today through mobile film showings and touring theatrical, operatic, and ballet troupes. The state encourages the development of grassroots folk arts.

China's rural population is organized in a three-tiered administrative system above the basic family unit. The production team, the lowest level, groups households for joint farm work on collectively-owned fields, owns the work tools, assigns tasks, and distributes income. The middle rung, the brigade, comprises a number of teams and generally administers light industries, clinics, and primary schools.

In 1985, after a five-year transition period, China's 56,000 people's communes were officially replaced by some 92,000 "townships" as the highest level of local administration. The townships are responsible for large-scale rural construction projects such as irrigation works, for forest and orchard management, and for the administration of hospitals and secondary schools.

The dismantling of the communes went hand in hand with the changeover from a centrally-planned, collectivized economy based on quotas and fixed prices to a semi-free market system based on contracts. Through 1985, mandatory quotas on most agricultural and rural sideline products—including grain, cotton, vegetables, hogs, and poultry—had been replaced by contract sales, and prices of many commodities were allowed to float freely.

However, disparities in geographical and climatic conditions and in technological development continued to cause regional imbalances. Further, large inequalities still exist between services and amenities available in the cities and those provided in the countryside.

In 1978, the government, acknowledging these differences and realizing that the livelihood of China's 800 million peasants must substantially improve if the country is to achieve its goal of modernization, reordered the nation's development priorities, shifting the emphasis toward raising the technological and income level of farming in China. The "contract responsibility system" was adopted, agricultural taxes were reduced, and the state's purchase prices for grains and other staples were increased by an average of 22%.

At the same time, the legitimization of township-, brigade- and even family-owned rural enterprises paved the way for what may become the most important and far-reaching revolution in China's economy: the industrialization of the countryside. Taking into account the need to improve living standards and economic stability in the countryside, the government hopes to shift as much as one half of the rural labor force out of farming and into manufacturing, forestry, and mining by the end of the century. Despite the persistence of many heartbreaking factors that have plagued the Chinese peasantry for so long—overpopulation, overtaxed soil, and a radically unpredictable climate—it can be said that perhaps for the first time in history the whole of the Chinese countryside is being mobilized primarily for its own betterment.

CHINA'S GEOGRAPHY

China's area of 3,692,244 sq. mi. (9,562,904 sq. km.) is greater than that of Europe or the continental United States. Its 49 degrees of latitude from north to south encompass a climate of great diversity, ranging from subarctic to tropical. Altitudes extend from 505 ft. (154 m.) below sea level at the Turpan Depression to the peak of Mt. Everest (in China, known as Qomolangma), at 29,028 ft. (8,848 m.) the earth's highest mountain. China's land border of 17,445 mi. (28,072 km.) is shared with Korea, the Mongolian People's Republic, the USSR, Afghanistan,

Pakistan, India, Bhutan, Nepal, Burma, Laos, Vietnam, Macao, and Hong Kong. Along the seacoast, the major bodies of water are the Yellow Sea, the East China Sea, and the South China Sea.

Formidable physical barriers—the wide Pacific Ocean to the east, the Himalayas and the Tibetan plateau (the "roof of the world") to the west, semi-arid steppes and barren deserts to the northwest, and rugged terrain and rain forests to the south—have insulated China from easy contact with other major cultures. Even within China proper, the gradual southward spread of Chinese civilization has been hampered by mountains and tortuous terrain. Some areas are still inhabited by unassimilated non-Han populations.

The topography of China is roughly divided into three tiers of elevation sloping downward from west to east. The mountains and highlands of the west with elevations above 2,000 m. give way to plateaus ranging between 500 to 2,000 m. and then to the plains and maritime regions which lie below 500 m. Much of the map of China is intersected by a grid of highlands which run east and west as well as southwest to northeast.

CLIMATE AND LAND USE

With its location at the extreme eastern end of the Eurasian land mass, China has a climate subject to seasonal patterns which alternate between the cold, dry winters brought by westerly winds from the arid regions of Siberia and Central Asia and a monsoon summer when warm, humid air comes from the Pacific. However, the north of China above the Huai River is drier than the south, with insufficient and erratic rainfall; here farming must depend upon irrigation. The Great Wall marks the border between settled agricultural China and the arid regions where herding and nomadism have been the distinctive way of life.

Within the Great Wall, the pattern of land use has been intensive agriculture; that is, a heavy reliance on human labor to cultivate land for maximum yields. This labor-intensive mode of production, evident not only in food crops but also in the cultivation of silk and tea, is closely linked with population growth and density. Agriculture is concentrated in the river valleys where both alluvial soil and water for irrigation are present. For most areas, water transport has been the cheapest and often—except in the drier north—the only means of carrying goods beyond local markets. River navigation has been less certain in the north and here is where roads and, more recently, railroads have been constructed. In the more mountainous terrain of the south, where river transport has been readily available, roads and railroads are still underdeveloped.

RIVER SYSTEMS

The three major rivers systems of China all have their headwaters in the western highlands. They flow to the east, falling precipitously to the plains and forming alluvial basins before emptying into the sea. The Yellow River

(Huang He), often called "China's sorrow," drains the northern quarter of China within the Wall. It is subject to excessive fluctuation and flooding as it carries a heavy load of silt from the loess regions of the northwest along channels which, as a result of man-made levees and silting by the river, now rise above the surrounding countryside so that any breach of the dikes results in disastrous floods. The lower channel of the river has changed its course frequently over the centuries, flowing either north or south of the Shandong Peninsula. It is not generally navigable. Recent flood control efforts have focused upon dams to extract silt and upon afforestation to prevent erosion.

The Yangtse River (Changjiang) is the third longest river in the world (after the Amazon and the Nile). Its drainage basin embraces about half of China's population and includes the major agricultural areas of China—the Sichuan plain and the lower Yangtse, which has long been termed "the land of rice and fish," denoting abundance of food. Major tributaries and lakes have served as natural means of controlling floods: the tributaries vary in times of peak flow and the lakes serve as reservoirs. Dam projects produce hydroelectric power and aid in flood control. As its channel is navigable by oceangoing ships as far as Wuhan, 600 miles from the sea, and by smaller craft as far as Chongqing, the Yangtse has served as a major transportation artery for central China. This easy access to the well-watered agricultural areas has made the Yangtse Valley a vital economic center since Tang China. Shanghai, at the mouth of the Yangtse, is China's largest port.

The West River (Xi Jiang) is a smaller river system which flows through a rugged terrain in south China. However, the delta areas around Guangzhou are well watered by the monsoon rains and the subtropical climate permits year-round crops. Guangzhou's access to this agricultural hinterland and its position near the mouth of the river makes it the major port of south China.

CHINA'S HISTORY

The cradle of Chinese civilization is thought to be the basins of the Wei, Luo, and middle Yellow rivers. According to Chinese tradition, the Xia Dynasty (2200–1700 BC) constituted the first Chinese state. Its successor, the Shang Dynasty (1700–1066 BC), which ruled over the valley of the Yellow River, left written records cast in bronze or inscribed on tortoise shell and bone, known as "oracle bones." The Shang was probably conquered by the Western Zhou Dynasty (1066–771 BC), which ruled a prosperous feudal agricultural society. In 770 BC, the Western Zhou abandoned their capital on the site of Xi'an and established a new capital farther east at Luoyang (770–256 BC). The new state, known as the Eastern Zhou Dynasty, produced the great Chinese philosophers, Confucius and Lao Zi (Lao-tzu). Between 475 and 221 BC, the Qin state gradually emerged as the most powerful of seven warring feudal states and brought about the unification of China. Qin Shi Huangdi, the first Qin emperor (221–210 BC), forcibly organized China into a hierarchy of prefectures and counties under centralized control. For defense against nomadic Mongolian tribes, he established the Great Wall by joining together previously built segments.

DIVISION AND REUNIFICATION

During the Han Dynasty (206 BC–AD 220), China expanded westward, the Huns in the Mongolian plateau were repelled, and contacts were made with Central and Western Asia, and even Rome. Under the later Han, Buddhism was introduced into China from India. Following the Han, three kingdoms (Wei, Shu, and Wu) contended for supremacy, and nomadic tribes from the north and west raided northern China. From the 4th century on, a series of northern dynasties was set up by the invaders, while several southern dynasties succeeded one another in the Yangtse Valley, with their capital at Nanjing. Buddhism spread during this period, and the arts and sciences flourished in the Yangtse region. China was gradually reunited, and work on the Grand Canal was begun under the Sui (581–618) and Tang (618–907).

During the Tang Dynasty, especially under Emperor Tai Zong (627–47), China emerged as a political and economic presence in Asia. Handicrafts and commerce flourished; a system of roads radiated from the capital (at the site of Xi'an); and successful wars were fought in Central Asia and Korea. Poetry and painting flourished, particularly under Emperor Xuan Zong (712–56). A period of partition under the Five Dynasties (907–60) was followed by the Song Dynasty (960–1279), which is distinguished for literature, philosophy, and the invention of movable type, gunpowder, and the magnetic compass. However, Mongol and Tatar tribes forced the Song to abandon their capital at Kaifeng in 1126 and move it to Hangzhou.

MONGOL, MING, AND MANCHU

In the 13th century, the great Mongol hordes under Ghengis Khan brought all of China under their control. Under Kublai Khan (1279–94), first ruler of the Mongols' Yuan Dynasty (1279–1368), the Grand Canal was completed and a system of relay stations assured safe travel. European merchants, notably Marco Polo, and missionaries reached the Mongol capital of Khan Buluc, on the site of present-day Beijing. The novel and the drama received substantial impetus under the Mongols.

After a long period of unrest, Mongol rule was succeeded by the native Chinese Ming Dynasty (1368–1644), which established its capital at Nanjing. During the reign of Cheng Zu (1403–24), the zenith of the Ming empire, the capital was moved to Beijing. In this period, China's contacts with the West began to expand: the Portuguese reached China in 1516, the Spanish in 1557, the Dutch in 1606, and the English in 1637. The Ming Dynasty was overthrown by the Manchus, non-Chinese invaders from the northeast, who established the last imperial dynasty, the Qing (1644–1911).

CHRONOLOGY OF
CHINESE DYNASTIES AND REPUBLICS

Xia (Hsia) Dynasty	**c. 21st–16th centuries BC**
Shang (Yin) Dynasty	**c. 16th century–1122 BC**
Zhou (Chou) Dynasty Western Zhou (Chou) / c. 1122–771 BC Eastern Zhou (Chou) / 770–256 BC Spring and Autumn Period / 722–481 BC Warring States Period / 403–221 BC	**c. 1122–221 BC**
Qin (Ch'in) Dynasty	**221–206 BC**
Han Dynasty Western Han / 206 BC–AD 23 Eastern Han / 25–220	**206 BC–AD 220**
Three Kingdoms Period* State of Wei / 220–65 State of Shu / 221–63 State of Wu / 222–80	**220–280**
Western Jin (Tsin) Dynasty	**265–316**
Eastern Jin (Tsin) Dynasty and Sixteen States Eastern Jin (Tsin) / 317–420 Sixteen States / 304–439	**317–439**
Southern and Northern Dynasties	**386–589**

SOUTHERN DYNASTIES	NORTHERN DYNASTIES
Liu Song (Sung) / 420–79	Northern Wei / 386–534
Qi (Ch'i) / 479–502	Eastern Wei / 534–50
Liang / 502–57	Northern Qi (Ch'i) / 550–77
Chen (Ch'en) / 557–89	Western Wei / 535–57
	Northern Zhou (Chou) / 557–81

Sui Dynasty	**581–618**
Tang (T'ang) Dynasty	**618–907**
Five Dynasties and Ten Kingdoms Period Later Liang / 907–23 Later Tang (T'ang) / 923–36 Later Jin (Tsin) / 936–46 Later Han / 947–50 Later Zhou (Chou) / 951–60 Ten Kingdoms / 902–79	**907–79**

*The Three Kingdoms Period, the Western Jin Dynasty, and the Eastern Jin Dynasty and Sixteen States are also known as the Six Dynasties.

Continued next page

Song (Sung) Dynasty
    Northern Song (Sung) 960–1126
    Southern Song (Sung) 1127–1279
	960–1279

Liao (Kitan) Dynasty	947–1125
Western Xia (Hsia) Dynasty	1038–1227
Jin (Jurchen) Dynasty	1115–1234
Yuan (Mongol) Dynasty	1279–1368
Ming Dynasty	1368–1644
Qing (Ch'ing or Manchu) Dynasty	1644–1911
Republic of China	1912–1949
People's Republic of China	Estab. 1949

The first century and a half of Manchu rule was a period of stability and expansion of power, with notable reigns by Kang Xi (1662–1722) and Qian Long (1736–96). The Manchus ruled as conquerors, but adopted Chinese culture, administrative machinery, and laws. Under Manchu rule, the Chinese empire included Manchuria, Mongolia, Tibet, Taiwan, and the Central Asian regions of Turkestan.

FOREIGN IMPERIALISM AND INTERNAL REBELLION

By the close of the 18th century, only one port, Guangzhou (Canton), was open to merchants from abroad, and trade was greatly restricted. Demands by the British compelled the reluctant Chinese court to accept increased trade. The opium trade was foisted upon China by the British, whose home markets clamored for Chinese goods. But the Chinese were interested in little that the British had to offer in exchange. China demanded that all foreign purchases be made with silver, threatening a serious drain on England's economy. Opium, produced in British-controlled India, filled the gap, however perniciously.

Chinese opposition to foreign opium imports led to the Opium War (1839–42) and China's defeat. By the Treaty of Nanjing (1842), the ports of Guangzhou, Xiamen (Amoy), Fuzhou, Ningbo, and Shanghai were opened, and Hong Kong was ceded to Britain. The Taiping Rebellion (1850–64), which aimed at the overthrow of the dynasty, laid waste to much of southern China. A second war (1856–60) with Britain, joined by France, resulted in the opening of Tianjin to foreign trade. Thereafter, the West dictated its terms to a moribund empire. Russia acquired its Far Eastern territories from China in 1858–60 and later obtained railroad rights in Manchuria and the lease of Port Arthur (now Lüshun). After the Sino-Japanese War of 1894–95, Japan obtained Taiwan, the opening of additional ports, and control of Korea. In 1898, Britain, France, and Germany leased Weihai, Guangzhou, and Jiao Xian (in Shandong Province), respectively. The Boxer Rebellion of 1900 was the last unsuccessful effort to expel foreign influence.

China's imperial government, mortally weakened by corruption and by its inability to compete militarily and economically with the West and Japan, had survived the 19th century only by dint of its own inertia. In 1908, the Empress Dowager, the most powerful figure of the Qing court, died. The revolution that finally overthrew Manchu rule began as a mutiny among troops in Wuchang on October 10, 1911. City after city repudiated the Manchus, and in February 1912, the child emperor, Pu Yi, abdicated.

NEW FERMENT IN REPUBLICAN CHINA

The new Chinese Republic, under its founder Sun Yatsen, entered upon a period of internal strife. Yuan Shikai, a former Qing general, seized power in 1912 and tried unsuccessfully to restore the monarchy. After his death in 1916, the Beijing regime passed into the hands of various warlords while Sun Yatsen consolidated his Nationalist Party (Guomindang) in Guangzhou.

China entered World War I on the side of the Allies in 1917. The Versailles Peace Conference at the conclusion of the war decided to transfer Germany's "rights" in Shandong Province to Japan. To protest this decision, a massive student-led demonstration erupted in Beijing on May 4, 1919. The incident sparked a nationwide movement involving demonstrations, strikes, and a boycott of Japanese goods. Workers and merchants joined with intellectuals in staging these protests. It was all to no avail, as the regime acted to interdict parades, speeches, and the dissemination of literature. However, what subsequently became known as the "May Fourth Movement" had undermined the credibility of the Beijing government and spurred the upsurge of contemporary Chinese nationalism.

The demands articulated during the May Fourth era included drastic domestic reforms such as the elimination of feudal relations, the wide-scale introduction of democratic policies and the promotion of science, and, in foreign policy, equal treatment of China by other nations. At the Washington Conference in 1922, the Chinese government succeeded in obtaining the abolition of certain foreign rights.

But the Republican government was rapidly disintegrating. In the south, at Guangzhou, the Guomindang, in tenuous alliance with the Communists, built a strong, disciplined party. After Sun Yatsen's death in 1925, his successor, Chiang Kaishek, unified the country under Nationalist rule and made Nanjing the capital in 1928. In 1927, a split developed between the Nationalists and the Communists, who sought refuge in mountain redoubts in provincial border areas. Their ranks severely depleted by Nationalist attacks, the Communists embarked on their arduous and now historic Long March during 1934–35. Gathering new recruits as they moved north, the Communists eventually reached Shaanxi Province in northwestern China, where—under the leadership of Mao Zedong—they set up headquarters at Yan'an.

THE STRUGGLE AGAINST JAPAN AND THE CIVIL WAR

Japan, taking advantage of China's weakness and factionalism, occupied Manchuria in 1931. Increasing Japanese pressure against northern China led in July 1937 to a Sino-Japanese War, which continued into World War II and saw Japanese forces occupy and brutally exploit most of China's major economic areas. Nationalist China, established in the southwestern hinterland with its capital at Chongqing (Chungking), mounted a largely ineffectual resistance, squandering large quantities of US and British aid, while the Communists fought the Japanese in the northwest, all the while winning the allegiance of large segments of the Chinese peasantry. Defeated in the Pacific theater, Japan evacuated China in 1945, and both Communist and Nationalist forces moved into liberated areas. The rift between the two groups erupted into civil war. Although supported by the US, whose mediation efforts had failed, the Nationalists steadily lost ground through 1948 and 1949. They were defeated by the Communists by early 1950 and fled to Taiwan, where they installed a government and remained in occupation of the island.

THE PEOPLE'S REPUBLIC OF CHINA—THE FIRST DECADE

Under the leadership of the Chinese Communist Party, Chairman Mao Zedong proclaimed the People's Republic of China (PRC) on October 1, 1949, at Beijing, the new capital. Rejecting both the traditions of China's imperial past and the weak, inept systems that dominated Chinese government in the first half of the 20th century, the new revolutionary government set out to restructure the country along socialist lines. During the First Five-Year Plan, from 1953 to 1957, a profound transformation occurred. By 1956, all significant industrial and commercial enterprises, including the banking industry, were nationalized and agriculture was collectivized. In September 1954, the First National People's Congress was convened; deputies were elected and the first formal constitution of the PRC was promulgated.

The highly centralized, technocratic development strategy of the 1950s, with its emphasis on heavy industry over light industry and on industry over agriculture, was based largely on the Soviet model and was carried out with Soviet aid in the form of loans and technology. But by 1956, the problems inherent in uncritically applying Soviet methods of industrialization to Chinese conditions had become apparent.

THE GREAT LEAP FORWARD

In 1958–59, the Great Leap Forward was launched, during which the Chinese experimented with indigenous approaches to development. Innovations included decentralization of authority and emphasis on local decision-making; equalization between the sexes, with former housewives engaging in production; and further collectivization of property through the establishment of rural people's communes.

However, the Great Leap Forward proved to be a period of intense upheaval and resulted in severe economic dislocations. These were compounded by the recall of all Soviet aid and technicians—owing to the Sino-Soviet dispute—as well as a series of terrible natural calamities. "Three years of hardship" ensued between 1960 and 1962, during which some 27 million people were reported to have died from hunger, disease, and climatic disasters. A period of restoration and retrenchment in economics and politics, therefore, followed.

THE CULTURAL REVOLUTION

After the economy had recovered in 1965, Mao Zedong again started to steer the country along the revolutionary path and gradually built up momentum for the Cultural Revolution launched in 1966. Through the Cultural Revolution, Mao apparently hoped to overcome the bureaucratic entrenchment in education, industrial management, and economic and agricultural development that had set in since the Great Leap, as well as to reform all areas of Chinese life in the egalitarian spirit of the movement. These hopes were thwarted by unexpected chaos and violence throughout the country, often fomented by groups of young militants known as "Red Guards," whom Mao himself had initially set into motion as the vanguard of the Cultural Revolution.

During 1966–68, "revolutionary committees" that included members of the military were established as the new organs of political power in an attempt to restore some order and end the factionalism that was dividing the country. By the late 1960s, the worst of the disruptions had ended, and major reforms in education, factory management, economic planning, and medical care began to take shape. Liu Shaoqi, previously titular head of state and second in command to Mao, had been dismissed from his Party and government posts and driven to his death early in the Cultural Revolution, while the 1969 Constitution named Lin Biao, an influential figure in the military, as Mao's heir and successor. Zhou Enlai, who had played a crucial role in healing the disruptive factionalism of the Cultural Revolution, remained on as premier.

THE 1970s: FROM TURMOIL TO STABILITY

Serious disagreements developed between Mao and Lin on issues such as the "Mao cult," fostered by Lin, and in foreign policy. Moving in a new direction, Chairman Mao and Premier Zhou Enlai advocated rapprochment with the US as part of a new international strategy of forming a broad global alliance to isolate the USSR. In 1971, Lin was killed in a plane crash while fleeing to the Soviet Union after failing in a coup against Mao.

The 1970s continued to be a complex period in Chinese politics. Zhou's protégé, Deng Xiaoping, earlier criticized for supporting Liu Shaoqi's relatively pragmatic and centrist approach to development, was reinstated in 1973 as vice-premier of the State Council. In 1974, as Zhou Enlai's health deteriorated, Deng assumed the responsibilities of acting premier.

Following Zhou Enlai's death on January 8, 1976, Deng Xiaoping once more came under heavy criticism for allegedly advocating capitalistic policies. By the spring, he was again removed from his leadership posts. In retrospect, it became apparent that a power struggle between the Zhou-Deng supporters on one side and the so-called "gang of four" on the other was the underlying cause of Deng's dismissal.

Mao Zedong died on September 9, 1976. Hua Guofeng, an apparent compromise candidate of the two factions, was simultaneously—and without precedent—named chairman of the Party, chairman of the Military Affairs Commission, and premier of the State Council. Mao's death was followed by considerable political turmoil in China. Jiang Qing (Mao's widow), Yao Wenyuan, Zhang Chunqiao, and Wang Hongwen (the "gang of four") were subsequently arrested and accused of conspiring to overthrow the government and attempting to usurp state power. In the summer of 1977, Deng Xiaoping was again rehabilitated and named to the positions of vice-premier, vice-chairman of the Party, and chief-of-staff of the People's Liberation Army. By late 1977, after more than a decade of confusion and disorder, stability had been restored to China under the leadership of Hua and Deng. The Cultural Revolution was officially declared "ended."

CURRENT DOMESTIC AND INTERNATIONAL DEVELOPMENTS

Under Deng's direction, a drive for rapid industrialization known as the "Four Modernizations" (of industry, agriculture, science and technology, and defense), earlier enunciated by Zhou Enlai, was finally launched in the year after Mao's death. Profound changes have since occurred in virtually every sphere of life, many of which reverse policies developed during the Cultural Revolution. In art and literature, traditional works have been rehabilitated and new works embodying diverse styles and content are being encouraged.

In foreign policy, China had developed trade relations with many Western nations during the early 1970s and fostered closer ties with developing countries. The PRC's entry into the UN in 1971 (replacing the Nationalist government on Taiwan as China's representative), together with US President Nixon's visit the following year, led many countries to establish diplomatic relations with the Chinese government in Beijing. While the PRC's relations with the USSR, never very close after the Sino-Soviet split of the late 1950s and early 1960s, continued to deteriorate, those with the US began to improve dramatically. Following Deng Xiaoping's visit to the US in December 1978, full diplomatic relations were established between the US and China on January 1, 1979. After normalization, the US opened an embassy in Beijing and consulates in Guangzhou and Shanghai. Trade pacts were signed and legislation for most-favored-nation status for China's commercial exchanges with the US was enacted by the US Congress on January 24, 1980. US President Reagan's visit to China in 1984 and Chinese President Li Xiannian's trip to the US in 1985 helped underscore improving ties between the two nations. Among the achievements of these exchanges was the signing, in July 1985, of a nuclear energy pact.

Tensions rose in Southeast Asia during the late 1970s, especially between the PRC and Vietnam. The PRC had played a major role in supporting the Democratic Republic of Vietnam during the Indochinese conflict of the late 1960s and early 1970s, but in 1978, as Vietnam's ties with the USSR became stronger, China withdrew all aid to its southern neighbor. Relations between the two countries continued to deteriorate, and, in February 1979, Chinese troops attacked across Vietnam's border. Chinese troops withdrew after 17 days of fighting, but numerous rounds of negotiations after the withdrawal failed to reach any semblance of a political settlement.

Through the 1980s, the significant trend in foreign policy in China was an increasing "secularization," that is, reducing the ideological content in dealing with other sovereign states. In addition, relations with the United States showed a growing maturity. Although potentially inflammatory incidents arose throughout the decade, China affirmed its basic intention to develop strong and friendly relations with the United States, not sacrificing the relationship over relatively small disagreements.

For its part, the United States tempered its response to China's policies in reaction to the Tibetan demonstrations which erupted in late 1987. These uprisings by some 2,000 Tibetan monks clamoring for Tibetan independence were decisively put down by Chinese forces, in a manner that was much criticized abroad. Although there was no question of tolerating what they regarded as foreign meddling or of allowing the Tibetan demonstrations to continue, the Chinese government was concerned enough about its image abroad that it made repeated public relations efforts to minimize the scope of problems in Tibet. Moreover, China has agreed to maintain links with the Dalai Lama, who is considered the spiritual leader of the Tibetan people. The Dalai Lama has expressed an interest in opening a dialogue with China, but his proposal — the equivalent of the "one country, two systems" formula for Hong Kong and Taiwan — has not been accepted by China.

Early in 1987, the Soviet Union reversed its longstanding policy of refusing to discuss the obstacles China sees between them and stated it would satisfy at least one of China's prerequisites (i.e., withdrawing from Afghanistan). China has since expressed willingness to go forward with discussions, even in the absence of satisfaction on its two remaining conditions: resolution of border disputes in North China, and Soviet withdrawal from Indochina. How far both sides are willing to go with this new phase in their relationship remains to be seen. But with a parallel course of reform being instituted in both countries, the two countries are apt to find a greater basis for constructive dialogue than in the past.

In September 1980, Zhao Ziyang, a protégé of Deng, succeeded Hua Guofeng as premier. The downgrading of Hua and the dramatic public trial, in late 1980, of the "gang of four" and other living former leaders deemed most responsible for the Cultural Revolution further strengthened Deng's leadership position in the Party. At the same time, the Politburo launched a reevaluation of Mao's role and Party history. In June 1981, the sixth plenary session of the CCP's 11th Central Committee formally stripped Hua of his remaining political power and named Hu Yaobang the new Party general-secretary (the post of "chairman" was dropped). The session also issued a resolution which applauded Mao's contributions to the Party's rise to national power and upheld him as a "great proletarian revolutionary," but faulted him for serious ideological and political errors in the last two decades of his life.

In 1987, Hu Yaobang was relieved of his post as general-secretary, and admitted to "making mistakes on major issues of party principle," when his views were seen as leaning away from the careful synthesis of "socialism with Chinese characteristics," and toward "bourgeois liberalism." Although deeper political problems were responsible for his removal, the publicized aspects of his downfall were still another manifestation of the pendulum which continues to afflict domestic Chinese politics: His experience was an example of the fine line that Chinese public figures tread between promoting economic reform and advocating Westernization in non-economic aspects of Chinese society. When Hu was dismissed, there were fears of retrenchment from the course of reforms laid by Deng and Zhao. But in time it became clear that Zhao had not wavered in his commitment to moving China forward; Hu was simply considered to have gone too far in his advocacy of political reforms. Subsequently, Zhao was appointed acting general-secretary and, in 1988, was named Party general-secretary. He relinquished his post as premier to Li Peng, a move which some have called a concession to more conservative elements in the Party (attributed mainly to Li's heavily Soviet-influenced background).

The campaign against "bourgeois liberalism" ebbed and flowed during the 1980s, resulting in the dismissal of prominent academics, such as Fang Lizhi, but not in their complete censure, as would have happened during previous political campaigns. The immediate flashpoints of this campaign were the recurrent student demonstrations in Beijing and Shanghai. These demonstrations for the most part demanded greater resources and autonomy for education but also, at the extreme, called for democracy, human right reforms, and the dissolution of socialism. The government banned further demonstrations, and further unrest was dampened but not eliminated.

CHINA'S CULTURE

The Chinese developed in relative isolation a civilization which has endured longer than any other in the history of the world. Its unique products—silk, porcelain, tea—have long been coveted trade commodities and the fabled splendors of far Cathay have excited the imagination of many travelers. Not only has Chinese culture left its indelible mark upon that of her neighbors—Vietnam, Korea, and Japan—but Chinese inventions such as the magnetic compass, gunpowder, paper, and printing have also had far-reaching impact upon the development of the West. Visitors from Marco Polo in the 13th century to Matteo Ricci in the 16th reported favorably upon a society which in many respects outshone the Europe of their own times. Columbus carried a well-thumbed copy of Polo's account with him on his voyages of discovery, and the Jesuit writings inspired Enlightenment thinkers with the idea of a country governed by a natural philosophy independent of revealed religion. Chinoiserie, a vogue for things Chinese which manifested itself in rococo furnishings and art, swept 18th-century Europe.

Chinese confidence in the superiority of their civilization was shattered during the 19th century, when internal problems brought on in part by a vastly increased population combined with pressures from an expansionist West led to repeated military defeats and the humiliating unequal treaties. The failure of traditional leadership in dealing with foreign aggression undermined the imperial institution, which was swept away in 1912. The search for a new political order was accompanied by an iconoclastic rejection of all aspects of the traditional society. Revolutionary changes have occurred, and repudiation of the "feudal" past has been a major theme in contemporary China. However, the distinctive features of Chinese culture which contributed to its unity and continuity are particularly resistant to change and remain the irreducible core about which a modern Chinese culture must be shaped.

LANGUAGE AND LITERATURE

The Chinese written language has served as the chief medium of cultural continuity for more than 2,000 years. The earliest records were inscriptions on Shang "oracle" bones and ceremonial bronzes of the second millennium BC. Even then, the symbols were sufficiently sophisticated so as to suggest long development, but only a few markings on Neolithic pottery exist as possible prototypes of earlier writing. The forms of Chinese characters, as the symbols are called, were standardized in 221 BC by the first emperor of the Qin Dynasty and remain in use to the present day. Some of the characters contain phonetic elements, but the script is not alphabetic. Since literacy is not tied to pronunciation, the written language remained unaltered, whereas the spoken language has changed much, as well as becoming differentiated among many regional dialects. The early association of writing with divination and the difficulty of achieving literacy doubtless contributed to the Chinese attitude of near veneration for scholarship. Successful candidates for public office achieved their positions of power and prestige by passing examinations based upon mastery of the Confucian classics. This common curriculum and the use of the classical style in all literature united all the educated Chinese across time and space and gave greater status to the written word. Paper with writing on it was once so respected that special "burial" receptacles were provided for its disposal. Calligraphy has been considered the highest of the arts, along with poetry and painting the special province of the scholar who has mastered the flexible strokes of the writing brush.

Classical literature included the Confucian canon, works of history, and *belles lettres*. The novel and drama, written in a vernacular form, were disdained by scholars and not considered authentic literature. The total literary production of the Chinese, although diminished by natural and man-made disasters, is so great that by the 18th century more books had been written in Chinese than in all of the world's other languages combined. From antiquity, the Chinese have been assiduous keepers of official archives. The purpose of amassing a formidable corpus of official dynastic histories is to draw lessons from the past. In the words of the 11th-century historian, Sima Guang, history is written so that "virtues might become examples and evils warnings." This didactic use of history, and of all literature, remains a part of the contemporary scene.

The 1919 May Fourth Movement not only gave impetus to a fervent nationalism but also spurred a "literary renaissance" which supplanted the classical literary language with a colloquial style (*bai hua*) more nearly akin to everyday speech. The vernacular literature movement succeeded because so many of the best writers of that period experimented with *bai hua* poetry, novels, essays, and short stories. They modeled their writing upon that of Gogol, de Maupaussant, Gorky, and Ibsen. Chinese vernacular novels, once deprecated, were now hailed as precursors to the modern *bai hua*: *Romance of the Three Kingdoms*, *Water Margin*, *Journey to the West*, and *Dream of the Red Chamber*. All writing in today's China, from newspapers to poetry, is now done in the vernacular, a style far easier to learn than the classical.

Linguistic reform continues in China with the promotion of a standard spoken form (*putonghua*) based upon the Beijing dialect. Far in the future is the hope of introducing an alphabetic written form. Meanwhile, simplification of the characters by reducing the number of strokes (often by adopting commonly used abbreviations) eases the still difficult task of achieving literacy (defined as mastery of about 3,000 characters). The ranks of the literate have burgeoned and, despite the anti-intellectualism of the Cultural Revolution decade, the written word continues to hold a special place in modern China. "Big character" posters and slogans have been the hallmark of every mass campaign from political purges to population control. Auspicious occasions—the lunar new year (now called the Spring Festival), weddings, birthdays—are commemorated with congratulatory scrolls and couplets. The calligraphy of political leaders as well as that of noted artists decorates public parks and monuments. If ever the written characters are discarded by the Chinese, a cultural break greater than that of dismantling the imperial government will have occurred.

MORALITY AND THE SOCIAL ORDER

The anti-Confucianism of the early Republican era attacked a time-honored ideology and way of life which had provided the rationale for a unified state and culture for millennia. Once the political structure which it supported was overthrown, the state orthodoxy lay exposed to the forces of revolution. The very class of intellectuals which had once been the defenders of the old order, now educated in a new curriculum and imbued with new notions of science, democracy, anarchism, or socialism as possible solutions to China's ills, led the attack against the authoritarian family system and traditional morality. The centrality of the family in Chinese society has long been noted. The well-ordered family represented a hierarchical society in microcosm, and the loyalty owed a ruler was an extension of the respect due a father. As a patriarch keeps his family in order, so a ruler maintains harmony in his realm. In practice, the ideal of mutual responsibility was skewed in favor of the superior in the hierarchy and there were few checks to the authority of either ruler or family head. When paternalistic state rule was eliminated, the authoritarian family came under attack by reformers seeking the emancipation of women and youth.

The Confucianism which dominated Chinese society for so long included a broad spectrum of ideas which changed and adapted to meet various circumstances. As a state orthodoxy, it had accommodated such diverse elements as the draconian legalism of the Qin, the metaphysical challenges of Buddhism, and survival under foreign conquest. Underlying the myriad forms of the tradition is the Confucian vision of man's capacity to establish a perfect harmonious society by cultivating virtue. If each individual cultivates a set of norms for correct behavior, then perfect harmony is possible in all of his relationships. The moral order becomes coterminous with the political order: the state must have an enlightened ruler who appoints capable ministers from among the most morally trained to help keep the world in order. The greatest values are order, harmony, and stability; changes which might bring about chaos are to be ruthlessly suppressed. Disorder in the realm means that the ruler risks loss of the mandate to rule; the successful overthrow of a dynasty gives legitimacy to rebellion. As dynasties rose and fell, the bureaucracy staffed by the class of scholar-officials maintained itself as the indispensable managers of society and the exemplars of moral probity and correct behavior. It was also their duty to guide and lead the masses of the less cultivated, by propagating Confucian ethics in family life, building memorials to the virtuous, and patronizing classical studies. In effect, it built a yawning gulf between the educated elite and the illiterate laboring classes, a gulf which still separates mental and manual work despite strenuous efforts by the post-1949 leadership to infuse a love of labor in the new socialist man.

The emancipation of women and the reduction of family and clan authority have made greater strides. Women were granted the right of divorce in the new marriage law of 1950, and families are no longer supposed to arrange marriages. However, the family unit remains strong even as the new society seeks to direct the loyalties and energies of the individual to the larger community and to the state. Grandparents are pressed into service as child-tenders while parents work, households pool their several paychecks and keep joint budgets, and in the expansion of "free" markets and family contract systems in the rural areas, the family again becomes the basic unit of production. In the conservative countryside, traditional values have greater resistance to change. The family planning program encounters difficulty among rural families who still prefer male children. Daughters still marry out of the family, removing themselves as sources of income and care for the aged parents.

The infusion of morality into the social and political order continues, although the Confucian ideology has been replaced by a new state orthodoxy of Marxism-Leninism-Maoism. The hierarchical social system gives way to the egalitarian ideal, harmony is shattered by class struggle, and efforts to replicate a past golden age find new directions in the dynamic of revolution. Enlisted in the struggle to build socialism are the party cadres, who represent the guides to the new morality. Education, art, and literature are to promote the new ideals just as the traditional culture had reflected the old. The blend of old skills with new modes of thought and behavior could very well produce a cultural amalgam to match the achievements of the past. In any event, the sense of cultural identification and national pride remains a powerful force of unity among the Chinese as they search for wealth and power in the contemporary world. The success of that venture will be reflected in a resurgent and revitalized culture which will, as did its antecedents, undoubtedly bear a distinctive Chinese mold.

POLITICS AND GOVERNMENT

MAO AND MARXISM-LENINISM

The concept of politics in the PRC continues to be described as the product of Mao Zedong's thought, which applies the ideas of Marx and Lenin to the concrete conditions of China. During the early 1980s, however, this formulation was being rendered with subtle yet important qualifications, many of which struck the theme that socialism in China is an evolving notion whose success depends on flexibility in light of actual conditions and imperatives.

Major elements from Chinese tradition found echoes in the Marxist-Leninist worldview that by the 1920s had become the dominant perspective of China's revolutionaries, Mao included. Marxism, like Daoism, stressed the interconnections and dialectical aspects of all human experience and knowledge. Like Confucianism, it placed social relationships at the core

POLITICS AND GOVERNMENT

Deng Xiaoping addressing the National People's Congress

of its political theory and linked these to a strong sense of historical periods and causality. The specific Marxist addition to this traditional orientation was the idea that throughout history there have existed social classes with differing material interests and ideologies, and that the struggle between classes is the substance of politics. Moreover, for Mao, as for Marx, politics was not limited to the realm of institutions and governmental processes. Personal and family life, education, artistic creation, morality, culture—all are understood in Mao Zedong's thought as expressions of the struggle between classes in the movement toward a more just social order.

MODERNIZATION AND REVOLUTION

Politics in post-1949 China has been marked by a continuing debate on how exactly to proceed toward a more just and equitable society. On the one hand, China, still economically backward, must modernize and create material abundance as a precondition for social equality. On the other hand, it must continue to revolutionize social conditions and relationships or risk the development of new forms of exploitation and injustice even in the midst of increased prosperity. Ideally, modernization and revolution should be carried on simultaneously, with revolutionary principles guiding economic development. In reality, the effort to mediate between those two goals has proved a complex and difficult task. At times, in the name of "making revolution," serious economic setbacks have occurred and social development itself has been blocked, as in the first half of the 1970s under the "gang of four." In the present period, China's leaders are once more trying to bring economic and social strategies into workable balance. One key example is the emphasis now placed on guaranteeing democratic rights and forms, seen as essential not only to social progress but to significant economic growth as well.

FREEDOM, DEMOCRACY, AND THE LAW

Under the leadership of Deng and his colleagues, the Chinese government has repeatedly pledged itself to the promotion of citizen's rights and democratic processes in its continuing effort to modernize by the end of this century. The new policy expressly permitted the staging of protests and the promulgation of laws safeguarding due process and the right to press grievances. Responding to the more open atmosphere, citizens moved to give greater vent to long suppressed grievances.

In the winter of 1978–79, demonstrations in Beijing, Shanghai, and other cities called for better housing, fuller employment, more educational opportunities, and acceleration of democratization. Sit-ins and marches were accompanied by outspoken *dazibao* or "big character posters." Posters have been periodically used since 1949 as a forum for airing personal injustices and demands. The wallposter phenomenon was curtailed in 1980 and prominent dissenters were detained or arrested. However, the official press continued to provide a limited arena for readers to debate policies and air criticisms.

In addition to a more open if still cautious approach to public debate, the Chinese government is adopting a massive body of legislation and formal codes. Key provisions of the Law on Criminal Procedure, effective January 1, 1980, highlight some of the ways the government is attempting to introduce democracy in the country. These provisions stress that all persons are equal before the law, and that no one has the privilege to be treated beyond or above it; they protect citizens against illegal infringement by any person or institution, and prohibit imprisonment without legal sanction and extortion of confession through torture. Such abuses are said to have occurred frequently during the Cultural Revolution.

Measures are being enacted to confer independence on judicial organs. Counterrevolutionary offenses are now being defined as "acts undermining the PRC with the aim of overthrowing the political power of the dictatorship of the proletariat and the socialist legal system" and prosecutions are limited accordingly. Every accused person will be entitled to legal defense, and trials must now be conducted publicly (although, in practice, justice continues to be meted out with consummate haste—severe felony cases are still reported to be handled within a space of four days, from arrest to execution).

The Fifth National People's Congress also announced drafting of the following new codes of law: a law of civil procedure; a new marriage law; a family planning law; a factory law; an energy law; and a law on environmental pollution.

A number of additional developments in the field of law include the opening of legal advisory offices in the cities; revitalization of the nation's law schools after 12 years of dormancy; the appearance of publications devoted to legal problems such as the two law journals *Legal Research* and *Democracy and Legality*; and an intensive campaign to popularize the due process of law in China through media as diverse as traditional opera and newspapers.

The Chinese government's stated objective is to relax and improve the country's social environment and to promote a participatory political system. At the very least, the new codes seek to make it more difficult for a group of officials to transgress laws—as was apparently the case during the Cultural Revolution. In a country without a tradition of uniform written laws and where arbitration and consensus have formed the basis for resolving grievances and assessing guilt or innocence, the PRC's legal codification of freedom and democracy comes as a potentially historic breakthrough.

The Communist Party of China (CPC). The leading political force in the PRC, as stipulated by the 1978 Constitution, is the CPC. Overall policy decisions in China—political, economic, and social—are made by the Party and its leadership. China's state government functions mainly to coordinate the national economy and preside over foreign affairs. In this sense, government is subordinate to the Party. Mao Zedong, chairman of the Party from 1935 until his death in 1976, was by virtue of that position the preeminent leader of the People's Republic. Mao was succeeded as chairman by Hua Guofeng in October 1976. On June 29, 1981, Hu Yaobang became general secretary; the post of chairman was eliminated to avoid overconcentration of power.

In the mid-1980s, the party began to consolidate its move away from the ideological themes of the Cultural Revolution and towards the practical goal of economic modernization. Beginning in November 1983, the memberships of 288,000 party members were placed under review. This action was aimed at weeding out the diehard leftist factions that stood in opposition to the new political and economic reforms. Several senior officials were demoted or sent into early retirement, culminating in the removal of Hu Yaobang from the Party leadership in January 1987. Many of these moves reflected Deng Xiaoping's goal of bringing adherents of his own policies into the party leadership.

In October 1987, the 13th Congress of the CPC convened in Beijing and presided over the formal retirement of Deng Xiaoping from the CPC Central Committee, together with the appointment of Premier Zhao Ziyang to the simultaneous post of General Secretary of the Party. Overall, the 13th Congress lent momentum to many of Deng's economic policies by endorsing several new departures toward the "Westernization" of the economy, including the increased reliance on market forces to balance supply and demand (a favorite theme of Zhao's), the ability of farmers to sell land-use rights, the use of stock and bond markets as legitimate means of raising capital for Chinese industry, and expansion of the relative size of China's private sector. As a modest balance to these changes, the five-member Standing Committee of the Politburo—the "inner circle" of China's leadership—consisted (apart from Zhao, as leader) of four relatively younger personages considered as moderates or conservatives relative to the new reforms: Hu Qili, Qiao Shi, Li Peng, and Yao Yilin. At the same time, departing from the Central Committee, along with Deng, were several of China's most durable leaders: President Li Xiannian; Chairman of the NPC, Peng Zhen; and chief-of-staff of the army, Yang Dezhi.

Various Party organs underwent considerable streamlining during the 1987 Congress; membership of the Central Committee was reduced from 209 to 172, while the formerly powerful Central Commission for Discipline Inspection had its membership reduced from 128 to 69.

The strongest leftist opposition to Deng and his policies has come from the ranks of the People's Liberation Army. Partly to consolidate power and partly to expedite modernization of the armed forces, a major drive to streamline the army was begun in May 1985. Certain generals were retired, and the number of active military personnel was significantly reduced.

The State Council. The 1978 Constitution declares that "the State Council is the central people's government and . . . the highest organ of state administration." It is headed by a premier and several vice-premiers. The premier is nominated by the Communist Party and approved by the National People's Congress, as are vice-premiers, ministers, and vice-ministers. The State Council coordinates the work of the ministries, offices, commissions, and special agencies, and draws up national economic plans and the national budget in accordance with Party priorities and strategies.

The National People's Congress (NPC). The highest organ of legislative power in China is the NPC. The Constitution stipulates, however, that the NPC is to function under the direction of the Chinese Communist Party. Deputies are elected by provinces and autonomous regions, cities under central government rule, the armed forces, and Chinese residents abroad. Specific NPC functions are to amend the constitution, pass laws, and examine and approve the state budget and final accounts.

The Standing Committee of the NPC. The Standing Committee is elected by the NPC as its permanent working organ. As such, the Standing Committee is empowered to convene NPC plenary sessions, interpret laws and enact decrees, appoint ambassadors and receive foreign ambassadors, and ratify treaties with foreign governments. The chairman of the Standing Committee, by right of the 1978 Constitution, can receive foreign envoys, and, with the approval of the NPC or full Standing Committee, promulgate laws and ratify treaties.

The Chinese People's Political Consultative Conference (CPPCC). The CPPCC is a consultative body with origins in the "united front" that predated the formation of the PRC in 1949. Its purpose is to provide a national platform of discussion for interest groups not directly represented in the NPC, including national minorities, professional societies, and minority political parties. In the mid-1980s, its ranks included prominent ethnic Chinese living overseas (including representatives from Hong Kong and Macao), as well as foreign nationals permanently residing in China.

The Supreme People's Court. The president of the Supreme People's Court is the only appointment not made on the direct initiative of the Party; that responsibility belongs to the NPC. Until the passage of the PRC's first national legal code in June 1979, the Court's function on the national level was negligible because of the local orientation of the Chinese legal system.

CHINA'S ECONOMY

China's economy is centrally planned and centrally controlled, although since the early 1980s a considerable degree of local initiative has been encouraged in most sectors. China has always been, and remains today, a predominantly agricultural country. For almost three decades prior to 1949, the incessant ravages of civil disorder, foreign economic rapacity and military aggression, and gross financial neglect had reduced China to a state of helpless dependence. The first task of the new government, therefore, was to establish a viable and relatively self-sufficient economy. By the early 1950s, mass starvation had been virtually eliminated and, by the end of the decade, China had begun to mobilize its vast natural and human resources to lay the base for industrialization and stable development.

ECONOMIC DEVELOPMENT UNDER THE PRC

During 1953–57, China's First Five-Year Plan introduced a stress on heavy industry. Economic development was aided by imports of machinery and other industrial equipment from the USSR and Eastern European countries. In return, China exported agricultural produce to them. A major geological prospecting drive resulted in the discovery of mineral deposits that provided a major thrust toward industrialization.

The "Great Leap Forward" of 1958–59 in industry and agriculture initially produced sharp gains, but the zeal for increased quotas quickly resulted in undue strain on resources and quality and produced severe economic imbalances. The Great Leap was followed by "three bitter years" of economic crisis (1959–62) brought on by bad harvests combined with the economic dislocation resulting from the Great Leap, and exacerbated by the USSR's withdrawal in the early 1960s of all technical and economic aid, upon which China's industrialization in the previous decade had largely depended. By 1961, the GNP had fallen to an estimated $81 billion, roughly the level reached in 1955.

By 1965, however, a readjustment of expectations coupled with a careful program of industrial investment caused the economy to recover its former production pace. China's trade patterns, meanwhile, had shifted sharply away from the USSR and toward Japan and Western Europe. China's trade with the Communist states fell from 69% of its total trade in 1959 to 26% by 1966. Although aggregate agricultural output and yield per acre had gone up, the expansion in agriculture lagged behind that of industry, necessitating huge grain imports from the West. Beginning in 1961, China had to import five to six million tons of grains each year from Canada, Australia, and other countries at an annual cost of about $300–400 million. The economic impact of the Cultural Revolution that began in 1966 was first felt in transport, industry, and public services. Factional fighting and other disruptions resulted in a drop in industrial production in 1967 estimated at between 10% and 20%. Good weather during 1966–68 prevented an agricultural slump but did not yield the abundance that might otherwise have occurred.

During the first half of the 1970s, China's economy registered relative gains in virtually all sectors. The country remained, by most measures, underdeveloped, and living standards were fairly spartan. Nonetheless, China was approaching levels of self-sufficiency—in food, primary industrial materials, and manufactured goods—far in excess of what had ever been achieved previously. Overall growth in trade and industry was spurred by dramatic increases in China's petroleum output. By 1980, the nation's oil fields—mostly located in remote northern regions—were producing 106 million metric tons of crude a year (compared with 5.5 million metric tons in 1960), providing ample quantities for export to Japan and elsewhere.

THE REASSERTION OF PRODUCTIVITY PLANNING, 1975–78

Political struggles among the leadership during 1973–74 indicated that basic policy disputes stemming from the Cultural Revolution had yet to be resolved. The "Anti-Confucius, Anti-Lin Biao" campaign pointedly called into question policies that perpetuated material incentives, sought major inputs from foreign technology, and returned to decision-making roles individuals who allegedly placed pragmatism above revolutionary doctrine. By early 1975, however, the staffs of major planning agencies had been restored to pre-Cultural Revolution levels and, in January, Zhou Enlai, addressing the Fourth National People's Congress, set economic policy on a course that was to remain generally intact throughout the remainder of the decade. The crux of Zhou's speech placed modernization at the core of China's economic development into the 21st century. He stated: "On Chairman Mao's instructions, it was suggested in the report on the work of the government to the Third National People's Congress that we might envisage the development of our national economy in two stages beginning from the Third Five-Year Plan. The first stage is to build an independent and relatively comprehensive industrial and economic system in 15 years, that is before 1980; the second stage is to accomplish the comprehensive modernization of agriculture, industry, national defense, and science and technology before the end of the century, so that our national economy will be advancing into the front ranks of the world."

The development goals embodied in Zhou's report, and the policies that were to proceed from it in the mid-1970s, marked a clear turning away from policies (since 1976 ascribed to the "gang of four") that regarded the pursuit of material growth *per se* as a betrayal of revolutionary ideals. Nevertheless, Zhou, and the leadership that in late 1976 succeeded Mao and Zhou, continued to stress continuity with past policies along with the necessity for continued revolution. Indeed, a number of policies that had their origins in the Great Leap and had developed in the course of the Cultural Revolution were reaffirmed and strengthened in the initial strategies evolved under Hua Guofeng and Deng Xiaoping.

THE 1978 TEN-YEAR PLAN

At the opening meeting of the First Session of the Fifth National People's Congress, held on February 26, 1978, Hua Guofeng put forth a new draft of a Ten-Year Plan (1976–85) originally drawn up in 1975. Hua's report specifically reiterated the thrust for development and modernization spelled out by Zhou Enlai in 1970 and 1975. The major points of emphasis, each consonant with policy themes brought into practice at various junctures since the early 1970s, were: 1) mass efforts in support of agriculture (including a goal of full-scale mechanization by the mid-1980s); 2) accelerated development of basic industries; 3) continued expansion of foreign trade; 4) vastly expanded efforts to achieve modern technology and scientific knowledge; 5) a strengthening of unified planning; and 6) a commitment both to improved living standards and to the principle "From each according to his ability, to each according to his work"—holding out the promise of continued, if not increased, use of wage policies as a source of worker incentives.

THE "FOUR MODERNIZATIONS"

In spring 1978, China's leadership announced the "Four Modernizations" program, an economic development strategy that would provide the country with a "powerful socialist economy" by the year 2000. The modernization thrust was to focus on agriculture, industry, national defense, and science and technology.

A dramatic enlargement of China's trade policies began in February 1978 with the signing of a 13-year (1978–90) agreement with Japan covering about US$20 billion in exchanges (largely Chinese oil and coal to Japan; industrial plants and technology to China). In the wake of the announcement of normalized US-China relations in December 1978, major US-China trade agreements were concluded, including the purchase of commercial aircraft from Boeing, the sale of Chinese petroleum to US refiners, and an arrangement by which Coca-Cola would be marketed in China. Major purchases from Canada, France, the UK, the Federal Republic of Germany, and other Western European countries were also concluded during 1978–79.

In another important departure from the pre-1976 period, greater emphasis was given to raising living standards for a population that had tolerated virtually no improvement in living conditions for two decades. Domestic consumer markets and housing were to be enhanced even if this meant slowing down the pace of industrialization. Heavy industry was de-emphasized in favor of agriculture and light industry.

In 1979, the government conceded that many of the 120 infrastructure projects called for in the 1978 Ten-Year Plan could not be completed by 1985. In fact, the Chinese acknowledged that they would be doing well to get all of those projects started by 1985. Most of the ambitious targets of the Plan were abandoned.

READJUSTMENT AND REFORM

Despite this reassessment, China has forged ahead with its economic liberalization and modernization. Domestically, the expansion of the "contract responsibility system" to include the urban sector and the lifting of some wage and price controls has fundamentally altered as well as considerably strengthened the grassroots economy. Although there will be a long way to go before every worker and peasant can afford the "four big things"—a color TV, stereo tape player, clothes washing machine and refrigerator—the income levels of many have already reached beyond this level. The country's Seventh Five-Year Plan (1986–90) takes account of the growing importance of middle- and high-grade consumer goods in the domestic economy, and recommends boosting production of household appliances, garments, furniture and building materials to meet the demand.

Foreign trade, investment, and technology will continue to play a central role in this crucial stage of China's development. The policy of "opening to the outside" has not changed in principle since its inception in 1979. The "Special Economic Zones" and the 14 Open Coastal Cities are still seen as the primary magnets for attracting much-needed infusions of foreign capital and technology. As of 1988, 4,000 enterprises using foreign investment have been established, comprising contracts valued at some $3 billion. However, the unrestrained optimism expressed initially by China's leaders has been tempered somewhat by the slowness with which foreign business has responded. In the second half of the 1980s, emphasis is expected to shift from the building of new plants to the upgrading of existing facilities and continued improvement of management techniques and quality control to improve efficiency. By substituting technical transformation for capital construction where possible, China hopes to keep up the pace of modernization while avoiding the waste and corruption that accompanied the first stages of reform. A $5.3-billion trade deficit in the first half of 1985 and the corresponding drop in the nation's foreign reserves had a sobering effect on China's economic planners.

In addition to calling for increased output of consumer goods, the Seventh Five-Year Plan calls for continued improvement in the industrial infrastructure, especially in the areas of energy and transportation. Construction of hydroelectric, nuclear, and coal-fired generating stations are the first priority. Increases in coal and oil production are also called for. Improvement of railway, highway, port, and civil aviation facilities and of telecommunications networks are of paramount importance.

To survive, China's economy must continue to grow, but growth *per se* was unacceptable if not accompanied by swift modernization of economic management processes and by reforms that lead to rational (rather than dogmatic) decision-making. A tacit underpinning for the new plan was the recurrent implication that modern methods (along with technologies) could be found in sources outside of China and, indeed, from within systems otherwise inimicable to Chinese socialism. Mao's China could go it alone. For Deng's China, the concept of self-sufficiency on all fronts is simply an impractical, if not absurd, ideal.

II

PLANNING
A TRIP
TO CHINA

CHINA'S TRAVEL POLICY

Today, virtually anyone who wants to visit China may do so. A few restrictions exist in the form of advance visa requirements and prearrival itinerary planning, the latter limitation created mainly by current shortages in hotel space and tourism personnel. Until recently one of the most closed societies in the world, China now readily acknowledges the economic and political benefits of international tourism and welcomes visits by foreigners within the bounds of "friendly exchanges . . . and serving China's modernization program."

China's central body for creating and coordinating national tourism policy is the National Tourism Administration (NTA), which was given ministerial status under the State Council in 1976. In 1984, NTA's central decision-making authority was reinforced by an administrative reshuffle that transferred most of the policy functions of the China International Travel Service and other tourism agencies to NTA. The purpose of the change was to broaden the base for tourism sponsorship among national and provincial organizations and thereby promote smooth, rational expansion within the tourism sector. In 1988, a new Tourism Commission was set up by the State Council, to be headed by vice-premier Wu Xueqian.

Rapid expansion in the early 1980s had created a host of problems for China's tourism sector. Hotels, travel facilities, organizations, and service staff were quickly taxed beyond their limits by the sudden onrush of tourists and labored under increasing bureaucratic pressures to generate more precious foreign exchange. The glow of enthusiasm that had engulfed the first tourist waves of 1977–78 had begun to fade.

In 1981, an NTA official acknowledged some of the persistent difficulties: "Problems remain in spite of improvements in service quality— bad manners on the part of some hotel attendants, bad service and bad environmental sanitation; unqualified guides and interpreters, who are unable to answer questions put forward by tourists. . . . Owing to bad management, rooms were often not provided promptly upon arrival of tourists during the busy season, schedules were often changed because of failure in obtaining plane tickets. Unreasonable charges were made at some places."

In 1982, the first major wave of new hotels began to enter service, while new sites were added to tourist itineraries in the hope of alleviating pressure on the nine major tourist centers—Beijing (visited by 80% of all foreign tourists), Shanghai, Guangzhou, Hangzhou, Guilin, Nanjing, Suzhou, Wuxi, and Xi'an.

By 1988, China had 1,000 tourist hotels, with over 300,000 beds, an increase of 50% over 1986. About 100 new hotels were to be added by 1990.

By 1988, the number of cities and scenic spots opened to foreign tourists has reached about 500, compared to the mere 40 or so accessible only a few years earlier. While fewer than 120 of these sites had yet to develop facilities capable of handling foreigners on a regular basis, the general direction of tourism policy remained clear—continued expansion with emphasis on a significantly broadened range of itineraries and options.

Tourists don "imperial" costumes for souvenir snapshot

Cities and Sites
Officially Open to Tourists (1988)

BEIJING MUNICIPALITY ▣ (including Changping, Daxing, Fangsha, Fengtai, Haidian, Huairou, Mengtourou, Miyun, Pinggu, Shijingshan, Shunyi, Tongxian, Yangqing, and Yanshan)

SHANGHAI MUNICIPALITY, TIANJIN MUNICIPALITY ▣ (including Dagong and Yancun)

ANHUI PROVINCE ▣ Anqing, Bengbu, Chaohu, Chuzhou, Fengyang, Fuyang, Haozhou, Hefei, Huaibei, Huainan, Huang Shan, Jingxian, Jiuhua Mountain Tourist Zone, Liu'an, Ma'anshan, Quzhou, Shexian, Suzhou, Tongling, Tunxi, Wuhu, and Xiuning

FUJIAN PROVINCE ▣ Chong'an, Fuzhou, Putian, Xiamen, Quanzhou, Zhangzhou

GANSU PROVINCE ▣ Anxi, Baiyin, Chengxian, Dangchang, Diebu, Dunhuang, Jiayuguan, Jinchang, Jingyuan, Jiuquan, Lanzhou, Linxia, Minqin, Minxian, Pingliang, Qingyang, Tianshui, Wenxian, Wudu, Wuwei, Xiahe, Xifeng, Yongjing, Yumen, Zhangye, Zhouqu

GUANGDONG PROVINCE ▣ Anding, Baishan, Baoting, Beisha, Boluo, Changjiang, Chaozhou, Chengmai, Conghua, Danxian, Dapu, Deqing, Ding'an, Dongfang, Dongguan, Fengkai, Fengshun, Foshan, Gaoyao, Guangzhou, Haifeng, Haikou, Hainan Island, Heyuan, Huaiji, Huidong, Huiyang, Huizhou, Jiangmen, Ledong, Lingao, Lingshui, Lufeng, Luodong, Maoming, Meixian, Qionghai, Qiongshan, Qiongzhong, Sanya (Yaxian), Shantou, Shaoguan, Shenzhen, Sihui, Tunchang, Wanning, Wenchang, Xingning, Xinxing, Xiqiao, Yunfu, Zhanjiang, Zhaoqing, Zhongshan (Shiqi), Zhuhai

GUANGXI PROVINCE ▣ Beihai, Beiliu, Binyang, Guilin, Guiping, Guixian, Hepu (Lianzhou), Jinxiu Yao Nationality Autonomous County, Lingshan, Liuzhou, Long'an, Longsheng Multi-Nationality Autonomous County, Luchuan, Nanning, Qinzhou, Qinchuan, Rongshui Miao Nationality Autonomous County, Rongxian, Sanjiang Dong Nationality Autonomous County, Wuming, Wuzhou, Xing'an, Yangshuo, Yulin, Zhuang Nationality Autonomous Region

GUIZHOU PROVINCE ▣ Anshun, Bijie, Chishui, Dafang, Dushan, Duyun, Guiyang, Huangguoshu Waterfall Scenic Region, Hongkou, Jiangkou, Kaili, Liupanshui, Pingba, Qianxi, Qingzhen, Shibing, Taijiang, Tongren, Xingyi, Zhenyuan, Zhijin, Zunyi

HEBEI PROVINCE ▣ Baoding, Beidaihe, Botou, Cangzhou, Chengde, Gangan Reservoir, Handan, Jixian, Kengtai, Langfang, Luanping, Nangong, Qinhuangdao, Shahe, Shashiyu, Shijiazhuang,

cont.

Tangshan, Xibaipo, Xingji, Yixian, Zhaoqiao Bridge, Zhaoxian, Zhuoxian, Zunhua

HEILONGJIANG PROVINCE ◼ Anda, Bei'an, Daqing, Fangzheng, Hailun, Harbin, Hegang, Heihe (Aihui), Hougang, Jiagedaqi Region, Jiamusi, Jiaojiang, Jixi, Mudanjiang, Nenjiang, Qiqihar, Qitaihe, Shuangcheng, Shuangya Shan, Suifenhe, Suihua, Tongjiang, Wudalianqi, Yichun, Zhaodong

HENAN PROVINCE ◼ Anyang, Buyang, Hebi, Jiaozuo, Kaifeng, Luohe, Luoyang, Nanyang, Pingdingshan, Puyang, Sanmen Gorge, Shangqiu, Wenxian, Xinxiang, Xinyang (Jigong Shan), Xuchang, Zhengzhou, Zhoukouzhen, Zhumadian

HUBEI PROVINCE ◼ Anlu, Danjiangkou, Ezhou, Gong'an, Hanchuan, Hong'an, Honghu, Huanggang, Huangmei, Huangshi, Jiangling, Jianli, Jingmen, Jingshan, Puqi, Qianjiang, Qichun, Shashi, Shishou, Shiyan, Songzi, Suizhou, Tianmen, Wuhan, Wuxue, Xiangfan, Xianning, Xiantao, Xiaogan, Yichang, Yingcheng, Yunmeng, Zhongxiang

HUNAN PROVINCE ◼ Anren, Anxiang, Binzhou, Changde, Changsha, Chenxian, Chenzhou, Dayong, Dong'an, Fenghuang, Guidong, Guiyang, Hanshou, Hengyang, Jishou, Jianghua Yao Nationality Autonomous County, Jinshi, Lengshuijiang, Lengshuitan, Lianyuan, Linfeng, Linli, Lixian, Loudi, Nanxian, Qiyang, Rucheng, Sangzhi, Shaoshan, Shaoyang, Taojiang, Taoyuan, Xiangtan, Xinhuang Dong Nationality Autonomous County, Xupu, Yiyang, Yizhang, Yongshun, Yongxing, Yongzhou, Yuanjiang, Yuanling, Yueyang (Dongting Lake), Zhijiang, Zhuzhou, Zixing

INNER MONGOLIA AUTONOMOUS REGION ◼ Baotou, Butha Qi (Zalantun), Chifeng (Hada), Dalad Qi (Shalinzhao), Dongsheng, Erenhot, Hailar, Hohhot, Manzhouli, Tongliao, Ulanhot, Xilinhot (Abagnar Qi)

JIANGSU PROVINCE ◼ Changzhou, Hai'an, Huaiyin, Lianyungang, Nanjing, Nantong, Suzhou, Wuxi, Xuzhou, Yancheng, Yangzhou, Yixing, Zhenjiang

JIANGXI PROVINCE ◼ Chongren, Dexing, Fengxin, Fuzhou, Ganxian, Ganzhou, Geyang, Ji'an, Jingdezhen, Jinggang Shan, Jiujiang, Le'an, Lu Shan (including Jinjiang and Yingzi counties), Nanchang, Nanfeng, Pingxiang, Qianshan, Quannan, Shanggao, Wanzai, Wuyuan, Xinyu, Xunwu, Yichun, Yifeng, Yihuang, Yingtan, Yiyang

JILIN PROVINCE ◼ Antu (Changbai Mountain Nature Preserve), Baicheng, Changchun, Gongzhuling, Hunjiang, Jilin, Liaoyuan,

cont.

Longjing, Meihekou, Siping, Tonghua, Tumen, Yanji

LIAONING PROVINCE ◼ Anshan, Benxi, Chaoyang, Dalian, Dandong, Fushun, Fuxin, Jinzhou, Liaoyang, Panjin, Shenyang, Tieling, Wushun, Yingkou

NINGXIA HUI AUTONOMOUS REGION ◼ Guyuan, Haiyuan, Lingwu, Pingluo, Qingtongxia, Tongxin, Wuzhong, Xijie, Yanchi, Yinchuan, Zhongning, Zhongwei

QINGHAI PROVINCE ◼ Gangca (Qinghai Lake, Niao Island), Golmud, Gonghe, Huangzhong, Huangzhou (Ta'er Lamasery), Ledu, Lenghu, Mangya, Xining

SHAANXI PROVINCE ◼ Baoji, Dali, Hancheng, Hanzhong, Huangling, Huayin, Liuba, Lüeyang, Mianxian, Nanzheng, Pucheng, Tongchuan, Xi'an, Xianyang, Yan'an

SHANDONG PROVINCE ◼ Changwei (including Anqiu and Linqu counties, and Weifang), Dezhou, Dongying, Jinan, Jining, Lingyi, Qingdao, Qufu, Rizhao, Shengli Oilfield, Tai'an (Tai Shan), Weifang, Weihai, Yantai, Zhaozhuang, Zibo

SHANXI PROVINCE ◼ Changzhi, Datong, Dazhai, Fanzhi, Hongdong, Linfen, Pingyao, Ruicheng, Taiyuan, Wutai, Yangquan, Yuncheng

SICHUAN PROVINCE ◼ Changning, Chengdu, Chongqing, Dazu, Deyang, Dukou, Emei Shan (including Emei County), Fengdu, Fengjie, Fuling, Guangyuan, Hongxian, Jiang'an, Leshan, Luzhou, Ma'erkang, Maowen Qiang Nationality Autonomous County, Mianyang, Nanchong, Nanping, Neijiang, Songpan, Suining, Wanxian, Wuxi, Wushan, Xichang, Xingwen, Ya'an, Yibin, Yunyang, Zhongxian, Zigong

TIBET ◼ Lhasa, Naqu, Naidong (Zedang), Nielamu (Zhangmu), Xigaze

XINJIANG UIGHUR AUTONOMOUS REGION ◼ Aksu, Artux, Changjie, Fukang, Kumul (Hami), Korla, Kashgar (Kashi), Kuqa, Shihezi, Shufu, Taxkorgan Tadjik Autonomous County, Turpan, Ürümqi, Yarkant (Shache)

YUNNAN PROVINCE ◼ Chihai, Chuxiong, Dali, Jinghong (Xishuangbanna), Kunming, Lunan (Stone Forest), Menghai, Lijiang Naxi Nationality Autonomous County, Qujing, Simao, Tonghai, Tongmao, Yuxi

ZHEJIANG PROVINCE ◼ Hangzhou, Huzhou, Jiaojiang, Jiaxing, Jinhua, Jinyun, Leqing (Yandang Shan), Lishui, Mogan Shan, Ningbo, Putuo (Putuo Mountain Tourist Zone), Qingtian, Quzhou, Shaoxing, Tiantai, Wenzhou

In addition to the above list, a number of other sites are accessible under a "special permission" requirement. Notable among them are selected tours along the Nepal-Tibet border, opened in 1985. Also listed as open to foreign tourists are th Yangtse River from Chongqing to Shanghai and segments of the coastline between shanghai, Qingdao, Yantai, Dalian, and Tianjin.

EXPANDING TOURIST VOLUME

The number of people visiting the PRC increased some 14-fold during the decade 1978–87. In 1987, 26.9 million persons visited the country, compared to 1.8 million in 1978. The vast majority of visitors (about 25 million, or 94%) were residents of Hong Kong and Macao. Foreign visitors (in all categories) totaled about 1.7 million, representing 6% of the total and a 16% increase over 1987 (compared with a 34% increase from 1985 to 1986). Of all foreign visitors in 1987, some 26% (91,100) were tourists hosted by CITS (up 6.9% over the 1986 total, but down from its 40% proportion of the foreign total in 1986); in 1987 CTS received 826,000 (up 38.8%), and China Youth Travel Service hosted 125,300 (up by an impressive 58%).

Two countries — Japan and the United States — accounted for about half of China's foreign visitors in 1987, with totals of 578,000 and 315,000 respectively. Other countries sending relatively large numbers of foreign visitors included Australia (58,600), the UK (83,000), the Philippines (57,600), Singapore (64,000), France (53,600), India (8,800), and the Federal Republic of Germany (60,000). In all, visitors from over 160 countries and regions traveled to China in 1988.

China's foreign exchange income from tourism totaled an estimated US$1.84 billion in 1987, up by 20% over the previous year. Visitors from the US and Western Europe spent an average of $1,000 per person during their stay in China.

CONVENTIONALIZING CHINA'S TOURISM

By 1988, some 500 Chinese cities (virtually ten times the number in 1976) were regularly receiving foreign tourists. Travel brochures now offer everything from sea cruises along China's coast to bicycle tours through the countryside, to mountain climbing in Tibet. During the early 1980s, the first tentative efforts to combine tourism with leisure and recreation were apparent with the opening of resort facilities at Xili Reservoir (north of Shenzhen) and Yanguo Village (north of Macao), the construction of three 18-hole golf courses, and the opening of an amusement park near Miyun reservoir, north of Beijing. China's numerous hot springs and spas were being refurbished to receive foreigners, while the beach resort at Beidaihe was used for the first time as a site for an international symposium—a welcome change from the bleak office blocks of Beijing or Tianjin.

Activities on the daily itinerary have also changed emphasis. Formerly, travelers would most likely spend the majority of their time visiting institutions, factories, communes, and other sites chosen to inform foreigners about key aspects of life in contemporary China. Now, historical monuments and museums are emphasized, and tour groups taken to special arts and crafts institutes in various cities are afterwards led straightaway to a tourist shop for a chance to buy samples of what they have just seen. Friendship Stores have proliferated throughout the country, as has the array of items being produced for tourist consumption. By the late 1980s, nearly 40% of China's tourism income derived from tourists' purchases of gifts and souvenirs.

INCREASING COSTS

China's official policy is to maintain costs for tourists at levels comparable to prices elsewhere in the world. During the early and mid-1980s, this policy caused drastic price increases and a startling rise in the number of services subject to separate billing (e.g., beer, soft drinks, and tea—formerly considered part of the prepaid hotel fare—are now charged as extras). More noticeable, perhaps, was the institution of a double standard of prices for Chinese and foreigners. Part of the point—not an unreasonable one—is that tourists should not be allowed to avail themselves unduly of China's low consumer prices, many of which are kept low through government subsidy and control. Thus, the new Beijing Duck restaurant is charging tourists a minimum of Y40 per person; railroads have joined airlines in charging special fares (in some cases double) for foreigners, and a system of "optional-at-extra-cost" excursions are being offered as add-ons to ostensibly prepaid group itineraries in major tourist cities. During the 1986–87 period, rates for hotels and other tourist services throughout the country were increased by as much as 40%. By 1988, however, the increased supply of hotel rooms was actually working to suppress hotel rates, while most other tourist rates had stabilized.

While the new policy promised a quick end to most bargain aspects of China travel, in most cases the increases seemed drastic only in comparison to previous levels in China: the new prices are rarely higher than what tourists are accustomed to paying elsewhere. And, when compared to costs in Tokyo or even Hong Kong, the price of travel in China still looks rather reasonable; e.g., about $100 per day for hotel, three meals, and sightseeing. Business travelers and others traveling individually, however, can expect to pay considerably more.

PROLIFERATION OF TOUR OPERATORS

Formerly, one had to have a special "in" or connection to find a way of getting to China. By 1988, however, China seemed to be dealing with anyone and everyone in the travel business, and visas were granted through a wide range of outlets, from the Smithsonian Institution to local garden clubs, to the travel agent down the block. In December 1986, some 400

Guilin Holiday Inn hotel

travel agents were invited to Beijing to attend the second China International Tourist Conference, sponsored by NTA. Subsequently, China tourism began to transform its role from that of a passive monopoly to a more aggressive international marketing posture. In 1988, NTA declared an international year of tourism in Beijing.

OFFICIAL TRAVEL CONTACTS IN THE PRC

Until 1983, authority for granting permission to visit China was vested almost exclusively in a discrete circle of central agencies in Beijing, the largest among them for tourist travel (with 172 branches and sub-branches throughout China) being the China International Travel Service (CITS, also known by its Chinese acronym LUXINGSHE). In 1983, a number of provincial and municipal branches of CITS also acquired the right to issue visas to foreign groups. Foreign groups receiving visas from local authorities are required to spend a reasonable portion of their touring within that locality (usually about a week), although other provinces as well as China's three major international entry/exit points—Beijing, Shanghai, and Guangzhou—could be included in these itineraries, Initial applications from all organizations, groups, and individuals must receive approval (usually transmitted in the form of an invitation to visit China) from one of these national agencies (or from one of their duly authorized branches).

China International Travel Service. The China International Travel Service carries out two functions. On the international level, it authorizes travel to China for general tour groups, i.e., those that come to China for nonprofessional reasons. On the domestic level, it makes all arrangements for travel within the People's Republic of China. Most tour groups should apply through a Chinese diplomatic mission abroad. The CITS national headquarters is a 6 East Chang'an Avenue, Beijing. (CITS branch offices are listed at the end of individual city sections in this book.)

In the mid-1980s, CITS began to open a number of representative offices around the world (including New York, London, and Paris), although the role of these offices was largely informational, with booking requests referred to commercial agents. CITS accredits (usually on an annual basis) a number of private travel agencies in Japan, Canada, the US, Latin America, and Europe, and through them, approves travel applications for general and specialized groups.

China Youth Travel Service. The CYTS Tours Corporation, an affiliate of the All-China Youth Federation, emerged in the mid-1980s as the second largest tour operator in China (after CITS). CYTS is uniquely authorized to offer discounted tours to youth groups under age 30 (minimum 15 per group). Youth programs include general tours, youth camps, and educational programs. But CYTS, through aggressive and creative marketing, has also become a leader in adult and specialized tour categories (e.g., law and medicine) where less expensive tours are also available. CYTS has 40 branches in China, as well as liaison offices in Tokyo and Hong Kong. Its head office is at 23-B Dongjiaomin Xiang, Beijing (tel: 54-1531, 54-1704; telex: 20024 CYTS CN; fax: 512-0571; cable: CHINAYTS).

Other PRC Agencies Authorizing Specialized Travel. A variety of organizations in China outside of the CITS sphere issue invitations to foreign delegations, although relatively few of these exchanges require parallel arrangements through government (or quasi-official) channels at the other end. Since 1979, a growing number of such exchanges have come about as the result of private initiatives. Cultural, scientific, and commercial exchanges that offer Chinese professional organizations contacts with their counterparts in the West and promise to broaden access to information in fields of mutual endeavor are being approved by Chinese bodies on local and provincial levels as well as on the national level. But while a growing number of foreign groups now visiting China bear an "official" label, few such delegations can expect any financial underwriting from the Chinese side. They are usually expected to pay their own way, generally on the same basis as a conventional tourist group.

The following PRC organizations (all with main offices in Beijing) have been among the most active in sponsoring visits by special-interest foreign groups:

▣ *All-China Sports Federation* (9 Tiyuguan Road, tel: 75-0624). This organization, through its affiliate, China International Sports Travel, invites foreign athletic teams, hosts sports-related private tours, sponsors international competitions in China, and authorizes television and film coverage of athletic events in China.

▣ *All-China Federation of Trade Unions* (10 Fuxingmenwai Avenue, tel: 36-7631). The ACFTU has been notably active as a sponsor of foreign trade union delegations of both leadership and rank-and-file composition.

▣ *All-China Women's Federation* (Dengshikou, tel: 55-4931). In addition to sponsoring visits of foreign women's groups to China, the Women's Federation has sent two delegations to the US, including one arriving in 1984 as guests of the US-China People's Friendship Association.

▣ *China Council for the Promotion of International Trade* (Fuxingmenwai Avenue, tel: 86-7504). The CCPIT's approximate counterpart in the US is the US-China Business Council. It arranges exchanges of business and commercial delegations.

▣ *Chinese Medical Society* (42 Dongsi Street West, tel: 55-0394). This agency invites medical delegations and is one of China's most active sponsors of visiting delegations from Western countries.

▣ *State Education Commission* (37 Damucang Lane, tel: 65-8731). This agency invites educational administrators as well as delegations from individual schools and universities.

▣ *Chinese People's Association for Friendship with Foreign Countries (YOUXIE)* (1 Taijichang Road, tel: 54-3190). This association invites cultural figures, orchestras, artists, dance companies, and other groups concerned with art, literature, and other cultural interests. YOUXIE maintains a consultative relationship with China-friendship associations in other countries, and sends its own delegations to North America and Western Europe for the purpose of promoting cultural and "people-to-people" ties with China. YOUXIE's staff is acknowledged as among the most polished of China's representatives assigned to host foreigners.

▣ *Overseas Chinese Travel Service* (2 Chongwenmen Xi Road; tel: 75-4912). This organization handles all travel requests and arrangements for overseas Chinese, whether born in China or not. Visitors of Chinese origin are generally accorded trips of longer duration. While in China, they may travel in smaller groups or singly, particularly if the purpose is to spend time with relatives.

PRC DIPLOMATIC MISSIONS ABROAD

In general, PRC diplomatic missions deal with governmental exchanges rather than with private travel requests, although special sections have been added in recent years to assist in travel arrangements for commercial

---

Directory of Major PRC Embassies Abroad

ARGENTINA ◾ Crisologo Larralde 5349, 1430 Buenos Aires

AUSTRALIA ◾ 247 Federal Highway, Watson, Canberra, A.C.T. 2602

BELGIUM ◾ 443-445, Avenue de Tervuren, 1150 Brussels

BRAZIL ◾ Embaixad Republica Popular da China, SES-Av. Das Nacoes-Lote 51, Brasilia, DF

CANADA ◾ 415 St. Andrews St., Ottawa, Ontario K1N 5H3

COLOMBIA ◾ Calle 71, No. 2A-41, Bogotá

DENMARK ◾ Oregaardsalle #25, DK 2900 Hellerup, Copenhagen

FRANCE ◾ 11 Avenue Georges V, 75008 Paris

FEDERAL REPUBLIC OF GERMANY ◾ Kurfuerstenallee 12, 5300 Bonn-Bad Godesberg

ITALY ◾ Via Bruxelles 56, 00198 Rome

JAPAN ◾ 4-33, Moto-Azabu, 3-Chome, Minato-ku, Tokyo

MEXICO ◾ Avenida Rio Magdalena 172, Colonia Villa Alvaro, Obregon, Mexico 20 DF

NETHERLANDS ◾ Adriaan Goehooplaan 7, The Hague

NORWAY ◾ Tuengen Alle 2B, Vinderen, Oslo 3

PERU ◾ Jr. José Granda 150, San Isidro, Lima

SWEDEN ◾ Bragevagen #4, 11426 Stockholm

SWITZERLAND ◾ Kalcheggweg 10, 3006 Berne

UNITED KINGDOM ◾ 49/51 Portland Place, London W1N 3AH

UNITED STATES ◾ 2300 Connecticut Ave., NW, Washington, DC 20008

VENEZUELA ◾ Qinta "El Oriente," Avenida El Paseo, Prados Del Este, Caracas

---

visitors and overseas Chinese. Since permission to visit China can be secured only from an appropriate host organization in Beijing (and not from a PRC embassy), inquiries regarding general travel—especially in the case of first trips—are likely to be redirected by the embassy to CITS. Chinese embassies issue visas, but only upon prior authorization from the PRC body or agency sponsoring the travel.

PRC diplomatic representatives may occasionally grant appointments to professional groups wishing to visit China. They may be helpful in framing a proposal, indicating the appropriate agency to write to in Beijing, and informally evaluating the merits of the application.

PRC Embassy in the US. The Embassy of the People's Republic of China in the United States plays an important role in evaluating travel and trade proposals. Once an invitation has been received from the host organization in China, the Washington office will also process visas. A copy of trade or travel proposals sent to China should be forwarded to the Embassy, with a covering request to discuss the proposal further.

The Commercial Section of the Embassy can provide assistance in making introductions in China and in ascertaining whether there is interest in the kind of business proposed.

PRC Consulates in the US. In 1988, the PRC had consular offices in Chicago, Houston, Los Angeles, San Francisco, and New York. Their addresses are:

Consulate General of the PRC, 104 South Michigan Avenue, Chicago, IL 60603, tel: (312) 346-0287.

Consulate General of the PRC, 3417 Montrose Boulevard, Houston, TX 77006, tel: (713) 524-4311.

Consulate General of the PRC, 502 Shatto Place, Ste. 300, Los Angeles, CA 90020, tel: (213) 380-2507.

Consulate General of the PRC, 1450 Laguna Street, San Francisco, CA 94115, tel: (415) 563-4857.

Consulate General of the PRC, 520 12th Avenue, New York, NY 10036, tel: (212) 330-7409.

PRC Consulates in Canada. The PRC has consular offices in Toronto and Vancouver. Their addresses are:

Consulate General of the PRC, 240 St. George Street, Toronto, ON M5R 2P4, tel: (416) 964-7575.

Consulate General of the PRC, 3380 Granville Street, Vancouver, BC V6H 3K3, tel: (604) 736-3910.

CHINA TRAVEL OPTIONS: GROUP TOURS AND INDEPENDENT TRAVEL

Group travel is the major mode of tourism in China. Preformed groups, traveling on a fixed itinerary and adhering to planned daily activities—including packaged sightseeing, dining, and hotel arrangements—make the most efficient use of China's limited tourist and travel facilities. Despite the apparent limitations of moving about in the company of 20 or 30 other travelers, China tour groups undoubtedly see more of the country—and at a lower cost—than would be possible on an unplanned, individual jaunt through the country. Even for local Chinese, travel within China is a formidable undertaking, with endless hours spent on getting travel information, on purchasing tickets, and on travel time itself. To these endemic problems, the foreign traveler must add the complications of pursuing these arrangements without much in the way of bilingual assistance or advice and must be prepared to arrive at a given destination without any advanced assurance of private transportation, a hotel room, or even a bilingual sightseeing program.

Nevertheless, there will remain those who regard travel in groups as anathema no matter what the relative advantages. Also, a variety of considerations—time constraints, special itinerary requirements, or the special personal or professional interests of a given China trip—might make group travel impractical or inappropriate. China has itself begun to recognize these realities in international travel and has, since 1983, begun to make formal provision for independent (or FIT) travel for foreign tourists. Costs for this mode of travel, although not prohibitive, can be substantially higher than for group travel and rather more time must be spent in advance planning, especially if a guide/interpreter is requested and if travel is contemplated during China's high season. But, by 1985, individual travel had become a viable option to group touring in China, opening new dimensions for exploration, discovery, and interchange.

CHOOSING A GROUP TOUR TO CHINA

Today, travelers seeking to visit China as tourists may do so simply by purchasing space from one of the hundreds of travel agents around the world now authorized to form China tour groups. For those willing to travel as part of an organized tour, the procedures are no more complex than for any long-range excursion. In some ways they are simpler, since all itineraries, hotels, meals, and sightseeing arrangements are included in the package and are standard for all participants in a given tour.

Genuine savings can accrue for China travelers choosing the group option: Depending on the package selected, group participants may save more than 50% of the cost they could expect to pay were they to follow the same route on their own. Moreover, savings in time and energy in China are not to be overlooked: the provision of prebooked hotel space, scheduled sightseeing programs, intercity transfers, dining plans, and ubiquitous attention from Chinese guides and interpreters can spare the China visitor several hours a day that might otherwise be expended on logistical hassles. It may well require another decade at least for China to build up a travel infrastructure and service sector capable of accommodating large numbers of individual foreign travelers. Until then, group travel will continue to offer a rational alternative for getting a look at China.

Indeed, most travelers in the 1980s will continue to visit China as part of a prearranged, organized tour group.

Groups usually consist of between 12 and 50 people and follow a fixed itinerary that includes from three to six cities. Tours spend as little as two days to as much as four weeks in China; in addition, most flight schedules include stopovers in Tokyo, Hong Kong, or other cities in Asia.

GROUP TRAVEL OPTIONS

Within the guidelines established by CITS, tours have become sufficiently varied in itinerary, cost, and duration to satisfy virtually every interest in China touring. Before signing up for one of the many trips now offered by airlines, travel agencies, and friendship organizations, it is advisable to do a little research on tours available during the desired time of travel. A careful assessment of your own interests and expectations, combined with knowledge of the options open to you, should enable you to select an itinerary that comes close to matching your "ideal" China trip.

Important variables in selecting a tour include the cities on the itinerary, the theme, if any, of the tour, time of year, length of time spent in China, international routings, and post-tour options. Tour costs, which used to be as predictable as the tours themselves, have lately become a major variable. Most group airfares are standardized, although the growing competitiveness of trans-Pacific routings can yield appreciable savings to the alert traveler. But "cheap" is a relative term, and many prospective travelers will remain unmoved over "bargain basement" packages that still hover around $2,000. Nothing can change the fact that a China trip must almost always involve travel over considerable distances, or the fact that in China most prices charged to foreigners are regulated by government agencies to ensure a fair return for the country.

Most general tours follow common itineraries (i.e., Beijing, Shanghai, Xi'an, Guilin, Guangzhou, and one or two other large east coast cities). In the mid-1980s, with the choice of cities steadily expanding beyond 500, many itineraries began to exhibit more variety and geographical range, with several pursuing specific themes (such as China's cuisine or folkcrafts) or fields of interest (archeology, education, medicine). A development in the opposite direction was the "mini-itinerary" trend, featuring tours of 6–12 days, with most visiting Beijing, Shanghai, and one or two other cities.

Types of Itineraries. Tour operators and travel agencies receive annual tour allocations from CITS, with authorizations usually given 9–15 months in advance. The final decisions as to itineraries in China are in the hands of CITS and subject to change (by them) at any time. While most groups cannot be 100% certain of their exact itineraries until they arrive in China (and sometimes not even then), tour allocations do specify departure dates, length of stay in China, and the number of days allotted to each city.

"Standard" itineraries range from 12 to 21 days in China and encompass three to five cities. Most tours include Beijing, although a recent CITS innovation is the "regional tour"—a euphemism for tours that skip Beijing altogether. The most common PRC entry and exit points and, thus, the first and/or last stops on most itineraries, are Beijing, Shanghai, and Guangzhou. CITS arranges all travel connections, hotel accommodations, meals, and most excursions. It is important to note, however, that CITS has become less eager in helping passengers make personal or professional contacts in the course of a tour, leaving tourists to their own devices for such purposes.

Most moderately priced tours follow the "east coast" itinerary, including Shanghai, Nanjing, Guangzhou, and another of the cities along the coastal route, such as Hangzhou, Wuxi, or Suzhou. Popular elements in more lengthy (and somewhat more costly) itineraries include Xi'an, the Silk Route region (Xinjiang and Gansu), Inner Mongolia, Yunnan (including Xishuangbanna), and cruises through the Yangtse River Gorges. However, as tourism has expanded in China, so has the range of sites open to foreigners. Cities and regions previously closed, such as Tibet, are opening their doors. Although first-time visitors to China will probably not want to miss Tian'anmen Square, the Great Wall, or Shanghai's exuberant street life, travelers with special interests (such as educators, health-care specialists, or archeologists), or with a penchant for exotic scenery or adventure, will want to take advantage of one of the alternative itineraries now available.

SAMPLE ITINERARIES

It is impossible here to detail all the itineraries now listed by CITS. The following sample routings will, however, give an idea of what to expect—and what to look for:

Standard "No Frills" China Tour (via Hong Kong)
18 days (15 in China)
Day 1—Depart San Francisco for Hong Kong (cross international date line)
Day 2—Arrive Hong Kong
Day 3—Fly to Beijing
Day 4–16—Travel in China: Beijing (4 days), Nanjing (3 days), Suzhou (3 days), Shanghai (2 days), Guangzhou (1 day)
Day 17—Depart Guangzhou via train to Hong Kong
Day 18—Depart Hong Kong for San Francisco

"Silk Road" Tour
20 days (19 in China)
Day 1—Depart New York for Beijing (cross international date line)
Day 2—Arrive Beijing

Day 3–19—Travel in China: Beijing (4 days), Xi'an (3 days), Lanzhou (2 days), Ürümqi (4 days), Shanghai (3 days)
Day 20—Depart Shanghai for New York

Special-Interest or Professional Tours. Some tour operators arrange tours in China for those with a particular interest, profession, or specialty to pursue. In these tours, a proportion of the time in the PRC is spent in meetings with professional counterparts for visiting institutions or sites of particular interest. The following is a sample itinerary for an archeological tour.

Archeological Tour
21 days (18 in China)
Day 1—Depart San Francisco for Tokyo (cross international date line)
Day 2—Arrive in Tokyo
Day 3—Tokyo
Day 4—Depart Tokyo for Beijing
Day 4–21—Travel in China: Beijing (4 days), Taiyuan (2 days), Kaifeng (2 days), Luoyang (2 days), Xi'an (4 days), Datong (2 days), Beijing (1 day)
Day 21—Depart Beijing for Tokyo
Day 22—Depart Tokyo for San Francisco

Tours for the Adventurous. One of the more salutary developments in China travel during the 1980s was a shift toward active modes of tourism, including camping, trekking, mountain climbing, wilderness exploration, and cross-country bicycling. Although retaining a group format and offering little if any savings over conventional group tours, these programs nevertheless offer far greater access to the Chinese countryside and to China's vast, rarely seen heartland. A growing number of these outdoor programs are being organized by the Chinese Mountaineering Association (9 Tiyuguan Road; tel: 75-3746) and its parent organization, the China Sports Service Company (6A Shangyuancun, Xizhimenwai; tel: 8316375), both headquartered in Beijing. Authorized foreign agents include Mountain Travel (Albany, California), China Passage (New Jersey), Adventure Travel Centre (Sydney), and the Society for Anglo-Chinese Understanding (London).

In 1981, the Xinhui Summer Camp opened in southern Guangdong Province, becoming China's first such facility for overseas youth and students. Initially intended for ethnic Chinese youth from the US and Canada, a three-week stay at the camp—which offers courses in Chinese language and culture plus a two-week tour of China—comes to US$1,630 (including the cost of travel between Hong Kong and Xinhui). Information about the camp is available from CTS or the Hong Kong Travel Bureau.

TOURING CHINA ON YOUR OWN

A foreign encounter in the Chinese countryside

In 1983, China raised the curtain on individual tourism. Addressing a tourism policy conference in October 1982, Han Kehua, director of China's National Tourism Administration, stated that China would begin accepting applications for visits by individual tourists with a view to expanding the proportion of individual tourists to 20–30% of China's total tourist volume by 1990 and to 30–40% by the end of the century. The vast majority of China's 1.5 million foreign tourist visits in 1987 were accounted for by group tour participants.

In the late 1980s, there were two distinct avenues available for foreign individual travel in China. The first method is the formal approach, through the auspices of CITS. CITS treats applications for individual travel in the same way it arranges travel for groups: itineraries are applied for in advance, CITS responds with a fixed schedule and price, the trip is paid for, and the visa issued. It is now possible to complete this process within two weeks, applying to CITS direct (through its offices in Beijing, Hong Kong, New York, or London) or through its travel-agent representatives.

For those who cannot (or will not) be pinned down in advance to a fixed schedule in China, there remains the quasi-sanctioned, "freelance" approach. This method is best begun in Hong Kong, where an individual visa (usually to Guangzhou or Beijing) is readily obtainable from CITS, CTS, CYTS, or a number of private agencies now issuing such visas. One-month tourist visas can also be issued by any Chinese consulate if one has a roundtrip air ticket or reservations at a hotel in China, providing that the trip does not take place during September and October, the peak travel season. There are also tour operators who can complete the necessary forms for you, for a modest fee. Obtaining the first sanctioned foothold within China is vital. From that point onward, authorizations and connections to other "open cities" in China are readily obtainable.

In 1988, a new travel option presented itself: Hertz International and CTS (Macau) will be promoting self-drive tourism packages in Guangdong and Guangxi provinces.

PLANNING AN INDEPENDENT CHINA TRIP

Along with the new freedom of individual travel comes the problem of deciding where to go, how long to stay there, what to see, and how to budget your money so that you can accomplish all that you want. For this reason, prior research and planning for your China trip becomes essential. First, think about the kinds of things you want to see: beautiful landscapes or gardens, historical relics, contemporary city life, life in the countryside, or pursuits of special interests. Of course you can see mixtures of these things or just pick a few places and see whatever there is to see without any specific goals in mind.

China is a very large country with great variations in living patterns, customs, and architecture, even among localities that may be only 50 miles apart. Thus, China's surprising parochialism allows you to see a variety of things within a relatively small radius, thus cutting down enormously on travel time and expense. Interesting groupings of cities would include the Shanghai, Hangzhou, Suzhou area; the Beijing, Tianjin, Chengde area; or the Luoyang, Xi'an, Kaifeng area. Each area has a unique scope and special appeal while still being varied enough to satisfy almost any general interest in China. For example, those whose interest is ancient history might want to visit the last group of cities along with Beijing. Fujian is one of China's most interesting provinces in terms of architecture and cities that still retain the aura of "old China." Beijing has virtually everything, so any amount of time spent there is bound to be rewarding. If your interest is beautiful landscapes and gardens, there is Hangzhou, Wuxi, Suzhou, Guilin, and the Taishan and Huangshan mountain areas. Huangshan is recommended only for the more adventurous, although it is easily one of the most beautiful places on earth. Kunming to the southwest, the Emei mountains, and the gorges of the Yangtse River are also recommended. If you seek a feel for old-world, untouched China, then smaller, less traveled cities are recommended. But be forewarned: these are also the difficult places to travel to and in, especially for those who do not speak Chinese. Wherever you choose to go, you can always make on-the-spot changes in your itinerary by acquiring visa extensions or travel passes or, if the city is on the "open" list, by merely purchasing a ticket. However, it's always best in China to plan ahead.

In general, the number of days spent in each city depends on how hard you want to push yourself, how much you want to see, and, of course, what means of transportation is used (arranging to take long-distance intercity trains by night can save hotel expenses and will provide more time in the cities themselves). As a general guide, one should allot a minimum of three days to Beijing, three days to Shanghai, two days to Xi'an, and two days to most other cities.

INDIVIDUAL TRAVEL
THROUGH CITS

As of early 1985, CITS was granting visas to individuals under its new "China-to-FIT" (Foreign Independent Travel) program. The following conditions apply:

1. Individual tourists must be in possession of a valid visa authorized by CITS and issued through a Chinese embassy or consular office (see listing above). Applications for such visas should be submitted (through a CITS overseas branch, an authorized CITS agent, or a PRC diplomatic mission) at least six weeks prior to the requested date of entry.

2. The proposed itinerary, with all dates, domestic connections, and cities requested, must be submitted and approved in advance of departure.

3. Advance deposits and payments for certain services indicated by the itinerary (e.g., hotels, intercity transportation, etc.) may be required. (See "Costs," below, for types of packages available.)

CITS officials indicate that each application will be considered on its merits subject to availability of hotels, domestic flights, interpreters, etc. To ensure speedy approval, applicants might do well to follow certain paths of least resistance that apply to China travel in general: try to avoid May, September, and October, the three most congested months for China travel; plan to use air connections where available for travel between Chinese cities, requesting train travel ("soft seat") for shorter links (under 500 km.) only.

Finally, travelers should note that CITS does not engage in the setting-up of professional or business meetings for visitors to China. Individual tourists are not expressly prohibited from engaging in such activities, but any special arrangements in this regard must be managed by the visitors themselves. As of 1988, all cities open to tourism are open to foreigners traveling independently (see p. 52 for list of open cities).

China travel contacts who may be consulted for further details on individual travel are listed in the section "From Your Country to China."

VISA APPLICATION (FACSIMILE) FOR CHINA

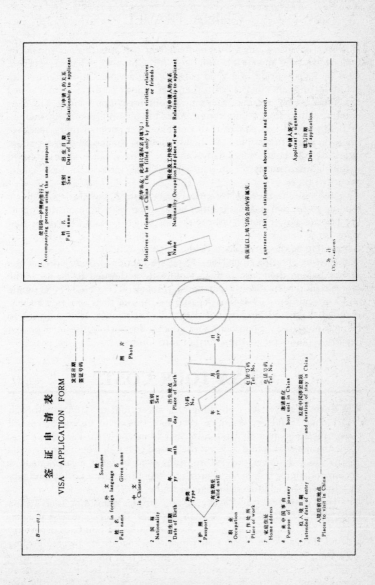

"FREE-LANCE"
CHINA TRAVEL

However impulsive one's reasons for going to China are, it should be understood that anyone planning to visit China for whatever purpose must be in possession of a valid passport and a valid Chinese entry visa before setting out. Since visas (other than transit permits) are not issued at China's border crossings, they must be obtained prior to entry. Travelers entering China from Hong Kong can readily obtain a visa to Guangzhou or Beijing usually as part of their purchase of a minimal tourist package (train or plane tickets plus 1–2 nights' hotel accommodations) for those cities. Tourist visas are normally valid for 30 days, but may be extended within China, usually for an additional 30-day interval, at local Public Security offices.

Visas specify the city (or cities) to be visited, but this too is not a binding restriction as long as other cities to be visited are on the "open" list (see above). Finally, visitors to most open cities should note that many sites outside of these cities may require a special travel permit (obtainable at the city's main Public Security office).

Visitors entering from Hong Kong are cautioned to ensure that the agency issuing their visa is in fact officially authorized to do so. If the visa has not been directly purchased through CTS or CITS, a simple check for authenticity before departure at one of their offices is recommended. It should also be noted that day trips into areas adjacent to Hong Kong (e.g., Shenzhen) and Macao do not constitute approved departure points for journeys further into China.

CHINA TOUR COSTS

There is as yet no such thing as a cheap tour to China—although competitive factors since 1980 have begun to impose downward pressure on both land costs in China and trans-Pacific airfares. Other variables affecting costs are the season of travel, length of time spent in the PRC, distances traveled in China (and by what means), grade of accommodations, number and length of stopovers outside China, and type of trip (i.e., special-interest or general tour).

Tour operators, travel agencies, and airlines sponsoring tours to the PRC will provide a listing of their trips for the upcoming year upon request. These listings, as a rule, include dates and points of departure, a detailed breakdown of the tour itineraries, and prices. Before deciding on a tour, you should find out what is included in the package and what is not. Since airfares have undergone frequent and sudden revisions in recent years, you should double-check all posted fares. (This rule also applies to prices cited in the *Guidebook*.)

GROUP LAND COSTS

When tour operators receive their group allocations for the PRC, they also receive a price tag from CITS covering all land costs in China. Hotel accommodations, three meals daily, tour escorts, and all surface and air transportation in China are arranged by CITS and included in the price of the package.

For 1988, land costs included in China tour offerings varied considerably—from a low of about $1,500 for 14 days in China (an average of $86 per day) to as much as $4,400 for 21 days, including a Yangtse River cruise ($209 per day). Tours that include Tibet can cost even more—up to $350 per day. Prices for the entire package may naturally vary among tour operators, owing to overhead and profit factors as well as actual costs for services provided. While standard CITS land charges to tour operators held fairly steady during the mid-1980s, the cost of "extra" services such as Great Wall excursions or "deluxe"-level Yangtse cruises placed upward pressure on prices. Moreover, many tour operators have opted to upgrade to newly available deluxe-standard hotels, thereby almost doubling the cost of accommodations. The "pinch" was most noticeable to seasoned China travelers from the 1970s who had grown accustomed to China's bargain rates. However, a tourist's day in China still costs less than it might in Tokyo or even Hong Kong.

Single-Occupancy Supplements. Hotel accommodations assigned by CITS are allocated on a double-occupancy basis. Single rooms are available at a surcharge of about $35 per day, although they cannot always be guaranteed in advance. Many tour operators advise passengers to request single occupancy upon arrival in each city. If space is available, the surcharge can be paid directly on the spot.

Items Not Included in the Tour Package Price. Land costs in China do not include meals or cultural events other than those arranged by CITS. Taxis and interpreter-escorts for individual sightseeing excursions are extra costs to expect (a car and driver can be hired for an entire day for about $40; daily fees for guides are about $35). Services of a personal nature, such as laundry, phone calls, and cables, are also charged as extra, as are alcoholic beverages. Of course, souvenirs, handicrafts, antiques, and other items purchased in the PRC add to the cost of the tour.

Since tipping is not practiced in China, there is no need to budget for these outlays for the PRC segment of the journey.

Costs for Non-China Itinerary Segments. Costs for non-China segments of the group itinerary are often the major source of disparities in China tour prices. Travelers should ascertain from travel agents exactly what additional services and amenities are offered in conjunction with each tour.

Excess baggage charges, passport and visa costs, and airport and departure taxes (e.g., Tokyo International Airport User's Tax, about US$7.50, and Hong Kong Departure Tax, HK$100) are not usually included in the tour price. The following are approximate guidelines for what to expect on most tours:

Accommodations. For cities outside of China, most packages include deluxe accommodations on a double-occupancy basis. For extended stays in Tokyo and Hong Kong, individuals should plan on daily hotel costs of at least $110 and $95 respectively (double occupancy).

Meals. Outside of China, group meal arrangements vary. Most tour prices include an "American" breakfast each morning at the hotel. Some tours provide dinner as well (on a table d'hôte basis), or a banquet at each city visited. An occasional "welcome drink" is also provided. Service charges at hotels and restaurants used by the group are usually prepaid.

Transportation. Transfers to and from airports and hotels are, as a rule, included in the tour price, providing tour group travelers utilize group air reservations. Individual travel arrangements are usually left to tour members and, as is the policy in China, there is no refund made for unused sightseeing and meal services. Group sightseeing excursions, including transportation and escorts, are provided as part of the overall cost of the tour. However, again, travelers must foot the bill for individual sightseeing, taxis, entrance fees, and personal interpreters as required.

COSTS FOR INDIVIDUAL TRAVEL

Costs for Individual Travel Hosted by CITS. Predictably, a host of variables apply to the pricing of individual itineraries, making generalized costs difficult to gauge in advance. The following are major internal factors that will have a bearing on costs in China:

—Open cities have been aligned into a three-tiered pricing system, with the "Golden Cities" of Beijing, Shanghai, Xi'an, and Guilin falling into the most expensive category (usually at least 10% higher than the others).

—Three general types of per-diem packages (with per-person double-occupancy hotel rates) are being offered:

1. *Full package:* Deluxe (or first-class) hotel, all meals, fully escorted sightseeing with private vehicle and a guide/interpreter. Cost: ca. US$165–240 per day per person (or roughly double the cost of group travel).

2. *Half package:* Deluxe (or first-class) hotel, all meals, half-day escorted sightseeing. Cost: ca. $100–150 per day per person.

Chinese opera

3. *"Mini" package:* Deluxe (or first-class) hotel, breakfasts, transfers only. Cost: ca. $55–90 per day per person. In the mid-1980s, the mini-package program was available for such cities as Beijing. Shanghai, Guangzhou, Xi'an, Nanjing, Guilin, Tianjin, Hangzhou, and Kunming. Most hotels used in those cities now have local CITS staff on hand to provide domestic travel bookings, interpreters, local sightseeing, and other services, which can be arranged and paid for on the spot.

The following are other important variables to account for when costing out an individual journey in China:

◼ There may be some latitude in the selection of hotels, although the choice will usually be limited to those in the higher priced categories (i.e., deluxe or first-class). But even within these echelons, individual hotel rates can vary by 50% or more (for current hotel rates, see hotel listings within individual city sections of the *Guidebook*).

◼ Intercity air (or rail) fares must be added to the above prices (for sample domestic airfares, see below).

◼ The arrangements for travel to and from China are of course the responsibility of the traveler, for whom group-fare reductions would not apply.

◼ The number (and pairings) of persons traveling together on a given itinerary—be it 2 or 6 or 18—will also affect price, to the extent that they can be booked in hotels on a double-occupancy basis and that fixed charges for cars with drivers, guides, etc., can be apportioned out among the participants.

◾ The time of year becomes a price factor, since travel in winter months (December through March) may be discounted and premium rates charged for certain locales at certain times (such as Guangzhou during the spring and autumn trade fairs).

◾ Visa fees, airport taxis, and services not provided in the package will be billed extra.

Costs for Free-Lance China Travel. The cost of traveling in China on your own, as anywhere else, can vary greatly depending on the distances traveled, the class of travel, and the level of accommodations. In China, however, other variables may apply: prices often depend on your status in China, your racial features (that is, Asian or non-Asian), and your nationality. For the purposes of this book, we will only discuss costs for non-Asian tourists from the West. This is the most expensive category; those who do not fit into it may expect to get by for somewhat less.

It is possible to travel in China for as little as $20 per day (see "Budget Travel in China" below), all costs included. But this level of travel is not for everyone.

A more realistic average for freelance China travel would be $60 per day and up, including room, board, and transportation. On the other end of the scale, it is possible—and indeed very easy—to spend $150 per day (not including gifts and other incidentals). These costs are calculated on the basis of an individual traveler on a two-week stay and visiting three major and relatively far-flung cities, such as Beijing, Shanghai, and Xi'an. A longer stay becomes cheaper on a per-diem basis, as would, of course, a trip by two people sharing the same hotel room. Most hotels in China are now priced between $20–50 per room per night, although some have now gone as high as $130 or more and for those willing to sacrifice on amenities, there are budget hotels. Three meals per day taken in hotel dining rooms should total about $9, which is the standard rate charged to foreigners.

Travel between most major cities by train (soft-berth sleeper class) will average between $50 and $100 for a single journey and less if one travels by hard sleeper class. Within a city, the cost of getting around somewhat depends on how the city is laid out. For example, in Changsha or Shanghai it is relatively easy to get around by public bus or by foot. But in Xi'an, most of the major tourist sites are outside the city, and in different directions from each other, almost obliging the short-term visitor to hire taxis. A similar situation prevails in Beijing, although at least there are inexpensive buses that connect to outlying areas.

AIRFARES

Group Inclusive Tour Fares (GIT). The China tour package price is usually broken down into the cost of airfare, land costs in China, and non-China stopovers and options. Most airfare prices quoted by tour sponsors are based on a Group Inclusive Tour (GIT) economy fare, which requires that a minimum of 10 persons travel together for at least 14 days and for not more than 35 days. The group must remain intact until the last stopover point in Asia. Passengers are allowed individual stopovers on the route home at no extra cost, providing they do not travel beyond their final Asian group destination or exceed the 35-day limit.

As of 1988, GIT fares from the US West Coast ranged from $1,203 (to and from the PRC during off-peak season) to $1,600 (for a standard San Francisco–Tokyo–China–Hong Kong–San Francisco routing during peak tourist season — June 1 to October 31). GIT fares for Pacific routings from the US East Coast are roughly $350 higher (to cover the "add-on" cost of travel to the West Coast).

Budget Fares. Since 1981, a variety of low-cost budget fares for groups were offered by the major airlines with direct trans-Pacific routes to China (e.g., CAAC, United, Northwest, and JAL). Budget fares are available to individuals as well as to groups, but carry more restrictions than GIT fares. For example, stopovers are not permitted, reservations are not accepted later than seven days or earlier than 21 days prior to departure, and cancellations are subject to a hefty 50% penalty. As of October 1987, the roundtrip budget (APEX) airfare between San Francisco and Beijing was $1,249 during low season (from November 1–March 30), and $1,311 during high season (from April 1–October 31); between New York and Beijing, $1,530 during low season, and $1,551 during high season. A few budget tour agencies purchase bulk tickets to Hong Kong and China, which can yield substantial savings.

Individual Inclusive Tour Fares (IIT). Those traveling in China with a tour group, but whose plans either before or after the China leg of the trip do not coincide with group-scheduled travel, are not eligible for GIT fares. (They should inform their travel agent *in advance* of their travel plans.) In many cases, the travel agent can arrange an Individual Inclusive Tour ticket (IIT) to accommodate separate itineraries outside of China. IIT fares are higher than GIT fares and vary according to mileage and stops. For example, if a traveler wishes to depart from San Francisco for Kyoto two weeks before the scheduled group departure and then join the group in Tokyo for the China leg of the trip, this can be arranged under an IIT fare plan. The cost (for off-peak travel) is approximately $200 more than the GIT fare. The 35-day maximum time also applies to IIT travelers. IIT travelers departing from the US East Coast should expect their fares to be about $400 higher than West Coast departures.

Economy Fares. Individual travelers such as business people might wish to take advantage of economy fares offered by most airlines. Economy-fare tickets carry few restrictions and are usually valid for up to a year. As of July 1988, the cost of a San Francisco–Beijing–San Francisco routing in this category was $1,900.

Excursion Fares to Hong Kong. An excursion-fare ticket to Hong Kong presents an option for the resourceful traveler who cringes at the high prices of airline tickets that often accompany all-inclusive tours. Excursion fares cover the cost of roundtrip airfare to Hong Kong—and nothing more. Many trans-Pacific carriers offer an "easy-fare" trip between San Francisco and Hong Kong for $850—considerably less than the GIT rate. Charter-flight operators were offering rates at as much as 10% below "easy fares," although scheduling restrictions and uncertainties must be weighed against these savings. Travel into China from Hong Kong can be arranged through a number of travel agents in Hong Kong who received group visas from CTS (see "The Hong Kong-China Connection," below).

BUDGET TRAVEL
IN CHINA

Rebecca Weiner

Travelling cheaply in China is more of a challenge than in many other countries because it means stepping out of an expected role. There's a chasm between what might be called "foreign guest rate"—planes, first-class trains, joint-venture hotels, and catered banquets—and "Chinese rate"—second class, multi-bed dorms, and ordering from the menu. Chinese people expect foreigners to travel foreign guest rate, along with the high Chinese officials, which means surrounding the tourist with buses and feasts, and protecting them from experiences that are too "exotic." Chinese rate serves most Chinese and the more intrepid tourists, and many Chinese are puzzled over how to regard foreigners who use it. Chinese rate means dealing with people who frequently do not speak English, hotels with no hot water, trains that are crowded, and sheets that are grey. And because Chinese-rate travel is not created for tourists, there are very few structures to ease the process. Once having purchased a hard-seat train ticket in order to have a chance to talk with the Chinese, the tourist may be drowned with questions from students of English or stared at by Chinese fellow-travelers.

The gap between Chinese- and foreign-guest rate is deliberate and huge. A soft-berth train ticket, for example, generally runs three times the hard-berth rate on the same train; a tourist hotel may cost 50 times the price of the Chinese hotels outside. And there is often nothing in between, nothing but four-star hotels and chilly dorm rooms, air-conditioned touring cars and carts. This two-caste system is enforced for a variety of reasons ranging from traditionally excessive care of guests, to lingering nervousness about tourists mixing with the rank and file, to a need for hard foreign currency. But whatever the reasons, the result is that there is virtually no middle level in Chinese travel. Those used to travelling mid-stream must choose up or down, paying for luxury or learning to pantomime and to wash in cold water.

Travelling Chinese rate has many rewards. It is possible travelling this way to see China for under $20 a day. More importantly, travelling Chinese rate means getting closer to the rhythms and emotions of China than a foreign guest rate tourist is likely to do. But just how much Chinese-rate travel is bearable is a matter of taste. Travel should be a pleasure, not an endurance contest. A tourist informed he could travel "Hard Seat" from Beijing to Ürümqi for the price of a movie ticket in New York replied, "Of course! But seeing a movie is a pleasure; travelling a thousand miles on Hard Seat is cruel and unusual punishment." The wise budget tourist comes prepared to enjoy meeting the Chinese people up close under travel conditions which are very different from those at home, but brings enough money to splurge now and again when the need for a private room is overwhelming.

This section will explore some of the special challenges and rewards of travelling Chinese rate for those who want to take the plunge. It may not always be easy, but it's always interesting, and guaranteed to create stories for the grandchildren.

EATING IN RESTAURANTS

There are no official restrictions on where foreigners can eat, but caution is advised. Chinese sanitary procedures are not as fastidious in the West, and most Western stomachs are not hardened to the variety of bacteria the Chinese encounter every day. When in doubt, check out the kitchen. Most smaller restaurants now use disposable balsawood chopsticks to prevent infection; it's a good idea to carry a pair of your own for places that don't. In most local restaurants the menu is on the wall. You pay when you order, buying tickets at one window and redeeming them for your food at another. It's a good idea to pay when you order even if not required, as a few restaurants are in the habit of grossly overcharging foreigners ("We gave you the large size. Whaddaya mean, you didn't order it? You already ate it!"). Even if no one in your party speaks Chinese, it's possible to get through a menu fairly well recognizing just a few characters:

肉	*ròu*, pork	牛肉	*niúròu*, beef	鸡	*jī*, chicken
鱼	*yú*, fish	豆腐	*dòfu*, tofu	菜	*cài*, vegetables
素菜	*súcài*, vegetarian	炒	*chǎo*, stir-fried	红烧	*hóng shāo*, braised
炸	*zhá*, deep-fried	汤	*tāng*, soup		

Either that, or look at other tables and point.

TRANSPORTATION

All plane travel is foreign guest rate, and given China's distances, is the only quick way to go. A flight from Beijing to Guangzhou, for example, runs about $160. A train-boat combination accomplishes the same trip for from $14 to $85, but takes six days. This means that tourists on a tight schedule cannot get cheaply from place to place. The rest of this section, dealing with surface travel only, is for tourists with some time to spare.

Surface travel includes trains, buses, riverboats, and coastal steamers, each under a separate authority. More Chinese want to travel than there are seats on trains and boats, and buying tickets on your own is complex. Unfortunately, unless you book your entire tour in advance through CITS (which charges exorbitant rates) it's impossible to buy or reserve tickets ahead, or even to buy roundtrip tickets. When you arrive in any town, the first order of business should be to find a hotel, and the next to make travel arrangements for your next destination. Only then can you be a relaxed tourist.

The easiest way to get tickets is to go to CITS. There are always English speakers, and they will buy tickets for you—three days in advance, for full price, in Foreign Exchange Certificates (FEC) only, plus a Y10 service charge per ticket. Travel counters in the large hotels will do the same, for a still-larger service charge. The alternative is to buy tickets yourself. It's cheaper and can be a sort of adventure, but can also be complicated and time-consuming. Before you go to buy tickets it's a good idea to ask other tourists or CITS how things are done in that town. In some cities, for example, train tickets are not sold at the train station, while hard class and soft class tickets may be sold at different addresses. In larger cities there may be special windows for foreigners and officials. If not, you'll have to brave the regular windows. Chinese lines can be shocking at first to those unfamiliar with sale day at Macy's; the best approach is to hold your breath and push. Once at the window, producing money and saying where you want to go is generally enough. If there are problems, in most any crowd there's at least one eager English-learner who'll be happy to translate.

Ticket prices are determined not only by class, but by who's buying. Non-Asian foreigners who do not work for China pay the highest rates, generally double the Chinese rate, payable in FEC only. Cashiers selling to foreigners on their own have been known both to ignore this rule, selling foreigners Chinese-rate tickets, and to abuse it, demanding triple or quadruple the Chinese rate. When travelling with local Chinese or with overseas Chinese, it is possible for one person to buy Chinese-rate tickets for a group. This can backfire, however. Zealous officials, especially on planes, have been known to confiscate Chinese-rate tickets held by foreigners.

Most budget tourists, when they can get tickets, prefer Hard Sleeper train tickets and 3rd or 4th class boat tickets. The differences between classes are:

Trains. Trains have five classes: Hard and Soft Sleeper, Hard and Soft Seat, and Hard Stand. Soft Sleeper (*ruǎnwò* 软卧) is four cushioned bunks to a private cabin with luggage space above. It is the only class where the train's loudspeakers can be shut off. Soft Seat (*ruǎnxì* 软席) is a car full of well-cushioned armchairs around tables with cheery plastic flowers. Both Soft classes have Western toilets at the ends of cars, are spanking clean, and have top service. But anyone Chinese who is not a top official is kept strictly out. A ride in Soft class guarantees separation from most Chinese people. Hard Sleeper (*yìngwò* 硬卧) is the preferred mode of middle-class Chinese travel. Padded bunks in three tiers fill most of the cars; a narrow aisle down one side has fold-out chairs and tables. Service staff bring hot water, but provide neither mugs nor toilet paper. If fellow passengers are rude, Hard Sleeper can be smoky or noisy, but it's generally not bad. Hard Seat (*yìngzuò* 硬座) is padded benches, generally overflowing with people standing in the aisles and chickens squawking in the luggage racks. Hard Seat in the daytime can be interesting, and, if you don't mind hawking and spitting or being asked a lot of questions, fairly pleasant. But Hard Seat at night, full of glazed eyes and heavy drinking, is only for the hardy or the financially desperate. Hard Stand (*zhànpiào* 站票), see below.

It can be difficult to buy Hard Sleeper train tickets, especially on short notice. One alternative is to buy a Hard Seat ticket and upgrade it on the train at the ticketmaster's bench, generally in car #8. Failing that, overnight passengers can spend a few *yuan* for a "tea seat" (*cházuò* 茶座), which means you get to have a seat to yourself in the dining car and drink cups of tea all night.

Riverboats have six classes. First Class is usually not sold to the public, consisting of two or three luxury cabins for the captain and visiting VIPs. Second Class has two beds, each with curtains, in a private, heated cabin, with a sink in the cabin and a Western toilet down the hall. First and second classes are cut off from the rest of the boat by iron bars. Third Class cabins have five bunk beds, heat, and a sink; Fourth Class cabins have ten beds, no heat, and no sink; and Fifth Class is one big cabin, with board beds and no linen.

Dispersed Seating (*sànxí* 散席), like Hard Stand on the trains, is a class created for people who need to travel but have no money and are willing to squeeze into the cracks. For prices so low they are essentially free, even by Chinese standards, passengers can and do sit in the halls and stairwells of the boats and unused freight cars of the trains, wrapped in quilts to keep warm in the winter and fanning themselves in the summer. Chinese etiquette would not permit foreigners to travel that way, and a few foreigners who have tried found themselves hustled onto Hard Sleeper, often at the expense of a Chinese person holding a legitimate ticket.

Oceangoing Boats have basically the same classes as the riverboats, except that Fifth Class has rentable linens and there is no Dispersed Seating.

ACCOMMODATIONS

Theoretically, Chinese law restricts foreigners to a list of state-approved hotels, most of which are both nicer and pricier than the Chinese ones. In practice, this law is strictly enforced in some areas but not in others. The best way to get a feel for an area is to walk up to a promising local hotel and ask for a room. Innkeepers know the lay of the land better than anyone, and if they give you a room, it's all right. It can be fascinating. Most local hotel-keepers speak no English, so communication becomes a challenging pantomime. Chinese inns may be outfitted with stone *kang* beds, bamboo walls, or single, communal fires around which all the guests gather at night. They are also generally under 1 *yuan* per bed. But on no account should pressure be put on innkeepers. They don't make the laws, and they face huge fines and loss of license if they take you in. All hotels listed in this guidebook are state-approved.

State-approved hotels (which are nearly always state-run) range from ratty to splendid, and vary in price by facilities and number of beds per room. In most large cities, there is a least one "cheap" hotel which has dorm beds for foreigners at under 10 *yuan* per night. In some, there is also a middle range of 2- and 3-bed rooms ranging from 20 to 40 *yuan* per bed. These hotels tend to become social centers for the international backpacking set, and one of the joys of budget travel is seeing again in Beijing the same group of Nigerians you swapped stories with in Wuhan. These hotels are listed under the heading "Budget Hotels" city by city in the China Tour section below.

Although some are quite nice, you should assume budget hotels will be spartan, with bunks and hall baths. It's a good idea to check the bed linen before retiring; if it hasn't been changed since the last guest, ask the service people to change it. Also, not all hotel clerks will volunteer information on the hotel's cheapest rooms, especially since reforms have based employee bonuses at some hotels on the total hotel income. It pays sometimes to take a few minutes to argue for a dorm bed if you want one.

In some cities there are neither state-approved dorms nor access to private inns. In that case, university guest houses are another option. Some require letters of introduction, some do not. Try calling the Foreign Affairs Office of a local college or university to ask if rooms are available. For this purpose, it is useful to request a general letter of introduction from any Chinese unit you may have access to, through a friend or job. Guest houses generally have fairly clean and quiet rooms for from 10 to 80 *yuan* a night. If all else fails, you may sometime have to spend full price for a Foreign Guest Rate room. In that case, bite the bullet and enjoy the color television.

Finally, a note on staying with families. Local laws will vary, and in some areas families can take in foreigners, sometimes with and sometimes without specific Public Security Bureau approval. Again, families will know the laws in their area. If invited by a family, it is appropriate to bring a gift. Something from your country or from some faraway part of China will be especially appreciated. But Chinese hospitality being what it is, you should take care that you are not more of a burden than the family has let on. In most areas, staying with families is still a bit out of the ordinary. If you are invited to a Chinese friend's hometown, unless the invitation is specifically to the house, you should expect to stay in a hotel.

FOREIGNERS AND OTHER FOREIGNERS

Foreigners are divided into price categories by race (Asian vs. non-Asian), and by status in China. Anyone working in China below a certain salary for at least six months gets a "white card," which allows payment in RMB at or near Chinese rates. Foreign students get student cards and even greater discounts. One white card-holder can generally spread the benefits around by picking up the tab at a restaurant or hotel, but tickets from place to place are harder. This may have some basis: transportation is heavily subsidized by the government, while hotels are not. There seems to be a feeling among many employees that it's all right for foreigners to escape the "foreign tax" at a hotel, but not on a train. There is reputedly a trade in forged white cards in Hong Kong, but reputedly also a network of Public Security Officers ready to catch anyone holding one.

Safety. Violent crime is virtually nonexistent in China, but theft is a large and growing problem. Budget tourists, on their own in local hotels and on the city buses, can be targets. A "safety pouch" for money and passport around the waist or neck is a good idea. Most budget hotels have lock-ups for valuables, and it's wise to use them. Most people in China are honest, but it's better to be safe than stranded.

WHEN TO GO

Choosing the time of year is probably the easiest thing to decide about your China trip. Of course, your personal schedule may make the choice for you. Otherwise, the chief factors to consider are climate, costs, Chinese holidays, and other seasonal events. Knowing travelers have made September and October the peak season in China owing mainly to the fine weather which prevails in most parts of the country at the time. Discounts and other incentives are now offered for "off" months—mid-November through mid-March.

CLIMATE

China, like the US, has a primarily temperate climate, with four distinct seasons. Similarly, China also encompasses a huge area, with temperatures and climatic conditions that vary across a wide spectrum of extremes. The north is bitterly cold in winter, while China's southern cities are sultry and humid in the summer months. As a rule, winter itineraries mercifully feature subtropical cities—like Guangzhou, Guilin, and Nanning—while northern cities—Harbin and Jilin, for example—are visited more often during the summer. Even the "temperate" city of Beijing (offered on most itineraries) can be uncomfortably hot in July and very cold in winter.

The following generalizations about China's climate can be made:

—Although rain and high humidity are common in summer throughout the PRC, the length of the rainy season is longer and the amount of rainfall considerably greater south of the Yangtse River.

—Winters are dry, particularly in the north and northeast where spring may also bring little rain.

Northeast. This area includes Shenyang and Harbin and comprises the huge northeast plain that extends some 960 km. (600 mi.) north-south. Summers are hot and dry, and winters bitterly cold; the climate overall is similar to that of Minnesota or southern Alberta.

North-Central. This region includes the middle and lower valley of the Yellow River, the intensively cultivated North China Plain, and the hills and mountains to the west. Cities in this area include Beijing, Zhengzhou, and Xi'an. Temperatures are roughly similar to those of Kansas and Nebraska, although there is year-round precipitation. Haze and dust storms can occur during late winter and early spring.

Southeast. The lower Yangtse Valley and the river's many tributaries are characterized by warm temperatures and substantial rainfall. Rice is grown in virtually all lowlands and the long growing season permits at least two crops a year in most regions. Climatic conditions are semitropical, comparable to the Gulf Coast (except that winter storms are rare). Summers are long, hot, and sticky, often subject to incessant rain. The fall is more pleasant, and winters are brief with cooler temperatures. Shanghai and Hangzhou are often overcast, damp, and drizzly during the winter.

HOLIDAYS AND SEASONAL EVENTS

China has only four official public holidays: January 1—New Year; May 1—International Labor Day; October 1–2—Anniversary of the Founding of the PRC; and Spring Festival—a three-day celebration of the traditional Chinese New Year, which occurs in January or February, according to cycles in the Chinese lunar calendar. Holidays in China are primarily occasions for family gatherings and outings and, apart from overseas Chinese, it is usually not worth planning one's trip to coincide with

TEMPERATURES AND PRECIPITATION IN CHINA

City	January	April	July	October
Mean Readings (minimum→maximum)				
Beijing				
°C	−10→1.7	6.2→20.5	21.7→31.7	6.7→20.5
°F	14→35	43→69	71→89	44→69
rainfall (in.)	.2	.7	9.6	.6
Shanghai				
°C	0.0→8.3	9.5→19.5	23.9→32.8	13.3→23.9
°F	32→47	49→67	75→91	56→75
rainfall (in.)	1.9	3.6	5.8	2.9
Guangzhou				
°C	9.5→18.3	18.3→25.0	25.0→32.8	19.5→29.5
°F	49→65	65→77	77→91	67→85
rainfall (in.)	.9	6.8	8.1	3.4
Guilin				
°C	5.0→13.1	15.0→23.4	24.5.→33.9	16.7→27.2
°F	41→55	59→74	76→93	62→81
rainfall (in.)	1.6	9.4	8.0	2.6
Changsha				
°C	1.7→7.2	13.3→21.1	25.6→34.5	15.0→23.9
°F	35→45	56→70	78→94	59→75
rainfall (in.)	1.9	5.7	4.4	3.0
Wuhan				
°C	1.1→7.8	12.8→20.5	25.6→33.9	15.6→23.4
°F	34→46	55→69	78→93	60→74
rainfall (in.)	1.8	5.8	7.0	3.1
Zhengzhou				
°C	−6.6→4.4	10.0→21.1	21.1→32.2	10.0→21.1
°F	20→40	50→70	70→90	50→70
rainfall (in.)	.4	.9	7.0	.7
Nanjing				
°C	−4.4→14.5	7.2→21.1	23.9→33.4	15.6→26.7
°F	24→58	45→70	75→93	60→80
rainfall (in.)	2.1	4.2	5.0	2.8
Shenyang				
°C	−16.7→6.6	7.2→12.8	21.7→25.6	3.3→14.6
°F	2→20	45→55	71→78	38→58
rainfall (in.)	.2	.8	9.2	1.0

nonpolitical holidays—although the crowded squares and parks generate a festive atmosphere, there is little in the way of organized public celebrations. In recent years, however, the government has been returning to formal public displays for the October First National Day and May Day. In Beijing especially these days are marked with considerable flourish and great public outpourings.

Traditional Western holidays such as Christmas have no official status in China and are generally not observed.

Beijing Holiday Inn Lido hotel lobby

III
GETTING TO
CHINA

VISA PROCEDURES
FOR CHINA TRAVEL

Persons seeking to enter China for the purpose of general tourism can do so without recourse to lengthy procedures or formalities. Valid PRC entry and exit visas are required of all persons traveling individually in China. PRC visas are usually authorized by an organ within China—PRC embassies and consulates abroad physically issue the visas, in most cases on direct instructions from the appropriate visa authority in China (e.g., CITS). But as of 1988, individuals can apply to PRC diplomatic offices directly for tourist visas.

By the mid-1980s, special restrictions continued to apply only to Western journalists (including photojournalists) and to citizens of a few countries that did not have full diplomatic ties with the PRC (e.g., as of 1988, South Korea, Israel, South Africa).

In a tentative but, perhaps, significant development, China began in late December 1984 to grant visas on the spot to foreigners arriving at Beijing Airport. A new visa office at the airport was added "to streamline the entry process for foreigners, especially those who wish to enter China as quickly as possible for business reasons." It remains unclear, however, whether the new policy applies to all business travelers as well as to tourists.

TOURIST VISAS

Tour Group Visas. Those traveling to China as part of a general tour group do not need to obtain an individual visa. Visas are granted to tours on a group basis, which means that the group's escort will be in possession of a "visaed manifest" listing the names and nationalities of all tour members. (Visa fees are now often included in the cost of the package.) Group visas for visiting the PRC are issued through the request of authorized China tour operators. The tour organizer or agent will supply prospective travelers with a Chinese visa application form (in duplicate, together with their passports) at a specified interval prior to departure (usually two months). Passports and applications are forwarded by the travel agent to the PRC embassy, whereupon approval is virtually automatic.

Individual Tourist Visas. Tourists planning to visit China on their own (that is, not as part of a pre-organized tour group) can usually apply for a visa through the travel agency from whom they are purchasing arrangements in China or through the Chinese consulate (see also below, "Touring China on Your Own"). Those making direct arrangements with a tourism authority in China can obtain PRC visa application forms from overseas CITS and PRC consular offices or from China Travel Service (CTS) offices in Hong Kong. Upon notification that a visa has been approved, visa forms should be submitted in duplicate, together with the applicant's passport, two passport photographs, and a processing fee ($7.00 for the US). Passports mailed to a PRC embassy are usually returned with a visa stamp in less than a week.

PROFESSIONAL AND
SPECIAL-INTEREST VISAS

In order to obtain visas for special-interest or professional (including business) visits, travelers must first secure an official invitation to visit the PRC. Such invitations may be in the form of a letter or telex, but they must be issued by a Chinese organization authorized to grant foreign visits—such as a Foreign Trade Corporation or one of its branches (see listing under Doing Business with China). Standard visas are issued for an initial stay of 30 days. Visas issued specifically for the Guangzhou Trade Fair are valid only in Guangzhou. These and other commercial visas can be extended should business circumstances require.

Acquiring Approval for Special-Interest Travel. Chinese approval of an application for special-interest travel (on the part of groups or individuals) will no doubt continue to rely on whether the applicants' interests or occupations have a clear counterpart in China and, by extension, on whether the Chinese counterpart seeks such an exchange.

In general, a short goodwill tour is the easiest to arrange. A wide variety of occupational groups has succeeded in gaining approval, with medical, educational, legal, and technical fields accounting for a significant share. Proposals that are vague, frivolous, or out-of-keeping with lifestyles in China will more than likely be rejected (or simply ignored).

Once a prospective group has been formed, a detailed letter requesting permission to visit China should be prepared and addressed to CITS or to a prospective PRC host organization. Letters should be submitted well in advance of the proposed time of departure; a one-year lead time is not unreasonable. The letter should include the following elements:

■ *Reason for the Visit.* Applicants should explain why, from the group's vantage point, they seek to make the trip; why the Chinese should invite this particular group; and the manner in which the trip will contribute to mutual understanding, friendship, and professional knowledge.

■ *One-Page Biographies of Participants.* Chinese travel authorities seek a clear sense of the composition and balance of a group and the relevance of each member to it. Biographies should be brief and should stress the applicant's work in professional or community organizations, as appropriate.

■ *Length and Time of Year of the Proposed Trip.* Inasmuch as most group visits to China last from two to three weeks, requests should be kept within these bounds. Proposals should include two alternate dates.

■ *Places to Be Visited.* Most groups, as a matter of course, travel to Beijing, Shanghai, and Guangzhou. Other cities commonly visited include Xi'an, Nanjing, Guilin, and Hangzhou. Requests to visit less frequented cities or regions should be rationalized in terms of the group's special focus.

■ *Requested Activities While in China.* Although a list of requested activities need not be exhaustive, proposals should logically include the kinds of institutions deemed relevant to the group's interest (e.g., universities, museums, hospitals, factories, historical sites). The more specific the list, the better, although the final itinerary will consist mainly of what's practicable from the Chinese end.

FROM YOUR COUNTRY TO CHINA

AUSTRALIA—CHINA TRAVEL

Measured by its population, both the volume and variety of Australia's exchanges with China are proportionally among the most extensive in the world. By the mid-1980s, some 60,000 Australians were visiting China annually, a total exceeded only by Japan and the United States. Just this past year, Australia's first Chinese National Tourist Office opened in Sydney. General tours to the PRC are conducted on a regular basis by the Australia-China Society, a China-friendship group that also sponsors cultural programs, trade symposia, and radio broadcasts. A news bulletin is published by the Society's Victoria branch (Fitzroy). An array of tour options, including bicycle tours and treks, is also provided by private travel agents. In mid-1984, Qantas and CAAC began operating nonstop services between Sydney and Beijing.

Australian-Chinese student exchanges have been ongoing since the early 1970s. Exchange agreements also exist between the Chinese and Australian Academies of Science.

CITS (Luxingshe) Representative in Australia ■ 55 Clarence Street, 11 Fl., Sydney. Tel: 294057.   Telex: AA 177886 CNTOS.

CANADA—CHINA TRAVEL

Canada established diplomatic relations with the PRC in 1970. Since then, successive governmental exchange agreements have been concluded annually. Canada sends only government personnel from various ministries on these missions. The government also monitors the student exchange program between the two countries. The Council for the Arts administers officially sponsored tours of Chinese cultural groups. In March 1978, in an event of major cultural significance, the Toronto Symphony Orchestra engaged in a major tour of Chinese cities. Additional exchanges are carried out through private channels, most of which are handled through Canada-China Friendship Associations active in 26 cities. Canadian Pacific Airlines organizes China tours for some 2,000 visitors annually. In 1988, an estimated 52,000 Canadians visited China, up 26.8% over 1987.

For Canadian business travelers, information on China trade is available from the China Desk, Department of External Affairs, East Asian Trade Division, 125 Sussex Drive, Ottawa, Ontario K1A 0G2; tel: (613) 992-6129. Free materials on Canada-PRC marketing practices are available

Guangzhou bicycle lane

on request. The Canada-China Trade Council, incorporated in 1978, is located at 133 Richmond Street West, Suite 310, Toronto, Ontario M5H 2L3; tel: (416) 364-8321.

JAPAN—CHINA TRAVEL

Japan's broad and multichanneled relationship with China—accentuated in 1978 by the signing of a treaty of friendship as well as a $20-billion long-term trade agreement with China—is reflected in a wide diversity of contacts between Tokyo and Beijing. The two governments regularly exchange delegations, but the Chinese also unilaterally invite opposition political parties, political leaders, and special-interest groups. Japan also has a number of friendship groups that sponsor private visits. Prominent among these is the Japan-China Friendship Association (Orthodox).

In December 1978, PRC officials announced an unprecedented decision (for China) to permit Japanese trading firms to open offices in Beijing and to receive long-term visas for their representatives. In a small but significant gesture, the Beijing Hotel in 1979 opened a special restaurant specializing in Japanese cuisine. Japan's Tokyo-based coordinating body for PRC trade is the Japan-China Association for Economy and Trade.

In 1987, China received 780,000 Japanese visitors, a 1,000% increase over 1979 and a 19.4% increase over the 1987 volume; Japan has by far and away the largest one-year allotment by the PRC to any single country, now accounting for about one-third of the total number of foreign visitors to China.

CITS (Luxingshe) Representative in Japan ■ 1-27-13 Hamamatsu-cho, 6 Fl., Minato-ku, Tokyo. Tel: (03) 433-1461. Fax: (03) 433-8653.

CHINA FRIENDSHIP ASSOCIATIONS
(Selected Listing)

AUSTRALIA	**Australia-China Society** 75 Quigg Street, Lakemba NSW 2195
AUSTRIA	**Die Botschaft der Volksrepublik China** Metternichgasse 4, 1030 Vienna
CANADA	**Federation of Canada-China Friendship Associations** Rm. 201, 2420 Douglas St., Victoria, BC V8T 4L7
COLOMBIA	**Asociación de la Amistad Colombo-China** Apartado Aereo 17028, Bogota
DENMARK	**Venskabsforbundet Danmark-Kina** Griffenfeldsgade 10, 2200 Copenhagen N
FEDERAL REPUBLIC OF GERMANY	**Deutsche-Chinesische Gesellschaft** Burg Str. 31-IV, O.G. Apt. 168, 5300 Bonn 2
FINLAND	**Finland-China Society** Erottajankatu 15-17, A 00130 Helsinki 13
FRANCE	**Association de Amitiés Franco-Chinoises** 51, rue de Rivoli, 75001 Paris
ITALY	**Associazione Italia-Cina** Via del Seminario 87, 00186 Roma
JAPAN	**Japan-China Friendship Association** 1-4 Kanda, Nishiki-cho, Chiyoda-ku, Tokyo 101
LUXEMBOURG	**Association Amitié Luxembourg-China Populaire** 28, rue Beaumont, Luxembourg City
MEXICO	**Sociedad Mexicana de Amistad con China Popular** Dakota 74 "A" Col. Napoles Deleg., B. Juarez C.P. 03810, Mexico 18, DF
NETHERLANDS	**Vriendschapsvereniging Nederland-China** Prins Hendriklaan 21, 3583 EB, Utrecht
NEW ZEALAND	**New Zealand-China Friendship Society, Inc.** 22 Swanson Street, Auckland
NORWAY	**Vennskapssambandet Norge-Kina** P. Boks 6823, St. Olavs Plass, 0130 Oslo 1
SWEDEN	**Swedish-Chinese Friendship Federation** Kungsgaten 80, 1 tr Og, 112 27, Stockholm
SWITZERLAND	**Société Suisse-Chine** % Ciba-Geigy AG, Klybeckstrasse 141, 4002 Basel
UNITED KINGDOM	**Society for Anglo-Chinese Understanding** 152 Camden High Street, London NW1 0NE
UNITED STATES	**US-China Peoples Friendship Association** National Office: 2025 Eye Street NW, Suite 715, Washington, DC 20006

Sports exchanges are popular between the two countries. They are sponsored by the appropriate national organizations as well as by universities, commercial enterprises, and military groups. Cultural exchanges are administered under a government umbrella organization but are usually initiated by private interests.

NEW ZEALAND—CHINA TRAVEL

Contacts between New Zealand and China have increased steadily since the two countries established diplomatic relations in 1973. By the early 1980s, some 5,000 New Zealanders were visiting China each year and in 1987, 10,900 made the trip. Several tours are sponsored annually by the New Zealand-China Friendship Society, Inc. The Society's national office is in Auckland, with 15 branches located throughout the country. Most of its tours are of about three weeks' duration. The Society issues a newsletter, *New Zealand-China News*, and publishes a brochure on China travel, *Helpful Information for China Tours*.

One of the most prolific writers on travel and cultural subjects among Beijing's foreign residents was Rewi Alley, a native New Zealander, who died in 1987.

SWEDEN—CHINA TRAVEL

Sweden was one of the first Western countries to acknowledge the People's Republic of China when it established diplomatic relations with the young country in 1950. In 1982, a total of 3,948 Swedes visited China; in 1987, 13,500. The Swedish-Chinese Federation (Svenski-Kinesiska Vänskapsförbundet) has been active for over 25 years promoting "friendship, knowledge, and understanding between the Swedish and Chinese peoples." The Federation, with main headquarters in Stockholm, maintains upward of 100 local branches throughout Sweden. Its membership of over 9,500 yields the highest ratio to total population of any China-friendship group in the world.

Study tours to China are a vital service of the organization, which conducted some 20 group tours in 1981. In addition to tours, other Federation services include importing Chinese products for sale in Sweden, lectures, cultural programs, and publication of the periodical *Kinarapport*.

UNITED KINGDOM—CHINA TRAVEL

The United Kingdom was one of the first Western countries to recognize the PRC after its founding in 1949, and the British have maintained a good working relationship with the Chinese since then. In fall 1979, former Chairman Hua Guofeng, on the first official visit to Western Europe by a PRC head of state, toured the UK and met with several of its leaders. Over the years, a great variety of British groups have visited the PRC, among them trade union groups, friendship delegations, sports teams, publishers, and technical delegations. By 1982, the volume of UK visitors to China reached 41,972; by 1987, the number had doubled. The UK has an official trade promotion organization called the Sino-British Trade Council, but the Chinese also deal with a private consortium known as the "48 Group," composed of a number of UK firms that were the first publicly to promote trade with China. Exchange agreements are reviewed annually by the two governments.

■ *The Society for Anglo-Chinese Understanding.* A number of private tours have been arranged each year since 1971 through the SACU, the British China-friendship organization founded in 1965. Membership in the Society is "open to all, irrespective of political affiliations, who are interested in the life and work of the Chinese people and support the aims and activities of the Society." SACU's 14 departures for 1984 included offerings for Tibet, Inner Mongolia, the Silk Route, and the Yangtse Gorges as well as a rail overland tour from Moscow to Guangzhou. Inclusive fares range from £1,200 to £2,000, with an average duration of three weeks for tours by air and 30 days for overland excursions via the Trans-Siberian Railway.

SACU's official tour booking agent is Regent Holidays, 13 Small Street, Bristol B51 1DE; tel: (0272) 211711. A number of other private tourist agencies in the UK offer China packages, including Sunquest Holidays Ltd. (specializing in overland routes), Bales Tours, and STA Travel (which organizes individual travel).

Periodicals on China published in the UK include *China Now* (produced by SACU) and the eminent scholarly journal, *China Quarterly.*

CITS (Luxingshe) Representative in the UK ■ China National Tourist Office, 4 Glentworth Street, London NW1. Tel: (01) 935-9427. Telex: 291221.

UNITED STATES—CHINA TRAVEL

Exchanges between the US and the PRC began officially in March 1971 when the US travel ban to China was formally lifted. The Shanghai Communiqué, issued in 1972, noted that exchange visits were an essential part of the process of establishing full diplomatic relations between the two countries. From 1972 until 1978, a total of about 35,000 persons from the US had visited China, with visa applications for the same period estimated at well over 1,000,000.

With the establishment of full diplomatic relations on January 1, 1979, PRC exchanges with the United States entered a new stratum. The first direct commercial air link between the two countries (San Francisco–Shanghai) was inaugurated in December 1979. By 1987, US visitors to China reached 315,000, a leap of more than 1,000% over 1978 and far exceeding the total number of US visitors to China during 1949–78 inclusive. Earlier projections of an annual volume of 500,000 US visitors by 1990 are now considered conservative by many analysts.

Thus, as of the mid-1980s, the US had become the second most important source of foreign tourism for the PRC (after Japan). Scheduled nonstop trans-Pacific services by Pan Am and CAAC began in April 1981. In mid-1981, CAAC opened an office in New York, its first in the Western Hemisphere. By 1986, nearly 500 private US travel agencies were offering tours to China, compared to the bare handful operating in 1978.

Quasi-Official Contacts. Three nongovernmental organizations, the National Committee on US-China Relations, the US-China Business Council, and the Committee on Scholarly Communication with the People's Republic of China, have handled what might be considered quasi-official exchanges in trade, science, technology, medicine, culture, and sports as well as exchanges of resident researchers, scholars, and students. Such exchanges and visits have been agreed to in principle by the two governments and are nominally hosted by them. Logistics and administration, however, are handled by the staff of the three organizations.

Within their areas of specialty, the three groups can advise on the likely success of a travel request, provide names of appropriate contacts in China, offer reports on previous visits in specific fields, and supply general background information. Delegations specifically organized by them, however, consist largely of officials or influential public figures, and are ostensibly not accessible to the general public.

◾ *The National Committee on US-China Relations, Inc. (NCUSCR).* 777 United Nations Plaza, 9B, New York, New York 10017. Tel: (212) 922-1385.

The NCUSCR facilitates and administers exchange visits agreed to by the US and PRC governments in the fields of education, international affairs, media and communications, government, and economic management and development. About half of the Committee's funds are provided by US government agencies (mostly USIA). Some of its major undertakings have included visits to China by the Philadelphia Orchestra (1973), a group of university presidents (1974), a group of congressional committee staff members (1978), and the Boston Symphony Orchestra (1979). Groups from China have included a martial arts troupe (1974), a television and film delegation (1979), a delegation from the Chinese People's Political Consultative Conference (1981), a delegation led by Deng Pufang on behalf of the disabled (1987), and a visit by He Dongchang, of the State Economic Commission (1987). General services of the National Committee include travel advice, briefing kits, seminars, and a newsletter, *US-China Relations — Notes from the National Committee,* describing its programs. Also available are lists of previous exchange groups who may be contacted for more specific information.

◾ *Committee on Scholarly Communication with the People's Republic of China (CSCPRC).* National Academy of Sciences, 2101 Constitution Avenue, NW, Washington, DC 20418. Tel: (202) 334-2718.

The CSCPRC is sponsored jointly by the National Academy of Sciences, the American Council of Learned Societies, and the Social Science

Research Council. It is supported in part by US government funding and administers exchanges in the natural sciences, social sciences, and humanities. Bilateral conference delegations are selected on the basis of prior negotiation with PRC co-sponsoring institutions.

Since 1979, the CSCPRC, through its National Program for Advanced Study and Research in China, has sent some 400 graduate students and scholars to China to conduct long-term research in the social sciences and humanities at Chinese universities and research institutes. Through its Visiting Scholar Exchange Program, the CSCPRC has exchanged scholars in all fields, including the sciences and engineering, for short-term lecturing and research initiation. The CSCPRC also co-sponsors bilateral conferences in a wide range of fields with Chinese counterparts. Through its Information Services Center and quarterly publication, *China Exchange News*, the CSCPRC disseminates information on US-China academic relations and Chinese developments in education and science.

▣ *The US-China Business Council.* Suite 500, 1818 N Street, NW, Washington, DC 20036. Tel: (202) 429-0340.

The USCBC is recognized by both governments as the US focal point for development of trade between China and the US. This organization is less directly connected to the US government than either the NCUSCR or the CSCPRC, as it derives its financial support from some 400 member corporations, banks, and smaller companies, and because the Chinese have been willing to move outside of government channels to engage in foreign trade and commerce. The USCBC assists members in formulating approaches to Chinese foreign trade authorities. It sponsors trade conferences (which have recently included Chinese participants), assists business persons in making appropriate contacts, sponsors commercial exchanges between the two countries (e.g., in 1988 and 1987 visits to the US by Jia Shi, Chairman of the China Council for Promotion of International Trade, and He Chunlin, Executive Director of the State Council Leading Group for Foreign Investment, respectively). The Council maintains an office in China (Suite 6036, Beijing Hotel).

The Council maintains special industry-wide committees and working groups to help promote US-China trade. Committees focus on telecommunications and electronics, importer issues, travel and tourism, engineering, legal issues, and mining and construction. Working groups sponsor activities concerning export controls and agricultural chemicals. The Council's bimonthly magazine, *The China Business Review*, has earned a reputation as one of the most authoritative and useful publications in the field, with incisive reports on key aspects of China's development. The *Review's* nonmember price of $96 per year unfortunately limits the range of potential subscribers. A listing of the Council's publications (including trade-related analyses, compendia, and directories) is available on request.

Private Travel. Since 1978, CITS has followed a policy of allocating the majority of its tourist visas to large commercial travel agents, who by 1983 were the direct or indirect (wholesale) suppliers of upwards of

A new Chinese-designed and built hotel

90% of US tourist visits to China. Agencies offering China tours now exist in virtually every major US city. Prior to 1978, the largest number of US citizens to visit China traveled under the auspices of the US-China Peoples Friendship Association (USCPFA), the longest established China-tour organizer in the US. Other organizationally based or ad hoc groups in the US have gained approval for tours through direct application to CITS. In 1979–87, such tours included artists, World War II veterans, religious leaders, overseas Chinese, trade union leaders, media specialists, women financial executives, and booksellers. A few groups also succeeded in arranging work-study tours of up to six months' duration in which participants could live and work with Chinese citizens in selected communes and factories. Another new departure during the early 1980s was summer-long Chinese-language study programs organized by the New York based Council on International Educational Exchange and by China Educational Tours of Boston, among others.

■ *US-China Peoples Friendship Association (USCPFA).* National Office: 2025 Eye Street NW, Suite 715, Washington, DC 20006. Tel: (800) 368-5883.

The USCPFA is recognized by the Chinese as the principal sponsor of "study" tours to the PRC for US citizens. A nonprofit educational organization founded in 1974, the USCPFA claims status and purpose similar to those of friendship organizations in other countries that are actively sympathetic to China. Its goal of promoting the development of "people-to-people" contacts between the US and China remained a focal point of its activities following the January 1979 normalization of diplomatic relations. The USCPFA publishes the bimonthly *US–China Review,* an appealing nonspecialist journal with a cultural and educational focus.

USCPFA tours are organized regionally and nationally and appeal to general as well as special interests. For 1986, the USCPFA offered 32 departures for some 500 visitors to the PRC. Most were organized into USCPFA China Study Tours for nonmembers ranging from $3,055 (high season) for 23 days roundtrip including Tibet (19 days China, 3 Hong Kong) to $1,770 (low season) for 21 days roundtrip (17 days China). (Prices do not include trans-Pacific airfares.) All USCPFA tours begin with a valuable predeparture China orientation, including lectures, films, and Chinese-language exposure.

CITS (Luxingshe) Offices in the US ■ China National Tourist Office,
East Coast: 60 East 42 Street, New York, NY 10165. Tel: (212) 867-0271.
Telex: 662142 CITSNYC. Cable: LUXINGSHE NEWYORK.
West Coast: 333 West Broadway, Ste. 201, Glendale, CA 91204. Tel: (818) 545-7505.
Telex: 910250 8906 CNTO LA. Fax: (818) 545-7506.

INTERNATIONAL ROUTINGS TO CHINA

While China may still seem "on the other side of the world"—psychologically and culturally—getting there is no longer an exotic or complicated procedure. Airline routes to China from points throughout the globe proliferated during the early 1980s, with new sea and overland connections adding to the array of choices for tourists.

MAJOR AIR ROUTES

The most common points of entry into China by air are Beijing, Shanghai, and Guangzhou. Since late 1978, when China's CAAC inaugurated regular charter air service connections between Hong Kong and Guangzhou, direct flights from Hong Kong to several other Chinese cities have been added, including Beijing, Shanghai, Hangzhou, Tianjin, and Kunming.

By 1988, more than 30 international carriers were authorized to fly into China. In addition to CAAC, major airlines now flying into Beijing include United, Japan Air Lines (JAL), Northwest Orient, Singapore, All Nippon Airways (ANA), Cathay Pacific, Canadian Pacific, Swissair, Air France, British Airways, Aeroflot, Lufthansa, Philippine Air Lines, Tarom, Thai International, Pakistan International Airlines (PIA), and Qantas.

North American Routings. Travelers beginning their journeys from North America may fly to China via either the Pacific or the Atlantic. A bilateral aviation agreement between the US and China took effect in 1980, with Pan Am beginning scheduled carrier service to Shanghai/ Beijing and San Francisco/New York three times per week. Many tour groups from the West Coast continue to utilize an intermediate stopover in Hong Kong or Tokyo. JAL offers direct flights from San Francisco and Los Angeles to Tokyo; CP Air flies from San Francisco via Vancouver to Tokyo and Hong Kong; and Northwest Orient flies from Los Angeles and Seattle to Tokyo and Hong Kong. Nonstop flying time between Los Angeles and Tokyo is about 11 hours; San Francisco to Hong Kong takes 14½ hours (nonstop, on 747-SP aircraft). Many tours now fly from the West Coast to Tokyo and then on to Beijing or Shanghai, and exit China via Hong Kong, affording tourists stopovers in both Tokyo and Hong Kong, while avoiding excessive backtracking within China.

Travelers from the US and Canada may also choose to fly to China via the eastern route across the Atlantic. This route is longer (total flying time is approximately 22 hours from New York) and requires an overnight layover in the home city of the airline and at least one additional stopover before reaching Beijing. As an example, passengers traveling on Air France first fly from New York to Paris, where they may stay overnight or connect directly on a flight to Beijing. Flights leave Paris for Beijing twice a week and take approximately 13½ hours, including a one-hour touchdown in Karachi.

European Routings. By 1984, CAAC had concluded reciprocal flight agreements with nearly a dozen European-based international carriers, with several additional accords expected to take effect in the near future. In Western Europe, the pioneers of China routings, Swissair (flying twice weekly from Geneva and Zurich) and Air France (twice weekly from Paris), have been joined since 1979 by British Airways (twice weekly from London) and Lufthansa (twice weekly from Frankfurt).

Individual travelers whose China itineraries permit exit and entry via Hong Kong may gain considerable savings by booking London–Hong Kong excursions through flight clubs or special charter offerings.

The major carriers from Eastern Europe are Romanian Airlines (Tarom), with direct flights from Bucharest, and Yugoslav Airlines, flying from Belgrade. Weekly nonstop service to Beijing is provided on Aeroflot (from Moscow).

Asian Routings. From Western Asia, direct flights to Beijing were offered in 1984 via Karachi (Pakistan International Airlines). Both Philippine Airlines (from Manila) and Thai International (from Bangkok) now offer direct services to Guangzhou. In addition, CAAC provides a weekly connection between Kunming and Rangoon, Burma. JAL's nonstop flights connect both Tokyo and Osaka with Beijing and Shanghai. As of early 1984, Pan Am, JAL, and Cathay Pacific (out of Hong Kong) were the only foreign carriers flying into Shanghai. A direct service from the African continent is provided by Ethiopian Airlines (flights originating in Addis Ababa).

Most travelers from Asia, however, continue to rely on the variety of connections into China available from Hong Kong (see The Hong Kong–China Connection, below).

OVERLAND BY RAIL

In 1979, for the first time in nearly 30 years, the railway route from London to Hong Kong was opened to the general public. Sunquest Holidays of London offers a 42-day excursion by train, called the "Central Kingdom Express." This marathon train trip begins in London and stops in Paris, Berlin, Warsaw, Moscow, Irkutsk, and Ulan Bator (in the Socialist Republic of Mongolia). In China, the group stops in Datong, Beijing, Nanjing, Shanghai, Nanchang, Changsha, and Guangzhou, with final destination Hong Kong. London's Society for Anglo-Chinese Understanding offers a more modestly priced overland journey taking 30–31 days. Travelers are flown to Moscow and from there proceed by rail to Beijing via Mongolia.

Individual travelers are now able to exit China on the Trans-Mongolian Express, which leaves Beijing once a week for Moscow via Ulan Bator; the entire journey takes one week. The Trans-Siberian Express also travels from Beijing to Moscow. It leaves Beijing twice weekly for the seven-day routing across the Siberian steppes.

CRUISE SHIPS

Many world cruise lines now feature shore excursions in China as highlights of their global voyages. During 1983, the M/S *Pearl of Scandinavia* offered 15 departures on its two-week China Explorer cruise, calling at Shanghai, Qingdao, Dalian, and Tianjin/Beijing. Air/sea inclusive fares from the US West Coast ranged from $6,888 to $3,058 per passenger. Holland America gives passengers on the SS *Rotterdam* an opportunity to visit Guilin or Guangzhou for three days or Beijing for seven days while the ship docks in Hong Kong. Travelers on the MS *Prisendam* Transpacific Cruise can choose between two tours to China while the ship calls at Hong Kong and Shanghai.

In June 1985, the Chinese passenger liner *Jianzhen* entered service between Shanghai and the Japanese ports of Kobe and Osaka. The service is operated by a joint-venture corporation, the China-Japan International Ferry Co. Ltd. Other cruise ships such as the Norwegian-American *Sagafjord* and the Royal Viking's *Sky* also call at China ports during their voyages.

A variety of passenger-liner services between Hong Kong and China have become available since 1980; see below for details.

THE HONG KONG–CHINA CONNECTION

Hong Kong has been called China's "window on the world" and the British Crown Colony is playing an ever-increasing role in China's exchanges with the outside world. For many years, the proximity of Hong Kong to China made it the major port of entry for travelers to China, as well as a primary outlet for Chinese export goods.

Individual travelers may choose to fly to Hong Kong and then enter

China from there. Once in Hong Kong, it is possible to join tours to China sponsored by the China Travel Service (CTS), the Hong Kong representative of China International Travel Service (CITS). Indeed, some tour operators in North America and Europe have been putting together lower-priced tour packages in conjunction with CTS and other Hong Kong-based tour operators.

By Air. Flights into Guangzhou from Hong Kong are available on scheduled and charter CAAC services which may be booked direct at the new CAAC office in Hong Kong (Gloucester Tower, tel: 5-211314) or through CAAC's agents. Throughout the year this 25-minute flight on a Boeing 737 or British Trident jet operates 3-4 times daily, with two flights operating seven days per week: departing from Hong Kong at 12:05 PM and 8:45 PM; and departing from Guangzhou at 10:40 AM and 7:20 PM.

By the mid-1980s, delays in connections for Hong Kong travelers going beyond Guangzhou were alleviated by the addition of new CAAC services linking Hong Kong directly with several other cities in China, including twice-daily non-stop service to Beijing as well as direct flights to Shanghai, Tianjin, Nanjing, Hangzhou, Guilin, Fuzhou, Xiamen, Chengdu, Haikou, and Kunming. CAAC charter flights to these and other destinations are added during Trade Fair or peak tourist periods. Cathay Pacific, a Hong Kong-based carrier, initiated services to Shanghai in 1981. Flight services to China from Hong Kong have proved so popular that in 1986, a Hong Kong–China joint venture called Dragonair inaugurated competing services to a number of south China cities. Early trip planning, especially during peak seasons, is strongly recommended.

By Rail. Trains provide the most common means of entry into China from Hong Kong. In April 1979, daily non-stop passenger service between Kowloon and Guangzhou was begun. By 1987, express trains were leaving Kowloon four times daily at 9:40 AM, 11:15 AM, 6:05 PM, and 7:38 PM. Tickets for the three-hour trip can be reserved in advance through CTS, and cost HK$135. Travelers are limited to one piece of luggage weighing 20 kg. (44 lbs.) and are charged HK$40 for each extra piece.

Many passengers still travel by the conventional train routing which requires a stopover and a change of trains at the Hong Kong/PRC customs before boarding a PRC train to Guangzhou. Luggage is transported between the two trains as part of the cost of the ticket. The fare is unaccountably more expensive than for direct service — HK$215 each way for foreigners — but is progressively reduced according to the number of passengers traveling together. Tickets may be purchased in advance. Trains leave Kowloon four times a day, with the entire journey requiring about four hours, including a lunch stop in Shenzhen on the PRC side of the border.

By Hovercraft. A favorite of frequent Hong Kong—Guangzhou travelers is the hovercraft service, which plies a route from Hong Kong Bay up the Pearl River estuary to the Chinese port of Huangpu; a 20–30 minute trip by taxi or bus completes the journey to central Guangzhou.

The British-designed hovercraft has a capacity of 60 passengers and travels at speeds of up to 40 mph, making the scenic (if somewhat blurred) journey in about three hours. The service operates three times daily, from Kowloon (Tai Kok Tsui Ferry Pier) at 8:40 AM, 8:50 AM, and 9 AM; and from Guangzhou (Zhoutonzha Pier) at 1:45 PM, 2:30 PM, and 3 PM. A single-journey fare is HK$145.

By Catamaran. Motorized catamaran service was added in 1986, docking at Guangzhou's districts of Beixiu and Li Wan Hu. The four-hour journey costs HK$122. Departures from Hong Kong are at 8:20 and 8:45 AM; the craft return to Hong Kong at 2 and 3:30 PM.

By Ship. Beginning in 1984, something akin to the original "slow boat to China" was available to China-bound passengers from Hong Kong.

◼ *Hong Kong-Guangzhou.* The 80-mile journey up the Pearl River is made aboard two steamers, the *Xinghu* and the *Tianhu*, which alternate to provide nightly departures (9 PM) from Hong Kong, with arrival at Guangzhou the following morning. Departures from Guangzhou for Hong Kong are at 9 AM daily.

Both ships are air-conditioned and provide dining and recreation facilities. Double-occupancy first-class cabins cost HK$130 per passenger.

◼ *Hong Kong-Xiamen.* Two ships, the *Gulangyu* and the *Jimei*, ply the 300-mile, 22-hour route between Hong Kong and Xiamen Island.

◼ *Hong Kong-Shantou.* The *Dinghu* offers alternate day service up the South China coast to Shantou. The 191-mile journey takes about 14 hours.

◼ *Hong Kong-Shanghai.* Weekly sailings between Hong Kong and Shanghai are provided by the tandem services of the *Shanghai* and the *Haixing*, with rates varying from HK$260 (economy class) to HK$845 (deluxe cabin) for the 60-hour voyage. Both vessels boast swimming pools and gourmet restaurants.

CHINA TOUR SERVICES FROM HONG KONG

China Travel Service. Since early 1978, the China Travel Service (CTS) in Hong Kong has been organizing trips to China. At first, CTS tours were limited to short excursions to Guangzhou and other southern cities. In 1978–79, however, CTS began dramatically to increase both the number and variety of its offerings. In 1981, CTS introduced tours for individuals and small groups of two to nine persons ("FITs").

CTS is headquartered at 77 Queens Road, Central District, Hong Kong Island (tel: 5-259121), with a branch office in Alpha House, 23-33 Nathan Road, Kowloon (tel: 3-667201). CTS organizes its own tours to China and moreover has enfranchised several local Hong Kong travel agencies to organize group tours. Most medium-sized travel agents in Hong Kong can provide travelers with the relevant information on these trips. A number of travel agencies in the US, Canada, and Europe have links with these Hong Kong agents and market the tours to the general public.

China tour services for non-Chinese are now also being offered through a new CITS branch in Hong Kong with offices at Units 601/605/606, Sixth Floor, Tower II, South Sea Centre, Tsimshatsui East, Kowloon (tel: 3-7215317; telex: 38449 CITS HX).

Following is a sampling of Hong Kong CTS/CITS tours offered to foreigners in 1985 (approximate rates in US dollars for single passengers; discounts apply for preformed groups of two or more persons traveling together):

1. **Guangzhou 3-Day Excursion.** Roundtrip by hovercraft. Departs Tuesdays, Thursdays, Saturdays. US$220.

2. **Guangzhou–Guilin 4-Day Excursion.** Roundtrip by hovercraft/train. Weekly departures (Wednesdays). US$390 per person.

3. **Beijing – Xi'an – Shanghai 9-Day Excursion.** Roundtrip by air. Three departures per month (consult CTS for dates). US$1,190 per person.

4. **Beijing–Xi'an–Chongqing–Yangtse River Cruise–Wuhan–Shanghai 13-Day Excursion.** Roundtrip by air. Departures April, July–October (consult CTS for dates). US$1,440 per person.

CTS/CITS China Travel Arrangements for Individuals. Both CTS and CITS now offer a wide choice for individual travel arrangements in China. Either organization can provide a China visa upon booking, through them, of a minimum package of travel services. Packages are mainly offered for Beijing, Shanghai, or Guangzhou (or for combinations of these cities). For travelers seeking the maximum amount of independence in China, the minimum predeparture arrangements would include the following:

1. **Beijing.** Visa, airport transfers in Beijing, one hotel night plus breakfast. Cost: US$179 (single); US$143 (two or more persons).

2. **Shanghai.** Visa, one airport transfer, one hotel night, one day's sightseeing. Cost: US$145 (single); US$95 (two or more persons).

3. **Guangzhou.** Visa, one-way transportation to Guangzhou (passenger's choice), arrival transfer to Guangzhou hotel. Cost: US$59 (if direct train); US$60 (hovercraft); US$63 (stopover train); US$78 (air).

Budget China Tours. Since 1980, low-cost China tours utilizing rail connections, charter flights, and budget accommodations have been available to youth and students and others willing to forego a modicum of comfort and special attention while in China. Two prominent operators in this field are the Hong Kong Student Travel Bureau (120/2 Des Voeux Road, tel: 5-414841) and China Youth Travel (151 Des Voeux Road, tel: 5-410975).

Visas. Two working days are usually required for visa processing for most excursions. Visas can also be processed in 24 hours on an "urgent" basis, requiring a surcharge of HK$120.

THE MACAO—CHINA CONNECTION

Since Macao's border gate crossing to China was opened to tourists in 1979, a number of short (1 to 3 days) but well-planned excursions to neighboring Zhongshan County have been offered by China Travel Service (Macao) Ltd. (Rua do Visconde, Paco de Arcos; tel: 3770).

Day trips to Zhongshan, which feature a visit to Cuihengcun, Dr. Sun Yatsen's birthplace, cost HK$320 per person. For longer visits, travelers may stay at the well-appointed Zhongshan Hot Spring Resort, which was completed in 1981.

PACKING FOR A CHINA TRIP

For visits to the People's Republic of China, just as to other parts of the world, a simple rule applies: bring twice as much money as might reasonably be needed and half as many clothes.

The Chinese are an informal people, eliminating the need to pack formal clothing, several changes in wardrobe, or any "special" items for a special occasion. Since the early 1980s, however, dress codes, as with many other things in China, have undergone subtle changes. For business occasions, suits or dresses have become the norm for Westerners, while T-shirts, jeans, and tennis shoes are deemed indecorous for events such as receptions, formal gatherings, or visits with ranking officials.

In most instances, however, women will find pantsuits, everyday dresses, and other casual clothing appropriate. They should minimize flamboyance in makeup and jewelry—such adornments will seem out of place in China. Shorts, halter tops, or other revealing clothes are frowned upon (sometimes literally). Men should choose a wardrobe of conservative color. For most visitors there is still no need to take anything more formal than one suit or sports jacket and, perhaps, one tie. On most occasions, shorts are acceptable for men in summer, as are jeans for men and women.

Only a few changes of clothing need be brought along. Laundry and dry cleaning services are excellent in China and are performed overnight in most hotels. Comfortable walking shoes or sandals are a must, perhaps with a dressier pair reserved for dinners or special occasions (women should avoid high heels).

The seasons must be taken into account, of course, and in cool weather it is better to wear several layers than to rely on bulky outer garments. In the winter, warm socks, thermal underwear, and headgear are recommended for both men and women. A sweater is appropriate for almost any time of year, as is a light raincoat. Cottons are most comfortable for hot weather.

Other practical items to include are:

Toiletries. Western brands of facial tissues, toothpaste, deodorant, shaving cream, and razor blades are not available, although Max Factor cosmetics and a few European sundries are now being sold at hotels in the larger cities. Inexpensive Chinese brands of mixed quality are available for some of these commodities. (As most Western brands can be replenished in Hong Kong and Tokyo, quantities carried in can be kept to a minimum.) Hotel rooms are amply supplied with soap and toilet tissue.

Pharmaceuticals. Bring prescription medicines, vitamins, aspirin, and other health and first-aid remedies as required on a regular basis. Women should bring along sanitary napkins and tampons, which are not generally available in China. As a precaution, cold and digestive medicines might be included. Mosquito repellent, tanning oil, and skin cream are optional.

Reading Materials. There are no longer significant restrictions on bringing Western magazines, books, and maps into China. Furthermore, since late 1979, periodicals such as *Time, Newsweek, Reader's Digest,* and the *International Herald-Tribune* have been offered for sale to foreigners in China's larger hotels.

Liquor and Tobacco. Since late 1978, Western spirits, wine, and cigarettes have been made available at a steadily increasing number of tourist locations (hotels, Friendship Stores, etc.) throughout China. They may be purchased with Foreign Exchange Certificates. Prices have been kept comparable to those in the West (indeed, a fifth of Johnnie Walker "Red Label" or a carton of Winston cigarettes could be purchased in Beijing at prices well below those in New York or London).

Cameras and Film. The rule about film in China seems to be that one can never have enough. Kodak and Fuji film have been on sale in China since 1979, although all types and sizes are not yet available and venues are as yet limited to hotels or other tourist byways in the larger cities. Time considerations usually do not permit developing, although one-day service for Ektachrome (but not Kodachrome) slides is now available from a few outlets in Beijing. An ample supply of batteries, flashbulbs, and, for the fastidious, replacement parts should also be brought along.

Electrical Appliances. Travelers who will not go out in public until they've shaved with an electric razor or have blow-dried their hair should take these and any other personal-care items along. Electric current in China is being standardized at 220v, 50 cycles, so travelers from North America with 110v equipment should bring a transformer and an assortment of adaptors (including an adaptor for rounded three-prong sockets). Even thus equipped, appliances with moving parts, such as shavers and tape recorders, will operate at about 80% of their normal speed if they have not been internally converted from 60 to 50 cycles. Battery-run equipment is of course not affected by these considerations. Transistor radios will pick up local stations. Voice of America and BBC news broadcasts can be picked up during the early morning hours on shortwave radios supplied in many hotel rooms.

Coffee, Tea, and Milk. Many people find the Chinese variety of instant coffee quite palatable. Nescafé instant along with some Brazilian and Japanese varieties (including canned brewed coffee) are being sold in larger cities. But those who are particular or are in frequent need should bring their own supply. And, ludicrous as it may sound, many travelers may prefer to bring their own tea, as the "black" varieties familiar to most Western palates (today produced mainly in India and Sri Lanka) are not readily obtainable throughout China. Fresh milk is available in most hotel dining rooms, but powdered creamers (in smaller than 50-lb. sacks) are not. Powdered milk (usually goat's) is sold throughout the country.

WHAT NOT TO PACK

"Street" drugs, pornography, firearms, inflammatory political or evangelical literature, and contraband are all absolutely forbidden.

IV

TRAVELING

IN CHINA

Steam engines remain the workhorses of China's rail system

GETTING ALONG IN CHINA: SOME UNWRITTEN RULES FOR CHINA TRAVEL

All visits to China are directly coordinated by the Chinese host organization that provided initial authorization for the trip. Upon arrival, the host organization assumes all responsibility for domestic travel and accommodations. In the case of tourists and most other foreign visitors, the responsible body for all travel logistics is the China International Travel Service (CITS).

"GUESTS" AND "HOSTS": PROCEDURES FOR GROUP TRAVEL

Most tour groups, including friendship groups and study tours, will be accompanied by professional guides and interpreters from CITS. Professional groups that have come to China to conduct seminars, discussions, or general business transactions often travel under the auspices of their Chinese counterpart organization. Official, government-hosted delegations will be accompanied by a ranking member of the host organization. This person fulfills both protocol and escort functions, and works closely with the visiting group's leader. Business representatives, by contrast, are left much more to their own devices, especially for any time not directly absorbed by business discussions or on-site visits.

Contrary to some lingering preconceptions of China travel, there is no rule that visitors be led around or observed during every moment of their stay in China. Guides and interpreters are conveniently provided at transfer points and for formal or prearranged segments of a visit, but their function in these instances is to expedite the visit and provide proper liaison between what are perceived as "guests" (the travelers) and "hosts" (the Chinese). At other times, foreign travelers are left pretty much on their own; language ability, sense of direction, and the time available are the only major impediments to tourist "wanderlust."

Arrival. Representatives of the host organization will be on hand to welcome visitors upon their arrival in China. In most cases, at least one staff person will be assigned to accompany the group throughout its stay in the PRC. These personnel serve as escorts, guides, and interpreters, and will have made all prior arrangements for the tour. Upon arrival at the preassigned hotel, people may go directly to their rooms (also preassigned).

For non-tourist groups, a meeting with the host is arranged shortly after arrival to discuss the proposed itinerary and work out details of the stay. Initial meetings with host representatives are important. They serve to acquaint escorts and guests, work out the itinerary, and generally set the tone for the visit. After guests are formally welcomed in China, a schedule is proposed. The Chinese usually prearrange trips in accordance with the interests of groups as may have been expressed in pre-tour correspondence. The schedule should be gone over in detail since it will be nearly impossible to make changes afterwards, especially those that involve alterations of travel dates between cities or appointments at particular institutions. Likewise, the Chinese rarely favor suggestions for splitting up into subgroups.

Group Leaders. The Chinese are sensitive to leadership responsibilities and will expect a visiting group—whether tourist or professional—to appoint a leader. Leaders of invited delegations are treated with special deference. A single room or suite is often set aside for leaders, and in some cases a chauffeured car will be provided for official duties. For their part, leaders are expected to assume responsibility for introductions at places visited and to act as intermediaries for complaints and suggestions. Leaders also serve as the first point of contact with Chinese personnel in making room assignments and working out schedule details.

Sticking to the Itinerary—and Flexibility. Visitors to China should bear in mind that the Chinese have no doubt attempted to prepare the details of their trip well in advance of arrival. These arrangements probably required considerable planning and bureaucratic jostling to find appropriate openings among the country's overtaxed tourist facilities. These advance efforts notwithstanding, the actual day-to-day itinerary of a trip may nevertheless be lacking full confirmation even by the time of a group's arrival in China. The order in which cities are visited and the number of days spent at each place are ultimately the responsibility of CITS, not the foreign tour operator. These decisions depend primarily on the availability of hotel and domestic flight space for the group and, apparently, on the ability of CITS to compete successfully for coveted space with a variety of other government entities (e.g., trade corporations and foreign affairs bureaus).

On occasion, the Chinese have exercised their right to add or delete cities without notice—usually a result of overbooking or poor communications (only tiny pockets of China's travel sector have been computerized). In such cases, a group may request to visit an alternative city of its own choice. CITS usually does what it can to offer some compensatory adjustment in the schedule (even to the point of offering to extend the overall length of stay in China). In all events, all requests for major itinerary changes should be made known on the day of arrival. The same rule applies when requesting changes in (or additions to) the schedule within a particular city: the sooner a request is made, the better the chances for its consideration. The leader should forward his or her group's specific sightseeing ideas to the Chinese escort, preferably in writing.

It is possible for individuals to drop out of scheduled activities and go sightseeing or shopping on their own. The group leader should be informed well in advance to ensure that a presentable proportion of the

A public park in South China

group remains available for any planned activities. No refunds are given for scheduled visits to sites, banquets, concerts, or other events which are missed. Individual excursions do not require an official escort. Indeed, the Chinese guides cannot be expected to provide direct assistance for personal outings.

In the case of requests for individual visits to non-tourist sites or for appointments with individuals within China, it is suggested that such requests be made in writing before arrival in China. Responsibility for assisting in these contacts does not fall within the purview of CITS.

Escort Procedures and Guides. A pattern of organization becomes apparent during the first few days of a stay in China. Escorts and interpreters will meet with the group at the outset of any planned activity, make the introductions at the institutions or sites visited, and help with any problems—from protocol to travel, from shopping to laundry—that may arise.

Unfortunately—for continuity's sake—tour groups can no longer expect to be in the company of the same guide throughout their trip. A shortage of "national" CITS guides—usually more experienced personnel attached to the CITS main office in Beijing—has meant that some groups are shuttled between local guides of each city visited on the itinerary. Moreover, each factory, school, museum, park, or other site maintains personnel who specialize in meeting "foreign friends." There will, however, be at least one interpreter assigned to the group at all times.

Most delegations have found translators to be quite competent (although the recent growth in tourism has occasionally caused students to be pressed into service before their training has been completed). All interpreters have a particularly grueling task, since they bear the major burden of making Chinese society comprehensible to the foreigner. They are called upon to translate briefings, speeches, signs, and conversations for many hours each day, often having to sift through a muddle of accents, jargon, and temperaments.

The guides assigned to tour groups by CITS vary, quite naturally, in personality and degrees of patience. Most will respond courteously to endless questions and do all in their power to keep tour members happy and comfortable. An aloof or surly guide is the rare exception—most tourists return from China with glowing reports of their solicitous and endearing escorts.

On-Site Briefings. When visiting a factory, school, commune, or other institution, the tour group or delegation is normally escorted to a room to have tea and receive a briefing from a "leading member" of the institution. Remarks usually take note of improved conditions since 1949, the effect of the current policy line, and general statistics. Guests are usually invited to ask questions as they tour the site. If time allows, the group may return to the briefing room for further discussion.

Questioning is always encouraged, but visitors should be sensitive about the style of questions and the areas probed. Unanswered questions should not be pursued beyond the bounds of courtesy. Reticence on the part of a spokesman should not be taken as a sign of evasion or deception. From the Chinese standpoint, briefings serve to fill a narrow, specific purpose. Most Chinese in this situation are not given to extemporizing and, lacking either information or the authority to give a complete answer, they will prefer to give none. Hosts at sites generally prefer to take all questions at once, answering them in as much detail as time and discretion allow. While this method works fairly well with larger tour groups, smaller delegations may seek to ask their questions one at a time so that appropriate follow-up inquiries can be made.

GUIDELINES FOR BEHAVIOR AND DECORUM

Under the special conditions imposed by escorted group travel, visitors should seek to exercise courtesy and patience. It is always best to try to relax and "flow" with the visit. A willingness to experience China on its own terms will result in a more satisfying visit, whether its purpose is business or general travel. The accumulated experience of certain visitors has produced guidelines that will facilitate positive relationships:

General Conduct. The Chinese expect their guests to behave as representatives of their own society and are respectful of cultural and national differences. Visitors should feel free to be themselves, to speak openly about differing political, economic, religious, or social beliefs. Spirited disagreements, however, should not be allowed to degenerate into remarks that are indiscreet or disrespectful toward aspects of Chinese society or particularly toward its leaders, past or present.

While Western manners need not be abandoned in China, some

restraint is advisable. The Chinese do not appreciate a hail-fellow-well-met style and are sparing in their use of direct physical contact. A courteous handshake is acceptable. As one gets to know the Chinese, greater familiarity becomes possible. Public displays of affection among members of visiting groups are also regarded as unseemly. Likewise, visitors should attempt to keep a pleasant demeanor and not show hostility or anger in public toward either the Chinese or fellow group members.

Norms of etiquette in the PRC do not differentiate between men and women, and members of both sexes are treated equally.

Punctuality and Protocol. Punctuality is expected for all business and social appointments. Except in extenuating circumstances, all planned activities and meetings should be attended. This is as important for general visitors as for business representatives. Even the most mundane arrangements may have required considerable preparation on the part of the Chinese. At many institutions, especially schools, guests are usually greeted upon arrival by applause. It is polite to return the gesture.

Smaller tour groups and delegations visiting an institution (or arriving at a negotiating session) should be cognizant of protocol requirements. The leader or senior member of the party should enter first since the Chinese will have lined up their hosts in protocol order. It is also appropriate to introduce group members individually after the Chinese have made their own introductions, noting those who may have special expertise in the subject at hand.

Voicing Complaints. Individuals should not be criticized or chastised openly. If complaints about arrangements must be raised, they should be broached first in private with an escort or interpreter. For example, if a group visits a commune and is advised that it is "inconvenient" to tour the local hospital, members should not insist on being taken there, even if they have just walked by it. When there is an opportunity, it may be mentioned in friendly terms that the group has a special interest in hospitals and hopes there may be another opportunity to visit one. If, indeed, another opportunity is available, efforts will be made to grant the request.

Expressing Gratitude. Tipping is strictly prohibited in the PRC; most Chinese would be insulted or at least deeply embarrassed if you attempted to tip them. The act of tipping, after all, implies a difference in status between the donor and recipient, and the implied servile relationship runs contrary to concepts of social and economic democracy in the PRC. Tipping is appropriate for servants, not workers, and in today's China there are only workers and no servants. For hotels and restaurants, the proper way to express gratitude for services rendered is to write a kind word in the suggestion book usually installed at the entrance.

In the mid-1980s, however, a modest amount of tipping practices began to come into practice, especially with hotel staff, taxi drivers, and tour guides. In late 1987, such practices apparently led to the issuance of new

A guardian from the neighborhood committee

anti-tipping regulations by NTA, threatening prosecution for severe of-
fenders among tourism service workers.

Modest tokens or mementos from home, such as magazines, emblems,
or lapel pins, may be offered to representatives of institutions visited on
the China tour. Such items are also appropriate as remembrances for tour
escorts.

In the case of officials or specially invited delegations, the proper
gesture of gratitude is to arrange a reciprocal banquet for the host organization at the end of the trip and, perhaps, to present the organization
with a collective gift. Such gifts might include plaques or banners commemorating the trip, technical or scientific books, tape recorders, calculators, and television sets. A few visiting delegations have been more
extravagant and have offered automobiles and computers. Donors should
be aware that Chinese import duties will be assessed for many items
brought to China as gifts. In all cases, such gifts are appropriate only when
presented in the spirit of collective mutual friendship and nothing more.
Personal gifts or those that bear the onus of charity are to be eschewed.

MEETING LOCAL CHINESE

In answer to the tourist's oft-asked question: yes, one can certainly approach the man on the street in China. The Chinese are friendly, warm
people. Visitors need not hesitate to walk into public places such as
shops, restaurants, and theaters (naturally, it is considered rude, as it
would be in any country, to wander uninvited into a house or private area).
If foreign visitors display an open, cooperative manner, the Chinese will
do the same.

Communicating with the Chinese. English and other foreign languages are now widely taught over radio and television in China. In larger cities, it is not uncommon these days for a Chinese student to approach visitors in a friendly attempt to polish up his or her foreign language skills. Usually, these conversations quickly develop into good-humored give-and-take discussions about the different lifestyles of foreign countries and will invariably offer some insights about life in China. A crowd may gather to observe—or to contribute. A particularly bold person may ask for a magazine, book, or other small article as a souvenir of the encounter. Such situations should be handled with discretion; it is perfectly polite to decline such requests.

The vast majority of Chinese outside metropolitan areas do not speak any foreign language. In all parts of the PRC, the dominant dialect is *putonghua* (or "common language"), a derivative of the Beijing dialect (sometimes referred to as "Mandarin"). The individual native dialect of each region (e.g., Shanghai, Guangdong, Hunan) is also used, making most Chinese people effectively "bilingual." Of course, any attempt to master some rudimentary Chinese phrases—no matter how horrendous the resulting pronunciation—might be helpful and certainly will be appreciated (see Chinese Phrases for Travelers in the Appendix).

A Note on Chinese Names. A basic feature of Chinese names is that the family name (usually one syllable) precedes the given name (usually two syllables). Thus, Zhang Huaming should be addressed as Mr. Zhang. The given name is used only by family members or close friends.

Neighborhood wedding, Beijing

A woman keeps her family name; hence, Miss Yu is still called Miss Yu after she has married. Mr., Miss, and Mrs.—as well as the ubiquitous *tongzhi* ("comrade")—are polite terms of address for the Chinese you may meet, including service people.

You may notice the Chinese referring to each other by nicknames. The most common is the prefix *xiao*, which means "small" and is used for young (or short) people, and *lao*, which is used for older, well-respected people—for example, *lao* Zhang. These are terms of endearment and should be used sparingly by Western visitors—unless the person in question genuinely is a close friend. A term often used between foreigners and their Chinese acquaintances is *lao pengyou*, that is, "old friend."

Official titles are generally eschewed in conversation. People in positions of authority may often be identified only as "responsible persons." A "cadre" (pronounced *kah-der*) may be any person with administrative functions.

Terminology. Terms for China in Western usage such as "Red China," "Mainland China," or "Communist China" may cause offense, as may references to Taiwan as the "Republic of China" or "Free China." The preferred name for China is the People's Republic of China or, simply, China. Formally speaking, Taiwan is Taiwan Province, a part of China.

CHINESE CUSTOMS PROCEDURES

China's customs formalities have tended to be rather exacting. Since late 1978, however, PRC officials have enacted measures to help simplify procedures for short-term foreign visitors.

The most important document the visitor must fill out before arrival is the Baggage Declaration Form. It requires an itemization of cameras, watches, tape recorders, jewelry, and other valuables being taken in. Visitors are given a copy of their completed form for presentation when leaving the country. Foreigners who are not residents of the PRC are allowed to bring in four bottles of liquor, 600 cigarettes, an unlimited amount of medicine for personal use, any personal effects, and an unlimited quantity of foreign currency. (For facsimile Baggage Declaration Form, see below.)

There is no restriction on film or still cameras, but professional film or video equipment (i.e., 16 mm. and 35 mm. cameras, and one-inch video recorders) is not allowed in without special permission. There are no restrictions on 8 mm. film cameras, half-inch videotape recorders, or tape recorders.

There are four cardinal rules to observe with respect to customs procedures:

1. Declare all items required by the Baggage Declaration Form. All personal possessions declared upon entry into China must be taken out

CUSTOMS OF THE PEOPLE'S REPUBLIC OF CHINA:
BAGGAGE DECLARATION FOR INCOMING PASSENGERS

NAME _____

NATIONALITY _____ PASSPORT NO. _____

FROM/TO _____

NUMBER OF ACCOMPANYING CHILDREN UNDER 16 _____

HAND BAGGAGE_____ Pcs. CHECKED BAGGAGE_____ Pcs.

Binding line — *Please read the NOTE carefully before you fill in this form*

ITEM	ENTRY		EXIT	
	Description & Amount			
CHINESE & FOREIGN CURRENCIES				
GOLD & SILVER ORNAMENTS				
TRIP NECESSITIES	BRAND	PIECE	BRAND	PIECE
CAMERA				
TAPE RECORDER				
VIDEO & MOVIE CAMERA				
OTHER ARTICLES DUE TO CUSTOMS PROCEDURES				
GOODS & SAMPLES	Yes/No	☐	Yes/No	☐
RECORDED VIDEO TAPE	Yes/No	☐	Yes/No	☐
PRINTED MATTER	Yes/No	☐	Yes/No	☐
ANTIQUES	Yes/No	☐	Yes/No	☐

DURABLE CONSUMER GOODS (PRICE$\geqslant$RMB50.00) AND GIFTS (TOTAL PRICE$\geqslant$RMB50.00)			
DESCRIPTION	BRAND	PIECE	CUSTOMS REMARK

IN ADDITION, ____ PIECES OF UNACCOMPANIED BAGGAGE

ARE TO BE IMPORTED THROUGH ____ WITHIN 3 MONTHS.

SIGNATURE: _____ DATE: _____

CUSTOMS REMARKS:

CUSTOMS ENDORSEMENT: _____

again. Customs officers at exit points are likely to ask to see such items, and time will be saved by having them readily available for inspection. In no case should items be given away—prevention of unauthorized gifts is, after all, the main point of the above regulations. Lost items should be reported as soon as they are found to be missing.

2. Do not attempt to bring in any contraband or other illegal items (e.g., weapons, drugs).

3. Save all currency-exchange vouchers and all receipts for major purchases (the latter may be required by customs people on your return home). If Chinese currency or Foreign Exchange Certificates are presented for reconversion upon exiting China, officials may ask to be shown proof that the amount to be reconverted was covered by official exchange transactions. Upon departure, the amount of money taken out must be noted on the original currency declaration form, and should correlate with the amount spent in China. Chinese currency may not be taken out of China (except in the form of FECs or Bank of China traveler's checks).

4. Items categorized as "cultural relics" may not be taken out of China without evidence that they have been officially approved for export. Proof consists of a wax seal or an export certificate from the Cultural Relics Administration, either accompanied by a receipt stamped "Foreign Exchange Purchase." Items covered by this regulation include fossils and all antiques—including old books, paintings, calligraphy, pottery and porcelain, metal objects, coins, furniture, fabrics, and handicrafts.

Special customs regulations apply to overseas Chinese, foreign citizens of Chinese origin, foreign citizens who are residents in China, and Chinese citizens who have been abroad to visit relatives; for details see "China Travel for Overseas Chinese" below.

MONEY IN CHINA

China's Currency. The official name for the currency of the People's Republic of China is renminbi (RMB—the "people's money"). It is denominated into the *yuan*. Within China, it is also informally counted out as *kuai* (unit). Notes in common use are printed in denominations of 1, 2, 5, and 10 *yuan*. The *yuan* is in turn divided into *fen* (cents); units of 10 *fen* are counted as *jiao* (also called *mao*). Paper notes are issued in 50-*fen* units (or 5 *jiao*), 20-*fen* units (2 *jiao*), and 10-*fen* (1 *jiao*). Coins are in denominations of 1, 2, and 5 *fen*.

The RMB is not traded on international markets and can be purchased or exchanged only within China. Rates of exchange fluctuate daily (see sample rates below). The RMB was devalued twice in 1986 against foreign currencies, adding nearly 30% to year-end exchanges for major currencies such as the US and Hong Kong dollars and the Japanese yen.

Foreign Exchange Certificates. A new system of Foreign Exchange Certificates (FECs) was introduced for use by foreign visitors in China

EXCHANGE RATES FOR CHINESE YUAN (RMB)*

COUNTRY	DENOMINATION	YUAN EQUIVALENT
Australia	A$100	300.17
Austria	Sch100	29.84
Belgium	BF10,000	996.98
Canada	CND100	304.32
Denmark	KR100	53.61
Finland	MK100	117.00
France	FF100	61.86
Germany (FRG)	DM100	208.43
Hong Kong	HK$100	47.55
Italy	L10,000	28.35
Japan	Y100,000	2,742.08
Netherlands	G100	185.12
Singapore	S$100	181.15
Sweden	Kr100	60.30
Switzerland	SwF100	253.80
United Kingdom	£100	624.85
United States	$100	371.27

*Yuan buying rates as of July 5, 1988. Source: Bank of China.

on April 1, 1980. The new certificates are intended to eliminate the direct use of foreign currencies in China for purchases of imported items such as cigarettes, spirits, film, cosmetics, Coca-Cola, and foreign publications. FECs are also required for the purchase of restricted exports such as antiques. FECs have also become the preferred means of payment by tourists for hotels, restaurants, and travel bookings made in China, as well as for all purchases in Friendship Stores and other retail outlets (such as large state stores). The certificates are sold at usual foreign-exchange outlets throughout the country—e.g., Bank of China branches, hotels, Friendship Stores—at equivalent RMB exchange rates as posted by the BOC (rates fluctuate daily and sharp upward or downward trends bear watching). FECs may be reconverted upon exiting China. Unlike RMB notes, FECs may be brought out of or back into the country. FECs are issued in seven denominations: 1, 5, 10, and 50 *yuan*; and 1 and 5 *jiao*.

The certificates have met with uneven success since their introduction, mainly because of the inability of many smaller outlets throughout the country to stock enough FECs to cover their transactions with foreigners.

Traveler's Checks. Traveler's checks from most of the world's leading banks and issuing agencies are now acceptable in China. Apart from protection against loss, they usually bring a slightly higher exchange rate than currency. More than 50 types of checks have been approved for use in the PRC. Both traveler's checks and foreign currency can be converted to FECs at Bank of China branches, Friendship Store, and hotels serving foreigners. Exchange service is also provided at most international transfer points within China.

Bank of China traveler's checks were introduced in 1978 (they are sold at the BOC's branches overseas for a small service charge). Other traveler's checks negotiable in China include Algemene Bank Nederland, American Express, Amsterdam-Rotterdam Bank, Arab Bank Limited (Amman), Australia and New Zealand Banking Group, Bank für Gemeinwirtschaft AG, Bank of America, Bank of New South Wales, Bank of Tokyo, Banque Bruxelles, Banque Nationale de Paris, Barclays, Bayerische Vereinsbank, Berliner Bank AG, Berliner Handels—und Frankfurter Bank, Citibank, Commercial Bank of Australia, Commerzbank AG, Commonwealth Trading Bank of Australia, Crédit Commercial de France, Crédit Lyonnais, Deutsche Bank AG, Dresdner Bank AG, Fuji, Grindlays, Handels—und Privatbank Ag, Hong Kong and Shanghai Banking Corporation, Lloyds, MasterCard, Midland, Mitsui, National Bank of Australia, National Westminster, Nederlandsche Middenstandsbank, Norwegian Travelers Checks, Rafidain Bank (Baghdad), Royal Bank of Canada, Royal Bank of Scotland, Rural and Industries Bank of West Australia, Société Générale (Paris), Société Générale (Belgium), Standard Chartered, Sumitomo, Swiss Bankers Travelers Cheque Centre (Berne), Swiss Credit, Union Bank of Switzerland, Swiss Volksbank, Thomas Cook, Vereins—und Westbank AG, and VISA.

Credit Cards. In fall 1979, Bank of East Asia/VISA Credit Cards were approved for use at the Guangzhou Trade Fair, setting the first such precedent for China. By the late 1980s, international credit cards could be used for purchases or to obtain cash advances at over 1,000 outlets in China, including Bank of China branches, several large hotels, and other tourist outlets in Beijing, Shanghai, Guangzhou, Tianjin, Hangzhou, Nanjing, Wuhan, and Kunming. As of mid-1987, there were over 100 shops, hotels, and other service establishments that accepted the American Express card for direct payment, but their use for shopping is still limited to a few of the larger state-run Friendship and antique stores. There are nine nationally accepted cards: MasterCard, VISA, Diners Club, American Express, East Americard-VISA, Federal Card, Million Card, and JCB Card; added to these in 1987 was the Bank of China's own Great Wall credit card, issued mainly to foreign residents by the bank's Beijing head office for use in China only. Most credit card cash advance transactions in China are subject to a 4% surcharge. But for most purchases in China, including items such as meals and CAAC airline tickets, cash remains the rule.

Letters of Credit. It is possible to arrange for letters of credit payable to foreign visitors in China through the Bank of China.

As of 1988, about 1,500 US banks had full correspondent relationships with the Bank of China, most of these relationships having been

US DOLLAR/YUAN EQUIVALENCIES*

US$	YUAN	YUAN	US$
1	3.71	1	0.26
2	7.43	2	0.53
3	11.13	3	0.80
4	14.85	4	1.07
5	18.56	5	1.34
10	37.12	10	2.69
20	74.25	20	5.38
50	185.63	50	13.46
100	371.27	100	26.93
200	742.54	200	53.86
500	1,856.35	500	134.65

*Rates as of July 28, 1988. Source: Bank of China.

formed in 1979. These included The First National Bank of Chicago, Manufacturers Hanover Trust, Chase Manhattan, Morgan Guaranty, Bank of America, United California, American Security, First National of Boston, Rainier National of Seattle, American Express International, Chemical, Citibank, Wells Fargo, Bankers Trust, Manufacturers National of Detroit, First National in Dallas, Crocker National, Provident National (Philadelphia), The Philadelphia National, First City National of Houston, Seattle First National, First National of Minneapolis, Security Pacific, Republic National of Dallas, Texas Commerce, and Continental Illinois.

Bank Accounts. Frequent travelers to the PRC, especially business people, may seek to open an account with the Bank of China. In Beijing, certain BOC branches are now authorized to open "special" accounts, mainly for use by foreigners resident in the country or by firms trading regularly with the PRC. These branches allow foreigners, upon departure from the PRC, to reconvert RMB deposits to foreign currencies. Inquiries may be made at the BOC Beijing Head Office at 410 Fuchengmennei Avenue.

HEALTH

Your physician or local public health authority should always be consulted before you leave for an extended trip. Touring China, even as part of an organized group, can be arduous, especially during the warmer months. Tourist days are long, and are usually compulsively filled with a number of planned activities, many of which may require a considerable amount of walking or even climbing (apart from the newer hotels, few Chinese buildings have elevators). Intercity travel days can be especially taxing, given long waits at airports and train stations and frequent shortage of adequate porterage services. Most itineraries allot little time for rest or relaxation. Not to be overlooked as a source of additional strain is the profound "remoteness" of China—its language, customs, food, and the look of its streets and cities. At first, at least, even the simplest transactions seem fraught with difficulty. So it helps, if at all possible, to try to embark on a China trip feeling fit and well-rested.

Since 1982, smallpox innoculations have not been required for entry into the People's Republic of China. Other shots are variously recommended by authorities and physicians, including cholera, tetanus, typhus, and gammaglobulin. In general, the PRC discourages travel by persons who are ill, pregnant, or of advanced age (all foreign entrants must fill out a health questionnaire prior to passing through immigration). Also, since early 1987, all foreigners planning to reside for a year or more in China must submit to testing for AIDS.

MEDICAL CARE IN CHINA

Many visitors have commented on the extraordinary concern shown by the Chinese for their guests' health and have praised the excellent care provided by Chinese hospitals and medical personnel. Medical services are available to visitors at hospitals and local clinics in all major cities and in the countryside.

The most common maladies afflicting travelers in China are respiratory problems such as head colds, bronchial conditions, and sore throats. Diarrhea or constipation may also be problems, and appropriate remedies should be taken along on the prior advice of a physician. Standard antibiotics and medications are available in China, but foreigners may have to spend a considerable amount of time and effort to obtain them. Visitors should be sure to pack ample supplies of prescribed medications. Women should take along sanitary napkins or tampons—although the guide may be able to supply the former, the latter are not yet publicly available in China.

Sanitary conditions are generally acceptable throughout the country. Tap water is not potable in China, even in the large cities. Hotel rooms are supplied with boiled water in thermos bottles or carafes. Ice is made from purified water and local beverages are safe. Restaurants take the sensitivity of their foreign guests' stomachs into account, and even meals prepared on rural communes will have been carefully supervised. Chinese cuisine provides built-in safeguards since two of its cardinal rules are use of fresh ingredients and cooking with extremely high temperatures.

Tour guides are extremely solicitous about health problems, and at first signs of illness will recommend seeing a doctor.

HOSPITALS

Should an illness require hospitalization, both Western and Chinese medicines are available. Visitors will be given their choice of treatment (it is in no case advisable, however, to go to China with the expectation of getting long-standing rheumatism or gallbladder disorders cured by herbs or acupuncture). The Chinese do not have Rh-negative blood, and their blood banks do not store it. Persons with this blood type should consult their physician before departing for China.

Some visitors may be put off by what may appear to be primitive medical facilities. There are no luxury hospitals in China, no carpeted waiting rooms, and few examples of the complex diagnostic equipment found in the West. Considering the barrier of language (although an interpreter will always come along to help) and the strange surroundings, it is natural to feel uncomfortable. Such qualms are unfounded, however, since Chinese physicians are well trained and their diagnostic techniques sophisticated, time-honored, and judicious.

In case of serious illness, it is possible to have relatives summoned; the Chinese will facilitate special invitations, visa clearance, and other necessary arrangements. At the same time, one should notify one's embassy in Beijing.

DOMESTIC TRAVEL
CONNECTIONS IN CHINA

Most travel by foreign visitors between the major cities of China is by air. Shorter intercity excursions are by train. Most foreign visitors will not have to buy their own tickets for air or train travel; the host organization handles all reservations, ticket purchases, and appropriate clearances with the public security bureau (a "foreigners check-post" is set up at all major airports and train stations).

CAAC DOMESTIC FLIGHT SERVICES

The Chinese airline, the Civil Aviation Administration of China (CAAC), has expanded its services greatly in recent years. Domestically, CAAC has more than 200 routes and uses an array of jet aircraft—Boeing 737s, 707s, 757s, British Tridents, and Soviet Ilyushin 62s and 18s—between the three major cities of Beijing, Shanghai, and Guangzhou, as well as between other points. Propeller planes such as the Soviet Antonov are used between small cities. The use of Boeing 747s began in 1980 on CAAC's international and Hong Kong routes and on the Beijing-Guangzhou run, with new equipment purchased from the US (including Boeing 767s and DC 9-80s) and Europe entering domestic service during 1984–85.

Air travel in China has become increasingly more comfortable (the Soviet planes are exceptions, with their notorious lack of legroom), and schedules more convenient. However, flights are almost always crowded, mainly with officials, People's Liberation Army personnel, and foreign tour groups. Flight departures remain subject to inordinate delays or even cancellations, mainly owing to lack of sophisticated weather instrumentation.

DISTANCES BETWEEN CHINA'S MAIN TOURIST CITIES

Shortest Railway Distance, in Kilometers

1,000 KILOMETERS = 621 MILES

	Beijing	Shanghai	Tianjin	Guangzhou	Nanning	Changsha	Shaoshan	Wuchang	Nanjing	Wuxi	Suzhou	Hangzhou	Jinan	Qingdao	Xi'an	Kunming	Chengdu	Chongqing	Zhengzhou	Shijiazhuang	Dalian	Shenyang	Changchun
Shanghai	1462																						
Tianjin	137	1325																					
Guangzhou	2313	1811	2450																				
Nanning	2565	2063	2702	1334																			
Changsha	1587	1187	1724	726	978																		
Shaoshan	1718	1216	1855	755	1007	131																	
Wuchang	1229	1534	1366	1084	1336	358	489																
Nanjing	1157	305	1020	2116	2368	1492	1521	1229															
Wuxi	1334	128	1197	1939	2191	1315	1344	1406	177														
Suzhou	1376	86	1239	1897	2149	1273	1302	1448	219	42													
Hangzhou	1651	189	1514	1622	1874	998	1027	1356	494	317	275												
Jinan	494	968	357	2536	2284	1558	1689	1200	663	840	882	1157											
Qingdao	887	1361	750	2677	2929	1951	2082	1593	1056	1233	1275	1550	393										
Xi'an	1165	1511	1302	2129	2381	1403	1534	1045	1206	1383	1425	1700	1177	1570									
Kunming	3179	2677	3316	2216	1501	1592	1503	1950	2982	2805	2763	2488	3512	3119	1942								
Chengdu	2048	2353	2185	2544	1829	1920	1831	1887	2048	2225	2267	2542	2019	2412	842	1100							
Chongqing	2552	2501	2689	2040	1325	1416	1327	1774	2552	2729	2771	2312	2523	2916	1346	1102	504						
Zhengzhou	695	1000	832	1618	1870	892	1023	534	695	872	914	1189	666	1059	511	2453	1353	1857					
Shijiazhuang	283	1266	420	2030	2282	1304	1435	946	961	1138	1180	1455	298	691	923	2865	1765	2269	412				
Dalian	1238	2426	1101	3551	3803	2825	2956	2467	2121	2298	2340	2615	1458	1851	2403	4417	3286	3790	1933	1521			
Shenyang	841	2029	704	3154	3406	2428	2559	2070	1724	1901	1943	2218	1061	1454	2006	4020	2889	3393	1536	1124	397		
Changchun	1146	2334	1009	3459	3711	2733	2864	2375	2029	2206	2248	2523	1366	1759	2311	4325	3194	3698	1841	1429	702	305	
Harbin	1388	2576	1251	3701	3953	2975	3106	2617	2271	2448	2490	2763	1608	2001	2553	4567	3436	3940	2083	1671	944	547	242

DOMESTIC TRAVEL

During 1986, CAAC witnessed the emergence of three competitors, with several other ventures in the offing. Hong Kong's Dragonair began scheduled services to Hangzhou, Xiamen, and Guangzhou. Shanghai Airlines set up operations in 1986 with plans to enter both domestic and international routings. United China Airlines (UCA), a new civilian airline in part operated by the air corps of the People's Liberation Army, began operating from Beijing's Nanyuan Airport; 14 domestic routings, to destinations such as Xi'an, Shanghai, and Lushan, were in place by the end of 1986.

Airports, whether new or old, are spartan, with vacant, unadorned waiting rooms. Each airport usually has a small retail shop (selling regional specialties) and a restaurant. The largest — and the least spartan — air terminal in China opened in Beijing in 1981; an airport hotel, covered ramps to the aircraft, automated baggage handling, and other modern amenities are part of the new complex. Other new airports have been built at Tianjin, Harbin, Ürümqi, and Guilin. Shanghai has the second largest. Since 1980, departing passengers on international flights have been required to pay an airport tax of Y10.

CAAC Flight Reservations. Independent travelers must either purchase their tickets through CITS (who will add a service fee) or at the local CAAC office, where the lines can be staggering. If you are going to a city that requires a travel pass, you must have the pass in hand before you can purchase a ticket. Requests for domestic flights should be made no later than 24 hours before the desired departure time (if possible, several days' notice is advisable to ensure a seat on the day requested). Domestic flights are not yet fully computerized, so advance booking of onward flights from your next destination can be problematic, if not impossible. CAAC prefers that you book the connecting flight when you reach your next point of departure, or else purchase an open ticket and confirm it in the next city.

If a reservation is canceled at least two hours prior to the scheduled departure time, a refund of the full purchase price less Y4 will be provided. If a reservation is canceled less than two hours before departure, a fee of 20% of the purchase price is deducted from the refund. China gets tough with "no-shows": passengers who fail to appear for their flight will forfeit the full purchase price; their ticket may not be transferred to another flight.

Fares. Below is a sample listing of CAAC's economy-class domestic fares. Fares were increased by 30% in mid-1987 and are subject to change without notice. Fares apply to all adults and children over 12 years of age. Children under 12 must be accompanied by a parent or guardian. The fare for an infant under 2 years old is 10% of the adult fare; a second infant and children between 2 and 12 years old are charged 50% of the adult fare. CAAC offers no excursion fares; foreign groups receive a 15% discount for domestic flights in off-season (December through February) and students (with ID) may apply for 50% reductions on outbound domestic flights from Beijing from July 15 to August 31.

CAAC DOMESTIC AND REGIONAL FARES*

		YUAN	US DOLLARS
Beijing to	Changsha	304	81.88
	Chengdu†	411	110.70
	Guangzhou†	553	148.94
	Hong Kong†	686	184.77
	Hangzhou†	274	73.80
	Nanjing	225	60.60
	Nanning	476	128.20
	Shanghai†	274	73.80
	Shenyang	143	38.51
	Wuhan	260	70.02
	Xi'an	240	64.64
Shanghai to	Changsha	205	55.21
	Chengdu†	425	114.47
	Guangzhou†	343	92.38
	Hong Kong†	480	129.28
	Kunming	517	139.25
	Nanjing	61	16.43
	Shenyang	384	103.42
	Xi'an	300	80.80
Guangzhou to	Guilin	129	34.74
	Hangzhou	308	82.95
	Hong Kong†	141	37.97
	Kunming	326	87.80
	Nanning	137	36.90
	Wuhan	194	52.25

*Fares in effect during 1988, subject to change. Conversion factor: Y1 =US$0.26
†First-class service available for 33% surcharge.

Baggage. Passengers are limited to 30 kg. (66 lbs.) of baggage in first class, 20 kg. (44 lbs.) in economy class. On domestic flights, passengers are allowed up to 20 kg. (44 lbs.) of baggage and 5 kg. (11 lbs.) of hand luggage. Excess baggage is assessed at 1% of the applicable one-way fare per kilo (2.2 lbs.).

CAAC personnel are scrupulous in their application of extra-weight charges. Passengers are thus advised to keep close tabs on their luggage weight, lest they suddenly find themselves being relieved of all reserve spending money on the last leg of their trip in China. In the case of tour groups, bags are sometimes weighed en masse, with the group collectively assessed for any cumulative overweight (in which case someone is bound to be left feeling resentful at having shelled out to transport someone else's jade elephant). The best remedy is to pack light before leaving and to try to limit purchases to items made of wicker, bamboo, or cloth.

RAIL SERVICES

Train travel affords an ideal means for taking in great stretches of China's remarkably varied countryside. Chinese trains are not notably comfortable, however, and service can be painfully slow. For example, "express" train service between Beijing and Guangzhou, a distance of 2,313 km. (1,436 mi.), takes 34 hours. All classes of rail fares have been steadily increased, so only the low classes will yield significant savings over air travel. For the Chinese people, however, trains provide the major means of long-distance travel, making rail travel an important component of the Chinese lifestyle. So the experience can be worthwhile — especially if it can be confined to under eight hours.

Classes and Services. The Chinese divide their trains into "hard seat" and "soft seat" coaches and "hard" and "soft" sleepers, with the "soft" categories reserved for foreigners and high-ranking Chinese such as army personnel and government officials. On long-distance trains there are sleeping coaches reminiscent of European trains, accommodating 32 passengers — four each in eight separate compartments, each with its own bunks, wood-paneled walls, fan, curtains, and a small potted plant. Such trains also have dining cars (as does the Guangzhou-to-Hong Kong train). Soft-class carriages are serviced by attendants who regularly mop the floors, clean woodwork, and serve tea and other beverages (unlike airplanes, trains serve beer and occasionally wine).

Most Chinese travel hard seat or hard sleeper, so if you view your trip as a chance to mingle with the average Chinese, or simply wish to save money, you could choose either of the hard categories. Hard seats can be very crowded and noisy, however, and tickets are no assurance that seats will in fact be available. Hard sleeper class is preferable (and costs *half* the price of soft sleeper), but these sections can also be noisy and congested. Soft seat is comfortable, quiet, and usually not very crowded. The ample compartments may allow you to stretch out on an empty seat and sleep. Soft sleeper offers the most privacy—four people in an enclosed cabin. But there is a tendency to segregate foreigners from Chinese in this class, leaving only a chance opportunity to meet up with Chinese during the journey.

Chinese trains generally run on time, and are at least more reliable than planes with respect to schedule. A long, ringing bell is the signal for departure. Most Chinese have few opportunities for long-distance train travel. Thus, a departure by rail is something of an event: as the train pulls out of the station, it is accompanied by martial music carried over loudspeakers in each compartment or coach. The music continues sporadically during the trip—dining, conversation, even slumber are frequently interrupted by loudspeaker announcements of stops, time, news reports, and interludes of music. It is possible to turn off the speaker system, either in the individual compartments, where the switch is located under the table, or near the door at the end of each car.

DOMESTIC EXPRESS TRAIN SERVICES
(From Beijing)*

DESTINATION	TRAVEL TIME	FARES (IN YUAN)		
	(approximate)	Soft Sleeper	Hard Sleeper	Hard Seat
Anshan	14 hours	116.00	61.40	38.50
Beidaihe	6 hours	56.00	29.20	17.70
Changcun	15 hours	135.70	71.90	44.90
Changsha	23 hours	175.50	93.00	58.20
Chengde	5 hours	17.30†	—	10.70
Chengdu	33 hours	212.00	112.50	70.40
Chongqing	45 hours	257.50	138.10	86.40
Dalian	19 hours	144.50	76.70	47.90
Daqing	20 hours	171.60	89.90	55.90
Datong	7 hours	56.70	30.20	18.70
Fuzhou	44 hours	276.10	141.50	88.60
Guangzhou	34 hours	235.20	124.50	77.80
Guilin	31 hours	217.40	115.10	72.00
Hangzhou	26 hours	179.30	95.00	59.40
Harbin	16 hours	158.40	83.80	52.40
Hohhot	14 hours	87.80	46.60	29.10
Jilin	23 hours	137.80	70.00	41.20
Jinan	9 hours	71.80	38.00	23.70
Kaifeng (via Zhengzhou)	13 hours	98.90	45.10	27.70
Kunming	59 hours	314.60	166.70	104.30
Lanzhou	33 hours	197.60	104.80	65.60
Luoyang	12 hours	103.10	54.80	34.30
Nanjing	19 hours	140.10	74.30	46.50
Qingdao	20 hours	117.70	59.20	37.10
Shanghai	23 hours	193.20	102.80	64.40
Shenyang	10 hours	107.30	57.00	35.70
Shijiazhuang	4 hours	50.00	21.70†	14.30
Suzhou	22 hours	158.40	83.90	52.50
Tianjin	2 hours	39.50	11.30†	7.60
Ürümqi	69 hours	365.80	194.00	121.00
Wuhan	18 hours	144.50	76.80	47.90
Wuxi	21 hours	153.80	83.70	51.10
Xi'an	21 hours	144.50	76.70	47.90

*All daily departures. Fares in effect during 1988, in many cases, slower trains available at lower rates. Fares subject to change and applicable only to train tickets purchased in China.
†Soft seat.

Railway Dining. Eating aboard Chinese trains can present problems, but the higher your class of travel the easier it is to obtain decent meals on the train. In soft sleeper class, an attendant will come by to take passengers' orders. Later, you will be advised of an appointed time to go to the dining car for your meal. Of course, you can also bring your own food, as many Chinese do. The alternative is to purchase a "box" lunch or dinner from carts pushed up and down the hard seat and sleeper sections of the train (this service is not available to those in soft sleeper). Individual dishes can sometimes be ordered but, more usually, you must pay a fixed amount for the "house dinner." Quality is very uneven. On some trains, only noodles are served.

Making Train Reservations. Using the Chinese rail system on your own is not a straightforward procedure. Under the glass of the main service counter in most hotels is a schedule for rail connections that serve the city. Many hotels or any CITS office can purchase tickets for you. A small service charge will be attached, but it is well worth the time saved waiting on line at train station ticket counters. If the hotel doesn't sell tickets (as is the case in most Beijing hotels) and the local CITS office is not inclined to be helpful (asserting, for example, that all trains leaving the city are fully booked for the foreseeable future), the train station may be tried as a last resort. But in some cities, even finding the correct booking office can be a problem. For example, in Guangzhou you have to go to CITS for train bookings going north of Zhengzhou, to the main station for trains leaving that day, and to another station clear across town for all other types of tickets. In Shanghai, the Heping (Peace) Hotel is the best place to buy tickets, but the Jinjiang Hotel and the railway ticket office on Beijing Road are also possibilities. In Beijing, a booking window for foreigners was opened at the main railway station in 1984.

For some connections, you will be presented with a choice of several different types of train services, and there is always a choice as to class of travel. There are "special express" (*te kuai*), "direct express" (*zhi kuai*— "modified express"), and "slow" trains. The differences in time can add up to a few hours, so it is important to know what the choices are.

LONG-DISTANCE BUS SERVICES

China as yet lacks a modern, long-distance highway system and intercity bus services exist mainly to supplement the railroads. Thus, there aren't many places in China where it is necessary to use buses for travel between cities. Exceptions include links between cities along the coast of Fujian, or from Hangzhou to Huangshan.

There are two types of long-distance buses: large, air-conditioned cruisers operated by CITS; and crowded, open-air public buses. The latter are tolerable if temperatures are moderate and if you are not carrying much luggage. Public buses are certainly a lot cheaper, although you will have to go to the bus station yourself to obtain a ticket. These buses can be substantially slower, too, as they often make a number of scheduled and unscheduled stops en route and may require frequent changes for long-distance journeys.

COASTAL AND INLAND PASSENGER SHIP SERVICES

Boat travel, either coastal or inland, can be one of the most pleasant ways to travel in China, although it will naturally take a bit longer to get anyplace by this means. Chinese boats tend to be much cleaner than the trains. This is especially true in the case of international-class vessels, such as the M.S. *Yangtse River,* which is a veritable floating pleasure palace, or boats that ply the East China coast between Xiamen and Hong Kong.

Boat tickets may be purchased at dockside or at the appropriate maritime ticket office. In some cities, CITS will purchase the tickets for you, although boat travel (apart from Yangtse Gorge cruises) has been slow to come under the purview of most local foreign-travel bureaus. It's best to purchase tickets early, and to obtain the best class available if comfort and privacy are of any consideration. The cheaper tickets afford few amenities, and may place you in an airless dormitory below decks. (See Shanghai city section and the Hong Kong–China Connection above for listings of passenger ship connections.)

Ferries cross major rivers, such as the Huangpu in Shanghai or the Pearl in Guangzhou. These inexpensive rides are recommended in leisure time, since they may allow exploration of areas not often visited.

GETTING AROUND IN CHINESE CITIES

Taxis. Taxis are available in most Chinese cities at rates of 50–80 *fen* per km. Surcharges, sometimes as much as 100%, may be applicable for return trips. Not all taxi drivers are as scrupulous as you'd expect, so it is always best to check the odometer to ensure that the assessed fare is correct. It should also be noted that fares are not related to the number of passengers. In some smaller cities, such as Suzhou, the best approach may be to hire a car for an entire day, in which case reasonable flat rates of Y25–30 will apply. In this way, you can secure convenient transportation, with the extra advantage of using your driver as a guide, and manage thus to cover an entire city in one day. Most cities also have three-wheeled taxis and tricycle pedicabs. These should theoretically be a lot cheaper than proper taxis, but might very well end up costing unsuspecting foreigners much more. In this respect, it's important to ascertain the fare before setting out. In Shanghai, motorized three-wheelers charge 15 *fen* per km. In other cities, and always in the case of pedicabs, the price is commonly established through negotiations with the driver.

As of 1987, Guangzhou and Beijing were the only cities where taxis could be hailed from the street (albeit with difficulty). Taxis in both cities now bear special license plates and other distinguishing marks.

Urban Buses. Even for those using taxis most of the time, there might be an occasion when you will need or want to take a bus, even just for the experience. If so, it's important to first purchase a bus map. These are commonly sold in front of train stations or in hotel gift shops. Bus maps are invariably in Chinese, although routes are denoted in Arabic numerals. The maps can be read alongside the street maps in this book. Otherwise, you may ask someone to point out where you are and where you want to go and work things out from there. Bus routes are traced with red and blue lines. Each dot on the line is a stop. Many cities now publish fairly detailed tourist maps in English, although bus routes are rarely indicated.

Buses can be crowded and seats are in great demand. If a large group is waiting at the stop, you can anticipate a mad rush for the door when the bus arrives. In these circumstances, it's best to stay out of the way and just wait for the crowd to clear. Once on board, there will be a ticket seller who will ask you where you want to go or what price ticket you wish to purchase. Usually, it's enough to say the name of the place and allow the seller to work out the fare. If you can't follow the transaction, just hold out your hand with some change in it and the conductor will take the required amount and give you a ticket. Fares are usually 5–25 *fen* per person, depending on the distance to be travelled. Usually, if the conductor observes that you are not familiar with the route, he or she will signal when you have reached your stop.

A new innovation has recently come to Beijing. State-operated "small public buses" (or minivans) stop at regular bus stops to pick up waiting passengers on the outskirts of town and drive up to the center of Beijing (Beijing Station or Qianmen). The minivan ride is faster than the regular bus but can cost as much as Y2.

Subways. China's first subway system now operates in Beijing and another is under construction in Shanghai. In Beijing, the subway, now complete, follows the line of the old city walls and extends to the western suburbs. (For more details, see Beijing section, below.) Rides on the Beijing subway cost 2–3 *jiao*. The subway operates between 6 AM and 9 PM. The equipment is spotlessly maintained and the ride is rapid, smooth, and quiet (a revelation to New Yorkers or Chicagoans).

Bicycles. In Beijing, Chengdu, and some other cities, you may rent bicycles, an option that is highly recommended if at all feasible. (Information on rentals is provided below in the Beijing and Chengdu city sections.) With a bicycle you can go just about anywhere you want and at your own pace. If you want to stop somewhere, look for a bicycle parking lot. If it's a pay lot, then wait for the attendant to give you a slip or tag. When you return, surrender the tag along with two *fen* for the parking fee.

Traffic rules are basically the same as in the US, but in China cycling is something more of a free-for-all. Be especially careful at street corners and traffic lights, as drivers often do not look carefully before making a turn and aren't required to stop before turning right at a red light. If traffic gets too heavy, just walk the bike as local people do.

Police Assistance. Other than its CITS offices, China has yet to set up a mechanism for providing assistance or information to foreign tourists. If you need assistance of any type, however, the Public Security Bureau (PSB—China's police) can be helpful. These are also the officials to be contacted for visa extensions and travel passes, as well as in cases of missing property. On the streets, PSB officers in the larger cities are being reoutfitted in tailored khaki-green uniforms with leather-peaked caps and belted jackets with gold trim. The demeanor of Chinese police is stern but accommodating. Officers who can't speak English can quickly seek out an interpreter.

URBAN SIGHTSEEING TOURS

In those cities open to foreigners, there may be as many as five Chinese organizations that handle tourism. In most cases, CITS will be your best bet, but some cities may only have a CTS office (mainly serving tourists of Chinese descent). Even in cities with both, CTS may be more helpful in terms of offering one- or two-day city tours at very reasonable rates. Prices per person may depend upon how many people are traveling together. In all cases, group touring may work out to be much cheaper than trying to visit the same sites on your own. Joining a group is certainly easier and will afford the benefits of a guide. There are also special Overseas Chinese Travel Service (OCTS) offices in many cities, with rates comparable to CTS. Information on these tour offerings is usually available at the city's overseas Chinese hotel. Even if the English of OCTS guides is less than intelligible, you can avail yourself of the transportation and perhaps the bilingual abilities of fellow tour members.

Aside from organized groups or taxi tours, you may simply wish to strike out on your own and on bicycle or on foot. In compact cities such as Changsha, this may indeed prove to be the best way to accomplish most of your sightseeing. There are very few restrictions on where foreigners can go within a city (as long as you avoid entering private areas or compounds), so you may generally feel free to walk anywhere. Moreover, walkers may proceed with the assurance that Chinese cities are among the safest in the world. Before you set out, however, take a card bearing the hotel's name in Chinese in case you get lost or decide to return by taxi (some hotels now automatically give out a bilingual address card upon registration). Many of the city sections in this book outline the most interesting walking tours, but you can just as readily follow your instincts. Consult a map and try either to follow a circular route or to walk parallel to a bus line. It's not always easy to find a taxi when you need one, so it's best to plan a means for returning to your starting point before setting out.

HOTEL ACCOMMODATIONS

For most travelers, hotel accommodations are prearranged and preassigned by CITS or other Chinese host organizations. China has been working hard to expand and modernize its hotel sector so that today the larger hotels in China in several respects approach deluxe or first-class international standards. The most reliable hotels in terms of comfort, amenities, and service are the establishments completed in the 1980s and under joint-venture agreements with foreign interests. Hotels such as the Great Wall in Beijing or the White Swan in Guangzhou rely heavily on Hong Kong-trained management and service staffs and thus more closely adhere to international standards than their wholly Chinese-owned counterparts. The joint-venture hotels are relatively expensive but they also have the singular advantage of accepting direct bookings from outside of China.

Hotels outside of this category vary considerably in standards and quality of services. While some newer, Chinese-built hotels, such as the Jinling in Nanjing, can be ranked among the better hotels in Asia, too many others have not risen from the standards to which they were first built some 30 years ago—as hardship posts for middle-level Soviet technocrats living in China. Thus it remains that most of the 1,000 Chinese hotels that serve foreigners are joyless edifaces, equipped with functional but homely appurtenances. The smaller or more remote the city, the less likelihood of finding innerspring (as opposed to straw) mattresses, air-conditioning, or hot and cold running water. And despite frequent exhortations from the hotel bureaucracy, overall standards of cleanliness and maintenance remain subject to gross, periodic lapses.

Newness in China does not automatically ensure greater comfort. Ancient, gardened guest houses made of teak and stone can prove far superior to an ill-maintained, 20-story high-rise with ricotta-cheese walls and biweekly elevator service. A new wave of luxury-style hotels, many being built with the help of US, Japanese, and Hong Kong developers, began to enter service in the mid-1980s. But even the availability of freshly brewed coffee, room service, and health clubs is not likely to make China's hotels a memorable part of one's stay in the country. It may take several years more before the gap between Western standards of efficiency and comfort and the Chinese hotel bureaucracy's ability to understand and meet those standards is appreciably narrowed. But at least it could be said that by the mid-1980s most China travelers could safely count on a good night's sleep, a hot bath, and a decent meal before setting out for the next day's sightseeing.

HOTEL RESERVATIONS IN CHINA

Advance Reservations. A select number of China's newer hotels now offer direct-booking service from outside of China through international hotel reservation networks to which all travel agents have access. These hotels include the Jianguo, Great Wall, Jinglun, Lido, and Fragrant Hill in Beijing; the Cypress in Shanghai; and the White Swan and China hotels in Guangzhou. Not surprisingly, space in these establishments is under great demand and many are booked up at least two or three months in advance, especially for peak months.

It's important to note, however, that the vast majority of China's tourist hotels are as yet neither equipped nor authorized to accept direct reservations from foreigners. Most of these hotels, rather, have direct links to CITS, which serves as their primary or exclusive booking agent. Thus, China tour packages sold by CITS, whether for groups or individuals, will automatically make use of these hotels unless a request is made for upgrading to one of the above-mentioned "joint-venture" hotels or state guest houses, as available from city to city. It should also be noted that travelers are rarely offered a choice when booking a CITS hotel. Indeed, although reservations can be confirmed well in advance of departure, the actual assignment of a specific hotel may not occur until the day of arrival in a given city. Thus it is that those not willing to pay the premium for a direct-booking hotel must take what they are given. Either of two developments could alleviate this problem: a nationwide, automated reservation system or a policy decision that allows all hotels to accept direct bookings. Neither is a likelihood for the remainder of the 1980s.

Reservations within China. Individuals traveling during peak seasons (April-June, September-October) or planning to visit cities with high tourist volumes (particularly Beijing, Shanghai, Xi'an, and Guilin) can expect to experience considerable difficulty in securing space at the hotel of their choice, especially if the choice is a deluxe or first-class hotel in a central location. The recommended approach is first to attempt to secure onward reservations through the hotels that accept direct bookings (see hotel listings in individual city sections, below) or through CITS. You will be assessed a fee for this service and may also be required to pay to have someone meet you at your point of arrival and escort you to the hotel. Despite the promised convenience, CITS greeting services are expensive and may not even happen: the guide designated to meet you may not show up or, more likely, may not be able to locate or identify you amidst the chaos of other arriving passengers. Probably the greatest drawback is that you cannot ordinarily choose the hotel you will be staying at, so you might end up at a location well outside of town. Most Chinese hotels will not accept reservations through any other means, but if one speaks Chinese, hotels have become increasingly willing to accept direct reservations.

For those arriving in a city without prior hotel bookings, the first step remains to ask CITS where space is available. In a few cities, CITS maintains a service desk in the airport or train station. The other option is to choose a hotel from among those listed in this book, engage a taxi to take you there, and make your case at the front desk. If you feel brave, you might even leave it to the judgment of the driver to take you to the nearest hotel with a potential vacancy. Often, if it is a small city, there are only one or two hotels set aside for foreigners, so at least the choice is made easier.

When registering at a hotel, budget-conscious travelers should inquire about room rates. Most hotels have a wide range of rooms and prices. If there are no rooms available within your requested price category, the attendant will usually try to help you find a hotel nearby that is suitable. People of Asian decent (e.g., Japanese, Filipinos, Thais) can stay at overseas Chinese hotels without difficulty. These hotels are usually very reasonable and often feature excellent food, including regional specialties. Offices of CTS and the Overseas Chinese Travel Service are usually housed in these hotels. Be prepared to be asked to surrender your passport, which will be returned on request. Checkout time is always noon. If you stay after that, there will be a half-day surcharge up to 6 PM and a full day's charge after that.

HOTEL SERVICES

Most large hotels now have postal, banking, telegraph, and telex facilities (outgoing but not incoming) on the premises. Arrangements for taxis, wake-up calls, and restaurant reservations may be made at the main desk or at service desks on each floor. Room service is available, but usually only for drinks and snack foods—heartier fare such as soup, club sandwiches, or eggs can be gotten only through ardent appeals to the service staff, usually on grounds of mortal illness or dire incapacity. Hotel shops sell snacks (lately including an array of imported sweets), sundries, and handicrafts.

Service Desks. Each residence floor normally has a service counter equipped to handle a variety of services. Laundry bags can be found in the room (behind the bathroom door or on the shelf in the closet) or can be obtained at the service desk, which usually offers excellent laundry and dry-cleaning services (laundry is usually ready in one day, dry-cleaning in two). The desk personnel will also take care of minor tailoring and repairs and can book long-distance telephone calls. Shoes left outside the room door will often be returned polished by the next morning (not recommended if you have only one pair of shoes). Service counters also sell snacks, cigarettes, mineral water, beer, Chinese liquor, and, in a few cases, ice (dispensed one cube at a time, like precious stones).

Storage. Most hotels in China permit guests to store anything from a small suitcase to a huge trunk in the hotel storage center. Rates average about 50 *fen* per day. Be prepared for an inspection of all goods you wish to store, and check time limitations, which may vary with each hotel.

Hairdressers. Hotels in the larger Chinese cities usually have a hairdressing and/or barber salon. Rates are low and the results are better than adequate. Blow dryers are becoming as popular in China's hair salons as they are in the West.

Chinese hairdressers provide a service that is, for most foreigners, an irresistible bonus: a head massage. Service fees are moderate.

HOTEL ROOM AMENITIES

The standard hotel room in China is simple, functional, and reasonably clean and comfortable. It is generally furnished with twin beds (double beds are almost unheard-of in China), a desk, easy chair, and bureau. A carafe of pre-boiled drinking water, a thermos of hot water for tea, and a container of loose tea are generally provided. Most rooms also have a telephone; some have radios; most now have TV sets, often with closed-circuit programming. Many hotels now offer "deluxe" accommodations— meaning more space, more furniture, and often a small refrigerator (usually turned off between occupancies so that by the time it gets cold enough to produce an ice cube you'll be well on your way to Inner Mongolia).

Electricity. While most electrical systems in China now operate at 220v, voltage in China may vary at times, occasionally dropping below 200v. Although small personal-care appliances should not be affected, larger, more complex machines may need a stabilizer. This can cause problems for visitors from North America (US and Canada) where the normal voltage is 110v; those who fail to ascertain the voltage in their Chinese hotel may thus end up with a detonated hair dryer or electric shaver. To avoid such "blow-ups," one should take along a transformer (220v to 110v).

Visitors to China should also be aware that there is little, if any, consistency in the size, shape, and performance of wall outlets. Some of the newer hotels are supplied with standard international (three-pronged) outlets. Adaptor plugs can be purchased at some hotels or Friendship Stores.

Lighting in hotel rooms is often inadequate, especially for reading or writing at night, and travelers who expect to do work in their rooms or do a lot of reading may wish to pack high-wattage bulbs for the trip. A small flashlight (with a few extra batteries) may also come in handy. Most transistor radios can pick up music from local stations and could provide pleasant diversion. Typewriters, calculators, and similar light office equipment may be hard to come by in China and should be brought along if a need for them is anticipated (in that light, business travelers might wish to pack a supply of carbon paper or even a portable photo-copier, since copying services are nonexistent in most Chinese cities).

POSTAL SERVICE
AND TELECOMMUNICATIONS

China maintains good mail and telecommunications links with the outside world. Telex and photo-telegraphic facilities are available for business transactions. Most communications services are available at hotels. In September 1986, international telecommunications rates were raised by an average of 50%.

MAIL

The following are current international postal rates (in RMB):

Postcard (airmail)	.70
Letter (airmail)	.80 for first 10 g.
Letter (surface)	.50 for up to 20 g.
Aerogram	.70
Small packets (surface)	.70 up to 100 g.
Small packets (airmail)	.70 + .20 for every 10 g. or fraction thereof

How Fast Is Airmail? Travelers should be aware of the inordinate time usually required for a postcard or letter from China to cross the sea. Postcards from China are particularly slow in arriving, sometimes taking 2–3 weeks to reach their destination. Letters with airmail postage should arrive in 6–10 days. If speed of communication is essential, travelers should consider placing a telephone call or sending a cable.

Sending Your Purchases Home. The Friendship Stores in Beijing and Shanghai, as well as PTT offices, are equipped to send large parcels overseas. International shipping rates are reasonable, but crating charges are high. Sending home large packages that require special crating is strongly discouraged, since it could take 3–4 months for the package to arrive—and may end up costing double or triple the value of the contents. Smaller packages of books or clothing can, by contrast, be mailed quite cheaply.

TELEPHONES

Long Distance. Long-distance calls to North America are charged at the rate of Y15 per minute, with a minimum three-minute charge. Long-distance calls may be booked at hotel service desks or at all PTT offices and usually take about 15 minutes to be completed. During peak hours (7–11 PM), however, an international call from one of China's large cities could take up to 1½ hours to complete. China's high rates can be avoided by reversing the charges or billing to an international credit card (neither method applicable to Hong Kong calls). The vast majority of China's long-distance operators are well-trained, persistent, and English-speaking.

Local Phone Calls. Although telephone services were expanding dramatically in the 1980s, China is still a long way from becoming a "telephone culture." Apart from activities in the foreign trade sector, most encounters are expected to be made face-to-face, with people commonly showing up at each other's homes or offices unannounced. Local calls can be frustrating, and often fruitless, for visitors to China. Coin-operated public phones were being installed throughout Beijing in 1983, but as of late 1985, there was but one pay phone in Shanghai—an antiquated model on display in a large department store—and it caused quite a stir among Chinese shoppers.

There are public phones in hotels and shops which display a metal sign with a sketch of a phone unit. Since homes are not usually equipped with phones, the few that exist are shared among a large number of people (e.g., one phone unit per apartment building).

Perhaps because of this relative shortage of phones, it could take 10 attempts to get through to the desired number. Your conversation would most likely begin with repeated shouts of *"Wei?" "Wei!"*—the Chinese way of saying "Hello, are you there?" The connection is often bad and the shouting could continue through the remainder of the phone call. Another irritating feature is that calls will be automatically disconnected after a lapse of 20 seconds of silence—if placed on hold, one is thus compelled to shout to oneself, whistle, or sing doggerels to keep the line open.

Try to avoid calling during *xiuxi* (rest) hours (about 12 noon–2 PM), when most of the switchboards close.

Callers should be aware that direct-dial calls will be billed by the minute even if no one answers. An unsuspecting soul in Guangzhou once was billed Y600 when he called overseas and let the telephone ring unanswered for 20 minutes. This can be avoided by hanging up promptly when there is no answer, or by calling via the international operator.

Cable. Telegram rates to overseas destinations vary considerably from country to country, but are generally expensive, at Y2.90 per word. The rate is doubled for "express" (four-hour) delivery and is halved for "regular cable" (night letter). International credit cards are accepted.

Telex. Telex facilities are available at main and branch post offices in large cities. A growing number of hotels now offer telex services, although most are equipped only for outgoing transmissions. In keeping with the Chinese practice of self-reliance, patrons are often expected to punch their own telex tapes. Rates to all overseas destinations, excluding Hong Kong, are Y14.40 per minute with a minimum three-minute charge.

INCOMING CORRESPONDENCE

Mail from North America or Europe generally takes 11–20 days to be delivered in China—almost twice the time of mail sent from China. For most tours, it is thus impractical to request mail from home. Since exact daily itineraries and hotels are rarely known prior to arrival in China, mail should not be addressed to hotels or cities. Mail for a tour group member should be addressed to:

Name of Individual, Name of Group, c/o Host Organization Head Office (e.g., China International Travel Service), Beijing, People's Republic of China.

Cables can reach the visitor in the same manner (the cable address of China International Travel Service is LUXINGSHE). Every effort is made to deliver cables promptly. For business travelers spending some time in one place, it is advantageous to register a cable address (annual charge is Y10).

Incoming telephone calls are connected by an overseas operator. Callers should instruct the operator to contact the host organization in Beijing in order to locate the delegation and the individual being sought.

TIME AROUND THE WORLD

When it's 12 noon in Beijing*, the standard time in the following cities is:

Amsterdam	5 AM	Montreal	11 PM**
Bangkok	11AM	Nairobi	7 AM
Beirut	6 AM	New York	11 PM**
Cairo	6 AM	Paris	5 AM
Chicago	10 PM**	Rio de Janiero	1 AM
Dallas	10 PM**	Rome	5 AM
Frankfurt	5 AM	San Francisco	8 PM**
Hong Kong	12 noon	Sydney	2 PM
Honolulu	6 PM**	Tokyo	1 PM
London	5 AM	Vancouver	8 PM**
Los Angeles	8 PM**	Zurich	5 AM

*Beijing time is standard throughout China.
**Of the preceding day.

CHINESE WEIGHTS AND MEASURES

Most of the PRC's international trade is conducted in the metric system, but the following Chinese weights and measures are still widely used in domestic transactions:

1 *jin* (catty) = 1.102 pounds = 0.5 kilogram
1 *dan* (picul) = 0.492 ton = 446.34 kilograms
1 *mu* = 0.1647 acre = 0.658 hectare
1 *li* = 0.5 kilometer = 0.311 mile

FOOD IN CHINA

O f the world's two great cuisines, the Chinese is as varied as, and, in fact, much older in tradition than, the French. The best Chinese chefs are masters at creating culinary triumphs from often mundane ingredients. Indeed, some of the most prized delicacies are said to have been concocted during times of famine from substances never before considered edible. The manner of serving even the simplest dishes appeals at once to the eye, the sense of smell, and the palate (see "The Cuisine of China," below).

But as with most great traditions in China, high praise must be tempered in one or another respect: in the old days, *haute cuisine* in China flourished under the patronage of the wealthy and aristocratic classes. With the disappearance of these groups, China's great chefs suddenly lacked consistent means of support. Furthermore, despite the government's efforts to sustain the old culinary traditions through vocational training programs, these could not compensate for skills and knowledge lost through profound disruptions in the old apprentice system. Thus, the absence of a demanding clientele, coupled with a profound social shift toward a cuisine that could be produced quickly and in large quantities and one that was compelled to make maximum use of local, mass-produced commodities, has resulted in a progressively less varied and less imaginative array of offerings.

In fairness, it should be noted that China's cuisine is not the only one in the world to have entered a decline in recent decades. And, in equal fairness, most travelers can still go to China with the expectation of being served healthful, palatable, well-prepared dishes—rarely brilliant but still distinguished by freshness of preparation (canned, freeze-dried, or frozen foods are virtually nonexistent) and by relative absence of chemical or synthetic enhancements (other than monosodium glutamate, known euphemistically in Chinese as "the essence of flavor").

HOTEL DINING

Dining in China can prove to be a nettlesome experience for those used to eating what they want, when they want. Generally speaking, most tour groups and visiting delegations will take most of their prepaid meals at their hotels (except for lunches on all-day excursions and banquets). Meals are served at designated times (usually 8 AM, 12 noon, and 6 PM), at preassigned tables, and from a menu preselected by the hotel cooks. Unless special requests are made, breakfast will be Western-style (eggs, toast, jam, coffee, a cake, or pastry); lunch and dinner are Chinese. It is usually possible to order a Chinese-style breakfast a day in advance, and if enough people to fill a table (eight or ten) request it. Diners are cautioned that "Western" cuisine in many hotels merely means Chinese food served in larger chunks and on large, individual plates; exceptions

FOOD IN CHINA

are the older "grand" hotels of Shanghai and Beijing, where the mixed grills and roasted fowls may still rival those served at London's Savoy 50 years ago. The hotel dining rooms will also be glad to serve Western food for lunch and dinner, again if the request is made well ahead of time and if enough persons in a group ask for it. It is often difficult to order individually prepared dishes (which in any case cost extra), although the large hotels will prepare special meals for visitors with special dietary requirements. In most cases, beverages, including beer and wine, are available at an additional cost (unless covered by a prepaid surcharge). Yogurt is sometimes available, at a small charge.

The argument runs that since the hotel staff has gone to considerable trouble planning menus for a tour group, the hotel will usually not refund the price of a planned meal that the tourist misses because of other arrangements.

For the sake of convenience, individual travelers will usually end up taking most of their meals at their hotels. One or more fixed-price house dinners are available as well as a range of Western and Chinese à-la-carte selections. Many newer hotels now offer buffets for breakfast and lunch. Hotel dining rooms tend to observe longer hours than restaurants, although it is still necessary to observe posted serving hours since few kitchens remain open continuously through the day or after 9 PM.

RESTAURANTS

Although it will entail an additional expense, eating at a local restaurant is highly recommended, both for atmosphere as well as for greater authenticity in their preparations, especially of local and regional fare, and for their wider array of offerings. If you wish to try a Chinese restaurant, you must first decide if you want a banquet-style repast or an average meal. The former requires a reservation; the latter requires only that you be in the restaurant early (usually 10:30–11 AM for lunch and 4:30–5 PM for dinner) and that you not be overly concerned about hygiene or crowds. Most of the country's best restaurants have set up separate sections for foreigners (including bilingual menus and, of course, price ranges that tend to inflate in translation). Group excursions to such establishments can be easily arranged by forming a party and making reservations through a tour escort, through the main service desk at the hotel, or at the restaurant itself (this usually requires a Chinese-speaking person). The custom is to establish a price range (Y20–30 per person is standard) and make advance requests for special dishes. (For recommended restaurants, see listings under individual cities.)

If you find yourself at a restaurant with no special provision for foreigners, you're certainly free to partake along with everyone else. If you can't find a seat, it is customary to stand behind the seats of people who look as if they might be finishing soon. The practice is not considered rude in China. Indeed, others will no doubt do this to you while you are eating. You can order from the menu by looking at the prices and asking questions or by simply pointing to what looks good on other people's tables. Some restaurants require diners to purchase tickets before eating. The tickets are collected by waiters who then bring the food. For these establishments, it's best to observe carefully what others are paying (and eating) before taking part.

The Chinese don't always use soap for washing dishes, so cleanliness is often a concern in public restaurants. For this reason, many local people carry their own chopsticks and are careful about selecting a place to eat. Westerners who reside in China tend to patronize hotel restaurants or the more expensive Chinese restaurants, as the food is usually better and the premises cleaner, quieter, and less crowded. Buying from most street stalls can be a health hazard, especially in neighborhoods near hospitals (where hepatitis may be endemic).

BANQUETS

It has been customary for the host organization in China to give a welcoming dinner in honor of visiting groups or delegations. Depending on the protocol required, the dinner can be an elaborate banquet—complete with formal invitations and a detailed seating plan—or a simple affair. In both cases, many of the same procedures apply.

All meals in China—including banquets—start at the announced time. Tardiness is considered rude. Formal dinners are timed to last about an hour and a half. Arriving guests are usually ushered into an anteroom and offered tea, hot towels, and about 10 to 15 minutes of light conversation with the hosts. The principal host will then signal that dinner is ready, and guests will be seated according to protocol. The host will preside, sitting at a head table (Chinese tradition dictates that the seat of honor faces the door), with the highest-ranking guests (i.e., the delegation's leaders) arranged to his left and right. It is customary for hosts to serve guests and for guests to at least attempt a nibble of everything they're served.

A typical setting will include a small plate, a pair of chopsticks resting on a holder (forks and knives are always available), and three glasses: for beer or soft drinks, wine, and maotai (a fiery 160-proof liquor) for toasts. Dishes are served according to a prescribed palate-stimulating sequence, starting with cold appetizers and continuing to 10 or more courses. A well-balanced menu will contain, at a minimum, the five basic tastes of Chinese cuisine (sour, hot, bitter, sweet, and salty). Dishes alternate between crisp and tender, dry and heavily sauced. Soup is usually served after the main courses; in the south, fried rice or noodles come last. Dessert is usually fresh fruit with pastries.

The Chinese have a simple rule for feeding foreign guests: serve them too much. It is polite to eat (or at least taste) a bit of each dish served, pacing oneself through the course of the meal. If by some odd chance there's only a bit of food left in a serving dish, leave it. An empty serving bowl implies that the host hasn't provided enough food.

In formal settings, it is impolite to drink alcohol alone, and thus toasts are usually offered either among neighbors or to the table as a whole. At banquets, it is appropriate for the tour leader to offer toasts to the entire assemblage. The host usually begins the toasts after the first course. Excessive toasting should be avoided, however.

Overt inebriation is frowned upon in China, although in the early days of China's encounters with foreigners, an assumption had somehow gotten around that Westerners wanted—even needed—to maintain a certain constant level of inebriation in order to function on a day-to-day basis. Thus, a group entering a hotel dining room for breakfast would be greeted by a staff frenetically snapping the tops off liter-sized bottles of beer. The obligatory beer-at-breakfast tradition has waned somewhat, although the earlier assumption about Westerners' lust for alcohol has been reinforced once again by foreigners' enthusiastic patronage of hotel "bars"—places that cater to the distinctly un-Chinese need to consume alcohol in the absence of food.

THE CUISINE
OF CHINA

Barrie Chi

PEOPLE may fiercely debate which national cuisine is the finest, but few will deny that Chinese traditional cooking ranks among the world's best. It certainly predates most of its rivals.

At the time of Confucius, in the 6th century BC, Gallic cuisine was still a crude ritual of roots and carcasses. Confucius may or may not have been a dedicated gourmet, but he did write extensively about sophisticated food preparation. Long before the first Western cookbook, China's foremost philosopher urged that meat be cut in long, thin strips and cooked with appropriate sauces. Furthermore, Confucius advised, the accompanying rice bowl must have polished grains or the meal would be a poor one.

STIR-FRYING AND CHOPSTICKS

Early styles of Chinese cooking developed from two important governing aspects of life in the Middle Kingdom. The first was religion. Daoism, which taught mankind to seek union with natural forces, encouraged a simple, vegetarian existence. Tender young vegetables are still an integral part of the Chinese diet. The second arbiter of Chinese cuisine was the country's chronic fuel shortage. Stir-frying small chunks of food over a hot stove for short periods of time is far more energy-efficient than baking. Even today, few Chinese kitchens have ovens.

To better accommodate food served in tiny, bite-sized morsels, chopsticks were devised. In large hotels and restaurants catering to foreigners, you will be supplied with forks and knives, but chopsticks do work better once you get the hang of them (see "How to Eat with Chopsticks," below).

WHAT CHINA EATS

It has been said that the French will eat anything once for the experience, but that the Chinese will eat anything out of necessity. Creatures and items considered totally repugnant in Western culture, such as sea slugs, snakes, bears' paws, and saliva extracted from birds' nests, are featured as delicacies in Chinese cuisine. And unless you're put off by the knowledge of what you're eating ahead of time, there's every chance you'll enjoy them. (Even to sedate Western palates, slugs or paws can be quite palatable.)

In China, fields are terraced for maximum yield and only those pastures deemed wholly impractical for cultivation are set aside for grazing. Thus the People's Republic produces few dairy products. With only a small proportion of its total land area (about 7%) suitable for farming, maintaining an adequate food supply for its huge population has always been a serious problem for China.

Millet, not rice, is the most widely cultivated grain, and soybeans are the most prevalent legume. Polished rice, although universally favored as a grain in China, remains something of a luxury commodity in many parts of the country. Throughout Chinese history, the pig and all its parts—from the choicest pork loin to the entrails—have eclipsed all other meats. Hogs, owing to their indiscriminate eating habits, can be raised virtually anywhere on very small parcels of land.

REGIONAL CUISINES

China's size and its sharp contrasts in climate have given rise to many different types of cooking. The five best-known Chinese cuisines today are Cantonese, Shanghai, Mongolian (and Shandong), Sichuan-Hunan, and Beijing. Cantonese cooking is probably the most familiar in the West. Egg rolls, chow mein,* *dim sum*, pastries and dumplings, and steamed fish are all indisputably Cantonese in origin. Shanghai fare is a little harder to pinpoint. One distinctive trait is the soya and brown-sugar sauce which often accompanies Shanghai's seafood and vegetable platters. Mongolian and Shandong cooking, on the other hand, owes little allegiance to traditional Chinese gastronomy. Muslim influences predominate, with lamb dishes and a fiery shishkebab the most renowned specialties. Also famous for its hot and spicy character is Sichuan-Hunan food. Legend has it that the steady drizzle and fogs of Hunan Province helped

---

*Literally, "fried noodles"—not the gummy chicken-and-vegetable concoction, allegedly invented in New York by an Irish seaman, which has taken the same name.

to inspire the hot chili peppers and flaming sauces of the region. Restaurant fare in Beijing is often an interesting hodge-podge of all of these cuisines, although certain items such as Beijing (Peking) Duck and steamed dumplings are identified with China's capital.

BORROWED FOOD

Some foods that we associate with China actually originated elsewhere. Tea was first grown in Southeast Asia and began trickling into China during the Six Dynasties period. Pistachio and lichee nuts came from Persia and India, respectively. The ubiquitous fried rice cakes are also Indian in origin. (The process worked both ways, however. Marco Polo took Chinese noodles back to Italy with him, where they were rechristened "spaghetti." Dumplings also have their generic roots in China!)

WHAT'S IN A NAME?

Many bona fide Chinese dishes have strange and wonderful names which can sometimes be misleading. Take "Red-Beaked Green Parrot with Gold-Trimmed Jade Cake," for example. This dish is in fact little more than spinach and fried beancurd. According to Chinese food lore, one long-ago, benighted chef in the service of Emperor Qian Long neglected to check the actual ingredients and came up instead with a freshly killed parrot garnished with a piece of jade. The chef was promptly beheaded. The worst you may suffer from indulging in such exotica is a bit of mental indigestion.

A TRADITIONAL BANQUET

Chinese banquets represent a special challenge. Not only is the food unfamiliar, but there's always so much of it. What to pass up and what to save room for are agonizing decisions. It used to be worse. In its heyday, the Imperial Palace was known to stage banquets with 80 to 100 dishes. Nowadays, hotels and elaborate private kitchens usually limit themselves to eight or ten courses.

The ritual, however, remains pretty much the same. At a traditional banquet, then and now, guests are typically greeted with a cup of exotic tea. Instead of hors d'oeuvres, you munch on lotus nuts, dried lichees, honeyed dates, and any number of small gingered fruits while your teacup is constantly replenished. Larger fruits such as pomelos, Hamai melons, Tianjin pears, and fresh lichees are also spread out on nearby tables.

Next come the cold dishes. Odd-sounding delicacies (drunken chicken, 2,000-year-old eggs, pickled celery cabbage) tempt your fancy, but remember, there's more. After the last marinated mushroom is bundled off, the first of many hot dishes arrives. It's usually something stir-fried and followed quickly by a heavy soup. Serious eating sets in with a sea cucumber dish or maybe a Beijing Duck. A clear, thin soup may come as a welcome relief before the next course—often a whole stuffed chicken—and at some banquets, a sweet dish may also be offered at this midway point. A well-garnished fish of impressive dimension is usually saved for last. Then, sadistically it would seem, there's still dessert!

TOASTING YOUR HOSTS

The traditional banquet drink is a heady brew made from sorghum grain, called maotai. Watch out—it's lethal. Chinese wines are gentler, but usually quite sweet and laced with strong aromatics. Whether or not you like either type, you'll probably drink several glasses for the many toasts given in the course of an evening. Chinese beer—more of a pleasantly bitter German-type lager—offers a potable alternative.

VARYING THE ROUTINE

After three weeks in the People's Republic, you may feel as stuffed as the banquet chicken, but good food is an essential part of Chinese hospitality. One way to vary hotel tourist fare is to eat in small, local restaurants. There are some drawbacks to this. The tablecloth and chopsticks are sometimes greasy and dirty. The cement floors are often littered with small bones and gristle. You may have to wait like everyone else for a table, but it's almost always worth the trouble. You'll catch a real glimpse of how the Chinese live and what they eat. The varieties of Chinese cooking are infinite. Only by exploring as many as possible will you get an idea of the astonishing array which makes up the cuisine of China.

HOW TO EAT
WITH CHOPSTICKS

Think of chopsticks as extensions of your fingers and the whole idea of eating with them will seem less foreign. Chinese food actually lends itself nicely to eating with long sticks. Everything is cut up into bite-size pieces beforehand. No one will ever ask you to carve up a pork chop or gracefully eat soft ice cream with them (the Chinese also use spoons and probably invented them).

Unlike Japanese chopsticks, Chinese chopsticks are blunt on the eating end (you can use either end for stir-frying in a wok) and come in a variety of materials. You've probably already seen the cheap wooden or plastic ones in your local Chinese restaurants. You might have to travel a little further afield to finger the elaborate ivory or silver sticks with intricate inlay designs, or the aluminum variety (for high speed?) now cropping up in Hong Kong. Chopsticks even come in smaller sizes for children and in giant sizes for cooking. But unlike short skis for beginners, short chopsticks will not hasten the learning process.

The best way to master chopsticks is to be very hungry with no tempting forks and knives anywhere nearby. Then, follow these directions:

☞ Pick up one of your chopsticks with the hand you write with. (Make sure the blunt, narrower end is touching the plate.) Pretend it's a pencil and place it in the V-shaped space between thumb and forefinger, resting it on the curved middle finger.

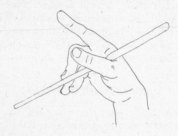

☞ Pick up the second chopstick with your other hand and place it between your forefinger and thumb, keeping the lower chopstick in place. Hold both of them quite close to the blunt end. Remember how it was easier to swing a heavy baseball (or cricket) bat if you clutched it closer to the middle? It's the same principle here.

☞ Try clacking the two ends together. Remember the top chopstick—the one held between thumb and forefinger—has more control and leverage. Use it to ferret out your first pieces of meat and vegetable. A good exercise is to practice picking up a small, thin coin by gripping it at the edges.

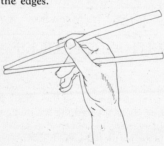

☞ Chopstick etiquette calls for plucking a single morsel from the dish and raising it to the mouth. In southern China, it's fine to raise the rice bowl to your lips and use the chopsticks to push rice into the mouth (a small quantity at a time). Holding the sticks with two hands—or using them to spear food—is bad form.

☞ Don't get discouraged. If more than one-fourth of humanity eats with chopsticks on a daily basis, so can you. It just takes practice.

CULTURE AND RECREATION FOR THE CHINA TRAVELER

Peking Opera actor before a performance

PERFORMING ARTS

China has a rich cultural heritage in the performing arts. Further, a renaissance of sorts in this area has been under way since 1978. New plays and operas and films are blossoming, while revivals and remakes of many prerevolutionary works now vie for center stage. And though a high degree of stylization (lots of posturing and broad gestures) still marks most Chinese presentations, performers' freshness and enthusiasm are contagious. You may not understand everything, but you will certainly be entertained.

At present, visitors to China usually enjoy a wide variety of performances during their two- or three-week stay. Apparently, tickets may soon come under the heading of "extra-cost option," but they're still worth it. No trip to the People's Republic is complete without a generous sampling of theater, music, and maybe even Chinese cinema.

Peking Opera. One of China's most famous art forms is the 200-year-old *jingxi* ("theater of the capital"). Other regions have also developed distinctive operatic styles. With its roots in musical forms dating from the Ming Dynasty, Peking Opera offers an intricate display of song, pantomime, dance, and acrobatics. The action swirls around four traditional characters and the many twists and turns of the plot are tunefully sung. (If you can get a hold of a plot synopsis beforehand, you'll follow these ins and outs far better. Your interpreter will have a hard enough time just keeping up with the lyrics.)

The four main characters are a scholar or statesman, a warrior or bandit, a principal female character, and a clown or a jester. All parts used to be played by men, but women have now pretty much taken over the roles which are rightfully theirs. Small drums open each scene, while stringed instruments, flutes, clackers, gongs, and, of course, loud crashing cymbals play throughout.

Peking Opera has undergone several changes in recent times. The first break with the past came in 1964 with the introduction of Western theater techniques. During the Cultural Revolution, only eight "model" operas, in which music, dance, and poetry were liberally infused with propoganda, were performed. The "models" are seen less often than new works or some of the traditional, marvelously complicated, and diverse prerevolutionary operas.

Old or new, Peking Operas run from 2½ to 3 hours with an intermission, but the verve and color are usually enough to sustain you throughout. More disconcerting may be the buzzing conversations throughout a performance. The fact is that no one can sensibly be required to sit still and remain attentive for four hours, so Chinese audiences are quite relaxed. Applause is reserved for a particularly stirring solo or a dazzling display of acrobatics. (Children and adults in China clap as a sign of welcome, but otherwise applause is rare.)

Theater. For most Chinese, plays are second in popularity to their beloved opera. But theater, too, is enjoying a resurgence. Many new works of the 1980s promote themes such as economic modernization or one-child families (entertainment in China has traditionally been spiced with politics), but the more historical material is well attended.

Playwright Cao Yu's new work is almost as popular as his famous 1930s trilogy, *Sunrise, Thunderstorm,* and *Peking Man,* all of which have played to packed houses in recent years. Guo Moruo, known also as a scientist and poet, died in 1978, shortly before his *Qu Yuan* made an impressive comeback in theater circles.

Western playwrights are also increasingly welcome. In 1979, Bertolt Brecht's *Galileo* was a nightly sellout in Beijing. In 1980, the first US play to be staged in China in 30 years was Arthur Miller's *All My Sons;* Miller's *Death of a Salesman* had its debut in Chinese in 1983, winning broad critical acclaim. *The Music Man,* a quintessentially American musical, was warmly received in 1987. And scholars are retranslating Shakespeare, banished during the Cultural Revolution, for the stage and for school texts. As part of this influx of Western drama, several US and European directors and theater consultants have been invited to teach backstage in China. The Chinese are interested in learning anything they can about new technology in props, lighting, and sound, and about Western acting techniques, especially in improvisational theater.

Improvisation actually goes back a long way in Chinese theatrical history. In the Song Dynasty, storytellers, singers, and comedians toured from city to city, tailoring their acts for each area. Centuries later, the People's Liberation Army and other troupes took the model plays of the Cultural Revolution to the countryside, changing the plots as they went along to focus on coal miners or fishermen or field workers.

Like the model operas, plays of the Cultural Revolution period are being replaced by traditional and modern works.

Music. From 1966 to 1978, most of the music performed or broadcast was strictly modern and strictly Chinese. Some people enjoyed recordings of Western music, but these were not encouraged. Times have changed. Now lots of Beethoven and Mozart and old Peking Opera can be heard on the radio. Composers Liu Shikun and Guo Zhihong have an enthusiastic following for their romantic, Tchaikovsky-inspired brand of music. Ma Ke, who wrote the famous score for the 1930s *White-Haired Girl*, has also found new favor. The Boston Symphony toured China in the spring of 1979, playing classical and Chinese selections before rapt audiences in several major cities. Isaac Stern followed that summer (his enthusiastic reception was recorded in a delightful US-made film, *From Mao to Mozart*).

The Haydn you hear while in China may sound a little different from the Haydn you're used to at home. Chinese music differentiates much less between pianissimo and fortissimo. Even those musicians who studied in the West sometimes have a hard time telling all the subtle shadings apart. Nevertheless, whether the music is Chinese or German in origin, an evening at Beijing's Central Philharmonic or at any other large city's symphony hall is usually a memorable experience. The love lavished on Western masterpieces by Chinese performers and audiences provides moving evidence of a deep-seated commonality existing between such ostensibly divergent cultures.

Other Entertainments. Dance troupes, puppet shows, and acrobatic acts also provide a diverting way to spend an evening. Sometimes all of them are combined into what is known as a live variety show. A former student at Beijing University calls these performances "Ed Sullivan without TV." Acrobats perform astonishing feats with chairs and rings and high wires. A master of ceremonies (who doesn't look anything like Ed Sullivan and is often female) then announces a well-known pianist or Peking Opera actor or a young vocalist. Colorful folk dances often follow. A popular variation in Mongolian, Hainanese, Khazakh, and other ethnic festival dances may accompany an elaborately costumed rendition of Thai, Korean, and even African dances. By all accounts, the Chinese versions are quite authentic. The puppets are also fun. Very similar to the French *guignol*, stock characters ingeniously draped in brilliant silks act out playlets that need no interpreters. Each region lends its own flavor to the variety shows.

A popular art form in China today is dance—including classical ballet. Never traditionally a part of Chinese dance, European ballet has been slowly integrated into the performing arts, thanks largely to the efforts of dancer-choreographer Dai Ailian. Among the first Chinese to

in Europe, Dai worked with Sadler's Wells and Cecchetti in
and returned to China with the dream of integrating classical
d the many native dances of China. Her Central Ballet Troupe
is r. rishing today.

Reservations and Ticket Purchases. The performing arts are far
more reasonably priced in China than in the West, but there are seldom
enough tickets to go around. If you're particularly interested in a performance, your best bet is to phone ahead. Waiting until you arrive in the
city where a given symphony or opera is playing may result in disappoint-
ment. (Your CITS guide will be happy to check the local papers for time
and place. You should leave the box-office transactions to someone who
speaks fluent Chinese.)

Since the Cultural Revolution, theaters have allocated a certain
number of tickets to each workplace so that, by rotation, everyone will
get a chance to enjoy acrobats or a night at the theater.

FILM

Movie houses are so packed that many Chinese simply wait for films to
be shown a few months later on television or at work. Chinese film-mak-
ing began at the turn of the century, reaching maturity with several
splendid social epics produced in the 1930s. During the 1980s, films
began to win back audiences through more realistic characterizations and
liberal injections of innocent romance, breezy social satire, and broad
humor. A subdued form of film-star idolization is now a major pastime
in China, with snapshots and film magazines on sale in virtually every
neighborhood market. Today, Chinese movies compete for audiences with
a growing range of US, Japanese, British, Romanian, Yugoslav, and other
offerings. In 1987, the Chinese produced 146 feature films and released 195
new full-length films. Many films during the 1980s retained the political
and social messages typical of the post-1949 genre, but a few have added fuel
to a raging current debate on the propriety of kissing on film. One movie
in 1979 apparently showed a couple mid-embrace; Chinese modesty has yet
to recover.

Most films shown to tourists are English-narrated documentaries on
China's modern accomplishments or travelogues on places like Guilin.
Old Charlie Chaplin movies or *The Sound of Music* and *Gone With the
Wind* (all sellouts in China) are usually both dubbed *and* subtitled in
Chinese.

NIGHTLIFE

There's been a lot more to do in China during evenings, especially since
the late 1970s. Despite recent innovations, however, China is not likely
to become known very soon for its effervescent nightlife. But in the
interests of foreign exchange and improved tourism, travel officials are
bending. Bars and cafés have begun to appear in large cities. Sophisticates

may find them less than exciting, but the change is significant in a society where only a few years ago Western forms of socializing were considered depraved and decadent in the extreme.

The bars are seldom even bars. Or at least they're not long and curved with brass rails underneath. Instead, most of them look very much like the cafés adjacent to them, except that the "bars" serve liquor and the cafés don't. Your martini may come in a water glass, but beer, Coke, whiskey, and coffee are now readily available.

The cafés are also learning to please Western palates. One recent Shanghai visitor recalls her surprise at the piped-in strains of Frank Sinatra singing "I Did It My Way" while she munched on a very creditable chicken salad. Some China travelers do get homesick for Western food and drink after several weeks. For them, these latest hotel amenities are a welcome respite. They are also convenient and pleasant places to meet with friends at times when the rest of the city has shut down for the night.

International Clubs. An older, more congenial meeting spot for foreigners is the International Club in Beijing, right next to the Friendship Store on Jianguomenwai Road. Shanghai also has an International Club, located on Yan'an Road, but its facilities aren't quite as lavish or extensive as those in the capital. At many of these clubs you can swim laps in the pool, play a number of racquet sports, and relax afterwards with a drink— served with chips and peanuts!—and a pleasant Chinese or American-style meal. Some clubs also have a film program. Midnight is the usual witching hour.

Social Dancing. Shortly after a campaign against Western "cultural pollution" shut down the dance halls in September 1982, social dancing was resurrected by a most unlikely patron: the government. Millions of people whose lives were disrupted by the chaos of the Cultural Revolution found themselves nearing middle age with few or no marriage prospects, and the government took it upon itself to play matchmaker, sponsoring social dances in towns and cities throughout the country. Gathering momentum, disco fever was officially sanctioned in early 1984 when dancing was publically endorsed by Party Secretary Hu Yaobang, and the craze is now sweeping China off its feet. In 1988, the break-dancing phenomena took hold in China, to the bemusement of the older generation.

Many newer hotels in the major cities have recently opened discos, and some, such as those in the White Swan Hotel (in Guangzhou) and the Great Wall Hotel (in Beijing) are flashy strobe-light and mirror affairs that would make even John Travolta feel at home. These discos, however, based on Hong Kong models and with cover fees to match, are generally off-limits to local Chinese.

THE MEDIA IN CHINA

Television. Television sets, although now mass-produced in China, are an expensive commodity. Nevertheless, virtually all city residents

CULTURE AND RECREATION

now have access to a "collective" television—one per apartment building or commune. By 1986, more than 87% of all households owned their own TV set, on a national average.

On weekdays, daytime programming is mainly educational fare, including courses from China's heavily subscribed Television University. News and entertainment shows begin at 9 AM. All media outlets in China—including television and radio—are state-owned and overseen directly by state (or Chinese Communist Party) bureaus, although many local stations now enjoy limited degrees of independence. A typical day's programming opens with the domestic news, which, in one of many contrasts with news broadcasts in Western countries, rarely resorts to sensational stories about accidents, murders, or the like. Instead, China's top story may be about a model steel factory in Anshan. The emphasis is almost always on positive rather than negative aspects of the country's society. After news from the home front, the spotlight is on the international scene, with footage from the US, Switzerland, Japan, or other countries. Occasionally, there's even a short spot on Wall Street trading activities.

A 20-minute documentary on another country might follow, such as a special on Canada's agricultural development. Finally, there's the evening broadcast feature. Sometimes it's a foreign film with Chinese dubbed in, though acrobatic displays broadcast live from Beijing or soccer games are also popular. After a news update, broadcasting ends for the night. By 1983, commercial advertisements, focusing more on industrial than consumer goods, were common adjuncts to more local and national programming. Only a few cities have more than one station (Beijing has three). All broadcasts are in Chinese.

Most large tourist hotels have now installed TV sets in their guest rooms. Many of these now offer free closed-circuit programming consisting of imported TV series and films, mostly in English and mainly of dubious quality.

Newspapers. Foreign-language periodicals are no longer hard to come by in China. Since late 1979, *Time* magazine, *Reader's Digest,* and a selection of other Western periodicals and newspapers (including the *Asian Wall Street Journal* and *International Herald-Tribune*) have been sold in big-city hotels, some arriving about a week after their issue dates. In June 1981, the long-awaited English-language *China Daily* began publication. Using major foreign wire services, the paper includes lively features, sports, and even foreign stock-exchange coverage. Some hotel lobbies and post offices also sell copies of local newspapers and magazines, including foreign-language editions of *Beijing Review, China Reconstructs,* and *China Pictorial.*

For people who can read Chinese, many different types of newspapers exist in the PRC. The nationally published *People's Daily* is one of the most widely read Chinese papers. The *Guangming Daily* is perhaps the most sophisticated publication, offering in-depth analyses of events and special sections on history, philosophy, and literature. Most cities also publish local papers, which are useful for their listings of ongoing cultural and sports events open to the public.

RECREATION

Sports. Spectator and player sports are very popular in China. At most factories and workplaces, workers spend part of the mid-morning break exercising to music. After work, many people play basketball, volleyball, and table tennis, and in warm weather they like to go for a swim (sometimes in excavation sites converted for the purpose). Most universities, communes, and even some factories have a gymnasium and many of them arrange competitive team events. Basketball courts are now ubiquitous in China, from Shanghai to Tibet—even on the grounds of Beijing's Imperial Palace. Volleyball is China's most popular participant sport, with many impromptu games played in a circle and without recourse to a net. Passers-by who chance on an informal match or game are almost certain to be enthusiastically welcomed should they care to join in. Indeed, these games can often produce the warmest and most spontaneous moments one can find on a China trip. But take care—although the competition is invariably friendly and polite, the play can be rough-and-tumble.

For golf enthusiasts, China now has three 18-hole courses: one at the Zhongshan Hot Springs Resort in southern Guangdong Province, another nearby in Zhuhai, and the third, opened sometime in 1986, near the Ming Tombs north of Beijing.

Beijing's International Club and the Friendship Hotel have Olympic-size swimming pools that are open from June until September. For these and other public pools, bathers must obtain a certificate of health from a Chinese clinic (your tour guide will direct you to one nearby). Only a badge of courage is needed for swimming in local lakes and rivers. And although women hold up half the sky in China, most of them don't swim. The men far outnumber the modest women—who are not usually comfortable wearing bathing suits in public—at China's lakes and beaches.

For travelers who like spectator sports, China has numerous indoor and outdoor stadiums. Be prepared for large, excitable crowds; the Chinese are as partisan sports enthusiasts as any in the world.

Tai Ji Quan. If you've ever taken a theater or dance class, you may know several of the Tai Ji Quan (T'ai Chi Ch'uan) exercises already. Old-age homes use the ancient Chinese discipline as a physical fitness program.

The West is only just beginning to discover the satisfactions of a regular Tai Ji workout. China has appreciated them for close to a thousand years. You can't help but notice Tai Ji's enormous following when you're visiting the People's Republic, especially during early morning.

The hundred or so different postures range from the very strenuous "low forms" to the upright, less energetic "high forms." The postures have wonderful names like "White Crane Spreads Wings" or "Needle at Sea Bottom." Others are more explicit—"Wave Hands Like a Cloud" or "Step Forward and Punch" give a clearer idea of what you're expected to do.

Tai Ji is actually a combination of the mental and the physical. Quiet concentration is essential, as is its Daoist-inspired breathing technique (Tai Ji is related to Qi Gong, a generic range of breathing exercises which have lately come into vogue all over the country). Coordination is second to the smooth, slow, balanced execution of the movement. In fact, the more slowly you move, the more adept you are considered to be. If you've done the postures correctly, you won't be sore or stiff afterwards, no matter how out of shape you are.

The discipline, actually a soft or "internal" form of Chinese boxing ("kung fu"), evolved from a variety of sources. The *Yi Jing (I Ching)*, the concept of yin and yang, and Daoist meditation all have had a hand in its development. A famous Daoist with a strong interest in the *Yi Jing* and the Confucian way is credited with formalizing the technique. Zhang Sanfeng is believed to have studied and taught Tai Ji during the Song Dynasty (960–1279).

There are many schools of Tai Ji Quan. Zhang began the Wudang school in Hubei Province; it, along with the Shaolin school (the forerunner of all East Asian martial arts, supposedly formed to toughen up the physically degenerate monks of Shaolin Monastery), serves as the basis for most modern-day forms and techniques. None is so unique that, even if you've practiced only one particular brand of Tai Ji before coming to China, you need hesitate to quietly join the turning, twisting, gently dipping Chinese while you're there and so begin your day with a feeling of exquisite calm.

☞ *Trying Tai Ji.* To learn Tai Ji Quan properly, you'll need a teacher. Only an experienced professional can give you the full sense of inner-breathing, cohesive movement, and gradual progression from high to low forms. If you want a bit more background or just need to brush up on some of the more complicated postures, Da Liu's booklet *T'ai Chi Chuan and I Ching* (Harper & Row, $2.50) is recommended.

You may want to try a few very rudimentary movements yourself to get a feel for the discipline. The First Series involves several basic steps as illustrated below.

No matter how complicated your program is, you always start out standing erect with both hands at your sides. Now relax. Your heels should be lightly touching as you sink slightly at the knee and then separate your feet (leading with the left foot). Straighten up gradually. Your feet should now be shoulder-width apart. Distribute your weight evenly between them (do this slowly, testing carefully the weight on each foot). Now raise your arms gently in front of you to shoulder height with your palms facing down. Bring your arms back to your sides and repeat the process once or twice as rhythmically and slowly as possible. Now reach up with your left hand to hold the bird's neck, while moving the right hand slowly downward to smooth the long, long plumage of the bird's

First Series of Tai Ji Quan

Two positions from
"Grasp the Bird's Tail"

---

tail. Slowly shift your weight to the left leg and, pivoting on your right heel, turn right. As you turn, raise your right arm, elbow bent and palm down, to shoulder level, and bring your left arm across your waist, palm up. Slowly drop your hands back to your sides. Repeat the movement turning this time to the left.

Chinese Games. No trip to China is complete without the obligatory pause to watch children perform native dances and martial arts in the schoolyard. It is disquieting to think that perhaps kids in China never spend their free time doing anything else. And what of their parents, after a hard day's work in the factory or office or rice field? China has few TVs and no late-night movies (most people are in bed by 10 PM anyway). But no one seems to miss them. Adults and children alike enjoy a wide variety of Chinese and Western games in their hours off.

☞ *Chess with Checkers.* Probably the best-known game is *Xiang Qi*, or "Elephant" Chess, which dates back to the 6th century AD. It's different from chess as you and Bobby Fisher know it. The pieces are red and black cylinders with markings on top—"like big fat checkers," one player remarked. Throughout the game, they are placed at the intersections, not on the squares, of a big black-and-white grid. Although the game looks like checkers, the moves correspond quite closely to those of the more familiar knights and rooks and kings. Like chess, the rules are fairly simple to master, but learning to play *well* is a far different matter.

The boards are made of flimsy paper and usually fall apart in a month or two. Many people just draw them on the ground or on a large piece of wood; others treasure ancient, carved boards of ivory or jade.

Whatever the surface, *Xiang Qi* is a sociable pastime. The game usually takes several hours and although only two can play, a crowd of kibitzers inevitably gathers round. The onlookers follow the moves closely, presumably so they can argue heatedly about them afterwards.

Chinese women do not usually play (or watch) *Xiang Qi*. Children have their own version of the game with animals (elephants take all).

The rules are less complicated, but the checkmate principle still applies.

☞ *Imports and Exports.* Kids don't play cards much. If they have to be indoors away from their beloved basketball or volleyball courts, they shoot marbles or twist long pieces of string into fantastic shapes. Cat's cradle was reportedly invented in China. Chinese checkers wasn't. (China is apparently beginning to import the game from the US).

Authentically Chinese distractions include *Jianzi* and Skipping the Rubber Band. *Jianzi* is a little like football—you change or make up the rules depending on what age group you're playing with. The only constant in a wide range of variables is the *jianzi* itself, which in its fancier form could easily be mistaken for a very large, old-fashioned badminton feather-cock. In its homemade form, the *jianzi* is a wad of old phone-book paper all balled up with bird feathers stuck in the top. China exports to Hong Kong and Singapore beautiful *jianzi* with elaborate feather tufts. Most kids would sooner be caught dead than playing with one on the street.

☞ *Rubber Jump Rope.* Skipping the Rubber Band may someday go commercial, too. For the moment, it's still dozens of thick rubber bands tied together to form a snake about four or five feet long. Obviously, the snake can be made to stretch much further than its dormant length. Two girls pull it out as far as it will go and hold it a few inches off the ground while a third jumps and twists in and out and over the rubber bands. As the snake moves higher and higher off the ground, the coiling and uncoiling become increasingly complicated. Chinese equivalents of "strawberry shortcake, cream on top" are recited throughout.

In an ominous portent, Japanese computer games have made their first encroachment on Chinese soil—in the courtyard of Guangzhou's Dongfang Hotel. Less conspicuously, perhaps, an army of Frisbee ambassadors has descended on China and it's now quite unusual to cross a Chinese park in summer without being buzzed by a flying plastic disc.

SHOPPING

Chinese guides, no doubt mindful of China's foreign-exchange needs, have become increasingly tolerant of their Western charges' penchant for shopping and will schedule at least a few group visits to local Friendship or department stores so that visitors can exercise their curious compulsions. China is not a consumer society and there is no equivalent of Fifth Avenue in New York, the Ginza in Tokyo, or the Champs Elysées in Paris. The emphasis in Chinese products is on the everyday and the practical, with the notable exception of some splendid handicrafts. The tourist will find that basic items are inexpensive, whereas few bargains are to be found in such common "Chinese" goods as silk, jade, jewelry, and antiques. In fact, such goods may be cheaper and available in wider varieties in Hong Kong. Standardized pricing—at least in the case of tourist purchases—is sadly becoming a thing of the past in China. Certain items available in Friendship Stores or hotel gift shops may be considerably less expensive in a neighborhood department store (although quality is not certain to be comparable). Still, the time and effort required to find the equivalent item may not be worth the savings. These days, it's possible to bargain in the free markets (especially for secondhand goods), but prices in all Friendship Stores and most local shops are fixed and nonnegotiable (possibly excepting a few high-ticket items). Specific shopping hints will be found in the shopping sections for individual cities.

FRIENDSHIP STORES

Friendship Stores have been established in the major cities specifically to sell export items to foreign visitors. Thus, they offer many products that do not circulate in the local economy (i.e., silk garments, handmade carpets, jewelry, or lacquerware furniture). Other advantages include sales personnel who speak foreign languages, uncrowded counters, facilities for packing and shipping large items home (e.g., in Beijing and Shanghai), and the helpful presence of tour guides.

However, the very attributes of Friendship Stores can also be disadvantages: visitors are deprived of the experience of mingling with Chinese shoppers. Also, mundane items that may be unusual outside of China (e.g., peasant clothing, posters, and everyday crockery) are not carried in the Friendship Stores.

LOCAL STORES

In most cities, major shopping areas are located close to the hotels. The best approach is to go out and explore them on your own. Prices are generally posted. If communication becomes difficult, Chinese shopkeepers will usually write out the price on a slip of paper.

Sales staff in Chinese shops can be counted on as among the most honest in the world. If visitors can't figure out the exact payment from the assortment of bills and coins, the sales staff will offer to extract the correct amount. Receipts are usually provided and, especially in the case of large purchases, should be retained for customs purposes.

Except in Friendship Stores, a number of items are rationed: cigarettes, cottons, and "luxury" fabrics such as silk. Local department stores or clothing shops abide strictly by these rules. If one is "waived off" from an item, offense should not be taken; it simply means ration coupons are required (in some cases, purchase of such items can be arranged with the help of the Chinese tour escort).

There is another aspect of shopping to keep in mind, especially in areas where foreign visits are less frequent. Even in the most crowded shops, Chinese patrons will courteously give way to foreigners, and staff will usually drop whatever they're doing to offer assistance. But expect to be stared at (in a friendly way) and even followed. This should not be interpreted as hostility or discourtesy but merely as an expression of understandable curiosity and interest. Under such circumstances, it's best to smile and persevere with one's shopping.

SHOPPING SUGGESTIONS

Antiques. Travelers who come to China expecting to find an antique-buyers' paradise are likely to be disappointed. First, antiques may be legally purchased only in licensed shops in Beijing, Shanghai, Guangzhou, Wuxi, Guilin, and some other middle-sized cities. Second, authorities have generally restricted sale of items older than 120 years. They regulate what is purchased by marking items with a special red or brown wax seal and requiring a special customs declaration form, issued at the time of purchase. Third, the Chinese keep a watchful eye on the international market prices of antiques and charge accordingly. Finally, the stores—especially in Guangzhou and Beijing—have been thoroughly "picked over" during the past several years as visitors to China have increased in number. This is not to say that the pursuit itself will not be rewarding. Prices for many of these items selling outside of China may be marked up by 1,000% or more by "exclusive" retailers. Moreover, the availability of many unusual "non-antiques"—jewelry, ceramics, and even paintings—may make the venture worthwhile.

A final caution: in China's more open commercial environment of the 1980s, foreigners may frequently come across urban "free markets"

Shopping for arts and handicrafts in Beijing's Friendship Store

where old artifacts are being offered for sale. If on the odd chance an item purchased turns out to be a genuine antique, it will more than likely be confiscated by Chinese customs, with considerable embarrassment added to the loss. Visitors to Tibet should be especially cautious with regard to such unauthorized purchases.

Items Recommended for Purchase. Following is a list of the most popular items bought in China over the past years and the best places to get them:

Rugs (Beijing, Shanghai, Tianjin, Datong, Lhasa)
Ceramics (Guangzhou, Foshan, Changsha, Jingdezhen, Wuxi)
Ivory (Guangzhou, Beijing)—note: as products from endangered species,
    illegal for US import
Bamboo and rattan wares (Chengdu)
Clay figurines (Beijing, Wuxi, Guangzhou)
Cloisonné, lacquerware (Beijing, Shanghai, Fuzhou)
Furniture (Beijing, Yangzhou)
Jewelry, including jade (Beijing, Shanghai, Guangzhou)
Silk (Hangzhou, Suzhou, Wuxi, Shanghai)
Embroidery (Changsha, Suzhou)
Furs and suedes (Beijing, Shenyang)
Scroll paintings (Beijing, Shanghai, Guilin)
Woodblock prints and stone rubbings (mainly Beijing)
Papercuts (especially Foshan, but available everywhere)
Mao-tai and other liquors (everywhere)—beware, mao-tai will leak through
    the bottle seal

Other Items to Look For. Chops (signature seals); postage stamp sets; miniature carvings in stone, cork, or wood; sandalwood fans; brushes and art supplies; knives; books; posters; acupuncture dolls; and clothing (don't despair—somewhere among China's vast population there are likely to be people who take the same size as you). Always look for the unusual: in Shanghai and Guangzhou, cold cream comes packaged in a charming double sea shell and is sold for about 30 *fen* ($0.20).

SHIPPING

Friendship Stores will ship any large item purchased from them, although the cost will not be cheap. Large items purchased elsewhere can be consigned through a Chinese overseas shipping agent (contact can be made through the hotel). If items are small, they can be posted from the city's main international post office (which has a customs office). Post offices also sell small packing boxes. Shipping is often faster than surface mail—which can take three months—and has the added benefit of being insurable.

RESTRICTIONS AND DUTIES
ON PRC PURCHASES

Import regulations vary widely from country to country and prospective travelers should consult their country's regulations before departing. In January 1980, the US Congress granted "most-favored-nation" status to China, substantially reducing the duties on a variety of items imported from the PRC.

Common Rules of Thumb. There is a general US ban on importing objects made of ivory (aimed at protecting Asian elephants), so Asian ivory may be confiscated by customs. Similarly, if you plan to purchase furs, you should check which are endangered species since there is a US ban on objects made from the fur or other parts of endangered species. Agricultural items such as seeds and plants may be held for inspection or quarantine and eventually denied entry.

Medical equipment and drugs purchased in China may be confiscated for inspection. Such items must be accompanied by full details as to their contents, manufacture, and instructions for use. Sometimes this extends to acupuncture needles and dolls, which have at times been sent to the FDA for examination.

Problem Areas. Challenges to the originality of artwork: this distinction is relevant since original artwork is duty-free, whereas mass-produced artwork carries a 25% duty. To be "original," the work should be the only one of its kind and should be signed. You can argue past the absence of a signature. If it's indeed original, hold your ground and make your case.

Challenges to the authenticity of antiques: certified antiques are duty-free, but duty on non-antique porcelain, bronzes, and jewelry can range from 25% to 110% of value, depending on the item. US customs requires a signed receipt from the dealer certifying that the item is more than 120 years old.

In the PRC, any old item officially sanctioned for export has a wax seal on it; these seals do not necessarily indicate that the item is a genuine antique, as is commonly believed. Their main function is internal: to show that the item has been approved for export out of China. The best way to keep the record clear for customs is to take down the name of the store from one of your guides and print it along with the description of the item on the sales receipt. If possible, have the shopkeeper print the age of the item on the sales receipt—otherwise, determine the age and print it yourself. Thus armed, you may argue forcefully at customs.

V

DOING
BUSINESS
WITH CHINA

CHINA'S NEW BUSINESS CLIMATE

Doing business with China is a complex and difficult undertaking. Communication—in both technical and human terms—is fraught with obstacles. Language barriers crop up everywhere. Letters go unanswered. Phone connections can be maddening. And true intent or a clear response seem forever elusive. The PRC trade bureaucracy, despite recent efforts to refine management practices, still functions with less than consummate speed and efficiency. Trade negotiations are often protracted, invariably expensive, and frequently bedeviled with large and small uncertainties. Yet, although business opportunities for the West are still relatively confined, two key factors are a cause for optimism. First, normalization of relations between the US and China and improved ties with the European Economic Community (EEC) have certainly eased many former constraints on trade. Second, recent changes in China's political and social atmosphere, combined with its ambitious goals for development and modernization, have resulted in an attitude of pragmatism and a willingness to adapt to international trade practices. The outlook for the mid-1980s remains guardedly favorable for traders able to combine prudence with determination.

In 1978, following the fall of the "gang of four" and on the strength of the third, and most durable, political comeback of pragmatist Deng Xiaoping, China embarked on a bold new program of economic modernization. Aimed at bringing China economically and technologically abreast of the Western industrialized nations and Japan by the year 2000, the program has been based on concurrently "opening to the outside" and "opening up the inside" (i.e., liberalizing the domestic political and economic systems). (See also above, the "Four Modernizations.")

While internal power struggles and uneven implementation of the new reforms have caused China's newly opened door to make some sudden and perplexing swings, the relative success and popularity of the reforms would seem to make any major retrenchment in the near future highly unlikely. Deng Xiaoping's visit to the Xiamen and Shenzhen Special Economic Zones in January 1984 did much to publicize the importance of economic reform coupled with foreign trade and investment in China's modernization drive. One result of this official sanction to engage in entrepreneurial activity has been the dismantling of the central government's monopoly on foreign trade, a trend that has spawned hundreds of new, specialized Chinese trading corporations. Ministerial, provincial, city, and even private corporations have been granted the authority to engage in trade directly with foreign companies, ensuring that the spirit of competition will infect every level of the new trade structure. This decentralization has caused some confusion among foreign businessmen, who must now analyze the relationships among various corporations, ministries, and end-users in order to identify an appropriate contract. It also, however, creates an atmosphere of increased opportunity, and gives the well-informed trader a greater degree of leverage in negotiations.

Decentralization has produced some unexpected results: unfamiliar with or reluctant to accept international business practice as the norm, and with no definitive arbiter of policy, the new trade corporations were without standard procedures or guidelines for dealing with foreign businesses. Responding to the call to bring some clarity and order to the chaos, China is speeding up the codification of laws governing contracts, patents, the management of joint ventures, accounting, and other areas where international participation demands explicit guarantees and standards.

CHINA'S FOREIGN TRADE STRUCTURE

Until recently, all of China's foreign trade was handled by the various Foreign Trade Corporations under the aegis of the Ministry of Foreign Economic Relations and Trade (MOFERT). Even after the adoption of reforms which nominally broke MOFERT's monopoly, most trade and investment deals must still pass through the hands of one or another MOFERT-related office at some stage of evaluation or implementation. However, there are now several other categories of trade corporations.

The most powerful of the non-MOFERT trade organizations are the specialized corporations that operate under the auspices of various ministries, or the State Council. Shipbuilding, petrochemicals, transportation, agriculture, and other specialized areas are covered, though not always exclusively, by the trading entities in this category.

Next are national-level corporations which represent producers of a particular product. These corporations usually need an initial sanction from MOFERT to begin operations, but after setting up shop, they may trade directly with foreign concerns. The largest and most successful of these integrated factory complexes represent textile producers. They are, with few exceptions, export oriented.

Occupying the lowest rung of the foreign trade ladder, with only limited power to authorize contracts with foreign companies, are the provincial and city trade bureaus. These organizations are something of a cross between a trade corporation and a local chamber of commerce, representing all interested business concerns in their area, rather than a particular category of product.

The proliferation of trade companies does not stop here, however. Many factories and even private individuals have set up their own corporations. While these organizations can help in initiating a deal, few of them have any real authority to finalize one, and all proposals sent to them must eventually be forwarded to one of the regional, national, or ministerial-level corporations for approval.

INVESTMENT ORGANIZATIONS

While China's door was never entirely closed to foreign trade, the direct investment of foreign capital, not to mention foreign ownership of enterprises on Chinese soil, was brought to a halt by the success of the Communist revolution in 1949. In the post-Mao era, as ideology and xenophobia have yielded to pragmatism, the way for making foreign investments in China has opened once again. As in the case of foreign trade, the situation has been growing increasingly complicated as restraints are eased and power is distributed.

At the national level, the China International Trust and Investment Corporation (CITIC) is the most powerful management body. Together with its subsidiary merchant bank, China Investment and Finance (CIF), CITIC is directly involved in setting up large-scale joint ventures, issuing bonds, and managing Chinese investment in both foreign and domestic enterprises, including the newly-opened CITIC Office Building in Beijing. For companies interested in investing in areas outside the SEZs, contact should be made with CITIC or a CITIC-connected organization.

Complementing, and sometimes competing with CITIC are several provincial and municipal-level "Trust and Investment Corporations." Through 1985, nearly every province and major city had set up an investment corporation of some kind, although few have any real authority.

There are many ways for companies to invest in China's modernization. Through the mid-1980s, the bulk of foreign investment has come in the form of contractual joint ventures and offshore oil exploration. Other options include compensation trade deals, equity joint ventures, and wholly-owned businesses. As of 1988, over 300 Sino-US joint ventures worth a total of $3.1 billion have been set up. US companies are the second largest investors in China, after Hong Kong, accounting for 14% of all foreign direct investment in China.

INVESTMENT PRIORITIES

Foreign investment is tied both directly and indirectly to China's modernization program. From the Chinese point of view, the most important advantage to be gained lies in obtaining the capital and know-how necessary for upgrading and expanding the infrastructure and modernizing the means of production. Transportation, energy, and telecommunications, as well as research, management techniques, and the tourist industry are all key areas.

Offshore oil exploration and recovery will continue to be a major investment opportunity, and bidding for inland oil leases began in 1986. It is estimated that China's total oil reserves are about 2.4 billion tons. In addition, the nuclear agreement signed by presidents Reagan and Li Xiannian in July 1985 is thought to be worth a projected $10 billion to US companies.

FOREIGN TRADE PRIORITIES

To achieve these goals, China needs not only foreign capital, but also machinery, raw materials, and technology. At present, raw materials, equipment, and chemicals account for about 60% of China's total imports. As the modernization drive accelerates, China will give even higher priority to technology transfers, with an eye towards speeding up in-house development of resource recovery techniques and reducing the costs of plant modernization. Both equipment and technology acquisition, through joint ventures, compensation trade, licensing agreements, and other means, will focus on several key fields through the 1990s. Energy: hydroelectric and nuclear power and fossil fuels (coal and oil); telecommunications: computerized switching systems, telephone units, etc. (the master plan calls for adding 25 million units by the year 2000; Guangzhou alone planned to purchase 60,000 telephone units in 1986); computers (hardware and software); transportation: railway modernization and port expansion are priorities; and food processing.

Sino-US trade reached a record high in 1987 of $10.3 billion ($3.4 billion in US sales to China and $6.9 billion in US purchases). In 1987, China's exports amounted to $38.2 billion, with about 16% going to US markets. Imports were valued at $41.7 billion, of which 8.7% came from the US. After Hong Kong and Japan, the US is China's third largest trading partner.

THE SPECIAL ECONOMIC ZONES

In 1980, as one important step in the process of "opening to the outside world," China established four Special Economic Zones (SEZ): one in Shenzhen, between Hong Kong and Guangzhou; in Zhuhai, near Macao; and in two former treaty ports, Shantou in northeastern Guangdong Province and Xiamen (Amoy) in southern Fujian. In 1988, Haiman Island was added to the list. The zones were set up not merely to promote local prosperity and generate foreign exchange, but also to serve as the testing grounds for new managerial and economic systems, and as classrooms where managers and administrators from other parts of China (including, presumably, recalcitrant Beijing bureaucrats) can learn the ways of international business. The SEZs, with Shenzhen in the vanguard, have already served China with many valuable lessons in Sino-foreign cooperation. China's contract law, for instance, which took effect on July 1, 1985, is based on the Shenzhen contract law promulgated 18 months earlier.

While from a purely economic point of view the SEZs have so far been less than a resounding success, the outlook is promising. The year 1987 was a good one for the SEZs: combined industrial output value rose to $5.35 billion, up 52% over 1986, and exports were up 114% to $2.74 billion, better than the national average.

In order to attract foreign capital and expedite the development of the SEZs, the provincial authorities which administer the zones offer the following preferential treatment to foreign investors:

Taxation. Joint ventures, partnership management, and wholly-owned foreign businesses pay a corporate income tax of 15% (18% lower than the national corporate rate). Companies with investments in excess of $5 million may be granted tax holidays of up to three years, or else enjoy a further income tax reduction of 20–50% and exemption from both the corporate consolidated tax (which can run anywhere from 1.5 to 65%)

and local surtax. Reinvested profits are not taxable, and import duties are waived for production equipment. Products made specifically for consumption outside of China are also tax-exempt.

Foreign Exchange. All after-tax profits may be repatriated. New reforms also allow businesses to use foreign currency as a means of exchange within the zones.

Marketing. Up to 30% of products may be sold on the Chinese domestic market; certain high-technology products and products made with Chinese materials on Chinese equipment are free from the 30% domestic sales ceiling.

Finance. Foreign banks may handle foreign exchange, loans, and other financial transactions.

Land Use. Renewable leases are initially limited to a maximum of 30 years for industry and tourism, and 50 years for commercial, residential, educational, scientific, and medical purposes. (For more detailed information on the SEZs, see individual listings in the Cities and Sites section, below.)

THE 14 OPEN CITIES

In April 1984, following Deng Xiaoping's declaration that the SEZs were a success and should be emulated, the State Council announced that 14 cities along China's coast, as well as Hainan Island, were to be opened up for foreign investment and trade. Dalian, Qinhuangdao, Tianjin, Yantai, Qingdao, Lianyungang, Nantong, Shanghai, Ningbo, Wenzhou, Fuzhou, Guangzhou, Zhanjiang, and Beihai were authorized to set up "Economic and Technical Development Zones" within their boundaries, empowered to sign agreements with foreign businesses, and entrusted with the overall management and administration of the zones.

The general guidelines adopted for running the open cities are similar to the policies in effect in the SEZs. But the SEZs are being built from the ground up, whereas modernization of existing facilities is the principal goal in the case of the open cities. Moreover, key differences exist in the range of investment opportunities offered and in the terms of preferential treatment. In the SEZs, investors can put their money into everything from industry and heavy construction to agriculture and tourism and enjoy the same special tax rate. In the open cities, investment has been generally limited to infrastructure projects, capital improvement of existing plants, and ventures specializing in high technology projects such as energy and telecommunications. Hotels and other service-oriented enterprises do not enjoy any special tax status. Furthermore, there are fewer categories of exemption from customs duties, even for enterprises engaged in production. In June 1985, the State Council announced plans to slow down investment in the 10 smaller cities in order to concentrate on developing the better-equipped cities of Guangzhou, Shanghai, Tianjin, and Dalian. Despite these less favorable conditions, through mid-1985 more than 200 contracts worth a reported $700 million had been signed.

Early in 1985, the Yangtse and Pearl River deltas, as well as a large area in the southeast corner of Fujian Province bounded by the cities of Xiamen, Quanzhou, and Zhangzhou, were declared Open Coastal Areas. Investment in these areas will focus on agriculture, forestry, aquaculture, textile manufacturing, and food processing. Tax incentives reportedly differ only slightly from those offered by the SEZs and open cities.

In addition, the Liaodong and Shandong peninsulas in northeastern China are slated for accelerated economic development in the near future. By 1990, most of China's coastline and nearly every provincial capital, coastal and inland alike, will be open for business.

ARRANGING A BUSINESS TRIP TO CHINA

Potential buyers and sellers must first be invited to visit China. To obtain an invitation, sellers or buyers must forward a formal application and business proposal to one of China's Foreign Trade Corporations (FTCs) or, in certain cases, other official bodies. Then they settle in for a long wait. Persistence and patience are the key.

There are other, less frustrating ways of getting your foot in the China door. Many FTCs now maintain permanent representatives in the US and Western Europe (see listings below). Special trade delegations to the PRC are organized regularly by US and European governmental and private agencies. Technical seminars with Chinese participants are sponsored by a wide variety of multinational corporations and other organizations. The formerly dominant Guangzhou (Canton) Trade Fair has given way to an increasing number of international trade exhibitions in both the PRC and major Western markets. Invitations to China's specialized trade fairs are now readily granted to all legitimate applicants engaged in that field of endeavor. The problem merely is to find out well enough in advance where and when a particular exhibition is to be held.

If more preliminary research is required, PRC embassy officials and government trade agencies (e.g., US Foreign Commercial Service) can be helpful in providing general (and usually free) advice. Agents for and consultants to the expanding PRC import-export business can often come up with even better firsthand information and personal contracts. The following more detailed explanations should be helpful to the expert and novice alike.

For those businessmen with relatively modest trade or investment objectives, it is possible to circumvent the cumbersome and time-consuming process of soliciting an invitation. Since the advent of independent travel in China, many traders, armed only with cash, credentials, and a tourist visa obtained in Hong Kong, have found that it is possible to make contact with their Chinese counterparts and occasionally conclude on-the-spot deals. Note, however, that most of those who have enjoyed success with this approach are experienced traders with established contacts. For the majority of businessmen and women, expert and novice alike, the more prudent procedures outlined below are still the surest strategy.

THE INVITATION

Whether you wish to buy or sell, the first step in establishing contact with the Chinese is to locate the appropriate Foreign Trade Corporation

168

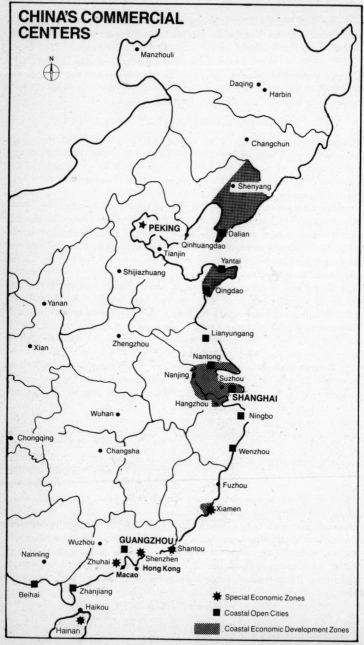

CHINA'S COMMERCIAL CENTERS

N

* Manzhouli
* Daqing Harbin
* Changchun
Shenyang
★ PEKING
Dalian
Qinhuangdao
Tianjin
* Shijiazhuang
Yantai
Qingdao
* Yanan
Lianyungang
* Xian
* Zhengzhou
Nantong
Nanjing Suzhou
Hangzhou SHANGHAI
* Wuhan Ningbo
* Chongqing
* Changsha Wenzhou
Fuzhou
Xiamen
Wuzhou GUANGZHOU Shantou
Nanning Zhuhai Shenzhen
Macao Hong Kong
Beihai Zhanjiang
Haikou
Hainan

✱ Special Economic Zones
■ Coastal Open Cities
▨ Coastal Economic Development Zones

Map ©1988, Eurasia Press

(FTC), industrial end-user corporation, or other government agency that handles commercial transactions for a particular commodity, service, or technology. The next step is to prepare a proposal and forward it to the appropriate office in China. First-time commodity sales negotiated entirely by mail are exceptions. Usually, foreign firms or individuals regarded as sound prospects will receive an invitation to visit the PRC to pursue negotiations.

PUTTING TOGETHER A PRC BUSINESS PROPOSAL

After the initial legwork has been done and the correct FTC or government agency is identified, the substance of your sales or purchase offering needs to be spelled out in detail. The form and content of the initial proposal is an important factor in eliciting a response. Although the final sale of products and services to and by the PRC depends more on the requirements of a given Five-Year Plan than the sales method employed, the well-informed trader will have a clear edge over the beginner.

If you wish to sell to China, the initial proposal should be straightforward, technically explicit, and sufficiently specific to permit a comprehensive evaluation by the Chinese.

Importers should include their exact requirements, along with detailed information about their company's history, product lines, and sales volume. Further data about the company, such as financial reports, bank references, and Dun and Bradstreet ratings, are considered useful.

Large firms should avoid including detailed descriptions of products or product lines other than those specific products or services to be traded. Extraneous information could prove confusing to the Chinese and ultimately counterproductive.

Chinese Translations. It is helpful, but not essential, to have the entire proposal translated into Chinese. It is definitely advantageous at least to translate the covering letter. There are good translation services available in most large US and European cities.

The Chinese themselves have set up translation companies specializing in technical materials. In China, the Nanjing-based Jiangsu Province Technological Materials Translation and Duplication Company opened in 1978. The China Council for the Promotion of International Trade (CCPIT) in Beijing now offers a fee-based English-to-Chinese translation service for foreign technical materials.

Multiple Copies. The FTCs and other central organizations distribute proposals to interested end-users. Chinese end-users (i.e., individual local factories and enterprises) now have considerable leverage in negotiating and even signing contracts. In large measure, the end-user will determine which firms will be invited to the PRC. You should send at least 20 copies of your proposal to the FTC or whatever other central organizations have been contacted initially. And if the appropriate end-users can be identified, you can also send them a copy as a backup. Approaching end-users directly, however, is a relatively new practice that has not yet been uniformly accepted. This tactic is generally not recommended for the novice China trader.

Copies of the proposal can also be sent to the Technical Exchange Department of the CCPIT and to the Center for Introducing Literature and Samples of New Foreign Products (also part of CCPIT). These organizations act in an advisory capacity and do not engage directly in commercial transactions. Additional copies of the proposal, or at least the covering letter, can be sent to the US or other appropriate embassy in Beijing and to the PRC embassy in your country. PRC embassies are reluctant to involve themselves directly in negotiations.

Waiting Time and Follow-Ups. It can take anywhere from 30 days to a year to get a response. A delay may mean that the proposal is not of immediate interest or simply that there is a backlog in China. The Chinese have been deluged with proposals from foreign companies since they announced the Ten-Year Development Plan for the National Economy in early 1978, and especially from US companies following normalization of US-China relations.

If you have not received a response within 90 days, however, it may be worthwhile to write again. The covering letter to a follow-up should always refer to the original proposal. There's no harm in providing additional information or samples at this juncture.

Technical Seminars. An effective lure in many sales approaches to China has been an offer by the foreign firm to conduct a technical seminar in Beijing or other appropriate city. Such a suggestion should underscore key developments in the manufacture and/or application of the product in question and should state the company's willingness to bring a team of highly qualified technical people to China. An invitation to a counterpart Chinese delegation to view plants, equipment, or technology in operation in one's home country is appropriate and, if accepted, could go a long way in helping to bond a relationship.

Technical seminars provide an excellent setting for acquainting the Chinese with the commodity or service you wish to sell. Although the overt purpose is educational exchange, the tacit understanding is that such seminars also function as sales presentations.

Sometimes these presentations are so successful that negotiations may begin on the spot (assuming the Chinese participants have secured prior governmental approval). In other cases, negotiations may have to wait until a second invitation to visit China is secured.

Before 1979, commercial seminars tended to emphasize "state-of-the-art" technology. More recently, the Chinese have been placing new stress on practical application of products. The most advanced labor-saving farm machinery, for example, may have limited applications on China's communes. Simpler and less expensive models and techniques have lately elicited greater interest from the Chinese.

PRC COMMERCIAL VISAS

Once an invitation to visit China has been received, the prospective visitor must apply for a PRC visa. Standard visas are issued for a maximum stay of 30 days. Visas are not renewable, although their time and geographic limits can be extended in China without difficulty should the situation warrant.

Visa application forms can be obtained from the PRC overseas commercial offices, the China Travel Service (CTS) offices in Hong Kong and Kowloon, or PRC embassies and consulates abroad. Visa forms should be submitted in duplicate, together with the applicant's passport, two passport photographs, and a processing fee ($7 in the US). Passports mailed to the local PRC embassy are usually returned with a visa stamp in less than a week. In December 1981, the PRC opened its first visa office in Hong Kong, a step calculated to speed up processing procedures for individual visas.

PRINCIPAL CHINA TRADE CONTACTS

CHINA'S PRINCIPAL FOREIGN TRADE CONTACTS

PRC Diplomatic Contacts in the US. Commercial Office, Embassy of the People's Republic of China, 2300 Connecticut Avenue, NW, Washington, DC 20008; tel. (202) 328-2526. Commercial sections are also attached to PRC consulates: 3417 Montrose Blvd., Houston, TX 77006; 1450 Laguna Street, San Francisco, CA 94115; 520 12th Avenue, New York, NY 10036; 502 Shatto Place, Ste. 300, Los Angeles, CA 90020; and 104 South Michigan Avenue, Chicago, IL 60603. (For addresses of other PRC embassies overseas, see Chapter II, above.)

China FTC Contacts in the US. Since 1981, a number of China's Foreign Trade Corporations have set up permanent representatives in the US. Offices in New York include the China United Trading Company, an umbrella organization which acts as MOFERT's US representative and coordinates the activities of the various Chinese trading companies operating in the United States: 1 Penn Plaza, Suite 1915, New York, NY 10119; tel. (212) 947-3140; CHINATEX at 209 West 40th Street, New York, NY 10018; tel. (212) 719-3251; MINMETALS, 1 Bridge Plaza, Fort Lee, NJ 07024; tel. (201) 461-3750; CEROILFOOD, 250 West 34th Street, New York, NY 10019; tel. (212) 947-2466; and ARTCHINA, Beijing Branch, 1133 Avenue of the Americas, New York, NY 10026; tel. (212) 398-1748. TECHIMPORT's office is at 3911 Bradley Lane, Chevy Chase, MD 20015; tel. (301) 654-6996.

PRC Diplomatic Contacts in Canada. Embassy of the People's Republic of China, 411-415 St. Andrew's Street, Ottawa, Ontario K1N 5H3 (for residents of eastern Canada); Consular Office to the PRC in Canada, 3380 Granville Street, Vancouver, British Columbia V6H 3K3 (for residents of western Canada); and 240 St. George Street, Toronto, Ontario, M5R 2P4.

China Council for the Promotion of International Trade. Technical Exchange Department, Fuxingmenwai Avenue, Beijing. Cable: COMTRADE BEIJING. The CCPIT is officially a "nongovernmental organization," although it functions as an important part of China's foreign trade structure. Working in conjunction with China's FTCs and ministries, CCPIT serves as a liaison between these organizations and their foreign counterparts. It does not engage directly in commercial transactions, although it has lately expanded its range of direct services to foreign traders, including introductions, legal advice, and translation services. Arbitration of contract disputes in China is handled exclusively by CCPIT's Arbitration Department; the Patent Bureau is also under its auspices.

Center for Introducing Literature and Samples of New Foreign Products. China Council for the Promotion of International Trade, P.O. Box 1420, Beijing. The Center's library keeps Chinese end users of foreign technology up-to-date on recent developments abroad.

China Resources Holdings Company Ltd. (CRC). 49/F, China Resources Building, 26 Harbor Road, Wanchai, Hong Kong. Cable: CIRECO HONG KONG. Telex: 73277 CIREC HX. The CRC represents the China National Machinery, Chemicals, Metals and Minerals, and Textiles Import and Export Corporations. The largest overseas branch of China's FTCs, CRC acts as a commercial liaison. The CRC is also authorized to extend invitations to Guangzhou trade fairs.

Foreign Trade Corporations. The FTCs are the direct negotiators between foreign trading interests and Chinese end users. Requests for an invitation to visit China for business purposes should be addressed to the appropriate FTC. The FTCs are organized according to the kinds of commodities they handle transactions for. An inventory of FTC headquarters is provided at the end of this section.

US CONNECTIONS FOR TRADE WITH CHINA

US Embassy in China. Foreign Commercial Service, Embassy of the United States of America, 3 Xiushui Beijie, Beijing, PRC (tel: 53-21831 x480).

Consulates-General of the US. Guangzhou: Dongfang Hotel, 11th floor (tel: 669900 x100); Shanghai: 1469 Huaihai Zhong Road (tel: 37-9880); Chengdu: Jinjiang Hotel, Renmin Nanlu (tel: 24481); Shenyang: 40, Lane 4, Section 5, Sanjing Jie, Heping district (tel: 29-0000).

US Department of Commerce. Office of the PRC and Hong Kong, East Asian and Pacific Affairs, Room 2317, Washington, DC 20030; tel: (202) 377-3583/4681.

Following normalization of US-China relations in 1979, the Department of Commerce became an invaluable source of information and advice. The Department's International Trade Administration publishes periodic reports and a useful handbook entitled *Doing Business with China*, available from the Government Printing Office in Washington.

In the early 1980s, the US Department of Commerce reorganized its foreign trade presence in China. Its functions are now represented by the Foreign Commercial Service, which maintains a separate building at the embassy complex (tel: 53-2831, x480).

US-China Business Council. 1818 N Street, NW, Ste. 500, Washington, DC 20036; tel. (202) 828-8300. The Council is recognized by both governments as the focal point for developing trade between China and the US. It is a private, nonprofit organization supported by approximately 400 member corporations, banks, and smaller companies. The Council assists members in contacting Chinese foreign trade authorities, and has information available on special trade delegations.

The Council also publishes a bimonthly magazine, *The China Business Review*, for members, and has an office in Beijing (Beijing Hotel, suite 6036). Formerly called the National Council on US-China Trade.

CANADIAN CONNECTIONS FOR TRADE WITH CHINA

Canadian Embassy in China. 10 Sanlitun Road, Beijing, PRC; tel: 52-3536.

China Desk, Asia Division. Department of External Affairs, East Asia Trade Division, 125 Sussex Drive, Ottawa, Ontario K1A 0G2; tel: (613) 992-6129. The China Desk provides information on China trade as well as materials on Canada-PRC marketing practices.

Canada-China Trade Council. 133 Richmond Street West, Ste. 310, Toronto, Ontario M5H 2L3; tel: (416) 364-8321. In China: CITIC International Building, Ste. 27E, 19 Jianguomenwai Avenue, Beijing; tel: 500-2255 x2765.

BUSINESS TRAVEL IN CHINA

DOMESTIC TRAVEL CONSIDERATIONS

Most business transactions in China do not require visiting more than one city. Should circumstances require additional domestic travel, you may be asked to make your own connections to other cities as well as any additional arrangements for your return flight home. (For general information on international connections to the PRC, see preceding section on traveling to China.)

For ticketing within China on both domestic and international connections, transactions must be conducted in person at a CAAC office. In Beijing: CAAC, 117 Dongsi Street; tel: 55-3245/0497; cable: CAAC PEK; telex: 22101 CAXT CN. In Guangzhou: CAAC, 181 Huanshi Road; tel: 66-2123 x904 (dom.), 66-1803 (int.). In Shanghai: CAAC, 789 Yan'an Zhong Road; tel: 53-5953 (dom.), 53-2255 (int.); cable: CAAC SHA. Although all international airlines operating in China maintain offices in the cities they serve, they are authorized only to make reservations; the actual tickets must be written by CAAC. Allow at least half a day for scurrying back and forth between the two offices.

CAAC links with principal cities have improved considerably in recent years. Several daily flights are available from Beijing to Shanghai and Guangzhou, most with first-class accommodations. Flight service has also picked up, with redesigned uniforms for crews, two varieties of beverages (nonalcoholic), the semblance of an in-flight magazine, and giveaways such as candy bars, little ceramic pots, and tiny address books. CAAC now has offices in Hong Kong and New York and throughout Western Europe and Asia.

COSTS

The costs for individual travel in China have rapidly increased since 1976. Beijing is China's most expensive city for foreigners (and the Great Wall Hotel one of the most expensive places to stay); the following itemization will give a sense of what a businessperson might be required to lay out during one day in the PRC's capital:

A Business Day in Beijing

ITEM	COST
Great Wall Hotel (room only, single occupancy)	Y440
Taxis (up to 100 km.)	Y96
Lunch at hotel	Y50
Laundry and dry-cleaning	Y15
Telex/telephone to US or Europe	Y50
Dinner at restaurant	Y75
Guide (half-day)	Y50

Some corporations now budget the total cost of sending a six-member delegation to China at $2,000 per day (including airfare); a budget of $200 (about Y744) per day for basic living expenses in China is now close to average. Indeed, for a 10-day business junket to China originating in the US or Western Europe, the prospective traveler must contemplate a total outlay in the range of $4,500, including airfare. It should be noted that the above costs do not include expenses for entertainment, liquor, incidental business expenses (e.g., mail, photocopying, etc.), or purchases of gifts or other items. If extensive travel by taxi (the only means of personal transport for foreigners) is required, those charges alone could exceed $50 per day. If the overall costs are a concern, an experienced travel agent should be consulted for detailed information.

SELLING TO CHINA

Once a firm is in possession of an invitation to visit China, the first question is, who should go? Your negotiating team should include technical personnel who can answer the most detailed questions about the company's product or service. Occasionally, an embarrassed company president has been forced to wire the home office to get the answers to his counterpart's rigorous inquiries.

The team should also have one person who is authorized to make on-the-spot decisions. This can make or break a sale, particularly when the issue is price. Companies occasionally lose sales because the negotiating team has to return home for consultations. This is all the more frustrating since sometimes the Chinese themselves will break off negotiations to consult with their superiors on key questions, while the foreign businessperson is left to wait in the hotel room until his Chinese counterparts return. Patience is essential for coping with these and other situations.

You should also be very sure that there is indeed a contract before trumpeting your success to the world. Several executives of top corporations have claimed to be in possession of deals worth hundreds of millions of dollars, only to admit later that they never really had a contract, but only a protocol or letter of intent.

The Chinese do not like to have details of their business negotiations discussed publicly, especially before a firm contract has been signed. In some cases, the Chinese may even have used a premature announcement to extract better terms from executives who did not want to tell stockholders that their billion-dollar deal had slipped away.

TRADITIONAL FORMS OF PAYMENT

Until 1978, the Chinese refused to accept foreign credits. They paid for their purchases either by cash on delivery, especially for smaller projects, or through deferred payments. Deferred payments have usually been handled through a credit or loan to the supplier. Although the Chinese have recently announced that cheap buyer's credits will be their preferred means of financing imports, the most common finance mechanism used to pay for foreign imports continues to be Letters of Credit (L/Cs).

Letters of Credit. China traders prefer to use their own contracts when they are making purchases by Letters of Credit. Profitable trading with the PRC under the L/C system requires you to have a good grasp of the deceptively simple Bank of China (BOC) financing mechanisms. As all PRC trade transactions are cleared through the BOC, the Chinese L/C system contains some pitfalls for the novice China investor, who must assume the onus of risk in the transaction.

Along with a shipment notice, the foreign exporter receives a sight draft to be drawn on the BOC's Beijing office. China is not a member of the International Chamber of Commerce and, although its L/C system closely parallels accepted practice, the Chinese are under no obligation to conform to the ICC Uniform Customs and Practices for Documentary Credits.

Another important characteristic of Chinese L/Cs for foreign exporters is that they are usually not confirmed, but merely advised. The foreign exporter has two options: to allow the advising bank to act as a collecting agent, bearing only limited responsibility; or to sell his L/C to the advising bank for a portion of the face value of the draft. If the investor adopts the first option, he must assume that the negotiations between the advising bank and the Beijing office will take about 20 days. The foreign exporter has thereby extended to the Chinese buyer roughly 20 days of interest-free credit. The alternative allows the exporter immediate payment; however, most banks will only buy the obligation for the negotiation of documents with recourse to the exporter.

Sometimes advising banks will assume a more direct role by issuing a "silent confirmation." By so doing, the banks assume responsibility for negotiating documents in the usual manner and then discounting the drafts without recourse to the exporter, assuming documents conform to all terms in the L/C. The advising bank then applies in good faith to the BOC for reimbursement. However, when the L/C stipulates that documents must conform not only to the terms of the L/C but also to a separate contract, most banks are unwilling to extend "silent confirmation." To avoid this complication, the foreign exporter may request that the BOC accept his certification that all documents in fact conform.

China will now accept payments in RMB, in the currency of the foreign contracting party, or in the currency of a third nation. Of course, the Chinese are prone to accept a currency of relatively easy convertibility and stability for evaluation of payment.

FINANCING SALES TO CHINA

If you're interested in exporting to China, you should carefully devise beforehand a financial package tailored to the budget-conscious Chinese. An attractive financial package can give you a distinct advantage over a competitor selling the same product.

As demonstrated by recent purchases, the Chinese prefer cheap buyer's credits. The three main variables to consider in designing a financing package for China are currency, maturity, and interest rates. The Chinese naturally seek the lowest possible interest rates and prefer dollar-denominated loans and favorable repayment schedules.

Long-Term Credits. The US Export-Import Bank began offering credit for exports to China in April 1980. Ex-Im offers credit to foreign nations on a project-by-project basis. Loans are made at an 8.75% interest rate for most purchases. Generally, 65% of the financing is provided by Ex-Im Bank, 15% by the buyer, and 20% by commercial banks at the floating prime rate. Applications for funding must come directly from the Bank of China and not from the companies interested in exporting to the PRC. Because China has a centrally controlled economy, the Ex-Im Bank wants assurance that the PRC government is committed to proposed projects and purchases in order to protect itself from contingent liabilities by entering into agreements with businesses for projects which China cancels. This is also seen as advantageous to American firms, for it will provide an indication of when the Chinese are serious about a project, which has not always been easy to determine. The Ex-Im Bank will continue to issue nonbinding "letters of interest" to US companies seeking equipment sales to China.

Short-Term Credits. Both US and European banks have access to the Eurodollar market to provide variable-rate, short-term Eurodollars at LIBOR (London Inter-Bank Offering Rate) market rates and some fixed-rate, medium-term Eurodollars. However, for short-term trade needs, most US banks can provide funds from their domestic fixed-rate dollar pool, or through access to fixed-rate institutional money at less than the LIBOR market rates. Dollar-denominated bankers' acceptances issued by US banks also provide low-cost, short-term financing at rates well below US prime.

You should also consider the possibility of offering 100% financing for Chinese purchases. Most Chinese imports have been financed for 85% of their value, with the Chinese importer making a 15% down payment in cash. The Chinese have been willing, however, to consider 100% financing for their purchases.

Bear in mind that the Chinese are exacting negotiators and will continue to scrutinize all their options before signing any trade agreements. Moreover, despite the recent proliferation of loans signed by the Chinese, they will undoubtedly continue to exert close control over China's expenditures.

INSPECTIONS AND ARBITRATION PRACTICES

PRC Inspections. Chinese insistence on purchasing the highest quality goods and holding sellers to the absolute letter of their agreement is reflected in an exigent guarantee clause. The guarantee period often extends to 12 or 18 months, beginning as soon as the cargo arrives at the Chinese port of entry.

Standard machinery clauses require the manufacturer to present a certificate of inspection regarding quality, specifications, performance, and quantity. The certificate is not considered final, and the contract usually requires an additional inspection by the Commodities Inspection Bureau when the goods reach China.

Western European and Japanese sellers marvel at the meticulousness and literalness of these inspections. European manufacturers have encountered Chinese complaints or refusals to accept newer models than those specified in the contract even when shipped at no extra cost. While other vehicle buyers are usually content to purchase small spare parts by weight, such as a kilogram of piston rings, the Chinese count them one by one. Steel pipe importers from other countries may X-ray the pipe at random for cracks, but the Chinese X-ray every inch and make claims for hairline cracks which most buyers ignore. In principle, every country does this, US manufacturers say; nevertheless, the Chinese seem for the present to be fussier than most.

Dispute Settlement. China's settling of foreign trade disputes is consistent with its claims settlement policy. Until very recently, the Chinese energetically avoided not only litigation but any third-party participation that carried overtones of adjudication. A standard clause provides that "all disputes in connection with this contract or the execution thereof shall be settled through negotiations." In the event that the negotiations fail, the case in dispute must be submitted to arbitration before the Foreign Trade Arbitration Commission in Beijing, unless both parties agree beforehand on a third country.

Some investors have been able to arbitrate disputes in Sweden or in Switzerland, and a recent contract with a US seller reportedly specified Canada as the arbitral forum. Occasionally, the contract will simply provide that arbitration will be held in an unnamed third country to be agreed upon by the parties. In recent years, the Chinese have become more willing to specify a third country, the arbitral body, and the rules of the arbitration proceeding. In at least one recent case, China not only agreed to arbitration before a named third-country body under International Chamber of Commerce rules, but also agreed that the contract would be governed by the law of that country.

The US-Sino bilateral trade accord signed in July 1979 commits the Chinese to adopting standard arbitration procedures.

PATENTS, TRADEMARKS, AND COPYRIGHTS

Foreign firms from the US and other countries with reciprocal trademark registration agreements may apply for Chinese trademark registration through the CCPIT or directly at the Trademark Office of the Administrative Authority of Industry and Commerce of the State Council, in Beijing. Trademarks are valid for 10 years from the date of registration and may be renewed for the same period. The application must be submitted in duplicate and accompanied by power-of-attorney forms, a copy of home registration (from applicants whose countries require this of China), certificate of nationality showing that the corporation is organized under the laws of the applicant's country, twelve prints of the trademark, and RMB 200.

As of 1988, China was not party to any international convention on copyrights, however, a draft copyright law was submitted to the Standing Committee of the 7th N.P.C. in 1988, which is expected to be promulgated in the near future. The 1979 Sino-US Trade Agreement, although it lacks Congressional ratification, calls for mutual protection of patents, trademarks, and copyrights; similar treaties have been signed with other countries. In August 1982, and again, more comprehensively, in April 1985, China promulgated trademark and patent laws that provided exclusive patent rights to foreign companies doing business in the PRC. China will issue three kinds of patents: normal patents which will last 15 to 17 years; utility-model patents covering minor inventions with a five-year term renewable for a second five years; and industrial design patents which also have renewable five-year terms. The Patent Office operates under the auspices of the China Council for the Promotion of International Trade, in Beijing, which also provides advice and legal assistance for Chinese patent procurement.

BUYING FROM CHINA

THE NEGOTIATING CLIMATE

Negotiations for buying Chinese products that involve design, labeling, and packaging details have sometimes seemed hopeless in the past. The new flexibility shown by the Chinese beginning in mid-1978 is encouraging. The Chinese now realize that they have to do a better job of meeting their buyers' needs if they are to increase their exports—and desperately needed foreign exchange earnings. But it will take time for such mandates from the top to filter down to lower levels.

Distance, not only in geography but also in a different business psychology, has made commercial ties exasperating at times. In the past, the Chinese have agreed to make changes, only to discover later that their slowness in meeting customers' requirements meant that products were already outdated by the time they had made the desired change.

Not all negotiations are difficult, especially after the importer has become known to the Chinese over a period of years. Chinese negotiators are willing to copy samples brought to them by importers, and they have begun offering exclusive US distributorships for some items, as they have done in Europe. The term of these arrangements has been limited, however. Problems have also arisen because the Chinese insist that the buyer purchase quantities that may exceed the maximum the buyer had in mind.

CONTRACT TERMS

China uses two standard types of contracts for sale of its goods. The one-page "sales confirmation" form contains only the bare essentials of the transaction. It names the buyer, the seller, and the commodity involved in the transaction. The form briefly describes the product's specifications and quality, and adds the unit price, total value, packing specifications, shipment date, loading port and destination, insurance (Chinese sales to the US are usually CIF or "C & F"), terms of payment, and shipping mark. Some "sales confirmations" also include a standard clause providing for final Chinese inspection of quantity, weight, and quality of the goods. The second common form, the standard "sales contract," contains in addition to all of the above clauses, items dealing with force majeure (which includes acts of government) and arbitration, as well as a variety of other stipulations relevant to each commodity or addressed to more general matters such as inspection, claims, and dispute settlement.

PAYMENTS

Letters of Credit. Where payment is to be made in cash on delivery, the standard payment clause in Chinese export contracts calls for the foreign importer to open a confirmed, irrevocable, transferable, and divisible L/C, payable at sight to the BOC. The clause requires that the L/C must allow for transshipments and partial shipments; that the L/C must reach the seller at a specified date—often 30 or more days before the date of shipment; and that it must remain valid 15 days after expiration of the shipment period.

The foreign importers' L/C differs in several important ways from that of the Chinese importers. Most important, the Chinese require that L/Cs in payment of their shipments be confirmed, while they are hesitant to confirm L/Cs when they are the buyers. In short, this means that the foreign importer cannot legally withhold payment on goods he feels are defective. Furthermore, foreign buyers are left without recourse for recouping losses incurred due to late shipments. All Chinese sales contracts now contain clauses providing for arbitration by the Chinese Foreign Trade Arbitration Commission in Beijing or by an arbitral body in a third country. According to the 1985 law covering Sino-foreign contracts, either side may apply for arbitration.

Inspection, Claims, and Dispute Settlement. What recourse do importers have if they believe they've received defective goods? The standard Chinese export contract provides that Chinese inspection of goods is final. Normally, the inspecting agency is the Chinese Commodities Inspection Bureau (CCIB), which maintains offices in the PRC's major ports and industrial centers. According to the CCIB, Chinese law requires inspection of only certain categories of products.

In practice, a buyer's claim is usually settled by bilateral negotiations with the corporation selling the goods. Negotiating claims may be time-consuming, and especially difficult if there is no tie-in to future business. Buyers have found PRC corporations reluctant to make cash payments, preferring instead to offer the customer some concession on new orders. The Chinese have, however, reimbursed buyers for large losses incurred by egregious error at their end, such as when dyed cotton cloth of the wrong color was shipped.

Delivery. One of the most common causes of dispute in international commerce is delay in delivery and subsequent loss to the buyer. Late deliveries have been a common problem in trade with China, though Chinese sellers have become more attentive to timing.

The delivery date in Chinese contracts is usually no more specific than a reference to a two-month period, such as "August-September." Another cause of delay is transshipment or transfer from one conveyance to another, which the standard Chinese sales terms are apt to permit. Conversely, the standard Chinese purchase contract does not allow transshipment of goods.

When delays occur, Chinese sellers have not only expected buyers to keep their L/Cs valid until they are able to ship the goods, but have also been unwilling to compensate buyers for any losses caused by the delay. Sometimes a tardy Chinese seller will agree to change the payment terms by cabling willingness to accept payment against documents presented in the US, in which case the buyer need not extend his L/C.

BUSINESS REPRESENTATION IN CHINA

Once a business relationship has been established with China, it is sometimes useful to have a representative remain in Beijing. The advantage to this is that the foreign business has someone on hand who can deal with any problems immediately and continue to develop contacts with Chinese people in the same field. A disadvantage is that in many cases there is very little business which actually needs doing in China. Although most travelers find China an exciting place to visit, for Westerners who spend extended periods in the PRC without much work to do, the allure frequently wears off. Life for a foreigner in a Chinese city is often—though not invariably—isolated, boring, and expensive. There are few outside sources of entertainment. Contacts with the Chinese, while always cordial, tend to be superficial. Office rates in Chinese cities, as well as salaries for interpreters and other support staff, are very high. Many companies have found that an effective compromise is to hire a resident overseas Chinese agent who represents several foreign businesses in the PRC or to open an office in Hong Kong rather than in China itself. Long-term residents of China should be aware of the personal income tax laws which now apply to foreigners living in the PRC.

PERSONAL INCOME TAX

An individual income tax law was announced at the meeting of the NPC in September 1980. The tax, which is aimed primarily at foreigners, is imposed on anyone earning more than Y800 a month who is in China for more than 90 days (183 days for U.S. citizens). Anyone who has lived in China more than a year is theoretically liable for tax on both income earned in China and from overseas sources. Residents of China for more than 90 days (or 183 days as the case may be) are taxed only on income earned in China. An agreement between China and the US to limit double taxation was signed in 1985. Salary and wages are now taxed at rates varying from 2.5% to 22.5%; income from compensation for personal services, lease of property, royalties, interest, dividends, and bonuses is taxed at a flat 20%. However, if the employer pays for housing costs directly, the amount is not taxed, nor are meal and accommodation costs borne by employers for their employees while temporarily outside of China. Other types of income may be taxed as specified by the Chinese Ministry of Finance. The tax is levied on the amount of monthly income over Y800, and, except for the initial Y800, there are no deductions.

TRADE FAIRS AND EXHIBITIONS

GUANGZHOU'S FOREIGN TRADE CENTER AND TRADE FAIRS

November 1979 marked the end of a 23-year tradition in the China trade. The internationally known Guangzhou (Canton) Trade Fair (or Chinese Export Commodities Fair) lost its central role as the dominant biannual series of exhibitions for foreign importers; instead, the large exhibition hall between the Dongfang Hotel and the Guangzhou train station, redesignated as the Guangzhou Foreign Trade Center, now hosts permanent displays of Chinese and foreign wares, as well as two general fairs per annum (on a much smaller scale than in the past) and a variety of specialized mini-fairs. These mini-fairs usually feature products from only one of China's FTCs as opposed to the former practice of presenting the wares of several related FTCs simultaneously.

Although considerably lessened in importance, the biannual Guangzhou Fair continues to function with a fall and spring session (October 15–November 15 and April 15–May 15, respectively). Sessions are staffed by literally thousands of Chinese end users and FTC representatives and thus continue to offer visitors a unique overview of what China is selling from year to year. These days, the Fair mainly services small and medium-sized purchasers of crafts and consumer goods, mostly from Southeast Asia. For these and others, the Fair's usefulness extends mainly to its convenience as an ordering or reordering center for China's standard export products. Attempts at deals any more complex than that are unlikely to get much of a hearing in the Fair's frenzied atmosphere.

A year-round foreign trade center is also slated for Beijing. Meanwhile, China's capital continues to expand its role as a major focal point for China trade since all of China's trade and economic ministries are headquartered there. By 1987, more than 500 foreign businesses had set up representative offices in Beijing.

For newcomers, Guangzhou's Foreign Trade Center and its variety of ongoing specialized fairs will continue to be extremely useful. Procedures for attending and doing business in Guangzhou probably won't alter much in the immediate future. Attendance at the majority of fairs will continue to be by invitation only and both established traders and "new friends" will undoubtedly have to apply to the appropriate FTC for at least a while longer. In the past, would-be fair goers were cautioned to allow two or three months' lead time for these preliminary preparations. You should continue to allow 10–12 weeks, if not more, for the invitation, visa formalities, and travel connections to be finalized. Although future fairs promise to be smaller and more focused, the ease of contact provided at these venues will continue to offer significant savings in time, energy, and costs to China traders.

DECENTRALIZATION OF FOREIGN-TRADE VENUES

The change in China's international trade venues has been inevitable. Recent compensation trade and joint-venture financing agreements, plus a variety of other negotiating techniques designed to cut through Beijing's ensnarling red tape, gradually outpaced the former trade fair's laborious and often inefficient methods. In the late 1970s, the Chinese realized they had to sharply step up sales to hard-currency markets. Decentralizing the process and vastly multiplying the points of contact for doing business were among the steps calculated to help expand business. Short-term results have been mixed. During 1987, China registered a trade deficit of $3.7 billion, down from $12 billion in 1986.

Mini-fairs are already being sponsored in other cities besides Guangzhou. The new China International Exhibition Center, the largest trade exhibition facility in China, is due to open in Beijing by March 1986. Elaborate exhibition and trade facilities aren't necessary for a focus on, say, carpets or furs. Such fairs have become a sine qua non for specialized commodity buyers. Shanghai, Tianjin, and Shenzhen, among others, have successfully brought together FTCs, Chinese merchants, and foreign buyers.

But the situation could change again rapidly. A good way to keep abreast of the latest trade developments is through *China's Foreign Trade*, an informative magazine in several languages available at most PRC embassies or from the China Council for the Promotion of International Trade in Beijing. Another excellent source is the US-China Business Council, publishers of the authoritative *China Business Review*. Two informative newspapers are the *Asian Wall Street Journal* (published daily in Hong Kong, weekly in New York) and the English-language weekly *Ta Kung Pao* (published simultaneously in Hong Kong and San Francisco). Additional publications and sources of information on the China market are listed in the China Travel Reading List (see Appendix).

OVERSEAS TRADE EXHIBITIONS

In 1980, China began promoting several major trade exhibitions in the US and throughout Western Europe. In most cases, PRC export officials are on hand to answer questions and initiate negotiations. Advance information on schedules of China's overseas exhibitions is available from the commercial sections of PRC diplomatic missions.

GUANGZHOU SERVICES FOR TRADERS

TELEPHONE INFORMATION AND SERVICES	Telephone
Long-distance (domestic)	113
Long-distance (international)	115

US CONSULATE-GENERAL	Telephone
Dongfang Hotel, 11th floor (new wing)	669900

GUANGZHOU FOREIGN TRADE CENTER AND EXHIBITION HALL — Telephone

Switchboard	330849	Retail shop	x770
Information	x745	Restaurant	x760
Customs	x769	Bookstore	x764
Banking and insurance	x765	Photocopying service	x211
Shipping	x768	Gate No. 1	x891
Post office	x766/7	Gate No. 2	x892
Telegrams and long-		Gate No. 4	x894
distance calls	x763	Gate No. 5	x895

CHINA NATIONAL IMPORT AND EXPORT CORPORATIONS

Guangzhou Branches	Cable	Telephone
Animal By-Products	BYPRODUCTS	886018
Shamian Nan Rd.		
Arts and Crafts:		
Main Branch, 2 Qiaoguang Rd.	ARTCANTON	334208
Export Department, GFTC Building	5050	330849
Ceramics Export Department, GFTC Building	POTTERY	330849
Cereals and Oils	CNCOFC	334154
2 Qiaoguang Rd.		
Chemical	SINOCHEM	885531
61 Yanjiang Xi Rd.		
Foodstuffs	FOODCO	861220
59 Yanjiang Xi Rd.		
Machinery	MACHIMPEX	885531
61 Yanjiang Xi Rd.		
Metals and Minerals	MINMETALS	776875
774 Dongfeng Dong Rd.		
Light Industrial Products	INDUSTRY	337522
87 Changdi Rd.		
Native Produce	PROCANTON	889215
486 Liu'ersan Rd.		
Textiles	CANTEX	331750
63 Wenming Rd.		

COMMERCIAL TRANSPORT SERVICES	Cable	Telephone
China National Foreign Trade		
Transportation Corporation		
Guangzhou Branch, Xiniu Rd.	0970	775393
Huangpu Sub-branch, Huangpu Port	ZHONGWAIYUN	779094

China National Chartering Corporation Erligou, Xijiao	SINOCHART	898745
Guangzhou Ocean Shipping Corporation 412 Huanshi Dong Rd.	COSCO	7765567
China Ocean Shipping Agency 22 Shamian Ave.	PENAVICO	882770

BANKING	**Telephone**
Bank of China	
Guangzhou Branch, 137 Changdi	889912

TRAVEL	**Telephone**
China International Travel Service (CITS)	
Main Office, 179 Huanshi Rd.	677856
Branch Office, Dongfang Hotel, Rm. 2366	669900 x2366
Air	
Civil Aviation Administration of China (CAAC)	
Ticketing, 181 Huanshi Rd.	661451/677462
Bookings (domestic)	662939
Bookings (international)	661803
Rail	
Guangzhou Railroad Station	
North Station, N. Renmin Rd.	777112
Information Desk, Zhanqian Rd.	333333
Kowloon-Guangzhou Railway (British section in Hong Kong)	
Kowloon Station, Hung Hom, Kowloon	Hong Kong 3-646321

HEAD OFFICES OF CHINA'S FOREIGN TRADE CORPORATIONS

China Film Export and Import Corporation (CHINAFILM)
25 Xinwai St., Beijing. Cable: CHINAFILM BEIJING.
Telex: 22195 FILM CN. Tel: 2015533

**China National Arts & Crafts Import and Export
Corporation (ARTCHINA)**
82 Dong'anmen Street, Beijing. Cable: ARTCHINA BEIJING
Telex: 22155 CNART CN. Tel: 55-8831

**China National Cereals, Oils and Foodstuffs Import and Export
Corporation (CEROILS)**
82 Dong'anmen Street, Beijing. Cable: CEROILFOOD BEIJING
Telex: 22281 CEROF CN. Tel: 55-8831 x221

China National Chemicals Import and Export Corporation (SINOCHEM)
Erligou, Xijiao, Beijing. Cable: SINOCHEMIP BEIJING
Telex: 22243 CHEMI CN. Tel: 89-9881

China National Complete Plant Export Corporation (COMPLANT)
28 Donghou Lane, Andingmenwai, Beijing. Cable: COMPLANT BEIJING
Telex: 22559 COMPT CN. Tel: 44-5678

**China National Packaging Import and Export Corporation
(CHINAPACK)**
28 Donghou Lane, Andingmenwai, Beijing. Cable: CHINAPACK BEIJING
Telex: 221490 CPACK CN. Tel: 46-2124

China National Foreign Trade Transportation Corporation (SINOTRANS)
Erligou, Xijiao, Beijing. Cable: SINOTRANS.
Telex: 22867 TRANS CN. Tel: 83-17733

China National Instruments Import and Export Corporation (INSTRIMPEX)
Erligou, Xijiao, Beijing. Cable: INSTRIMPEX BEIJING
Telex: 22304 CIIEC CN. Tel: 83-17733

China National Light Industrial Products Import and Export Corporation (INDUSTRY)
82 Dong'anmen Street, Beijing. Cable: INDUSTRY BEIJING
Telex: 22282 LIGHT CN. Tel: 55-8831.

China National Machinery and Equipment Export Corporation (EQUIPEX)
16 Fuxingmenwai Street, Beijing. Cable: EQUIPEX BEIJING
Telex: 22186 EQUIP CN. Tel: 36-8541

China National Machinery and Equipment Export Corporation (EQUIMPEX)
16 Fuxingmenwai Street, Beijing. Cable: EQUIMPEX BEIJING
Telex: 22186 EQUIP CN. Tel: 36-8541

China National Metals and Minerals Import and Export Corporation (MINMETALS)
Erligou, Xijiao, Beijing. Cable: MINMETALS BEIJING
Telex: 22241 MIMET CN. Tel: 89-0931

China National Native Produce and Animal By-Products Import and Export Corporation (CHINATUHSU)
82 Dong'anmen Street, Beijing. Cable: CHINATUHSU BEIJING
Telex: 22283 TUHSU CN. Tel: 55-4124

China National Publications Import and Export Corporation (PUBLIMEX)
Chaoyangmennei Ave., P.O. Box 88, Beijing. Cable: PUBLIMEX BEIJING
Telex: 22313 CPC CN. Tel: 440731

China National Technical Import Corporation (TECHIMPORT)
Erligou, Xijiao, Beijing. Cable: TECHIMPORT BEIJING
Telex: 22244 CNTIC CN. Tel: 89-0931

China National Raw Materials Textiles Import and Export Corporation (CHINATEX)
82 Dong'anmen St., Beijing. Cable: CHINATEX BEIJING
Telex: 22280 CNTEX CN. Tel: 55-8831

China Council for the Promotion of International Trade (CCPIT)
Fuxingmenwai Street, Beijing. Cable: COMTRADE BEIJING
Telex: 22315 CCPIT CN. Tel: 86-7229

Bank of China
410 Fuchengmennei Ave., Beijing. Cable: HOCHUNGKUO BEIJING
Telex: 22254 BCHO CN. Tel: 66-5325

VI
FOR TRAVELERS
WITH SPECIAL
INTERESTS

Visiting
China's Schools

John Israel

"A MISCELLANY OF EDIFYING ADVICE FOR THE INTREPID
SCHOOLMARM ABOUT TO EMBARK UPON A TEACHERS'
TOUR OF THE PEOPLE'S REPUBLIC OF CHINA"

THOSE who are about to embark on a China trip expecting to unearth some heretofore unsuspected aspect of official policy are bound to be disappointed. Talmudic China analysts in government and academia devote their lives to ferreting out every nuance concealed between the lines of the *People's Daily*. A brief tour is not likely to reveal very much about high-level policy and official attitudes that cannot be gleaned from the written word.

The most important thing you can bring back—something that a desk-bound expert cannot match—is a feeling for the realities of China. Visitors will see China's schools not as abstract models but as living institutions where human teachers interact with flesh-and-blood students. After meeting these people, each with his or her own personality and perceptions, one will never again find oneself thinking of the Chinese as undifferentiated "blue ants." The sense of China as a living reality may be an intangible benefit, but it is an invaluable one. If you come back with nothing more than this, the trip may be deemed a success.

But you should come back with a great deal more. One way to learn as much as possible is to take the broadest possible view of education, which is in fact the Chinese view—that education is not confined to schools but permeates the whole social order. In addition to institutions that are "educational" in the narrow sense, your group may visit townships (formerly known as communes), factories, clinics, homes, theaters, bookstores, restaurants, museums, and tourist attractions. You will observe people at work and at leisure, in groups and individually, reading, strolling, and playing poker. You will see political posters and billboards, as common as commercial advertising is in the United States. Once you realize that education is all pervasive, you will be sensitive to one of the fundamental realities of contemporary China and will be better able to evaluate what you see in the schools you visit.

BRIEFINGS

On a typical China education tour there will be few days on which you fail to visit at least one school and many days on which you visit two. At each school, you will be greeted at the gate by your hosts, including, perhaps, the principal or chancellor and his or her assistants and possibly some teachers. At famous and frequently visited institutions such as Beijing University you may be hosted by a representative of the school's office of foreign affairs, usually a staff member well versed in receiving visitors. You will be ushered into a conference room, seated around a table, furnished with tea and cigarettes, and treated to the standard fare of China visitors, the "brief introduction." The "BI" is a 10–20 minute discourse on the history of the school, its academic structure, and its vital statistics. Almost invariably there will be some mention of national, political, social, and educational goals, which recently have emphasized support for the post-1976 leadership, recovery from the depredations of the "gang of four," and construction of a strong modern socialist state by the year 2000. You will hear, in either general or specific terms, that the institution you are visiting is overcoming obstacles and doing its part in reaching these goals. In recent years, briefings have been more factual and less rhetorical. In some cases, printed handouts have cut the time necessary for presentation of facts and figures.

What you learn beyond the brief introduction depends upon how thoroughly you have prepared for the trip, the acuteness of your observations, your aggressiveness in seeking out information, and a bit of luck. There are two kinds of information that you should have when you start out. One is the kind of general background on education that you can acquire from preparatory reading (see list at end of this section). Even more important, however, if you want to probe deeply, are up-to-date reports on educational conditions in various parts of China during the period immediately preceding your visit.

Fortunately, such material is available in translated press accounts and radio broadcasts regularly published by American governmental agencies. For example, the Foreign Broadcasting Information Service provides daily verbatim news reports from radio stations all over China. These are available in major university libraries, or your group leader can request a file of translations on Chinese education from the National Committee on US-China Relations. A careful reading of these will make it possible to go beyond the formulaic generalities of the brief introduction. You may have learned, for example, that policies presented by your hosts as centrally approved and nationally enforced are so controversial that "bitter and prolonged struggles" are taking place in schools all over China. Such information from Chinese sources will enable you to ask incisive questions with some assurance.

Sometimes even a simple query may lead to a startling reply. For example, a member of our group once asked an innocuous question about the number of books in the school library and drew the answer that there were not very many, since the Red Guards had burned the library to the ground during the Cultural Revolution.

CLASSROOM TOURS

Some of your questions may have to wait, for immediately after the brief introduction you probably will be taken on a tour of the school. In the classroom, you are on familiar turf and can draw freely from your own teaching experience. What is the teacher-student ratio? In a given classroom, it is likely to be on the order of 1:40 or 1:50. What teaching methods are used under such conditions? From your own experience and reading on Chinese educational traditions, you will not be surprised to learn that the teacher resorts to that time-tested rote education that Chairman Mao derisively called "stuffed duck" learning. You might also take note of the conventional physical layout, the teacher's desk facing a neat alignment of old-fashioned wooden desks. Both the tone in which the teacher speaks and the attitudes of the students will tell you much about the learning experience even if you do not understand a word of Chinese. You may also look over students' shoulders or borrow one of their books, which will be especially interesting if you are observing an English-language lesson. Your school hosts will probably try to include such a class on your tour.

You should take careful note of the decorations and displays on classroom walls and elsewhere on the school grounds. You may be surprised to find Benjamin Franklin staring at you from a bulletin board in a school yard. (Franklin is admired as a paragon of science and patriotism.) If you have time, ask for translations of some of the attractive, multi-colored displays adorning school courtyards. If there is no time to obtain a translation, take a close-up photo and get help from a Chinese-reading friend when you return home. And don't forget to seek out English-language displays: the words will be familiar, and the contents will tell you much about official values in China's school system.

WHO DECIDES
WHAT YOU WILL SEE IN CHINA

Your itinerary will probably be a compromise between what your group asks to see and what the Chinese want—or find it logistically possible—to show you. Well in advance of departure for China, your group leader should compile a "shopping list" of members' interests, general and specific. This will be sent to your Chinese hosts; then you sit and wait. Do not expect to learn details of your itinerary until you arrive in China. In some cases, even the cities you will visit will remain a mystery until you have crossed the border.

Most Americans want to see what is "typical" or "average" or at least a spectrum from best to worst. Your hosts, understandably, want you to see their proudest achievements. "Key schools" favored with government subsidies, hand-picked teachers, and selected students may represent a small proportion of all the schools in China, but will account for a disproportionate number of the schools you visit. It is easy to find out whether or not a specific institution is a key school; just ask.

Arriving in China, you will be met by your chief guide and interpreters from the host organization, and they will be joined in each city en route by local guides or interpreters. You will soon discover that despite the highly centralized Chinese political structure, many decisions are made on the local level. Your centrally appointed guides can be invaluable in handling problems, requests, and complaints, but they, like you, are guests in strange cities and must defer to their local hosts.

To illustrate: On its final day in Chengdu, my group visited a local Temple of 500 Buddhas. This was a 500-Buddhas temple to beat all 500-Buddhas temples, and we spent three hours there, first picnicking among the ancient artifacts, then gawking at the exquisitely carved and painted Buddhist saints, each of them uniquely different from the other 499. That evening we overheard our chief guide on the phone, long distance, to our next city, Wuhan:

"But you can't take them to a 500-Buddhas temple. They've just been to one!"

Next afternoon we checked into our Wuhan hotel and were taken to—you guessed it—Wuhan's Temple of 500 Buddhas.

Although it is difficult to add to your itinerary or to exchange one institution or attraction for another, it is sometimes possible to cancel a visit in favor of free time. In the packed agenda of a China trip, that is no small blessing. For example, having visited an industrial exhibition just before leaving Shanghai, we were about to be taken to a handicraft exhibition just after we got off the plane in Beijing. Instead, we requested—and got—free time to shop, stroll, and rest. Such changes are easiest to arrange in instances when an entire commune or school is not geared up and waiting to entertain its foreign friends.

Difficult though it may be to change your itinerary, you may find it easy to adapt scheduled visits to your special interests. You should try to inform your group leader and guides of your particular needs in advance, e.g., a desire to visit an art class or to meet with a professional counterpart. But even if things cannot be arranged in advance, opportunities may arise at the school. Most groups are too large for everybody to visit the same classroom at once, so you will have to split up anyway. After the brief introduction, it is perfectly all right for the group leader to ask one of the hosts if members may visit a particular kind of class. If such a class is in session, they will probably be happy to accommodate you.

While walking through the school, you will generally be free to stop, ask, and look, provided that you do not hold up the group. For example, one of our group's most fruitful encounters occurred during an impromptu visit to a teacher's lounge, where we were able to talk informally to the teachers and even to ask questions about their teaching schedules (which were posted on the blackboard). My wife's curriculum-developers group gained permission on several occasions to break up into three or four units to talk informally with counterparts—master teachers, administrators, curriculum specialists, etc. Pursuing your own interest will be beneficial to your group as well as to you when you return to your hotel and compare notes with colleagues who had different kinds of encounters.

USE OF CAMERAS AND TAPE RECORDERS

Your hosts would not take you to an institution or tourist site if they were not prepared to have you record your experience. Cameras and tape recorders may generally be used without special permission. In fact, frequently visited schools are so accustomed to camera-happy foreign friends that you can often take photos at point-blank range without distracting your subject. Flash photos are permitted at dramatic performances, both school and professional. The only educational and cultural sites where photos sometimes are forbidden are certain museums—either because exhibits are not yet in their final, approved form or because authorities find it profitable to monopolize or merchandise photographic rights. At the Terra Cotta Army Exhibit outside of Xi'an, I have seen a heavy fine levied on the spot against a tourist who violated the injunction.

EDUCATIONAL SOUVENIRS

In a country where politics rather than the marketplace determines the price, the more educational the commodity, the cheaper the cost. For a few dozen yuan you can fill your suitcase with souvenirs that will dazzle your friends, fascinate your students, and make you the most popular show-and-teller in your school.

You can buy all sorts of picture books readily comprehensible to non-Chinese readers, as well as English-language translations sold in Friendship stores and hotels. Equally educational and even cheaper are the colorful political posters that sell for 11 to 40 *fen* in bookstores and special poster shops. (When we returned, we held a Chinese poster exhibit that was warmly received.) Postage stamps, available in all major hotels, reveal much about political values and esthetic standards. Games can be useful as well. Among the not easily found but highly prized items in 1978 was an anti-"gang of four" dartboard. Models, charts, and English-language publications on acupuncture can be purchased on the ground floor of the Shanghai Friendship Store, among other places.

There is no limit to souvenirs save your own ingenuity. Beer labels have become such a tourist favorite that some hotels will furnish, on demand, new ones that never have touched a bottle. Even toilet paper wrappers, if properly read, have a story to tell.

AFTER YOUR RETURN

Some method for sorting out and building upon your group experience is highly desirable. You may exchange slides, notes, or taped transcriptions by mail or you might want to get together for a day or two's reunion or "debriefing." By then, your photos will have been processed, your notes typed, and you will be able to exchange experiences in conveying your knowledge and enthusiasm to the unfortunate majority of your fellow citizens who have not yet been to China.

Before flaunting your expertise to groups of friends and fellow citizens, you will want to catch up on Chinese press translations for the period since your visit. Remember that anything you have seen or heard may be overtaken by new developments. For example, one of my favorite slides, taken in a Guangzhou middle school, was a scale model of a rural "sister school" with which the urban institution generously shared its superior teachers, books, and curricular materials. My audiences were invariably impressed with this effort to bridge the gap between modern cities and backward rural areas. Then I found a translation of a recent newspaper article criticizing such arrangements as grossly inefficient and announcing a new policy of concentrating educational resources in the cities.

WHAT TO READ BEFORE THE TRIP

If you are looking for a single, comprehensive, authoritative volume on contemporary Chinese education, forget it. Such a book has yet to be written. However, with a little industry you can assemble a collection of materials that will fill the bill. To begin with, the philosophical and psychological assumptions that guided Chinese education through the Cultural Revolution are brilliantly elucidated in Donald J. Munro's *The Concept of Man in Contemporary China* (1977), especially Chapter 5, "The Role of the Schools." To trace permutations of policy from 1949–1976, see Ronald N. Montaperto's essay, "China's Education in Perspective," in *China's Schools in Flux*, edited by Montaperto and Jay Henderson (1979). For a useful overview of education in the PRC, see Part One of Thomas Fingar and Linda A. Reed, *An Introduction to Education in the People's Republic of China and U.S.-China Educational Exchanges* (1982), available from the National Association for Foreign Student Affairs, 1860 19th Street, N.W., Washington, D.C. 20009. A historical perspective on Chinese universities can be found in my own "The Idea of Liberal Education in China" in *The Limits of Reform in China* (1983). For the secondary school scene, see Stanley Rosen, "Obstacles to Educational Reform in China," *Modern China* 8:1 (January 1982), pp. 3–40.

When it comes to critical analysis of Chinese education since the death of Mao, Suzanne Pepper is without peer. Working out of Hong Kong, Pepper skillfully utilizes written sources, refugee interviews, and firsthand material collected on China research trips. Consult her articles: "Education and Revolution: The 'Chinese Model' Revised," *Asian Survey* 18:9 (September 1978), pp. 847–890; "Chinese Education after Mao," *The China Quarterly* 81 (March 1980), pp. 1–65; and "China's Universities," *Modern China* 8:2 (April 1982), pp. 147–204. In addition, try to lay your hands on a file of *Chinese Education*, which has appeared quarterly since 1968. The journal features translations from Chinese books, periodicals, and newspapers, with preparatory essays by authorities in the field. Issues of particular interest include spring-summer 1979 ("Educational Policy after the Gang of Four"), winter 1981–82 ("Encyclopedia of Education, 1980"), and summer-fall 1981, a translation of a Chinese world history textbook.

See also the section on education in F.M. Kaplan and J.M. Sobin, *Encyclopedia of China Today*, 4th edition (1988). Finally, the National Committee on US-China Relations, 777 United Nations Plaza, 9B, New York, New York 10017, is an excellent source for all kinds of information, including up-to-date lists of other educational tour groups and their reports, topically defined packets of newspaper clippings and press and radio translations, and a five-page "Bibliography on Education in China." The National Committee will also prepare comprehensive China briefing kits.

FOR TRAVELERS WITH SPECIAL INTERESTS

China's
Health Care
Facilities

Ruth Sidel, Ph.D., and Victor W. Sidel, M.D.

RECENT VISITORS to China—particularly those who lived there in the 1930s and 1940s and those with knowledge of other technologically less developed countries—usually express amazement at the remarkable changes which have taken place in the health of the Chinese people. Before 1949, it was estimated that life expectancy at birth was about 35 years and two children out of five were dead before their fifth birthday. In the words of a Canadian hotel manager who returned to Shanghai in the early 1970s after an absence of 25 years:

> I searched for scurvy-headed children. Lice-ridden children. Children with inflamed red eyes. Children with bleeding gums. Children with distended stomachs and spindly arms and legs.... I looked for children covered with horrible sores upon which flies feasted. I looked for children having a bowel movement, which after much strain, would only eject tapeworms. I looked for child slaves in alleyway factories. Children who worked twelve hours a day, literally chained to small press punches. Children who, if they lost a finger, or worse, often were cast into the streets to beg and forage in garbage bins for future subsistence.

Of course, he did not find them. Life expectancy at birth in China is now estimated at 68 years, and infant and childhood mortality rates are among the lowest in countries at China's level of technological development. In addition, observations of visitors provide evidence of a vigorous, healthy people. Many, indeed probably most, of these improvements in health are due to the fundamental social changes which have taken place in China: the availability of an adequate diet, adequate sanitation, safe water supplies, and adequate clothing and shelter. But reforms in health care and medical services are also important in determining the physical well-being of a people, and are of course extremely important in improving the quality of their lives.

SURVEY OF CHANGES SINCE 1949

Over the past four decades, as is now well known, the People's Republic has fundamentally reorganized China's health services. In a country possessing extremely limited personnel and facilities for modern medicine (and those few concentrated in urban areas), a radical and rapid change has been achieved.

Following the establishment of the PRC in 1949, a National Health Congress in Beijing set down four basic principles for health work: serving the workers, peasants, and soldiers; putting prevention first; coordinating the practices of traditional Chinese and Western medicine; and integrating public health work with mass movements. From 1949 to 1965, large numbers of doctors and middle-level health workers (assistant doctors, nurses, and midwives) were trained. During the same period, large numbers of new hospitals were built; in 1965, a Ministry of Health official reported that each of China's 2,000 counties had at least one hospital. A number of medical schools and other "centers of excellence" were established.

At the same time, the government was also fostering mass participation in health care and preventive medicine. Through the "patriotic health campaigns," sanitation was improved and pests such as flies and mosquitos were largely wiped out. Opium addiction was brought to an end and venereal diseases were essentially eliminated through campaigns conducted by locally recruited and briefly trained workers with community support. Vast numbers of people participated in campaigns against schistosomiasis and other parasitic infestations. Mobile health teams brought initial measures of preventive medicine to isolated areas.

Despite this enormous effort, by 1965, China's professional medical services were still woefully inadequate. There was only one doctor for every 5,000 people (compared to one per 600 people in the US) and one hospital bed for every 1,000 people (compared to one per 100 in the US). And the personnel and facilities, while far more equitably distributed than before 1949, were still relatively concentrated in urban areas.

In June 1965, foreshadowing the Cultural Revolution, Mao Zedong criticized the Ministry of Health for its sparse provision of services in rural areas, its emphasis on theoretical knowledge and the length of its training program, and its lack of attention to research on the prevention and treatment of common disease. In response to this criticism, and as a result of policies generated during the Great Proletarian Cultural Revolution (1966–76), many professional policies which are standard in industrialized countries were largely abandoned and replaced by much more vigorous attempts at the popularization of medical services. Over one million "barefoot doctors" (part-time paramedical workers trained in diagnostic and treatment techniques) and three million rural health aides were trained, and local cooperative medical care systems to organize and finance care were developed and expanded in the rural areas. Urban medical workers were rotated into the countryside. Medical schools were closed for several years; when they reopened in the early 1970s, they adopted radically altered methods for selecting and training students.

In the years since the end of the Cultural Revolution, and particularly since the beginning of the "Four Modernizations" campaign, the pendulum has swung back towards methods of selecting and training students which more closely resemble those found in the US and other technologically-developed countries, and greater emphasis is currently being placed on technological improvement, particularly in hospitals. There is said to be one doctor for every 1,500 people and one hospital bed for every 500 people, a rapid increase but nevertheless still far short of the ratios found in the industrialized countries. As a result of changes in the structure of the rural areas, the economic base that supported the barefoot doctors and the cooperative medical care systems has largely disappeared. Health statistics in China as a whole have continued to improve, but there are said to be areas, particularly rural ones, that are being left behind in China's progress.

HEALTH CARE IN RURAL AREAS

Until the recent restructuring of the rural economy, attempts had been made to have health care available at each level of rural organization. The smallest subdivision of a Chinese rural community was the production team, with a membership of 100–200 people. Members of a production team lived close to one another, usually in one or more small villages, forming the basic social unit in the countryside. A group of teams, usually 10–20, combined to form a production brigade. A typical commune, which was the basic economic unit from the 1960s to the early 1980s, was composed of 10–30 production brigades. The township, which has replaced the commune as the lowest level of formal state power in the rural areas, is analogous to the "neighborhoods" in the cities.

Health care for the production teams was provided by barefoot doctors and health aides who dealth with problems of sanitation under the supervision of the barefoot doctors. The barefoot doctors provided health care and medical care, including health education, preventive medicine, and the treatment of minor illness, in their sparsely equipped health stations. They also provided care in the fields, taking their medical bags with them while participating in agricultural work. They were paid, like other members of the commune, through distribution of crops and through work points; these were given for medical work in the same way as for agricultural work. The production teams chose volunteer health aides, whose primary role was to teach people about sanitation and to collect night soil and ensure that it was adequately stored before being used as fertilizer.

In recent years, many barefoot doctors have been upgraded to "rural doctors" and the term "barefoot doctor" is no longer recognized by the Ministry of Health. With the shift to the rural responsibility system (under which land is farmed under contract), many rural doctors now engage in fee-for-service practice and the cooperative medical care systems and health aides have disappeared in many areas.

Health facilities at the brigade level varied widely in different parts of China. Care at this intermediate level is now provided by rural doctors. The health stations are generally furnished with an examination table, a desk, a few chairs, a medicine cabinet stocked with traditional and Western medicines, and an acupuncture chart. Midwives also work out of these health stations.

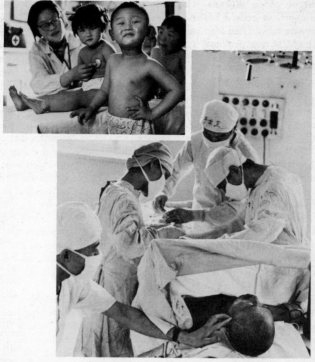

Preschool children receive checkups in Shanghai health care center; a sophisticated operation uses electronic acupuncture anesthesia

Many large townships have their own hospital facilities to which patients are referred from the local health stations; these are staffed with regularly-trained doctors, assistant doctors, and nurses.

At the highest rural level, county hospitals serve patients referred from the lower levels or who come directly to them. Traditional Chinese medicine as well as Western-type medicine are offered. The level of technology in these facilities is improving rapidly but is still considerably below that of facilities in the cities.

HEALTH CARE IN THE CITIES

Health care in China's cities, as in the countryside, is provided at each organizational level. The smallest unit in the urban area is usually the "lane." The lane health station, which may serve from 1,000 to 5,000 people, is near the residents' homes; its major functions are preventive work — including health education and immunization, birth control, and the treatment of minor illnesses. Health workers at the lane level are local housewives or retired health personnel; during the Cultural Revolution they were called "Red Medical Workers." Health care is also provided in factories. Most factories have a central clinic as well as health stations in individual workshops; some large factories have in-patient hospitals for short-term stays.

The backup institution for lane and factory health stations is the "hospital" (which often has no beds and thus might be more appropriately termed a clinic); until recently, it was called the "neighborhood hospital," but the relatively autonomous structure of the neighborhood that emerged in the 1960s and 1970s has been replaced by a more hierarchical structure and the hospital now is much more directly controlled by the district and higher levels of the Ministry of Health. These hospitals, which may serve as many as 50,000 people, are generally staffed by physicians fully trained in both traditional and Western medicine and by "middle" medical workers (nurses, technicians, and assistant doctors). They are the referral centers for the local health stations and in turn refer patients to better-equipped district and specialty hospitals. Facilities for simple laboratory tests and X-rays are available, however, the equipment is usually sparse and relatively outdated. In addition, these hospitals act as centers for public health work in the neighborhood. These are usually highly-organized efforts that have proven extremely effective.

Hospitals in China's cities range from these small neighborhood institutions to technologically-sophisticated research and teaching hospitals. Intermediate hospitals, with rapidly improving technology, include those at the district level and at the municipal level. Beyond these are higher-technology referral hospitals, often specialized. In Beijing, for example, there are research-oriented specialized hospitals functioning under the aegis of Chinese Academy of Medical Sciences. One of these, Peking Union Medical College Hospital, is the center of its own medical school; it is located near the Beijing Hotel and serves English-speaking foreign visitors.

TRADITIONAL CHINESE MEDICINE

Efforts have been made over the past 30 years to combine China's traditional medicine (zhongyi, "Chinese medicine") with modern scientific medicine (xiyi, "Western medicine"). The visitor is often shown a variety of Chinese medical techniques. Acupuncture and moxibustion are both based on a complex theoretical system of meridians running over the surface of the body with hundreds of points along them related to specific internal organs or functions. Insertion of needles at these points (acupuncture) or burning an herb that is shaped into a cone and held over them (moxibustion) is used to treat a wide variety of medical problems. In addition, acupuncture may be used to suppress pain during a number of surgical operations, mainly of the head and neck. Called "acupuncture anesthesia" during the Cultural Revolution, this technique does not provide total pain relief; it is still considered experimental and is used only with the patient's consent and cooperation.

Even more widespread than the use of acupuncture is the use of herbal medicine. Herbal treatments are frequently preferred to alternative Western-type medications, because herbal formulations are cheaper and usually have no side effects. They are often combined into multi-ingredient prescriptions.

Exercise is another important element in Chinese health therapy. The visitor will usually be able to observe both individuals and groups practicing the slow, postured, traditional exercises of Qi Gong (breathing exercises) and Tai Ji Quan, or doing Western-type calisthenics. Although most medical schools in China now concentrate predominantly on "Western medicine," there still exist a number of schools of "Chinese medicine" and visitors may be able to arrange visits to them.

THE CURRENT SCENE

Since the late 1970s, China's new leadership has shifted much of the emphasis in medical care toward "modernization." Many doctors from China have gone to the United States or other industrialized countries for specialized training and those who have returned are developing specialty practices similar in many ways to those in the countries in which they were trained. The technological resources required for this shift to increasingly specialized practice, together with the changes in economic structure in China, may be placing in jeopardy some of the remarkable improvements in public health and in the efforts to distribute basic medical care to remote or poor rural areas. The emphases on primary care, on mass movements for health, on barefoot doctors and other indigenous health workers, and on bringing together traditional Chinese medicine and Western medicine— emphases that made China's health care system a model for many developing countries in the 1970s—now appear to be disappearing. On the other hand, life expectancy in China continues to improve overall and cancer, heart disease, stroke, and accidents—the most important causes of death in industrialized countries—are now becoming the leading causes of death in most areas of China. This is a remarkable, if somewhat ironic, testimony to the health achievements of a country that is still in many ways appropriately classified as a "developing country."

VISITS TO HEALTH FACILITIES

Visits to health care facilities are usually included in tours of China for general visitors and often even in non-health-related specialized tours. The briefing at the beginning of the visit may not, however, describe that facility's place in the overall structure of the health care system. While the changes in the facility that have occurred since 1949 and often the changes since the end of the Cultural Revolution in 1976 may be covered in detail, aspects of current functioning such as referral patterns, staffing patterns, payment for services, and quality of care issues are usually given less attention. The briefing is usually followed by a tour of the facility, during which the visitor may note, for example, the level of technology, the availability of both "Western medicine" and "Chinese medicine," open wards or multi-bedded rooms, and a number of relatives present in the rooms. Careful preparation for the visit and submission of questions in advance can help avoid the frustration that occurs when there is insufficient time for discussion of important elements in the services provided. It is also important to request clarification of terms that may be used differently in China, even such simple ones as "doctor" and "hospital."

WHAT TO READ BEFORE THE TRIP

The Chinese Ministry of Health has summarized many of China's health statistics and its health care organization in *Public Health in the People's Republic of China 1987*. Health care professionals may also wish to review recent issues of the *Chinese Medical Journal*, published monthly in separate Chinese and English editions. China also publishes a number of booklets on medical care in English.

Sources of information written outside China include: *Away With All Pests* by Joshua Horn (1971), a firsthand account by a British surgeon who practiced in China from 1949 to 1964 and witnessed the extraordinary changes that were made (Monthly Review Press, New York); *The Health of China* by Victor W. Sidel and Ruth Sidel (1983), a history and analysis of the recent evaluation of China's medical care system (Beacon Press, Boston); *Primary Health Care: The Chinese Experience* (1983), the report of a seminar sponsored by the World Health Organization (Geneva) and *Child Health in China* by Mary E. Young and Andre Prost (1985), prepared as a working paper for the World Bank (Washington, DC). There are many books and articles on traditional Chinese medicine; an excellent starting point is *The Web That Has No Weaver* by Ted Kaptchuk (Conghom and Weed, 1984). For a recent analysis, see also *Chinese Medicine* by Manfred Porkert (William Morrow, 1988).

Advanced students receiving instruction in microsurgery

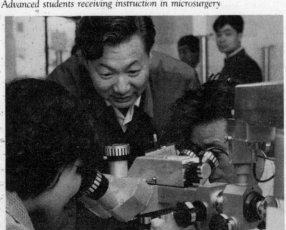

FOR TRAVELERS WITH SPECIAL INTERESTS

Religion
in China

Franklin J. Woo

AMERICANS who are interested in China may find it helpful to bear in mind the phrase of Frederick W. Mote of Princeton University: culturally speaking, he said, there is a "cosmological gulf between China and the West." Those who tour China are apt to be disappointed if they look for their own image in the people of that historically very different land.

Religion has never had the same status in China as it has in Western society. Chinese journalists from the People's Republic who recently toured the United States were amazed to discover so many churches in the cities and towns they visited. In every hotel room was to be found—like the ubiquitous thermos in Chinese hotels—the Gideon Bible. From these signs, the Chinese visitors concluded that Americans, not having all the answers to the hard questions of life, still have to resort to a father writ large in heaven.

Religion does not have a special place in today's China. Furthermore, religion is generally regarded as superstition, an opiate of the people, and a tool of the ruling class to keep power and privilege.

However, in the 1980s, organized religions in China again began to flourish after a decade of ultra-leftist attempts of the Cultural Revolution to suppress them. Today the Chinese Communist Party recognizes five religions: Buddhism, Islam, Daoism (Taoism), and two forms of Christianity (Catholicism and Protestantism) which developed separately in China.

THE CHINESE ORIENTATION

In China, formal religion—such as it was—was woven into the total fabric of life. As an eminent Chinese sociologist, C.K. Yang, remarked, religion in China is diffused rather than institutionalized. One has to look for signs of it in daily life rather than in church buildings or ceremonies. Although there are a number of active mosques, shrines, temples, and churches in China today, religious practice is not confined to them.

Confucius, the famous Chinese sage who lived in the 6th century BC, was once asked what he thought of life after death. He answered that he had not solved the mysteries of this life, let alone those of the next. Chinese religion, generally speaking, is notably down-to-earth. The spiritual roots of Chinese religion are traditionally found in the systems of thought embodied in Confucianism, Buddhism, and Daoism (Taoism). Their common emphasis is on how to live life in the here-and-now and how the individual (always in community) can relate meaningfully and harmoniously to other humans and to nature. Religion is thus more ethical than theocentric, more practical than theoretical. For a people who over the centuries were preoccupied with producing enough food merely to stay alive, how could it have been otherwise? Religion had to be oriented toward this world, and it is precisely in this mundane relationship to the everyday activities of life and in the relationships between people and environment that the sacred dimensions of life are to be found. In the words of Tu Wei-ming of Harvard, there is no "ontological gap between heaven and earth" in Chinese life.

JUDAISM AND CHRISTIANITY IN CHINA

Judaism. Judaism's role in Chinese history has been minor, albeit colorful. Records of Jewish settlement in China extend back to the year 950, when 70 Jewish families were listed in the city register of Kaifeng in Henan Province. Probably originating in Persia, Kaifeng's Jews erected their first synagogue there in 1163. The community remained intact through the 18th century, by which time its members had been totally assimilated into the Chinese ethnic and social fabric. By the early 20th century, however, apart from a handful of aging citizens still practicing some Jewish rites (including the proper slaughtering of pigs), vestiges of Kaifeng's Jews had all but vanished. In the decades prior to 1949, substantial numbers of Jewish migrants from Russia and Central Europe had established prominent Jewish communities within the foreign settlements of Tianjin and Shanghai but, here again, scant physical evidence of these now dispersed groups has survived to the present day [readers are referred to the best current work on the subject in English: Michael Pollack, *Mandarins, Jews, and Missionaries: The Jewish Experience in the Chinese Empire* (1980)].

Christianity. Christianity made four major attempts to enter China. The first was by the Nestorians, who came from Persia through the route of the silk trade in the 7th century; Judaism and Islam also came to China by the same route. The second attempt was headed by Father John Montecorvino of Rome in the 13th century. Then came the Jesuit Matteo Ricci in the end of the 16th century who brought, along with his religion, astronomy, mathematics, and physics to the Imperial Court—the Chinese were interested in modernization even then. Protestant and Roman Catholic missionaries came in large numbers during the 19th and 20th centuries, almost in parallel with Western expansionism. Christianity and imperialist economic and political interests penetrated China and together enjoyed special advantages in the imbalanced relations between a technologically backward China and a technologically advanced West.

Beijing's Nantang Cathedral

With the Communist victory of 1949, Mao Zedong announced at Tian'anmen in Beijing that the Chinese people had finally stood up—the culmination of a 150-year effort to rid themselves of foreign domination and exploitation and a decaying social order. Through the Communist-led revolution, they gained the dignity and pride that go with selfhood, an important aspect of the religious dimension of life. To some degree, Chinese Christianity was also part of the struggle for the selfhood of the Chinese people, as it attempted to stand up against the domination of the churches of the powerful West and their well-intentioned missionaries. Thus it was that the Protestant churches in China for over a century strove to be self-governing, self-supporting, and self-propagating.

CURRENT DEVELOPMENTS

In the Protestant churches in China today that same effort is known as the "Three-Self Patriotic Movement." Within the Marxist revolution, Chinese Christians in this movement have made a concerted effort to identify themselves with the hopes and aspirations of their own people. For Roman Catholics in China there has been a similar movement (although belated, because of the previously anti-Communist stance of the Vatican), which formed the Chinese Catholic Patriotic Association. Comparable groups also exist for other religious adherents such as the Muslims, Buddhists, and Daoists. All of them are religious organizations, but they are focused on political action to bring about a better social order for the welfare of all Chinese people.

Where, then, are the spiritual roots of China to be found today? As we have said, they are traceable to Confucianism, Buddhism, and Daoism; also to Islam, Christianity, and within the last half-century, to Marxism-

Leninism and Mao Zedong Thought (however interpreted). Religion in China, perhaps more so than elsewhere, exists as the realm of human values set amidst the urgent material needs of the people. As Gandhi once said of India, "For the hungry, God comes in the form of bread." The human values, both Chinese and Western, which are expressed in the gigantic effort to provide food, clothing, shelter, medical care, education, and a meaningful life for the people constitute the essence of religion in China today. It is a concern for social justice as much as for religious piety.

REVIVAL OF RELIGIOUS FREEDOMS

Visitors to China will find opportunities to visit places of worship and to participate in religious services. With the policies of the "gang of four" no longer dominant, religious freedom is again being revived in China. Since 1979, more and more churches, mosques, temples, and shrines are reopening, after being closed down with the onset of the Cultural Revolution in 1966. Today more and more Chinese are participating in public worship as well as in the more popular form of gathering in small private groups at home or elsewhere. Also in fall 1979, the first interreligious delegation from China came to the United States to attend the Third Assembly of the World Conference on Religion and Peace at Princeton, New Jersey. The delegation of 10 included Buddhists, Muslims, and Christians. In 1981, a delegation of church leaders, both Catholic and Protestant, participated in an international meeting in Montreal, Canada. Another unprecedented international Christian meeting, *Nanjing '86*, took place in China in May 1986 when 144 participants from 22 different countries including China participated. More recently, Protestant leaders have visited Hong Kong, Japan, Great Britain, parts of Europe, Scandinavia, countries in Africa, India and the Philippines. Christians in China have also received delegations from many of these countries, including Bishop Desmond Tutu of South Africa. Though there has not been any official religious census, estimated figures for the different religions in China today are as follows: 100 million Buddhists, 20 million Muslims, three million Catholics, and at least 4.5 million Protestants. Protestants in Zhejiang Province, one of the smallest provinces in China, alone claim 1,300 churches and 800,000 Christians.

In China today, interreligious cooperation takes place through the organ known as the Chinese People's Political Consultative Conference (CPPCC). Here religious adherents and all people of goodwill interact in the political arena to bring about what each segment of Chinese society regards as the welfare of all Chinese people. In the CPPCC, religious believers gather with members of the various democratic parties of China, returned overseas Chinese, national minorities, socialist workers, peasants, intellectuals, and people in the arts and literature to deliberate upon the welfare of China and the Chinese people. Usually more than 2,000 people from all walks of Chinese life attend the national meetings of the CPPCC.

THE RELIGIOUS SPIRIT IN EVERYDAY LIFE

Travelers to China should seek signs of the religious dimension of existence, its truly human aspect, in the quality of Chinese society in general. They should look for signs of the sacred in the common courtesy, the kindness, and the tenderness of the Chinese people. They should see the divine in the relationships of people that cut across the generations, in respect for and care of the young and the aged within the family. Although more and more religious places in the usual sense have come into being here and there, religion in China remains, as always, more diffused than institutionalized.

Roman Catholics visiting China should realize that the relationship between the Catholic Church in China and Rome has been strained since 1957–58 over the issue of the appointment of bishops and largely because of the then overtly anti-Communist policies of the Vatican. To date, there is still no official relationship between the Catholic Church in China and Rome. This situation was worsened by the Pope's unilateral elevation (1981) of a bishop in Guangzhou (Canton) to archbishop without consultation with the Chinese Church. Religious people, concerned with reconciliation, should be sensitive to the political ramifications of religious beliefs as have been shown in China's history.

Since the restoration of the policy of religious freedom in 1979, open public worship is increasing rapidly among Buddhists, Muslims, and Christians (Protestants and Catholics). Though progress has been slow, in the 1980s there have been renewed interest in Confucianism in the People's Republic. There are in China today some 5,000 active Protestant churches plus 17,000 home congregations; there are now more than 1,000 Catholic churches. To provide new and younger men and women to the aging leadership of the churches in China has been the main preoccupation of the China Christian Council in recent years. They are moving forward in Chinese selfhood towards governing well, supporting well and propagating well their religious life within Chinese society. If you wish to participate in religious services or see some places of worship while in China, ask your guides about those that are open to visitors. For further information about Christians and churches in China, write to:

Catholic:	Protestant:
Mr. Liu Bai-nian	Mr. Han Wenzao
Assistant Secretary	Associate General Secretary
Chinese Catholic—	China Christian Council
Patriotic Association	169 Yuan Ming Yuan Road
Beijing, PRC	Shanghai, PRC

RELIGIOUS CURRENTS IN THE 1980s
Randy J. LaPolla

Protestantism. Throughout the 1980s, a new church has been opening somewhere in China on the average of every two days. The Chinese

Christian Three-Self Patriotic Movement renewed public activities in Shanghai during Easter 1979. In September of that year, public services began to be held in Shanghai.

Before 1949, there were said to be between 700,000 and 1,000,000 Protestants in China. There are now 300,000–400,000 active churchgoers, whose numbers are increasing rapidly. It is estimated that there may be another group just as large as this who are believers, but for political or other reasons do not partake in organized religious activity. It is also thought that about 60% of the believers have kept up their faith because of a Christian family background, and that most other adherents have had some contact with believers. Some of the young people, however, clearly come on their own, either out of curiosity or for some personal reason.

Most large cities have at least several hundred Protestants, but the majority live in Shanghai and in Henan, Shandong, Anhui, Fujian, and Sichuan provinces. Development has been more rapid in South China as well as in the Chinese countryside, both areas, in which Protestantism had its historical roots. Even so, most Protestants in the countryside participate in family/home (*jia ting*) associations that take the place of a church or, if they are nearby, travel to the city each week for services.

Before 1949, a large number of sects functioned within the scope of Protestantism. Now these have all been joined into the Three-Self Movement, but some sectarian distinctions have been retained. For example, two baptism services and five communion services are variously practiced, as well as the foot-washing service of the church members with a Brethren Church tradition. The church has also developed to suit the needs of today's China. There are now services on Saturday night for those who work on Sundays. There are women's groups, Bible classes, prayer meetings, and groups for young people. The current view is that the church before 1949 was too foreign in its orientation, and that many church members colluded with foreigners in their attempts at cultural and material domination of China. Therefore, the sinicization of the church is seen as a positive trend.

Seminaries have also reopened. The first to resume training was in Nanjing in 1980; it was followed by Shenyang in 1982; Beijing in 1983; and Chengdu, Fuzhou, and Shanghai in 1984. By 1987, there were 11 Protestant seminaries in China, with a combined enrollment of 600 students. In general, new candidates for the seminaries must be baptized high-school graduates who have passed an entrance test and have been recommended by their local churches. However, because the seminaries have only recently reopened, there are few young pastors in China. To fill the gap, the church also runs one-month short courses to train assistant clergy. There is also a correspondence course operated out of Nanjing. There are religious presses in Nanjing, Shanghai, and Fuzhou that publish Bibles, correspondence-course texts, and other books. Between 1981 and 1984, some 1,400,000 copies of the Bible (photocopied from an early vernacular version published in the 1920s) were printed. The United Bible Societies in 1987 has established through the Amity Foundation of China a $6.9-million printing plant outside of Nanjing to print Bibles and other literature.

Catholicism. The first national congress of the Chinese Catholic Patriotic Association was held in May of 1957, with some 260 representatives from 200 provinces participating. This was a mass organization with elected representatives. There were fewer than 200 bishops in China after 1949, so the Chinese community began choosing its own clerical leaders in 1958, but all were excommunicated by the Vatican. The second representative congress was held in January 1962, and the third in May 1980. At this last conference, a constitution was adopted and officials were elected, with Zong Huaide selected as chairman. All members of the organization who were persecuted during the Cultural Revolution were rehabilitated, and many returned to work in the Church. Later, a separate Representative Congress of Lay Catholics was also set up under the direction of Zhang Jiasu, who was also the head of the Chinese Conference of Bishops.

There are now six Catholic seminaries in China: the National Shenzhe College in Beijing, the East China Shenzhe in Shanghai, the South Central Shenzhe in Wuchang, the Southwest Shenzhe in Chengdu, the Northeast Shenzhe in Shenyang, and the Beijing City Shenzhe in the suburbs of the capital. There is a combined total of about 150 students in these seminaries; they are allowed to attend if they are single, baptized high-school graduates who have the approval of their parents and can pass the entrance exam. There is also a school in Jinan, Shandong, that serves as a preparatory school for those interested in entering the seminary. China now has 40 bishops, about 1,000 priests, about 1,300 nuns, and, although there are no precise figures, about 3,000,000 lay Catholics (about the same number as in 1949). Outside the city of Shanghai the huge Sheshan Philosophical and Theological Institute, under the leadership of Bishop Jin Luxian, was opened in October, 1982.

The church now publishes Bibles and missals, and also publishes the magazine *Catholic Church in China*. At present, the Bible is printed in classical Chinese, which is no longer regularly taught in Chinese schools, but a vernacular edition is being prepared.

Contemporary circumstances must be viewed together with Catholicism's long but uneven history in China. There were contacts as early as the 7th and 13th centuries, but it wasn't until the 16th century, with the dominance of the Portuguese and later the coming of Matteo Ricci, that Catholicism acquired a foothold in China. By the year 1700, there were an estimated 300,000 Catholics in China, although all of the priests were foreign. In 1724, the French took control of the Chinese Church and banned the worship of ancestors and Confucius. This caused the emperor to ban Catholicism, thus halting the growth of the religion in China. The imperial ban lasted for 120 years, up to 1844, but even after that the Vatican continued to forbid ancestor or Confucius worship, so the religion retained a distinctly foreign cast.

This was the time of the large imperialist division in China, so China was split into different religious districts: the French in the Central Plain area; the German in Shandong and Shanxi; the Italian in Hunan, Hubei, and Gansu; and the American in Guangdong. The Japanese also sent priests into the northeast. These religions had an expressly colonial orientation, serving the imperialist goals of the various countries. In the 1930s, after the Japanese set up the puppet government of Manchukuo, the Vatican was the first after Japan to recognize the puppet regime and ordered the Chinese Catholics not to interfere with the Japanese.

The Vatican opposed the Chinese Revolution and some Catholic groups organized armies to fight against the Communists. Upon founding of the PRC in 1949, the Vatican ordered Chinese Catholics not to read newspapers, not to wear red scarves, not to participate in any Communist organized or approved activity, and to generally oppose the new government in any way they could. To this day, the Vatican and China still have no formal ties.

Buddhism. Although vigorously suppressed during the Cultural Revolution, Buddhism has been experiencing a tremendous resurgence in the 1980s. Millions of yuan are being invested by government and other sources in rebuilding temples all over the country. The rebuilding campaign serves two functions: in addition to increasing the number of Buddhist centers, it also adds to the number of tourist sites in China, thus promoting the development of China's tourism sector. Now almost all medium-size and large cities have local Buddhist associations.

The All-China Buddhist Association has its headquarters in Beijing's Guangji Temple. The association oversees the restoration of temples, the organization of Buddhist activities, and the publishing of Buddhist books and its magazine, *The Sound of the Dharma.* They also operate the Buddhist academies. Academies now function in Nanjing, Beijing, and Wuhan; there are also preparatory schools in many cities for those wishing to enter the academies. The academies train students in Buddhist theory and restoration of cultural artifacts. To enter an academy or even to just become a monk, candidates must be high-school graduates of at least 18 years of age who have their parents' or unit's permission and can pass the entrance exams.

As each local Buddhist association in China has a relatively large degree of autonomy, the nature and scope of Buddhist practice can vary greatly between cities. In Chengdu, for example, an old practice survives where each of the 5,000 or so lay Buddhists is registered and assigned to one of the 200 or so monks, who is then responsible for the training of that individual. In Wuhan, most of the 300–400 Buddhist clergy are women, as is the case in Changsha, but in Zhenjiang there is only one woman serving along with 50 or so monks.

There are three main types of religion that carry the name "Buddhist" in China: one is practiced mainly by elderly women, often illiterate, who go to the temples to burn incense and kow-tow to a statue, asking that some request be granted. The second type is represented by those who seriously study Buddhism, at home or in one of the Buddhist academies or schools, and whose main practice is meditation. It is this form that is organized and developing. Most temples in the Han areas are Chan (Zen) or Jingtu (Pure Land) temples; several are a combination of these two sects.

Chan Buddhism is said to have been brought to China from India through Guangdong in the 5th century by Boddhidharma, although it evolved into a distinctly Chinese form of Buddhism, having adapted considerably to Chinese ways of thinking and practice. The word "Chan" means "meditation," the principal practice of most Chan Buddhists. Chan is distinguished from Japanese Zen in that it no longer recognizes all of the old sub-sects of Chan that still differentiate Japanese Buddhists, and in that the Chan still retains monastic disciplines (e.g., forbidding marriages and consumption of alcohol).

There is a third religion referred to as "Buddhist," but more accurately designated as Lamaism. Lamaism developed as the result of the spread of Buddhism into Tibet around the 7th century. Buddhist traditions then merged with the native animistic religion and developed along a path quite different from Chinese Buddhism. Although there are a few Lamaist temples in Han areas of China, the sect is mainly practiced in Tibet and Inner Mongolia. Lamaism also had a rebirth after the Cultural Revolution, although the resurgence has mainly been confined to Tibet. Although temples are also being rebuilt in Inner Mongolia, there has been no upsurge of young people going into the monasteries as witnessed in Han China, where more than half of all the Buddhist monks these days are young and educated.

Islam. Possibly the largest of China's organized religious groups, the Muslims consist mostly of millions of Hui minority people. Although Muslims are scattered all over China, the largest concentration is in northwest China. The Muslims too have received large subsidies in recent years to rebuild mosques. In cities such as Hohhot, Xi'an, and Beijing, the restored mosques have become very active. Although Muslim communities can and do receive funding from the state, they try to be as self-reliant as possible. There is a very active Chinese Islamic Association, with headquarters near Niu Jie in the southwest part of Beijing.

Confucianism. Some historically notable Confucian temples have been preserved or restored, including the Kong (Confucius) family home in Qufu; and the 1980s have witnessed renewed interest in Confucian philosophy. Nevertheless, there has not been any visible rebirth of religious activity associated with these temples or with Confucius worship. The only visible evidence of ancestor worship is efforts to construct more elaborate graves or tombs in the countryside.

Judaism. Although there are a few traces of an ethnic Chinese Jewish community in Kaifeng and of 20th-century settlements of Russian Jews in Northeast China, there are now virtually no practicing Jews among the indigenous population in China. (Information on Jews in China may be obtained by writing to the Sino-Judaic Institute, 3197 Louis Road, Palo Alto, CA 94303.)

FOR TRAVELERS WITH SPECIAL INTERESTS

China's Arts and Handicrafts

Roberta Helmer Stalberg, Ph.D.

TODAY'S travelers to China will have the good fortune of arriving in the midst of a nationwide campaign to expand and modernize the production of arts and handicrafts. Greater emphasis is now being placed on traditional forms, with a new stress on individual and aesthetic values. Developments since 1977 also augur a more flexible and eclectic attitude in the area of fine arts. Once again, scenic landscapes and bird-and-flower still-life studies are being painted in the style of the old masters, although these now frequently contain modern subject matter. The visitor's enjoyment and appreciation of China's art, new and old, will be enhanced by a basic knowledge of how Chinese art evolved.

A GLANCE AT THE HISTORY OF CHINESE ART

During China's Neolithic period, which spanned the 8th to the 2nd millennia BC, finely executed styles of pottery appeared, foreshadowing the development of ceramics as a major Chinese art form. The wares, exhibiting a high level of craftsmanship, were ornamented with incised or painted geometric motifs, linear designs, or stylized animals and fish. Along with the shapes of the *li* and *ding* ceramic tripods of this period, these forms set important stylistic precedents for later times.

The appearance of bronze metallurgy in the 2nd millennium BC, during China's first historical dynasty, the Shang, marked the end of the Neolithic period in China. A skilled class of Shang craftsmen produced ritual objects of clay, bronze, jade, and wood for the homes and tombs of rulers and nobles. Shang pottery, which still exists in Chinese museums, approaches the technical level of porcelain. These high-fired wares were sometimes glazed, and their incised geometric or zoomorphic motifs are also seen in Shang bronze ritual vessels. The ritual vessels were designed to hold food or liquor offered at sacrifices to the ancestral spirits, who consumed the "essence" and left behind the food itself. The magnificent bronze vessels of this age demonstrate a metallurgy so technologically advanced that it has not been surpassed since. These imposing objects, often covered with a rich green patina, can today be seen in museums throughout China. Their gruesome animal and human forms still awe travelers.

In the 11th century BC, northwestern invaders defeated the Shang rulers and established the Zhou (Chou) Dynasty, which endured for 800 years. Bronze vessels continued to be used in sacrificial rituals but were also produced for commemorative purposes. Bronze casting maintained a high quality, while decorative motifs became more linear and abstract. After the 9th century BC, Zhou art was increasingly influenced by the vigorous animal designs of the Central Asian nomads, which were more realistic than Chinese forms. From the 5th to the 3rd centuries BC, during an age known as the Warring States period, the strict rituals of the feudal Zhou society were abandoned, and elegant green-glazed stoneware, gold and silver inlays in bronze, and lacquerware, already highly developed, acquired a new, fluid grace.

THE HAN DYNASTY

Realism reached full flowering in Chinese art during the Han Dynasty (3rd century BC–3rd century AD). During this powerful and cosmopolitan period, China's borders were pushed westward almost to Persia, where more realistic design elements originated and were gradually carried back to China. Carved and painted tomb-wall bricks depict active scenes of daily life. The tombs of the Han—and of the short-lived Qin (Ch'in) Dynasty preceding it—contained vast quantities of ceramic figures created to assist and accompany the spirits of the dead. In 1974, an army of realistic, life-sized clay warriors and their mounts was discovered in Xi'an near the tomb of the founding emperor of the Qin Dynasty, Qin Shi Huangdi (Ch'in Shih Huang Ti).

In the Han, dragons, tigers, birds, and snakes were used in art as part of an elaborate system symbolizing seasons, directions, and natural elements. Dragons were thought to possess the power to change shape and size at will and to control the rain. Because of this limitless ability to control natural forces, the dragon's might paralleled the emperor's power on earth, and in the Han the dragon became the official emblem of the emperor and his sons. The Han also brought a heightened appreciation of the aesthetic value of jade in addition to its value for ritual purposes. The art of silk production, which had developed in China in the shadows of unrecorded time, flourished in the Han, and lengths of gossamer-thin silks, patterned silk brocades, and silken embroidery were carried along the "Silk Road" through Western Asia to clothe Rome's patrician matrons.

After the fall of the Han in the 3rd century AD, Daoist and Buddhist beliefs played an increasingly important role in developing a new Chinese aesthetic, which was primarily concerned with nature. During the 350-year period of political instability which followed the end of the Han, literati painters gradually abandoned the turbulence and cruelty of court intrigues and turned instead to philosophical speculations amid the natural beauties of mountain and stream. With Buddhism—which had been transmitted from India by the 1st century AD—and Daoism as their metaphysical basis, these artists developed a complex vocabulary of landscape elements whose influence continues to the present. This new system of aesthetics, which determined value by beauty rather than moral or practical worth, was to usher in great changes in Chinese art. While art had previously been used almost entirely to convey moral teachings, the breakdown of Confucianism and rise of Daoism brought a reevaluation of the purpose and value of art.

In the 6th century, six principles required for artistic excellence were proposed by Xie He (Hsieh Ho), and these important concepts, strongly Daoist in inspiration, have been the touchstone of all later painting. Briefly stated, Xie He proposed that the artist must first perceive and attune himself to *qi*—the cosmic "breath" or force of nature which animates and energizes all things. When properly attuned, the painter can invoke or recreate nature's energy through the act of painting. Landscape paintings were important because they portrayed a physical realm while also implying an imaginary world of the spirit. This magical second world is always suggested in landscape painting.

THE GOLDEN AGE OF TANG

The Tang Dynasty was founded in the 7th century. The first half of this 300-year period was a time of unparalleled political stability, economic well-being, and military expansion, and the resultant flourishing of art and culture led later ages to call the Tang China's Golden Age. Buddhism continued to influence art, particularly in painting and monumental sculpture, which can still be seen in caves and temples all over China. The cosmopolitan court could sample the commodities of India, Arabia, Persia, and Southeast Asia. An unprecedented wealth was revealed in bronze and gold mirrors, jewelry, ornaments, and vessels, which often evidenced Near Eastern motifs and metalworking techniques. The realistic style continued in vigorous funerary figures with polychrome glazes depicting camels and horses, Central Asian and Indian merchants, musicians, dancers, and mounted polo players. Even the ceramic vessels of the Tang demonstrate confidence and vitality in their expansive shapes and boldly colored glazes.

Tang painting continued to develop the techniques which would come to fruition in the succeeding Song Dynasty. Buddhist paintings of deities and sages were an important genre in the Tang, much influenced by Indian elements, while a purely Chinese tradition of figure painting flourished at court under the direction of the Tang Imperial Academy. Few Tang landscape paintings exist besides those on the walls of tombs and Buddhist caves, but it appears that Tang painters were perfecting two techniques which would be maintained in all later landscape painting: a fluid, clearly outlined pattern with careful color washes, and a more forceful use of bold outlines and layered washes. Wu Daozi (Wu Tao-tzu), who lived in the 8th century, was the greatest of Tang painters. Although none of his paintings is extant, admiring descriptions by his contemporaries confirm his extraordinary force and realism.

THE SONG DYNASTY:
LANDSCAPE AND CERAMIC ART

In contrast to the expansive confidence of the Tang, the succeeding Song Dynasty was a time of exclusivity and deep nationalism. The Song was the greatest age of Chinese painting. At court, the Imperial Academy imposed a rigidly defined vocabulary of form and subject. Emperor Hui Zong (Hui Tsung) himself set the tone of purity, elegance, and restraint which was the keynote of academy painting. Imperial Academy painters were conservative and, following the example of past masters, generally produced bird-and-flower still-life scenes using meticulously clear detail.

Painters of the Northern Song (10th–early 12th centuries) showed an entirely different style, however. Their landscapes were immense, monumental, and realistic works which fairly pulsed with intensity. Fan Kuan, one of the most famous Northern Song landscape painters, created overwhelming mountains and jagged precipices of intensity and realism. A different mood is conveyed in the paintings of the Southern Song school. Influenced by a softer climate, these painters created mountains girded in mist, with a greater luminosity of sky and water. They also developed a more intimate, informal, less monumental style. The works of the 13th-century painter Ma Yuan reveal the soft intimacy tinged with melancholy which characterized Southern Song landscapes.

In ceramics, the Song was a time of consolidation of earlier technique and refinement of form and color. Potters had perfected the production of stoneware bodies by the time of the Han Dynasty, while green and polychrome glazes were refined during the Tang. Also during the Tang came the discovery that mixing the white plastic clay called kaolin with almost equal proportions of a white feldspathic powder called *petuntse* produced translucent, resonant, and thin-bodied wares of true porcelain. Porcelains were glazed with a liquid mixture of the same feldspathic formula as the body and then high-fired at a kiln temperature of 1300° C or more. At that temperature, body and glaze fused completely, becoming totally vitrified. It was left to the Song potter, however, to create the fine porcelain vessels whose classical elegance and exquisite glazes are prized today by collectors.

During the Song there were literally thousands of kiln sites spread throughout northern and southern China. Fine porcelains of bluish-white hue were produced in the important Jingdezhen kilns in Jiangxi Province. White and greenish-tinged Ding (Ting) porcelains were produced for court use, and thus were designated *guan (kuan)*, "official" wares, as were the crackled, gray-blue glazed Ru (Ju) wares and the finest of the Jun (Chun) wares, whose aqua glaze was splashed with purple or scarlet. Perhaps the most famous of Song ceramics are the green-glazed celadons made at Longquan (Lung-ch'uan) in Zhejiang Province, as well as at other kilns.

Throughout Chinese history there runs a vigorous parallel tradition of folk craftsmen who used inexpensive and common materials to create fresh and lively wares to suit local tastes. Folk artists usually worked on such projects during agricultural slack seasons, fashioning dough, wood, clay, and common stones for their own use or for sale to their peers. True rag paper had been discovered in AD 105 and was further refined in the Tang. By the Song, this excellent and inexpensive material was commonly used by folk artists—and increasingly by literati landscape painters. Folk-art products were often designed for use at traditional festivals and ceremonies. Such crafts were almost entirely made by hand, as opposed to those requiring elaborate tools or mechanical techniques. Folk wares such as papercuts, lanterns, kites, and umbrellas; baskets and chests; stoneware and ceramics; toys, figurines, and puppets of clay, wood, and dough; embroidered, woven, and batiked goods; and woodblock prints of New Year's paintings and Door Gods have been a continuing source of vitality and imagination throughout the development of Chinese art up to the present.

THE MONGOL INVASION AND
THE YUAN DYNASTY

In the 13th century, the Song Dynasty fell before the Mongol invaders from the north. Under the century-long Yuan Dynasty which the Mongols established, China turned from the elegance and restraint of the Song to a lavish decorative style. Craftsmen at Jingdezhen had adopted and developed the technique of painting designs in red or blue under a final glaze, and these wares, especially the blue-and-white, were highly prized throughout the world.

Most scholar-painters (*wen-ren*) of the Yuan Dynasty lived in seclusion away from the Mongol court. One exception was the great calligrapher and landscape painter Zhao Mengfu (Chao Meng-fu) of the 13th to 14th centuries, who served at the court of Kublai Khan. In addition to his landscapes, he is famed for his paintings of horses.

MING THROUGH QING

The Ming Dynasty reestablished Han Chinese rule in the 14th century. Painters at the Ming court specialized in bird-and-flower pictures of great detail and delicacy, while the school of literati painting (*wen-ren hua*) developed personal styles within the boundaries of tradition.

During the Ming, special kilns were established at Jingdezhen for the production of imperial wares, and soon the town eclipsed all other pottery centers in the quantity and quality of its output. Fluid white porcelain vessels and figurines were produced at the Dehua (Tehua) kilns in Fujian Province. The underglaze technique was perfected, and robust new decorative techniques such as overglaze enamel were developed.

Cloisonné enamelware, introduced from the West in the Yuan and developed during the Ming, was produced by soldering wires, usually of copper, onto a metal base to create cells (*cloisons*) which were filled with colored enamel pastes. The pieces were then fired, and afterwards the surface was finely polished to remove any roughness. The final touch was the gilding of the exposed wires. Cloisonné enamelware displayed the Ming taste for richly colored florals and the use of the cobalt blue background seen in porcelain during this same period.

The Qing (Ch'ing) Dynasty, established by the Manchus in the 17th century, was the last of China's imperial dynasties and the great age of decorative arts. The Manchu court initiated a spirit of conservatism, although the individualistic style of landscape painting was preserved by painters among the aristocracy. Ceramics reached a perfection in technique, as seen in "*famille rose*" and "*famille verte*" enamels. The 19th century, however, brought gradual decay as sheer technique replaced creative force. Imperial workshops produced lacquerware, jade, and other luxury items for court use according to rigid specifications, but elaborate decoration, although masterful, could not conceal the artistic decline. Many luxury items were also produced for export, and showed a growing influence of European decor.

By the early 20th century, most of China's guilds and workshops were merely producing pieces for export using foreign designs and colors or were mechanically turning out quantities of mediocre, uninspired products for domestic use. Skilled craftsmen needed the patronage of the court or commissions from wealthy merchants to survive, because their techniques were time-consuming and required expensive materials. When these two sources of support were lost, craftsmen were reduced to making small items such as jewelry, chopsticks, and mahjong pieces—often sold as curios to Westerners—in order to subsist. As a result, standards declined and motifs dwindled to a few themes such as fat Buddhas and languid goddesses. A century of foreign domination, culminating in a decade of Japanese occupation, had smothered the last embers of vitality in the old crafts.

ART IN THE NEW CHINA

Such was the situation when the new government set about to revive the native arts and crafts industry in 1950. First, research institutes were established in important craft centers throughout the country to preserve traditional arts while modernizing techniques. Master craftsmen were gathered together to transmit ancient skills to a new generation of China's youth. During the process, feudal or superstitious elements were removed from the old designs, and new symbols were drawn from the government's

Renowned landscape artist, Li Keran

promotion of socialist realism and from legends and folk traditions. Old production centers were revived, including the famous Longquan kilns which had lain idle for some 300 years. Today, talented youngsters with an aptitude for design and drawing are again being selected to study in research institutes and art schools, and this generation will preserve and refine China's ancient craft traditions.

In fine arts, the 20th century had brought both foreign influences and a spirit of innovation. The Shanghai School of painting, which took shape in the second part of the 19th century, encouraged artists to employ traditional techniques to express their inner feelings. China's most famous modern painters belong to this school, which by the late 19th century had become the leading force in Chinese painting. Qi Baishi (Chi Pai-shih), born in 1863 into a peasant family in Hunan Province, pared his subjects to their barest essentials. His unconventional paintings of birds, flowers, shrimp, and insects capture the vitality of these humble creatures. Except for a few creative figures like Qi Baishi, however, by the early years of this century Chinese painters were not producing original or distinctive works.

In the years following World War I the level of social ferment increased in China. In the late 1920s, a new movement for social change emerged in the cities, and the development of the woodcut was part of this drive. Influenced by a powerful European style, the new woodcuts presented a sharp contrast to all preceding Chinese art. They answered a social need and provided a means for artists to criticize social conditions during this turbulent period. Inexpensive and easy to produce, woodcuts were the perfect vehicle for social criticism.

In the 1930s, the Communists established an academy of art at their base in Yan'an and promoted woodcuts to disseminate information and stimulate public morale during the anti-Japanese war. Woodcut artists also began to incorporate folk elements.

In the period since 1949, great woodcut artists have emerged, while the style of traditional landscapes has also been maintained. Landscapes now incorporate elements of the new China: red flags, modern tractors, and vast bridges appear among mountains clothed in mist. Famous painters have preserved the tradition of the Shanghai School, and animals are a popular subject, from yaks to donkeys, owls, and goldfish. Peasant painters, too, have been actively experimenting with folk forms derived from papercuts and New Year's woodblock pictures. The peasant paintings of Huxian near Xi'an reveal bustling, colorful, rural scenes and have won international acclaim. No new national style in the fine arts has appeared as yet, however, and no one style has taken a distinct prominence over the others. China's artists are still searching for a mode that combines the old and the new. The outcome of the experiment remains to be seen.

MUSEUMS TO VISIT IN CHINA

Thanks to government support of systematic archeological excavations, vast quantities of artifacts are being discovered every year in China. Today's travelers are in a unique position to enjoy the new discoveries, which are sometimes placed on display in Chinese museums even before official records and photographs have been published. China has a number of impressive museum collections, both in major cities such as Beijing, Shanghai, and Guangzhou and in provincial capitals. The provincial museums house art and archeological finds gathered throughout the province, and a number of these collections are outstanding. Below is a brief survey of some of China's more important museums.

BEIJING

The Forbidden City, once the home of China's emperors and royal family, is now a public museum for the enjoyment and education of China's people and foreign visitors. The present walled palace used to be incorporated within a much larger walled area known as the Imperial City, but the walls had deteriorated by the beginning of this century and were removed. The various courtyards and halls of the Imperial Palace, now also known as the Palace Museum, are arranged along a central north-south axis, at the rear of which are the Imperial Gardens, constructed during the Ming Dynasty. The Forbidden City was designed to represent the universe in microcosm, with the emperor, like the polestar, as its pivot. Constantly in a state of renovation because of its immense size and complex architecture, the Palace Museum now houses permanent exhibitions as well as special exhibits of paintings, ceramics, and archeological discoveries. Travelers should ask their guides about special exhibitions being held within various parts of the Palace Museum at the time of their visit. A permanent collection at the Bao He Dian (Hall of Preserving Harmony) contains excellent examples of Shang bronzes and carved jade, and Song, Ming, and Qing porcelains and paintings. Many of these pieces were taken from the Qing imperial collection.

The collection of the Museum of Chinese History in Beijing contains many reproductions among its artifacts. The exhibitions range from Paleolithic times to the present, including ancient pottery, bronze vessels, tomb figures, and rubbings. A very exciting recent addition is the exhibit of life-sized terra cotta soldiers and horses discovered near the tomb of the Qin emperor Qin Shi Huangdi.

SHANGHAI

Here travelers should plan to visit the exceptional collection of the Museum of Art and History. If you have time to visit only one museum in China, make it this one. Here, visitors can view fine Shang and Zhou bronzes, including a very large *ding* tripod, rare Shang pottery, Han terra cotta tomb wares, Buddhist sculpture, Song celadons, Yuan paintings, and Ming and Qing cloisonné, lacquerware, porcelains, paintings, and calligraphy. The museum also exhibits arts and crafts from all parts of the country which have been produced since 1949. The exhibits are beautifully displayed, and paintings are housed in climate-controlled cases.

GUANGZHOU

The Guangdong Historical Museum is housed in an especially lovely building, a striking five-story pagoda of Ming date. Visitors can see a broad spectrum of ceramics, from Neolithic artifacts to modern pottery produced in the nearby Shiwan Ceramics Factory. Also on display are prehistoric tools discovered near Guangzhou, tomb figurines, bronze bells, and rubbings. Visitors also frequently make a side trip to nearby Foshan, a traditional craft center for centuries, where a Daoist temple today contains exhibits of iron bells and incense burners, large papier-mâché statues, and intricate ceramic friezes.

PROVINCIAL MUSEUMS

China's outstanding provincial museums are located in Xi'an, Changsha, Taiyuan, Hangzhou, Nanjing, and Wuhan.

The Shaanxi Provincial Museum in Xi'an contains a particularly exciting collection, partly because Xi'an was an important cultural center at numerous times in Chinese history. Many capitals were located in or very near this city, including the magnificent cosmopolitan Tang capital of Chang'an. Housed in a former Confucian temple, the museum contains fine examples of stone carving, including Tang chargers, tigers, rhinoceroses, and a large Buddha. On the museum grounds is a collection of more than 1,000 stone stelae from the Han to Qing dynasties which provides a record of the development of classical calligraphy. Called the "Forest of Stelae," this collection also includes stone inscriptions of the

Bronze wine container from tomb in central China

complete texts of the Twelve Confucian Classics, finished in the 9th century.

At the Hunan Provincial Museum in Changsha, visitors will find the magnificent discoveries from Han Tomb No. 1 at nearby Mawangdui. Delightful lacquer vessels, patterned and embroidered silks, wooden tomb figurines, and the well-preserved female corpse found buried in the tomb are now on view at the museum. Also on display is a silk painting depicting the underworld, the human realm, and the celestial sphere, using symbols of the southern religious tradition.

The Shanxi Provincial Museum in Taiyuan contains a fine collection of stone carvings from many periods, as well as Buddhist stone sculpture and printed sutras.

In Hangzhou, the Zhejiang Provincial Museum contains an extensive collection of pottery and paintings of different ages.

The Jiangsu Provincial Museum in Nanjing displays prehistoric pottery, Shang bronzes and jewelry, Han ceramic wares, wall paintings from a Song tomb, and Qing paintings.

The collection of the Henan Provincial Museum in Zhengzhou contains Neolithic pottery, Zhou lacquerware and bronzes, Han tomb figures, Tang bronzes, and Song porcelains.

Visitors to the Hubei Provincial Museum in Wuhan will see an interesting collection of ceramics as well as archeological discoveries from a 5th-century BC tomb, including large bronzes, gold jewelry, and vessels.

FOR TRAVELERS WITH SPECIAL INTERESTS

China's Archeological Treasures

Annette Juliano

FOR the visitor with a particular interest in art and archeology, China offers an array of unforgettable experiences. In every part of China, museums, architectural monuments, and archeological sites evidence the richness of over 7,000 years of continuous creativity—from Neolithic times to the present. Into the 1980s, more sites and monuments are expected to be opened to the public as the Chinese government continues extensive programs of restoration and preservation to make these treasures available both to the Chinese people and to foreign visitors.

The science of archeology was first introduced to China from Japan and the West in the first half of the 20th century. Some of the earliest digs in northern China during the 1920s uncovered Neolithic villages and the now world-famous Bronze Age capital Anyang, along with a nearby cemetery containing five royal tombs. By 1949, this new science, supported by the government and the universities, took firm hold. Government support—coupled with major national construction projects to build canals, reservoirs, and housing—produced a veritable flood of new finds from under the earth. The last 30 years have been enormously productive. Old sites were reworked and many new ones discovered. Vast amounts of hitherto unknown and often unprecedented material have been uncovered. As a result, the history of China's ancient cultures is being rewritten.

With few exceptions, most cities on the visitor's planned itinerary will have important local or provincial museums, often filled with recent archeological finds; perhaps a tomb opened to the public with a small attached exhibit hall and palaces or temples. Be prepared: sometimes unexpected treasures are found in the most unlikely places. The following discussion summarizes briefly the various kinds of experiences a visitor interested in art and archeology can expect in China.

ARCHEOLOGICAL SITES

Generally, visitors are not taken to excavations in progress. More likely are sites which have been completely excavated and turned into museums. An example is the site of Banpo, a Neolithic village outside of Xi'an. Among the most worthwhile excursions are visits to Luoyang with its two small tombs from the Western and Eastern Han Dynasties (206 BC–AD 220) and to the Tang tomb of the Princess Yongtai (about 42 miles west of Xi'an), who died in AD 706. As one walks down the entrance ramp, the air cools rapidly. In all three tombs, some of the *mingqi* (usually clay and sometimes wood objects made specifically for burial with the deceased) are left in their original positions, providing the visitor with some tangible insights into these underground burial chambers and ancient burial practices in China. The Han tombs are less lavish in scale and decoration than that of the Princess. Two exhibit halls stand near the Tang tomb. The first contains objects removed from the tomb, including some gold ornaments, jade plaques, and ceramic wares; the second has some of the contents from nearby tombs not yet open to the public.

Yongtai's tomb is one of 17 satellite tombs that surround a large tumulus marking the burial site of the Tang emperor Gaozong (who died in 683) and his wife, Empress Wu (who died 21 years later). The satellite graves marked by smaller mounds contain relatives and mistresses of the imperial family. The approach to the imperial tumulus consists of a "spirit" road lined with stone ostriches, flying horses, courtiers, and two armies of barbarians (with their heads knocked off). Spirit roads like this and those that have been preserved near the Ming and Qing tombs are characteristic of imperial burial sites.

East of Xi'an is the large tumulus of Emperor Qin Shi Huangdi. In 1974, archeologists discovered a set of gigantic pits containing an army of life-size clay warriors and horses, estimated to total over 6,000 pieces. Recently even more striking clay figures have been unearthed from two additional pits found to the north of the first group. Many of these figures exhibit exceptional sculptural qualities, particularly the kneeling bowman poised on one knee ready to fire his crossbow. One pit apparently contains only 68 pottery figures, all of officers and officials. This small group may be the "command center" for the entire army guarding the east face of Qin Shi Huangdi's burial mound. Although the imperial tomb itself has not been opened, archeologists doing test excavations at the site in 1984 and 1985 found convincing evidence that the tomb is intact. If this proves to be the case, it may turn out to be one of the greatest archeological finds of the century, outshining even the 1922 discovery of Tutankhamen's burial treasures.

The Chinese have built an enclosure over sections of the pits which have been excavated. Visitors are able to see clay figures in their original positions and states, half hidden by soil, fragmented but recognizable. An auxiliary building houses the fully restored examples.

When visiting an archeological site or museum, groups of visitors will

A partial view of the Qin Dynasty archeological digs near Xi'an

be met and briefed on-site. These briefings usually provide a general introduction with pertinent statistics. Occasionally, such briefings will be given by an archeologist or someone knowledgeable about the site, offering an opportunity for more technical questions or discussions.

MUSEUMS

Most archeological treasures are housed in an impressive network of thousands of museums all over China. Each province has a central museum which brings together artifacts drawn from all parts of the province. Many of these provincial-level museums are quite large and have become well-known for the exceptional quality of their collections; an example is the Shaanxi Provincial Museum in Xi'an and the Henan Provincial Museum in Zhengzhou. A veritable treasure trove resides in the Shanxi Provincial Museum in Taiyuan, a city recently opened to foreigners. Aside from the sumptuous array of cloisonné, porcelains, and paintings, there is an extensive collection of Buddhist stone carvings from the 5th to the 10th centuries. Colossal stone Buddhas and animals litter the main entrance courtyard along with Buddhist stelae stacked against the enclosure walls.

In addition to these provincial repositories, many smaller towns and cities maintain local or municipal museums to preserve artifacts uncovered in the immediate vicinity. A good example is the Luoyang Municipal Museum. Because of their more modest scale, local museums are often more manageable for the visitor with limited time. One of the most delightful museums of this type is the Zhengzhou City Museum, located in the Zhengzhou Workers Park. Collections include superb examples of Neolithic pottery from nearby Dahe village and early Shang bronze vessels. Around the back of the main buildings is an astonishing sight—several headless stone statues of bodhisattvas stand lashed to wooden stakes. Rows of bodiless heads rest on a stack of hollow clay tiles excavated from a Han Dynasty tomb. Many of the objects in the courtyard were discovered locally (some during the Cultural Revolution) and brought to the museum, which lacks sufficient display space at the moment.

Buddhist temple compounds are places where collections of objects are likely to be tucked away. The Longxing Temple near Shijiazhuang has at least three buildings filled with local discoveries and art treasures ranging from ancient bronzes to Song, Yuan, and Ming porcelains. Several examples were unearthed in 1974 and 1977. The Xiangguo Monastery near Kaifeng in Henan and the Huayan Monastery in the city of Datong in Shanxi also have fine collections. Similar situations probably exist in other Buddhist temples.

Museums do present challenges to the visitor. Most only provide labels and explanatory materials in Chinese. Tour guides and museum staff are quite willing to provide assistance here. However, they cannot be expected to translate every label in the museum. Since museums are generally dimly lit, flashlights are useful for closer scrutiny.

ARCHEOLOGICAL TREASURES

Pottery tile from a tomb near Deng Xian, Henan Province; early 6th century AD.

ARCHITECTURAL MONUMENTS

Untold numbers of architectural monuments dot the Chinese landscape. Visitors will be taken to selected monuments accessible to the cities on the planned itinerary. The Chinese will not usually allow visitors to see monuments which have not been completely or partially refurbished. Many requests are turned down for this reason.

The visitor's experience can run the gamut from magnificent palaces and temples to pagodas and bridges. All can be interesting and informative. For example, the road to the Great Wall is straddled by a magnificent stone gateway built in the Mongol period (1345), certainly worth a short stop. The surfaces of the vaulted arc are covered with excellent low-relief carvings of the four heavenly kings, Buddhas, and mandalas. Southeast of the city of Shijiazhuang in Zhao Xian stands the handsome Anji bridge built in the Sui Dynasty (c. AD 605), famous for its daring conception, structure, and elegance. This single-arch bridge is 50 m. (164 ft.) long and constructed with 700 tons of stone. Original relief carvings of dragons piercing clouds and monster masks are preserved in a nearby museum. Besides the stone pagodas in Xi'an, Kaifeng boasts the "Iron Pagoda," built in 1049. The 13-story pagoda is constructed of masonry and faced with tiles glazed in deep browns and greens, which appear from a distance to be rusted iron. The tiles have stamped designs of *apsaras*, Buddhas, dragons, and musicians.

It is possible to see two types of Buddhist temples: compounds composed of several wooden buildings, and rock-cut temples. Two interesting wooden compounds are the Longxing Monastery in the town of Zhengding near Shijiazhuang and the Huayan Monastery in Datong. The Longxing Monastery covers an area of 5.2 sq. km. (2 sq. mi.) and most of the fine buildings date from the Song and Qing dynasties. In the chief temple is a 21.6-m. (71-ft.) bronze image of Guanyin (the Bodhisattva of Mercy).

At Datong, the Huayan actually consists of two monasteries, the upper and lower. The lower monastery contains an exquisite wooden building constructed under the Liao in 1038. The decoration, the frescoes, and particularly the sculpture, are superb. Some of the greatest Buddhist sculpture in China can be found in the rock-cut temples of Longmen near Luoyang and Yungang near Datong. Yungang, one of the earliest such sites, has 21 caves carved from a sandstone cliff and ranging in date from the mid-5th through the 6th centuries AD. Colossal, powerfully conceived images, 6–12 m. (20–40 ft.) high, fill the five earliest caves, Nos. 16–20. The carved limestone cliffs of Longmen rise up on either side of the Yi River about 14.4 km. (9 mi.) from Luoyang. The majority of caves are on the western cliffs. If time allows, a small group of later Tang caves can be visited on the opposite side.

Another important group of Buddhist temples which may soon be open to the public is located on Wutai Mountain in Shanxi.

MISCELLANEOUS

The city of Kaifeng, which remains a cultural center where handicrafts flourish, provides a contrast to other Chinese cities. Intensive urbanization is just beginning. It offers an undisturbed atmosphere of old houses, cobblestone streets, and thatched roofs. In Kaifeng's embroidery factory, the workers produced an exquisite silk embroidery reproduction of a famous Song painting in the Palace Museum in Beijing, "Life Along the River on the Eve of the Qingming Festival." Twenty workers took five years to complete the task.

Various kilns have also been opened to visitors. The most famous, which has been producing porcelains for centuries, is Jingdezhen in Jiangsu.

Many excursions hold surprises. For instance, Taiyuan in Shanxi has a small, late Buddhist temple, still used by a few practicing Buddhists. The main hall contains a sutra library with about 5,000 texts, some illustrated with Ming paintings of exceptional quality.

For additional information, travelers should consult the comprehensive survey of Chinese art by Michael Sullivan, *The Arts of China* (University of California Press, 1977 ed.); two booklets published in the People's Republic of China, *New Archeological Finds in China* (Foreign Languages Press, Beijing, 1972) and *New Archeological Finds in China (II)* (FLP, Beijing, 1978); and Annette Juliano, *Treasures of China* (Richard Marek Publishers, 1981).

Several articles dealing with specific archeological finds appeared in popular magazines in the late 1970s. For the unprecedented finds at the Qin Shi Huangdi site, consult the April 1978 issue of *National Geographic* and the November 1979 issue of the *Smithsonian*. In July 1979, *Archeology* covered the Tang imperial burial grounds outside of Xi'an, particularly the large stone sculptures along the Tang emperor Gaozong's spirit road and the tomb of the Tang princess Yongtai.

FOR TRAVELERS WITH SPECIAL INTERESTS

China Travel for
Overseas Chinese

Janet Yang

CHINA is strengthening the bonds that link it with its millions of "sons and daughters" around the world. Persons of Chinese origin living outside of China—no matter what their citizenship or country of birth—are accorded a special status and welcome as visitors to the People's Republic. The PRC now actively encourages their contacts with relatives in China. Recently, too, growing numbers of overseas Chinese have established commercial relationships in China.

While overseas Chinese may participate in any general tour program, a variety of travel options is available especially for them. Beginning on August 1, 1985, overseas Chinese were no longer required to obtain visas or exit permits for visits to China. They need only carry valid passports from their country of permanent residence or a certificate issued by the Chinese government. Travel agencies in Hong Kong and throughout the world also offer tour packages expressly designed for overseas Chinese groups.

Within China, overseas Chinese are often accommodated at hotels set aside for their use. Amenities are usually somewhat simpler than in hotels designated for non-Chinese, but rates are also lower.

Overseas Chinese seeking to go to China individually or in small groups to visit relatives or to engage in private business should write directly to the Overseas Chinese Travel Bureau or the China Travel Service (CTS), Beijing, PRC. Most visa departments at China's embassies and consulates now include special divisions for overseas Chinese. CTS branch offices in Beijing, Guangzhou, Shanghai, and other cities maintain special bureaus to assist overseas Chinese visitors.

VISITING RELATIVES IN CHINA

Your reunion with long unseen relatives in China is likely to be one of the most joyous experiences of a lifetime. Unlike other foreign visitors, you have a dual purpose and perspective: you are simultaneously a tourist traveling to a vastly varied and fascinating nation and a Chinese returning to your birthplace or to the home of your ancestors. You will have special opportunities to learn what life is like in the People's Republic today.

Your visit may well be an extraordinary event for your relatives, too. For a solid week prior to my family's trip to China, the village where my uncle and cousins live underwent considerable renovation in preparation for our arrival. Electricity was rewired, walls repainted, leaks repaired. Our "coming-home" dinner of freshly killed chicken and rare vegetables was an exceptional feast. Furthermore, a batch of color photos of our family that had been confiscated during the Cultural Revolution as "bourgeois" was suddenly returned. The welcome to overseas Chinese visitors is clearly not confined to the family circle; as in our case, the local authorities are usually made aware of your arrival and are eager to make a good impression.

Touring China with Your Chinese Relatives. In order to take full advantage of the brief time you have with your relatives, it's possible to arrange for them to accompany you on your travels through the rest of China. Our sponsorship provided our relatives with their first opportunity to tour their own homeland. They stayed in hotels for the first time in their lives, visited sites they'd never seen before, and ate food they'd never imagined existed. Needless to say, touring with our Chinese family immeasurably enhanced our enjoyment of the trip.

When traveling with your relatives, be prepared for some awkward moments. Minor complications may arise due to differences in customs and in standards of living. For the most part, however, visiting overseas Chinese are received with courtesy and lots of friendly curiosity.

GIFTS FOR RELATIVES

It has become commonplace for overseas Chinese to bring their relatives massive quantities of gifts. Many items or commodities readily available in the West are still either unaffordable or unobtainable in China. Gift-giving to relatives in China is perfectly permissible, although special regulations are in force to limit excesses or abusive practices.

The best way to find out what your relatives really want is, of course, to ask them. They aren't likely to be shy in responding. Undoubtedly at the top of their lists will be household appliances such as television sets (color is preferred), tape recorders, radios, cameras, and sewing machines. Current income levels in China make such items prohibitively expensive except for those people receiving remittances from relatives abroad.

Since the demise of the Cultural Revolution in 1977, scientific and technical books and articles, English dictionaries, textbooks, and other learning materials are especially appreciated by students and teachers.

You might also consider bringing some canned delicacies—e.g., pickled vegetables, meat, and fish—to add variety to daily fare. Although dutiable at 200%, shark's fin, sea cucumbers, abalone, or dried scallops would provide a savory treat that may not have been experienced for years.

For those of your relatives who work in an office, a calculator or a portable English typewriter could prove invaluable.

A final word on gifts. Although you obviously want to satisfy your relatives' needs as fully as you can, it may not be possible for you to furnish *all* the things they ask for. Do not be disconcerted if they seem to have little conception of precisely how much their suggested gifts cost, in terms of time or money. Perhaps you can gently remind them that your visit in itself is quite a sizable gift.

PRC Duties on Gifts. In spring 1978, China set forth definitive rules for duties on items brought into and out of the country by overseas Chinese. These rules still apply, although they should be checked for periodic minor revisions. The four categories of visitors to whom these rules apply are defined by China as:

1. Overseas Chinese (Chinese-born, with Chinese citizenship, but living abroad).

2. Foreign-born Chinese (those of Chinese descent possessing foreign citizenship and living abroad).

3. Foreigners residing in China (foreign-born, with Chinese citizenship, living in China).

4. Chinese citizens with a visitor's visa (usually short-term).

DUTY-FREE ITEMS, UNRESTRICTED

Educational materials (e.g., books, newspapers, periodicals, educational films, slides, language cassettes)

Birth-control devices, pills

Jewelry, gold and silver items, precious stones (e.g., pearls, jade, diamonds)

Other items immune to taxation include those defined as "basic necessities used in day-to-day living"; arts and crafts items purchased in China and accompanied by receipts and certificates of currency exchange; printed matter.

DUTY-FREE ITEMS, RESTRICTED

	ITEM	QUANTITY
1	Coats	3
2	Underwear	20 pieces
3	Other clothing items	40 pieces
4	Bedding	1 set
5	Woolen and knitted garments	4 kg. (8.8 lbs.)
6	Scarves (including head scarves)	6
7	Shoes, socks, and stockings	6 pairs
8	Fabrics (narrow width)	30 m. (32.7 yd.)
	Woolen fabrics (double width)	5 m. (5.4 yd.)

9	Food (not including luxury goods or delicacies)	50 kg. (110 lbs.)
10	Cigarettes	600
11	Liquor	4 bottles (size unspecified)
12	Medicines	Y50 in value
13	Ginseng, tonics (for medicinal purposes)	50 g. (1.75 oz.)
14	Toiletries	Y100 in value
15	Watches†	1
16	Bicycles†	1
17	Radios (not including phonographs or tape recorders)†	1
18	Sewing machines†	1
19	Electric fans†	1

*Quantities indicated may be brought into or out of China duty-free. The following exceptions apply to quantities to be brought out: fabrics, 15 m. (16 yd.); food, 25 kg. (55 lbs.) medicines, Y25; and toiletries, Y50.
†A maximum of two items from this list of five can be brought in duty-free.

Different regulations apply to persons traveling to China more than once a year. Your local Chinese embassy can provide details.

Of the first 14 items above, quantities valued at more than Y200 cannot be brought in at all. For example, three coats with a total value of Y199 may be brought in duty-free; five with a total value of Y199 will be allowed, but duty will be charged for two of them; a single coat valued at Y225 may not be brought in. Allotments are halved for children under 16.

DUTIABLE ITEMS, RESTRICTED

	ITEM	QUANTITY
1	Watches	1
2	Small calculators	1
3	Tape recorders or phonograph/radio components	1
4	Cameras	1
5	Musical instruments	1
6	Ginseng, tonics	150 g. (4.2 oz.)

SCHEDULE OF DUTIES

ITEM	DUTY RATE (percentages of assessed values)
1 Grains, flour, cereal products	20%
2 Medical supplies, scientific instruments, calculators	20%
3 Medicines, drugs (animal or plant origin)	50%
4 a. Machines for home and office use; tape recorders; cutlery; hand tools; agricultural tools (including accessories, spare parts)	50%
b. Television sets (including accessories, spare parts)	50%
c. Athletic equipment, musical instruments	50%
5 Foodstuffs and beverages (non-delicacies)	100%
6 Antlers, musk tonic, ginseng (for medicinal use)	100%
7 Cotton and linen fabrics and blends	100%
8 a. Radios, phonographs (including accessories, spare parts)	100%
b. Bicycles (including accessories, spare parts)	100%
9 a. Clothing fabric of wool, silk, synthetic, and blends; woven goods; leather, fur, plastic	150%
b. Cameras (including accessories, spare parts)	150%
10 a. Delicacy foods (e.g., bird's nest soup, shark's fin, sea cucumber, abalone, dried scallops, dried fish maw, fish lips)	200%
b. Tobacco, liquor	200%
c. Cosmetics	200%
11 Watches, wrist and pocket (including accessories, spare parts)	200%

Note: All items not included on the above list are considered dutiable at 100% of their value. Appeals may be made to have these duties waived. In such cases, however, assessed taxes must still be paid upon entering China; in case of a favorable ruling by customs officials, money will be refunded.

華僑回國旅行
凌波譯

中國正在加強與其分佈於全世界成百萬的「中華兒女」聯繫。中國政府歡迎居住在國外的中國人——不論其國籍或出生地——以特別旅客的身份回大陸探訪。中國政府現主動地鼓勵他們與在中國的親戚聯繫，最近不斷增加的華僑們已與中國建立了商業關係。

華僑回國探訪，除可享受一般的旅遊節目外，同時還能得到多種的旅行安排。自一九八五年八月一日起，凡欲回國探親、經商、旅遊的華僑，只要持用有效之外籍護照或中國政府所簽發的出入境許可證明便可免簽證而立即入境。

在中國，華僑經常被安排在專供他們使用的旅館住宿。設備較一般外國人所住之旅館簡單，收費亦較低。旅館附設的餐廳經常供應道地的中國風味的食物。

海外華僑若欲以個人或小家庭爲單位回國探親或純爲私人業務，可以直接寫信給中華人民共和國，北京，中國旅行社。其在北京、廣州、上海和其他城市都有分社，且有一個特別部門爲華僑服務。大部份中國大使館和領事館的簽證組址也包括了一個爲華僑特別服務的部門。如欲探訪邊遠地區的親人，須在中國境內申請許可。

回國探親 回國與多年不見的親人團聚是人生何等榮事，與其他外國遊客不同，華僑有雙重目的，能同時以遊客身份在一個非常不同而又迷人的國家旅行，又以一個中國人身份回到他的出生地或祖先的老家。他們將有較多的機會來了解今日中國大陸同胞生活的情形。華僑們的來訪對其親人來說也算是非常特殊的事情。在我家去大陸旅行前一整星期，我叔叔和堂兄弟等住的村子爲了準備我們的到來很徹底地整修了住房，重新接上電，粉刷牆壁，修補漏洞。我們的團圓飯是一頓少有的盛宴。包括一隻現殺的雞和稀有的蔬菜。除此之外，在文革期間被沒收的一批被視爲中產階級代表的全家福彩色照片突然間也被退回來了。同時地方官員通常非常明瞭華僑的來訪，而且希望他們留下好印象。

由親人陪同在中國旅行 爲了利用與親人相處的有限時間，很可能安排他們一起到外地去旅行，對於在旅行中因爲風俗習慣、經濟條件等的差異可能出現的情況要有準備。大陸人民見到回國探親的華僑都表示熱烈的歡迎和友善的幫助和好奇。

贈送親友禮品 華僑回國帶一些禮品贈送親友是很平常的事。很多在西方很普遍的東西在中國不是他們買不起就是買不到。當然，問親友們自己才是最好辦法得知他們的需要，他們不會因爲不好意思而不說。毫無疑問的，他們列出項目頭幾樣一定是家庭用品。譬如：電視機（彩色更好）、錄音機、收音機、照相機和縫衣機。以中國目前收入水平尚無能力購買這些東西除非收到海外親人匯款。

自七六年「四人幫」垮台後，科學技術書籍和期刊，英語書刊（包括英語字典、英語會話錄音帶）及其他學習材料，特別受到教師和青年學生的歡迎。華僑也許考慮帶一些罐裝食品——如泡菜、肉類和魚類——能增加他們每日食物的種類。雖然稅率高達百分之二百，如魚翅、海參、鮑魚、干貝是他們多年沒嘗過的鮮美滋味。計算機或手提英文打字機對坐辦公室的親友很有價值。談到禮物最後一點，雖然華僑們都想盡全力滿足親友的需要，但不太可能完全達到他們的要求。依時間和金錢看，如果親友對所需要的禮物費用沒有一點概念，也不必爲難自己了。

稅率 對華僑帶進或帶出的物品，中國在一九七八年春，制定了確定稅率。這些條款今後可能有某些修改。以下四種身份華僑適用於這些稅率：

1 華僑（中國出生，持有中國公民權，但定居國外者）
2 國外出生之中國人（那些承襲了外國公民權且定居國外者）
3 居住中國的外國人（國外出生，具有中國公民權且定居中國者）
4 中國人持有觀光簽證者（通常爲短期）

有限制免稅物品

	品　名	進　口　數　量*
1	外套	3 件
2	內衣	20 件
3	其他衣物	40 件
4	寢具	大約一套
5	羊毛和針織衣服	4 公斤
6	圍巾（包括頭巾）	6 條
7	鞋類、男襪、女絲襪	6 雙
8	布料（窄幅約三十六吋寬）	30 公尺
	雙幅或四十五吋寬幅羊毛料	5 公尺
9	食物（不含上等食品）	50 公斤
10	香烟	600 支
11	酒類（不規定大小瓶）	4 瓶
12	藥物	50 人民幣值
13	人參、補品（普通藥用）	50 公克
14	化粧品	100 人民幣值
15	手錶†	1 隻

16	自行車†	1 部
17	收音機†不含唱機或錄音機	1 台
18	縫衣機†	1 台
19	電風扇†	1 台

　　＊以上指定數量可免稅帶進口或出口。以下例外只適用於帶出口之數量：布料，十五公尺；食物二十五公斤；藥物，廿五人民幣值；化粧品，五十人民幣值。

　　†最多只能五種中選兩樣免稅。

　　對每年去中國旅行一次以上的華僑，制定有不同的繳稅條款。中國駐外大使館均能提供詳細的資料。

　　在上表中，第1至第14項，數量總值約超過人民幣200元，就不許進口。例如：三件外套總值人民幣199元，可免稅進口；如果五件外套，總值人民幣199元，可以進口，但需繳超過的兩件稅款。如果一件外套值人民幣225元，則不許進口。第15至第19項所列物品，只要不超過規定數量，可以帶進中國。如果數量超過規定，但總值低於人民幣200元，可以帶進口，但需酌情繳稅。上列條款適用於成人，對於16歲以下孩童，可攜帶進口數量則減半。

無限制免稅品

　　教育材料，如書籍、報紙、期刊、教育影片、幻燈片和語言卡式錄音帶。

　　避孕藥物與用具。

　　珠寶類，金、銀和寶石，如：珍珠、玉、鑽石。

　　其他能免稅品，包括能説明是每日必需品；在中國買的藝術品和手工藝品則需附有收據和現值證明；印刷品。

有限制加稅品

	品　名	數　量
1	手錶	1 隻
2	小型計算機	1 個
3	錄音機或唱機或收音機	1 部
4	電視機	1 台
5	照相機	1 架
6	樂器	1 個
7	人參，補品	150 公克

稅率表

品　名	稅　率（根據略估價值）
1　穀類、麵粉和食用穀類	20%
2　醫藥用具、科學器材、計算機	20%
3　藥劑、麻醉藥（來自動植物）	50%
4　家庭和公司使用之機器；錄音機； 刀劍類；手工具；農業工具　（包 括附件和零件）	50%
電視機（包括附件和零件）	50%
運動器材、樂器。	50%
5　食物和飲料（非熟食）	100%
6　獸角，麝香補品，人參（藥用）	100%
7　棉和疏布或混紡布料	100%
8　收音機，唱機（包括附件，零 件）	100%
自行車（包括附件和零件）	100%
9　毛料、絲料、人造纖維和混紡 紡織品、皮革、毛、塑膠皮、	150%
照相機（包括附件和零件）	150%
10　熟食（燕窩湯、魚翅、鮑魚、 干貝、乾魚肚、魚脣）	200%
烟草，酒類	200%
化粧品	200%
11　手錶和袋錶（包括附件和零件）	200%

　　上表於一九七八年八月發佈，所有物品不在上表之內以１００％稅率爲準。特殊情形不適用以上稅率時，則需在進入中國時繳納大約價值的稅款；海關如果決定合適的稅則將退回稅款。

VII

THE CHINA TOUR: CITIES AND SITES

Chinese teenagers on a Sunday outing

Anshan

saddle mountain

traditional spelling/Anshan

ANSHAN, the site of China's largest iron and steel complex, is located in Liaoning Province, about 80 km. (50 mi.) southwest of Shenyang, the provincial capital. This city of over one million people produces 25% of China's annual output of steel (35.6 million metric tons in 1981) as well as agricultural machinery, construction materials, chemicals, textiles, porcelain, and electrical appliances.

Anshan lies, appropriately enough, on the same latitude as an important US steel center, Youngstown, in Ohio. Its climate, however, is more like that of Minneapolis: hot, dry summers and bitterly cold winters, when temperatures rarely rise above freezing.

ANSHAN IN HISTORY

Anshan's history is synonymous with the development of iron and steel. Organized iron mining and smelting began about 100 BC. There was some expansion of activity during the 10th and 11th centuries, but a superstitious Qing Dynasty emperor curtailed operations for fear of disturbing some ancestral graves about 10 miles away.

The modern development of Anshan began with the rediscovery of iron ore deposits by the Japanese in the early 1900s and the introduction of open-hearth furnaces in 1935.

In 1945, Anshan was occupied by the Soviet army, which began the systematic dismantling and removal of power generating and transforming equipment, electric motors, and all new or undamaged machine tools. Conditions worsened during the civil war (1946–49), when control of the town seesawed back and forth 11 times between the Communist and Guomindang forces.

The Chinese are extremely proud of Anshan's role in producing most of the steel used in the PRC's initial industrial expansion during the 1950s. Today, the iron and steel complex sprawls over an area of about 13 sq. km. (5 sq. mi.), its smokestacks, blast furnaces, and cooling towers dominating the city's northwestern skyline.

HIGHLIGHTS FOR TRAVELERS

An effort has been made to enliven the drab, rather polluted city by laying out broad avenues and roundabouts, and numerous lovely parks.

Climate		Jan	Feb	Mar	Apr	May	Jun	Jul	Aug	Sep	Oct	Nov	Dec
Temp.	°C	−11.9	−9.1	1.9	10	15.5	21.3	14.1	21.1	16.3	8.3	−1.1	−9.7
	°F	10.5	15.5	35.5	50	60	70.5	57.5	70	61.5	47	30	14.5
Precip.	mm.	76	76	102	152	178	203	279	254	178	152	127	76
	in.	3	3	4	6	7	8	11	10	7	6	5	3

二一九公园

February 19 (Eryijiu) Park. This attractive park in the city's eastern sector takes its name from the date in 1948 when the People's Liberation Army finally gained control of Anshan.

千莲山

Thousand Lotuses Hill (Qianlian Shan). The poetic name of this 10th-century Buddhist hermitage derives not from actual lotus flowers, but from the lotus-like cloud formations wreathing the hilltop. From the Immortal Terrace, at the mountain's summit, one can take in panoramic views of the city. Today, religious ceremonies are still conducted in the Buddhist and Daoist monasteries on the hill.

汤岗子温泉公园

Tanggangzi Hot Springs Park. Located about 10 km. (6 mi.) southeast of Anshan, this park was once a fashionable resort where the wealthy and the powerful maintained private villas. Today, the park houses a sanitorium for steelworkers and is a popular spot for Sunday outings. Water from the hot springs gushes out at the rate of 600 metric tons a day and maintains a constant temperature of 23°C (73°F) year-round. It contains over 20 minerals and is said to be beneficial for treating rheumatism.

Other sites of historical interest in Anshan include the Zhonghui Temple, the Western Tower, and the Dragon Spring Temple.

HOTEL ACCOMMODATIONS

鞍山宾馆

Anshan Guest House (121 Shengli Road; tel: 25993; telex: 24403). Located in the city's center, the Anshan Guest House has 72 rooms and suites, each with a color TV and radio. Prices range from Y40 to Y65.

The hotel has both a Chinese and a Western restaurant as well as a dance hall, post office, barbershop, and currency exchange counter. CITS has an office at the hotel.

Another lodging possibility in Anshan is the **Shengli Guest House**, also located in the center of town. There is a hotel at the hot springs as well, but Western tourists are usually directed to downtown lodgings.

中国国际旅行社
CITS (Luxingshe) Office in Anshan ■ Anshan Guest House. Tel: 24403/24908

Beidaihe

north of the Dai River

traditional spelling/Peitaiho

BEIDAIHE is located in Hebei Province on the Bohai seacoast—four-and-a-half hours northeast of Beijing by train or 30 minutes by plane. This delightful city of 17,000 is one of China's best-known resort areas. The beaches stretch for 10 km. (6 mi.) from the outlet of the Daihe River to Jinshan Hill. The Lianpeng Hills provide a lush green backdrop to this peaceful, seaside town—altogether a rare commodity in China.

The Han emperor Lin Chi built a terrace here, but Beidaihe did not become a summer resort until the 1980s, when English engineers discovered its bathing advantages while building the Tianjin–Shanhaiguan railroad. Foreigners and wealthy Chinese soon began buying up the land and building villas. During the Boxer Rebellion in 1899, many of these villas were burned down, but the Manchu government had them rebuilt. By 1949, some 350 cottages had been constructed in the area, although many were closed down in the 1950s due to lack of clientele.

Subsequently, the government declared this a vacation area for workers and a large number of sanatoriums and rest homes were built. It also became a favorite vacation spot for political leaders, who kept individual estates here for their personal use. Jiang Qing (Mao's widow and the most notorious member of the "gang of four") had a large villa here, replete with expansive gardens (now known simply as Villa No. 125).

BEIDAIHE'S BEACHES

There are three main beaches: East, West, and Middle. The East Beach is reserved for "model workers" and army members, whose two-week vacations, including food and travel expenses, are partially subsidized by the state. The area is dotted with rest homes for workers suffering from arthritis and other chronic diseases, who come to Beidaihe for three to six months to convalesce. They receive full pay and free medical treatment while at Beidaihe. (Some 60 of these sanatoriums were closed down during the Cultural Revolution in 1967, and only reopened in 1979.) The Middle Beach is used by various PRC ministries to house top-level officials and guests of the state. The West Beach is the exclusive preserve of the China International Travel Service, and umbrellas with its logo can be seen at the six beach houses in this area.

From June to September, bus loads of tourists arrive daily to enjoy the beach and the surrounding scenery. There are individual changing rooms

Climate		Jan	Feb	Mar	Apr	May	Jun	Jul	Aug	Sep	Oct	Nov	Dec
Temp.	°C	-4.2	-1.7	4.7	13.2	19.7	24.4	26.6	25.8	20.9	14.0	4.6	-2.2
	°F	24.5	28.9	40.4	55.7	67.4	75.9	79.8	78.4	69.6	57.2	40.2	28
Precip.	mm.	76	76	76	102	152	229	330	279	178	152	102	76
	in.	3	3	3	4	6	9	13	11	7	6	4	3

with good showers and, if you forgot to pack for the beach, you can borrow a sedate, Chinese-style bathing suit free of charge. There are some recreation rooms for Ping-Pong and billiards. Both Western and Chinese cold drinks are available and the local ice cream is a must.

Swimming at Beidaihe is not for the timid. The beach descends sharply into the water and, while the breakers do not extend more than 6 m. (20 ft.) from the shore, the waves can be moderately rough. Bamboo rods mark off the swimming area and a double line of fishing nets is set out along the perimeter to keep out sharks and jellyfish (none of these present much of a danger, but the Chinese like to be absolutely certain). Chinese lifeguards always swim amidst the bathers.

The town area is decidely more like the Hamptons on New York's Long Island or Brighton in England than any Chinese city. But there is no noisome commercialism or radio music, and gone also are the noises of urban China. The heat of Beijing and the hectic pace of China travel are quickly forgotten as you sit in a rattan chair and absorb the sounds of the birds, the rolling surf, and the gentle rustling of the leaves.

HIGHLIGHTS FOR TRAVELERS

The beach is Beidaihe's main attraction, but there are a few other attractions in the town itself. If you are staying for a few days you might want to arrange a side trip to Shanhaiguan or Qinhuangdao.

莲花石公园

Lotus Rock Park (Lianhuashi Gongyuan). This is a small park on the crest of a hill above the West Hill Hotel. Its main point of interest is a Republican-period stele from 1919 erected on a turtle with a dragon's head (symbol of longevity). Nearby is a copper bell used during the Ming Dynasty to call Buddhist monks to worship. On the edge of the park is a gray stone house, looking somewhat like a military fortress. It used to belong to Lin Biao, the former army chief-of-staff who was exposed as a traitor and died in a plane crash while fleeing to the Soviet Union in 1971. It is said that Lin was heliophobic and lived on the first floor of the house with all the windows shuttered.

观音寺（古刹）

Ancient Temple of Guanyin (Gucha Guanyin Si). Near Lotus Rock Park is a small group of 300-year-old temples which have recently undergone renovation.

鹰角亭

Eagle Pavilion. Towering above the beach is a structure from which one can take in the entire Beidaihe panorama. For an impressive view of the Beidaihe sunrise, visitors can walk up to either the Eagle Pavilion or the Seaside Pavilion, located on the tip of the Coupled-Peak Hill.

Chinese holidaymakers on the beach at Beidaihe

HOTEL ACCOMMODATIONS

西山饭店

Xishan (West Hill) Hotel (Xiyi Rd.; tel: 2678; 2338 ext. 364; cable: 0518). Located near the beach, the Xishan has about 150 rooms, including several suites. Double room rates are Y42, suites are Y70. All rooms have telephone, color TV, and private bath. Some have refrigerators. The hotel has a magnificent auditorium and dance hall, as well as the obligatory shops, post office, barbershop, Chinese restaurant, and open-air tea room.

中海滩宾馆

Zhong Hai Tan (Central Beach) Guesthouse (30 Xijing Rd.; tel: 2398, 2445, ext. 626). The Zhong Hai Tan has 100 double rooms at Y42. All have private bath and telephone and some have color TV. This hotel is also by the beach, with open-air tea tables, a Chinese restaurant, post office, barbershop, and currency exchange.

Small groups may be assigned to separate bungalows, each with three bedrooms, wide verandas, and private dining and living rooms. A staff of two lives in the back and is always on hand. The service is incomparable —perhaps the most gracious in all of China.

CUISINE

The Chinese go to resorts for the same reasons everyone else does: to relax, enjoy the scenery, and eat, eat, eat. Beidaihe does not disappoint them. There is an abundance of seafood, with the crabs especially recommended. The natives reportedly eat jellyfish, but these have not been seen on any menu presented to foreigners. Vegetables are fresh, and pork, beef, and chicken are in good supply, but it is the fish dishes that tend to win the accolades.

Beihai

北 海

north sea   *traditional spelling/Pakhoi*

QUIET, picturesque, and far from the beaten track, the ancient fishing town of Beihai overlooks the South China Sea at the extreme southern tip of the Guangxi Zhuang Autonomous Region. Established over 2,000 years ago, during the Qin dynasty, Beihai became an important trading center during the Song Dynasty. In that era, seafaring Arab merchants came here to barter African ivory, gold, and rhinoceros horn for Chinese silks, ceramics, and pearls. As a "treaty port," Beihai was opened to foreign interests under the Agreement of Chefoo in 1876. The city still bears the architectural stamp of its colonial past — that curious mix of Chinese and European influences typical of many south China ports.

One of China's most important fishing bases, nearby Beibu Gulf is among the world's four most productive fishing zones, with over 500 species of fish and 43 varieties of shrimp. The city is best known, however, as a source of natural pearls. There is archeological evidence that the people of Beihai have been diving for pearls since the Former Han Dynasty (2nd century BC). Indeed, nearly all of Beihai's current 168,000 inhabitants make their living directly or indirectly from the sea.

That centuries-old economic pattern began to change dramatically in 1984 when Beihai was declared one of China's 14 Open Coastal Cities, chiefly because of nearby offshore oil deposits. However, Beihai is rich in other exploitable natural resources, not the least of which is its 10 miles of beautiful beaches. Industrial development and large-scale extraction of mineral and porcelain-quality clay deposits await only the expansion of transportation, power, and other essential infrastructural facilities. To date, the city has signed contracts worth over Y70 million with foreign businesses. Of this total, however, Y50 million will go towards hotel construction and beachfront development. A recently completed rail link with Nanning and a soon-to-be-completed jetport should do much to awaken Behai from its economic slumber.

There is little to see or do in Beihai that in and of itself is worth the detour, although once in Beihai, the oceanographic museum/aquarium shouldn't be missed. Beihai's chief charms are the slow, tropical pace of life; the warm, maritime monsoon climate; and the everyday sights and sounds of an ancient, almost forgotten port town.

Climate		Jan	Feb	Mar	Apr	May	Jun	Jul	Aug	Sep	Oct	Nov	Dec
Temp.	°C	13.1	13.8	17.5	21.9	25.8	27.1	28.3	28.2	27.0	23.8	19.8	15.2
	°F	55	56.8	63.5	71.4	78.4	80.7	82.9	82.7	80.6	74.8	67.6	59.3
Precip.	mm.	152	203	254	279	381	508	457	406	330	203	152	127
	in.	6	8	10	11	15	20	18	16	13	8	6	5

Fishing off the beach, Beibu Gulf

Beijing

BEIJING, the capital of the People's Republic of China, is, like any great metropolis worthy of the designation, its own universe. And while many of its elements are common to other Chinese cities, the sum of this city—its scope, its grandeur, its presence in history—has no equivalent in China or anywhere else in the world.

Beijing is a shadowy city of pale yellows and greys. The hazy sunlight of the North China Plain is diffused by billions of dust particles borne by prevailing winds from Central Asia. The monumental palaces of the Forbidden City and the massive grey and beige halls of the Chinese central government loom as remote fortresses in the blurred light. Then, in the

246

北京

northern capital

traditional spelling/Peking

Modern housing
frames Beijing's
Temple of Heaven.

middle sky, appearing almost subliminally at first, are great swatches of
crimson and yellow—the banners, placards, and painted slogans that speak
of national pride, of world revolution, and of long life to the people, to
the government, and to the Communist Party of China. Intense individual
purpose and strident public exhortation combine to make up the special
chemistry of Beijing. But with all of its bustle and the haranguing
billboards, the city is a curiously quiet, self-absorbed place.

Beijing is not only the political and administrative center of the
People's Republic of China, it is also China's single greatest repository of
monuments and treasures from the imperial era. It is also the second-largest

247

and fastest growing municipality in today's China, the home and workplace of 9.3 million people. The city proper extends over 16,800 sq. km. (6,486 sq. mi.). It is divided into 10 districts (including four urban districts) and nine counties.

Beijing's Population. Western city dwellers might remark at the fact that some 42% of Beijing's population belong to the agricultural sector. This reflects a notable feature of Chinese planning which seeks to make the big cities as self-sufficient as possible in food production. Beijing's rural population occupies the several thousand square miles of dun-colored suburbs that have been annexed to the municipality. They are organized into 269 townships and state farms. A small proportion of Beijing's population (about 4% in 1984) consists of minority nationalities: Muslims predominate, but observant visitors will frequently catch glimpses of other minorities—Tibetans in their colorful flowing robes, Uighurs from the far western province of Xinjiang in their distinctive black-and-white caps.

Living Standards. Living standards of Beijing residents have improved dramatically in the 1980s. Even casual observers will note visible yearly improvements in housing, transportation, clothing, food distribution, and consumer products. Official statistics for 1983 indicated that 91% of households in the industrial and service sectors owned TV sets, while 41% had tape recorders and 29% washing machines. Living space was 5.7 sq. m. per capita, rising by about 8% each year. Average household expenses for the same year came to about Y600.

Modern factories have been built in the southeastern suburbs to avoid adding industrial fumes to the prevailing dust-bearing northwesterly winds. Pollution nevertheless is a problem in the capital, mainly due to coal residues from home heating and diesel wastes from buses and trucks.

Climate. Beijing lies at approximately the same latitude as Philadelphia and Madrid. Beijing's climate forces one to wonder why anyone ever chose this place as a site for prolonged human habitation. The preferred time of year to visit Beijing is during September and early October. During this short period, Beijing remains dry and warm in the daytime and cool in the evenings. It then undergoes an abrupt transition to winter, when temperatures often drop well below freezing. By late winter, the dry earth is fanned by brisk northern winds that swirl dust everywhere. Temperatures moderate in late March and April, when trees begin to display a pale green patina—a miraculous appearance in an otherwise bone-dry vista. Most summers are oppressively hot and humid, interrupted by periods of heavy rainfall.

Climate		Jan	Feb	Mar	Apr	May	Jun	Jul	Aug	Sep	Oct	Nov	Dec
Temp.	°C	−4.7	−1.9	4.8	13.7	20.1	24.8	26.1	24.8	19.9	12.8	3.8	2.8
	°F	23.5	28.6	40.6	56.6	68.1	76.6	78.9	76.6	67.8	55	38.8	37
Precip.	mm.	76	76	76	102	152	203	305	254	178	152	102	76
	in.	3	3	3	4	6	8	12	10	7	6	4	3

Beijing today retains many facets of its antiquity, but has subordinated them to intensive urban development. Most of the formerly walled town in the heart of the city (including its basic street plan) dates from before the 16th century. In 1958—to the dismay of many Western sinophiles—the old walls and several gates of the Imperial City were dismantled brick by brick to make way for a number of new buildings and monuments. The subway system began operations in 1969 and was completed in 1984. It is laid out along the lines of the old city walls.

Beijing's Internationalization. Inevitably, with all the changes in recent years, Beijing is becoming more internationalized. Preservation of dominant edifices from the past, combined with the present government's patriotic desire to impart a Chinese look to new architecture and planning elements, will ensure that Beijing will keep its distinctive aura. But the recent boom in the volume of foreign visitors and residents is also a phenomenon that the city welcomes and seeks to encourage, with the result that Beijing is steadily losing the parochial, isolated aura it had maintained up to only a few years ago. By late 1985, the city had over 50 hotels with about 20,000 beds to handle an annual influx of nearly 700,000 foreign guests. Thousands of foreign residents now work in Beijing's 126 embassies, 500 foreign commercial offices, and 75 news agencies.

Traffic. Although Beijing has a central business district headquartered in downtown Wangfujing Street, scattered neighborhood markets and shopping centers help somewhat to diffuse urban congestion. But rush-hour traffic jams continue to plague the main arteries; despite major efforts in recent years, the road network is not sufficiently developed to cope with the rapidly increasing number of buses, goods vehicles, and bicycles. A major new superhighway connecting Beijing to Tianjin and adjacent seaports is due for completion by the end of the decade. It is designed to handle traffic at speeds of up to 120 km./hour, or about twice as fast as any surface transportation now available in China.

BEIJING IN HISTORY

Early History. The discovery of fossil remains, tools, and other artifacts at Zhoukoudian, where Peking Man made his home, indicates that the area just southwest of present-day Beijing was inhabited as early as 500,000 years ago. But it was not until the early years of the Western Zhou (c. 1066–771 BC) that there were historical records of a settlement called Jicheng (Reed Town) arising on the treeless, marshy banks of the Yongding River.

During the Warring States Period (403–221 BC), the town became the capital of the Kingdom of Yan. Destroyed by the armies of Qin Shi Huangdi, founder of the Qin Dynasty (221–206 BC), the town was not rebuilt until the Han Dynasty (206 BC–AD 220), when it was made a provincial center called Yan. Situated on the northern frontiers of ancient China, Yan was the scene of many clashes between invading nomads and imperial troops, and for nearly 300 years it remained largely under nomadic control.

In AD 610, the Sui Dynasty emperor Yangdi ordered the construction of a waterway extending from the Yangtse River northward to the area around Beijing in order to speed supplies to his armies in their campaigns against Korea; this was the start of the Grand Canal, which by the 12th century connected Beijing to fertile regions over 1,000 miles to the south.

The Imperial Era. Measures taken during the Tang Dynasty (617–907) to prevent further incursions by northern nomadic tribes gave new strategic importance to the town on the edge of China's North Central Plain. Now renamed Youzhou, the town also thrived as a center of commerce and handicrafts. During the period of turmoil that ensued, the Khitans, a northern tribe that subsequently established the Liao Kingdom (947–1125), razed Youzhou and built their capital on top of the site. The largest of the five Liao capitals, the new city of Khitan was laid out in a grid pattern, with the emperor's palace occupying the center of the square. The name Khitan, or Khitai, is thought to be the origin of "Cathay," the name by which China was known in medieval Europe.

In 1125, the Liao were defeated by a Manchurian tribe known as the Jurchen, who established the state of Jin. The city was made the Jin capital and renamed Zhongdu (Central Capital). Less than 100 years later, the Mongols under Genghis Khan swept down from the north and took the city after repeated attacks. In the final battle the palaces were set ablaze and burned for a month.

When Kublai Khan, founder of the Yuan Dynasty (1279–1368), set out to build a new capital on the site, he shifted the center of the city to what is today Beihai. He constructed imposing palaces, boulevards, and even a canal which linked up with the Grand Canal—then China's main north-south inland artery—so that boats bearing tributes from the south could sail directly to the capital. The new city was named Dadu (Great Capital) and, for the first time, served as the political center of all China. Marco Polo, who visited the city during its Mongol renaissance, gave a grandiloquent description of life in "Khan Buluc (Baliq)" in his *Travels*.

The Yuan Dynasty was overthrown in 1368 by Zhu Yanhang, leader of a peasant revolt, who founded the Ming Dynasty (1368–1644). He established his capital elsewhere, and Dadu was given the name Beiping (Northern Peace). In 1402, Zhu's son inherited the Dragon Throne and moved the capital back to the city which he renamed Beijing (Northern Capital). Prior to the move, great sums were spent on constructing palaces and temples which gave the city a scale and splendor it had never known before. An important part of the expansion involved the resettling—by imperial decree—of thousands of people in the capital from other parts of China, particularly Shandong Province.

In 1644 the city changed hands twice in rapid succession. First, a peasant leader, Li Zicheng, held Beijing for 43 days. Then, the Manchus seized the city and made it the capital of the Qing Dynasty for the next two and a half centuries (1644–1911). Beijing's characteristic insularity was perhaps at no time more pronounced than under the Qing emperors,

Tian'anmen Square memorial rally for Zhou Enlai, 1976

for whom the city functioned increasingly as a barrier against external realities. Mainly by dint of the services required by the imperial court, Beijing became one of the largest cities in the world. Extensive renovation and expansion was carried out on the 780 palaces, pavilions, and temples of Ming times. New gardens and lakes of unsurpassed beauty and elegance were created. Within the city walls were three "seas"—Beihai, Zhonghai, and Nanhai; beyond the city walls to the west were the secondary palaces of Changming Yuan, Yuanming Yuan, and Qingyi Yuan. Yuanming Yuan was the favorite imperial residence of Qian Long, the emperor with the longest reign in all of Chinese history (1736–95). His reign marked the height of splendor for the Qing Dynasty, but it also brought the beginning of its decline. At the conclusion of the Opium Wars in 1860, British and French troops overran the capital and destroyed Yuanming Yuan by fire.

Beijing's Revolutionary Tradition. The roots of the modern revolutionary movement in Beijing can be traced to the invasion of the city by 17,000 British and French troops in 1860, an event that ushered in five decades of Western expansionism and hastened the end of the imperial dynastic system.

Belatedly the Chinese government attempted various reforms. The most notable effort came in 1898 when a group of ministers tried to modernize the government by forming a parliament and strengthening the armed forces. The "reform movement" failed, however, bringing to power more extreme factions, whose rallying cry became "Expel the barbarian!"

The extremists found an effective political and military ally in the Boxers, a secret society founded in the late 18th century to foment popular rebellion against imperial reign. The Boxers at this time narrowed their objective to ejecting foreigners and entered into a dubious alliance with the imperial government. In 1900, Boxer and imperial troops besieged the foreign legations in Beijing for 45 days; Western forces retaliated, the Manchu rulers were forced to flee, and the Boxer Rebellion was crushed. The Western powers imposed a huge indemnity and yet another "unequal treaty" on the powerless Manchu rulers, thereby further bankrupting the country.

As the imperial system disintegrated, Beijing, the imperial capital, suffered a similar fate. When provincial warlords refused to forward to the capital the taxes they had collected on behalf of the central government, officials in Beijing were reduced to exacting tolls at the city gates as a means of ensuring a flow of national revenue.

Beijing in the 20th Century. The overthrow of the dynastic system by Sun Yatsen's 1911 Revolution led to the first attempts to lay the foundations for a modern nation. Factionalism continued, however, and in 1912, Yuan Shikai, a former Qing general, usurped Sun's position and established a new government in Beijing. Chaos ensued as lingering traditional values conflicted with new forces of social and political change.

On May 4, 1919, some 300,000 youths rallied in the capital to denounce the Beijing regime's weak response to continuing humiliation at the hands of the Western nations and Japan, specifically the decision of the Versailles Peace Conference to transfer Germany's "rights" in China to Japan. The sentiments and ideas expressed by the May Fourth Movement were to influence Chinese politics profoundly. For the next 30 years, a series of worker's strikes and student demonstrations in the capital underscored the growing desire among many of the Chinese people to see their country emerge as a modern, strong, and sovereign nation.

When Sun Yatsen's Guomindang (Nationalist) Party moved its capital to Nanjing in 1928, the name of the capital was changed back to Beiping— the name it had been given 600 years earlier. Nine years later, the city fell into the hands of the Japanese after the attack at Marco Polo Bridge just outside the city. It was not until the end of World War II that the city reverted to Guomindang control.

Victory over the Japanese did not mean an end to violence in Beijing. Civil strife continued, prices soared, and unemployment rose to unprecedented levels. On May 20, 1947, the students of Beijing once again took to the streets, this time to inveigh "against civil war, against starvation." The movement soon spread nationwide, effectively winning millions over to the side of the Communists.

In January 1949, the residents of Beijing lined the streets to give the Communist troops a tumultuous welcome. On October 1 of that year, from atop Tian'anmen, the Gate of Heavenly Peace, Mao Zedong proclaimed the founding of the People's Republic of China. From that day on, the fortunes of this historical city have been on the rise.

ECONOMY AND CULTURE

Since 1949, Beijing's industrial development has been rapid and diverse. Although the city still ranks behind Shanghai as a manufacturing center, Beijing has become a major producer of textiles and synthetic fibers, petrochemicals, automotive and agricultural equipment, and light and heavy machinery. Recent growth has emphasized the manufacture of communications and electronics equipment, as well as advanced military weapons.

Expansion is itself an important industry in Beijing. Over 150 major new residential complexes have been built since 1949, and new construction since 1960 has enlarged the city's original area by one-third. New housing has increased at an average of about two million sq. m. (21 million sq. ft.) of floor space per year, with 95 million sq. m. added since 1949. Other large public works projects include a vast underground network of air-raid shelters, a subway, several national museums, and monumental structures such as the Great Hall of the People and the Mao Zedong Memorial Hall at Tian'anmen Square. Major projects—and their maintenance—employ large segments of the work force.

In 1949 the city's population of two million was served by only 49 streetcars and five buses. The rich traveled in their private cars and rickshaws, the poor walked. Today, the rickshaw, a symbol of human exploitation in China, is nowhere to be seen. By 1984, there were over 3,000 electric and gasoline-fueled buses, as well as a 30-km. (18-mi.) subway.

The new Beijing International Airport, completed in October 1979, has two 3,200-m. (10,496-ft.) runways capable of handling jumbo jets. A modern dome-shaped terminal and 300-bed hotel for passengers in transit were completed in early 1981. To facilitate motor transport, freeways and overpasses are being added annually throughout the capital. Of special interest to foreign visitors are the tour taxi companies that now operate in the city with fleets totalling 2,900 vehicles (many imported from Japan and the Soviet Union).

The city's thousands of fruit and vegetable stands, noted for their colorful, artistic displays, are nearly all supplied by the surrounding region, where some 111,300 hectares (275,000 acres) are under cultivation. The area southwest of Beijing is extremely fertile, and the creation of reservoirs and irrigation systems has assured a continuous food supply.

Beginning in 1978, many free markets for fruit and vegetables began to reappear, the result of liberalized economic policies. For Beijing residents, the free markets—selling meat, peanuts, fish, poultry, and sometimes pets, furniture, and even toys—have become a popular shopping alternative. Two of the largest free markets (there are 45 in all) are located at Beitaipingzhuang, north of the Beijing Hotel (about 15 minutes away by car) and opposite the Beijing Film Studio, and at Baiwanzhuang, next to the Foreign Languages Press. Beijing's first indoor free market opened in 1984 on Zhongguancun near Beijing University.

Institutions related to the arts and culture are flourishing as well. Beijing now has 11 museums, six exhibition centers, 22 public libraries, 96

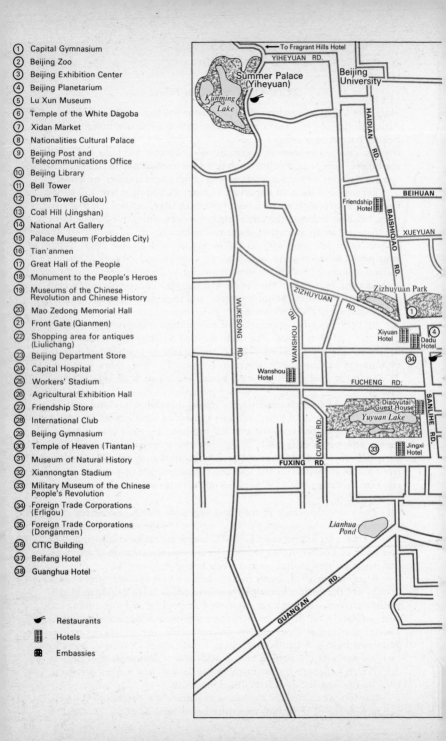

1. Capital Gymnasium
2. Beijing Zoo
3. Beijing Exhibition Center
4. Beijing Planetarium
5. Lu Xun Museum
6. Temple of the White Dagoba
7. Xidan Market
8. Nationalities Cultural Palace
9. Beijing Post and Telecommunications Office
10. Beijing Library
11. Bell Tower
12. Drum Tower (Gulou)
13. Coal Hill (Jingshan)
14. National Art Gallery
15. Palace Museum (Forbidden City)
16. Tian'anmen
17. Great Hall of the People
18. Monument to the People's Heroes
19. Museums of the Chinese Revolution and Chinese History
20. Mao Zedong Memorial Hall
21. Front Gate (Qianmen)
22. Shopping area for antiques (Liulichang)
23. Beijing Department Store
24. Capital Hospital
25. Workers' Stadium
26. Agricultural Exhibition Hall
27. Friendship Store
28. International Club
29. Beijing Gymnasium
30. Temple of Heaven (Tiantan)
31. Museum of Natural History
32. Xiannongtan Stadium
33. Military Museum of the Chinese People's Revolution
34. Foreign Trade Corporations (Erligou)
35. Foreign Trade Corporations (Donganmen)
36. CITIC Building
37. Beifang Hotel
38. Guanghua Hotel

Restaurants

Hotels

Embassies

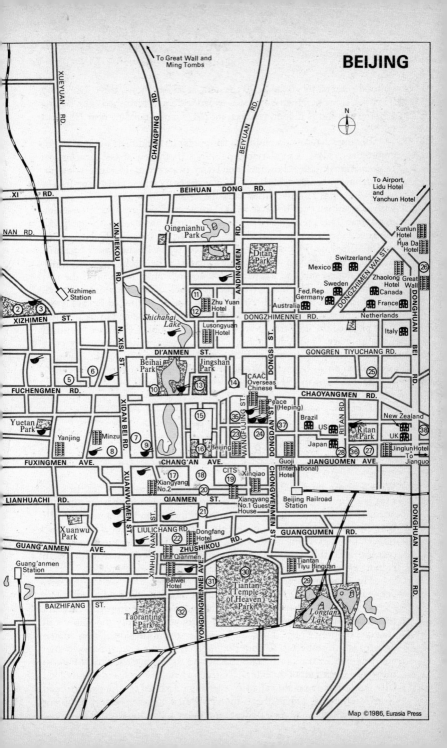

cultural centers, 99 cinemas, 20 theaters, seven stadiums, three gyms, and 33 parks, some of which have been expanded and refurbished. The Beijing Library, housing 11 million volumes, moved to a new building near Ziheyuan in 1987.

Beijing's artisan community is famous for its handicraft work. Carpets, embroidery, silks, ivory carving, paintings (both new styles and classical reproductions), jade, cloisonné, and lacquerware are of the highest quality. A museum has been established to display the best of these arts and crafts.

Beijing has 51 universities and colleges and 32 branches of universities with a combined enrollment of 94,000 students. There are also 189 research institutes. The prestigious Beijing University (nicknamed "Beida") and Qinghua University are located in its northwestern suburbs. Beida, founded in 1898, had its original campus in the center of Beijing (near Shatan). In 1952, Beida merged with Yanjing University, which had been administered by Americans and financed by Boxer indemnity funds until the revolution in 1949. The faintly "Ivy League" look of Beida's present campus extends from its Yanjing inheritance. Mao worked in the old Beida Library in 1918 and it was on that now-defunct campus that he and other intellectuals planned the important May 4th demonstrations of 1919 (see "Beijing's Revolutionary Tradition," above). The university's students and faculty played a central role in organizing national resistance to the Japanese occupation until the end of World War II. Qinghua University, ever since its establishment in 1911, has been considered the MIT of China.

HIGHLIGHTS
FOR TRAVELERS

With a history of 3,000 years, Beijing is extraordinarily rich in historical sites and cultural relics. Indeed, the entire area within the city limits is one grand historical relic. The layout of Beijing is quite symmetrical. Just imagine three rectangles, one within another. The lengths of the two smaller rectangles run north-south, while the length of the largest runs east-west. To the south side of the largest rectangle is attached a fourth rectangle—slightly longer in length and narrower in width.

The innermost rectangle forms the Forbidden City—once the residence of Ming and Qing emperors, now a museum and public park. The second rectangle outlines the former boundaries of the Imperial City. Of the vermilion brick walls which once surrounded it, only the south wall (the one running along Chang'an Avenue on the north side of Tian'anmen Square) is still standing. Within the Imperial City lie several parks: Beihai and Jingshan in the north; Zhongshan and the People's Cultural Park in the south. Once part of the Imperial City and lying just west of the Forbidden City is a large compound called Zhongnanhai (named for the two artificial "seas"—Zhonghai and Nanhai—found within it). Today, high government officials, including members of the State Council, live and work in this area.

The outermost rectangle follows the former Outer City wall. In the area between the Inner City and Outer City walls are located government buildings, market districts, and old residential areas.

A north-south axis, 8 km. long, runs through the center of Beijing. It begins at the Bell Tower and Drum Tower to the north, crosses the peak of Jingshan Hill, enters the Forbidden City through the Shenwumen Gate, exits through the Wumen Gate and Tian'anmen Gate, continues through Shengyangmen Gate in the southern wall of the Inner City, and ends at Yongdingmen Gate, the southern entrance to the Outer City. The Forbidden City was positioned at the dead-center of this axis to symbolize the central authority of dynastic rule.

The rest of Beijing hinges on the north-south axis. East and west of the main axis are found, in perfect symmetry, park for park, market for market. Most of the city's larger avenues run north-south, parallel to the main axis, while smaller streets and alleys (*hutongs*) run horizontally.

Beijing, of course, has expanded far beyond the old city limits. Today, it is ringed by a near suburb and a far suburb. In the first zone, immediately outside the former Outer City, are found new housing, factories, schools, and government buildings. On the outer fringes of this zone are farms which produce vegetables and fruit for consumption by the urban population. The far suburb is more extensive, and comes under the administration of several communes and state farms. In this area is located most of Beijing's heavy industry.

In April 1985, Beijing municipal authorities announced that 14 formerly off-limits rural and industrial areas outside the city would be opened to foreigners. The areas include the Miyun Reservoir, 75 km. (47 mi.) northeast of Beijing, where a large amusement park, complete with bumper cars, a rotating rocket, and ferris wheel, opened in August 1984. The master plan for the park includes a ballroom, restaurants, and a racecourse. The 13 other counties and districts include Daxing, Tongxian, Shunyi, Pinggu, Fengtai, Yanshan, Fangshan, Yanqing, Changping, Huairou, Haidian, Shigingshan, and Mengtougou (see map, p. 259).

FOR TRAVELERS ON A BUDGET

ON YOUR OWN IN BEIJING

Arrival. If you arrive in Beijing by train, the first challenge is to get out of the train station. There is no special foreigner's exit at the Beijing station, as there is in Shanghai and many other cities; all passengers must proceed down the stairs and up the long corridor towards the exit. Follow the crowd—or simply allow yourself to be swept along with the throngs rushing to make local transport connections. Upon exiting the station you must present your ticket to an attendant at the departure door, who will put it through a machine for invalidation and return it to you. Then walk straight out the door and towards a small trailer-type kiosk directly ahead (there will no doubt be a long line by the time you reach it). That is where you get a taxi. Get in line and tell the dispatcher where you want to go.

Chinese and foreign tourists ascend the Great Wall.

BEIJING ENVIRONS

N

Miyun

★
Beijing

Pinggu

Shanyi

Fengtai

Tongxian

Yanshan

Daxing

Map ©1988, Eurasia Press

If you are lucky, a driver may approach you directly and ask you where you want to go. If your destination is convenient for him, he might decide to take you, even though you haven't properly waited your turn.

If you prefer not to deal with taxis, you could try the buses, but you have to walk a bit (north on the main street, in the same direction you walked upon leaving the station) to get to the bus stops for buses #1, 4, 9, and 37. Buses #103, 104, 10, and 20 stop just northwest of the station. The only hotels easy to reach without a change are the Jianguo Hotel (#1, 4, or 9), the Overseas Chinese Hotel (#103 or 104), and the Xiyuan Hotel (#103). The Beijing Hotel is about one-half mile from the closest #1 or 4 stop. Unfortunately, most of the city's other hotels require one or more bus changes (more than we can cope with in this section).

If you arrive by air, the taxi stand is just inside the airport lobby's main exit doors. (You should change money in the airport—a Bank of China desk has been set up inside the customs area—if you've just arrived in China.) Lately, airport cab drivers have become more aggressive, approaching passengers directly as they emerge from customs. The cab ride is expensive (Y40 or more to the center of town), but the expense may be worth it, considering the alternatives—two low-frequency buses: a CAAC staff bus that often refuses to take foreign passengers, and bus #315, which terminates at the Northeast Terminal. Both may cost hours of precious time and may leave you nowhere near your ultimate destination.

Hotels. It's best to select a hotel in advance from among those in the hotels listing in this section, and give the name to the taxi driver (many carry street directories). Except in peak seasons (April–May and September–October), many of the less expensive hotels are willing to accept guests without prior reservations. In the busier seasons, visitors might do well to proceed directly to one of the city's three Hotel Information Centers or to the Beijing CITS office (addresses listed in the Beijing Directory at the end of this section).

For travelers with a week or less to spend in Beijing, the location of a hotel can be as important a factor as its rates. As is common in many cities, Beijing's cheapest lodgings tend to be those situated on a perimeter far from the center of the city—the **Evergreen Hotel** (Guanlianjin Binguan), operated by the China Youth Travel Service and located in the northwest suburbs, is about an hour's bus ride from Tian'anmen; Beijing University's foreign-student residence, **Shao Yuan Lou,** is about 45 minutes from the city center; and the **Heilongjiang Guesthouse,** situated on the road to Badaling and the Great Wall, can take over two hours to reach by public bus. Shared accommodations at these locations are available at US $10–25 per night, compared to the US $30–50 rates that prevail at a wide selection of older hotels in the central district (see specific listings in the Beijing hotels section).

Getting Around the City. After you've checked into your hotel and rested up a bit, purchase a local street map with bus routes marked (detailed maps for Beijing are now available in English and are also sold outside of China in Chinese bookshops). Use your map along with the *Guidebook* to work out some sensible daily itineraries—Beijing is a spread-out city and major sites may be hours apart, especially if you are relying on public transport. You have the choice of going by taxi, public bus, or tourist bus. An extremely useful innovation is the new "minibus" routes in the city, which operate from 8 AM to 5 PM. Passengers can flag down the buses anywhere along the route and get off at any point. Current routes are as follows: 1. From the train station to Beihai Park, passing Dongdan, Wangfujing, the Art Gallery, and the Forbidden City. 2. From the train station to the zoo along Chang'an Boulevard, turning at Lishi Lu and up through Baiwan Zhuang. 3. From the main train station to the Yongdingmen train station. 4. From the zoo to the Summer Palace along the route of the 332 bus line. Fares are 50 *fen* for up to three stops; Y1 for up to six stops; and Y1.50 for over six stops. Buses on these routes are spaced at 5- to 15-minute intervals.

One easy and inexpensive way to get to some of the key attractions outside of the city is to make use of the buses that leave from Congwenmen every day between 7–8 AM. They are run by the Capital Cab Company and cost from Y2.50–7 for day-long excursions to the Great Wall and

surrounding areas; the Western Hills, including Xiangshan and the Summer Palace; the Eastern Tombs; Zhoukoudian; or Tanzhe Si, including Jietai Si. All buses return in the late afternoon.

For the sites inside the city as well as for some in neighboring suburbs, you may be able to manage quite well by taking public buses or walking. There are also several bicycle-repair shops that rent bicycles in the city (the best are listed in the Beijing Directory at the end of this section). Cycling is by far the best way to feel a part of your surroundings, although bicycling along Beijing's more crowded thoroughfares can be perilous. (For more information, see Touring Beijing without an Escort, below.)

In 1984, the train station opened a special ticket office for foreigners, at which time CITS dispensed with its train ticketing service for individual travelers, although international train reservations and ticketing (i.e., on Trans-Siberian and Trans-Mongolian trains) are still handled by CITS at the Chongwenmen Hotel. The new domestic train ticket office is located in the rear (northeast corner) of the station. It can be found by walking through the main doors and to the back of the lobby between the escalators, then turning left, through the waiting room for international passengers; the ticket office is in Room 103 inside and is identified by signs in English. Seats can be reserved 6–10 days in advance and purchased up to five days in advance. International flights on CAAC can be booked at the Beijing Hotel. Domestic plane tickets may be purchased at the CAAC office, just north of the Overseas Chinese Mansion and just east of the Art Gallery, at 117 Dongsi Xi Jie. It is important to note that here, as elsewhere in

China, reservation systems are not yet fully computerized, with one effect being the inability to book anything beyond the initial leg of a trip out of the originating city. Thus, for example, if you are purchasing tickets in Beijing for a train or plane trip that will include stops in Xi'an, Shanghai, and Guangzhou, you may only be able to reserve a seat to Xi'an, where you will then have to book your next onward leg.

故宫
THE IMPERIAL PALACE

Also known as the Forbidden City (*Zijin Cheng*), the Imperial Palace (*Gugong*) complex is an abiding symbol of traditional China. Although it is China's most imposing architectural masterpiece, it is characterized by simple lines and elegant decoration.

The construction of the Imperial Palace was truly one of the great feats of human history, comparable to the pyramids or China's own Great Wall. The site of the present-day structure was originally chosen by Mongol rulers of the Yuan Dynasty (1279–1368), but the buildings were completely reconstructed by Yong Le (1403–24), the third Ming Dynasty emperor. Between 1406 and 1420, literally hundreds of thousands of workers participated in erecting these palaces. Sacked and looted by Manchu armies during the overthrow of the Ming Dynasty in 1644, the complex was restored to its original splendor under the Qing (notably by Emperor Qian Long, 1736–96). New additions in the northern sector date from the tyrannical rule of the Empress Dowager Ci Xi (1835–1908).

Located in the heart of Beijing, the Imperial Palace covers an area of 101.2 hectares (250 acres). It is surrounded by a wide moat (today, sections of it are used for boating) and protected by a wall 10.7 m. (35 ft.) high,

marked off by towers at each corner. The entire complex includes six main palaces, as well as many smaller buildings, together containing over 9,000 rooms (some of which may soon be converted into hotel space for foreigners). Nearly all of the buildings stand two stories high, flanked by courtyards with dimensions proportionate to the importance of their former inhabitants.

The palace grounds are divided into two sections. In the foreground are three public halls from which the Ming and Qing emperors conducted important state ceremonies. The rear part of the complex is composed of three main palaces, a few smaller "east" and "west" palaces, and the Imperial Gardens. In this setting, the 24 emperors divided their time between affairs of state and their families, rarely if ever leaving the palace complex.

From the Dragon Throne the 24 "Sons of Heaven" ruled the nation with an absolute authority rarely paralleled in human history. An imperial decree ordained that no building in Beijing could be taller than the palace. No commoner or foreigner could enter the palace complex without special permission, on pain of death, which forced the poor to make long detours around the sprawling grounds. Only since the establishment of the People's Republic of China in 1949 has the Forbidden City—now converted into a public park—been open to ordinary people.

The Imperial Palace formerly housed the emperor, his consort, other wives, concubines, eunuchs, ministers, favored court officials, and thousands of artisans and servants. The 9,000-room complex was a vast treasure house of precious art objects and rich architecture until it fell into disrepair after 1911. Crateloads of its valuable art and jewels were looted during the Japanese occupation of Beijing in the 1930s and by the Guomindang forces in 1949 before their retreat to Taiwan. Many treasures remain, however, and are today on display for the visiting public at the Palace Museum.

At least a full morning or afternoon is required even for a superficial overview of the Imperial Palace. It is open from 8:30 AM to 4:30 PM daily.

午门

Meridian Gate (Wumen). This massive gate, surmounted by five pavilions, is the main entrance to the Forbidden City. Originally built in 1420, it was restored in 1647 and again in 1801. From the heights of this imposing structure, also known as the Gate of the Five Phoenixes, the emperor reviewed his armies. Here prisoners were trooped past him so he could decide which were to be pardoned and which were to die. From Wumen, too, the Son of Heaven announced each year's new calendar (in China, where the science of astronomy originated and was always highly esteemed, even the designation of months and days of the year was the emperor's personal province). The gargantuan doors to the gate are festooned with wooden carvings and a set of lion's-head knockers.

Beyond the Meridian Gate is a courtyard, traversed by the Golden Water Stream (Jinshui He). Five marble bridges crossing the stream lead to the Gate of Supreme Harmony.

太和门

Gate of Supreme Harmony (Taihemen). Smaller than the Meridian, this gate is guarded by two striking, stylized bronze lions, symbolizing the power of the empire. Three sets of stairs (the central flight was used exclusively by the emperor) lead to three carved marble terraces, each supporting a main hall.

Beyond the gate is a huge courtyard, designed to accommodate 90,000 people during imperial ceremonies.

太和殿

Hall of Supreme Harmony (Taihedian). Built in 1420 and restored in 1697 during Emperor Kang Xi's reign, the hall is 35 m. (115 ft.) high, and covers an area of about 2,400 sq. m. (2,843 sq. yd.). It is the tallest and largest of the palace buildings, and was used by the emperor on state occasions.

The Hall of Supreme Harmony is filled with art treasures of symbolic significance. The 18 bronze incense burners represent the 18 provinces of imperial China. A nine-dragon screen behind the emperor's throne symbolizes both longevity and the unity of earth and heaven. At its base are the two elephants of peace. The gargoyles—half-tortoise, half-dragon—also signify longevity and immortality, while the grain measure and sundial denote imperial justice and righteousness. In imperial times, the huge gilded copper cauldrons always contained water in the event of a fire. The roof is supported by 20 columns; the central six are decorated with the Imperial Dragon. In this grand setting, with incense burning and sacred bells ringing, the emperor conducted important affairs of state, full of pomp and ceremony. In 1917 this same courtyard was the scene of a ceremony conducted jointly by Western and Chinese troops to celebrate the end of World War I.

中和殿

Hall of Perfect Harmony (Zhonghedian). Passing through the Hall of Supreme Harmony, one descends a flight of steps into one of the largest courtyards of the palace, which precedes the Hall of Perfect Harmony. Originally built in 1420, the hall was restored in 1627, and further renovated in 1690. Here the emperor donned formal regalia before entering the Hall of Supreme Harmony, and here he performed such ceremonies as examining seeds for the new planting, greeting foreigners, and delivering addresses to the imperial children (with several wives and several thousand concubines, they would often comprise a huge assemblage).

保和殿

Hall of Preserving Harmony (Baohedian). This hall was built in 1420, rebuilt in 1625, and repaired in 1765. In 1789, it became the site of the "Palace Examinations," the highest level of the nationwide imperial examination system—ostensibly the origin of all modern meritocracies. Successful candidates were awarded the title of *Jinshi* ("scholar"). Graduates of the system were appointed to high positions in government and administration throughout the empire, and their wealth and status were assured. Although

THE IMPERIAL PALACE

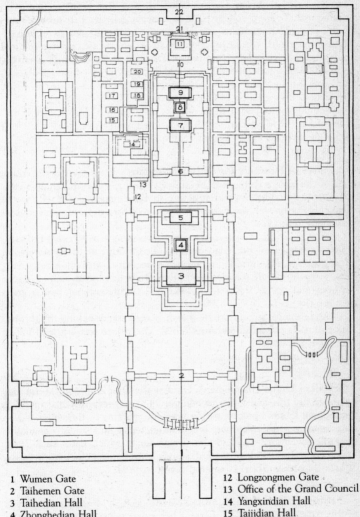

1 Wumen Gate
2 Taihemen Gate
3 Taihedian Hall
4 Zhonghedian Hall
5 Baohedian Hall
6 Qianqingmen Gate
7 Qianqinggong Palace
8 Jiaotaidian Hall
9 Kunninggong Palace
10 Imperial Gardens
11 Qingandian Hall
12 Longzongmen Gate
13 Office of the Grand Council
14 Yangxindian Hall
15 Taijidian Hall
16 Tiyuandian Hall
17 Changchungong Palace
18 Yikungong Palace
19 Chuxiugong Palace
20 Laijingchan
21 Shunzhenmen Gate
22 Shenwumen Gate

tainted by corruption, the system did provide a modicum of upward mobility in traditional Chinese society.

The original throne is surrounded by some fine bronzes. The hall's anterooms have been converted into museum galleries that display relics of the imperial households and gifts presented by foreign governments. Most of these gifts were never opened and remain encased in their original wrappings—as if to underscore imperial disdain for the barbarians' effrontery. There are also some 5,000-year-old embroideries and funerary objects, including a magnificent group of bronze charioteers, discovered in 1969. The famous Flying Horse of Gansu is exhibited in this section.

Behind this hall is the flight of steps known as the "dragon pavement," dating from the Ming Dynasty. It was carved from a single 200-ton block of marble quarried in the Beijing region.

乾清宫

Palace of Heavenly Purity (Qianqinggong). Visitors enter the courtyard of this palace through the Gate of Heavenly Purity (Qianqingmen), the longest-standing original structure in the compound. The Palace of Heavenly Purity itself was burned and restored three times after its original construction in 1420.

From the Ming (1368–1644) to the early Qing (1644–1911) Dynasty, emperors resided in this palace and handled routine affairs of state from these quarters. The surrounding terrace is decorated with gilt incense burners, a few miniature temples, and other symbolic objects such as bronze tortoises and cranes (longevity), a sundial (righteousness), and a grain measure (justice).

Inside the palace, an ornate dragon screen stands behind the throne. The ceiling is carved in stunning relief. The palace was last used for an "imperial" occasion in 1922, when the child emperor, Pu Yi, last of the Qing Dynasty line, was married.

交泰殿

Hall of Union (Jiaotaidian). Used by the Qing emperors for birthday celebrations, this hall was first built in 1420 and reconstructed in 1655. Traditional China's preoccupation with the marking of time bordered on an obsession. On display here is one of ancient China's most remarkable scientific inventions—a clepsydra (water clock) which dates back 2,500 years. On the west side of the hall stands a mechanical clock made by the Works Department of the Imperial Board in 1797.

坤宁宫

Palace of Earthly Tranquility (Kunninggong). Ming empresses lived in this palace, built in 1420. Later, Qing rulers used it as a place to offer sacrifices. An eastern side-room was used as a bridal chamber by the last Qing emperor.

东宫、西宫

East and West Palaces. To the east and west of these main halls stand a total of 12 palaces used as libraries, living quarters, and so on. Today they house exhibitions that include furniture, jewelry, and other household items. Usually only one or two rooms are open for inspection at any given time.

御花园

Imperial Gardens (Yuhuayuan). Beyond the palaces are the Imperial Gardens, which cover 7,000 sq. m. (8,400 sq. yd.) and were originally landscaped during the Ming Dynasty. The pines and cypresses are several hundred years old. On the grounds are statues, rock gardens, pebble walkways laid out in intricate designs, and an artificial hill (built in 1538) adorned with a cave, waterfall, and pavilion.

Before leaving the Imperial Palace grounds, visitors will be escorted to the boutique located near the rear entrance. Some of the finest reproductions made in China, as well as precious stones and artifacts, are sold here. Visitors leave the palace through the Chengguangmen—a simple portal guarded by two bronze elephants—and the Shunzhenmen. Beyond the massive Shenwumen (Gate of Divine Pride), buses wait for the return trip to the hotel.

THE IMPERIAL PALACE VICINITY

煤山或景山

Coal Hill (Mei Shan or Jing Shan). Coal Hill is situated directly opposite the exit gate of the Imperial Gardens. Now more commonly called Jing Shan (Prospect Hill), it is entirely artificial and was used by the emperors to bring a little of the countryside into the flat plain of Beijing. They stocked the area with hares and other small game. The park was built in the 13th century and covers 23 hectares (56.8 acres). Earth excavated in digging the moat around the Imperial Palace was used to create Coal Hill.

Closed "for renovations" during the Cultural Revolution, it was reopened to the public in March 1978. Sites in the park include five white pavilions, the Beautiful View Tower (Qiwanglou), and the Pavilion of Everlasting Springs (Wanchunting). A breathtaking view of the Imperial Palace and the full expanse of the capital can be gained from the summit.

北海公园

Beihai (North Lake) Park. Closed during the Cultural Revolution "for renovations" until March 1978, this park, named for one of the three imperial lakes on its grounds, is the loveliest in Beijing. Its beauty is subtle and can best be appreciated on a weekday when the park tends to be less crowded. The Bridge of Perfect Wisdom (Zhichu Qiao), one of the park's famous landmarks, links Qionghua Island on North Lake to the southeast shore. On this island stands the prominent Tibetan-style White Dagoba (Baita), built in 1651 to commemorate the visit of a Dalai Lama. Damaged by the 1976 earthquake, it has since been reinforced. Covered corridors, pavilions, and terraces in the park have all been repainted. Views from the Dagoba include: to the north, the lake, with the Ministry of Defense building to the left, a portion of the original Beijing University campus to the right, and in the distance the Bell Tower and the Drum Tower; to the south, the magnificent panorama of the Gugong and, beyond that, the high-rise apartment buildings that trace the line of Beijing's former wall. Also restored to its original splendor is the famous Nine-Dragon Wall (Jiulongbi), a screen 5 m. (16.4 ft.) high and 27 m. (88.6 ft.) wide with nine dragons formed of variegated glazed bricks on each side.

The park itself is said to date back to AD 300. A pleasure palace was built on this site under the Liao Dynasty, a thousand years ago. The lake was created during the 12th-century Jin Dynasty and deepened in 1951. It was in Beihai in 1260 that the Yuan emperor Kublai Khan established his palace—a place immortalized in Coleridge's poem "Kubla Khan." Today it is the best preserved ancient garden in China.

Beihai Park is now arguably Beijing's most popular spot for recreation and, increasingly, romance. Rowing on Beihai Lake is a favorite activity of Beijing's youth, and in the evenings, young couples dot the wooden benches on the lakeside and throughout the park. On summer evenings, impromptu dancing, to music provided by cassette tape recorders, sometimes takes place as well.

中南海

Zhongnanhai. Zhongnanhai is the combined name for "middle sea" and "southern sea," two lakes which flank the Imperial Palace to the west. Before his death in 1976, Mao Zedong lived and worked here, and his home is sometimes opened for viewing by Chinese visitors on special occasions. Zhongnanhai still serves as home for some of China's highest leaders and as headquarters of the Central Committee of the CCP, so it is not normally accessible to tourists. Beginning in 1981, however, a few specially invited guests, usually foreign government officials, were being received by Chinese government leaders in Zhongnanhai. Gates punctuate the north, west, and south walls of the compound. The main south gate is on Chang'an Avenue, about half a mile west of Tian'anmen Square. A flagpole and two armed guards mark the entrance.

天安门广场
TIAN'ANMEN SQUARE

Just as the Forbidden City represents the insular nature of China's imperial past, Tian'anmen, the Gate of Heavenly Peace, symbolically declares China's openness to the world and to the future. The square in front of Tian'anmen is the largest public square in the world. Originally built in 1651, the square was quadrupled in size in 1958 to its present 40.5 hectares (100 acres) during a massive citywide reconstruction program. Each flagstone is numbered so that parade units can line up in their assigned places. Ceremonial gatherings of a million or more people in the square are not uncommon, the latest one occurring on October 1, 1984, marking the PRC's 35th anniversary.

Great Hall of the People, Tian'anmen Square

Several important monuments and buildings are situated around the square's perimeter. These are described below.

天安门

Gate of Heavenly Peace (Tian'anmen). This massive stone gate with its wooden roof was built in 1417 and restored in 1651. A stream spanned by five sculptured white marble bridges flows at the foot of the gate. The central portal is dominated by an immense portrait of Mao Zedong. On top is a rostrum where, on special occasions, China's leaders present themselves to the people. Inscribed on plaques on each side of the portal are two slogans: on the left, "Long Live the Unity of the Peoples of the World!" The grandstands below, with a capacity of 20,000, are used by official guests reviewing parades or participating in celebrations.

人民英雄纪念碑

Monument to the People's Heroes. In the center of the square is an obelisk 36 m. (118 ft.) high, a tribute to heroes of the Chinese Revolution. The cornerstone was laid by Mao Zedong and the structure was completed on May 1, 1958. A bas-relief depicts key episodes in the revolution (the sequence begins on the east side). The obelisk carries two inscriptions. One, in Mao's calligraphy, states, "The People's Heroes Are Immortal." A second, longer text is one of the rare public examples of Zhou Enlai's calligraphy.

毛主席纪念堂

Mao Zedong Memorial Hall. Few men in world history have had the impact of Mao Zedong. His stature as an international figure and as the preeminent leader of the People's Republic of China is symbolized by the Memorial Hall. Facing the Gate of Heavenly Peace, behind the Monument to the People's Heroes, it occupies the most prominent location in the square.

The cornerstone for the Memorial Hall was laid on November 24, 1976, by Mao's immediate successor as Communist Party Chairman, Hua Guofeng. The 30.5-m. (100-ft.)-high building was inaugurated on September 9, 1977, the first anniversary of Chairman Mao's death.

Its flat, low-tiered roof with golden-yellow glazed tile cornices is supported by 44 granite pillars. In the entrance hall is a white marble statue of Mao Zedong seated; a magnificent Chinese landscape in subdued colors, painted by the renowned artist Huang Yongyu, furnishes a backdrop. Inside the mausoleum itself, Mao's body may be viewed lying in a crystal sarcophagus, draped with the red flag of the Communist Party of China.

The Hall is now open to all residents with an identification card or to individual foreign visitors with a letter of introduction from their host organization. Tour groups who wish to visit the hall may do so through prior notification to CITS. Chinese are admitted between 7–11 AM on Tuesdays, Thursdays, and Saturdays. Foreigners are admitted between 8 AM–12 PM on Mondays, Wednesdays, and Fridays. Decorous attire is encouraged (e.g., no shorts, jeans, sneakers, or bright colors). Photographs are prohibited inside and visitors are expected to maintain a respectful silence while in the building. The experience, no matter what one's political views, promises to be both moving and memorable.

前门

Front Gate (Qianmen). The gate, recently refurbished to better complement the Mao Zedong Memorial Hall, was originally built in the 15th century by the Ming emperor Yong Le. Each year, during the winter solstice, the emperor exited through Qianmen on his way to pray at the Temple of Heaven.

人民大会堂

Great Hall of the People. On the western side of the square is the Great Hall of the People, referred to in some older guides as the National People's Congress Building.

The Great Hall extends 310 m. (1,017 ft.) from north to south and contains a 100-m. (328-ft.)-long marble hall. It was completed within the space of just ten months during 1958–59 by mobilizing cadres, professionals, students, and workers to participate in its construction. Its main assembly room can accommodate 10,000 people. On the occasion of Richard Nixon's visit to China in 1972, 5,000 guests dined in one of its giant-size banquet halls. The structure also contains reception rooms—named after each of China's 27 provinces—where high-ranking leaders conduct interviews with foreigners.

中国历史博物馆、中国革命博物馆

Museum of Chinese History and Museum of the Chinese Revolution. Two large buildings dominate the eastern side of Tian'anmen Square. These are the Museum of Chinese History (covering the period up to 1919) and the Museum of the Chinese Revolution (covering the post-1919 period). The Museum of the Chinese Revolution closed its doors completely in 1966 for a period of 12 years. When it reopened in 1978, a pictorial exhibition on the life of Zhou Enlai became a major attraction for Beijing residents and visitors. On October 1, 1979, the museum's permanent exhibition—a retrospective of the founding and development of the Chinese Communist Party—went on display.

The Museum of Chinese History began welcoming viewers to its revised exhibits in October 1976. Here the development of China from the dawn of civilization until the 20th century is portrayed within a Marxist framework. Accordingly, the evolution of man and society is broken down into the primitive (communal), slave, feudal, capitalist, and socialist epochs.

Two retail shops on the premises sell unusual gift items and paintings, many of them contemporary. An excellent museum guidebook with explanatory notes is available here.

中山公园

Zhongshan Park. This park flanks the western side of the Imperial Palace. Its lovely gardens contain an amphitheater, covered wooden walkways, well-manicured lawns and shrubs, and a teahouse beside a pond. First laid out in 1421 for the imperial household, today this park affords a quiet place in the downtown area to relax from the rigors of sightseeing. It is open daily from 8 AM to 9 PM.

劳动人民文化宫

People's Cultural Park. Located to the east of Tian'anmen Gate, People's Cultural Park contains many trees, rock gardens, and ponds. Its pavilion features an orange tile roof and some very well carved gargoyles. Millions of Chinese came here in January 1976 to view the ashes of Zhou Enlai and pay respects to the former premier. Memorial meetings for deceased leading figures are customarily held in this park.

Movies and cultural performances are held here on weekends and holidays. There is boating in summer and skating in winter on the moat of the Imperial Palace at the northern end of the park. It is open daily from 8 AM to 9 PM, admission 5 *fen*.

民族文化宫

Nationalities Cultural Palace. Less than a mile and a half west of Tian'anmen stands a large, mosaic-tiled rectangular structure with a 13-story tower. It is trimmed in green and topped by a turquoise roof. This is the Nationalities Cultural Palace, dedicated to the cultural contributions of China's 55 minority peoples. Completed in 1959, it contains four sections: a cultural center, a theater, a library, and a museum with 18 exhibition halls. In 1979, a restaurant and dance hall opened here. In 1980, one floor of the Cultural Palace was converted into hotel rooms as Beijing struggled to keep up with the influx of tourists. A highly recommended gift shop on the second floor of the main building offers some dazzling costumes and ornamental items produced in minority areas.

China's national minorities are accorded an important status by the

PRC government. While the Han (Chinese) people make up 94% of China's population, the remaining 6% of minority peoples inhabit nearly 60% of China's territory, giving them political significance well beyond their numbers.

北京动物园

Beijing Zoo. The zoo is a 15-minute ride by car from Tian'anmen. In the Ming Dynasty, it was the site of an imperial park. A zoological garden was established here during the Qing Dynasty, but by 1949 only a dozen or so animals remained. Today, following expansion, the Beijing Zoo boasts more than 2,000 animals of 300 species. Some of the more prized are giraffes, lions, polar bears, roe deer, and gibbon apes. Another major highlight is the zoo's superb outdoor bird sanctuary. One of the two musk oxen given to China by President Nixon (in exchange for the two pandas now in the Washington Zoo) is still alive here. China's most celebrated native animal—the giant panda, native to Sichuan Province—is represented in the Beijing Zoo. The lesser panda, a smaller, rust-colored species, tends to be overshadowed by its more glamorous cousin.

A map of the zoo is sold at concession stands on the grounds. The large domed building across the street is the Beijing Planetarium. Entrance fees to both the zoo and the planetarium are 10 *fen*.

白塔寺

Dagoba Temple. This temple is southeast of the zoo, off Fuchengmennei Dajie. Not much is left of this Yuan Dynasty site except for the pagoda and a few other structures. It is interesting because it is a prime example of the Nepalese-style architecture made popular by Kublai Khan's court architect, who designed a number of temples in the city.

北京大学

Beijing University. Since Beijing is also a center of education, tours are likely to include one of the city's renowned universities. Beijing University ("Beida") was founded in 1898 near Coal Hill in the downtown area. Many of its students took part in the May 4th Movement of 1919 and organized numerous activities to resist the Japanese occupation of the 1930s and to support the revolution which succeeded in 1949. In 1952, Beida merged with Yanjing University, a private institution with strong American connections, and in 1953 Beida moved to the more spacious Yanjing campus, its present location in northwest Beijing between the zoo and the Summer Palace. The university may be reached in a half-hour's drive from Tian'anmen.

It was at Beida that the debates which gave rise to the Cultural Revolution in 1966 began. During that period, many of the most noted professors, under attack by Red Guards, publicly confessed their guilt for putting academic pursuits ahead of revolutionary ideals. By 1977, however, most were restored to their former posts and their research and academic achievements were receiving vocal support from the highest echelons of China's new leadership. In 1978, Beida's 3,000 students were augmented by several thousand more who had taken the first nationwide university entrance examinations held in China since 1966. By 1984, more than 10,000 undergraduates and hundreds of graduate students had been enrolled after passing the stiff entrance examinations. That number was expected to double by the end of the decade. The foreign students' dormitory, Shao Yuan Lou, occasionally rents rooms or dormitory space to visitors on a daily basis (see "Budget Hotels" below).

中国国家图书馆

National Library. China's new National Library, located near the Friendship Hotel, opened in October 1987. This structure, the second largest library in the world, houses 14 million books and pamphlets. Its 7,000–8,000 reader capacity is four times the amount handled in the old quarters near Beihai Park. The National Library has contacts with libraries in 114 countries.

雍和宫

Yonghe Gong (Palace Temple). Located in northeast Beijing, the Yonghe Gong has become one of the city's most active Buddhist temples. Built as a palace in 1694, the structure was rededicated as a Buddhist temple in 1723 and was given over to Lamaist practitioners in 1744. The complex consists of a consecutive chain of five halls, the last of which houses a spectacular 18-m. (59-ft.) Maitreya Buddha carved from a single sandlewood tree.

The Yonghe Gong can also be reached via public buses #13, 44, and 116 (the latter being the most direct).

首都图书馆

Capital Library. Located on a side street adjacent to the Yonghe Gong, the library is located in an ancient complex that once comprised the Guozijian, established in 1306 as the highest academy of learning in imperial China. Next to the library is a Confucian temple. The stone stelae in the temple courtyard list the names of candidates who successfully passed the imperial examinations.

牛街清真寺

Niu Jie Muslim Temple. A few minutes' walk south of the Yanjing Hotel, the Niu Jie was built in 996 and remains as Beijing's oldest and largest mosque. The Niu Jie is set in the midst of the capital's largest Muslim community, most of whom are members of the Hui minority. As an active center for prayer and religious activities, the mosque maintains a solemn atmosphere and does not always welcome casual visitors. Its interior is worth noting for its unusual mixture of Chinese and Arabic motifs.

法源寺

Fayuan Si. Located near the Niu Jie mosque, the Fayuan temple is a Tang Dynasty legacy that was completed in 696. The large complex includes an impressive collection of Buddhist antiquities, among them some of the rarest religious treasures in China. Its library contains 120,000 rare volumes. The temple also houses the Beijing Buddhist Academy and serves as publishing center for the Chinese Buddhist Association.

白云观

Baiyun Guan. Beijing's largest and only extant Daoist temple, the Baiyun was built during the 8th century (713–741). The complex includes six major halls and is worth visiting in sequence with the Yonghe Gong or Fayuan Si to note the contrast between Daoist and Buddhist symbolism and ornamentation. The Baiyun is located just south of the Yanjing Hotel.

潭柘寺

Tanzhe Si. First built during the Jin Dynasty (265–316), Tanzhe Si is Beijing's oldest temple, situated about two hours west of the city. Built on the side of a hill, it follows the contours of the hill, so the experience is like climbing a hill and visiting a temple at the same time. The temple is set out on a large site. An interesting pavilion off to the side has a small channel for water set into the floor. In old times, a rivulet of spring water was used to float wine cups on leaves and carry them down to fellow imbibers sitting along the winding path that the channel creates. There is a small lake behind the temple.

戒台寺

Jietai Si. On the way to Tanzhe Si, Jietai Si was built in 622 and remains as one of only three initiation platforms left in China. Also built on a hill, the temple runs sideways, but the main gate still faces south as required by Buddhist tradition. The 10-ft.-high platform is in the northwestern part of the temple. There is also a Mahavira Hall, with a Thousand Buddha Hall behind it. Throughout the temple grounds (up the hill) are a number of small Liao and Yuan dynasty pagodas.

北京古观象台

Guguanxiangtai Observatory. Originally built in the Ming Dynasty, the observatory has recently been restored to its original state. This massive grey stone structure sits astride a modern highway overpass on Jianguomennei Dajie (about midway between the Beijing Hotel and the Friendship Store). A collection of ancient astronomical instruments—many from the period when China led the world in astronomy and related sciences—are arrayed on the structure's rooftop.

卢沟桥

Marco Polo Bridge (Lugouqiao). The bridge, named "Reedy Moat Bridge" in Chinese, is located southwest of Beijing. When Marco Polo visited here in 1290, he described the bridge in such effusive terms that it has since been nicknamed the Marco Polo Bridge. The original bridge was washed away by a flood in 1698, but a faithful replica was built in its place. The white marble bridge is 235 m. (770 ft.) long, supported by 11 arches. When it was widened in 1969, the original balustrades, adorned with miniature stone lions, were retained.

The bridge was the site of the 1937 attack which preceded the Japanese occupation of Beijing.

天坛
TEMPLE OF HEAVEN

L ocated in the southeastern section of Beijing, the Temple of Heaven (Tiantan) is a masterpiece of 15th-century architecture, built according to the most advanced principles of mechanics and geometry available at the time. Inside the gates are three main structures: to the north is the Hall of Prayer for Good Harvests; in the center is the Imperial Vault of Heaven; to the south is the Circular Mound Altar of Heaven. The whole complex is set within an extensive park enclosed by walls. Auxiliary buildings in the park today house a barracks, a radio station, and an open-air theater.

Each year in old China, on the day before winter solstice, the Son of Heaven emerged from the Forbidden City through Qianmen (Front Gate). His procession moved through Beijing's hushed streets with great ceremony. Commoners (and foreigners) remained hidden behind shuttered windows, careful to maintain utter silence.

After the emperor arrived at the Temple of Heaven, he would first meditate in the Imperial Vault and then make his way to the Hall of Prayer for Good Harvests. On the morning of the solstice, he would return to the Imperial Vault and then proceed to the Mound Altar to pray for good harvests and perform sacrificial rituals amid burning incense and tinkling bells. This ceremony was last performed in 1913 by the warlord and would-be emperor Yuan Shikai.

The Hall of Prayer for Good Harvests (Qiniandian) is set on a triple-tiered round marble terrace, each tier surrounded by a balustrade 11 m. (36 ft.) high. The temple is surmounted by a cone-shaped roof made of 50,000 brilliant blue-glazed tiles (representing the sky), culminating in a gilded sphere. Not a single nail was used in the construction. The interlaced wooden frame is supported by 28 columns hewn from trees brought from Yunnan. Four immense support pillars in the interior are painted with fanciful designs. The roof, remarkably, is supported only by an articulated skeleton, without any ceiling joists.

The Imperial Vault of Heaven is a simpler version of the Hall of Prayer. Its main feature is the circular echo wall surrounding the hall's outer courtyard. Two people standing at opposite points along the wall can hear one another speak without raising their voices. The three large stones that pave the central stairway leading up to the main temple, known as the Three Echo Stones, display further acoustic oddities. A single shout or handclap at the first stone produces a single echo; a double echo is produced on the second stone; and on the third, three echoes. (The effect is due to the distances of the stones from the walls, producing measured variations in the sound reverberation.)

Finally, there is the Circular Mound Altar, consisting of three marble terraces symbolizing earth, the mortal world, and heaven.

Numerologists will be interested in certain patterns revealed in the temple's architecture. The four main pillars supporting the Hall of Prayer represent the four seasons, and the 12 interior posts the months of the year. In ancient days, the Chinese divided the day into 12 two-hour periods, represented here by the outer ring composed of 12 pillars. The imperial number, nine, signifying heaven, recurs in the design of the Mound Altar. The flagstones on the upper terrace are arranged in concentric circles in multiples of nine; i.e., the first circle has nine stones, the second 18, and so on to a total of 243 in the 27th and outermost ring.

The main hall was built in 1420, first restored in 1751, and then again in 1889 following a fire. After 1949, scientists analyzed the paint pigments and wooden structure in order to recreate its original splendor as exactly as possible.

The altar was built in 1539 and enlarged in 1749. Renovations costing the equivalent of $353,000 were completed in 1978. These included the addition of three pavilions and the transfer of a long, covered corridor originally situated in a government compound.

颐和园
THE SUMMER PALACE

The Summer Palace (*Yiheyuan*) lies 11.2 km. (7 mi.) northwest of Tian'anmen Square in Beijing's Haidian district. The palace grounds occupy a vast park (one of four protected by the state) of 280 hectares (692 acres.) The grounds are demarcated by Longevity Hill to the north and Kunming Lake to the south. The lake, which is used for swimming and boating in the summer and skating in the winter, occupies three-quarters of the total park area.

There actually were two "summer palaces"—so named because they served as the summer residences of the imperial households. The original Yuanming Yuan palace was built by the Jurchen Tatars in the 12th century near the present site of Qinghua University. The entire complex was looted and burned to the ground in 1860 by British and French troops as a pressure tactic to make the imperial court "see reason." The most precious objects were sent abroad to Queen Victoria and Napoleon III. A marble arch, several fractured pillars, and a wall, strewn across an isolated patch of land surrounded by agricultural communes, are all that remain of this legendary suburban palace which is reputed to have surpassed even today's Summer Palace in splendor.

The extant Summer Palace was constructed in 1888 by the erratic and Machiavellian Empress Dowager Ci Xi, using funds originally intended for the imperial navy. (This palace was also destroyed by Western troops during the Boxer Rebellion of 1900 but was restored in 1903.) Ironically, the empress used part of the funds to erect an extravagant marble boat that sits on the edge of the palace's Kunming Lake. Ci Xi was also responsible for the beautiful Painted Gallery, a wooden walkway decorated with exquisite landscapes that girds the north shore of the lake. Unfortunately, when it was "retouched" in 1979, much of the subtle detail of the original paintings was lost.

After entering the walled grounds through a red gate, the visitor passes a number of buildings, each with its own lyrical name: the East Palace Gate (Donggongmen), guarded by a splendid bronze lion; the Hall of Benevolence and Longevity (Renshoudian); the Garden of Virtuous Harmony (Deheyuan); the Hall of Happiness and Longevity (Leshantang); and the Hall of Jade Billows (Yulantang). Some have been open to the public only since 1979. Formerly used as elegant apartments for members of the royal family, these buildings still contain the original jewel-encrusted furniture and precious art objects.

Longevity Hill is the focal point of the Summer Palace. The panoramic view from the summit is well worth the climb. From here the visitor gazes out at the 17-Arch Bridge, the Jade Belt Bridge, and a lovely stone pagoda perched on a distant hill. The glazed golden tiles of the palace roofs, shimmering in the sunlight, have inspired countless Chinese paintings.

Atop Longevity Hill, overlooking Kunming Lake, is the Listening to the Orioles Pavilion Restaurant (see "Beijing Cuisine" below). Throngs of Chinese spend their Sundays boating along the lake and its channels and picnicking along its shores. On National Day (October 1) and May Day (May 1) the park is festively decorated. A number of shops that sell paintings, craft items, books, and magazines operate throughout the grounds of the Summer Palace. The best shops, located within the compound which houses the Listening to the Orioles Restaurant, these days feature items such as hand-painted T-shirts. A small villa, operated by Club Med, opened on Nanhu Island in 1986.

长城
THE GREAT WALL

Rising and falling in concert with the ridges of the northern hills and undulating far off into the distance, the Great Wall consistently exceeds visitors' expectations. The only man-made object visible from satellites in orbit, the wall remains one of man's most remarkable accomplishments. The amount of brick and stone employed to construct the Great Wall could circumscribe the earth with a dike eight feet high.

The wall's construction began during the Warring States Period (403–221 BC), when separate sections were built in scattered strategic areas. Following China's unification under the first Qin emperor, Qin Shi Huangdi (221–206 BC), 300,000 men—many of them political prisoners whose bodies are buried in the wall—were put to work connecting the segments into one huge rampart of stone and earth.

From the 6th to the 14th centuries, the wall ceased to be an effective

barrier against determined invaders, who discovered that bribing the sentries was their most effective weapon. The Ming emperors tried to make it an effective fortification again by reinforcing it with cement and stone.

Scholars estimate that the Great Wall with all its branches once stretched for 10,000 km. (6,200 mi.), from the Yalu River in the northeast to Xinjiang in the northwest, passing through an expanse now covered by 16 Chinese provinces. Today it measures 6,000 km. (3,750 mi.), from the Shanhaiguan Pass near the Bohai Sea to the Jiayuguan Pass in the Gobi Desert.

The section at Badaling, 75 km. (46.8 mi.) northwest of Beijing, which is ritually visited by virtually all tourists to the capital and by vacationing Chinese, dates from the Ming Dynasty (1368–1644). It is broad enough to accommodate five cavalrymen or 10 infantrymen marching abreast. The average height is 6.6 m. (21.5 ft.); width is 6.5 m. (21.3 ft.) at the base and 5.5 m. (18 ft.) at the top. Watchtowers, built at regular intervals, were used as beacon towers.

The Great Wall has suffered serious damage from wind and water erosion, as well as man-made destruction. Between 1970 and 1974, an army unit stationed at Gubeikou destroyed some 3,000 m. (9,840 ft.) of the wall and used the stones to construct barracks. Local peasants and miners followed the army unit's example. In 1979, a special commission was established to preserve this national monument. One of its first decisions was to arrange for the reconstruction of the section at Gubeikou—by the very army unit that had destroyed it. Opened in 1985, this section of the Great Wall is in a remote area northeast of Beijing.

Less crowded than Badaling, the area can be reached by train via Huairou, long-distance bus or even by taxi. Continuing incidents of vandalism are prominently reported in the Chinese press, with due opprobrium heaped upon the culprits. A restoration committee has begun a public campaign to raise funds to rebuild more of the Great Wall. Begun in mid-1984, the campaign is being conducted by Badaling and five Beijing newspapers. So far, a 500-meter section at Badaling has been fully restored, with work on nearby sections in the course of early 1987. Their slogan is "Love our Motherland and rebuild the Great Wall."

Special trains, as well as excursion buses and cars, connect Beijing and the Great Wall. Approximately two hours are required each way. The route traverses agricultural communes, market towns, and extensive rock quarries, finally reaching the wall at the rock-strewn foothills of the Yanshan Mountains, which once marked China's northern frontier.

Standing atop the Great Wall at Badaling, the visitor looking through slots and over parapets can imagine the terrible battles which were fought here hundreds of years ago.

It is customary for tourist groups to break up the return from the day's outing with a lunch stop and visit to the Ming Tombs.

Helicopter tours of the Great Wall and the Ming Tombs, begun on a trial basis in March 1985, are now being offered to foreign tourists as part of a packaged excursion to the Great Wall and the Ming Tombs. Departing every morning from the Lido Hotel, passengers are transported to Sha He Airport in the northern suburbs, where they board a helicopter for the hour-long flyover. After getting a bird's eye view of the Wall, groups debark at the Ming Tombs for a quick tour of the Sacred Way. They are then driven to the Great Wall and returned to the Lido before 2 PM. The cost for the half-day excursion is Y150 per person. For information and reservations, contact the CTS Helicopter Desk in the lobby of the Lido Hotel (tel: 500-6688, ext. 3388).

慕田峪长城

Mutianyu Great Wall. This newly restored section of the wall was reopened in April 1986. Mutianyu was itself an important fort built to defend the border against northern raiders. It is located in Huairou County, 79 km. northeast of Beijing; its name derives from the nearby village of Mutianyu. This segment of the wall is 2,500 m. long and is studded with 22 watchtowers. The towers are believed to have been designed by Qi Jiguang, a Ming general who led many victorious battles in southeast China. The architectural style—particularly the shape of the lookout openings at the top of the towers—was contrived to resemble a traditional fence design of that region.

The area is heavily forested and blessed with many natural springs. The wall itself is built directly onto the mountain slopes, and its inclines are steeper than those of the Great Wall at Badaling. At its sharpest gradient, the wall runs to a height of more than 1,000 m. It is reached by a climb of 1,200 steps, conveniently laid out with frequent rest stops. The view from the top is nothing less than spectacular.

Mutianyu at this point in time has yet to be heavily commercialized in the manner of Badaling. One actually has the feeling of viewing the wall in its natural setting, without being pressed by crowds and hawkers at every step.

Mutianyu is, however, less accessible than Badaling. For most foreign tourists, the easiest approach is to hire a car for the day. For the more intrepid traveler, and for those on a budget, there is bus service from Beijing, mainly intended for Chinese tourists. Tickets must be purchased one day in advance at the ticket office of Dongzhimen Long Distance Bus Line. Buses depart daily at 7:10 AM and return at 4 PM. A stop at Yansai Lake is also included. The cost is Y4.

A restaurant serving both Chinese and Western food has been opened at Mutianyu, although many visitors prefer to bring a picnic lunch. A cableway is being planned in cooperation with Hong Kong company.

十三陵
THE MING TOMBS

Maintaining an imperial tradition that originated in the Zhou Dynasty (c. 1066–221 BC), the Ming emperors selected the location and design of their tombs while they were still alive. The selection of sites, based on the prevailing winds and the water level, ensured that only benevolent spirits were inhabiting the area. Of the 16 Ming emperors, 13 chose to be buried in this serene valley (*Shisanling*) just north of Beijing.

神道
The Sacred Way. The road to the tombs, which branches off the route to the Great Wall, was once a 6.4-km. (4-mi.)-long sacred way, forbidden to all but the emperor's funeral cortège. The road begins at a five-arched

marble gate, built in 1540. A mile further down stands a three-arched gateway, the Dahongmen (Great Red Gate).

The emperor's body was carried through the central archway. Only on this one occasion was the center door opened. Just beyond the gate sits a huge stone tortoise (symbol of longevity) with a 9.1-m. (30-ft.) stele mounted on its back. The stele, the largest such tablet in China, was inscribed by the fourth Ming emperor at the time of the death of his predecessor, Yong Le, in 1424. This tortoise marks the beginning of the famous Avenue of the Animals. Lions, camels, elephants, horses, and two sets of mythical (or at least unrecognizable) beasts, 12 statues in all, line either side of the road, alternately standing and kneeling. Iron fences now ward off tourists.

Beyond the animal figures stretches a series of 12 stone human statues, dating from the 15th century: four military men, four civilian officials, and four obedient retainers, all with stately postures and fixed stares—an honor guard for the dead emperor. A legend says that an emperor of the later Qing Dynasty wanted to transport the statues to line the road to his own tomb. One of the emperor's ministers was told, in a dream, that the statues were eternally loyal to the Ming emperors and therefore should not be moved. The Qing emperor took this as a warning that if the statues were disturbed, a wind of death would blow down from the Ming Tombs upon the capital, and he abandoned the project.

长陵

Chang Ling. Of the 13 tombs, only two have been excavated, those of Chang (the burial name for Yong Le, 1403–24), and Ding (Emperor Wan Li, 1562–1620). The Chang Ling tomb is the largest and best preserved of the tombs; it served as a model for the remaining 12.

Visitors enter through a red gate which opens onto a courtyard. From here they pass under the Gate of Eminent Favors (Lingenmen) into a second courtyard, in which stands the marble Hall of Eminent Favors (Lingendian), surrounded by pine trees (another ancient symbol of longevity). The roof of the hall is supported by 32 giant tree columns. Beyond this hall is a third courtyard, where the visitor will see a simple stele with the inscription *Da Ming*—Great Ming. This marks the passage to the sepulcher.

定陵

Ding Ling. Also known as the Underground Palace, this is the first imperial tomb to have been excavated in China. The work was completed over a period of three years (1956–59). Ding (Emperor Wan Li) was buried here in 1620 with two of his wives in a deep marble vault located four stories underground (on the hottest of summer days the vault remains mercifully cool). The entrance to the grounds is marked by a large red gate with a magnificent bronze lion. Gigantic marble doors stand at the entrance to the first of the three burial chambers. (After burial, a "locking stone," similar to the modern "police" lock, was rolled in front of the tomb itself.) Inside are three coffins. Twenty-six chests of jewelry and other artifacts were discovered at the foot of the coffins, and many of these finds can be viewed in the two exhibition halls constructed aboveground.

The vast, tree-shaded grounds surrounding the tomb are dotted with stone picnic tables and seats. Tour groups are usually served a lunch at "Ding Ling's Restaurant" (not, you may assume, named by Ding Ling) within the underground complex.

乾隆墓（裕陵）

Emperor Qian Long's Tomb. In 1978, the tomb of the Qing emperor Qian Long (1736–96), located about 100 km. (62.5 mi.) east of Beijing, was opened to the public.

Known as Yu Ling, the tomb is on a grander scale and of higher artistic quality than most imperial tombs. Construction began in 1743 and cost 90 tons of silver. The wood used was the durable, fragrant, close-grained *nanmu*. Some logs weighed up to 20 tons.

The tomb is, in effect, an underground palace, similar to the tomb of Ding Ling. Nevertheless, Yu Ling has distinctive architectural features. Flanking the roadway leading to the tomb are eight pairs of stone sculptures depicting civil officials, military officers, horses, *qilin* (a mythical animal of good omen), elephants, camels, *suanni* (mythical monsters), and lions. Each figure was carved from a single stone block. The largest weighs about 43 tons.

The underground palace contains three stone halls and four pairs of stone gates, all arched. The overhanging eaves, tile gutters, ridges, and animal-shaped ornaments on the gate corners are in white marble. Each

gate weighs about two tons and contains a Bodhisattva, each with a different mien. The inner walls and arched ceilings of the gateways and halls are decorated with four celestial guardians (also called Deva kings), seated statues of gods and Buddhas, carvings of potted flowers, and small three-legged tables to hold incense burners and Buddhist scriptures.

The coffin of Qian Long lies in the innermost recess of the underground palace. It was placed over a well that never runs dry.

TOURING BEIJING

WITHOUT AN ESCORT

Most guided tours of Beijing will show you the city's main sights through the sealed windows of a bus. But much of the city's charm lies hidden in quiet neighborhoods and narrow back alleys where tour buses do not go. To increase your enjoyment of Beijing, you might want to familiarize yourself with a few of the main landmarks and, referring to the city map, go out exploring on your own.

Taxis. The quickest way to cover Beijing's great distances is by taxi. Rates are based on distances traveled (as registered on the car's odometer or by electronic meters now being installed), plus waiting time. The per-km. rate varies from 50 to 80 *fen*, depending on the size and model of the taxi (a dubious policy since passengers rarely have a choice—and must settle for whatever car is offered). Rates remain quite reasonable; the minimum fare is roughly Y2. Taxi stands at the large hotels offer the best bet of getting a cab, since they now control the lion's share of the city's taxis. Nevertheless, a shortage of both cars and trained drivers can still cause waits of 15–30 minutes for cabs. It's thus best to call ahead and book a taxi well in advance of when it's needed. The major fleet serving foreigners is the Shoudu (Capital) Taxi Company; the line for its English-speaking dispatchers is 55-7461 (see Directory at the end of the Beijing section for a list of major taxi stations and their telephone numbers). Restaurants catering to foreigners can call a taxi for you, but for other kinds of outings it is better to arrange for your driver to bring you to your destination and wait for you (at a minimal charge) rather than trying to call after your visit is over. In 1984, Beijing taxis began to sport roof markers and special red license plates (until then, taxis were indistinguishable from other cars in the city). Beginning in 1985, taxis could be hailed along major thorough-fares.

Rental Cars. If you wish to hire a car and driver for the entire day, the simplest approach is to call CITS at 512-1122. Chauffeured buses or minibuses can also be hired by calling 86-3661.

The Beijing Hired Cars Company has a fleet of various sizes and descriptions, including trucks and motorized tricycles. Its 35 stations throughout the city provide 24-hour service. The company also runs tour buses that depart daily from Qianmen Station going in four different directions: (1) to the Great Wall at Badaling, the Ming Tombs, and back to Qianmen; (2) to the Temple of the Sleeping Buddha, Xiang Shan (Fragrant Hills), the Summer Palace, and back to Qianmen; (3) to Xi Shan (Western Hills), the Temple of the Sleeping Buddha, Xiang Shan, and back to Qianmen; and (4) to the Qing Dynasty Eastern Tombs and back to Qianmen.

Public Transportation. Public transportation in Beijing consists of buses, trolley cars, and the subway. The subway starts at the railroad station in the east and runs under Qianmen out to the steel mills in the far west of the city and north to Xizhimen (near the zoo). The cost is 20 *fen*. The subway is used chiefly by commuters during rush hours. More useful to those touring the city are the 58 bus and trolley routes within Beijing, supplemented by 68 bus lines out to the suburbs and beyond. Buses are jammed during rush hours and holidays, but if you can get a seat—the

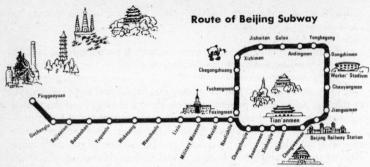

Route of Beijing Subway

Reprinted from *China Reconstructs* (December 1981)

Sketch Map by Liao Zengbao

practice seems to be on the decline, but some Chinese still make a point of giving up their seats as a courtesy to foreigners (and to children)—the view of Beijing from the bus window shows the city much as the Chinese themselves see it day-to-day. Fares run from 20 to 30 *fen*, depending on how far you go. City maps show bus routes, and the staff at the front desk of your hotel will help you figure out an appropriate route. The city's new "minibus" system, introduced in 1984, offers a happy medium between taxis and buses (see "On Your Own in Beijing," above).

New long-distance telephone center, Chang'an Boulevard East

Bicycles. There is no better way to explore the city at your own pace than by bicycle. A letter of introduction from CITS sometimes is required to rent a bicycle at the Jianguomenwai Bicycle Repair Shop, located around the corner from the Friendship Store, although cash deposits, passports, and driver's licenses are now generally accepted as collateral. The charge for renting a bicycle for a full day is roughly Y1. The shop is open from 6 AM to 6 PM.

Beijing has the largest bike population of any city in the world—nearly three million. With so many bikes, the problem is not necessarily traffic, but parking. You cannot leave your bicycle wherever you choose, but must park it with an attendant in a designated parking area. The attendant gives you a slip of paper or a wooden tag which you hand back along with the parking fee of 2 *fen* when you return to collect your bicycle.

WALKING OR BICYCLING TOURS

The following tours cover some of the districts close to the main hotels. The first three are convenient to the Beijing Hotel; the fourth begins near the Minzu Hotel; and the fifth is relatively close to the Qianmen Hotel. Except for the first tour (for which you should allow three hours if on bicycle, six hours if on foot), each tour can be completed in an hour or less.

TOUR ONE: Around the Imperial City. The Imperial City, with the Forbidden City at its core, comprises several parks and the former offices and residential quarters of the imperial household staff. It was once surrounded by a massive wall and a moat, which were demolished in 1933, except for the stretch running along the north side of Tian'anmen Square.

The first intersection west of the Beijing Hotel marks the southeast corner of the Imperial City. Heading north on Dong'anmen Street, you come to **Reed River (*Gepu He*),** once part of the drainage system for the moat. Across the river, to the west, is a small, red-walled compound, the ancestral hall of the Manchu emperors known simply as **The Hall (*Tangzi*).** It is now closed to visitors. On the west side of Dong'anmen Street, about 500 meters north, is the old Western-style brick building which used to be the **Peking Union Church.** The next alley north leads to the former **Mahakala Monastery,** dedicated to the Great Black Deva, the patron saint of Mongolian Lamaism, a branch of Buddhism. Originally a palace built for the Prince Regent Dorgon, the building was converted into a monastery in 1691, the only Lamaist monastery in Beijing where services were conducted in Mongolian instead of Tibetan. Although closed to the public at present, a few of the magnificent halls and the walls around them are visible to the curious.

The next main intersection to the north was the site of **East Peace Gate (*Dong'anmen*),** the eastern entrance to the Imperial City, which led directly to the eastern gate into the Forbidden City. The emperor's kitchen used to stand between these two gates.

Continuing north on Dong'anmen Street, between the former campus of Beijing University on your left and coal storage sheds on your right, you reach **May Fourth Avenue (Wusi Dajie)**. The street name commemorates the May Fourth Movement of 1919 in which students from Beijing University demonstrated against the Chinese government's acquiescence to Japanese demands after World War I. The four-story building on the northwest corner of this intersection was once a student dormitory. The university abandoned the site in the late 1930s and the building now houses the editorial offices of a number of academic journals.

One kilometer north of this intersection is the northeast corner of the Imperial City. About halfway there, on the left side of the street, is a television factory on the site of **Lofty Blessings Monastery (Songzhu Si)**, the former printing house for Tibetan and Mongolian liturgical texts until the first half of this century. Many of the old buildings dating from the 17th century are still visible over the wall.

At the next major intersection, turn west onto Di'anmen Street, once the northern boundary of the Imperial City. The **Gate of Earthly Peace (Di'anmen)** once stood at the next intersection, less than a kilometer ahead. It faced the magnificent **Drum Tower (Gulou)**, 800 meters to the north. The Drum Tower, built in 1420, was given its name because a drum was beaten here to summon officials to their predawn audiences with the emperor. Just behind it, slightly to the right, is the **Bell Tower (Zhonglou)**, dating from 1745. Until 1924, the watches of the night were sounded from this tower.

Continuing west on Di'anmen Street, you pass **Ten Temples Lake (Shichahai)** on the right. This artificial lake, created 700 years ago for the emperor's pleasure, flows south into Beihai Park. At the next main intersection, one kilometer to the west, turn south down **West Ten Storehouses Avenue (Xishiku Dajie)**. The wall of the Imperial City actually turned south another short block farther west, but by taking this turning you will pass right by **North Church (Beitang)**—officially consecrated as St. Xavier's Cathedral in 1889—the largest Catholic church in Beijing until the revolution in 1949, and now a school.

After crossing the wide east-west road where Xishiku Avenue ends, you reach Fuyou Street. Along your left runs the wall that surrounds **Middle and South Seas (Zhongnanhai)**, that part of the former imperial park which now houses the offices of the State Council, the administrative center of the Chinese government. Fuyou Street leads south to Chang'an Avenue. Turn left toward Tian'anmen Square and you will pass the freshly varnished **New China Gate (Xinhuamen)** standing at the entrance to Zhongnanhai. A kilometer to the east is the **Gate of Heavenly Peace (Tian'anmen)**, formerly the main entrance to the Imperial City. Continue straight on from here to the Beijing Hotel. The total length of this tour is 10 km.

TOUR TWO: Wangfujing and Dongdan. On the east side of the Beijing Hotel is the city's major shopping street, known by the old name of Wangfujing, meaning "Well of the Princes' Palaces." The name dates back to the 19th century, when the aristocracy lived in this part of the city and controlled one of the sweet-water wells in Beijing. The well's underground channels are thought still to exist, and rumor has it that they are used as escape routes in times of turmoil.

Foreigners once knew Wangfujing Street as Morrison Street—named for Dr. George Morrison, the correspondent for the *London Times* who lived near the well earlier in this century. Before 1949, most of the foreign community lived just south of Wangfujing Street, and their patronage stimulated the growth of stores dealing in luxury goods and Western imports. When Wangfujing was renovated in the 1950s, the foreigners left, but the shops stayed. (For a listing of the more interesting shops along this street, see "Shopping" section below.)

About 200 meters north of the Beijing Hotel, on the west side of the street, are located part of the editorial offices of *People's Daily (Renmin Ribao)*, China's official national newspaper. The paper, usually only six pages, is always posted on the display boards at either side of the entrance. On this site, the Qing government once published the *Capital Gazette (Jingbao)*, a daily record of government decisions for the perusal of all officials. Only in the first half of the 20th century did independent newspapers flourish in China.

A bit further up the east side of the street is a small lane leading to the **Peking Union Medical College Hospital** (until 1985, known as Capital Hospital). Founded in 1906, the hospital was supported from 1915 until 1949 by the Rockefeller Foundation, which spent $7 million on the construction of the large complex of Chinese-style buildings still in use today. The best hospital in Beijing, it treats foreign outpatients in the old section and inpatients in the new wing off Dongdan Street. The building decorated with modern bas-reliefs on the north side of the lane is part of the **National Art Academy (Zhongguo Meishu Xueyuan).**

Within the next block north on Wangfujing, on the east side of the street, come the entrances to the **East Wind Market (Dongfeng Shichang).** Originally a parade ground for Manchu troops, the site was made into a permanent market in 1903 when small merchants were forced to vacate their stalls two blocks east to make way for a wider road. Besides several hundred separate stalls, the market had many restaurants and a few small theaters. All these were nationalized in 1956, and a new building to house the market went up in 1969.

Leaving East Wind Market by the northern entrance, turn right into **Goldfish Alley (Jinyu Hutong),** named for the goldfish sellers who once had their shops there. The lane leads out to Dongdan Street, in front of the Peace Hotel—the first hotel built in Beijing after 1949. Dongdan means "East Single," and refers to the single decorated wooden arch that once stood at the south end of this street. As you turn onto Dongdan

Street, you see the **Red Star Cinema (Hongxing Yingyuan)** on your right. The four-story building was built in 1906 as the headquarters of the Beijing YMCA, established by American missionaries. By 1920, the YMCA had a Chinese membership of 2,500, but it was disbanded after 1949.

Nearby, on Xiaoxunhutong, stands another site of Chinese Christianity, but this one is still in operation. **Rice Market Church (Mishitang),** a fairly small building designed partly in traditional Chinese style, was one of the three or four Protestant churches built by Chinese Christians independently of foreign missionaries. Of the two Protestant churches in Beijing now conducting Sunday services, this is the more important one. Indeed, Rice Market Church is now deemed the center of the Protestant faith in China. The church takes its name from the rice market which was located here before the church was built in 1915. Services are conducted on Sundays at 9 AM and on Saturdays at 7 PM.

South of the church you pass the new wing of Beijing Union Hospital and reach the intersection of Dongdan Street and Chang'an Avenue. Turn right past the large vegetable and meat market and follow the service road parallel to Chang'an Avenue back to the Beijing Hotel. The total length of this tour is 3 km.

TOUR THREE: Around the Forbidden City. A tour of the Forbidden City is a must for visitors to Beijing, but a walk around the perimeter of the Forbidden City can be almost as interesting as a walk through it.

The point of departure for this tour is the arched gateway of **South Moat (Nan Chizi),** the second street west of the Beijing Hotel. The ditch just north of the gateway is **Reed River (Gepu He).** Directly north of it, on the right, is the red wall surrounding the **Imperial History Compendium (Huangshi Cheng),** the archives containing all the documents issued by China's emperors. The documents are still stored in 152 copper chests in the main hall, a remarkable building that was designed to be fireproof and has miraculously remained unharmed by fire since it was completed in 1536.

Farther north, a block short of the main intersection at **East Peace Gate Avenue (Dong'anmen Dajie),** is an alley leading to the former **Mahakala Monastery** (see Tour One). At the north end of South Moat, across the way and to the left, stands **East Flowery Gate (Donghuamen),** the eastern entrance to the Forbidden City. Instead of continuing north on **North Moat (Bei Chizi),** cross the causeway in front of the gate and head north along the dirt path which runs all the way up the east side of the Forbidden City. Along this path, facing onto the moat, is a row of interesting old houses. The path will bring you through a grove of willow and plum trees to the north side of the Forbidden City and to the **Gate of Divine Military Prowess (Shenwumen),** the northern gate of the Forbidden City. Where the path stops, cross the causeway to the far side of the moat and continue west under the shadow of **Coal Hill (Jing Shan).** At the little restaurant by the northwest corner of the moat turn left and follow Beichang Street, which runs parallel to the west side of the Forbidden City.

Some 800 meters down the street is a cross street that used to connect

West Flowery Gate *(Xihuamen),* the west gate of the Forbidden City, with the imperial pleasure grounds of **Middle Sea (Zhonghai).** Turn left toward the gate, cross to the inner side of the moat, and walk along the base of the wall to the southwest corner tower and the **Right Tower Gate** *(Queyoumen).* Passing through this small gate, you find yourself standing before the **Meridian Gate** *(Wumen),* the southern entrance to the Forbidden City. From this point you can either turn east around the corner tower and end up at Donghuamen (where you first crossed the moat), or walk straight south toward Tian'anmen. The total length of this tour is 6 km.

TOUR FOUR: South of Xidan. Xidan, the main intersection on the city's west end, is west of the Beijing Hotel along Chang'an Avenue. Like Dongdan to the east, Xidan was once marked by a single large arch, removed earlier this year to accommodate traffic. This tour leads south of Xidan, ending up at the Minzu Hotel, 500 meters to the west.

The street running south from Xidan, Xuanwumennei Street, is a stretch of small shops and restaurants (see Shopping and Cuisine sections). At the south end of this street is **South Church** *(Nantang),* the Roman Catholic cathedral. The present building dates only from 1904, but the site has been associated with the Catholic church since the eminent Jesuit missionary Matteo Ricci purchased the land in 1605. The Chinese considered the site tainted because it was next to the **Gate of Proclaimed Military Prowess** *(Xuanwumen),* the so-called Gate of Death through which convicts passed on their way to execution. Ricci bought it because it was the only site a foreigner could purchase. The small chapel he built was enlarged in 1650 and was called the Church of the Immaculate Conception. Over the next 250 years, the church was destroyed and rebuilt three times. The last attack was led by the Red Guards in 1966. Closed for the next five years, the cathedral was reopened only in 1979. It has become the main place of worship for several thousand Chinese Catholics. The present bishop of Beijing, consecrated in December 1979, is Michael Fu Tieshan. Sunday mass is conducted at 9 AM.

Walking west to the next main street running north, you pass a complex of old Western-style buildings on your right. These were built when the Republic of China was founded in 1912 to house China's short-lived parliament. The parliament was dismissed after 12 years of corruption and intimidation, and the buildings were converted into a law school. Before the parliament buildings were constructed, the site was occupied by the stable for the emperor's elephants.

At Minzu Gong Nan Street, turn north. On the east side of the street, about 250 meters up, is the entrance to **Human Hair Alley** *(Toufa Hutong).* Legend says that this narrow passage got its name in 1625 when the shock of an explosion at an arsenal on this spot blew the hair off the men who were unloading kegs of gunpowder. It is a fact that an explosion occurred on this spot and killed some 500 people.

Continuing north on Minzu Gong Nan Street, you arrive at the **Nationalities Cultural Palace** *(Minzu Wenhua Gong)* and the Minzu Hotel.

For those returning to the Beijing Hotel by bus, the stop for Bus #1 is located at Xidan. The length of this tour is 2.5 km.

TOUR FIVE: Qianmen and Dazhalan. The district known as Qianmen takes its name from the imposing double gate standing at the south end of Tian'anmen Square. Prior to 1553, **Front Gate (Qianmen)** was the southern entrance to the capital city. As the city expanded southward, the shantytown in front of the gate was officially incorporated into the city and walled in as the Outer City. After the Manchus conquered Beijing in 1644, they banished all Han Chinese residents to the Outer City. Very quickly, Qianmen became the business and entertainment hub of the city, free of the aristocratic touches of the palaces located within the Inner City. To reach Qianmen from the Beijing Hotel, take Bus #2 two stops south; from the Qianmen Hotel, walk to Hufangqiao and take Bus #2 four stops east.

The gates of Qianmen were first built in the early 15th century. The present superstructure dates from 1905, when the gate was restored after the Boxer Uprising of 1900. The larger gate on the north side of the street is the main gate; the one on the south side was an outer gate.

Running south from Qianmen is Qianmen Road, which has for centuries been a main shopping district (several of the more interesting shops are described in the Shopping section below). This commerce also spilled over into the side streets. The first three lanes off the west side of Qianmen Road once had English names given to them by foreigners earlier in this century. The first was called Lantern Street after the lantern makers who had their shops there; the second, Jade Street; and the third, Silk Street. Silk is still sold in the third lane, now called by its Chinese name, **Dazhalan** (which literally means "large wicker gate").

The entrance to Dazhalan is just south of the bicycle parking lot on the west side; the crowds of shoppers jostling in and out make it easy to spot. The chief silk shop along Dazhalan was, and still is, **Auspicious Wealth Fabrics Stores (Ruifuxiang),** an old store with a marble porch standing 50 meters down the right side of the lane. With its unusual Western-style interior—a central well surrounded by balustrades—the store was considered one of the wonders of Beijing.

Dazhalan was famous for other products besides silk. **Shared Benevolence Hall (Tongrentang),** 75 meters down the south side of the lane, is still the best-known Chinese herb medicine shop in Beijing.

Dazhalan also has a long history as an entertainment district. In the 19th century, five of the largest opera theaters in Beijing were located here.

Dazhalan is a short lane, barely 300 meters in length. At the intersection with **Coal Market Street (Meishi Jie),** you can either turn north and then east again through the back streets and make your way back to Qianmen Road, or you can follow the continuation of Dazhalan southwest to Hufangqiao, from where it is just a block south to the Qianmen Hotel. The total length of this tour is 1.5 km. (2 km. to the Qianmen Hotel).

HOTEL
ACCOMMODATIONS

In 1986, Beijing received over one million foreign visitors, an increase of about 25% over the previous year. Government estimates envision two million overseas tourists in 1990 and an astonishing 4.3 million by the year 2000. Since the vast majority of China's foreign visitors include Beijing on their itineraries, inordinate pressure has been placed on the capital's limited hotel capacity. A lack of hotel space in Beijing meant that overall expansion of tourism in China could not be brought off without first opening the Beijing bottleneck.

In the mid-1980s, formidable efforts in local construction, combined with an avid pursuit of foreign investment, resulted in a doubling of the city's hotel rooms to over 17,000. By 1990, the city's hotel-room total was officially projected to reach 40,000. Nearly one dozen large hotels were expected to enter service during 1986–87 alone. By 1988, in fact, it was felt that Beijing could for the first time surmount the crest of its tourism boom and would have adequate space for all tourist arrivals.

Major new hotels expected for 1988–89 include the China World Hotel, a 750-room extravaganza at the China World Trade Center, sponsored by the Shangri-La group (rates starting at about US$90); the Chanfugong Center Hotel, a 25-floor, 512-room luxury venture with Japanese backing, at Jianguomenwai; the Olympic Hotel, a 500-room, US-financed hotel in the Western Suburbs (twins will be in the Y150–200 range); the Yugang Hotel, a 30-story Hong Kong joint venture going up near the Huadu; the Huayuan Hotel, an 800-room structure in the first-class category in the Western Suburbs (Huayuan Lu, Bei Taipingzhuang); the Olympic Hotel, a 14-story, 380-room joint venture between the China Sports Service Corp. and Hong Kong's Seylla Corp.; and the Taiwan Hotel, at 5-19 Jinyu Hutong, a 300-room, first-class facility with rates (US$80–100) and services aimed at the level of the Minzu. Thought to be coming in early 1989 are the Jinguyang Hotel, near the Jinglun on Hujiao Lu; and the Xizhimen Center Hotel, backed by Beijing's Capital Iron and Steel Company.

By 1988, these efforts could be said to have successfully transformed the Beijing hotel sector from a "take what you can get" situation to one where comfortable accommodations in the city are more or less assured and where even a degree of selectivity with regard to cost and location can be applied. The new generation of hotels varies somewhat in the range and quality of services and facilities offered, although each provides a standard of comfort well above the previous norm: central air-conditioning, hot showers, a choice of restaurants, adequate elevator service, and well-planned transport connections. The ubiquitous use of deep-pile carpeting is another notable feature of the new hotels, causing them to be known in some circles as the "Static Inns." (Beijing's dry climate contributes to a quick build-up of static electricity, especially after crossing one of these hotels' long, carpeted hallways—to avoid a shock, readers are advised to use *The China Guidebook* for pressing elevator buttons.)

Room rates for most upper-level Beijing hotels rose dramatically in 1986, with many now priced at over US$100 per day (per room). Also, several hotels are now following international practice by adding a 10% service charge to most items on the bill.

[Beijing's hotels are ranked below according to four categories: *Superior*— indicating facilities and services generally adhering to first-class international standards. Most of these hotels were built with foreign participation and can be booked directly from outside of China. *First-Class*—the best of Beijing's Chinese-built and managed hotels and including most of the hotels under contract to CITS for its tour groups. *Standard*—older hotels that have been renovated or upgraded at least in part to receive foreign guests; most rooms are air-conditioned and have Western-style baths. *Budget*—low-cost facilities that usually offer dormitory space and mainly serve overseas Chinese guests but have been known to accept foreigners.]

SUPERIOR HOTELS

北京饭店

Beijing Hotel. The most prestigious address for foreign visitors to the capital remains the Beijing Hotel. The 910-room hotel consists of three wings (with a fourth, "deluxe" wing built in 1986; *see below*). The west wing, built in the early 1950s in "grand" Soviet-style, has a rather gloomy lobby, a large ballroom still used for state banquets, and wood-paneled guest rooms. Formerly reserved for Chinese guests, its rooms were renovated in 1979 to accommodate foreigners.

East Wing. The 17-story, centrally air-conditioned east wing, completed in 1974, is still among the country's most modern and commodious hotel facilities and a landmark in Beijing. Its location is excellent: Wangfujing Street, Beijing's main shopping district, is around the corner; Tian'anmen is just two (albeit very long) blocks away. The east wing is used exclusively by foreign guests, but only rarely by tour groups. Important business delegations and invited political, governmental, or cultural-exchange delegations now comprise the majority of east wing clientele. A good number of the rooms have been converted to office-residences for foreign banks and traders. Floor-by-floor renovation of the east wing began in late 1986.

Rooms in the new wing are comfortable, reasonably clean, good-sized, and feature drapes that are electrically controlled. An increasing number are being furnished with color TV sets and multi-band radios, and most now have small refrigerators. Balconies off some rooms offer a spectacular view of Beijing, particularly rooms that look west over the golden, winged rooftops of the Forbidden City and the hills beyond (rooms whose numbers end in 44, 43, 39, 38, 37, or 36).

A number of retail shops are situated in the east wing lobby: an arts and crafts shop (near a large world map); a pharmacy selling traditional Chinese medicines; and an always busy cashmere boutique that features a fine array of handsome Chinese-made sweaters at bargain prices. The east wing's café-bar, still one of Beijing's foremost spots to see and be seen, serves ice cream, sandwiches, Coca-Cola, tea with lemon, coffee with milk, and Chinese and Western liquor. A Japanese-style sing-a-long bar (Karaoke) has been opened off the east lobby; a large screen behind the volunteer singers depicts scenes to conjure the mood of the lyrics. Admission is Y50.

Middle Wing. In the lobby of the old middle wing, the food shop sells fruits, baked goods, sweets, liquor, and cigarettes, and the souvenir boutique stocks a variety of scarves, stationery items, leather and fur goods, and artwork. The hotel's book and magazine kiosks have been relocated here. The post office and a branch of the Bank of China (mainly for currency exchange) are located along the corridor joining the middle and east wings.

West Wing. The old west wing was substantially refurbished—inside and out—in 1982. The hallway connecting the middle and west wing now has a carpeted coffee shop, offering a quiet alternative to the often raucous atmosphere of its east wing counterpart (the chairs, however, rank among the most uncomfortable in China, with a tendency to hurl you forward into your coffee). A new telex facility in the west wing lobby is the largest and most modern in Beijing. A new restaurant across the hall serves first-rate Sichuan dishes.

The hotel's spacious main dining room is located at ground level in the easternmost corner of the complex. Lunch and dinner specials are usually excellent: Sichuan, Cantonese, Huaiyang, Tanchie, Japanese, and Western dishes are prepared. There has been a gradual improvement in the quality of service. (For example, coffee is poured soon after guests sit down to breakfast and tablecloths are now changed regularly.) The dining room is open 7–8:30 AM for breakfast; noon–2 PM for lunch; and 6–8:30 PM for dinner. An "after-hours" restaurant, open 24 hours a day, has been relocated in the middle wing just east of the coffee shop, directly to the north of the main dining room. What may be the best Japanese restaurant in China is located at the east end of the second floor (new wing).

北京饭店贵宾楼

Distinguished Guest Building (Guibinlou). The fourth building in the Beijing Hotel complex, this new wing is located immediately to the west of the three-building Beijing Hotel complex old west wing, and is called Guibinlou (Beijing Hotel Distinguished Guest Building). The new wing consists of 287 guest rooms and has two below-ground levels (where banquet/meeting rooms will be located) and 10 floors above ground. It is a deluxe facility, offering all of the services generally associated with superior-class hotels. Room rates are comparable to those at the Great Wall Hotel and thus more expensive than the Beijing's other wings.

Regrettably, the Beijing Hotel is not available for direct booking by foreigners. You will need a Chinese contact—and a high-placed one at that—to secure accommodations here.

Address: 33 East Chang'an Avenue, corner Wangfujing Street

Telephone: 500-7766

Telex: 22426 BHCTL CN (hotel guests may now be contacted by telex; be sure to include room number; fees are now assessed for incoming telexes—to be adjusted according to whether the news is good or bad?)

Post Office: Monday–Saturday, 7:30 AM–7 PM; Sundays, 8 AM–4 PM

Cable PEKINGHOTEL, 6531 BEIJING

Bank: Foreign exchange desk, Monday–Saturday, 7:30 AM–10 PM; Sundays, 8–11 AM, 2–5 PM

Taxis: Order at the taxi kiosk in the front parking lot

Rates:

EAST WING	MIDDLE WING	WEST WING
Double room (2 beds): Y230	Double: Y315	Double: Y250
Two-room suite: Y474	Two-room suite: Y850	Suite: Y450–525
Large suite: Y750		

建国饭店

Jianguo Hotel. Beijing's first joint-venture hotel (with the Hong Kong/ British Peninsula Group which managed the hotel until November 1987) looks astonishingly like a Holiday Inn that's been uprooted from California's Pacific Coast Highway. Located a few blocks east of the Friendship Store, the Jianguo offers amenities that would be de rigeur for any modern American hotel but come as disarming anomalies in the context of today's Beijing: a coffee shop (called "The Greenery") that serves freshly brewed coffee plus an array of exotica (for China) that includes thick cheeseburgers, tossed salads, and milk shakes; a bar (named "Charlie's") that actually has a bar, serving correctly mixed drinks; a delicatessen, featuring imported meats and cheeses; an indoor swimming pool; and crisp, efficient service throughout. Needless to say, the Jianguo, which opened in early 1982, has taken Beijing's foreign community by storm. But, once again, its singular appeal seems to stem from the fact that virtually everything inside the place (including some of the management staff) is unabashedly foreign.

Designed by Clement Chen & Associates (a San Francisco-based firm), the Jianguo's thick wall-to-wall carpeted rooms are furnished with imported American beds, lamps, dressers, and touch-dial phones. Although the hotel does not offer 24-hour room service (Rome was not built in a day), each room has a refrigerator stocked with cold drinks, including White Horse scotch and Coca-Cola. And the Jianguo's bakery must rank as the most chic in China, turning out croissants, cheesecake, and *challah*.

The well-appointed, candle-lit restaurant (Justine's) offers Moët champagne, shrimp cocktail, onion soup gratinée, New Zealand sirloin, duckling glazed with orange, and prawns in garlic butter. Desserts range from a cheese plate to lemon mousse to ice coupé. Breakfast is served from 6:30–9 AM, lunch from noon–2:30, and dinner from 6:30–10 PM. Brunch is served on Sundays. Reservations are necessary for Justine's. The Four Seasons Restaurant in the east wing serves Beijing's finest Guangdong-style cuisine. A very good, rather expensive Japanese restaurant, the Nakabachi, features authentic fare prepared by Japanese chefs.

Telegraph, telex, long-distance telephone, and bank services are available and a rather ordinary basement shop offers handicrafts and books.

The Jianguo was the first hotel in Beijing to accept direct individual or group bookings from outside of China; it can be booked through Swiss-Belhotel or through Cathay Pacific.

Address: 5 Jianguomenwai Dajie
Telex: 22439 JGHBJ CN
Rates: Twins: US$85–100
   Suite: US$185

Telephone: 500-2233
Cable: 6677 PEKING
Fax: 500-2871

长城饭店
The Great Wall Sheraton Hotel. An immense high-rise facility with 1,007 rooms, the Great Wall opened in December 1983 and immediately set itself apart from all rivals as the most flamboyantly modern hotel in Beijing. A multiple 21-story glass and concrete structure, the Great Wall boasts a number of "firsts": a six-story-high atrium, glass-enclosed elevators, a rooftop cocktail lounge, tennis courts, a heated indoor swimming pool and health club, an acupuncturist, an underground garage, a cinema/theater, and iced tap-water in the bathrooms.

The Great Wall Hotel

The hotel also boasts about its Cosmos Club—with the only overseas band in town, a French restaurant, and a ballroom that can seat 1,200 (or hold 1,800 cocktail imbibers). An array of business services are available to guests and the Great Wall is among the few hotels in town offering limousine service and 24-hour room service. A great convenience are the three airline offices on the premises: CAAC, Lufthansa, and Thai. But the Great Wall's services and striking facade don't come cheap—it is easily one of the most expensive hotels in China.

The Great Wall looms over eastern Beijing, in the Chaoyang district (near the National Agricultural Exhibition Center). It is situated at about a 25-minute drive to the airport; the ride to Tian'anmen can take from 15 to 40 minutes, depending on traffic. The Great Wall accepts direct bookings from outside of China and accepts credit cards for payment of room bills. It joined the Sheraton chain in 1985.

Address: 6A Donghuan Bei Road   *Telephone:* 500-5566
Rates: Twins: US$110–140   *Telex:* 22002 GWHBJ CN
     Suites: US$200–850   *Fax:* 500-1938

中国大饭店

China World Hotel (1 Jianguomenwai Avenue; tel: (861) 500-5258; telex: 210087 CWTC CN; fax: (861) 59-1769). Under the Shangri-la International China Management, Ltd., the China World Hotel promises to be much more than just a hotel. It is billed as a convention and exhibition center, with deluxe accommodations for 1,000, convention facilities for 3,000, and 7,300 sq. meters of exhibition space. Due to open in early 1989, the hotel complex is part of a new China World Trade Center, which includes a 39-story office tower, a smaller office building, an underground shopping plaza, parking lot, a smaller business-class hotel, the **Trader Hotel,** and two 30-story residential apartment buildings for foreign business personnel. Among the hotel amenities are central air-conditioning, international dial-direct telephones (with an extension in the bathroom), stocked refrigerator and minibar, tea- and coffee-maker in each room, 24-hour room service, dry cleaning services, and a tourism office. Their Executive Center supplies business services including telex, facsimile, and photocopying, as well as secretarial, translation, and courier services. A Fitness Center, with a sauna, massage, two squash courts, bowling, indoor pool, and fully-equipped gymnasium are available for recreation. Three restaurants (Chinese, Japanese, and Continental), discothèque, coffee shop, pub, and lobby lounge provide dining and entertainment; full banquet and meeting facilities will be at hand for all business needs.

京伦饭店

Jinglun (Beijing-Toronto) Hotel. One of the newest of Beijing's modern, Western-style hotels, the Jinglun has the distinction of management provided by the highly reliable Nikko Hotels International system. Most staff were trained through a special course run by service experts from Hong

Kong and Japan. Construction came about through a joint Chinese-Canadian venture, which explains the hotel's name. So if you are now prepared to find the restaurant crowded with sushi-eating Mounties, you shouldn't be surprised to learn that they were probably booked by CITS, which also has a contract with Jinglun for tour groups, although unlike many other CITS-affiliated hotels, the Jinglun can also be booked directly from outside of China through Japan Air Lines/Nikko hotel chain.

The Jinglun starts life with many advantages, not the least of which is its location on Beijing's central axis, between the Friendship Store and the Jianguo Hotel.

The Jinglun is a 12-story structure with 659 rooms. Facilities include an indoor pool, sauna, shopping arcade, bar, coffee shop, Western and Chinese dining rooms, and banquet and meeting rooms. All the rooms are equipped with closed-circuit TV, central air-conditioning, refrigerators, and alarm clocks. Each is designed with a bay window over-looking the building boom of east-central Beijing. Special winter rates.

Address: 3 Jianguomenwai Dajie (next to Jianguo Hotel)
Telephone: 500-2266   *Cable:* 5650 BEIJING
Telex: 210011/210012 JLH CN   *Rates:* Y350–370 ($95–100)
Fax: 500-2022

崑仑饭店
Kunlun Hotel. The 30-story Kunlun, managed by the Shanghai-based Jinjiang Group, was officially opened on October 1, 1986. Its location directly across from the Sheraton-managed Great Wall Hotel is no coincidence: the hotel is clearly meant to compete with its joint-venture neighbor. Indeed, the Kunlun is almost the mirror image of the Great Wall, distinguished mainly by its dun-colored facade. Services and accommodations have been designed to be on a par with or to exceed those offered by the Great Wall, while room rates are slightly lower (which would rank the Kunlun as the second most expensive hotel in China). All 1,005 double rooms are air-conditioned and equipped with a refrigerator, mini-bar, and large closets; bathrooms feature full-size bathtub and shower, heat lamps, and extension phones. There are also 25 two-room suites, six three-room luxury suites, and a five-room "Presidential Suite." Guests who dine at the hotel have a choice of four cuisines: Shandong, Cantonese, Japanese, and French. The Japanese restaurant has authentic tatami rooms, while the revolving rooftop restaurant (apparently a sine qua non for new Beijing hotels) features French cuisine in a Louis XIV setting.

The Kunlun boasts a 200-car underground garage, the first rooftop heliport in Beijing (overflights of the Great Wall and Ming Tombs are offered), and "the first true nightclub in Beijing" (the Great Wall has "only a disco"). Sports facilities include tennis courts, a swimming pool, a gym and a fully-equipped health club. Also on the premises are a barbershop, a beauty salon, and a huge, high-priced shopping arcade.

There is a ballroom, as well as several meeting rooms (simultaneous translation services are available).

Address: 21 Liang Ma Qiao, Chaoyang District
Telephone: 500-3388 *Cable:* 2745
Telex: 210327 BJKLH CN *Rates:* Twins: US$115–140

兆龙饭店

Zhaolong Hotel. Another addition to Beijing's new "hotel row," the 22-story Zhaolong is a modern glass high-rise situated near the foreign embassy district, about 1 km. south of the Great Wall and Majestic hotels. Although Tian'anmen Square is at least an hour-and-a-half walk away, footweary tourists needn't despair: taxis are readily available, and the #113, #350, and #402 buses all stop nearby. In non-rush hours, the ride into town should take about 20 minutes.

With only 270 rooms, the Zhaolong is much smaller (and a bit cheaper) than most of its nearby competitors, yet offers many of the same luxuries and services. The hotel is centrally air-conditioned, with in-room climate controls; all rooms are equipped with a refrigerator/mini-bar, color TV (closed-circuit programming), and telephone; and bathrooms are surfaced in marble and feature Japanese-made fixtures. In addition to the nine dining rooms, each offering a different Chinese regional or Western cuisine and decor, there is a 24-hour coffee shop and a bar. Amenities include a swimming pool, sauna, bank, post office, hairdresser, and shopping arcade. Telex and other business services are available.

The Zhaolong began operations in spring 1986.

Address: 2 Gongren Tiyuguan Beilu, Chaoyang District
Telephone: 500-2299 *Rates:* Standard: Y220–230
Telex: 210079 ZLH CN Suites: Y560–3,500
Cable: Zhaolong Beijing

北京丽都假日饭店

Holiday Inn Lido Beijing. Opened in early 1984, the Holiday Inn Lido is an attractive, deluxe-level hotel situated about 20 to 40 minutes by car from Tian'anmen in northeast Beijing, just beyond the Jianguomenwai embassy district. Lacking the brassiness of the Great Wall and without some of the more elegant touches of the Jianguo, the Lido nevertheless offers one of the more acceptable places to stay in the capital. In 1986, however, guests began to complain of inattentive service and poor maintenance. In that year, the management was pushing ahead with ambitious development projects, including six apartment towers for foreign residents and an office block.

With spacious public areas and a modern yet quietly tasteful decor, the Lido maintains 1,000 guest rooms and a good array of services calculated to attract business people and individual travelers. Amenities include secretarial services, 24-hour cable and telex, babysitters and cribs, bowling alleys, an indoor swimming pool, sports center, sauna, and tennis courts.

The Lido has a good Cantonese restaurant, the Marco (Western) restaurant, two coffee shops, and a highly popular and trendy disco called Juliana's. Guest rooms, however, are smallish and appointments have a decidely synthetic, cut-rate feel to them, which may stem from the fact the hotel is of modular construction—room units are manufactured in Singapore and then assembled in Beijing. Plumbing performance seems endemically erratic. Abandoning imagination for kitch, the hotel selected a panda for its logo and practically assaults you with the cloying little creature on every doorway and appurtenance.

The new Business Center opened in 1988, offering bilingual staff for translation and secretarial services, and "urgent message" service outside of office hours. Private offices there can be rented by the half-hour, hour, or full day.

As at the Jianguo and Great Wall, accommodations at the Lido can be booked direct from outside of China through the HOLIDEX Reservation System.

Address: Jichang and Jiang Tai Roads *Fax:* 500-6237
Telephone: 500-6688 *Rates:* Standard: US$90
Telex: 22618 LIDOH CN Superior: US$100
Cable: 8333 Suites: US$195–380

拉马大亚洲宾馆

Ramada Asia Hotel. Managed by Ramada International, this joint venture with the Beijing Asia Hotel Company is located in the embassy area near the Worker's Stadium, only 30 minutes from the airport. The Ramada Asia Hotel is scheduled to be completed in December 1988. It will feature 300 rooms and 90 furnished apartments. Facilities include a swimming pool, health club, disco, business center, meeting rooms, and an adjoining office block with a shopping arcade. Several restaurants, banquet facilities, and lounges will be available for dining and meetings.

北京香格里拉饭店

Shangri-La Hotel Beijing. The Shangri-La Hotel Beijing, which initiated operations in October 1986, is arguably one of the most pleasing and comfortable hotels in Beijing. The Shangri-La is a joint venture between the China National Metals and Minerals Corporation and Shangri-La Hotels International. It describes itself as an international-class hotel, with a formidable investment budget of $80 million. Rates are in the upper range. It is located in the western suburbs, about 45 minutes from the Erligou Trade Negotiation Center.

The hotel consists of a seven-story west building and a 24-story main building. The West Building, with 76 guest rooms and 44 offices, opened on October 1, 1986. The Main Building, with 666 guest rooms and 40 suites, was fully operational by March 1987. Rooms in the main building are somewhat larger.

The hotel features three restaurants: Chinese and French, plus a coffee shop; three cocktail lounges; a disco called Xanadu; a gourmet corner selling take-out cakes and other delicacies; a grand ballroom and 13 function rooms; and a shopping arcade replete with a US-style drugstore. In addition, there is a business center, health club, heated indoor swimming pool, hairdresser, and medical clinic. Services provided include 24-hour room service, same-day laundry and valet service, and babysitting. The Shangri-La maintains its own fleet of 250 taxis.

Guest rooms are attractively furnished with imported furniture and fixtures. All rooms are equipped with a mini-bar, color TV, in-house movies, telephones in both bedroom and bathroom, international direct dialing, air-conditioning, and bedside control panels.

American Express, Diner's Club, and Visa will be accepted for direct payment. Travelers can book direct through all Shangri-La International reservations offices. Special winter rates available.

Address: 29 Zizhuyuan Road
Telephone: 831-2211/890-931
Telex: 222322 SHABJ CN
Rates:

Cable: 1123 SHANHTLBJ
Fax: 802-1471

WEST BUILDING
Standard/single: Y372; standard/double: Y409; two-room suite/single: Y1,078–2,790
Office units range from Y296 for a simple unit to Y706 for an executive office suite.
MAIN BUILDING
Standard/single: Y518; standard/double: Y558; suites/double: Y1,078–2,678

钓鱼台国宾馆

Anglers' Rest (Diaoyutai) State Guest House. Few hostelries in China can match the grand, elegant appointments of the Anglers' Rest, which, prior to 1979, had been set aside for visiting heads of state and other prominent guests of the Chinese government. In recent years, CITS has allocated space at the Diaoyutai for deluxe-level private tours and delegations. Guests can usually count on a private suite and superb, personalized service from a staff that often outnumbers the clientele. Situated amidst the Sanlihe diplomatic residential complex, the surroundings may seem a bit rarefied to visitors seeking a more authentic taste of daily life in Beijing. But for those who come to China in the faith that "living well is the best revenge," the Anglers' Rest is the appropriate choice.

Address: 2 Fucheng Road
Telephone: 86-6152/86-8831
Telex: 22798 DYTGH CN

Rates: Double: US$140
Suites: $300–500

丽晶钓鱼台饭店

Regent Diaoyutai Hotel. Located in the courtyard of the state guesthouse, the Regent will accommodate travelers of less exalted rank. The hotel is due to be completed in 1990 and its 262 rooms will be located in a low-rise building containing several restaurants and lounges, a business center, and health spa, as well as a revolving exhibition of Chinese art.

香山饭店

Xiang Shan (Fragrant Hill) Hotel. The Xiang Shan Hotel, designed by the Chinese-American architect I. M. Pei, promised to become one of China's most sumptuous and stately hotels when it opened in early 1983. Located in a lovely suburban park popular with Beijing residents, the Xiang Shan's pristine white exterior conveys an almost forbidding, fortress-like aspect. But its striking and understated interiors convey a master's touch — the Xiang Shan succeeds as no other hotel in China in combining a Chinese sense of line and form with Western ingenuity in uses of light and space. Skillfully integrated with formal gardens and external landscaping, the total effect of the Xiang Shan is almost unsettling in that it may be the only new structure in China where design and mood seem to have taken precedence over function. But the hotel's development contained a tragic flaw — responsibilities for construction and maintenance were parceled out to two separate engineering units which apparently failed to communicate with one another. Not surprisingly, the Xiang Shan quickly began to fall apart at the seams. By late 1984, only strenuous efforts by the local management began to get the place working again.

Rooms are large (24' x 13') and are appointed with rareties such as double beds and American bath fixtures. All rooms (except 178 through 191) look out on delightful garden or mountain settings. Notable facilities include a large outdoor swimming pool, atrium coffee shop, bar, health club and conference rooms (which rent at a rate of Y30 per hour). Table d'hôte in the restaurants is unremarkable.

Regrettably, the Xiang Shan's location appears to have limited its appeal (at least as evidenced by its rather empty look during its first years of operation). Although the Xiang Shan is unparalleled as a conference site, the required 40-minute drive into town will prove an impediment to visitors whose schedules require daily visits to central Beijing. But the surrounding countryside, which includes several significant shrines and monuments, offers splendid opportunities for walkers and climbers (who can seek the aid of a just-constructed ski lift).

Address: Xiang Shan Park
Telephone: 256-5544
Cable: 7391
Telex: 222202 FHH CN

Rates: Single rooms: Y223
Double rooms: Y260–446
Suites: Y1,360

北京国际饭店

Beijing International (Guoji) Hotel. Situated directly across from the train station, the Beijing International, which opened in December 1987, is the most centrally located new hotel in Beijing. Designed and built without foreign assistance and operated directly by the National Tourism Administration of China, the 32-story, 1,049-room hotel will accept advanced bookings for both individuals and tour groups.

Every guest room has a panoramic view of the city, and is equipped with modern bath facilities, color TV, direct-dial phone, and individual climate control. Guests can choose from among 12 Chinese and Western restaurants (including yet one more revolving rooftop bar). For night owls, there is 24-hour room service. Other amenities include banquet and meeting facilities with simultaneous translation services, indoor swimming pool, sauna, tennis courts, bowling alleys, and a shopping arcade. Banking, postal, and travel services are also available.

Address: 9 Jianguomenwai Dajie
Telephone: 512-6688
Telex: 211121 BIH CN

Rates: Single: $70–105
Double: $95–115

首都宾馆

Capital Guesthouse. Distinguished by its superb location, the Chinese-built and managed Capital Guesthouse is yet another addition to the deluxe hotel category. Opened on October 1, 1987, the 20-story tower has 300 guestrooms and suites, while a separate, three-floor section houses 120 offices. Two levels underground comprise a 100-car parking garage.

The hotel has 14 restaurants and banquet halls, with a combined seating capacity of 1,400, serving Chinese, Western, and Japanese food; coffee shop and bar; and 24-hour room service is offered. Business services are also provided (telex, copying, typing), as well as a bank, a post office, and a rare and valuable amenity — a CAAC booking office. Other facilities include a swimming pool, tennis courts, bowling alleys, billiard room, exercise room, sauna and steam rooms, and a shopping arcade.

Guest rooms, of course, have all the standards for a hotel of this category: air-conditioning, color TV, and refrigerators. Room rates are pegged at "slightly less" than the Great Wall Hotel. (The Capital Guesthouse is not to be confused with the former Capital Hotel, recently subsumed under the Xiyuan Hotel as its east wing.)

Address: 20 Dongjiaomin Lane
Telephone: 54-1231

Telex: 210305 CHE CN
Cable: 6172

王府井饭店

Palace Hotel Wangfujing. The Palace Wangfujing has been rebuilt as a joint venture with the Hong Kong branch of Kumagai Construction Co. (Japan). Management is under the care of the Philippines' elegant Manila Hotel. The Palace's greatest asset, perhaps, is its superb central-city location. The Palace is a 15-story Chinese-style structure with a green-tiled roof. It reopened in October 1987. The number of guest rooms is 600, including suites. Floors 14 and 15 comprise luxury suites with separate elevator access.

Most of the hotel's facilities are located in three underground levels, including the lobby (graced by a cascading waterfall). Restaurants include the now standard triad of Chinese, French, and Japanese; plus coffee shop, bars, and banquet halls.

Direct bookings are permitted.

Address: 5A Yong'an Xi Road
Telephone: 500-5333

Telex: 210370 KGBJ CN
Fax: 500-5651

龙泉饭店

Dragon Spring Hotel. Nestled in a delightful garden setting, the Dragon Spring opened in June 1987 as part of the Moevenpick (Swiss) and Radisson (US) chains. Located in the Western Hills, about 45 minutes from town, the hotel comprises 235 rooms and suites, laid out among three "villages" linked by an enclosed walkway.

The hotel is located 35 minutes from the Summer Palace. Room amenities include air-conditioning, minibars, refrigerators, color television, international direct-dial telephones, and fresh fruit platters. For dining, there are two restaurants, two bars, and a Garden Terrace which features ice cream direct from Switzerland. Other facilities are a convention hall, six banquet rooms, a heated swimming pool, tennis courts, gymnasium and health club, jogging track, billiard room, and solarium. Moevenpick also plans a second hotel in Beijing, now under construction at Beijing Airport, in concert with Radisson and CITIC, scheduled to open in the fall of 1989. Special winter rates available.

Direct bookings are available through either of the two managing chains.

Address: Shui Zha Bei Lu, Men Tou Gou
Telephone: 877-3366   *Rates:* Single: US$75
Telex: 222293 DSHBJ CN   Doubles: US$80–85

FIRST-CLASS HOTELS

天平饭店

Tianping Hotel. A joint venture between Lee Gardens International Group of Hong Kong and the Legal Exchange Services Company, the Tianping is expected to open in early 1990. The hotel will have 252 rooms and 120 suites, and offer comprehensive legal services for business travelers. Other facilities will include function rooms, a business center, health club, beauty salon, three restaurants, and a lobby lounge. The 15-story building will be located in the commercial center of Beijing.

香港澳门中心

Hong Kong-Macau Center. This 500-room hotel, managed by Swissôtel, is scheduled to be completed in 1989. A joint venture of the Hong Kong and Macau Affairs Office of the State Council and China Benefit Investment of Hong Kong, the Hong Kong Macau Center will offer apartments, offices, and shops in addition to its hotel rooms in central Beijing.

北京希尔顿酒店

Beijing Hilton. In 1988, this hotel was under construction in the embassy area, adjacent to the Oriental Arts Theatre. Scheduled to be completed in 1989, the 400-room hotel is a joint venture of the Oriental Arts Building Company and the Indar Group of Hong Kong.

假日美景园饭店
Holiday Inn Grandview Garden (Grandview Garden Park). Designed as a "no-frills" alternative to other Western-built hotels in Beijing, this five-star 500-room hotel will offer Holiday Inn quality with prices attractive to the budget-minded traveler or business traveler. Among the facilities will be a Chinese restaurant, a Western restaurant, coffee shop, health club, swimming pool, business center, and banquet room. Due to be completed in 1990.

金光中心饭店
Jinguang Centre (Chaoyang Road and North Donghuan Road). Scheduled to open in mid-1989, this 52-story tower will contain a four-star hotel in addition to office space and 240 apartments. The 150,000-square-meter complex is located near the embassy district. On the premises will be nine restaurants and lounges, the Dynasty Club, a business center, swimming pool, fitness center, billiard room, games room, shopping arcade, and function rooms. New World Hotels of Hong Kong will manage this new complex together with Huawei Center, a new office and apartment complex located in Xidan.

假日王宫场饭店
Holiday Inn Crowne Plaza Beijing. This 400-room hotel will be located at the intersection of Wangfujing and Dengsikou streets. Scheduled for opening in 1990, its facilities will include two restaurants, health club, swimming pool, and banquet room for up to 300 persons.

北京新代饭店
Beijing New Era Hotel. A new Sino-Japanese joint venture located on the Western outskirts of Beijing, the Beijing New Era Hotel is due to open in August 1990. It will feature 762 rooms and rental office space.

田园荘饭店
Tianyuanzhuang Hotel (West Yuanmingyuan Road; tel: 289661). A joint venture with the Japanese Xinhuo Industrial Co., the Tianyuanzhuang is located somewhat past Beijing University. Its 154 rooms are equipped with color television, refrigerator, air-conditioning, and telephone, and the hotel provides transportation services. Beijing Agricultural University supplies fresh produce daily to this pastoral setting. The chef prepares requests and daily specials from the nearby fishing pond; visits to the nearby farm can be arranged. *Rates:* Single: Y100; double: Y100/150; suite: Y250.

紫薇宾馆
Ziwei Hotel (40 South Shijingshan Road; tel: 876931; telex: 222619 ZWH CN; cable: 8031; fax: 876845). Only a five-minute walk from Beijing's western subway line is the Ziwei Hotel. With one transfer, this line goes directly to the center of the city. A joint venture with the Hong Kong/China Tourist Hotel Management Co., the hotel offers such amenities as central air-conditioning, minibar, and color television. Facilities include a Communications Center, banquet hall, disco, and bars. *Rates:* Double: Y135; suite: Y225.

友谊宾馆

Friendship Hotel. In the early 1950s, the Soviet Union sent thousands of experts and technicians to Beijing. To accommodate this special community, the Chinese built the Friendship Hotel complex in the northwestern suburbs.

Today the Friendship Hotel's buildings house a variety of people. Chinese inhabit apartments in the northernmost section; foreign residents working in Beijing and their families live in the southern blocks; in between are a series of buildings recently refurbished for tourists, mainly groups booked through CITS. All guest rooms are air-conditioned, with private bath.

Facilities are excellent. Several dining rooms serve fine Beijing cuisine and fairly good Western-style dishes; snack shops and grocery stores are scattered throughout the compound; other shops include a bookstore, an arts and crafts boutique, a carpet outlet, and a photography store. A Japanese-style refreshment bar was added in 1986; it includes a laser video—vocal system that allows customers to watch their own singing performances on closed-circuit TV. New in 1988 is a Suzhou-style garden, with a restaurant offering Suzhou-style cuisine.

This "small city" also contains a beautiful Olympic-size swimming pool (open from June 1 to September 15), tennis courts, a huge theater (with Chinese film showings on Fridays), a café, and a clinic.

The main drawback of the Friendship Hotel is its location—some 25 minutes from downtown by taxi (when it is not rush hour). The hotel has started its own shuttle-bus service to downtown, charging Y1–2 per trip.

Address: 3 Baishiqiao Road, Haidian District
Telephone: 89-0621   *Rates:* Double rooms: Y93–160
Cable: 2222   Suites: Y200–300

华都饭店

Huadu Hotel. A large new hotel of Chinese design and construction, the Huadu began receiving guests in August 1982. Located about 9 km. northeast of the city center and 22 km. from the airport, the Huadu is adjacent to the Sanlitun embassy district. The hotel is mainly used for CITS tour groups, and certainly ranks as one of Beijing's best facilities in that category, and these days emerges as something of a bargain overall.

The hotel suffers from being set in the midst of several massive residential construction sites, turning even the most meager attempt at a neighborhood stroll into an ordeal of dust and bad footing. Its 522 rooms are distributed among six attached five-story buildings. The public areas are large and pleasantly laid out, lending the aspect of an island of calm (in a sea of construction). Both the service and food are commendable, given the newness of the place.

Address: 8 Xinyuan Nan Road   *Rates:* Single: Y120 (small)
Telephone: 500-1166   Single: Y160 (large)
Telex: 22028 HUADU CN   Suite: Y425
Cable: 5431

民族饭店

Minzu (Nationalities) Hotel. The Minzu, located 3 km. (2 mi.) due west of Tian'anmen, reopened in mid-1984 after being closed for over a year for a complete overhaul and modernization. Happily, many of the same experienced staff have returned (they had spent the year studying). So has the excellent cuisine standard in the Minzu's Western and Chinese restaurants. More remarkably, menu prices have not gone up very much. Both restaurants will eventually be open 24 hours per day, solving the problem of where to eat at off hours in this part of town.

The Minzu's 615 rooms are quite comfortable, with carpeting, closed-circuit TV, central air-conditioning, radios, and Western-fitted bathrooms. The tenth floor now includes a gym, billiards room, and other services.

Address: 51 Fuxingmennei Avenue   *Rates:* Standard: Y172–242
Telephone: 601-4466   Suites: Y377–612
Telex: 22990 MZHTL CN

西苑饭店

Xiyuan Hotel. Adjacent to the Erligou Trade Negotiation Center (garments, light industry, etc.) about 12 km. northwest of Tian'anmen, the Xiyuan is ideally located for traders on a quick visit to Beijing. Also nearby is the Beijing Industrial Exhibition Hall, the zoo, and Beijing and People's universities.

East Wing. Known for a few years as the Capital (Shoudu) Hotel, the Xiyuan's east wing is the most dominant edifice in northwest Beijing: a gleaming 27-story tower topped by a revolving restaurant that—unlike the Great Wall's—actually revolves.

Opened in October 1984, the structure has 749 rooms, including a large number of suites. All are equipped with closed-circuit TV and other conveniences. There is also an indoor pool, a gym, a sauna, a massage room, and 13 dining rooms, including a Muslim restaurant decorated with rugs and other artifacts from Xinjiang. The service personnel wear costumes to match the decor. On the 26th and 27th floors, which revolve once every hour, there is a restaurant and bar with music and dancing. Glass elevators and innovative lighting make for a gleaming atmosphere similar to that of the more expensive Great Wall Hotel.

The Xiyuan is owned by the Beijing Municipal Hotel Corporation. The new wing was partly financed with foreign loans and was built largely with imported materials. It is under joint management with the Jinling Hotel in Nanjing and the Dongfang Hotel in Guangzhou. The staff have all received at least nine months of training, and will receive further training on the job. The management advises confidently that rooms can be booked directly up to three years in advance. Major credit cards are accepted for direct payment of hotel bills.

West Wing. Accommodations consist mostly of two- and three-room suites, but there are also singles and four-room suites. The complex of seven three- and four-story buildings was originally built in the 1950s, but recently underwent extensive renovation. There are now 343 rooms, all with air-conditioning, TVs, telephones, and private bathrooms. Most of the old wing's rooms are now being let out on a long-term basis as residences and offices for foreigners.

Address: 5 Erligou, Xijiao
Telephone: 831-3388

Telex: 22831/2/3/4 XYN CN
Cable: 8766 BEIJING

Rates: **EAST WING**
Twins: Y250
Suites: Y275–2,700

WEST WING
Twins: Y80
Standard Suites: Y95

燕京宾馆

Yanjing Hotel. One of Beijing's new-generation hotels, the 20-story, 507-room Yanjing Hotel opened its doors in 1981. Rather massive by Chinese standards, the building was originally planned as an office complex for foreign firms. Midway through its construction, the structure was changed into a hotel (which might explain the odd placement of plumbing facilities and light switches). Its location—about 5 km. west of Tian'anmen—is advantageous, especially for visitors with business in both central and west Beijing.

All rooms are equipped with closed-circuit color television and overhead shower facilities and, like the public areas, are air-conditioned (though insufficiently). Both food and service are of a good standard. Clientele include tour groups and business people, with a large proportion coming from Japan. As yet, the Yanjing has no facility for direct booking.

Address: 19 Fuxingmenwai Avenue
Telephone: 86-8721
Telex: 20028 YZHTL CN
Cable: 1500

Rates: Standard: Y105 (stall shower)
Standard: Y115 (bathtub/shower)
Two-room suite: Y220

东方饭店

Dongfang Hotel. The original, 70-room Dongfang Hotel is more than 30 years old. It opened at the same time as the Beijing Hotel, but was used only by Chinese travelers. That building is currently being renovated, and a new 17-story tower was scheduled for completion by late 1987. The tower will feature 252 moderately-priced guest rooms, mostly standard size (only 24 suites). All will be modern, with air-conditioning, color TV, bedside controls, and imported bathroom fixtures. Access, however, will be limited since 200 of these rooms have already been reserved on a four-year basis by a Singapore tour company. The 70 rooms in the original building will remain available, although they will not be quite up to the standards of the new tower's rooms.

There will be two Chinese restaurants, two Western restaurants, a coffee shop, bar, and teahouse. The 17th floor will serve as an observation deck, offering drinks and snacks. The hotel is said to have two chefs in the "special class" (that is, higher than first-class category) who specialize in Shandong and Sichuan cooking. The hotel will also have business services (telex, etc.), a beauty parlor, massage, sauna, exercise room, and disco.

Address: 11 Wan Ming Road (north of the Beiwei Hotel)
Telephone: 33-1431   *Cable:* 1432
Telex: 222385 DFH CN

和平饭店
Heping (Peace) Hotel. Built in 1952 for the Asian Pacific Region Conference, the Peace Hotel was Beijing's first post-1949 hotel. Overshadowed (almost literally) by the neighboring Beijing Hotel, it has been one of the city's best-kept secrets ever since. It was closed during the Cultural Revolution and reopened in 1980 as a clean, modern, air-conditioned hotel mainly used by business travelers. The hotel was closed in early 1986 for construction of a new 18-story tower, and was still closed in 1988. After this metamorphosis, it is expected to emerge as a first-class facility with 300 air-conditioned rooms (including 30 suites), all equipped with TVs, refrigerators, and bedside control consoles. There will be a selection of restaurants, two-way telex, business services, and a taxi stand. Direct bookings will be permitted.

The Peace Hotel enjoys an almost unrivaled central location. It is situated within a peaceful courtyard just steps from Wangfujing Street, Beijing's main shopping thoroughfare, and just west of Dongdan, another important shopping street.

Address: 3 Jinyu Hutong (Goldfish Alley No. 3, Dong Cheng District)
Telephone: 55-8841   *Rates:* Twins: Y165–195
Cable: 5131   Suites: Y350

New hotels in Beijing due to open in the summer of 1988 include the **Changsha Hotel** (East Wuyi Road); **Huatian Hotel** (Shaosan Road); and **Hudie Mansion** (Wuyi Road).

STANDARD HOTELS
蓟门饭店
Jimen Hotel. The Jimen Hotel, located in the western suburbs of Beijing, opened on October 1, 1986. This hotel is convenient to many of Beijing's higher educational institutions, including the Aeronautical Institute, Beijing Medical University, and Beijing Foreign Languages Institute. It is 10 km. from Tian'anmen Square. It consists of 160 rooms, of which 63 are suites. All are carpeted and have private bathrooms, air-conditioning, color TV, and telephones.

There are two Chinese dining rooms, specializing in Shandong cooking (Western food is available only at breakfast). There are meeting rooms, small banquet rooms, bar, shop, foreign exchange and postal desks, beauty parlor, and massage services; a taxi stand, telex, copier, and typewriter room are planned. Foreign guests will be able to book directly.

Address: Xueyuan Lu, Haidian District
Telephone: 201-2211   *Rates:* Standard: small Y66; large Y80
Telex: 222325 JMH CN   Suites: small Y108; large Y120
Cable: 5636

新侨饭店

Xinqiao (New Citizen) Hotel. This Soviet-style, six-story hotel, located southeast of Tian'anmen in the former foreign legation quarter, used to be an exclusive haunt of foreign journalists, businessmen, and other "China hands." Its location—about midway between the Beijing Hotel and the railway station—is superb. This, combined with its relatively low rates and experienced staff, still makes the Xinqiao something of a "find" among Beijing's hotels.

Rooms are just large enough to accommodate twin beds, a desk, and two easy chairs. A dining room on the sixth floor serves some of Beijing's best Chinese dishes and provides a splendid view of the city. A Western and a Japanese restaurant are to the far left of the main lobby. Other services include a coffee shop, which provides light snacks; and a foreign exchange desk, open daily from 7:30 AM to 5:30 PM. Guests should not neglect to stop at Rosenbec, a new Western-style bakery/cafeteria that runs along the eastern side of the hotel building. Pizza, hamburgers, and croissants are featured.

As with so many Beijing hotels, the Xinqiao is hoping to capitalize on the current tourist boom by raising a new annex in the rear, expected to catapult the Xinqiao into the first-class stratum in 1988. The original section is to operate undisrupted through the current construction, which should be completed in 1991.

Address: 2 Dongjiaomin Lane   *Rates:* Standard: Y133–189
Telephone: 55-7731   Suites: Y210
Cable: 0145

前门饭店

Qianmen Hotel. The venerable Qianmen underwent profound renovations during 1985–86. By completion in January 1987, the 30-year-old hotel was displaying a pretense towards elegance, with a marble-faced lobby and a counter marked "Concierge." The hotel's 406 new rooms and suites are centrally air-conditioned and connected by a new telephone system. Furnishings are pleasant and bath fixtures bear the mark "American Standard." There are Western and Chinese restaurants (the latter among Beijing's better hotel restaurants), a coffee shop, and dining rooms for tour groups.

The Qianmen is situated at a deceptively distant 2 km. from the Front Gate (Qianmen) of Tian'anmen and the Mao Zedong Memorial Hall. Nevertheless, it is in an excellent neighborhood for walking. Next door is the Beijing Opera Institute and across the street are the editorial offices of *The Guangming Daily*, one of China's most influential newspapers. Within one square mile are antique shops, old-style houses, and a variety of busy neighborhood stores and restaurants.

A direct-booking system is planned, but is not yet in place.

Address: 175 Yong'an Road *Rates:* Standard: Y132
Telephone: 33-8731 Suites: Y260–312
Telex: 222382 QMHTL CN

长春园饭店

Changchunyuan Hotel (5 Xiyuan Caochang, Haidian District; tel: 283094; cable: 3023 BEIJING). Located across the street from Beijing University on the former site of the Changchunyuan (Soothing Spring) Royal Garden, the hotel is managed by the Ministry of Commerce and prides itself on its small size (76 rooms, including suites), its many services (bar, arts and crafts store, and beauty parlor), and reasonable prices. Opened in 1987, the Changchunyuan is a comfortable and inexpensive alternative to the city's deluxe hotels. All rooms are air-conditioned. *Rates:* Double: Y85; suite: Y170.

北京西直门饭店

Xizhimen Hotel. The 150-room Xizhimen Hotel opened in September 1986. It is located 7 km. from the city center in the western suburbs, near the zoo, Beijing Exhibition Center, and Xiyuan Hotel. The hotel was built as a joint venture with an entity from Inner Mongolia, and the lobby therefore features two large paintings of the Mongolian grasslands. In addition, of the two Chinese restaurants, the first-floor establishment will feature Mongolian barbecue. Other hotel facilities include a bar, foreign exchange, post office, shop, beauty parlor, billiard and electronic game rooms, medical clinic, meeting rooms, and a taxi stand. Business services will also be provided (telex, typing, and photocopying).

Rooms at the Xizhimen are all standard size—no suites. They are comfortably and attractively furnished, and all have air-conditioning, color TV, and telephones. There are two types of rooms—those with full bathroom (60 units) and rooms with a small stall containing shower and toilet (90 units).

The Xizhimen has to be considered one of the best hotel bargains in the city as it offers both low rates and pleasant surroundings. Direct bookings are accepted.

Address: Beixiaguan, Haidian District
Telephone: 802-2744 / 802-1155 *Rates:* Double: Y60
Cable: 4379

燕翔饭店

Yanxiang Hotel. Adjacent to the more fashionable Lido, the Yanxiang is simple, yet quite modern and comfortable. With the completion of the new wing in February 1985, the Yanxiang more than doubled its capacity, and now accepts direct overseas booking. All rooms are air-conditioned, carpeted, and provided with telephones and radios, and closed-circuit TVs have been installed in the older sections of the hotel. There is a Western-style coffee shop as well as a Chinese-style teahouse, where one can wile away the hours sipping green tea and playing Xiang-Qi (Chinese chess—boards and pieces provided). A Chinese restaurant at the rear features an exotic array of wild game.

Other facilities include a shopping arcade, an indoor swimming pool, a health club, and a barbershop. The courtyard has a pleasant garden and meals are well prepared and inexpensive. The hotel is a 15-minute drive from the airport, with about twice that amount of time required to reach the center of Beijing.

Address: 2A Jiangtai Road, Dongzhimenwai
Telephone: 500-6132   *Rates:* Standard: Y85–210
Telex: 210014 YXH CN   Suites: Y410
Cable: SWAL BEIJING 5046

陶然宾馆

Taoran Guesthouse. This small, faintly charming hotel opened in June 1986. It is a joint venture with Guangzhou Guesthouse. It is situated in Taoranting Park, which is a spectacular setting in summertime: weeping willow trees surround a small lake, where local citizens enjoy themselves boating and fishing.

The hotel itself has only three stories, with 132 guest rooms (including four suites). The lobby has impressive marble floors and Guangzhou-style ponderous, carved wooden furniture. Facilities will include a post office, bank, and shop. Rooms are somewhat plain but are large and comfortable. All are air-conditioned and equipped with refrigerators and color TV.

Currently only the Chinese restaurant (Yang Chang Jiu Lou) is open, specializing in Cantonese dishes. But the manager advises that his chefs will gladly prepare Western food on request. A Western restaurant, coffee shop, and bar were opened in 1987.

The hotel has its own taxi stand—an essential feature given its location within the park.

Address: Taiping Avenue   *Telephone:* 54-9796
Rates: First-floor rooms: Y80; second/third floor: Y110; suites: Y220

北纬饭店

Beiwei Hotel. The Beiwei Hotel, located south of Tian'anmen Square in a residential area close to Taoranting Park, was opened to foreign visitors in 1978 after serving for years as a hotel for Chinese guests. Rooms are small and spartan, but rates are commensurately fair.

The hotel was being refurbished in 1985–86, resulting mainly in the addition of a fifth floor and redecorating of the lobby (with splendid new murals) and dining room (where clusters of artificial grapes now hang from the ceiling). The Beiwei has 226 air-conditioned rooms (instead of the previous 176), most with private baths.

The Beiwei now has one dining room serving both Chinese and Western cuisine. Entrees range from Y2–7. Shops on the first floor sell souvenirs, arts and crafts, liquor, daily necessities, fruit, and candy. Recent additions are a barbershop, money exchange, and taxi stand.

Address: 13 Xijing Road
Telephone: 33-8631   *Cable:* 3362

Rates: **Floors 1–4**	**Floor 5**
Standard: Y68	Standard: Y80
Large: Y90	Studio suite: Y140
Suite: Y140	Two-room suite: Y221

南华酒店

Nanhua Hotel. The Nanhua Hotel is a small (49-room) hotel that opened in July 1986. It is located in an area which will assuredly please those seeking a firsthand look at the daily life of Chinese people. The Nanhua, set right in the midst of an area of small alleys and courtyard houses, has many rooms with small balconies that look directly into the surrounding dwellings.

Rooms are small but attractively appointed. All have air-conditioning, color TV, and bedside control panels. There is a Chinese restaurant specializing in Huiyang cuisine (Western food is served at breakfast only). There is also a very cozy bar, which serves a selection of imported liquors at curiously high prices (Y13 for a shot of Jack Daniels or Black Label; Y13 for a glass of Dynasty wine). The staff are young and seem enthusiastic and eager to please.

Address: 11 Nan Hua East Street (a five-minute walk from the Qianmen Hotel), off Hu Fang Road, Xuanwu District
Telephone: 33-7916; 33-2619   *Rates:* Standard room: Y120
Telex: 222430 NHHCC   Suite: Y200

日坛宾馆

Ritan Guesthouse. Conveniently located in Beijing's eastern embassy section, the Ritan has large, bright rooms, many with picture windows overlooking Ritan (Altar of the Sun) Park. Displaying some of the faded grandeur of Beijing in the 1920s, the rooms are appointed with lace curtains, carpets, and posh upholstery. All have private bathrooms, air-conditioning, TVs, and telephones. Chinese and Western dining rooms feature dishes prepared by prize chefs. Overseas bookings can be made by mail.

Address: 1 Ritan Road   *Rates:* Standard: Y120
Telephone: 500-2288   Large: Y180
Telex: 21007 RTH CN   Suite: Y350
Cable: 5956

天坛体育宾馆

Tiantan Tiyu Binguan (Temple of Heaven Sportsmen's Inn). Located near the northeast corner of the Temple of Heaven Park (about 4 km. from Tian'anmen) is this inconspicuous, 25-year-old, four-story brick building. Renovated in 1981 and again in 1984, this simple guest house caters to international sports delegations and individual athlete-travelers. Situated in a pleasant neighborhood, the Sportsmen's Inn is only 10 minutes from Chang'an Boulevard by public bus.

The 120 air-conditioned, mostly white-washed, high-ceilinged rooms have telephones, TVs, and baths. The small rooms are in fact quite tiny.

Two restaurants offer Western breakfasts from 7–9 AM and Jiangsu-style dishes at lunch (12–2 PM) and dinner (6–8 PM). Postcards, stamps, film, drinks, and handicrafts are sold in the small shop on the first floor. Long-distance calls are available, but there is no telex. A taxi stand was added in 1986.

Address: 10 West Tiyuguan Road
Telephone: 75-2831
Cable: 3128

Telex: 222283 CIST CN
Rates: Single: Y45
Double: Y68–100

首都机场宾馆

Capital Airport Hotel. A modern, functional facility, the Capital Airport Hotel is convenient for transit passengers and those who have early-morning flights out of Beijing and may want a few extra minutes of sleep. Besides the 210 guest rooms, facilities include a bar, a bank, and a beauty parlor. Reservations can be made from abroad, but only by cabling at least one week in advance. Closed during 1988 for renovations.

Address: Airport Road
Telephone: 55-8341 x3017
Cable: 6333 Beijing

Rate: Twin: Y56
Deluxe twin: Y70
Suite: Y140

大都饭店

Dadu Hotel. One of the least appealing of the old hotels, the Dadu is now mostly used by provincial cadres in Beijing on official business. All rooms come with private bath and are equipped with air-conditioning, TVs, and telephones. The singles are small, while the suites feature a sitting room big enough for 30 and a tiny bedroom. The hotel restaurant is undistinguished.

Address: Chegong Zhuang Dajie
Telephone: 89-0981
Telex: 222447 DDH CN

Rates: Small double: Y80
Suite: Y250

万寿宾馆

Wanshou Guesthouse. Built in the 1950s, the Wanshou is a small, clean, well-kept hotel featuring large, high-ceilinged rooms and peaceful surroundings. All rooms have private bathrooms and are equipped with air-conditioning, TVs, and telephones. Both Chinese and Western food are available.

Address: 12A Wanshou Road
Telephone: 81-2901

Rates: Standard: Y70
Suite: Y150

竹园宾馆

Zhuyuan (Bamboo Garden) Hotel. Originally the residence of the postal minister of the Qing Dynasty (and later inhabited by Kang Sheng—infamous cohort of the "gang of four"), this small complex of guest houses with its peaceful bamboo gardens and rockeries began accepting tourists in March 1982. Hidden down a narrow alleyway just northeast of the Drum Tower (Gu Lou), this new hotel caters to overseas business people, tourists, and government officials. Its limited accommodations (11 single rooms and four suites) were expanded to include an additional 24 rooms in a building in back. Although the rooms are small and simply furnished, each is air-conditioned and has a color TV. Some rooms are done in striking Chinese decor.

Address: 24 Xiaoshiqiao, Jiugulou West Street
Telephone: 44-4661
Cable: 3428
Telex: 22033 BBGH CN

Rates: Single: (old building) Y80
Single: (new building) Y200
Suites: Y300–380

紫玉饭店

Ziyu Hotel. Opened in March 1984, the Ziyu is one of several former courtyard residences converted for hotel use in recent years. Set in a neighborhood undergoing rapid and noisy reconstruction, the Ziyu is less than restful. Amenities are relatively modern. The original 125 rooms all face one of the many small, flower-filled courtyards, and all have private bathrooms, air-conditioning, TVs, and telephones. A new wing added in 1986, however, lacks even the modest attempts at charm and comfort of the original structure. The staff is friendly and efficient. Both Western and Chinese (Shandong and Sichuan) food are well prepared, but dining-room hours are limited.

Address: 5 Huayuan Cun, Fucheng Road
Telephone: 89-0191
Telex: 22078 ZIYU CN

Rates: Twin: Y75
Suite: Y130

民族文化宫客房服务部

Nationalities Cultural Palace Hotel. This hotel, not to be confused with the Minzu (Nationalities) Hotel, is located on floors 3–9 of the Nationalities Cultural Palace itself. Opened in 1980 to accommodate foreign tourists, this hotel has 44 newly painted, air-conditioned rooms (the newest on the sixth, seventh, and eighth floors), all of which are carpeted and equipped with TVs. The total of 44 rooms consists of 32 singles, 10 two-room suites, plus two huge deluxe rooms. Guests, who are mainly long-term residents, must take their meals at the Minzu Hotel.

Address: Fuxingmen Avenue   *Rates:* Standard: Y96
Telephone: 65-3231, x311   Large: Y127
                                 Suites: Y237

华侨饭店

Huaqiao Fandian (Overseas Chinese Hotel). Not to be confused with the Huaqiao *Dasha* (Overseas Chinese *Mansion*), the Huaqiao Fandian is a grade upwards in comfort, although it too offers few mansion-like amenities. Located in east-central Beijing, just a few minutes (5 km) from the railway station, the Huaqiao has 145 rooms with private bath, wall-to-wall carpeting, color TV, and air-conditioning.

There is a good Chinese restaurant, barbershop, shopping arcade, and taxi service.

Address: 5 Santiao, Beixinqiao   *Rates:* Single: Y110
Telephone: 44-6611   Twin: Y125
Telex: 210336 BOCH CN   Suite: Y185

BUDGET HOTELS

桥园宾馆

Qiaoyuan Hotel. The Qiaoyuan, apart from being one of the most reasonably priced (and most spartan) hotels in town, is also one of the liveliest—its clientele is a mixture of youthful budget travelers from around the world, and the hotel management and staff seem to welcome the atmosphere of conviviality. The Qiaoyuan is only about 6 km. from Tian'anmen Square. It can be reached easily from the railway station by taking bus #20 to the last stop and then walking a few minutes; other convenient bus routes are #106 and #116.

The Qiaoyuan has 207 rooms, including five rather grim-looking 20-bed dormitories (Y8 per bed). Most of the remaining rooms are tiny two-bed chambers with baths at Y36. All guest quarters are air-conditioned.

The restaurant serves Western food at breakfast (the French toast is recommended) and dinner, with Chinese cuisine featured at lunch. Its terrace is popular in the evening as a meeting place for sharing information and experiences about China travel. Among the usual facilities are a very helpful CITS desk in the lobby and a taxi stand. CITS organizes daily minibus trips to the Great Wall, leaving directly from the Qiaoyuan.

A new 12-story, standard-class wing of the Qiaoyuan was scheduled to open behind the present structure in late 1987. The double-room rate will be Y60.

Address: Dongbin He Road, Yong'anmen District
Telephone: 33-8861 x217
Rates: Double room (with private bath): Y36; bed in 15-space dormitory: Y8

飞霞饭店

Feixia Hotel. Opened in 1984, the Feixia is an inexpensive, 111-room hotel located approximately 4 km. west of Tian'anmen (10 minutes via the #48 bus line, which stops at both the railway station and Tian'anmen Square). It is in the midst of a complex of high-rise apartment buildings, directly behind the central government TV complex. There are 91 standard rooms, each with three beds that rent at Y9 per bed; standard rooms have no bathrooms. There are 20 "first-class" rooms, with two beds and private bath, at Y55 per day. All rooms have air-conditioning and TV. First-class rooms have telephones; there are public phone booths on each floor for other guests. Though furnishings are of budget quality, the rooms are of good size and seem reasonably clean and comfortable.

Other facilities at the hotel include foreign-exchange counter, taxi stand, CAAC booking counter, a small food shop, a Chinese restaurant, and an arts and crafts shop. Small as the Feixia is, its reservations system is computerized, and guests may book directly.

The restaurant, located in a separate building opposite the hotel, specializes in Muslim cooking. In addition to an à la carte dining room, there are banquet and private dining rooms where one can arrange such specialties as a "Whole Lamb Banquet" or a "Whole Duck Banquet."

Address: Building No. 5, Xili Xibiangmen, Xuanwuqu
Telephone: 34-1470   *Cable:* 0056

华侨大厦

Huaqiao Dasha (Overseas Chinese Mansion). The Overseas Chinese Mansion has long served as the capital's center for overseas Chinese visiting relatives in Beijing (it is not to be confused with the more expensive Overseas Chinese *Hotel*). The Chinese dining room serves good food at moderate prices.

Address: 2 Wangfujing Dajie Beikou
Telephone: 55-8851   *Cable:* 5588
Rates: Dormitory bed: Y10; double room (no bath): Y35; triple (no bath): Y54
     Standard room (with bath): Y85; triple (with bath): Y96; suite: Y150

惠中饭店

Huizhong Hotel. The 16-story Huizhong is a rather pleasant, even cheery addition to the capital's lower-priced hotels. Although it began operations in December 1985, it had not "officially" opened as of 1986. The Huizhong thus far has been catering mostly to tour groups from Hong Kong and Macao. All nationalities are welcomed, however, and direct bookings are accepted.

All 342 rooms are equipped with air-conditioning, telephones, color TVs, and carpeting. There are 26 two-room suites (with bath), and 26 single rooms with bath. All other rooms use shared bath facilities (bathing conditions are said to be particularly favorable for women, as female guests are few and need wait less to use the facilities). Rooms are of decent size and comfortably furnished.

The Huizhong has three Chinese restaurants; Western food is available at breakfast. The second-floor dining room is decorated in the manner of the Summer Palace, with a dragon fountain and walls covered with paintings and calligraphy. It specialized in "Qingting" (Imperial Court) cooking. Currently this restaurant is used mainly for banquets, but an à la carte menu is being prepared.

Other facilities include a taxi stand, money exchange, shop, massage, barber shop, and copying machine. A post office counter opened simultaneously with the installation of a telex in 1987.

Address: 120 Zhushikou Xi Dajie   *Rates:* Single (without bath): Y45
Telephone: 301-2255   Single (with bath): Y70
Cable: 3592   Suite: Y90–120

百乐酒店

Park Hotel. The Park, a small but airy hotel with 120 rooms, received its first guests in September 1987, with full completion in early 1988. Built with Hong Kong investment, the Park boasts a marble-faced lobby and lounge; a disco; a business center; a billiards room; car rental/transportation arrangements; and a clinic. The hotel's three restaurants offer Sichuan, Western, and Korean cuisine. All rooms at the hotel have air-conditioning, private bath, television, and international direct-dial telephones. The Park Hotel, located next to the Temple of Heaven, is 15 minutes from Beijing's shopping and business center.

Address: 36 Pu Huang Yu Lu   *Cable:* 8877
Telephone: 721-2233   *Rates:* Twin: Y90
Telex: 22968 PARK CN

乐游饭店

Le You Hotel. The six-story, 146-room Le You opened for business on May 1, 1985. Unfortunately, like so many Chinese-built structures, it gives the appearance of having in fact opened several decades ago. For a hotel of this category, however, it offers a surprising range of services. In addition to the standard post office, beauty salon, shop counter, and taxi stand, facilities also include telex and copy machines, a travel service desk, and a medical clinic. One service lacking at present is a bank counter, although one is planned in the future.

There is currently one Chinese restaurant at the Le You featuring Guangdong and Shandong cuisine (dinner served until the wee hour of 11 PM). A Japanese restaurant was scheduled to open in 1986 and a Western (French) restaurant by the end of that year. There is also a bar, with imported liquors served at half the price of the joint-venture hotels. Rooms at the Le You include three price categories: standard rooms, suites, and some very inexpensive, dormitory-type facilities for budget travelers. They are also rather sparsely furnished, although adequate. All are air-conditioned, carpeted, and have color TV. A drawback are the tiny bathrooms in all but the Y96 rooms.

The Le You is located 6 km. southeast of Tian'anmen, and 4 km. from the Temple of Heaven. It is convenient to many public bus lines.

Address: 13 Dong San Huan Nan Road, Chaoyang District
Telephone: 78-4752/4761   *Telex:* 20078 POTCO CN
Rates: Dormitory (four beds): Y10–15; standard: Y70–80; large: Y100; suite: Y150

光华饭店

Guanghua Hotel. Also designated as the "Beijing Center for Foreign Apprentices," the Guanghua maintains 83 private rooms for foreign visitors. Recently refurbished, most rooms are air-conditioned, with TV and private bath. Bookings should go through CITS, or may be made in advance through the mail. Closed in 1988 for renovations and due to reopen in early 1989.

Address: 38 Donghuan Bei Road   *Rates:* Standard: Y45 (no bath)
Telephone: 59-5142   Standard: Y72 (bath)
                                                                          Suites: Y85–115

京华饭店

Jinghua Hotel. Opened in 1985, the Jinghua is clean, comfortable, and very reasonable. All rooms now have private bath, air-conditioning, TVs, and telephones. There is a Chinese restaurant and a bar/disco.

Address: Yongdingmen waixiluyuan, Nanli
Telephone: 76-1331   *Rates:* Standard: Y40
Cable: 2857 Beijing   Large: Y51
                                                          Suite: Y102

鹿松园宾馆

Lusongyuan Guest House. One of Beijing's classic "courtyard" hotels, the Lusongyuan is located just a few blocks northeast of the Forbidden City. Despite its central location, the area immediately surrounding the hotel is rather quiet, making for a peaceful and relaxing setting. The formerly undistinguished restaurant has recently retained the services of master chef Tang Guoxing, whose specialty is a roast chicken prepared from a recipe passed down from an ancestor who served in the imperial kitchens of the Qing court.

Address: 22 Banchang Lane   *Rates:* Singles: Y67
Telephone: 44-0436   Double: Y73–94
                                                          Suite: Y109

北京大学招待所（勺园楼）

Beijing University Guest House/Shao Yuan Lou. Although situated about 45 minutes from Tian'anmen on the campus of "Beida," this simple facility is highly recommended on the basis of its university setting. Rooms are furnished with two cots and a desk, lamp, and chair. Bath facilities are shared. Inexpensive meals are available in the foreign students' dining room, also a good place for meeting students and resident foreign academics.

Address: Beijing University
Telephone: 28-2471 (ask for Shaoyuan Zhaodaisuo)
Rates: Twin (no bath): Y24; twin (with bath): Y45–67
　　　Air-conditioned suites: Y80–120

Other budget-level hotels in Beijing, listed according to their proximity to the center of town, include:

京丰宾馆
Jingfeng Guesthouse

Address: 71 Fengtai Road, Fengtai District
　　　Distance to train station: 20 km
　　　Distance to airport: 45 km
Amenities: Rooms with private bath, air-conditioning, color TV,
　　　telephone, bank.
Telephone: 37-2411
Rates: Single: Y75; twin: Y70; suite: Y120

芙蓉宾馆
Furong Guesthouse

Address: Ba Li Zhuang, Shilipu, Chaoyang District
　　　Distance to train station: 10 km
　　　Distance to airport: 28 km
Amenities: Rooms with private bath, air-conditioning, color TV, telephone,
　　　Chinese restaurant, shop, bank.
Telephone: 59-2921
Rates: Twin: Y72; suite: Y120

清华园宾馆
Qinghuayuan Guesthouse

Address: 45 Chengfu Road, Haidian District
　　　(near Beijing and Qinghua universities)
　　　Distance to train station: 27 km
　　　Distance to airport: 35 km
Amenities: Rooms with private bath, air-conditioning, color TV, telephone,
　　　dining room, post office.
Telephone: 256-2420
Rates: Twin: Y54–72; suite: Y150

回龙观饭店
Huilong Guan Hotel

Address: Changping Rd., Deshengmenwai (northern suburbs)
         Distance to train station: 31 km
         Distance to airport: 29 km
Amenities: Rooms with private bath, air-conditioning, color TV, telephone,
         health club (with massage), photo service, beauty salon, post office,
         bank; Chinese and Western restaurants.
Telephone: 291-3931   *Telex:* 210083 BHLGH
Rates: Twins: Y86–100; suite: Y255

花园饭店
Garden (Huayuan) Hotel

Address: Huayuan Nanlu, Haidian District
         Distance to train station: 32 km
         Distance to airport: 13 km
Amenities: Rooms with private bath, air-conditioning, color TV, telephone,
         massage and postal services (not connected).
Telephone: 66-9656
Rates: Twin: Y120

钟园饭店
Zhongyuan Hotel

Address: 16A Zaojunmiao, Haidian District
         Distance to train station: 32 km
         Distance to airport: 19 km
Amenities: Rooms with private bath, air-conditioning, color TV, telephone,
         bank, Chinese restaurant.
Telephone: 81-9459
Rates: Twin: Y70

In addition to the above listing, Beijing also has numerous low-cost guest houses, many of which may yield to gentle persuasion and accept foreign guests. Some have actually become quite popular with students and other budget travelers. Among these are the **Xuanwu Men Hotel,** at 30 W. Qianmen Ave. (tel: 34-1930); the **Yanshan Guest House,** at 56 Haidian Road (tel: 28-2394); the **Wannianqing Guest House,** near Zizhuyuan (tel: 89-1331); and the **Inner Mongolia Guesthouse,** at Meisuguan Houjie, Dongcheng.

BEIJING

CUISINE

Of course, there is Beijing Duck. But there is also a wide range of other specialties to try—virtually the entire gamut of China's many and varied cuisines are represented in Beijing's restaurants, limited only by the availability of local ingredients. Some of the capital's finest dining spots specialize in Shandong, Sichuan, Hunan, Cantonese, Mongolian, Shanghai, and other regional styles of cooking.

Northern or Beijing cuisine is naturally generic to most of the city's

Coffee-lounge, Great Wall Sheraton, Beijing

restaurants. Local cuisine features dishes such as pickled consommé, bird's nest soup, steamed and fried dumplings (*jiaozi* and *guotie*), braised fish in sweet red sauce, batter-fried shrimps, chili-fried pork, and for dessert, apples, bananas, or beaten egg whites enveloped in molten toffee, sprinkled with sesame seeds, and solidified in bowls of water at the table.

All of this can be washed down with some excellent beers, such as Beijing, Qingdao, and Waxing brands, or some good Chinese wine (made from sorghum or grapes), many tending to be sweet. The most highly regarded is the semisweet Shaoxing, usually warmed before serving.

Beijing has 400 restaurants and snack bars catering to over a million people a day. This actually represents a smaller volume than a decade ago, but urban reconstruction, damage by earthquakes, and changing residential patterns have taken their toll. The resultant overcrowding is being remedied, however, with the opening of many new restaurants. In any event, from the traveler's viewpoint, there is certainly no shortage of fine restaurants to choose from. In this section we can only introduce a few—as with any large city, the best insights into the ever-changing restaurant scene are to be gotten from local denizens upon arrival. Most restaurants discussed below have separate rooms for foreigners which are quieter and more comfortable than ordinary Chinese dining rooms. Throughout (in Beijing anyway), decor tends to be simple by international standards.

As a word of caution, most Beijing restaurants close their doors very early, usually around 7 PM.

Many of Beijing's hotel restaurants (discussed under individual hotels, above) offer fine versions of local and regional cuisines. Most do not require reservations and have staff that speak English. Moreover, for visitors with limited time in Beijing, the extra time and travel involved in visiting an outside restaurant may just add pressure to an already busy schedule. Some hotel dining rooms remain open "late"—until 8 or 9 PM.

BEIJING (PEKING) DUCK RESTAURANTS

The art of preparing Beijing Duck became popular in the 15th century, although the dish had existed much earlier as a delicacy for the aristocracy. The cooking process is a long and complicated one. For starters, the duck is scalded in boiling water, coated with molasses, pumped with air, and then hung up to dry for as long as 48 hours. Then it is slowly and evenly roasted over a fire of date, peach, and pear wood until it turns a golden brown color and looks almost lacquered. In this state, the shiny creature is carried to the table on a platter for presentation and approval (applause is appropriate—not for the duck, but for the kitchen staff). Next, the bird is sliced before the guests, who then dip their portions into a sweet bean sauce, and wrap them with pieces of green onion into paper-thin pancakes. The most favored morsels are the duck's skin.

The original Beijing Duck restaurant was opened in 1866 by a man called Yan Quanren, near Qianmen, the South (or "Front") Gate. Today the state and several former restaurant owners jointly manage a veritable chain of Beijing Duck establishments.

To supply restaurants of the capital with this famous fowl, a substantial number of agricultural communes in the Beijing vicinity rapidly nourish ducks to the desired plumpness through the method of force-feeding (it's probably best to have a duck farm visit *follow* the dinner).

It's necessary to reserve well in advance at any of the Beijing Duck restaurants.

全聚德
"Big Duck" Restaurant (The Qianmen Roast Duck). The Big Duck is located on the site of the original Beijing Duck restaurant, just south of Qianmen. It is the best establishment of its type, but its prices keep rising steeply, and some "precious" ingredients, such as "silver ear" fungus, now cost extra (perhaps, you'll think, just as well).

Address: 32 Qianmen Street
Telephone: 701-1379

北京烤鸭店二店
"Sick Duck" Restaurant (The Beijing Duck). The Sick Duck acquired its nickname from its proximity to the Capital Hospital. It is located in an alley off Wangfujing, one block north of the Beijing Hotel. The atmos-

phere is pleasant, due to recent renovations, but the prices here also climb continually. An average meal costs Y60–200.

Address: 13 Shuaifuyuan
Telephone: 55-3310

北京烤鸭店

"Wall Street" Duck (New Beijing Duck). Originally, this popular place had 30 employees with diners crowded into a three-story edifice. In 1979, it moved to new seven-story quarters—resembling a modern apartment building. Here it has 41 dining rooms and a seating capacity of 2,500. Over 40 different traditional duck dishes are prepared at the Wall Street Duck. Unfortunately, prices are sky-high, and sometimes reservations will not be accepted without prior agreement to run the bill to a minimum of Y50 per person (including drinks). Large tourist groups are now shuttled through the Wall Street Duck with assembly-line precision. As a result, service has become perfunctory and rather rushed. In all events, the Wall Street Duck is hardly a haven for quiet dining.

Address: Xinhua Nan Street, near Qianmen
Telephone: 33-4422

NORTHERN CUISINE

仿膳饭庄

Fang Shan ("Imitation Imperial") Restaurant. Fang Shan is a favorite dining spot in Beijing both for its setting and its cuisine. It is picturesquely located in Beihai Park at the edge of the North Lake. The chefs here recreate the food eaten by former emperors and empresses (a dream of the last empress led to the sesame seed biscuits stuffed with minced pork which are still served in the Fang Shan today). Tour groups have come here for three days of nonstop dining on the most exotic foods imaginable. In the event that reservations are secured (be sure to put in a bid the moment you arrive in town), count on spending at least Y50 per person for the ersatz "imperial" treatment.

Address: Beihai Park
Telephone: 75-1024

听鹂馆

Tingliguan (Listening to the Orioles Pavilion). This splendidly located restaurant overlooks Kunming Lake in the Summer Palace. Dishes include dried fish in sweet sauce, velvet chicken, dumplings, and other typical northern-style dishes. Service is leisurely.

Address: Summer Palace (Yiheyuan)
Telephone: 28-3955

日坛公园饭店

Ritan Gongyuan (Temple of the Sun Park) Restaurant. Those who crave a hot dog will find a reasonable facsimile at this restaurant (open to foreigners only), which also serves dishes such as dumplings, shrimps with pepper, and breaded pork and chicken slices.

Address: Ritan Park, north entrance (north of the Friendship Store)
Telephone: 59-2648

萃华楼饭庄

Cuihualou Restaurant. Every dish served here is a delicacy, and the variety available is large: shrimps, pork, vegetables, and soups are prepared in different ways, some northern- and others Shanghai-style. The unusual house dessert is a mixture of almond beans and fresh fruit, a fine coolant in summer.

Address: 60 Wangfujing (a 15-minute walk north of the Beijing Hotel)
Telephone: 55-2594

MUSLIM CUISINE

民族文化宫

Minzu Wenhua Gong (National Minorities Palace) Restaurant. This fine restaurant is located in the Nationalities Cultural Palace, next door to the Minzu Hotel. A variety of unique dishes is served here, including the best lamb in the capital.

Address: Fuxingmen Avenue
Telephone: 66-0544

北京烤肉季

Beijing Kaorouji (Beijing Grille). Guests can dine here outdoors in summer on a veranda overlooking Shichahai Lake. But the tasty barbecued mutton strips which give the restaurant its name are prepared only in the colder seasons. The chef is also adept at cooking a variety of delectables on request. (No pizza with anchovies, please.)

Address: 14 East Qianhai Dongyan
Telephone: 44-5921

东来顺饭庄

Donglaishun Fanzhuang. The Donglaishun is just one of five fine restaurants housed in and managed by the East Wind Market Complex, which is a 15-minute walk north of the Beijing Hotel. It serves the best Mongolian "hot pot" in the capital, offering it even during the summer. Copper cauldrons of sizzling broth are placed in the center of the table. Diners dunk paper-thin slivers of mutton and vegetables into the broth and then dip them into a mixture of hot and spicy sauces (practice your chopsticks *before* attempting the hot pot). The restaurant also serves an exemplary Beijing Duck.

Address: 16 Donghuamen
Telephone: 55-0069

鸿宾楼饭庄
Hongbinlou (Important Guests' House). Crispy fried dumplings (*guotie*) are as popular here as the shashlik, hot pot, and other Mongolian dishes. Recent patrons argue that its Beijing Duck is the best in town—and certainly cheaper than those offered at the "official" duck restaurants.

Address: 82 West Chang'an Avenue, near the central post office
Telephone: 65-6404

SHANDONG CUISINE

丰泽园饭庄
Fengzeyuan (Horn of Plenty). Tradition and reputation rank the Fengzeyuan as one of the finest restaurants in Beijing. Diners can choose to be treated to such subtle Shandong delicacies as braised shark fins, snowflake prawns, salted sea cucumbers, duck marrow soup, and braised asparagus. Its "silver thread rolls" are famous throughout the country (theoretically, each roll has 1,000 threads, but apparently no one has ever managed to refrain from eating long enough to count them).

In 1980, the Fengzeyuan Restaurant became famous throughout China when it was revealed in the Chinese newspapers that the Minister of Commerce, Wang Lei, had frequently dined on the restaurant's finest dishes and paid very low prices. The case—first exposed by a young cook at the restaurant—became one of China's most talked-about scandals.

On a subsequent visit, the Fengzeyuan was found to be overpriced and below expectations in both service and cuisine.

Address: 83 West Zhushikou Street
Telephone: 33-2828

同和居饭庄
Tongheju. Shandong's delicate cuisine also lives up to its reputation at the Tongheju. Some of the regional specialties featured here are juicy duck slices with pepper, savory egg-white froth, batter-fried shrimps, abalone with mushrooms, and crabmeat with vegetables.

Address: 3 South Xisi Street, north of Xidan
Telephone: 66-6357

SICHUAN CUISINE

四川饭店
Sichuan Restaurant. Formerly known as the Chengdu, this restaurant is notable for its hot, spicy food and old-world atmosphere. Several single-

floor pavilions are linked by cobblestone courtyards in the style of traditional China. Each wing contains several small dining rooms. One section offers a fixed-price banquet at reasonable rates, but tourists will need perseverance to gain entry to this part of the restaurant.

Its offerings include spicy, crisp chicken, fish in red chili sauce, prawns spiced with ginger and garlic, duck smoked in tea leaves and camphor, and chicken cooked with peppers and peanuts.

Address: Xuanwumennei Street
Telephone: 33-6356

峨眉饭店

Emei Restaurant. This is an old Sichuan restaurant relocated next to the Temple of the Moon Park. It is truly a "people's" restaurant—there is no special section for foreigners, but the waiters and waitresses are very obliging and sign language may be an effective means of ordering. Cold dishes and beer, bottled or draft, are selected at the front counter. If you feel adventuresome, order typical Sichuanese dishes such as *Mapo Dofu* (pock-marked beancurd) and *Ganshao Yu* (fish fried in chili sauce).

Address: Lishi Road and North Yuetan Street intersection
Telephone: 86-3068

力力餐厅

Lili Restaurant. One of Beijing's finest Sichuan restaurants, probably second only to the Sichuan Restaurant itself, the Lili specializes in spicy bean curd, fiery pork with peanuts and chilis, and hot spicy noodles.

Address: 30 Qianmen Road
Telephone: 75-2310

蜀乡餐馆

Shuxiang Restaurant. A ten-minute walk away from the Beijing Hotel (only five minutes from the Xinqiao Hotel), the Shuxiang offers a wide variety of spicy Sichuan dishes in a typical Chinese atmosphere.

Address: 40 Chongwenmennei Street
Telephone: 54-1715

SHANGHAI CUISINE

镇江饭馆

Zhenjiang Fanguan. Delectable Shanghai favorites such as crisp spring rolls, jumbo shrimps in a mouth-watering red sauce of wine, ginger, and brown sugar, sharks' fins in chicken puffs, and sweet-coated fried whole fish are served at the Zhenjiang.

Address: West Chang'an Avenue and Xidan intersection
Telephone: 66-2115

淮扬餐馆

Huaiyang Restaurant. The Huaiyang offers authentic Shanghai and Jiangsu cooking. Its seafood dishes are especially recommended.

Address: 217 North Xidan Street
Telephone: 66-0521

老正兴菜馆

Laozhengxing Caiguan. Located in the middle of the Qianmen shopping district, this restaurant serves good Shanghai cooking, especially seafood dishes.

Address: 46 Qianmen Road
Telephone: 75-2686

松江餐厅

Songjiang Canting. The menu at the Songjiang Restaurant covers a range of southern-cooking styles, and the clientele sometimes includes leading members of the municipal government whose offices are located directly across the street.

Address: 10 Taijichang Road
Telephone: 55-5222

CANTONESE CUISINE

广东饭店

Guangdong Fandian. Cantonese specialties here include turtle, poached fish, and fresh bamboo shoots. And dog.

Address: Xijiao Market, facing the Beijing Zoo
Telephone: 89-4881

YUNNAN CUISINE

康乐饭店

Kangle (Happiness and Enjoyment). Yunnan steamed chicken in herbs, Shanghai shrimps in sizzling rice, prawns or duck with walnuts, and deep-fried winter melon with dates and bamboo shoots are just a few of the items on the Kangle menu.

Address: 259 Andingmennei Road, north of Jiaodaokou
Telephone: 44-3884

VEGETARIAN CUISINE

北京素菜餐厅

Beijing Sucai Canting (Beijing Vegetarian Restaurant). Here the menu reads like that at any ordinary Beijing restaurant; for example, roast duck, steamed fish, and fried chicken are featured. However, vegetables alone are used in the preparation. Most remarkable is that the food on each dish also visually resembles duck, fish, chicken, etc. The platters are a marvel to the eye and taste splendid as well. The principal ingredients used are fresh vegetables, beancurd, nuts, and spices.

Address: 74 Xuanwumennei Street, south of Xidan
Telephone: 65-4296

WESTERN CUISINE

世界之窗餐厅

Windows on the World. This deservedly popular new restaurant, located on the 28th and 29th floors of the CITIC Building, is a joint venture between CITIC and Fuhua Enterprises (Maxim's Restaurants) of Hong Kong. It opened in October 1985 and rapidly established a reputation among Beijing's foreign community for attentive service and well-prepared food. "Windows" has a total seating capacity of 500, and comes by its name honestly—the corporation is a bonafide member of the World Trade Center Association.

The Chinese restaurant, by far the larger of the two, has a bright, airy feeling and a great view of the city (ironically, the view from the Western Restaurant one floor above is largely obstructed by a walled balcony). As might be expected, the specialty is Cantonese cuisine. The menu features Barbecued Suckling Pig, Panfried Prawn and Chicken Balls in Phoenix Nest, Sauteed Diced Pork with Cashew Nuts, and Dim Sum; a specialty of the house is Fortune (Beggar's) Chicken, which must be ordered six hours in advance. A Beijing "noodle-pulling" demonstration takes place nightly at 7:30 PM. A seasonal menu, reflecting market availability, is also offered and changes on a weekly basis. Prices are generally moderate, and dishes may be ordered in either standard (serving four people), or medium (six to eight) sizes. If you avoid the more expensive items, such as Braised Shark's Fin Superior (Y580), you can enjoy a most satisfying dinner at an average cost of Y35.

The Western restaurant is much smaller, and the mirrored walls and muted tones give it a more intimate feeling. Here you may indulge your craving for Western food with such dishes as onion soup, escargot, Caesar salad, rack of lamb, or beef Wellington. For dessert there is Crêpes Suzette or a wonderful chocolate soufflé. Finish with an Irish Coffee Diablo, prepared and flamed at your table.

Prices are higher here; an average dinner will run about Y55. At lunchtime a buffet is offered at Y20.

Other facilities at Windows include two small bars, although most of the one on the 28th floor has been appropriated for extra dining space to accommodate the high demand. Dinner is served until 10 PM.

Address: CITIC Building, 19 Jianguomenwai (adjacent to Friendship Store)
Telephone: 500-2255, x.2828; 500-3335

Preparing Beijing Duck

北京展览会餐厅

Beijing Exhibition Hall Restaurant. The Beijing Exhibition Hall complex, built and formerly used by the Soviets, is a landmark in the capital because of its towering church steeple. The former Moscow Restaurant still serves Russian borscht, caviar, chicken Kiev, fish or shrimps in cream sauce au gratin, beef Stroganoff, goulash, and steak. All served with a faint Chinese cast, but fine as a change of pace.

Address: Beijing Exhibition Center, Xizhimenwai Street
Telephone: 89-4454

国际俱乐部

International Club. An extensive selection of well-prepared European dishes is available at the International Club. The menu ranges from hamburgers to elaborate fish dishes. Chinese dishes are also featured.

Address: Ritan Road, near the Friendship Store
Telephone: 52-1084

友谊餐厅

Youyi (Friendship) Restaurant. Located just north of the Friendship Hotel, the Friendship Restaurant serves low-priced and acceptable Western food to Chinese patrons in one half of its large dining room (the other half serves good Chinese dishes).

Address: 3 Baishiqiao Road
Telephone: 89-0621 ext. 1602

JAPANESE CUISINE

白云日本餐厅

Baiyun Japanese Restaurant. Inside the Chinese-Japanese Friendship Guest House, at 7 Houyuan'ensi near Jiaodaokou, is this very authentic and very good Japanese restaurant. Built by the Segagakai Party of Japan, everything about the restaurant, from the building to the chef, is definitively Japanese. The prices also reflect this circumstance, however.

Telephone: 44-1036, ext. 264/265

"MASSES'" RESTAURANTS

While these establishments cannot match the fancier ones above in food, service, or decor, the cuisine is at least of an acceptable standard, and the prices are more modest.

东风市场餐厅
Dongfeng (East Wind) Market Restaurant. This highly typical Beijing masses' restaurant is on Jinyu Hutong at the north end of the market area. The dishes are highly spiced and cooked with a liberal use of oil; the plates of assorted cold cuts simple but delicious; the beer warm and flat; and the wait long. The upstairs dining room offers a better selection, but the downstairs is one of the few spots in town that stays open all night.

都一处烧麦馆
Duyichu Shaomai Restaurant. Located just down the way from the Big Duck Restaurant, this restaurant at 36 Qianmen Road specializes in *shaomai*, juicy pork dumplings served in the bamboo racks in which they are steamed.

华东西方咖啡店
Huadong Western Pastry Shop and Cafe. The Huadong, on Dongdan Street north of Chang'an Boulevard, serves a variety of homemade pastries (European style), hot dogs, coffee, and other refreshments. Cakes can also be ordered by phone (55-5401); prices range from Y6–20. The second floor has music and air-conditioning. The Huadong is open from 7 AM to 10 PM.

清风包子餐厅
Qingfeng Baozi Restaurant. The specialty at this restaurant, just a few doors east of the Xidan intersection at 122 West Chang'an Avenue, is *baozi*—steamed dough stuffed with pork and vegetable filling. *Hundun tang* (wonton soup) is also served.

人民餐厅
Renmin Canting (People's Restaurant). This busy restaurant at 17 Liangshidian Street, a lane that runs parallel to Qianmen Road, just south of Dazhalan, serves snacks and *jiaozi* (dumplings) downstairs and full meals upstairs.

山西烧面馆
Shanxi Xiaomianguan (Shanxi Noodle Restaurant). In this small eatery at 16 Dong'anmen Road, just west of the north end of Wangfujing, noodles are served Shanxi style with lots of vinegar.

燕京饭店
Yanjing Restaurant. Adjacent to the west wing of the Yanjing Hotel (19 Fuxingmen Avenue) stands a new "masses'" restaurant famous for its "sweet and sour fish." In contrast to the run-down dinginess of most masses'

restaurants, the Yanjing has lace curtains, white tablecloths, music, and clean linoleum floors. Opened in March 1981, it quickly became a "hangout" for the offspring of higher officials who come here for a leisurely, moderately priced meal or a few beers. (tel: 86-8721).

义利快餐

Yili Fast Food Restaurant. The Yili, at 145 Xirongxian Hutong (corner of Xidan Nan Lu), is Beijing's first Hong Kong-style fast-food establishment, offering a wide range of tasty Western and Chinese dishes. Although wholly Chinese-owned, most of the equipment (including a soft ice-cream machine) is imported. The Yili has quickly become very popular, although it is a bit expensive by local standards.

肯德基家乡鸡店

Kentucky Fried Chicken (Qianmen Street). China's first branch of the enormous U.S. fast food chain opened in Beijing in November 1987 amidst a clamour of hype and ceremony appropriate to the historical moment. Located just opposite the Mao Memorial, the Beijing branch of KFC, with seating for 500, is in fact the world's largest restaurant in the Colonel's universe. Average meals cost about $1.75, expensive for China, but not high enough to put off throngs of Chinese patrons, whose main problem is negotiating through the large cuts without benefit of chopsticks.

NIGHTLIFE AND ENTERTAINMENT

After the revolution of 1949, a curtain of Puritan prudishness descended on the once lively if seamy entertainment world of Beijing. The ubiquitous teahouses and wineshops disappeared, and not a trace remained of the pleasure houses of the past. Social dancing flourished briefly during 1979–81, but was officially proscribed in late 1982. In 1983, discos were opened within the confines of the Jianguo, Great Wall, and Huaqiao hotels, but as "tourists only" establishments. Most hotels still maintain cafés for late-night imbibers.

While outlets for socializing remain limited, Beijing's cultural offerings are more numerous than ever: 11 museums, six exhibition centers, 22 public libraries, 96 centers for cultural activities, 99 cinemas, seven stadiums, and 33 parks. For Chinese and foreigners alike, the most popular form of entertainment in Beijing now is the theater, with selections ranging from traditional Chinese opera to Chinese productions of Chekhov and Arthur Miller. Musicians, acrobats, and athletes all draw large crowds, and there are never enough tickets to go around. The only tickets that are relatively easy to obtain are tickets to the cinema. Foreign visitors should first try to secure reservations through CTS, although cinema box offices will sell tickets to foreigners provided they come early enough. In Beijing, everything sells out.

CULTURAL PERFORMANCES FOR TOURISTS

Traditional Chinese cultural performances include opera, music and dance, and acrobatics.

Chinese Opera. Chinese opera is a marvelous mix of acting, singing, dancing, acrobatics, and mime. If the piercing singing style, accompanied by clashing cymbals and gongs, is difficult for most foreigners to appreciate, the visual impact of the gorgeously costumed characters is instantly appealing. The story is usually a classical tale depicting the struggle between good and evil—although a few companies have experimented with modern subjects.

Of the eight opera companies in Beijing, four specialize in "Peking Opera." The best known of all Chinese opera styles, Peking Opera has a relatively short history, emerging as a distinct form from its central China antecedents only around 1830. Since then, Peking Opera has undergone many changes at the hands of great performers like Mei Lanfang (1894–1961), who broadened the medium and introduced a host of new styles. The four Peking Opera companies are the China Peking Opera Company (Zhongguo Jingju Tuan), the Beijing Peking Opera Company (Beijing Jingju Tuan), the Beijing Experimental Peking Opera Troupe (Beijing Shiyan Jingju Tuan), and the Beijing Wind-and-Thunder Peking Opera Troupe (Beijing Fenglei Jingju Tuan). All but the last have toured abroad.

Other kinds of opera performed in Beijing include *kunqu*, one of the oldest forms of Chinese opera; *ping* opera, a northern style; *bangzi* or "rattle" opera, a local style; and *yue* opera from the south. For each of these forms there exists a separate opera troupe.

The major opera theaters are Capital Theater (Shoudu Juchang), Wangfujing, tel: 55-4877; February Seventh Theater (Erqi Juchang), Zenwumiao, tel: 86-6262; Guanghe Theater (Guanghe Juchang), Qianmen Roushi, tel: 75-1892; Labor Theater (Laodong Juchang), Working People's Cultural Palace (Laodong Renmin Wenhua Gong), tel: 55-0474; People's Theater (Renmin Juchang), Huguosi Street, tel: 66-2249; and Tianqiao Theater (Tianqiao Juchang), East Beiwei Road, tel: 33-0513.

Music and Dance Concerts. The spectrum of music and dance performances is broad, ranging from concerts by the Central Philharmonic Orchestra to rousing performances of traditional Mongolian and Uighur folk dances by the Central Nationalities Song and Dance Troupe (Zhongyang Minzu Gewu Tuan).

Bejing also boasts two Western-style opera and ballet companies: the Central Opera and Ballet Company (Zhongyang Geju Wuju Tuan), which relies mostly on Western techniques and repertoire; and the China Opera and Ballet Company (Zhongguo Geju Wuju Tuan), which is experimenting with indigenous forms to create a distinctly Chinese style. Both companies toured the United States in 1978.

Besides the theaters already mentioned, the main concert halls are Beijing Exhibition Hall Theater (Beijing Zhanlanguan Juchang), Zhanlan

Teenage acrobatic troupe from Changchun

Road, tel: 89-4455; Beijing Workers' Club (Beijingshi Gongren Julebu), Hufang Road, tel: 35-5390; Concert Hall (Yingyue Tang), Zhongshan Park, tel: 55-5059; and Nationalities Cultural Palace Auditorium (Minzu Wenhua Gong Litang), Xidan, tel: 66-2530.

Acrobatics. Acrobats have been the most popular entertainers in China for at least 22 centuries! After the 1949 revolution, the China Acrobatics Troupe (Zhongguo Zaji Tuan) was one of the first groups organized by the government. It began strictly as a team of traditional acrobats, then expanded to include animal acts in 1958. The other big troupe is the Beijing Acrobatics Troupe (Beijing Zaji Tuan), specializing in a local style called Tianqiao (Bridge of Heaven) acrobatics—named after the district outside the Temple of Heaven where acrobats used to perform in imperial times. Since they are among the best in the country, these two troupes are often sent on tour. But visitors to Beijing can still see performances by the troupes organized by each of the city's districts.

Acrobatic shows are performed at Beijing Gymnasium (Beijing Tiyuguan), Tiyuguan Road, tel: 75-7381; Capital Gymnasium (Shoudu Tiyuguan), Baishiqiao Road, tel: 89-0281; and Workers' Gymnasium (Gongren Tiyuguan), Chaoyangmenwai Street, tel: 59-2961.

MASS CULTURE

Theatrical events of varying kinds, movies, and sports events are all popular with the Chinese people.

Popular Theater. After opera, the favorite theater entertainment in Beijing is *quyi,* "the art of verse." *Quyi* is basically storytelling and comic dialogue, China's version of the standup comic routine. The Beijing Quyi Troupe (Beijing Quyi Quju Tuan) plays in theaters around the city and sometimes contributes skits to variety and acrobatic shows.

Basketball drill at Beijing Physical Culture Institute

Beijing also has three Western-style drama companies, but the reliance on melodramatic Soviet socialist realism does not sit well with most Western audiences. The China Children's Drama Company (Zhongguo Ertong Yishuju Tuan) is also based in Beijing.

One theatrical form well worth seeing in China is puppet theater. Combining traditional puppetry with modern techniques, the China Puppet Drama Troupe (Zhongguo Mu'ou Yishuju Tuan) plays to packed houses whenever it performs. Unfortunately, this troupe has no permanent theater.

Movies. Beijing has some 100 full-time movie theaters, but movies are also shown in theaters, clubs, auditoriums, factory and school cafeterias, and even parks. The majority of the films are Chinese-made, heavy on theatrics and overt political messages. Among the few foreign films that are shown, Charlie Chaplin's are the best-known and the best-loved.

Film showings are often arranged in hotel auditoriums; the Friendship Hotel, for example, shows films every Friday night and supplies earphones with English translations. But you might want to try your luck at a public cinema. The following are within easy reach of some of the main hotels: Capital Cinema (Shoudu Yingyuan), West Chang'an Avenue, tel: 65-6575; Changhong Cinema (Changhong Yingyuan), Renmin Shichang Street, tel: 44-1160; Dahua Cinema (Dahua Yingyuan), 82 North Dongdan Street, tel: 55-0125; Zhonghua Cinema (Zhonghua Yingyuan), South Tianqiao Street, tel: 33-3586.

Sports Events. Beijing hosts a large number of national and international sports events of high caliber. China is strongest in Ping-Pong and volleyball, but basketball, soccer, and gymnastics are all popular spectator sports. The mammoth Workers' Stadium (Gongren Tiyuchang) in the city's northeast suburb, completed in 1961, can hold 80,000 people.

SHOPPING

When the imperial court moved to Beijing in the 15th century, it brought along an army of craftsmen to make its luxuries and necessities. By 1593, an official claimed that "today all possessions under heaven are amassed in the capital." Beijing still retains something of that reputation four centuries later.

Distinctive Beijing craft goods include cloisonné, jade, carved ivory, and lacquerware, all handicrafts which flourished in response to the demands of the imperial court. The same is true of lanterns, embroidery, and carpets. Beijing carpets, usually woven of soft wool, are not as durable as the costlier carpets from the nearby city of Tianjin, but they include a larger array of patterns.

Besides these palace crafts, Beijing also offers a range of folk crafts: batik cloth, kites, silk flowers, and figurines made of clay, glass, or shiny silk floss.

Antique and art collectors will find what they are looking for in specialty shops in the Liulichang district. Those interested in picking through more ordinary secondhand goods may try the commission shops (*xintuo shangdian*) scattered throughout the city. For such items as used watches, porcelain, and clothing, visit the commission shops at 113 North Dongdan Street and 12 Dongwenmennei Street in the east end, 128 Di'anmenwai Street near the Drum Tower in the north end, or 119 Qianmen Road in the city's southwest sector.

Prices. In the late 1970s, prices ceased to be uniform throughout China, or even within a given locality. An item sold in a tourist shop may

be less expensive in a neighborhood store located off the beaten path. However, there is little time for comparison shopping, and the attractive jade earrings or bamboo basket seen at a "foreigners' shop" in Wangfujing Street may not turn up elsewhere. So it may be best to suppress the bargain-hunting instinct and to "seize the moment." In all events, haggling is not generally acceptable in China, especially in state-owned establishments. In smaller, out-of-the-way shops, however, bargaining is known to occur. For antiques and high-priced items, some "friendly inquiries" about price might even be advised. If there are serious qualms about cost, the best solution is not to buy.

FRIENDSHIP STORE

友谊商店

Beijing's **Friendship Store** on Jianguomenwai Avenue (about one mile east of the Beijing Hotel) is the largest of its kind in China. Its third or top floor sells furniture, paintings, cloisonné, jade, ivory, silk hangings, pottery, and other fine art and handicraft items. A wide selection of carpets is sold in a separate shop at the back of this floor. The second level stocks an array of cloth items, from the finest silks to synthetic textiles, clothing, and scarves. Furs, luggage, toiletries, and toys can also be purchased on the second level. The first or ground floor is filled with a variety of imported and domestic edibles, from pastries to meats and fish, and a wide range of wines, spirits, and tobacco. Attached to the main "supermarket" is a florist and pet shop.

Even if Beijing is the first stop in China, it may be best to shop at the Friendship Store, since many items found there may not be available anywhere else in the country (except quite possibly in Hong Kong). It is also the only place in Beijing (and for that matter, one of the few in all of China) that will take care of packaging, customs clearance, and shipping, even for items purchased elsewhere. There are no bargains in the shipping charges, however, which may run as high as Y600 per cu. m. (35 cu. ft.).

The Friendship Store is open from 9 AM to 9:30 PM daily (subject to seasonal variations); its Bank of China Branch is open to exchange money from 9 AM to 7 PM.

DEPARTMENT STORES

百货大楼

Main Department Store (Baihuo Dalou), 255 Wangfujing Street, tel: 512-6677. On the west side of Wangfujing, set back from the street, is the largest and best-stocked department store in Beijing. Three floors of merchandise cover a total area of 12,600 sq. m. The first floor carries daily necessities, foodstuffs, and electrical goods. Piece goods, watches, stationery, and musical instruments are sold on the second floor, and clothing and shoes on the third. Except for a few Japanese-made luxury goods, such as color televisions and watches, everything is Chinese-designed and Chinese-made.

东风市场

Dongfeng Market (Dongfeng Shichang), 130 Wangfujing Street, tel: 55-8351. Across the street from the Main Department Store, behind the shops on the east side of Wangfujing, is the Dongfeng Market. Originally a series of separate stalls, the market complex was rebuilt as a unified store in 1969. The market has three entrances off Wangfujing, and a fourth at the north end. Under one roof you will find a full range of merchandise, ranging from hardware to clothing. At the north end are a baked goods counter and a bookstall stocked with foreign books—mostly antiquated science textbooks. The best place in town to have luggage repaired is in a stall next to the market's chop shop (also highly recommended). The luggage stall will also affix wheels to your existing pieces.

西单百货商场

Xidan Emporium (Xidan Baihuo Shangchang), 120 North Xidan Road, tel: 66-2406. This department store in the west end of the city is Beijing's newest, completed in the mid-1970s. Although slightly smaller than the store on Wangfujing, it offers a more attractive setting for the full range of daily necessities, yard goods, clothing, and hardware. It is located east of the Xidan intersection, a 15-minute walk from the Minzu Hotel.

SHOPPING DISTRICTS

In addition to the Friendship Store and large department stores, there are innumerable specialty shops scattered throughout the city. Moreover, since 1984, a new shopping phenomenon has been emerging in the capital: night markets, which are now flourishing at the major shopping areas of Zhongguancun, Xidan, Wangfujing, Di'anmen, and Dong'anmen, among others. Instantly popular, many markets have grown to 100 or more stalls, selling clothing, housewares, food, and other items, usually at bargain prices. Many remain busy until 10 PM or later, with neighboring shops also staying open to keep pace. Below, grouped by district, are some shops which may be of interest to foreign visitors.

王府井

Wangfujing. The main shopping district in Beijing, Wangfujing is just around the corner from the new wing of the Beijing Hotel. As you turn onto the street from Chang'an Avenue, the large, modern building on your right, at No. 212, is the **New China Bookstore** (Xinhua Shudian), the main branch of China's national bookstore chain. Although only Chinese-language books are sold here, there is a good selection of posters, postcards, and wall maps on the second floor. Books in foreign languages are sold past the intersection on the left. At No. 200 is the **Beijing Arts and Crafts Service Store** (Beijing Gongyi Meishu Fuwubu). The third and fourth floors comprise a small Friendship Store specializing in crafts of high quality, including furniture and jewelry, and some rather grisly-looking furs. The first two floors, open to the Chinese public, sell less expensive art and craft items. Pottery, paper, and art supplies are sold on the first floor; linens, embroidery, and figurines on the second. Although the lower two floors close at 6 PM, the upper floors stay open until 8 PM for tourist groups.

Farther north, on the same side of the street, is the **China Fur and Leather Clothing Store** (Zhongguo Pihuo Fuzhuangdian) at No. 192. This store, catering to foreigners only, has a good selection of coats, jackets, vests, hats, and gloves, and is prepared to make any of these items to order.

At the corner of the next block is the **Lantian Style Shop** (Lantian Shizhuangdian), No. 178, a branch of a clothing store chain specializing in larger sizes. Women's fashions are found on the street floor, men's fashions upstairs. The styles are quite limited. There are two watch stores on the same block, the **Seiko Watch Store** at No. 174 and the **Capital Clock and Watch Store** (Shoudu Zhongbiaodian) at No. 170. The Seiko store, for the Chinese, is one of the most fascinating attractions on Wangfujing. The contrast with the Chinese watch store is striking. Between the two, at No. 172, is the **New China Children's Goods Store** (Xin Zhongguo Ertong Yongpin Shangdian), which carries the largest selection of children's clothing and toys in Beijing.

Just south of the first entrance to Dongfeng Market are two stores called **Tongshenghe,** No. 158, and **Shengxifu,** No. 156. Tongshenghe is the latter-day version of a shoe emporium established on this site at the beginning of the 20th century by a Tianjin hat and shoe merchant. A competitor by the name of Shengxifu, not to be outdone, set up his own branch right next door. After both stores were nationalized in 1956, they agreed upon a division of labor: shoes at Tongshenghe and hats at Shengxifu. North of Dongfeng Market is the **Capital Medicine Shop,** No. 136, the largest pharmacy dispensing traditional Chinese drugs in Beijing.

At the intersection of Wangfujing and Dong'anmen Street, cross to the west side of Wangfujing and proceed south. At No. 231 is the **Musical Instruments Store,** which stocks both Chinese and Western instruments, but specializes in traditional Chinese wind instruments.

Farther south at No. 255 is the **Main Department Store,** which has been described above. In the next block, at No. 261, is the **Wangfujing Seal-Engraving Store** (Wangfujing Kezi Menshibu). This store sells elaborately carved stone seals and inscribes them to order.

The **Arts Store** at No. 265 sells mostly scroll paintings in classical styles and tomb rubbings. A few doors south, at No. 289, is the **Beijing Paintings Shop** (Beijing Huadian), which carries a good selection of works by contemporary artists in both traditional and modern styles, including the occasional oil painting.

Continuing south, you come to an electrical and audio equipment store at No. 295, a good place to see what the Chinese produce in terms of radios, record players, and televisions. Finally, just before reaching the Beijing Hotel at the south end of Wangfujing, there is the **Hongguang Photographic Equipment Store** (Hongguang Zhaoxiang Qicai Shangdian), at No. 299. The store carries film, albums, photographic supplies, and the latest in the state of the photographic arts in China.

琉璃厂

Liulichang. Since the 18th century, Liulichang has been Beijing's mecca for collectors of old books, art, and antiques. Nearly obliterated during the Cultural Revolution, the area is now enjoying a flurry of urban renewal under the stimulus of foreign tourism. Renovations were virtually complete as of mid-1985 and by late 1988, the entire district around Liulichang was being embellished with new restaurants and small hotels, creating an *ersatz* cultural district for tourists.

Some of the more famous shops described here may change names and locations in the next few years. Many of the restorations have stayed true to the original styles, and have somewhat succeeded in retaining the neighborhood's original appeal.

Liulichang runs east-west, south of and parallel to Qianmen Street in the city's southwest. From the Qianmen Hotel, it is one kilometer due north, and can be reached on foot or by taking bus #14 two stops. From the Beijing Hotel, the district is best reached by taxi. Taxis should be retained for the return trip.

At the entrance to Liulichang Dong Street, the complex of old and new bookstores at No. 115, facing the small parking lot, is operated by **China Bookstore** (Zhongguo Shudian). The shop to the left of the passageway into the courtyard is called **Literary Elegance Retreat** (Wenya Sui) and sells Chinese books in print on cultural and historical topics. To the right is **Hall of the Star of Literature** (Wenkui Tang), selling old Chinese books as well as some paintings and rubbings.

The large courtyard behind is graced with galleries on both sides. The one on the left, the **Sea of Books** (Wenyuan), sells new and used Chinese books; the one on the right, the **Chinese Painting Gallery** (Zhongguo Yiyuan Hulang; tel: 33-7281), sells an eclectic collection of scroll paintings by contemporary artists along with writing brushes, inkstones, and related handicrafts. At the far north end, the **Educated Youth Service** (Zhiging Fuwu She) sells cheap new and used books.

Glorious Treasures Studio (Rongbaozhai), at No. 19, is justly the most renowned store in Liulichang. Founded as a paper store and woodcut workshop in the 17th century, Rongbaozhai continues to train craftsmen in the tradition of woodblock-printed notepaper and watercolor reproductions that are indistinguishable from the originals. The reproductions are displayed in the west half of the store, while a remarkable collection of watercolor originals hangs in the east half. The shop does its own scroll mounting and will accept commissions; the work takes from two to three weeks.

A block farther west of the Glorious Treasures Studio (on the opposite side of the street) at No. 78 West Liulichang Street (tel: 33-3276) is the **Artistic Seal Carving Shop** (Cui Wen Ge). Another "chop" store is the **Seal Carving Shop** (Yin Hen Lou) located in its new storefront at 35 South Xinhua Street. This store (located just a one-minute walk south of the China Bookstore complex) has been producing coveted chops and seals for more than 80 years. The Seal Carving Shop usually requires a minimum of three days for seal-carving work.

西单

Xidan. Xidan is an old commercial area in the west end, second only to Wangfujing in popularity. It is just east of the Minzu Hotel, two stops from the Beijing Hotel on bus #1, and six stops from the Qianmen Hotel on trolley #102.

Most of Xidan's interesting shops are on the right side as you walk north. The shoe shop at No. 178 has a good selection of shoes and sandals for men, women, and children. Ballet slippers are sold two doors up at No. 174. The **Xidan Chopstick Store** (Xidan Kuaizi Shangdian) at No. 160 is the only one of its kind in Beijing. Besides a wide assortment of chopsticks, the shop sells craft items ranging from walking sticks to good-quality porcelain—especially tea sets. Fans are featured in the summer months.

Past the alley decked with ads for the Hongguang Cinema is a complex of old shops linked by covered corridors: first a food store, then a bookstore with used books in the back and a good selection of posters and postcards in an alcove in the south wall. A Western-style ice cream parlor upstairs serves refreshments throughout the day. Continuing north past the knitting shop at No. 139, you come to **Xidan Emporium** (Xidan Baihuo Shangchang), one of the largest in this part of the city.

If you are walking back to the Xidan intersection, cross over to the west side of the street and take a look at the produce market at No. 195. You will get an idea of what is in season and what is available to the average Beijing shopper. Among the other stores between this point and the intersection are a pharmacy at No. 215, selling both Western and Chinese traditional medicines, and a glass and mirror store at No. 227.

前门

Qianmen. A tangle of old stores selling all sorts of merchandise has flourished along Qianmen Road and down its narrow side streets for centuries. To get to this shopping district from the Qianmen Hotel, walk east one kilometer to the traffic lights and turn north up Qianmen Road. From the Beijing Hotel, take bus #20 three stops heading west.

The first store on the west side of Qianmen Road is the oddest turn-of-the-century building in the district. This three-layered wedding cake in green is now the **Qianmen Clock and Watch Repair Shop** (Qianmen Zhongbiao Shoulibu). Behind it, facing the small parking lot, is the **Beijing Silk Store** (Beijing Sichou Shangdian) at No. 5.

At the head of the line of shops running down the other side of the street is the **Xinsheng Musical Instruments Store** (Xinsheng Yueqidian), No. 18 Qianmen Road, specializing in traditional Chinese percussion instruments—gongs, chimes, bells, cymbals, and the biggest drums sold in Beijing. Two doors down, at No. 22, the **Spring Fragrance Tea Store** (Chunxiang Chazhuang) offers a wide assortment of teas dispensed from floor-to-ceiling wooden chests of drawers. Besides loose tea, you can buy tea leaves that have been compressed into blocks and shipped from China's mountainous southwest. At No. 28 is **Hall of Eternal Youth** (Changchun Tang), a pharmacy dispensing traditional Chinese medicines.

Next door at No. 32 is the original **Beijing Duck Restaurant,** and beyond that, three masses' restaurants—Lili, Duyichu, and Laozhengxing.

At this point you will be across from a bicycle parking lot fenced in with advertising billboards. Between the lot and the **Qianmen Stationery Store** (Qianmen Wenhua Yongpin Shangdian) is a small lane leading into the old shopping district called **Dazhalan.**

Continuing south on the west side of Qianmen Road, you come to the **Hunan Pottery Store** (Hunan Taoci Shangdian) at No. 99. Hunan Province is a major producer of pottery and porcelain, some of which is exported abroad. This retail outlet offers pieces—from tea sets to garden stools—that have fallen slightly short of export standards. A few doors down at No. 119 is one of Beijing's many commission shops, this one carrying everything from used furs to pure junk.

Although the Qianmen shopping district stops at the first set of traffic lights south of the gate—the Zhushikou intersection—there are a few interesting shops further south. The **Jingdezhen Artistic Porcelain Store** (Jingdezhen Yishu Ciqi Fuwubu), No. 149, is a must for lovers of fine china. The kilns of Jingdezhen in the central province of Jiangxi have been turning out high-quality blue-and-white ware for centuries. Finally, at the end of the lane next to No. 130 on the east side of the street, there is a theater costume workshop where you can buy stage props and costumes that are used in Chinese plays, operas, and ballets. Little of the stock is on display, so an interpreter would help a great deal.

The famous Wei-Wei

BEIJING DIRECTORY

HEALTH AND EMERGENCY SERVICES	Telephone
Peking Union Medical College Hospital, North Dongdan St.	55-3731, ext. 251/274
Police Emergency	110/500/1110

TELEPHONE AND TELEGRAPH SERVICES	Telephone
Information (local calls)	174
Information (long-distance calls)	115
Long-distance (domestic, Chinese-speaking)	113/173
Long-distance (domestic, English-speaking)	55-3536
Long-distance (international)	115
Beijing Post and Telecommunications Office, West Chang'an Ave.	66-6215
Domestic telegraph information	66-7895
International telegraph information	66-4800

FOREIGN EMBASSIES	Telephone
Australia, 15 Dongzhimenwai, Sanlitun	52-2331/6
Brazil, 27 Guanghua Rd., Jianguomenwai	52-2740
Canada, 10 Sanlitun Rd., Sanlitun	52-3536
Finland, 14 Liangmahe Rd.	52-1817
France, 3 Dongsan St., Sanlitun	52-1331/3
Germany, Federal Republic of, 5 Dongzhimenwai, Sanlitun	52-2161/5
Italy, 2 Dong'er St., Sanlitun	52-2131
Japan, 7 Ritan Rd., Jianguomenwai	52-2361
Mexico, 5 Dongwu St., Sanlitun	52-2574
Netherlands, 14 Liangmahe Rd.	52-1131
New Zealand, 1 Dong'er St., Ritan Rd.	52-2731/4
Sweden, 3 Dongzhimenwai, Sanlitun	52-3331
Switzerland, 3 Dongwu St., Sanlitun	52-2736
United Kingdom, 11 Guanghua Rd., Jianguomenwai	52-1961/4
United States, 3 North Xiushui St., Jianguomenwai	53-2831
Consular Office, Bruce Bldg., 2 East Xiushui St., Janguomenwai	53-2831

TRAVEL	Telephone
China International Travel Service (CITS)	
Head Office, 6 East Chang'an Ave.	51-21122
North America Department	51-22138
Beijing Branch Office, Chongwenmen Hotel	51-22211
FIT (independent travelers) Head Office, Chongwenmen Hotel	
Room 1302; FIT Branch Office, Huadu Hotel, Room 5102	51-22006
China Travel Service (CTS)	
Head Office, 8 Dongjiaominxiang	55-3491

Air

Civil Aviation Administration of China (CAAC)	
Beijing Branch Office, 117 West Dongsi St.	55-2515

Hotels

Beijing Hotel Company	
Qianmenwai Roushi Jie	55-0681
Beijing Hotel Information Desk	
Beijing Railway Station	516-7766

Rail

Beijing Railroad Station	55-4866
Guang'anmen Railroad Station	36-1183
Xizhimen Railroad Station	89-2668
Yongdingmen Railroad Station	33-0031

Local Transportation

Shoudu (Capital) Taxi Company (English-speaking dispatchers)	55-7461
Beijing Taxi Company	78-2561
Beijing Travel Service Taxi	75-5246
Beijing Auto Service Co.	59-4290
Taxi stations (also at all major hotels and restaurants):	
Wangfujing	55-0221
Dongsi	44-1056
Qianmen	65-4007
Xidan	65-6406
Bicycle Rental	
Jianguomenwai Bicycle Repair Shop	59-2391
Dongsi Bicycle Rental	44-1056
Xidan Bicycle Repair Workshop	
Xuanwumenei Dajie	65-4005
Xidanliaoyuan Bicycle Repair Service (24 hours)	
Xidan Bei Dajie	66-7928
Dongsishitiao Bicycle Rental	44-3613

POINTS OF INTEREST	Telephone
Agricultural Exhibition Hall, North Donghuan Rd.	58-2331
Beijing Exhibition Center, Xizhimenwai St.	89-0661
Beijing Gymnasium, Tiyuguan Rd.	75-7381
Beijing Library, Wenjin St.	831-5566
Beijing Planetarium, Xizhimenwai St.	89-3003
Beijing Zoo, Xizhimenwai St.	831-4411
Capital Gymnasium, Baishiqiao	89-0281
Friendship Store, Jianguomenwai Ave.	59-3531
International Club, 21 Jianguomenwai St.	52-2144
Lu Xun Museum, Gongmenkou Xisantiao	66-7033
Military Museum of the People's Revolution, Fuxing Rd.	86-3580
Museum of Chinese History, Tian'anmen Square	55-8321
Museum of the Chinese Revolution, Tian'anmen Square	55-6155
Museum of Natural History, Tianqiao Rd.	75-1254
National Art Gallery, Wangfujing St.	44-2098
Nationalities Cultural Palace, Fuxingmen Ave.	65-3231
Palace Museum, Jingshanqian St.	55-5031
Summer Palace, Yiheyuan Rd.	28-1931
Temple of Heaven, Tiantan Rd.	75-4368
Workers' Stadium, Chaoyangmenwai, Tiyuchang Rd.	59-2961
Xiannongtan Stadium, Xiannongtan	33-8801

Changchun

長春

eternal spring   *traditional spelling/Changchun*

CHANGCHUN, the capital of Jilin Province since 1954, is situated on the Yitong River in the central part of China's northeast plain. A city of 1.5 million, it is known as the first center of China's automotive industry.

Visitors to Changchun have noted the city's wide, tree-lined avenues and its large administrative buildings topped by prominent watchtowers. Much of Changchun was developed under the Japanese military occupation of 1933–45 when the city was the capital of the puppet state "Manchukuo."

In 1953, work on China's first automobile factory began in Changchun. The plant produces trucks and automobiles, including the famous "Red Flag" limousines. The city's industry also includes machine tools, electric motors, textiles, and food processing. The Changchun Film Studio ranks among China's most famous.

Changchun's Jilin University and the Chinese Academy of Sciences are among the most active centers in the country for historical, archeological, botanical, and literary studies.

Changchun's tourist attractions include Nanhu (South Lake) Park, with facilities for swimming, boating, and skating in winter; Children's Park, with its peony and waterside pavilions, music teahouse, and rollerskating rink; and Xinlicheng Reservoir.

HOTEL ACCOMMODATIONS

长白山宾馆

Changbaishan Guest House (12 Xinmin Street; tel: 53551; cable: 9119 Changchun). Located in the center of Changchun, the Changbaishan has 244 standard double rooms and 54 suites (Y50 to Y100). All bedrooms have private bath, phone, and TV, with electric fans provided in summer. The hotel also offers a Chinese restaurant, banquet hall, Western restaurant, post office, currency exchange, and souvenir shop.

春谊宾馆

Chunyi Guest House (2 Stalin Street; tel: 38495). The dark corridors of the Chunyi Guest House lead to surprisingly comfortable, bright, large-windowed rooms with handsome furniture and two double beds, an unusual amenity in China. Most rooms (Y40 to Y80) have a private bath, color TV, air-conditioning, refrigerator, and telephone. The hotel is conveniently located across from the train station. The CITS office is housed here.

Accommodations are also available at the **Changchun Guest House** (10 Xinhua Rd.; tel: 22661/28540).

中国国际旅行社
CITS (Luxingshe) Office in Changchun ■ 12 Xinmin Rd. Tel: 52401
Cable: 1119 CHANGCHUN   Telex: 83028 CITSC CN

Changsha

long sandbank

traditional spelling/Changsha

CHANGSHA, the capital of Hunan Province, is a flourishing regional center for culture and education. Situated in south-central China on the lower reaches of the Xiang River, Changsha lies 525 km. (326 mi.) northwest of Guangzhou and 1,350 km. (840 mi.) south of Beijing. It is one of three principal stops on the Beijing-Guangzhou railway line (12 hours from Guangzhou, 26 from Beijing). The municipality of greater Changsha has an area of 3,989 sq. km. (1,540 sq. mi.); the central city occupies 218 sq. km. (84 sq. mi.). Greater Changsha supports a population of 4.4 million.

Changsha owes its contemporary significance to two factors: the intensively cultivated alluvial lowlands, which are among the most beautiful and productive in China; and the major role the city played in the life and political career of Mao Zedong.

Mao was born in neighboring Shaoshan and moved to Changsha in 1912 to attend high school. His observations of life in this area served as the basis of the most important of his early political essays, "Report on an Investigation of the Peasant Movement in Hunan."

CHANGSHA IN HISTORY

The site of Changsha was inhabited as long as 3,000 years ago. Metallurgy, textile handicrafts, and lacquer work have flourished here since the Spring and Autumn and Warring States periods (770–221 BC).

The city was known as an important educational center as early as the Song Dynasty (c. 10th century AD). Yuelu Academy was founded here in 976 as one of the country's four imperial academies of higher learning. A large encircling wall with nine gates (portions of which are still standing) was built during the Ming period.

In 1904, an "open-door" treaty established Changsha as a foreign trade port. Afterwards, large numbers of Europeans and Americans began to take up residence in the city. Foreign influences were soon manifested in the establishment of churches, educational institutions—including a college (now a medical center) set up by Yale University—and a number of small export factories.

Mao Zedong was a student in Changsha from 1912 to 1918. It was here that his conversion to Communism began. Local guides relate that during this period Mao matured politically from a naive country lad who had never read a newspaper to a questioning student, progressive teacher, and local

Climate

		Jan	Feb	Mar	Apr	May	Jun	Jul	Aug	Sep	Oct	Nov	Dec
Temp.	°C	4.7	6.1	11.0	16.8	21.6	25.9	29.4	28.8	24.4	18.3	12.5	6.8
	°F	39.2	42.9	51.8	62.2	70.8	78.6	84.9	83.8	75.9	64.9	54.5	44.2
Precip.	mm.	152	152	203	279	304	381	254	203	178	178	152	127
	in.	6	6	8	11	12	15	10	8	7	7	6	5

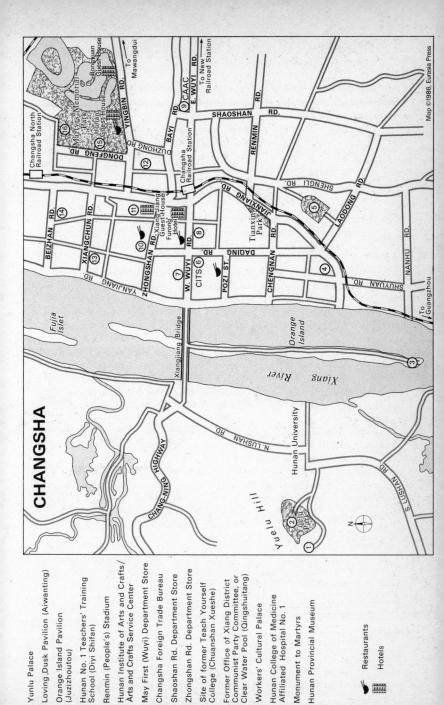

CHANGSHA

① Yunlu Palace

② Loving Dusk Pavilion (Aiwanting)

③ Orange Island Pavilion (Juzizhoutou)

④ Hunan No. 1 Teachers' Training School (Diyi Shifan)

⑤ Renmin (People's) Stadium

⑥ Hunan Institute of Arts and Crafts/ Arts and Crafts Service Center

⑦ May First (Wuyi) Department Store

⑧ Changsha Foreign Trade Bureau

⑨ Shaoshan Rd. Department Store

⑩ Zhongshan Rd. Department Store

⑪ Site of former Teach Yourself College (Chuanshan Xueshe)

⑫ Former Office of Xiang District Communist Party Committee, or Clear Water Pool (Qingshuitang)

⑬ Workers' Cultural Palace

⑭ Hunan College of Medicine Affiliated Hospital No. 1

⑮ Monument to Martyrs

⑯ Hunan Provincial Museum

Restaurants

Hotels

Map ©1986, Eurasia Press

political organizer. One of his first jobs was editing the local *Xiang River Review*. Many of the sites associated with those days are still indispensable parts of the visitor's itinerary.

Changsha suffered acute damage during the Sino-Japanese War (1937–45), and much of it remained in ruins until after the establishment of the PRC in 1949. By 1952, reconstruction and rehabilitation were well under way and important industrial construction had begun.

ECONOMY AND CULTURE

Changsha served as a major trading center for more than 2,000 years. Prior to the 20th century, most commercial activity stemmed from agriculture. Hunan has traditionally been a surplus food producer, annually furnishing about 15% of China's total rice crop.

An early boost to development occurred when Changsha was linked by rail to Hankou (now a part of Wuhan) and Beijing in 1908, providing an impetus for the growth of modern light industry, particularly textiles and food processing. Today, the city's economy has diversified to include machine tool, chemical, and electronics industries. A new railway terminus was completed in 1977.

River transportation plays a significant role in Changsha's economy. Although its cargo facilities have yet to be modernized, Changsha remains the busiest port on the Xiang River. Food grains, construction materials, coal, and timber account for about 70% of the freight handled. Shipments arrive in long, graceful, flat-sailed cargo boats or on low-riding, utilitarian barges.

Culturally, Changsha is noted for its marionette and shadow-puppet theater. A recent attraction is the important Western Han (206 BC–AD 24) tomb discoverd at Mawangdui in 1972. The site contained some outstanding and superbly preserved artifacts which are now on display in Changsha's Hunan Provincial Museum. The city's major educational centers are located on the west bank of the river at the base of Yuelu Hill. These include Hunan University, Hunan Teachers' College, and the Central-South Institute of Metallurgy. Changsha also boasts 13 hospitals and an Institute of Chinese Traditional Medicine.

HIGHLIGHTS
FOR TRAVELERS

Focal points for visitors still include the historical sites associated with Mao Zedong and his early revolutionary activities (e.g., the schools he attended and the house he lived in), the local museums, and the surrounding countryside.

Vegetable farming, near Changsha

Museums. The **Hunan Provincial Museum** (3 Dongfeng Road, tel: 23866). Located in Martyrs' Memorial Park in the northeast section of town, this museum was formerly known mainly for its collection of documents dealing with revolutionary history. Although the documents are still there, most attention now focuses on the relics unearthed from Han Tomb No. 1 at Mawangdui, a site just 3.2 km. (2 mi.) east of the museum. Excavated in 1972, the tomb yielded two spectacular finds. The first was the perfectly preserved corpse of a woman about 50 years old, apparently the wife of a royal personage, who lived during approximately 193–141 BC. Organs removed from her body are on display. Details of her life have been deduced from material found in her stomach and other medical evidence. The body itself is housed in the basement of the museum and may be viewed through a plexiglass skylight.

When unearthed, the body was wrapped in more than 20 layers of silk and linen. Draped over the inner coffin was the second major find: a silk painting in three layers depicting scenes of the underworld, human society, and the celestial sphere. Some details derive from legend, others from the society of the time. The painting retains its brilliant colors, with figures outlined by a single flowing line and colored with mineral pigments of vermilion, azurite, and malachite. (The museum is located one block north of the main gate of Martyrs' Park, on bus route #3.)

Visitors interested in arts and crafts should look in on the **Hunan Ceramics Museum** (tel: 22737) and the **Museum of Chinese Traditional Painting, Pottery, and Porcelain** (tel: 25898), both located in the same building at Zhanlanguan Rd.

岳麓山公园

Yuelushan Park. Yuelushan—"the hill at the foot of the sacred peak"— is the last of 72 mountain groupings of the Hengshan range, with its summit at 295.4 m. above sea level. Among the hill's principal pavilions is the Aiwan Ting (Admiring-the-Dusk Pavilion), built in 1792 by the dean of Yuelu Academy (the "Aiwan Ting" signboard at the entrance uses Mao's calligraphy). White Crane Spring (*Baihequan*) has a small pavilion overlooking the spring; its teahouse uses the spring water to brew its famous "Cloud and Fog" tea. Yuelu Palace on Yuelu Peak was built in the Ming Dynasty (c. 14th century) and also has a pleasant teahouse. The "Drum-Sounding Ridge" is located behind the palace—if you stamp hard on the rock, it produces a drum-like sound. Near the palace, look for a large bronze bell stuck in a tree (unfortunately, we haven't received a satisfactory explanation for this curiosity).

Lushan Temple, one of China's oldest extant Buddhist temples, was founded in AD 268 during the Western Jin Dynasty. Two trees in front of the temple are very old indeed—the one on the left was planted during the Ming Dynasty; the tree on the right is reputed to be 1,700 years old. Seriously damaged during the Cultural Revolution, the temple is now being repaired and is to be restored to the custodianship of the local Buddhist association. One hall, opened in 1983, contains a statue of the Goddess of Mercy. Scattered around the mountain are the graves of martyrs of the 1911 revolution. (To reach Yuelushan, take bus #5 three stops from the bridge.)

岳麓书院

Yuelu Academy. Built in 976 (Song Dynasty), Yuelu was one of China's four imperial academies of higher learning during that period. Located at the foot of the mountain behind Hunan University, the site is now being restored to its original form.

第一师范学校

First Normal School. Located six stops west of the Xiangjiang Guest House on bus #1, the First Normal School was attended by Mao from 1914 to 1918 and is still an active middle school.

烈士公园

Martyr's Park. A large park with a man-made lake, the park's features include several pavilions, boating, an open-air movie theater, an exposition hall, a chrysanthemum garden, and a restaurant that serves fish from the lake. (Bus #3 stops at the front and rear of the park.)

望麓园

Wanglu Yuan. Mao opened a cloth factory here in 1922 as a funding base for Communist activities. The factory failed, but the building survived as a center for political work. Mao lived here during 1926–27 when he prepared his seminal "Hunan Peasant Report." (The building is located around the corner from the Xiangjiang Guest House, up Jianxiang Lu to the second left at the end of the street.)

清水塘 (中共湘区委员会旧址)

Qingshuitang. (Former office of the Hunan Party Committee.) As Party Secretary, Mao lived here from October 1921 until April 1923 together with his first wife, Yang Kaihui. One of their children was born here. To the right over the hill is a large exhibition hall featuring histories of Mao's early years and the life of Xiang Jingyu (a famous woman leader in the early period of the Communist movement), as well as an exhibit on Changsha's archeological history. (Qingshuitang is located in a small building behind a pond just east of the Xiangjiang Guest House, past the bridge on the left.)

天心阁

Tianxin Ge. This is the only remnant of Changsha's ancient city wall. Perched on the highest point within the city, the wall was purportedly first built during the Han (Western Han) Dynasty, although the gun portals are known to have been added in the 1850s. The pavilion on top of the wall was originally built during the Qianlong period (early 19th century) as a star-gazing platform. Most of the wall was gone by the 1920s and its pavilion burned down in 1938. During the mid-1980s, a park and restored three-story pavilion were under construction.

桔子洲

Juzizhou. Orange Island is in fact the "long sandbank" from which Changsha takes its name. Lying midstream in the Xiang River, it runs almost the length of the city. Orange Island Pavilion (*Juzizhoutou*), at its southern tip, affords a view of river traffic.

Active Religious Sites. Since 1980, Changsha has witnessed a strong revival in religious activity. Detailed information is available from the Government Office of Religious Affairs (tel: 22777). The main active institutions are described below.

开福寺

Kaifu Temple. First built in 896 (Tang Dynasty), the premises of this ancient Buddhist site were occupied by a factory during the Cultural Revolution. The factory has not yet fully moved out and the temple has not officially reopened but they do admit visitors, as one hall (the Mahavira) has been restored (in 1985, the entire area was turned into a protected park). There is a Sakyamuni mural and two boddhisattvas. There are also 18 arhats (clay figures) and a Goddess of Mercy statue behind the mural. The temple is a nunnery of the "pure land" sect; some 40 nuns and two monks (the only ones in Changsha) live there. Services are held at 4 AM and from 7 to 9 PM.

To reach the temple, take bus #11 to the last stop and walk north to the corner (Chaoyang Lu). Turn right and look for the temple on the left. It is old and in terrible disrepair, but quite interesting for that reason. Enter through the factory and bear left. There is no telephone in the temple, but you may call the factory at 23385 and ask for the head monk (*jieyuan fashi*).

长沙教堂

The Changsha Catholic Church is located just south of Kaifu Temple on Changchun Xiang. The church now offers services early every Sunday morning. Take bus #11 to Fandi Lu (Beizhan Lu) and walk east; or board bus #2 from the intersection of Zhongshan Lu and Dazhai Lu (Cai'e Lu) for two stops and then walk west and north. The **Protestant Church** is very near to the Catholic Church on Waixiangchun Jie. Services are held Sunday mornings at 8:30. The **Moslem Temple** is not far down Sanxing Jie (off Wuyi Lu) on the right. There is also a Daoist temple outside of the city in Changsha County.

CHANGSHA WALKING TOUR

Walking west from the Xiangjiang Guest House on Zhongshan Lu (to the right), you will first come upon the site of the **Hunan Self-Study University,** established by Mao and others in 1921 to train Communist cadres. By the time it was shut down (by the Nationalists) in November 1923, the university had over 200 students. Walking west, the next sites are the **Zhongshan Lu Department Store;** the **Youth Palace;** and a park-like recreation center with movies (indoor and outdoor), an exhibition hall, a skating rink, and a science game section. Across the street is the **Youyicun Restaurant,** one of the best in the city. Walking south from here along Huangxing Lu (Daqing Lu), you will pass many small shops to **Wuyi Square** and the arts and crafts store on the southwest corner. A little farther south on Huangxing, at #43, there is a theater (costume) shop. The northeast corner of the square has a shop selling stationery supplies and musical instruments. Just to the east is Changsha's main bookstore. From the square you can walk to Cai'e Lu and north back to the hotel; or take bus #16 two stops or bus #12 three stops east to the Friendship Store and the Shaoshan Lu Department Store. Southwest of the square, across from the Friendship Store, is the Tourism Products Service Center, another department store. In front of the Friendship Store is the stop for bus #1, which will take you back to the hotel in two stops.

HOTEL
ACCOMMODATIONS

湖南芙蓉宾馆

Hunan Lotus Hotel (Wuyi Road; tel: 26246; cable: 1652; telex: 98119 HNCST CN). Completed in 1987, the Lotus has nearly 300 rooms, including 13 suites. The standard single rooms cost Y60 per night, while doubles are Y80, and the suites fetch Y120. All rooms have air-conditioning, and closed circuit TV, plus the usual amenities. In addition to a Chinese and Western restaurant and dance hall, there is a conference hall that seats 500 people, and a raft of shops and services. The Lotus is located near the railroad station.

湘江宾馆

Xiangjiang Hotel (267 Zhongshan Rd; tel: 26261; cable: 6666; telex: 98131 XIANG CN). Located in the heart of town, the Xiangjiang offers 270 rooms, including 36 triples and 14 suites. Rates range from Y45–Y50 for singles and doubles to Y80 for a suite. Students can get dormitory lodging much more cheaply.

The hotel is divided into two buildings. The older section, built in the 1950s, has been undergoing renovation recently, and may become more desireable than the newer section. The new structure was built in 1978. It is clean and comfortable, with air-conditioning and TVs in all rooms, but it is hardly extravagant. There is a service desk on each floor where guests can buy cold drinks and beer.

The dining room offers Chinese and Western food and converts into a "bar" each night. A large auditorium shows movies on Saturday nights. Two large maps in the lobby list bus routes and tourist sights. Buses stop right outside the hotel. The train station is easily reachable by bus.

蓉园宾馆

Rongyuan Guest House. Situated on Hongyu (Red Rain) Lake off Bayi Rd. (tel: 267294; service desk: 267801), the Rongyuan is 2 km. from the train station and 22 km. from the airport. The residence complex consists of three buildings in park-like grounds with 196 beds. Built in 1980, but only recently opened to foreigners, it offers three categories of rooms: first class—queen-size bed with TV, refrigerator, and balcony with view: Y65 (single rate); second class—queen-size bed but no TV, refrigerator, or view: Y35 (single); third class—a double room at Y40, also with no TV or refrigerator. All rooms have heating and air-conditioning and are furnished simply, although the hotel is notably clean and well main-

A new rail line traverses hilly Hunan Province.

tained. Interesting dining rooms are set around a small indoor garden with a sliding roof. One resembles a cave. Meals—either Chinese or Western— are billed at a flat rate of Y18 per day. The park-like grounds are heavily wooded and feature numerous gardens and lurking clay animals. Although an altogether pleasant place, the Rongyuan's amenities do not quite compensate for its location well away from almost everything that's interesting in Changsha.

岳阳宾馆
Yueyang Guesthouse (Yueyang county; tel: 23011). The Yueyang, with its 267 rooms featuring air-conditioning with individual controls and minibar, is a joint venture hotel overlooking the lake. Three restaurants provide dining for guests. *Rates:* Double: Y90; triple: Y60; suite:Y360.

湖南宾馆
Hunan Guest House (9 Yingbin Rd.; tel: 26331). Formerly Changsha's major hotel, the venerable Hunan no longer welcomes foreign guests.

Other hotels for resourceful travelers include the **Changsha Hotel** (116 Wuyi Rd.: tel: 25029); and the **Yunwu Hotel.**

HUNAN
CUISINE

Hunan cuisine, like that of neighboring Sichuan, is noted for its liberal use of the hot chili pepper grown in south-central China. Smoking with chilis, a distinctly Hunanese method of cooking, results in such popular dishes as smoked chicken in tangerine-peel sauce and smoked chunks of pork fat.

Tourists whose meals are confined to the hotel dining room may not have the opportunity to savor the region's renowned peppery dishes. Apparently the hotel is under instructions to refrain from challenging its guests' palates and, as a result, blander versions of Hunan fare are the rule. The alert tour group will try to make a special request of the kitchen or to negotiate an evening at a local restaurant with the tour guides. The **Youyicun Restaurant** (225 Zhongshan Rd. West; tel: 24257) near the Xiangjiang Guest House offers delicious Hunan-style bacon and pork served with bean curd and cabbage. Visitors to Changsha would be remiss not to have a go at the **Huogongdian Restaurant** at 145 Pozi Jie (tel: 23591), famous for its "malodorous" bean curd and other snack foods and one of Mao's favorite eating places. The structure had originally been built during the Five Dynasties Period as a temple for worshipping the god of fire (a fact obviously well noted by the present chef). Also recommended is the **Changdao Restaurant** on West Wuyi Rd. (tel: 26211).

SHOPPING

The people of Changsha and Shaoshan produce an array of distinct regional handicrafts. The embroidery is justly famous. Hotel shops display crafts

such as miniature sampans made from shells. Pottery and ceramics are also recommended (especially the tiny figurines) as are eiderdowns (quilts and pillows filled with duck feathers) and down vests. Attractive, hand-painted wooden tea containers are a local specialty. The best selections are to be found at Changsha's new seven-story Friendship Store, located in front of the Shaoshan Lu Department Store at the northeast corner of the intersection of Shaoshan Rd. and Wuyi Rd., two stops east of the Xiangjiang Guest House on bus #1. Opened for business in late 1983, the store features items for foreign purchase on its second and third floors. A fine array of handicrafts is also featured at the Arts and Crafts Service Center at 92 Wuyi Rd. (tel: 22253).

Visitors can also browse through an interesting array of inexpensive goods at Changsha's major department stores: Shaoshan Lu Department Store (23 Shaoshan Rd.; tel: 22125); the Overseas Chinese Store (25 Shaoshan Rd.; tel: 26539); and the Zhongshan Lu Department Store (148 Zhongshan Rd.; tel: 24621).

中国国际旅行社
CITS (Luxingshe) Office in Changsha ■ Furong Hotel, E. Wuyi Rd. Tel: 98132.
Cable: 2002 CHANGSHA. Telex: 98132 HLHCT CN.

Changzhou

changeless district

traditional spelling/Changchow

CHANGZHOU, a peaceful riverine town that lies astride the Grand Canal just north of Lake Tai—about halfway between Shanghai and Nanjing—has maintained its ancient reputation as an important textile center through to the present day.

Although Changzhou's urban area covers 94 sq. km. and has a population of about a half million, the city's influence reaches well beyond those confines. It controls several surrounding counties, so that the entire territory that falls under its jurisdiction extends for 4,211 sq. km., with some three million inhabitants. Changzhou lies in a subtropical belt within Jiangsu Province, so it has a mild climate that is warm and wet for about half the year. The average temperature is 14°C (57°F); average annual rainfall is about 1,000 mm.

Although it has no civil airport, Changzhou is easily reached by train or, for those with more time, by a new, scheduled Grand Canal boat service from Wuxi (the 37-km. voyage takes 3½ hours; the fare for foreigners is Y40).

CHANGZHOU IN HISTORY

Changzhou has a known past that dates to 500 BC. During its 2,500 years of recorded history, it underwent several name changes: it was known as Yanling in the Zhou Dynasty; as Piling in the Han Dynasty; and as Lanling during the Jin Dynasty. In AD 589, Emperor Wen of the Sui Dynasty gave the name of Changzhou to the region.

Early on, Changzhou became famous for its textiles and fine-tooth combs. With the advent of the People's Republic of China, the city was gradually transformed into an integrated economic area, so that today some 443 industrial enterprises produce textiles, building materials, and light industrial goods. Every year for the past three decades the city's industrial output was reported to have risen by an average of 10–13%. In 1983, the total value of production reached Y4,325 billion, 59 times the volume of 1949. Because of its rapid growth in recent years, Changzhou was named one of the 10 "mid-sized economically developed 'star' cities" in China. Lately, Changzhou has been promoting tourism and has begun to repair and reconstruct many scenic points within its boundaries. It is also adding new services to accommodate visitors.

Climate		Jan	Feb	Mar	Apr	May	Jun	Jul	Aug	Sep	Oct	Nov	Dec
Temp.	°C	1.9	3.7	8.6	14.6	20.3	24.4	28.2	28.2	23.0	16.8	10.6	4.2
	°F	35.4	38.6	47.4	58.2	68.5	75.9	82.7	82.7	73.4	62.2	51	39.5
Precip.	mm.	254	254	330	330	305	356	279	279	305	254	203	178
	in.	10	10	13	13	12	14	11	11	12	10	8	7

HIGHLIGHTS
FOR TRAVELERS

天宁寺

Temple of Heavenly Tranquility. First built in the late Tang Dynasty (901–4), the temple was destroyed several times, most recently during the Cultural Revolution, but has since been resurrected. The existing buildings date to the late 19th century, while the interiors are all new. Currently, a hall of 500 arhats is being renovated.

One of the four largest temples in southern China and local headquarters for the Buddhist Association, this sanctuary now houses some 40 monks and has a lay membership of about 10,000 Buddhists. It is an active temple, where the monks sit in meditation at least six hours a day, and have special periods twice a year when they meditate 12 hours a day and do not sleep for as long as 14 days.

During the 6th and 19th months of the Chinese Lunar calendar, major gatherings are held, open to both members and nonmembers. Throughout the year, visitors are admitted from 1 to 5 PM daily.

宫梳名篦

Changzhou Palace Combs Factory. The production of combs in Changzhou goes back 1,500 years to the Jin Dynasty (AD 265–420). Today, the city maintains the factory (at 109 Nanheyan Road; tel: 3208) to produce this special type of comb which, over the years, has accumulated 12 national and international handicrafts medals.

The combs, handmade of boxwood or other natural materials, come in 1,000 varieties and fall into two categories: daily-use combs and those used as artistic ornaments (which feature designs depicting scenes of human or animal representations). They are purported to be especially beneficial to people with dry hair since they diminish static electricity. The Palace Combs Factory's 368 employees turn out about 12 million combs per year, one third of which are exported.

文笔塔

Pagoda of the Waiting Bush. Built during the Northern Song Dynasty, between 976 and 984, this structure stands seven stories and 48.38 m. high. From atop the pagoda you can view the entire city.

红梅阁

Red Plum Pavilion. One of the largest parks in Changzhou (37 hectares), this area was first constructed during the Tang Dynasty (889–904). Throughout the park, surrounding the pagoda and pavilion, are thickly planted red plum trees. During blossom time, the scene is quite spectacular.

Parks, Museums, and Other Attractions. Other parks in Changzhou worth visiting are Yizhou Park, with a pavilion built in honor of the Northern Song poet Su Dongpo, and the Jin Park, designed during the Kang Xi period of the Qing Dynasty (1667–1672). Other sites to visit are the Changzhou Museum, built in the style of the Song Dynasty and housing a collection of artifacts from the area dating from the Western Zhou Dynasty to the present; and the memorial hall for Hui Nantian, one of the six great painters of the early Qing Dynasty. This hall displays his works as well as those of other artists.

A major industrial facility open to the public is the Changzhou Tractor Manufacturing Center in Xinzhazhen (tel: 23986, 25685). The factory has a worker population of 1,356 producing some 3,300 walking tractors per year, many of which are exported to over 40 countries.

Bicycle Rentals. Changzhou is one of the few municipalities in China where foreigners can readily rent bicycles. The rate is Y4 per half-day; the agent is CITS, Changzhou branch.

HOTEL ACCOMMODATIONS

白荡宾馆

Baidang Guest House (1 Yingbin Road; tel: 26169; cable: 4101). The Baidang Guest House sits astride Baidang Lake. It has 58 standard rooms, 10 suites, and one deluxe suite. Price range from Y45 to Y96, and all rooms are equipped with air-conditioning and color TV. On the first floor is a shop, currency exchange desk, and taxi stand, and there is a coffee shop on the fourth floor. The dining room is in a separate building located directly to the right of the main entrance. There are meeting rooms and an auditorium. Service at the Baidang is notably good.

常州宾馆

Changzhou Guest House (9 Changsheng Lane; tel: 26971; cable: 6333). Located in the city center, the Changzhou Guest House features a 300-year-old Suzhou-style garden, as well as a restaurant, auditorium, recreation room, and shop. It has 38 standard rooms, four triples, four suites, and a deluxe suite, all with private bath, air-conditioning, and TV. Some rooms have refrigerators.

公园路招待所

Gongyuan Road Hostel (271 Dongda Street; tel: 5577, 4395). Located in the city center, the Gongyuan Road Hostel has 21 rooms with private baths, as well as 67 rooms with shared facilities for budget-minded travelers and students. There is also an inexpensive restaurant.

小营前招待所

Xiaoyingqian Hostel (tel: 4981). The Xiaoyingqian is also centrally located, with 80 rooms, all reasonably priced and featuring air-conditioning, color TV, and private bath. The hostel also has rooms with shared baths at cheaper rates.

中国国际旅行社
CITS (Luxingshe) Office in Changzhou ■ 103 Dong Dajie. Telephone: 24886, 24046 (night phone: 24046, 24981). Cable: 0057 CHANGZHOU.

Chengde

承德

to inherit virtue

traditional spelling/Jehol

CHENGDE, once a mountain retreat for the Qing emperor Kang Xi and his concubines and eunuchs, can offer a highly rewarding two- or three-day sojourn out of Beijing for those seeking an unharried, contemplative look at a major junction in the history of the Manchu Empire. Located 256 km. (159 mi.) northeast of Beijing (about five hours away by train), Chengde has a modest role in the contemporary context as a distribution center for forestry products, medicinal plants, and fruits. Its historical importance is marked by the remains of Emperor Kang Xi's summer palace and gardens (now a public park) and some of the country's most unusual Chinese and Tibetan temples.

Daily rail services connect Beijing with Chengde: trains depart Beijing and Chengde twice daily for the seven-hour trip. The single fare (soft-seat) is Y17.30. Connections are also available by air and by long-distance bus, departing from Qianmen and Chongwenmen in Beijing.

CHENGDE IN HISTORY

Chengde used to be known as Jehol—after the warm springs of the nearby Wulie River, a tributary of the Luan River. Inhabited since prehistoric times by non-Han minority peoples, Jehol also functioned as Imperial China's administrative center for eastern Mongolia. In 1703, Bishushanzhuang ("mountain hamlet to flee the heat") was built along lines similar to that of the Summer Palace in Beijing, with a vast park surrounded by 24.8 km. (15.5 mi.) of battlements. Construction was completed in 1780 during the reign of Emperor Qian Long. In an effort to strengthen the Qing court's ties with the Tibetan clergy and their Mongolian adherents, Emperor Qian Long had a whole series of Lamaist temples replicated, including a copy of Lhasa's Potala. By the early 19th century, the town's population had swollen to some 780,000 (compared with today's 30,000 residents).

Originally, Kang Xi's "summer city" had an important strategic function. It promoted consolidation of his empire's rule over the Mongolians and helped ward off threatening influences from Tsarist Russia. About 100 km. north of Chengde (in what is now Weichang County), Kang Xi had first constructed a huge walled area of over 10,000 sq. km. that was nominally set aside as an imperial hunting ground but provided a more important role

Climate		Jan	Feb	Mar	Apr	May	Jun	Jul	Aug	Sep	Oct	Nov	Dec
Temp.	°C	−4.7	−1.9	4.8	13.7	20.1	24.8	26.1	24.8	19.9	12.8	3.8	2.8
	°F	23.5	28.6	40.6	56.6	68.1	76.6	78.9	76.6	67.8	55	38.8	37
Precip.	mm.	76	76	76	102	152	203	305	254	178	152	102	76
	in.	3	3	3	4	6	8	12	10	7	6	4	3

as a military encampment and training center. Later, when a more commodious site for a summer palace was selected at Jehol, the Qing court had become more preoccupied with its civic and cultural image. They wanted an imperial residence that was set apart from the Ming-influenced palaces of Beijing. Thus, at Jehol they did away with the sweeping eaves and ornate woodwork that characterized most Chinese buildings from the imperial era. The architectural style at Jehol was kept simple yet elegant.

But a stroke of summer lightning cast a pall over the place. In 1820, Emperor Jia Qing was killed in a thunderstorm near the palace. Jia Qing's successor, Emperor Dao Guang, was hopelessly corrupt and became so enmeshed in court intrigues that he never dared to leave the confines of the Forbidden City in Beijing. The Manchu court abandoned the mountain retreat at Jehol, returning only once in 1860 when Emperor Xian Feng fled there to escape the Anglo-French troops' invasion of Beijing. Xian Feng also died in the Jehol palace, after which the Manchu rulers permanently abandoned the site. During China's Republican era, Chengde became the capital of the newly formed Jehol Province, a region largely dominated by warlords. During 1933–45, much of the area was occupied by Japan.

HIGHLIGHTS FOR TRAVELERS

Today you can flee the heat or the swarms of foreign tourists to the south and enjoy several hours poking around the nine temples on view, the famous Wenjinge library, Kang Xi's palace and pavilions, and the lovely park, all a short drive northwest of the town. Of the 11 temples built between 1713 and 1780, nine remain. The first group of temples is east of the park: the Chinese-style Temple of Universal Love (1713); the partially destroyed Tibetan Temple of Universal Goodness (also 1713); the Temple of Universal Joy (1766)—which has an unusual double terrace and double roof of yellow tiles; and the Ili Valley Temple (1764).

The second group of historic structures is found north of the park. From east to west, they are the Temple of Universal Help (1760), whose Tibetan statues sharply contrast with the Chinese architecture; the Lamaist-inspired Temple of General Peace (1775); the Potala-like structure which is Chengde's largest temple, measuring 199,094 sq. m. (239,000 sq. yd.); the Xumifushou Miao (1780), a temple with a distinctive, glazed-tile pagoda inside; and finally, the Shu Siang Si (1774).

HOTELS AND SHOPPING

Hotels in Chengde which currently receive foreigners are the **Qiwang Hotel** (Bishushanzhuang; tel. 4385), which has doubles for Y160; **Yunshan Hotel** (outside Bishushanzhuang; tel: 5649), offering doubles for Y150 and suites for Y300; **Rehe Villa** (tel: 2528), located near Puning Temple, with doubles for Y65; and the **Dehuai Guesthouse** (near Dehuai Gate, just outside Bishushanzhuang; tel: 3810), which has doubles for Y65.

Another option is to stay in Mongolia yurts, inside Bishushanzhuang (tel: 2269). These are typically concrete yurts with air-conditioning and private bathrooms at Y110/130 for double occupancy.

A new countryside guest house with traditional Chinese courtyard.

Visitors to Chengde should be mindful that there are very few taxis and only a few motorized three-wheelers available in town. The buses to the outer temples are few and far between, and when they come they are very, very crowded. There are a total of five bus lines in the city.

Shopping. The Friendship Store is in the small square in front of Dehuimen, one of the entrances to the park, just east of Lizhengmen. There are also a number of shops along Nan Yingzi Dajie (the liveliest part of town), including an arts and crafts shop and the Number One Department Store, both just across from the City Hotel. Chengde is famous for its silk, *nanmu* tables, *hehuanmu* wood carvings, rugs, and haw (Shanzha) products.

中国国际旅行社
CITS (Luxingshe) Office in Chengde ▣ 11 Zhonghua Rd., Dongkou. Tel: 3502/3401.

Chengdu

establish the capital   *traditional spelling/Chengtu*

CHENGDU is the capital of China's most populous province, Sichuan, and an important industrial city in southwestern China. A dynamic and colorful city graced with a gregarious, outgoing population, Chengdu must be ranked among China's most rewarding urban destinations. Located in one of the country's richest agricultural plains—Sichuan produces more rice than any other province in China, and one of the largest wheat crops—Chengdu has 180,000 hectares (445,000 acres) of land under cultivation, and is an important producer of rice, wheat, sweet potatoes, tea, medicinal herbs, tobacco, and silk.

By rail, Chengdu is 2,048 km. (1,272 mi.) from Beijing. Situated at an elevation of 126.1 m. (414 ft.), it has a temperate climate and abundant rainfall in the summer.

The population of Chengdu is 3.85 million—divided among two city districts, three suburban areas, and two outlying prefectures—with a total area of 3,861 sq. km. (1,490 sq. mi.). About 1.4 million persons reside in the city center.

Chengdu is pleasantly laid out with broad streets and many public parks. The older parts of the city have narrow streets, lined by two-story brown-and-white stucco dwellings with balconies of sculptured wood. The old city wall was pulled down in the early 1960s.

ON YOUR OWN IN CHENGDU

Chengdu now has two major hotels for foreigners: the **Chengdu Hotel** completed in 1984, and the venerable **Jinjiang Guest House.** Although less modern than the Chengdu, the Jinjiang is much better situated, especially for visitors intent on seeing the city on their own. The Jinjiang is on the opposite side of town from the train station, reachable on a direct, eight-stop ride on bus #16, which departs from the front of the station. The #16 proceeds along Renmin Road, which forms a north-south axis through the center of the city. It is thus the most useful of Chengdu's bus lines. Taxis, motorized three-wheelers, and pedicabs are also available just outside the train station. The airport is just about the same distance away from the hotel, but to the southwest; there are many flights to Chengdu from major cities, including Beijing, Shanghai, and Hong Kong. Since there are no convenient buses into town from the airport, you are fairly well obliged to take a taxi.

Climate		Jan	Feb	Mar	Apr	May	Jun	Jul	Aug	Sep	Oct	Nov	Dec
Temp.	°C	7	10	14.5	19.5	23	25.5	29	30	25	19	14	10.5
	°F	44.6	50	58.1	67.1	73.4	77.9	84.2	86	77	66.2	57.2	50.9
Precip.	mm.	15	20	38	99	142	180	142	122	150	112	48	20
	in.	.6	.8	1.5	3.9	5.6	7.1	5.6	4.8	5.9	4.4	1.9	.8

Chengdu has the advantage of being one of the few cities in China that still allows foreigners to rent bicycles. The main bicycle rental is a few doors north of the Jinjiang Guest House on Renmin Road. There is another a bit further north and around the corner to the left at 33 Hongzhaobi. No deposit is necessary, but some formal identification is. Much of the city can be seen on foot or using a combination of bus #16 and a bit of walking. You can also use a bike to trace the walking tours outlined in this book. For outings to sites in the far north of the city, local buses are recommended (specific bus lines are listed in the section that follows). To visit sites further out from the city, try locating a group at the hotel that might be visiting the same place. Otherwise, you can sign up for a one- or two-day trip organized by CTS or CITS. Hiring a car to visit distant sites is possible, but can be very expensive.

CHENGDU IN HISTORY

Until 1949, Chengdu's reputation rested more on its ancient history than its modern development. Some 2,000 years ago, during the Zhou Dynasty, the kingdom of Shu moved its capital to this site. Later, during the Han Dynasty (206 BC–AD 220), the brocade trade brought so much prosperity that the city became known as Jincheng (Brocade Town) and earned the nickname "storehouse of heaven." It became the "city of hibiscus" during the Five Dynasties Period (907–960), when a local feudal lord had those colorful flowers planted atop the town wall.

Subsequent centuries saw little change, and Chengdu thus remained comparatively underdeveloped until 1949 when the new government decided to build it up as a regional industrial base.

ECONOMY AND CULTURE

Traditionally a center for handicrafts and brocades, the city is still known in China for its fine silks, bamboo products, and herbal medicines. But Chengdu today also has a solid industrial base. Since the early 1950s, industial output has increased several hundred fold and the number of factories has increased from the original 10 to about 2,000. The work force numbers 500,000. Industries include metallurgy, coal mining, machine building, aluminum, and electronics (including computers). Natural gas is abundant in the region.

Chengdu is the chief cultural center of southwestern China. It is the home of Sichuan opera, which has a tradition of close to 2,000 years. Characterized by a combination of music, dance, and acrobatics, Sichuan opera is more earthy and lighthearted than its Peking counterpart. A delightful diversion is promised by the city's Children's Opera Troupe, which performs at the Wangjiang Theater. Performers and musicians are all between the ages of five and 14.

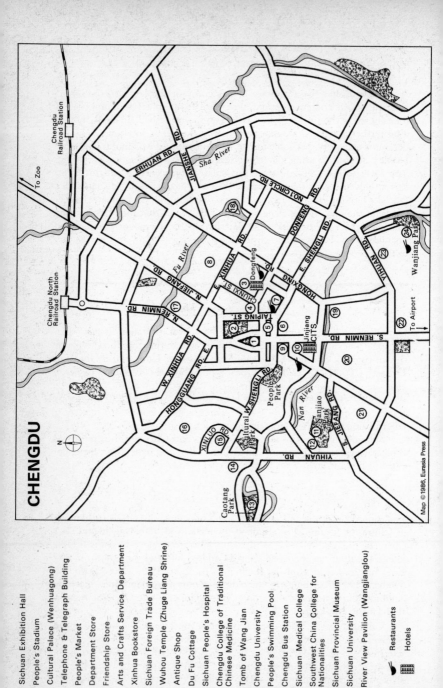

CHENGDU

Map © 1986, Eurasia Press

1. Sichuan Exhibition Hall
2. People's Stadium
3. Cultural Palace (Wenhuagong)
4. Telephone & Telegraph Building
5. People's Market
6. Department Store
7. Friendship Store
8. Arts and Crafts Service Department
9. Xinhua Bookstore
10. Sichuan Foreign Trade Bureau
11. Wuhou Temple (Zhuge Liang Shrine)
12. Antique Shop
13. Du Fu Cottage
14. Sichuan People's Hospital
15. Chengdu College of Traditional Chinese Medicine
16. Tomb of Wang Jian
17. Chengdu University
18. People's Swimming Pool
19. Chengdu Bus Station
20. Sichuan Medical College
21. Southwest China College for Nationalities
22. Sichuan Provincial Museum
23. Sichuan University
24. River View Pavilion (Wangjianglou)

🍴 Restaurants

🏛 Hotels

Chengdu has more than a dozen institutions of higher education, including the nationally famous Sichuan University, established in 1927. South Renmin Road bisects the campus of Sichuan Medical College and its adjoining hospital complex, previously a major missionary educational enterprise called West China Union University and staffed mainly by Americans and Canadians.

Religious Activities. In the 1980s, China has been witness to a renaissance of religious activity of all types, and Chengdu is one of the places where this resurgence has been most evident.

The headquarters and main sanctuary of the Chengdu Catholic Patriotic Association is at 29 Ping'anqiao Street, just northwest of the exhibition center. The church was built in 1884 in beautiful Italian revival style reminiscent of cathedral architecture in Europe or America. The cathedral reopened in 1979. In 1984, its seminary resumed teaching, with over 30 students. Services are held daily at 6:30 AM, and all are welcome to attend. At Christmastime, as many as 2,000 people turn out for Mass. The Protestant Church is located just northeast of the exhibition center, on Dingxiang Street just off Jiefang Zhong Road. Although more modest in structure than the Catholic sanctuary, this church is equally as active, and also has a seminary. The 10 AM Sunday service is often crowded, so visitors should plan on arriving early.

There are about 200 monks and 5,000 lay Buddhists in Chengdu. The lay Buddhists register and are assigned to a monk, who is then responsible for teaching that person about Buddhism. The two main Buddhist temples are listed in the "Highlights" section, below.

HIGHLIGHTS
FOR TRAVELERS

Chengdu's annual lunar New Year (January-February) lantern festival dates back 1,300 years. The more than 20,000 elaborate designs for the festival include birds, an arrangement of swan and fish lanterns floating on a pond amidst lotus blossoms, and the figure of an elephant carrying grain.

杜甫草堂

Du Fu Cottage. The great Tang poet Du Fu (712–70) lived in Chengdu for three years and composed over 200 poems here. During the Song Dynasty (960–1279), a shrine was built on the site where his modest house used to stand. The spot is marked by a small stream. A painting exhibition inside the shrine attempts to evoke the poet's moods. Many contemporary figures, including Mao Zedong, Zhu De, and Guo Moruo, have written couplets in praise of Du Fu. (The cottage can be reached from town on bus #35 west to the last stop, then bus #1 five stops west.) The cottage is open daily from 7 AM to 6 PM (tel: 25258).

武侯祠

Zhuge Liang Shrine (Wuhou Ci). Zhuge Liang (181–234), also known as Wu Hou, was a renowned military strategist and statesman in the early Three Kingdoms Period (220–65). The shrine to his memory was built during the Tang Dynasty (618–907) and reconstructed during the early Qing Dynasty (1644–1911). Mao sent new cadres here to study his writings. Renovation took place in 1952 and it is now a "protected treasure" of the state.

The Du Fu and Zhuge Liang shrines are both situated within sprawling but charming parks, dotted with pavilions and filled with lush greenery, flowers, and ponds. The shrine houses a delightful teahouse where apples and hard candies are served. The adjacent park has a superb bonsai collection. The shrine is open from 7 AM to 6 PM (tel: 26397).

望江楼

River View Pavilion (Wangjianglou). This three-story wooden structure in the architectural style of South China stands near the Nine-Arch Bridge at the edge of the Jin River. The surrounding park is known for its bamboo forest containing 120 species of that family. The park dates to the end of the Ming Dynasty (1368–1644). Hours are from 7 AM to 6 PM (tel: 27552).

宝光寺

Precious Light Monastery (Baoguangsi). With origins in the later Han Dynasty (c. 2nd century AD), this Buddhist temple of colossal proportions is located in a park in the city's northern suburb. In 881, the temple provided refuge for the Tang emperor while in flight from the Hangchao rebellion. Today, it still houses 500 arhat statues and other Buddhist art treasures, including several paintings executed by emperors and a fine collection of contemporary works by Xu Beihong and Zhang Daqian. Just outside the temple is a delightful peasant market featuring straw crafts—almost worth the trip in itself. Individual travelers should note that access to the temple's main collection is limited to groups (which may be joined through the CITS office at the Jinjiang Guest House). (Express buses to the monastery are available at the main railway station.) The monastery is open to visitors from 8 AM to 6 PM.

都江堰和青城山

Dujiang Dam and Green City Peak. Situated about 40 km. (25 mi.) northwest of Chengdu, this engineering marvel, conceived and designed by Li Bing, dates back to 250 BC. Designed as a mammoth irrigation project, Dujiang Dam checks the Min River, which flows down from Green City Peak. A trunk canal was cut through the mountain and a water distribution network set up to irrigate 1.3 million hectares of land. Expansion has been undertaken since 1949, and the whole system today irrigates well over 6.67 million hectares (16.5 million acres), including the Chengdu region.

Visitors are taken to an exhibition room in the Dujiang Dam Pavilion to watch a film tracing the history of the irrigation network.

二皇寺

Two Kings Temple (Erhuangsi). During the Qin Dynasty (221–206 BC), Emperor Qin Shi Huangdi appointed Li Bing as the ruler of Sichuan. Along the face of Yulei mountain, not far from the Dujiang Dam, a multi-tiered Daoist temple complex was erected to commemorate the benevolent rule of Li Bing and the son who succeeded him. Seated in pavilions near the mountaintop are two imposing, larger-than-life painted statues of father and son. They overlook the rushing river below. A second stature of Li, found in the river only a few years ago, had been cast into the waterway by peasants at the time of his death to ensure the project's permanence. Today, Daoist monks work as waiters in the temple's bamboo-furnished teahouse.

王建墓

Tomb of Wang Jian. Wang Jian was a soldier of fortune in the late Tang Dynasty (618–907) who became a prince and was given the posthumous title of emperor. His tomb, located in Chengdu's northwest, is 23.4 m. (77 ft.) long and divided into three burial chambers supported by 14 double arches. In the center chamber, where the sarcophagus reposes between two rows of stone figures, a frieze depicting musicians and courtiers runs around the east, south, and west walls. The innermost chamber contains a life-size statue of Wang Jian sitting on a dais. A rich collection of relics dating from the late-Tang and early-Five Dynasties periods was found in the tomb, which has been designated a "protected treasure" of the state.

文殊院

Wen Shu Yuan. An important—and still active—Buddhist site, the Wen Shu (Manjusri) temple has had a stormy history: it was first built during the Tang Dynasty, destroyed by fire during the Ming, and last rebuilt under the Qing (1691). The temple consists of five main halls which house collections of both Chinese and Asian artifacts. Today, the Wen Shu is one of the most active Buddhist centers in the country and offers training for young monks (candidates must be at least 18 years old and must pass an entrance examination as well as have their parents' permission). The temple is also headquarters for both the Sichuan and Chengdu Buddhist associations. The site is open daily from 8 AM to 8 PM.

青羊宫 (文化公园)

Qing Yang Gong. The Qing Yang (also known as Cultural Park) is the oldest and largest Daoist temple complex in Chengdu, established during the later Han Dynasty. The extant structures—including the two bronze sheep at the entrance—all date from the latter half of the Qing Dynasty. A two-month-long flower festival, with origins in the Tang Dynasty, is still held here each year, beginning on the 15th day of the second lunar month (February/March). The festival is a cultural outpouring, featuring opera and theater performances along with displays of flowers (the crab apple and plum blossoms are renowned throughout China), crafts, and birds. (Qing Yang is easily reached by bus #35, east from the Jinjiang Guest House, last stop.) The complex is open from 7 AM to 6 PM (tel: 23637).

人民公园

People's Park. This centrally located park is a popular gathering place for residents of Chengdu. A large bamboo teahouse, erected on a terrace, is one of its more attractive features. Three Olympic-size swimming pools in the park are open only to permanent residents. The zoo is open from 8 AM to 6 PM daily (tel: 22021).

成都动物园

Chengdu Zoo. The giant panda is a denizen of Sichuan so, not surprisingly, Chengdu's zoo boasts one of the best panda displays in the world, among other rare species. (Reachable by bus #9, on the way to Baoguangsi.)

四川省博物馆

Sichuan Provincial Museum. Chengdu's principal museum, located just south of the Jinjiang Guest House, displays some 1,800 artifacts of historical and (secondarily) aesthetic interest. The first floor's exhibition rooms range from prehistory to the pre-1949 era. The second floor focuses on revolutionary history, from the 19th century to the present. The museum is open daily (except Mondays) from 8–11 AM and 2–6 PM (tel: 52158).

HOTEL ACCOMMODATIONS

成都饭店

Chengdu Hotel (Dongfeng Rd., corner of Sanduan Rd; tel: 43312; telex: 60164 COHOT CN). Local people are especially proud of this newly opened 15-story hotel, which is seen as a symbol of Chengdu's contribution to China's modernization program. Entirely Chinese-built, at a cost of Y20 million, the Chengdu has 258 rooms: 118 standard-rate doubles, 130 lower-rate triples, and 10 suites (unusually for China, both Chinese and foreigners are accepted at the same rates for the same level of accommodation). All rooms have private baths; the standard rooms and suites also include refrigerators, telephones, closed-circuit TVs, and balconies. There is a banquet hall, 11 meeting rooms, a Chinese/Western restaurant, a Sichuan specialty restaurant, a bar, a health-food restaurant, a coffee shop, a teahouse for listening to music, and a shopping arcade.

The main desk will help guests with transportation and other requests. Located about 3 km. from the center of town, in its eastern section, the hotel is convenient to #21, #2, and #4 bus lines. To reach the heart of the city by foot, turn left after exiting the hotel and walk straight. You might want to explore the hotel's lively surrounding residential area.

锦江宾馆

Jinjiang Guest House (36 South Renmin Road; tel: 24481; telex: 60109/10 JJH CN; cable: 4481). The Jinjiang occupies a rather somber looking building built in 1962 in the socialist-realist style. Its 487 rooms were renovated floor-by-floor beginning in 1983. All renovated rooms have air-conditioning and refrigerators. The triples do not have private baths.

Facilities include a bank; rooms for chess, billiards, and film-showing; a tea house; a dance hall (on the ninth floor); Chinese and Western restaurants; one-day laundry service; and Chengdu's tennis court. The CITS office is conveniently located on the first floor (Rm. 129) and can help with plane and train reservations.

The hotel has 368 doubles (Y140), 68 triples (Y144), 26 suites (Y150), and four deluxe suites (Y300–Y800).

Taxis: Available at rates of 60 *fen*/km., Y1.20/hour, or Y30/day
Discounts apply after first 100 km.

陕西会馆

Shaanxi Huiguan (36 Shaanxi Street; tel: 22687). In traditional China, *huiguans* were special inns which served as gathering places for travelers from a specific city or province. To counteract homesickness, the inns prepared dishes from home and employed staff who spoke the dialect of the native region. This *huiguan* was established for Shaanxi people in 1663, then destroyed, and rebuilt twice: once during the Qian Long period of the Qing Dynasty, and again after the Cultural Revolution, in 1981. It now functions strictly as a hotel/restaurant (you'll be welcome even if you're from New Jersey or Yorkshire). It has 35 simple rooms with no air-conditioning, but with an exceptional restaurant. The building itself is quite appealing, constructed in the old courtyard style, and is even closer to the center of town than the Jinjiang Guest House.

Located in the center of the city, it is about 3 km. from the train station and 10 km. from the airport. Rates range from Y75–Y110.

东风饭店

Dongfeng Hotel (31 Zongfu Street; tel: 61115). The Dongfeng Hotel is another of Chengdu's smaller hotels, also located in the center of town. The Dongfeng has 26 double rooms (Y140) and eight suites (Y250), all with private bath, telephone, and either color or black-and-white TV.

CUISINE

Although best known abroad for its hot, spicy dishes, the region's cuisine is just as famous in China for its refined and varied flavors, often enhanced by the use of medicinal herbs and flower petals. Among the well-known dishes are soft-fried lotus flowers, orchid-petal chicken strips, duck cooked with medicinal herbs, *mapo dofu* (bean curd cooked in a spicy-hot meat sauce) and street vendor's noodles. A banquet of regional specialties can be prearranged at the famous Furong Restaurant (27 S. Renmin Rd.; tel: 4004), within walking distance of the Jinjiang Guest House. Other fine restaurants are the Chengdu (Shengli Zhong Rd.; tel: 7301); the Shaanxi Huiguan (Shaanxi Rd.; tel: 28496); and the Wangjianglou (near the Pavilion on Wangjiang Rd.; tel: 7552). For late-night snacks, the Jinjiang Guest House's "noodle bar" stays open til 10:30 PM.

An interesting underground (bomb shelter, in fact) restaurant/coffee shop is called the Huaxi Restaurant, just east of the Jinjiang Guest House along the river. Downstairs there are several rooms lying off a central corridor, so there is the choice of dining in privacy or in a room with local people. The Huaxi is usually smoky, warm, and crowded, but the food is inexpensive and good. Western dishes are available, along with several types of ice cream and drinks. The workers are all formerly "waiting-for-work" youth. There is also a similar, although smaller, establishment at the south end of Yanshikou.

SHOPPING

Chengdu, once known as the "storehouse of heaven," still lives up to that name. Embroidery, brocade, lacquerware, bamboo and plaited straw goods, cutlery, and pottery all make excellent purchases. These may be found at the People's Market, north of Yanshikou at the west end of Dong Dajie (formerly Shengli Lu). Similar items may also be found at the Friendship Store; on the third floor of the Chunnan Shop on Chunxi Rd.; and at the

Chengdu Department Store, on Shengli Zhong Rd., one of Chengdu's main shopping areas. Specialty shops include the Arts and Crafts Service Center and Shibeijia, a cultural products store, both at the north end of Chunxi Rd. (tel: 6817); and the Antiques Shop at Shangyechang (tel: 22787). The two main hotels also boast large stores, as does the Chengdu Exhibition Center, which is in reality a giant crafts emporium. Aside from these places, Renmin South and Central roads are both excellent shopping areas. Be sure to visit Renmin Road South, which has an interesting night market, selling artworks, among other goods.

A stroll through Chengdu's old-fashioned covered marketplaces and along its bustling, colorful shopping arteries will give the visitor a glimpse of Sichuan's distinctive lifestyle. Not only are most buildings constructed of bamboo, but almost every store is stocked with an array of basketware. Amid the stream of bicycles and buses, visitors will also spot an occasional pedicab—a tricycle supporting a hooded passenger seat and pedaled by a driver. Chengdu is one of China's few cities where this form of local transportation is still available for hire.

中国国际旅行社
CITS (Luxingshe) Office in Chengdu ■ Jinjiang Guest House, 180 S. Renmin Rd.
Tel: 29474/25042 Cable: 8225 CHENGDU Telex: 60154 CITCD CN

Chongqing

repeated good luck

traditional spelling/Chungking

CHONGQING, the largest city in Sichuan province, is the most important industrial city of southwest China and a key regional transportation hub. The city owes its early development and rapid recent growth to its location at the confluence of the Jialing and Yangtse rivers—about 2,400 km. (1,500 mi.) upstream from Shanghai and 1,055 km. (660 mi.) southwest of Beijing—and at the juncture of major north-south land routes.

Physically, Chongqing resembles the superstructure of a gigantic ship. The old city (pop. 800,000) is set on a peninsula, rising in tiers from 190 to 700 m. against the high, steep slopes of a mountain wedged between the two rivers. The narrow lanes in this older sector often merge into flights of steps connecting the various levels of the town. The newer sector to the west embraces industrial areas developed within recent decades, and has more open space, trees, and large buildings. Today, greater Chongqing covers an area of 9,800 sq. km. (3,783 sq. mi.), comprising nine districts and four counties, and has a total population of 6.5 million.

Chongqing's ambiance is unlike that of any other city in China. Covered outdoor marketplaces, juice stands, black-tiled wooden houses built along winding pathways, the people's suntanned appearance—all combine to give this city the flavor of a Chinatown in Southeast Asia.

Unfortunately, Chongqing's climate is one of the least appealing in all of China, as suggested by its local nickname—"furnace of the Yangtse." Summers are hot and humid, with temperatures rising to the mid-30s C (mid-90s F). From May to September, heavy rain falls four days out of 10. In autumn and winter, frequent changes in temperature tend to give rise to dank, foggy days. For the weather sensitive, early spring is about the only time to visit Chongqing.

CHONGQING IN HISTORY

Little is known of the early history of Chongqing. Records indicate, however, that the city was the capital of the Ba Kingdom—a non-Han polity that had a coiled snake (*ba*) as its totem—as early as the 12th century BC. It was known as Bajun during the Qin Dynasty (221–206 BC), when it was already an important trading center. The city was named Jiangzhou during the Han Dynasty (206 BC–AD 220) and renamed Yuzhou in the Sui Dynasty (581–618). Apparently it was not until the 12th century that the city

Climate		Jan	Feb	Mar	Apr	May	Jun	Jul	Aug	Sep	Oct	Nov	Dec
Temp.	°C	7	10	14.5	19.5	23	25.5	29	30	25	19	14	10.5
	°F	44.6	50	58.1	67.1	73.4	77.9	84.2	86	77	66.2	57.2	50.9
Precip.	mm.	15	20	38	99	142	180	142	122	150	112	48	20
	in.	.6	.8	1.5	3.9	5.6	7.1	5.6	4.8	5.9	4.4	1.9	.8

received the name Chongqing—to commemorate the "repeated good luck" of its prince, who went on to become Emperor Zhao Dun of the Southern Song Dynasty (1127–1279). Chongqing became a treaty port in 1891, but the few foreigners who came to this isolated outpost made little impact.

Chongqing's modern development began in 1928 with a planned program of street widening and industrialization. The major growth spurt came in 1938, when Chongqing became the wartime capital of Chiang Kaishek's Guomindang government. Whole industrial plants, universities, and service facilities were moved from the war zone along the eastern coast into the districts adjoining Chongqing. Local deposits of coal provided the energy base upon which rapid industrialization could proceed. By 1945, nearly two million people were jammed into the municipality. Even Japanese bombing failed to slow the city's growth, although the ensuing civil war did inflict damage.

Chongqing in the Revolution. Although Chongqing was the Nationalists' seat of government during World War II, the Communists were also openly active in the city. The last years of the war witnessed a degree of cooperation in the form of a united front against the Japanese. During the course of the war, Zhou Enlai, Dong Biwu, Ye Jianying, Deng Yingchao, and others were in Chongqing as Communist Party representatives. Their headquarters in Red Crag Village is now a tourist site. Local residents particularly remember the work of Zhou Enlai, who directed the *New China Daily*, headquartered in Chongqing, and who engaged in various anti-Guomindang activities. Mao Zedong himself came to Chongqing on August 28, 1945, to negotiate an ill-fated truce with the Nationalists.

ECONOMY AND CULTURE

Chongqing fell to the Communists in November 1949, one month after the official declaration of the founding of the People's Republic of China, and repair and expansion of the city's industrial base began soon thereafter. Growth was accelerated by improved navigation on the Yangtse and by the construction of new railroads linking the region to a national rail network. Rebuilding, street widening, and construction of cable railroads have somewhat altered the city's eastern and older sections. More dramatic changes during recent decades have occurred in the western half of the city. A 300-ft. hill was leveled to provide space for a new stadium and several major government and cultural buildings. Trees were planted and parks laid out to give the new section a more attractive and more open appearance.

Chongqing's comprehensive industrial base embraces steel, machinery, chemicals, power, textiles, and light industry. Its machine-tool plants now produce complete sets of equipment for small and medium-sized factories. Over 2,600 factories now account for 90% of the total value of industrial and agricultural production.

Cultural and educational institutions include the Sichuan Academy of Fine Arts, the Chongqing Workers' Palace of Culture, and several universities and technical schools.

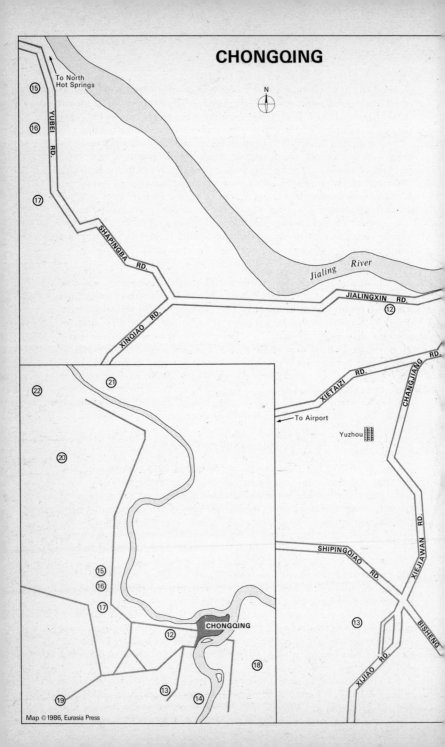

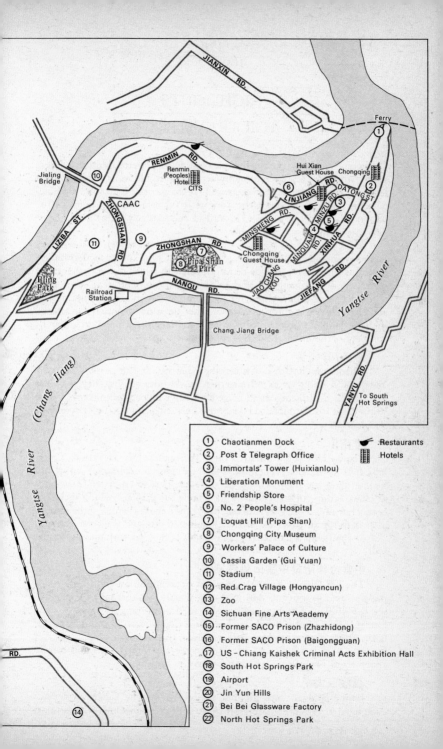

① Chaotianmen Dock
② Post & Telegraph Office
③ Immortals' Tower (Huixianlou)
④ Liberation Monument
⑤ Friendship Store
⑥ No. 2 People's Hospital
⑦ Loquat Hill (Pipa Shan)
⑧ Chongqing City Museum
⑨ Workers' Palace of Culture
⑩ Cassia Garden (Gui Yuan)
⑪ Stadium
⑫ Red Crag Village (Hongyancun)
⑬ Zoo
⑭ Sichuan Fine Arts Academy
⑮ Former SACO Prison (Zhazhidong)
⑯ Former SACO Prison (Baigongguan)
⑰ US – Chiang Kaishek Criminal Acts Exhibition Hall
⑱ South Hot Springs Park
⑲ Airport
⑳ Jin Yun Hills
㉑ Bei Bei Glassware Factory
㉒ North Hot Springs Park

🍴 Restaurants
🏨 Hotels

◀━━━━━━━━━━━━━━━━━━━━━━━━━▶

HIGHLIGHTS

FOR TRAVELERS

▶━━━━━━━━━━━━━━━━━━━━━━━━━◀

Chongqing lacks many of the historical attractions offered by other Chinese cities—there are few ancient monuments, and its old walls and most of its temples have long since been destroyed. Yet to consider it merely a jumping-off point for a cruise down the Yangste River or a trip to Chengdu (the provincial capital, 504 km. [313 mi.] to the south by train) would be to discount its interest considerably.

The city provides a glimpse of Chinese life rarely seen by foreigners. It conveys an image of having been bypassed in China's urban modernization programs which have already transformed (with mixed results) other cities such as Beijing, Shanghai, Wuhan, and Chengdu. The steep stone steps of the old city meander through neighborhoods which are unkempt, gritty, and often lacking in running water or other amenities. Tunnels and air-raid shelters, built for protection from Japanese bombs during World War II, still pepper the rock face of the upper town.

朝天门（码头）

Chaotianmen Dock. Chongqing's harbor, at the point where the Yangtse and Jialing rivers join together, bustles with activity. Tugs tow lines of junks piled with cargo, and barge after barge unloads onto trucks. Some heavy cargo is still unloaded by laborers balancing bamboo poles over their shoulders.

枇杷山

Loquat Hill (Pipa Shan). This is the highest hill (elevation 208 m. [682 ft.]) in the city proper and a favorite spot for cooling off during hot summer days and nights. Local people come here to enjoy tea, play cards or chess, strum guitars, or just walk among the gardens (which include a bonsai nursery). Foreigners are usually taken to the tea garden at the summit after dark for an overview of the illuminated city and the river activity. The city museum is located on the grounds of the park surrounding Loquat Hill.

中美合作所集中营旧址展览馆

The US-Chiang Kaishek Criminal Acts Exhibition Hall. This building was used as a prison during World War II. Visitors may be taken to see the display of torture instruments used on Communists here by the former "Sino-American Special Technical Cooperation Organization," set up in 1942. The exhibition hall is west of the city. The second stage of the visit entails a ride up Gele Hill to see the former cells and torture chambers at two prisons which now serve as museums.

嘉陵江大桥

Jialing Bridge. Until the highway bridge over the Yangtse River was completed in 1981, the Jialing Bridge was one of Chongqing's few transport links with other parts of the country. Constructed during 1963–66, it is 150 m. (492 ft.) long and 60 m. (196 ft.) above mean river height. The bridge affords a good view of river traffic and of the city itself.

红岩村

Red Crag Village (Hongyancun). Formerly the clandestine headquarters of the Southern Bureau of the Central Committee of the CCP and the Chongqing Office of the 8th Route Army, it is better known as the former residence of Zhou Enlai, who lived here from 1938 until 1945. Zhou led the delegation sent by the CCP to negotiate with the Guomindang government. The residence sits on a bluff overlooking the Jialing River. English-speaking guides explain the assembled artifacts and memorabilia.

温泉

Hot Springs. The North Hot Springs are located in a large park which looks out over the Jialing River. Visitors can soak for hours in one of the 40 baths filled with mineral water maintained at a temperature of 38°C (100°F), or swim in one of three Olympic-size pools fed by the hot springs.

The South Hot Springs, located 20 km. (12 mi.) south of the city in a scenic setting of pavilions, lakes, and landscaped gardens, offer the same facilities.

四川美术学院

Sichuan Fine Arts Academy (tel: 25423). A visit to the Sichuan Fine Arts Academy at Huangtongping, set in splendid woods in a leveled mountain area, is a highlight on the China itinerary. The academy was originally established in the liberated areas of Shaanxi Province in 1940 but was moved to the southwest a decade later. In 1953, it was restructured as the present Sichuan Fine Arts Academy and has become one of China's most important training centers for artists.

On exhibit at the academy are not only outstanding works created on the premises, but also a dazzling series of oil paintings by China's leading artists.

重庆市博物馆

Chongqing City Museum (tel: 55449). Located on Pipa Shan Rd., the museum focuses on the region's natural history, ancient history, and revolutionary history. Hours are 8–11:30 AM and 3–6:30 PM.

Theaters. Chongqing has two major theaters—the Chongqing Theater on Wuyi Lu Kou (tel: 42733) and the Renmin Theater on Xinhua Rd. (tel: 41931).

The Yangtse at Chongqing

HOTEL
ACCOMMODATIONS

人民宾馆
Renmin Hotel (175 Renmin Rd.; tel: 351421; telex: 62187). Opened in 1953, this massive, grand-looking hotel on the southern bank of the Jialing River is Chongqing's main hotel for foreigners. A huge auditorium between its two wings is modeled after Beijing's Temple of Heaven. All of the Renmin's 142 rooms are heated and most are air-conditioned. Services include three shops, a bank, and a post office. Chongqing's CITS branch is also located here. The downtown area may be easily reached via public bus #13. Taxis are available at 60 *fen*/km. or Y30/day. The hotel was completely renovated in 1988.

Rates: Doubles: Y160 per room; small suite: Y300; large suite: Y528.

重庆宾馆
Chongqing Guest House (235 Minsheng Rd.; tel: 46771/47662; telex: 62122). This elaborate structure is located in the northwest section of the city (reachable on bus route #1), across from the former office of the *New China Daily* where Zhou Enlai worked during World War II. The Chongqing underwent extensive renovation in 1985, and reopened in spring 1986.

重庆饭店

Chongqing Hotel (41-43 Xinhua Rd.; tel: 43233; telex: 62193 CKHCL CN). The prewar Chongqing Hotel reopened in 1987 after extensive renovations. Centrally located, the Chongqing boasts a superb restaurant.

渝州宾馆

Yuzhou Guest House (2 Youyi Rd.; tel: 23829). A former state guest house reserved for high government and Party officials, part of this pleasant compound now accepts tourists when there is an overflow at the Renmin Hotel and the Chongqing Guest House. Situated in a walled compound with its own garden, the Yuzhou can accommodate 400 people. Its main drawback is its distance from town—about 15–20 minutes by bus. Rates range from Y45–80, with a deluxe suite available at Y650.

小泉宾馆

Xiao Quan Hotel (tel: 8533). Situated near the Southern Hot Springs (about one hour's drive from town), the Xiao Quan is set in a lovely rural area. It has 168 rooms, with many of the baths supplied with piped-in spring water. Amenities include a swimming pool, dance room, and air-conditioning.

重庆扬子江假日酒店

Holiday Inn Yangtse Chongqing (Dianziping, Nanping xiang, Nan An district). Located in the new financial district near the Yangtse River 50 miles from the airport, the Holiday Inn Chongqing is scheduled to open in 1990. The 383 rooms including King Leisure rooms and Presidential Suite, have a view of the Yangtse River. Each is equipped with air-conditioning, radio, color TV, minibar and refrigerator. Banquet facilities for up to 300 are available. Sichuan Hot Pot Restaurant, Western restaurant, and coffeeshop provide dining. For evening entertainment there is a Lobby bar, sky lounge bar, and disco. Recreational possibilities include health club, games room, shopping arcade, and outdoor pool.

Chongqing's first modern hotel, the **Lu You Dalou,** was scheduled to open in early 1988 with 500 guest rooms.

沙平饭店

The **Shaping Hotel** (84 New Xiaolongtan Street, Shaping District; tel: 664196) also welcomes foreign guests. *Rates:* Double: Y130; suite: Y250–300.

For budget travelers, the **Huixianlou,** near the Jiefang Memorial on Minzu Road, offers Y9-dormitory beds; however, its facilities are lacking in hygenic conditions.

CUISINE

The food in Chongqing, as in all of Sichuan Province, is highly spiced, characterized mainly by chilis and peanuts. The hot peppers, however, do not mask other flavors but subtly enhance them. Those who like spicy food should be sure to mention this to the local guides, since hotels will normally serve dishes adapted to foreign tastes, resulting in a selection of bland, if not banal, dishes. Some of the special dishes of the region include cold noodles in chili sauce (*dan dan mian*), Chef Zhang's fat duck (*zhangpang ya*), bean curd in hot, spicy meat sauce (*mapo dofu*), "husband-and-wife" lungs (*fuqifeiyan*), local dumplings (*cahou shou*), and twice-cooked pork (*huiguo rou*). A fiery version of pickled raw vegetable salad is often eaten as a side dish.

There are few restaurants catering exclusively to foreigners. Some of the restaurants popular with local residents are Lao Sichuan (15 Bayi Rd.; tel: 46644), Yuexiangcun (Minzu Rd.; tel: 41526), the Minzu Road Restaurant (Minzu Rd.; tel: 41675), the Chongqing (Xinhua Rd.; tel: 43996), and the Xijiao (1 Qianjian Zhi Rd.; tel: 23106).

SHOPPING

The city's Friendship Store (tel: 47425) is located on Minzu Rd. across from the Liberation Monument (Jiefang Bei). Special items here include gold and silver filigree jewelry, colorful masks, and ceramic cups with bamboo decoration.

The streets radiating from the monument in the center of town constitute the downtown shopping area. Starting at the Jiefang Bei and winding along Zhongshan Road, one passes attractive shops with imaginative window displays. The Foreign Languages Bookstore sells old prints. The arts and crafts stores carry small bamboo objects such as water pipes and calligraphy brushes and holders, as well as decorated ink stones, jewelry, embroidered goods, and lacquerware.

The main shopping area is also dotted with colorful food markets and numerous cafes, some of which stay open until midnight. The largest markets are at Jiefang Bei and Shangqing Si (both very active between 8–9 PM). A 24-hour market operates adjacent to the railway station.

中国国际旅行社

CITS (Luxingshe) Office in Chongqing ◼ Renmin Hotel. Tel: 51449.

Cable: 4015 CHONGQING. Telex: 62126 CCITS CN.

Dali   大　理

Special Report by John Israel

OFFICIALLY opened to foreign visitors in March 1984, Dali, in north-west Yunnan Province, had already established a reputation among the handful of special delegates and foreign experts lucky enough to receive permission to travel there. Former Party General-Secretary Hu Yaobang visited Dali in 1981 and termed it "the Pearl of the Yun-Gui Plateau." That was no overstatement. As one old Yunnan hand remarked, "Dali is so charming it makes you whimper."

Dali is located 415 km. west of Kunming toward the southern end of a 50-km.-long stretch of highway that cuts through the terraced paddy-fields along the western shore of Erhai Lake. With the snowcapped Cangshan Mountains on one side and deep, blue waters on the other, the drive from Xiaguan at the south end of Erhai to Shapin at the north is a picture postcard panorama. Off the main road runs a network of cobblestone and dirt paths, beckoning visitors to explore the picturesque villages of the Bai minority that inhabits the region. Adding an enchanting touch to an already enchanting scene are the Bai women in red velvet vests, blue aprons, and flowery headdresses. Nowhere in China do the natural landscape and the human landscape blend more harmoniously.

Because of its isolation and dearth of modern facilities, Dali has thus far been frequented more by young independent travelers—especially Europeans—than by tour groups. Rumors that a modern airport was about to be built have caused these adventurous souls sleepless nights, filled with apparitions of paunchy Americans and rich Japanese overrunning their Shangri-la. Sooner or later rumor will become reality, and Dali could go the way of Guilin; but for the moment it is something special—reserved for those who are prepared to accept paradise on its own terms.

Although open, the Dali area remains remote. Most visitors arrive after an arduous, albeit scenic, 11–12-hour journey, most of which follows the old Burma Road of World War II fame. Buses leave daily at 7 AM from the West Gate Station in Kunming and depart from Dali and Xiaguan at the same hour for the return trip. Tickets (ca. Y14 each way) should be booked in advance at both ends. For travelers staying near the Kunming railroad station, there are also said to be daily buses from the Kunhu Fandian. During the lunch stop en route, I recommend that you cross the highway from the bus depot, turn right, and walk to the nice little Muslim restaurant just up the street.

Climate		Jan	Feb	Mar	Apr	May	Jun	Jul	Aug	Sep	Oct	Nov	Dec
Temp.	°C	9.6	11.0	14.4	17.8	19.3	19.5	20.1	19.8	18.3	15.7	12.7	10.2
	°F	49.2	51.8	57.9	64	66.7	67.1	68.1	67.6	64.9	60.2	54.8	50.3
Precip.	mm.	8	18	28	41	127	132	196	198	97	51	56	15
	in.	.3	.7	1.1	1.6	5	5.2	.7.7	7.8	3.8	2	2.2	.6

Xiaguan. Fifteen km. before you get to Dali, you reach Xiaguan. Located at the southern tip of Erhai, Xiaguan serves as the center of communications for the region. Xiaguan also boasts the only modern hotel in the area, the Erhai Binguan. The city suffers, however, from industrial pollution and is virtually devoid of charm. Travelers prepared to endure spartan accommodations are advised to stay in Dali.

Xiaguan is the point of departure for boat trips that take visitors to temples and other scenic points along the lake. There is also a five-hour excursion that covers the length and breadth of Erhai without making any stops. A short distance out of town to the southwest is a hot spring and just off the road (about 5 km. to the north) is the Shegu Ta (Snake Bones Pagoda). Halfway between Xiaguan and Dali is the little settlement of Qiliqiao (Seven Mile Bridge) from which dirt roads and trails lead to the waterfall at Qingbixi (Clear Blue Stream). Even out of season, when the waterfall is dry, the view of Erhai framed by pine-studded cliffs is worth the 90-minute walk.

HIGHLIGHTS FOR TRAVELERS

Most of the area's major sights, as well as the most scenic parts of the countryside, are located north of Dali. Just outside of town are Dali's three landmark pagodas, dating to the Tang and Song periods. In the same area are paths leading to Huang Long Tan (Yellow Dragon Lake) and the Zhong He Monastery, both in the foothills of the Cangshan Mountains.

Local Markets. Just past the 32-km. mark (18 km. north of Dali) a cobblestone road to the east leads to Xizhou, scene of a colorful daily market (8 AM to noon). An even larger and more varied market is held Monday mornings in Shapin, some 35 km. north of Dali. ("Go shoppin' in Shapin, buy from Bai.") Dali itself has a market day on the 2nd, 9th, 16th, and 33rd days of the lunar month. Dali's marble market and factory, open daily, are also worth visits.

Local markets are dwarfed by the Third-Month Fair, held between the 15th and 25th days of the Chinese lunar calendar—usually in April. Here, members of a dozen or so nationality groups set up shop in a tent colony. Here, machine-made goods are increasingly displacing native wares. It is debatable whether it is worth a special effort to hit Dali during the fair since the level of noise and congestion takes a quantum leap during the period, matched by a marginal decline in Dali's generally high level of civility.

Dali by Bicycle. The best way to see the Dali plain is by bicycle. Bikes can be rented from the Number Two Hostel in Dali or from the Happy Bicycle Rental next door. The latter is run by an attractive and accommodating group of private entrepreneurs, who offer, as an added enticement, a free map of the area. Alas, bicycles are no longer in the kind of shape they were when these places opened for business in 1984. Check out your vehicle for misaligned pedals, brakes, and other problems before you set off.

Bicycles offer freedom and mobility, allowing you to explore the back roads, villages, and temples between the highway and the lake. A delightful day begins with a trip to the Xizhou market. Have lunch at the Shicheng Fengwei (Historical City Local Specialties Restaurant). The regional noodles, called *ersi*, are excellent, as is the shredded pork and hot peppers *(lajiao rou si)*. After lunch head toward the lake. Charming villages and little temples dot the countryside and, with luck, you may discover a picture postcard scene of little fishing boats, fishermen mending nets and weaving traps, and lovely Bai women. Leaving the lake, work your way north and west to rejoin the highway near Zhoucheng (past the 38-km. mark), an exquisitely preserved little town whose residential architecture eclipses even Dali's. From there peddle back to Dali as the late afternoon sun casts a golden glow over the rice fields.

Bai sister and brother, Dali

HOTELS AND RESTAURANTS

The only hotel in Dali open to foreigners is the **Number Two Hostel**. Spartan but adequate accommodations run from Y15 yuan a bed in a double in the new wing to Y3 a bed in a five-bed dormitory off the courtyard of the old wing. Since the hot water in the new wing depends upon solar heat, you might well choose a bathless room and bathe yourself in the large washroom in the old wing, a convivial meeting place for backpackers from all over the world. Better yet, go to the public bathhouse next door (open until 7 PM) where, for a couple of *yuan*, you can soak your weary bones in an enormous tub, followed by a creditable Chinese massage. Unfortunately, this luxury is limited to male bathers. Women can only content themselves with a small tub with lukewarm water, but they are permitted to take advantage of the massage service.

You can take your meals in the hostel's dining room, but few do. It is far more fun to try some of the little restaurants that have sprung up around the hostel. For a breakfast treat, try the "Please Take a Rest and Drink Tea" lunchroom up the street at 10 Huguolu. There, in a captivating courtyard decorated with local artwork (including the owner's poetry), you can feast on an oversized portion of banana pancakes. The place is also open for lunch and dinner and features other dishes learned from itinerant foreign guests. Like everything else in Dali, the food here is reasonable, but prices vary according to the whim of the proprietor and his wife, so ask before you order.

A hundred meters down the street from the hostel is a place advertised by a large "Coca-Cola" sign. Here the prices are right, the portions are huge, the potato-tomato-egg dish is the best in town, and the accommodating hosts are happy to play your cassettes while you dine. They have, however, been known to run out of Coca-Cola. Another 100 m. down the street and across the main drag is the Peace Cafe, whose enormous menu includes spaghetti, hamburgers, and salads as well as all manner of Chinese cuisine. The chef will also cook to order whatever ingredients you care to bring in.

The Garden Restaurant (99 Yuer Lu), the first of the new generation of Dali's private enterprise eateries, no longer gets the rave reviews it received in earlier editions of this book. Although I still have a warm spot in my heart for the friendly Wen family that runs this charming little place, my culinary experience in April 1986 was not up to the level of 1984. My enthusiasm was further dampened by the discovery of a piece of broken glass in the rice. Most foreign travelers have deserted the Garden for places nearer the hostel. The Wens remained optimistic, however, and were busily expanding and remodeling.

Reports on Dali's Muslim restaurant — which features "pork chops from cow"— are negative.

Xiaguan Hotels. If you crave modern conveniences, stay in Xiaguan at the Erhai Hotel (Erhai Binguan, 140 Renmin Jie, tel. 5347). In the new wing you can choose a single, double, or triple at Y20, Y12, and Y8 per bed or a bathless quadruple at Y5. The old wing has bathless rooms ranging from Y5 to Y8 per bed. The best bargains in the hotel are the Y40 suites which offer two bedrooms (one double bed, one single) and a sitting room elegantly appointed in furniture of carved wood and Dali marble.

If you find the Erhai Binguan filled, try to get to Dali, for the other hotel in Xiaguan, the Number One Hostel, is as spartan as the Number Two but without any of its charm. The only thing that the Number One has that its sister facility lacks is a phone number (5681). To get the Dali facility, just ask the operator for the Dali Di-er Zhoudaisuo.

丽江
LIJIANG

A seven-hour bus ride to the north takes you to Lijiang, center of the Naxi nationality group. Here one stays in the Number One Hostel, where prices range from Y4 a bed in four-person dormitory rooms to Y32 for a double with bath off the newly constructed rear courtyard.

Repairing fishing nets by a Yunnan lake.

The new part of town where the hostel is located is architecturally featureless; the local cuisine is inferior to Dali's; and the Naxi women, who top off otherwise exotic costumes with "Mao caps," fall short of Bai standards. Nonetheless, Lijiang is well worth the trip. The old section of town is charming, and the surrounding countryside is spectacular. Rent the hostel's solitary jeep (sits six, costs 60 *fen*/km.) and drive out to the village of Baisha. (You can also do it by bike, but bicycle rentals are outrageous and the country roads are taxing.) In Baisha, visit Dr. Ho Shan-hsou (He Shixiu) at the Clinic of Chinese Herbs in Jade-Dragon-Snow Mountain of Lijiang. The affable, English-speaking doctor will give you a blow-by-blow account of his eventful life, from encounters with US aviators during the Second World War to his struggle for survival during the Cultural Revolution. Baisha also has a local temple with some exquisite Ming Dynasty murals, if you can find somebody to open the place up for you. Continue your drive to the Yufengsi (Jade Peak Temple), one of China's rare Red Sect Lamaseries, where colorfully dressed Red Lamas are happy to pose for photographs.

Lijiang hosts a livestock fair in April and a general fair in August.

From Lijiang you can connect to the Chengdu–Kunming railroad at Jinjiang. Reserve a seat on the 6:50 AM bus run by the Lijiang District Transportation Co. (Lijiang Diqu Yunshu Gongsi). You can also get a bus from the main terminal, but that is twice as far from the hostel. You will arrive in Lijiang in time for dinner at one of the open-air restaurants across from the station and a cup of tea at the adjacent outdoor teahouse, before catching the evening express to Chengdu.

Dalian

great link

traditional spelling/Talien

DALIAN (formerly known in the West as "Dairen") lies at the southern tip of the Liaodong Peninsula in northeast China. It is the country's third largest port engaging in foreign trade. Although the city is located only about 500 km. (310 mi.) east of Beijing, the train route must cover an additional 1,450 km. (900 mi.) in its journey around the Bohai Gulf.

Northernmost of China's 14 Coastal Open Cities, Dalian's Economic and Technical Development Zone is situated in nearby Maqiaozi Village. A site for 100 new factories has already been readied in the zone, and port expansion at Dalian and the new Dayao facility is well underway. Through mid-1985, 92 contracts, worth approximately Y1.1 billion, had been signed with foreign investors. Dalian is one of the four "priority open cities," which means that in 1986 Dalian will continue to pursue its present course of rapid economic development in the midst of reduced growth rates elsewhere.

This city with a population of 4.6 million is known for both its industry and scenic setting. Round green hills form a backdrop on three sides. The deep blue bay to the south is skirted by four excellent beaches.

Construction of Dalian's ice-free port began in 1899 and was completed in 1930 by the Japanese. Under the terms of the 1945 Yalta Agreement, control of the city passed from Japan to the Soviet Union, which assisted in the construction of vast munitions plants and the completion of Dalian's network of underground defense shelters. The Soviet occupation ended in 1954, but the Soviet presence still lingers, as evidenced by the bilingual street signs and the cenotaph on Stalin Square.

On the way to Dalian, the train passes through fields of sorghum and soybeans. The outskirts of the city are dominated by factories that produce diesel engines, ships, machine tools, chemicals, textiles, refinery products, processed food, and blown glass. Famous for the wide variety of apples it produces, Dalian is popularly known within China as "the homeland of apples."

HIGHLIGHTS FOR TRAVELERS

Sightseeing in Dalian usually includes the port, some factories, and the beach resorts. The port employs about 13% of the population and its ice-free harbor receives ships from over 100 countries. Modern dock facilities can handle containerized shipping and oil and coal from northeast China. In

Climate		Jan	Feb	Mar	Apr	May	Jun	Jul	Aug	Sep	Oct	Nov	Dec
Temp.	°C	−4.2	−1.7	4.7	13.2	19.7	24.4	26.6	25.8	20.9	14.0	4.6	−2.2
	°F	24.5	28.9	40.4	55.7	67.4	75.9	79.8	78.4	69.6	57.2	40.2	28
Precip.	mm.	76	76	76	102	152	229	330	279	178	152	102	76
	in.	3	3	3	4	6	9	13	11	7	6	4	3

addition to touring the factories, visitors are often taken to see new residential neighborhoods for workers, affording a view of daily life in the city. Recreational areas such as Tiger Park (Laohutan) and the beaches are quite popular, especially in the summer.

HOTEL ACCOMMODATIONS

大庆宾馆

Dalian International Hotel (9 Stalin Road; tel: 238238; telex: 86363 DTH CN). Opened in February 1988, the Dalian International Hotel is part owned by a Hong Kong company and managed by Carrington Hotel Management. This first joint venture property in Dalian has 380 rooms. Hotel facilities include a dim sum café and a Western restaurant, a disco, singalong bar, sauna, gymnasium, health club, and business center. Rooms are equipped with minibar, in-house movies, and direct-dial telephones. Room rates are $55–95.

大连丽晶饭店

Dalian Regent Hotel. Scheduled to open in April 1988, the Dalian Regent has been designed for the leisure crowd, rather than business travelers. It has 220 rooms and will be managed by the Japanese Dai-Ichi hotel chain.

富丽华大酒店

Furama Hotel Dalian (74 Stalin Road; tel: 239128; telex: 86441 FRAMA CN). The Furama Hotel, opened in January 1988, is a joint venture with Hong Kong's Pearl International Hotels. Located downtown, the 500-room hotel has four restaurants, a disco, health club, indoor pool, business center, and an Artist's Corner which features contemporary works of Chinese art. Room rates are $50 and up.

大连九州假日饭店

Holiday Inn Dalian (18 Shengli Square, Zhongshan ward; tel: 230668; telex: 86383). Located in the main city square, the Holiday Inn Dalian opened in 1988. It faces the main thoroughfare leading to the harbor and is only 10 km. from the airport. The hotel has 226 rooms, as well as apartment units containing 60 apartments. Rooms are provided with air-conditioning, color TV, video, refrigerator, and minibar. In addition to Japanese and Chinese restaurants, and a coffeeshop, their specialty Chinese restaurant serves Dalian, Sichuan, and Cantonese cuisine, with the focus on seafood. Banquet facilities up to 180 are available, as is a business center. For recreation, there is a health club with a sauna, and a games room including billiards and ping pong.

棒棰岛宾馆

Bangchuidao Guesthouse (on the coastal road, southeast of the city; tel: 235131; telex: 86236 DBCIG CN). This 10-building guest house is attractively situated in a forested area near a beach with the same name. Seven of the 10 buildings are villa-type structures. Building 9 is larger, with spacious rooms classified as large suites, suites, and single rooms. Building 8 is a self-styled "international club" with game rooms. Building 9 has facilities for swimmers, providing hot baths and boating and fishing gear.

大连宾馆

Dalian Guesthouse (4 Zhongshan Square; tel: 23111). Located in the heart of the city, the Dalian Guesthouse has about 100 rooms. Its chefs prepare a wide spectrum of seafood delicacies ranging from consommé of sea-cucumber to sliced snapper with sea bream.

大连饭店

Dalian Hotel (6 Shanghai Rd.; tel: 23171). The clientele of this seven-storey hotel consists mainly of overseas Chinese. The hotel is conveniently located in the center of the city (near Zhongshan Square) and is equipped with a barbershop, currency exchange counter, and taxi stand.

南山宾馆

Nanshan Hotel (56 Fenglin Street, Zhongshan District; tel: 28517; cable: 5103). Located in the center of the city, the Nanshan Hotel has some 120 rooms, with prices ranging from Y40 (for a single) to Y210 (for a deluxe suite), with the majority of rooms renting for about Y100. All have private bath and color TV. The hotel restaurant serves Chinese food.

大连友谊 宾馆

The Dalian Friendship Hotel (137 Stalin Rd.; tel: 24121) has 154 rooms and suites, and offers Chinese and Western food.

CUISINE

As one might expect, Dalian's culinary specialties revolve around seafood. The Haiwei Restaurant (85 Zhongshan Rd.; tel: 27067) is a genuine seafood-lover's haven, serving over 600 different seafood dishes. Among its specialties are yellow croaker in sweet-and-sour sauce, phoenix shark's fin, soft-fried sea conches, and pike in soybean sauce. The Huibin Restaurant (3 Jinbu Jie; tel: 35362) serves Beijing cuisine and is noted for its Beijing Duck and sea-cucumber stew. For those who favor Sichuan dishes there is the Sichuan Restaurant (230 Tianjin Jie; tel: 24614).

中国国际旅行社
CITS (Luxingshe) Office in Dalian ■ 1 Stalin Square. Tel: 28751/335795.
Telex: 86252 FERTC CN.

Daqing

great celebration

traditional spelling/Taching

DAQING—the site of China's most famous oil field—is situated in the northeastern province of Heilongjiang, approximately 1,085 km. (675 mi.) northeast of Beijing—about 12 hours by direct train. In a pattern reminiscent of 19th-century boomtowns of the American West, Daqing has been transformed within a few decades from a virtually uninhabitable swampland into a major economic center with over 600,000 people.

After 1949, exploratory drilling began with technical assistance from the Soviet Union. When the Soviet Union withdrew its technicians in 1959 as a consequence of the Sino-Soviet split, the Chinese pressed on independently and on September 26—a few days before the 10th anniversary of the founding of the PRC—the No. 3 Exploratory Well yielded oil. Daqing became China's key model for industrial development because of its worker discipline, skillful planning, managerial efficiency, and the triumph of spirit over circumstance. Daqing also produces natural gas.

HIGHLIGHTS FOR TRAVELERS

Daqing has no central downtown urban section but consists instead of a cluster of small communities, including over 50 scattered villages, each with its own shopping and service facilities. As a model agro-industrial complex, the state-run enterprise of Daqing was deliberately developed this way in order to combine industry and agriculture, promote communal self-reliance, and avoid the congestion and pollution plaguing modern cities. Oil workers' family members participate in production by raising crops and running small workshops in the vicinity of their homes. Throughout Daqing, women can be seen engaged in all types of skilled and semi-skilled industrial production. Pioneer Village, built and administered entirely by women, has comprehensive school and medical facilities.

HOTEL ACCOMMODATIONS

大庆宾馆

The **Daqing Guest House,** constructed in 1975, consists of 110 rooms in two sections joined by a courtyard. The hotel is spartan but comfortable. The usual tourist amenities are provided: banking and postal services, a café, and a souvenir stand. The food at the hotel is particularly good—some people claim it is the best hotel food north of the Yangtse. Long-term guests are forewarned to pack a pair of tennis shoes—the hotel is surrounded by basketball courts and the friendly staff is always eager for a match.

Climate		Jan	Feb	Mar	Apr	May	Jun	Jul	Aug	Sep	Oct	Nov	Dec
Temp.	°C	−19.7	−15.8	−4.8	6.5	14.7	20.2	22.5	21.2	14.2	5.8	−6.2	−16.0
	°F	−3.4	3.6	23.4	43.7	58.4	68.3	72.5	70.1	57.5	42.4	20.9	3.2
Precip.	mm.	8	8	18	28	69	84	183	170	64	36	28	15
	in.	.3	.3	.7	1.1	2.7	3.3	7.2	6.7	2.5	1.4	1.1	1.6

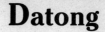

great togetherness   *traditional spelling/Tatung*

DATONG, an industrial and mining center with a population of 850,000, is situated in northern Shanxi Province on an arid plain 1,216 m. (3,990 ft.) above sea level. A dusty, dun-colored place, Datong exhibits as dramatically as any town in China the remarkable ability of an organized, mobilized population to convert the cruelest of environments into a productive, largely self-reliant urban center. Strategically located just south of the Great Wall and the border of Inner Mongolia, Datong serves as a major rail juncture for north-central China. It is about 270 km. (167 mi.) and six hours west of Beijing by train.

Datong's coal industry (Shanxi is China's leading coal-producing province) grew rapidly during the 1920s when coal was used to fuel the steam engines formerly built in the city. Today, both industry and agriculture have become considerably diversified, and Datong now produces cement, soda, and light industrial products (notably shoes, whose manufacture grew out of the hide trade with Inner Mongolia, and carpets). Datong is also home to the world's last operational steam locomotive factory.

DATONG IN HISTORY

Datong first became important in the 4th century when the Toba invaders from Central Asia conquered and unified northern China, establishing the Northern Wei Dynasty (386–534), with Datong as its capital. The Toba were a Turkic people much more sympathetic to the ideas of Buddhism than the indigenous Han aristocracy, who espoused Confucianism and Daoism. During the Northern Wei Dynasty—a period of war and social upheaval— Buddhist concepts of personal salvation and paradise became popular among the lower classes and Buddhism was adopted as the state religion.

It was the Northern Wei conquerors who began carving the man-made caves at Yungang, near Datong, in AD 460. Although the work continued under the Sui and the Tang, the town itself declined in importance after the Northern Wei moved their capital to Luoyang in 494. A brief renaissance occurred under the Liao (907–1125). Datong remained an important frontier town under the Jin (1115–1234) and was further fortified under the Ming in 1372.

Climate		Jan	Feb	Mar	Apr	May	Jun	Jul	Aug	Sep	Oct	Nov	Dec
Temp.	°C	−0.8	1.8	8.1	13.6	19.3	25.2	26.8	25.8	19.1	13.6	6.6	0.6
	°F	30.5	35.2	46.5	56.4	66.7	77.3	80.2	78.4	66.3	56.4	43.8	33
Precip.	mm.	76	76	76	102	152	203	305	254	178	152	102	76
	in.	3	3	3	4	6	8	12	10	7	6	4	3

HIGHLIGHTS FOR TRAVELERS

In Datong itself, there are four major sites of interest to visitors.

九龙壁
Nine Dragon Screen (Jiulong Bi). This exquisite Ming Dynasty screen composed of multicolored glazed tiles is set in the midst of a courtyard in the town center. A pool runs the length of the screen, and when a breeze ripples across the water, the reflected imperial dragons appear to writhe.

上华严寺
Upper Huayan Monastery. This plain and somewhat austere temple (one of the two largest in China) was built by the Liao and later rebuilt by the Jin. It contains five large Ming Buddhas and some lively Qing frescoes on the rear wall. There are about 10 other lesser Qing buildings in the area.

下华严寺
Lower Huayan Monastery. Located near the Upper Huayan, this monastery was also originally constructed under the Liao. All of the present buildings, except for the small library, date from the Ming and Qing. The library has been declared a national monument and it contains a number of exquisite Liao frescoes and sculptures.

善化寺
Shanhua Monastery. This monastery in the southern part of Datong was constructed in the 8th century under the Tang. Originally the complex consisted of ten buildings covering an area of 13,900 sq. m. (16,624 sq. yd.), but now only four remain, all dating from the 12th century. Note the square wooden pavilion, two stories high. It is a faithful reproduction of Liao architecture.

For those seeking a place to relax, there is the People's Park located northwest of the monasteries; and for shoppers, there is the Red Flag Bazaar, located directly south of the People's Park.

HOTEL ACCOMMODATIONS

云冈饭店
Yungang Hotel (21 Yingbin East Rd.; tel: 36202). The Yungang was hurriedly opened in July 1985 before it was finished and, indeed, was showing such signs of wear and tear that a new manager was required. This hotel, with 150 rooms (300 beds) with bath, has been designated to accommodate CITS tour groups. It has a dining room and a coffee shop.

大同宾馆
Datong Hotel (Yingbin Road; tel: 32333/32409). Located in a residential area just south of the Huayan and Shanhua monastaries, the Datong has 150 rooms, all reasonably priced and while the facilities are less than luxurious, all rooms have telephones and most have a private bath. Chinese and Western food is available. The Datong is six km. from the railroad station and 55 km. from the airport.

A giant sandstone Buddha at Yungang

云冈石窟
YUNGANG CAVES

Visitors to Yungang would do well to read up on the rich cultural history of the site prior to departure. Unfortunately, little useful information is provided by local guides or literature.

The Yungang Caves are located 16 km. (10 mi.) west of Datong, at the base of the low-lying sandstone Wuzhou Hills. Most were carved under the Northern Wei between 460 and 494.

The advent of the Northern Wei marked a new high point in Chinese art and culture. The Wei introduced a period of stability and, through an intelligent series of laws on marriage and land distribution, created a "melting pot" of Han and non-Han peoples. Major treatises on agriculture and river transportation were written in this period, while painting, calligraphy, and poetry all developed a new vividness and grace. But the greatest achievement of all was Buddhist grotto art.

The art of cave temples originated in India and first appeared in China at Dunhuang. However, the carvings at Dunhuang are in terra cotta, whereas those at Yungang are the earliest examples of stone carvings in China. The 53 caves—including 21 major ones—contain 51,000 bas-reliefs and statues, ranging in height from just a few centimeters to 17 m. (55 ft.). A number of different influences can be seen: Indian (draperies, shortened skirts, and headdresses); Persian and Byzantine (weapons, lions, and beards); and Greek (the trident and the curling acanthus leaves).

From east to west, the main caves fall naturally into three groups:

Caves 1 to 4. At the far eastern end are the first two caves, somewhat removed from the others. The square floor-plan indicates that they were built quite early. The first cave has some bas-reliefs of the life of Buddha, while the second has a delicately carved pagoda at its center. Cave 3, the largest at Yungang, contains a basic triad of a large Buddha flanked by two bodhisattvas. The elegance of their garments and the use of high relief is reminiscent of some of the carving at Longmen (near Luoyang), indicating that the Datong figures may have been created under the Sui or early Tang.

Beyond the fourth cave are a small ravine and a monastery, consisting of several temples. The monastery dates from 1652. Historical writings suggest that there may once have been as many as 10 monasteries in these hills, but today there is no trace of them.

Caves 5 to 13. Caves 5 and 6 mark the high point of Yungang art. In the fifth cave, a colossal Buddha (16.8 m. [55 ft.] tall) is seated in serene contemplation. Both caves, but particularly cave 6, are richly carved with episodes from religious stories and processional scenes. The interiors of these two caves have fortunately been preserved from the elements by the twin towers at their entrances. Caves 5, 6, and 7—the latter has six bodhisattvas and two lions in high relief—were restored in 1955. Cave 8 contains a number of foreign influences: a Vishnu seated on a bull, a Shiva, and a guardian bearing a trident.

Caves 7 and 8 form a pair, as do caves 9 and 10, also richly carved. Each of the latter two contains front and back chambers and fine bas-relief work at its entrance. Cave 11 was decorated in 483, in honor of the imperial family. It contains 95 large carvings and hundreds of tiny bodhisattvas in niches around the wall. The bas-reliefs in cave 12 provide valuable information on the architecture and musical instruments (borne by the flying *apsaras*) of the period. Cave 13 has another colossal Buddha, his arm supported by another figure and an enormous halo around his head.

Caves 14 to 21. The first two in this series are badly eroded, though they still contain thousands of tiny bodhisattvas in niches around the walls. The next five caves, the oldest at Yungang, were all carved in 460 during the reign of Emperor Wen Chang. Each contains a colossal Buddha whose countenance is austere and divinely remote. The early carving in these caves has a geometric, linear quality, and the decoration is not as rich or bold as in later caves.

After 1949, the caves were declared historic monuments, and the steady erosion by wind and water was slowed down through judicious tree planting and the construction of protective barriers. Unfortunately, little can be done to restore the ravages of early 20th-century art thieves and smugglers. Hundreds of statues were beheaded and a number of bas-reliefs removed. They now reside in the art museums of Japan, Europe, and North America.

大 足   # Dazu

great fulfillment   *traditional spelling/Tatsu*

DAZU ranks among the most important Buddhist archeological sites in China. It is the repository of more than 50,000 stone carvings dating from the 9th to the 13th centuries AD. Dazu's remote location, isolated in the hills 160 km. (100 mi.) northwest of Chongqing, has not only kept it a "secret" to China scholars and travelers but has also preserved it from being destroyed.

In 1982, with the opening of a new highway to Chongqing, Dazu was declared ready to receive a steady volume of visitors. The Chongqing branch of CITS (located in the Renmin Hotel) now arranges overnight excursions to Dazu for foreigners at a rate of Y70 per person (includes transportation, meals, lodging, and guide/interpreter services). For overseas Chinese, the excursion fee is Y17 (Saturday departures only). The direct bus ride from Chongqing to Dazu takes three hours.

HOTEL ACCOMMODATIONS
大足宾馆

Dazu Guest House (51 Guangdong St.; tel: 100). The Dazu Guest House has 70 double rooms (Y28) and four suites (Y48). There is taxi service, currency exchange, and a Chinese restaurant.

HIGHLIGHTS FOR TRAVELERS

Dazu is unique among the other famous Buddhist grottoes in China (such as Dunhuang and Yungang), which were built before the late Tang period. Dazu's iconography (carved during the 400 years after this period) presents Buddhist figures as human beings and depicts scenes from everyday life. Dazu's artists eschewed the often fearsome and supernatural aura attached to earlier versions of these figures, signalling a significant departure from earlier Buddhist art both in form and in content.

北山

Beishan. Dazu's sculptures are distributed among 40 different sites throughout Dazu County, although the majority are concentrated at Beishan (North Hill) and Baodingshan (Treasure Peak Mountain). Beishan, also called Longgangshan (Dragon Mound Hill), is 2 km. from Dazu town. In 892, Wei Junjing, the military commander of eastern Sichuan, selected this area for a stronghold and fortified it for the storage of arms and grain. Wei also ordered the construction of Beishan's first Buddhist shrine.

Climate		Jan	Feb	Mar	Apr	May	Jun	Jul	Aug	Sep	Oct	Nov	Dec
Temp.	°C	7	10	14.5	19.5	23	25.5	29	30	25	19	14	10.5
	°F	44.6	50	58.1	67.1	73.4	77.9	84.2	86	77	66.2	57.2	50.9
Precip.	mm.	15	20	38	99	142	180	142	122	150	112	48	20
	in.	.6	.8	1.5	3.9	5.6	7.1	5.6	4.8	5.9	4.4	1.9	.8

Today, Beishan is most famous for its 250-m.-long "Buddha Crescent," where some 10,000 figures have been sculpted. Chiseled into 290 niches, this endeavor took more than 250 years to complete (from the late Tang to the Song Dynasty). "The Wheel of the Universe" or Grotto 136 is considered the most outstanding and best preserved of the Beishan grottoes. Besides the intricately carved stone wheel, which housed a number of sacred sutras, and which symbolizes the cycle of man's life and the limitless power of Buddhism, this grotto contains some 20 figures. Perhaps the main attractions here are the bodhisattvas Manjusri and Samantabhadra, who sit astride a lion and an elephant, respectively. In Buddhist tradition, the image of the two who subdued wild animals suggests the triumph of good over evil. Visitors should not miss grottoes 125 and 245. Located in the former is a large sculpture of the bodhisattva Guanyin (Goddess of Mercy). She is standing, wearing flowing robes, and clasping prayer beads. The 2.6-m.wide Grotto 245 incredibly houses more than a thousand minute figures illustrating scenes from the sutras, including pagodas and temples, phoenixes rowing boats, dancing sparrows, musicians and orchestras, and dragons and snakes pulling chariots.

宝鼎山

Baodingshan. Another 10,000 figures—sculpted in just a seven-decade period (1179–1249)—are located at Baodingshan, 15 km. northeast of Dazu. Built under the direction of the famous Southern Song Dynasty (12th century) monk Zhao Zhifeng, most of the carvings are concentrated in a "Big Buddha Crescent." Unlike Beishan, where figures are grouped haphazardly, Zhao's project was carefully planned (in fact, his miniature model still stands). One of the most extraordinary pieces of workmanship at this site is the huge Sleeping Buddha. Only the upper part of the reclining Buddha's body is visible and that in itself measures more than 31 m. long.

The Yuan Jue (Total Awakening) Grotto is famous for its carving of a kneeling deity surrounded by Buddhist followers, a motif unique in Buddhist art. The remaining cave walls are carved into temples, trees, mountains, flowers, and heavenly and earthly beings. A series of ten scenes recounts the life of a herdsman. Another series entitled "Parental Love" shows a woman's pregnancy, her child's birth, nursing, and her son's marriage. Apart from the ingenious skill of the artists in creating such lifelike figures and scenes, their use of natural light is also worth noting. In the Yuan Jue, for example, they designed a huge window that illuminates details of the carvings with almost stereoscopic effect. Perhaps even more astonishing is the drainage system. When it rains you can hear water trickling through "invisible" pipes. But a close look under the clouds, trees, and pagodas will reveal a complete system that empties all of the roof water into a fountain located on the head of a dragon—from there it disappears underground.

中国国际旅行社
CITS (Luxingshe) Office in Dazu ■ Courtyard of the Government Organization
of Dazu County

Dunhuang

DUNHUANG is located in the northwest desert corridor of Gansu Province, near the Xinjiang border to the east and the Qilian mountain range to the west. This 2,000-year-old town was once an important caravan stop on the Silk Road linking Central Asia with China. Today, it attracts visitors mainly because it is the site of one of the most priceless troves of Buddhist art the world has ever known—the Mogao Caves.

Despite China's new enthusiasm for tourism, access to the caves is by no means easy. The new Dunhuang Airport, expanded in 1988, has doubled its former capacity. Air routes have been opened between Dunhuang and Ürümqi, in addition to Lanzhou, enabling direct access to Dunhuang from either direction. Although still relatively remote, devotees of Buddhist culture can now visit Dunhuang much more easily. The grottoes are located an additional 25 km. (15 mi.) southeast of the town.

Dunhuang itself is a prosperous town boasting a number of shops, a bank, and a cinema. Because tourism is new to Dunhuang, visitors should be prepared for friendly but curious stares from the local populace.

► HIGHLIGHTS ◄

► FOR TRAVELERS ◄

Although the Mogao Caves are the main attraction of the region, visitors should leave time for a drive to the old Yangguan and Hongshan mountain passes 62 km. (40 mi.) southwest of Dunhuang. Until the area was blocked off by the Mongols in the 14th century, these passes served as China's gateway to the Western world, not only for trade, but also for ideas. Christianity, Islam, and Buddhism all came to China along this route. Han Dynasty (206 BC–AD 220) beacon towers, which formerly warned the populace of invaders and marked the route for camel caravans, have been almost obliterated by drifting sand. The camel, so well adapted to desert conditions, is still commonly used here.

Climate		Jan	Feb	Mar	Apr	May	Jun	Jul	Aug	Sep	Oct	Nov	Dec
Temp.	°C	−15.2	−12.2	0.7	10.8	18.9	23.4	25.7	23.8	17.4	8.2	−2.6	−12.0
	°F	4.6	10	33.2	51.4	66	74.1	78.2	74.8	63.3	46.7	27.3	10.4
Precip.	mm.	15	8	13	38	28	38	18	25	15	43	41	10
	in.	.6	.3	.5	1.5	1.1	1.5	.7	1.0	.6	1.7	1.6	.4

The Dang River runs beside the new Gansu-Xinjiang highway. It has recently been diverted from its original course to protect the 16 West Caves at Nanhutian, all that remain of an earlier legacy of Buddhist grottoes. In 1975, the Dang River Reservoir was constructed in an effort to control annual summer floods. This reservoir, together with a network of irrigation channels, is the source of most of the region's water and electricity.

The area surrounding the Yangguan Pass was marshland 1,000 years ago, and the grasslands to the south formerly supported a fine breed of wild horse. Accumulating sand gradually transformed the whole area into desert. Since 1949, as part of the effort to bring more land under cultivation throughout China, considerable portions of the Gansu desert have been reclaimed through irrigation, as is evident in the fertile land of Shanshui Gulley, which today provides the bulk of the region's produce. New grass-lands have been created as grazing ground for sheep, cattle, and donkeys, as well as horses. Nanhu Commune alone has reclaimed hundreds of hectares in recent years.

Nearby are the ruins of the ancient Han town of Shouchang, where potsherds, bronze coins, arrowheads, and even pearls from old necklaces have been found in the sand. From atop one of the Han beacon towers near the Hongshan Pass, one can survey the entire area—pasturelands, reservoirs, houses, roads, and the still unconquered golden desert.

莫高窟
THE MOGAO GROTTOES

The Mogao Grottoes, the oldest Buddhist shrines in China, are located 25 km. (15 mi.) southeast of Dunhuang in a river valley between the Sanwei and Mingsha mountains. The caves are open to visitors from April to November. According to a Tang inscription, carving was begun in AD 366 by a monk named Yue Zun who was traveling through the area and saw a vision of a thousand golden Buddhas. Over the next 1,000 years, hundreds of caves were carved out of the steep sandstone cliffs in a layered honeycomb pattern and connected by wooden walkways and ladders.

After the 14th century, the grottoes were abandoned. They were accidentally rediscovered in 1900 by a man named Wang Yuan, who took refuge here while fleeing famine in Hebei Province. He stumbled upon the hidden monastery library, a priceless collection of scrolls, documents, embroideries, paintings, and sutras which had been left behind by the monks who inhabited the caves until they were driven out by the invading Western Xia in 1036. Due to lack of interest by the decadent Manchu government, Wang sold crateloads of priceless artifacts and historical documents to British and French sinologists. Plunder by warlords, local officials, Guomindang soldiers, and—not least of all—Western collectors continued unabated until 1949.

The desert cliffs above the grottoes stand in stunning contrast to the green valley below but furnish virtually no protection from the elements. The interiors of all the caves have been severely damaged by wind and water erosion and many of them have collapsed. Today, 492 grottoes are still standing.

Each cave has an identifying marker, with number, date, and dynasty. Eight dynastic periods are represented: Northern and Western Wei, Sui, Tang, Five Dynasties, Song, Western Xia, and Yuan.

Most of the caves are rectangular or square-shaped, with coffered ceilings. Many contain daises surmounted with statues of Buddha and other figures. The walls are filled with niches, some of them so deep they form additional grottoes. The Northern Wei and Tang caves have been best preserved and, with the exception of the Song grottoes, are generally larger than the caverns of the other dynasties.

Because the sandstone here did not take well to fine carving, the smaller statues are made of terra cotta, coated with a form of gesso, and brilliantly painted with mineral pigments. While a few of the cave walls and ceilings are bare, most are covered with vivid murals. As in the grottoes later carved at Yungang (near Datong) and Longmen (near Luoyang), the main themes are the life of Buddha, various religious stories, and tales from Chinese folk mythology. The murals are also an invaluable source of information on the architecture, scientific and cultural achievements, foreign contacts, dress, and everyday life of Chinese society during this 1,000-year period. The scenes depict people hunting, fishing, cutting timber, making pottery, forging iron, and making wine. There are also portrayals of weddings and funerals, celebrations in teahouses and inns (including figures of musicians and acrobats), processions of visiting foreign dignitaries, merchant caravans from the West, as well as some rather grisly paintings of the torture of prisoners.

The caves exhibit the distinct artistic styles of the various dynasties, the most notable of which are the Northern and Western Wei, the Sui, and the Tang.

NORTHERN AND WESTERN WEI DYNASTIES (386–557)

The grottoes of this period (sometimes called the Sixteen Kingdoms) are filled with delicately carved statues whose broad faces show prominent cheekbones, thin lips and eyebrows, and noses set high on the face—the latter indicating Indian influence. The earlier Wei faces, in xiao style, were originally painted vermilion, with chalk-white nose and eyes. But the vermilion oxidized, and the subsequent configuration of white features on a black background resembles the shape of the Chinese character xiao, meaning "small." Later Wei carvings depict figures wearing wide hats and elaborate dress, but in general the slender Wei figures are draped in clinging, light robes, and the heads seem large in proportion to the bodies.

Wei grotto ceilings are decorated with geometric patterns and animals and figures from Chinese mythology, such as Fuxi—a legendary emperor of China, the Royal Lord of the East, and the Queen Mother of the West—whose chariot is pulled by a dragon and a phoenix. Certain symbols simultaneously represent both points of the compass and the seasons, such as the Somber Warrior (north, winter); the White Tiger (west, autumn); the Green Dragon (east, spring); and the Scarlet Bird (south, summer). The latter is usually depicted as a pheasant, quail, or phoenix.

SUI DYNASTY (581–618)

These grottoes are located to the north of the Wei caves, and the Sui artists in some instances may have painted over Wei carvings. Side niches are deeper than those in the Wei caves, and usually comprise two designs motifs. Sui heads and torsos, elongated in proportion to the rest of the body, convey an aura of majesty. All figures are draped in Chinese robes; there is no Indian influence in the Sui grottoes. Ananda, the young disciple of Buddha, appears for the first time. The lotus flower motif occurs frequently in the ceiling murals. Stories from the Jataka (life of Buddha) provide the main themes for the Sui wall paintings.

TANG DYNASTY (618–907)

The niches in the Tang grottoes are divided into tiny, separate rooms, constructed on three levels, and the figures are seen in transit between one level and the next, through small connecting passages. Many of the paintings bear signatures although the sculptures are unsigned. The Tang statuary includes colossi (as in grottoes 96 and 130), and the cave walls of this era are completely covered with lively, urbane paintings (as in grottoes 152, 171, 172, and 320).

The Buddha, depicted as a majestic personage radiating goodness and compassion, appears as Amitabha Buddha the Immeasurable, or Maitreya the Future Buddha. The Bodhisattvas, richly ornamented, were often modeled on local officials and lords (as were attendants in much Christian art). Warriors and Lokapalas (celestial guardians) are well-muscled, bellicose, and bare-chested, and their armor and helmets symbolize honesty and determination (grottoes 45, 194, and 420). The faces in the processions of devotees and in servant retinues express a wide range of emotions.

The lithe bodies and flowing robes of the Tang figures suggest an element of sensuality influenced by Persian and Indian art. The mandalas and other decorative patterns are no longer geometrical, but full of curlicues and arabesques, also the result of Persian and Indian influence.

LATER DYNASTIES

Since little space remained to carve out new caves, later dynasties resorted to either painting over or enlarging and restoring the art in the earlier caves. Although the latter practice was particularly true of the Song (960–

1279), there is one magnificent original Song mural in Grotto 361, a landscape in relief called "Wutai Mountains," which depicts the terrain, towns, roads, temples, and travelers of this area. A nine-story tower and five pagodas near the center of the cliffs also date from the Song.

During the Yuan Dynasty (1279–1368) nine new caves were carved and others were restored. These caves are characterized by circular altars and—for the first time—frescoes.

THE GROTTOES TODAY

In 1961, the government established the Dunhuang Cultural Research Institute and soon after declared the 16 West Caves of Nanhutian and the Mogao Grottoes to be national treasures. An exhibition hall in a courtyard at the foot of the caves contains artifacts from the grottoes, such as oil lamps, earthenware plates, jars, and water pitchers, all tinted with mineral pigments, as well as tools used by the sculptors and artists. Only a handful of original documents and silk fragments remains (most are in museums in Britain and France), but these have proven invaluable as historical and archeological records.

One of the priorities of the research institute was to prevent further flood damage to the West Caves. A new trunk canal, built to divert the Dang River to the north of these grottoes, succeeded in keeping recent floods from reaching the caves.

In 1963, five wooden Tang and Song pavilions at the Mogao Grottoes were rebuilt, and the exterior walls of the caves were reinforced with concrete colonnades. Windows, doors, walls, and cornices were constructed to prevent further erosion from wind and drifting sand. Foundations have been laid under many of the statues, humidity regulators have been installed, and preservative glue has been applied to many murals to prevent further flaking and peeling. Where possible (as in Grotto 220), surface murals of later dynasties have been removed intact to expose the earlier murals underneath and also to preserve the more recent works. Four- and five-story walkways have been erected to facilitate access to every cave in the 1,600-m. (5,248-ft.) cliff face.

Unfortunately, taking pictues inside the caves is prohibited.

HOTEL ACCOMMODATIONS

敦煌宾馆

Dunhuang Guest House (Dong Da Jie; tel: 2324/2492; cable: 2464). Opened in July 1981, the original building has 30 rooms. An annex with 100 rooms was completed across the street in 1983. The hotel is open only during the tourist season (ca. March 15–ca. Nov. 15). Rates range from Y41–Y53, with inexpensive dormitory accommodations available. The Dunhuang is just a short walk from the center of town.

中国国际旅行社
CITS (Luxingshe) Office in Dunhuang ■ Chengguanzhen. Tel: 2325/2497.

Emei Shan

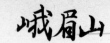

the lofty eyebrow mountain   *traditional spelling/Omei Shan*

MT. EMEI (Emei Shan) in Sichuan Province is famous throughout China for its magnificent snowcapped peaks, intriguing underground caves, rivulets, waterfalls, and dense, lush forests. Its highest peak rises abruptly from a plain to 3,099 m. (10,164 ft.) above sea level.

One of four famous "Buddhist mountains" in China, Mt. Emei lies about 168 km. (105 mi.) from Chengdu, the capital of Sichuan Province. Daoist temples were built on the mountain as far back as the Eastern Han Dynasty (2nd century), and Buddhist temples have been constructed from the advent of Buddhism at the end of the 1st century until the founding of the People's Republic in 1949. The mountain became a sacred place for pilgrims from all over the country. Worshippers would take several days to make the ascent, stopping for the night in one or another of the numerous temples or monasteries. After 1949 the mountain remained a popular summer excursion place. During the Cultural Revolution, a number of the temples were looted by Red Guards. Following extensive renovations, they were reopened to visitors in 1978.

The breathtaking view from the top of Mt. Emei has for centuries been a source of inspiration to painters and poets, including the famous Tang Dynasty poet, Li Bai (Li Po, 701–762), who wrote that "Emei is loftier than the western heaven." Nevertheless, the high cliffs and peaks are often shrouded in clouds and mist. In spring and summer, the mountain is carpeted by rhododendrons of various kinds and colors.

Nearby is the colossal 12th-century Sitting Buddha of Jiading, 120 m. (394 ft.) high. It is cut out of the rock face overlooking the Min River.

HIGHLIGHTS FOR TRAVELERS

Climbers start their ascent of Emei Shan at Baoguo Temple, originally constructed in the 6th century but entirely rebuilt in the 17th. There are two paths to the Jinding (Golden Summit), named after a glistening bronze hall that once crowned the main peak of Mt. Emei. The 44-km. (27.5-mi.) northern path, the shorter of the two, is wide and easy to follow. The southern path, 63.5 km. (39.5 mi.) long, is more rugged and winding. Because it is easier to go up than to come down, most people ascend by the southern route and return on the northern one. Foreign tourists are usually taken only as far as the first few temples. In winter, they may be prohibited for reasons of safety from climbing even this far.

The northern route passes Bailongdong (White Dragon Cave), Wan-

Climate		Jan	Feb	Mar	Apr	May	Jun	Jul	Aug	Sep	Oct	Nov	Dec
Temp.	°C	7	10	14.5	19.5	23	25.5	29	30	25	19	14	10.5
	°F	44.6	50	58.1	67.1	73.4	77.9	84.2	86	77	66.2	57.2	50.9
Precip.	mm.	15	20	38	99	142	180	142	122	150	112	48	20
	in.	.6	.8	1.5	3.9	5.6	7.1	5.6	4.8	5.9	4.4	1.9	.8

EMEI SHAN

niansi (Temple of Myriad Ages), and Zhanglaotai (Immortality Terrace). The southern route passes through Fuhusi (Crouching Tiger Temple), Qingyinge (Clear-Sound Pavilion), Jiulaodong (Nine Immortals Cave), and Yuxiansi (Temple of Meeting Immortals). The two paths converge and lead to the Xixiangchi (Elephant's Bathing Pool), so-called after the legend that Bu Xian, a Buddhist monk of the Western Jin Dynasty (265–316), passed here on a flying elephant which he washed in the pool before resuming his flight.

The path continues to Leidongping (Thunder Cave Terrace), a small stone temple in which the thunder god was supposed to live, and finally to the Jinding—the Golden Summit itself. Jinding is reputed to be extremely beautiful at sunrise. In the old days some people jumped off this mountain peak in the belief they would thus encounter the Bodhisattva.

For nature lovers, Emei Shan is abundantly filled with plants and animals. Over 60 different varieties of azaleas grow here, and rare animals such as serows, silver pheasants, fadedleaf butterflies, and bearded frogs can be seen along the paths up the mountain. Groups of monkeys often delight travelers by displaying their antics in hope of being awarded food.

HOTEL ACCOMMODATIONS

峨嵋宾馆
Emei Guest House (35 Zhengbei St.; tel: 2452/2846). Located in the center of town, the Emei Guest House has two singles and 28 doubles, all with private bath, TV, and telephone. There are also 74 triple rooms with shared bath.

ON YOUR OWN IN EMEI SHAN

by John Israel

There are many ways to "do" Emei Shan—a massive formation with a complex network of trails and a motor road. However, pilgrims and hikers should be able to glean some useful information from the following travel notes (based on a visit in June 1983):

You reach Emei Shan by railroad, generally by taking the Chengdu-Kunming express about three hours south of Chengdu and getting off at the Emei station—I boarded one of the fleet of tourist buses that met the train. For Y1 the bus took me to Baoguosi (Requiting the Nation Temple), which is the region's center for tourism.

保国寺
Baoguosi. Though one can stay in the temple, I was directed to the Hongzhushan (Red Candle Mountain) Hotel, where single rooms were available for Y24. I opted for a Y3 dormitory—a spartan but clean four-bed accommodation. It was a five-minute walk to the hot showers, which opened at 4 PM. I dined in the temple, mainly for the atmosphere, but discovered much better food at bargain prices (Y1 for breakfast, Y2 for lunch or dinner) in the hotel dining room.

I recommend that you waste no time nailing down a room, for tourists are numerous and Baoguosi's capacity is limited. I encountered some Chinese who arrived late in the afternoon and had to walk far into the countryside to find lodging with local peasants. Another admonition: Secure a travel permit in advance. You also need a mountain permit, which you get by displaying your travel permit to the authorities at Baoguosi.

A final detail: The ticket window at the railroad station opens for about an hour before the arrival of trains but is closed after the train pulls in. The most convenient way to get a return reservation, according to the clerk at the hotel, was through the tourist bus driver who takes you to Baoguosi, but he was nowhere to be found. The price for ignorance is time, so instead of taking a direct bus to Leshan the next morning, I first had to go to the train station, make my reservation, and wait nearly an hour to continue my journey to the site of the famous Buddha colossus.

乐山

Leshan. The bustling town of Leshan is about an hour's ride from Baoguosi at the confluence of the Min, the Dadu, and Qiangyi rivers. The famous Buddha is on an island in the middle of the Min and can be reached by a bus that crosses a bridge not far from the terminal, or via ferry, which is about a 20-minute walk. If you get hungry en route, succulent roast duck, a local specialty, is old along the street, or for six *jiao* you can buy 15 steamed dumplings garnished with as much good Sichuan hot pepper sauce as you can bear.

From the ferry pier on the island, you climb up a steep road and through the Lingyun Temple to a vantage point for viewing the Buddha. By descending the stairway carved into the cliff you can see the statue from different perspectives. If you enjoy exploring ancient ruins, the Lingyunshan Pagoda, dating from the Tang Dynasty, is just a 10-minute walk from the Lingyun Temple. It takes a bit of scrambling to climb the unlit and unrepaired staircase inside the pagoda, but the view, framed by a gaping hole in the brick wall, is magnificent. In another direction there is a bridge to an adjacent island, where you can visit the Wuyou Temple. A ferry from the far end of Wuyou Island takes you back to Leshan.

If you arrive in Leshan by mid-morning, you should have time to take in the local sights in a single day. Should you wish to extend your stay, however, there is an inexpensive hotel next to the bus terminal.

Ascending Emei Shan. I caught the last bus back to Baoguosi around 4:30 PM, and began my ascent of Emei Shan the next morning. It is possible to start hiking directly from Baoguosi via the trail that goes past the Fuhusi (Crouching Tiger Temple). You can save time, however, by taking a bus to Jingshui and beginning your climb from there. Baoguosi's bus system is a little tricky: besides the special buses for tour groups, public buses from Baoguosi branch out all over the region. However, be sure you get accurate information. There are two ticket windows, for different companies, at the crossroads pavilion near the temple. Some destinations are served by both, so it pays to double-check. In my own case, I was on my way to breakfast when I discovered that the earliest bus to Jingshui was at 7:10 AM, not at 8 AM as the clerk at the Red Candle had led me to believe. I barely had time to grab my pack and hop on board but, I can testify, the pork with hot peppers at the Mingshui station is worth an hour's ride on an empty stomach.

From Jingshui you climb to the Wanniansi (Temple of Myriad Ages), where you have a choice of two routes. The one to the right, via Huayan Peak, is shorter, but I took the circuitous one to the left where, I was told, I might encounter the famous Emei Shan monkeys. Sure enough, late that afternoon, on the fog-shrouded, pine-studded cliffs near Yuxiansi (Meeting Immortals Temple), I ran into a large troop of them. These waist-high mendicants can get nasty if teased, but you can avoid trouble by carrying any food you have for them in your hands. If you reach into your pocket, you're asking for trouble, because the monkeys are likely to close in for an intimate inspection to see if you are holding anything back.

洗象池
Xixiangchi. I reached the Xixiangchi (Elephant's Bathing Pool) temple in time for dinner. The mess hall abuts on the bathing area, and a grimy haze enveloped the mob of grubby hikers crowded around greasy, food-splattered tables. The scene was reminiscent of a Dickensian workhouse—if not of Danté's portrayal of the wretched in Hell. The food was worthy of the setting. I pushed aside an utterly inedible plate of pork and onions and made a meal of seaweed soup and boiled rice. At Y4 for a bed in a double room, the temple's accommodations were reasonable, and the breakfast of hot, sweetened soybean milk and crullers was adequate. But for dinner I strongly recommend that you try one of the little trailside eateries.

From the "Elephant" hostelry to the Jin Ding (Golden Summit) temple is a morning's hike. For Y7 I got a single room off a spacious lounge and with a magnificent view. Unfortunately, the peak was wrapped in fog and I could see nothing. Around 4 PM it began to clear, and everybody ran outside to take in the natural drama of mountains and valleys appearing and disappearing in the windblown fog. During the night the wind became so intense that it blew a pane of glass out of my window!

万佛顶
The Summit at Wanfo Ding. The next morning I hiked to the highest point on the mountain, the Wanfo Ding (Myriad Buddhas Peak), less than an hour from Jinding. The primitive ridge trail was more reminiscent of an American mountain wilderness than were the manicured walks and stone steps below Jinding, and the views were worth the hike. However, with cramped legs and an incipient cold, I was reluctant to trek down for my overnight at the Wanniansi, from which I had planned to hike to Jingshui the next morning to catch a bus to the train. Instead, I decided to walk only the 6 km. to the roadhead at Jieyindian (Reception Hall) and catch transportation back to Baoguosi. I flagged down a bus that was pulling out just as I arrived and rode nonstop to my destination. There were only a couple of other passengers, and the driver refused to accept a fare since it was a tourist bus making a return trip, not a public conveyance. I cannot guarantee that all hikers or hitchhikers will be so fortunate, but one or two regularly scheduled buses go down the mountain each day.

The dusty tourist scene at Baoguosi was less idyllic than the wooded refuge of Wanniansi, but I welcomed the hot shower and good food at the Red Candle. The next morning I picked up my ticket at the Emei station and boarded the express back to Kunming.

A few final words of advice:

■ *Emei Shan and Leshan are worth the trip.* In terms of historic traditions, evoked by calligraphic inscriptions carved into cliffsides, Emei Shan takes a back seat to Shandong's Taishan. For scenic splendor, neither Emei nor Tai matches the reputation of Anhui's Huangshan. But both the cultural and natural attractions of Emei are impressive. Even without the sidetrip to Leshan—which should not be missed—Emei is a living center of Buddhism. The temples house state-run hostels, but an endless stream of pilgrims comes to worship at their altars and to burn votary paper along the mountain paths. The wooded slopes are quite lovely, as are the views from the higher portions of the trail—which brings me to my next point:

■ *If you can, go when the weather is clear.* The best month, by all accounts, is May. By the time I arrived—in the second week of June—the summer clouds were closing in, bringing fog and drizzle which turned dirt paths to mud, made stone steps treacherously slippery and, but for a stroke of luck, nearly robbed me of my hard-won summit vista. In winter, the snow-covered mountain may be closed to tourists for reasons of safety.

■ *Don't seek Daoist solitude on a Buddhist mountain.* Emei Shan was one of the most intensely social outdoor experiences of my life. The paths overflowed with people—Chinese tourists, cadres passing through on "official business," young people from Hong Kong, and hundreds of little old ladies on pilgrimages. Westerners were rare: in three days I encountered only four of them. The sight of a back-packing foreigner is enough to turn heads, and one who speaks a few words of Chinese will have all the companionship he or she desires—at times more than he wants. On the whole, I greatly enjoyed my friends of the road, especially a former army officer with whom I ate several meals, drank countless cups of wine, and exchanged poems in the time-honored literati tradition. He would write a verse in elegant classical style, extolling the glories of the scenery or the virtues of friendship. I responded, as best I could, in English, at first trying to capture the spirit of the ancients:

> Outside the lacquered walls
> The pitter-patter raindrops fall.
> Inside, we eat a simple meal.
> Good wine, good friends,
> When will we meet again?

. . . but soon falling back into doggerel:

> Borrowed paper, borrowed pen,
> Far from home and wife,
> Drinking with a new-found friend,
> My God, what a life!

■ *Do not underestimate Emei Shan.* Though the 3,099-m. (10,164-ft.) peak would hardly pique the curiosity of Sir Edmund Hillary, and though young and old can make it, the hike to the top is strenuous. Not without reason are tourist groups generally restricted to a circuit of temples on the lower slopes.

Do not set out for the summit unless you are in good condition, clad in the appropriate footgear, and traveling light. My notion of traveling light was a large frameless backpack that held camera, reading matter, trail food, bath towel, long underwear, several changes of clothes, toilet articles, and medical supplies for any emergency. The Chinese idea of traveling light is a walking stick or umbrella and a tiny hand or shoulder bag containing toothbrush, washcloth, sweatshirt, and an extra pair of socks. Try to go as close to Chinese style as you can, with a decent backpack and a camera as your concessions to foreign standards. To deal with the wind chill factor at higher elevations, you can rent enormous stormcoats at the temples near the summit. All kinds of edibles, boiled water, tea, and soft drinks are readily available along the route, so you needn't carry food or drink. If you are fastidious, take your own cup and chopsticks.

The Chinese idea of appropriate footwear—ranging from sneakers to straw sandals—is a bit on the light side for my tastes. My preference was for sturdy, water-resistant hiking boots—the subject of frequent comment along the trail—with a pair of those lovely black cloth Chinese shoes for overnight use. Whatever you opt for, make sure it is appropriate for walking on steep slopes of slick stones and slimy mud.

◼ *Do not overestimate Emei Shan, as you may be led to do by available literature* (see *Mount Emei—A Fairyland,* Sichuan People's Publishing House, 1983). Some of the trail distances, according to my calculations, are considerably overestimated, and the sample itineraries call for base-to-summit round trips of up to five days. Though one could easily spend much longer rambling around the temples, enjoying the scenery, or engaging in drinking and poetry contests, a reasonably strong hiker should require no more than a day and a half up (the long way) and a day down (the short way), starting and ending at Jingshui, with half a day to rest and enjoy the summit area.

Add another day for Leshan and—excluding the days of arrival and departure—you have four full, strenuous, but utterly enchanting days in the Emei Shan area.

佛山 **Foshan**

Buddha hill

traditional spelling/Foshan

FOSHAN is one of China's most important folk-crafts centers and often features in tourist itineraries as a day trip from Guangzhou. A small city lying at the juncture of two tributaries flowing into the Pearl River (Zhu Jiang), Foshan is 28 km. (17 mi.) southwest of Guangzhou and connected to the provincial capital by a major highway (30 minutes by taxi or an hour by public bus).

FOSHAN IN HISTORY

Historical records show that the area was settled as early as 4,500 years ago. By the 4th century AD, it was the site of a thriving fishing village called Jihua Xiang. The name Foshan was given to the town in the Tang Dynasty (618–907). According to one of the stories about how the town received its name, a Buddhist monk from Kashmir traveling through the area in an earlier epoch brought along three statues of Buddha which he enshrined on a hilltop. After he returned to India, the shrine collapsed and the statues disappeared. Then, in the Tang Dynasty, one of the statues turned up—an event which was considered miraculous—and led to the townspeople constructing another Buddhist temple on the site and changing the name of the town to Foshan. In any event, Foshan became a well-known religious center from the 10th century onward.

During subsequent centuries, Foshan flourished as a handicrafts center, one of four such centers in classical China (the others were Zhuxian in Henan, Jingdezhen in Jiangxi, and Hankou in Hebei). After the Opium War (1839–42), Foshan was eclipsed by Guangzhou and it did not develop into a modern industrial city until after 1949. These days, increasing export trade is turning Foshan into something of a boomtown, as evidenced by widespread construction activity.

ECONOMY AND CULTURE

Foshan's economy has traditionally been based on its handicrafts—especially pottery, metal casting, silk weaving, and papercutting. The tradition of pottery making began in the village of Shiwan (which is practically an extension of Foshan) about 1,500 years ago. By the Tang Dynasty, Shiwan pottery was already fairly famous and, beginning in the 14th century, much

Climate		Jan	Feb	Mar	Apr	May	Jun	Jul	Aug	Sep	Oct	Nov	Dec
Temp.	°C	13.1	13.8	17.5	21.9	25.8	27.1	28.3	28.2	27.0	23.8	19.8	15.2
	°F	55	56.8	63.5	71.4	78.4	80.7	82.9	82.7	80.6	74.8	67.6	59.3
Precip.	mm.	152	203	254	279	381	508	457	406	330	203	152	127
	in.	6	8	10	11	15	20	18	16	13	8	6	5

of the ware began to be exported to Southeast Asia. However, Shiwan pottery did not acquire its distinctive characteristics until the early Qing Dynasty (1644–1911), when artisans concentrated on producing realistic animal and human figures.

About 1,000 years ago, the village of Nanpu (now a suburb of Foshan) developed the art of metal casting. Many of the bells, weapons, tripods, and statues produced by the early artisans are still to be seen in temples in the vicinity of Guangzhou. After 1949, the industry was modernized, and the metal casting factories around Foshan today produce tools and household hardware as well as artistic metalwork and reproductions of old decorative pieces.

Silk weaving became an important cottage industry during the Tang Dynasty. Local weavers were much in demand for their brocade and *liangchou* (gambiered silk gauze), a soft, light fabric which made the coolest and most comfortable garments for wear during China's hot and humid summers.

The art of papercutting became a specialty of Foshan during the Ming Dynasty (1368–1644). Using only small, pointed scissors, Foshan's artisans turn out astonishingly intricate freehand designs, both large and small, that are framed as pictures or used to decorate lanterns and books.

HIGHLIGHTS
FOR TRAVELERS

Most visitors to Foshan will tour one or another of the town's handicraft factories. Perhaps the most popular is the Shiwan Ceramics Factory, just 20 minutes by bus from Foshan. Here, one can observe the seven steps of the process: designing, making the mold, shaping, polishing, painting, firing, and glazing. There are about 20 ceramics factories in Shiwan producing everything from earthenware cooking vessels and flower pots to glazed tiles and superb statues of animals and humans.

A tour of the Red Brocade Factory, the largest of Foshan's modern plants where silk is woven, painted, and dyed, can also be requested.

The ornate Temple of the Ancestors (Zu Miao) in Foshan is not to be missed. This Song Dynasty (960–1279) structure is built entirely of interlocking wooden beams: no metal or nails were used in its construction. The temple consists of seven parts, some of which were built in 1372 during the reign of the Ming Emperor Hong Wu. The Ten-Thousand-Blessings Terrace (Wanfutai), dating from 1658, is now used as a stage for theatrical performances during temple festivals.

Inside the main temple is a massive bronze statue of the god called the Northern Emperor (Beidi), also known as the Black Emperor (Heidi). Beidi was supposed to rule over water and its inhabitants, especially fish, snakes, and turtles. Since South China was prone to floods in ancient times, people often sought to appease Beidi by honoring him with temples and carvings of snakes and turtles. Under the tiled eaves of the temple are many such animal figures, undoubtedly placed there for good luck. Somewhat gaudily restored, the temple also houses many statues dating from the Ming Dynasty.

HOTEL ACCOMMODATIONS

佛山市
Foshan Hotel (64 Zumiao Rd.; tel: 87930/87923; cable: 2388). Located in the center of town, the Foshan has 215 rooms, all with private bath, air-conditioning, and color TV. The usual amenities include a restaurant, coffee shop, foreign exchange, and taxi service.

佛山华侨大厦
Overseas Chinese Mansion (14 Zumiao Rd.; tel: 86511). Built in 1962, the Overseas Chinese Mansion (distinguish from *hotel* of same name, below) has 134 large rooms, and relatively extensive services — a foreign exchange desk, shops, taxi station, hairdresser, and an array of dining facilities. The six dining halls serve excellent cuisine, featuring fresh fish and vegetables from nearby farms.

佛山华侨饭店
Overseas Chinese Hotel. This hotel has 52 double rooms, 26 triples, and seven suites, with prices ranging from Y45–Y75. Most rooms have private bath, telephone, and color TV.

旋宫酒店
Rotating Palace Hotel (Zumiao Rd.; tel: 85622; cable: 3288). Located 1 km. from the railway station, the Rotating Palace has 100 double rooms (Y60–Y70) and two deluxe suites (Y500). All rooms are air-conditioned, with closed-circuit color TV, telephone, piped-in music, and carpeting. There are Chinese and Western restaurants and the usual services.

CUISINE

In addition to regional Cantonese cooking, Foshan restaurants often feature local minority dishes. Two restaurants deserve mention for their ambiance as much as for their cuisine. The Hero's Pavilion (Qunyingge) Restaurant is built in local minority style and set in the middle of Xiuli Lake in Zhongshan Park. (Note that the restaurant is open only from 8 AM to 3:30 PM). The Plum Garden (Meiyuan) Restaurant, located near the Temple of the Ancestors, also serves diners in an attractive garden setting.

Tour groups to Shiwan are generally taken to the Capital of Ceramics (Taodu) Restaurant for lunch. Centrally located near the colorful marketplace, right across from the bus station, the Taodu has eight dining halls on three floors with seating capacity of 1,200. The third floor is reserved for foreign tourists; Chinese dine on the two lower floors. Seafood is the specialty here.

中国国际旅行社
CITS (Luxingshe) Office in Foshan ■ 75 Fenjiang Nan Rd. Tel: 87923
Cable: 2300. Telex: 44773 FSBRA CN.

Fuzhou

wealthy district

traditional spelling/Foochow

FUZHOU is the ancestral home of millions of overseas Chinese whose forefathers emigrated in earlier centuries to form Chinese trading communities throughout the world. Today Fuzhou is the capital of Fujian Province and a city of 1.6 million people. The central town, with an area of 1,040 sq. km., is situated on the northern banks of the Min River on China's southeastern coast, some 600 km. (380 mi.) southwest of Shanghai. Fuzhou is also known in China as "Three Hills"—after Pingshan, Yushan, and Wushan—and as "Banyan City." Over the centuries, Fuzhou has drawn visitors to its unusually hot (up to 70°C) and sulfuric medicinal springs. Fuzhou's climate is mild and pleasant: summer temperatures average 28°C (82°F). During the April to September monsoon season, typhoons are fairly common.

Once effectively isolated from the rest of China by its geographical setting, Fuzhou now has scheduled air and rail links to other major points in the country. In addition, coastal passenger ships connect Fuzhou with Shanghai. Departures are scheduled every five days with fares for the two-day voyage ranging from Y82 (deluxe class) to Y27.30 (third class).

FUZHOU IN HISTORY

Fuzhou's history extends back over two millenia to 202 BC, when King Gou Jian of Yue named the city Ye and proclaimed it the capital of the new state of Minyue. Heavily settled during the 6th century, the town was named Fuzhou under the Tang in 725. Fuzhou became the capital of an autonomous state at the beginning of the 10th century, during the Five Dynasties and Ten Kingdoms period. The city walls were erected during the early Ming Dynasty and fortified during the Qing, when the town became the focus of a struggle between the loyalist Ming general Zheng Chenggong (Koxinga) and the Manchu forces.

During the early 19th century, an official from Fuzhou named Lin Zexu led the first serious Chinese military campaign against foreigners seeking to introduce the opium trade—efforts that led directly to the outbreak of the First Opium War. In 1842, however, the Treaty of Nanjing compelled China to establish Fuzhou as an open port. From 1861 onward, Europeans began to settle on the southern bank of the Min River opposite the town. Fuzhou's economy was—and is today—largely based on agriculture (rice,

Climate		Jan	Feb	Mar	Apr	May	Jun	Jul	Aug	Sep	Oct	Nov	Dec
Temp.	°C	10.3	10.3	13.2	18.3	22.7	25.0	28.8	28.3	26.3	21.7	17.9	12.9
	°F	50.5	50.5	55.7	64.9	72.8	77	83.8	82.9	79.3	71	64.2	55.2
Precip.	mm.	152	152	203	279	304	381	254	203	178	178	152	127
	in.	6	6	8	11	12	15	10	8	7	7	6	5

sugarcane, tea, and oranges are the main crops). Fishing is also a thriving industry. In the 1920s, papermaking, machine-building, and chemical industries were introduced. After Fujian was designated as one of China's "autonomous economic zones" in 1979, industries such as food processing and radio and television assembly for export also sprung up. In 1984, Fuzhou was designated as one of 14 Coastal Open Cities, and an Economic and Technical Development Zone was set up 13 km. from the city in the ancient port town of Mawei. Through mid-1985, more than Y75 million (about $27 million) in foreign capital had been invested in more than 250 projects, including 20 joint ventures. Major infrastructure improvements include construction of a power plant, a reservoir, and a highway network (not yet complete).

Fuzhou has a significant handicrafts industry. Particularly well-known is its prized "bodiless" lacquerware, which began to be produced early in the 18th century. (The removal of wood or copper forms beneath the layers of hardened lacquer makes the finished products lightweight, or "bodiless.") Today, two factories employing over 1,000 skilled workers can hardly keep up with the demand for Fuzhou's special lacquerware—regarded as one of the "three treasures" of Chinese crafts. Another popular handicraft produced in Fuzhou is cork sculpture, often rendered in glass-enclosed miniature landscapes which have become Friendship Store staples throughout China. Other local crafts include Shoushan stone carvings, Longan wood figures (people and animals), combs made from animal horn, painted umbrellas, and printed silk.

A notable feature of contemporary Fuzhou is its large Christian population. This community includes an active, 2,000-member Protestant church (Methodist in origin) with six ministers, a youth organization, and twice-daily services on Sundays and Saturdays.

HIGHLIGHTS FOR TRAVELERS

The northern and southern parts of the town are linked by two magnificent stone bridges which meet on Nantai Island, midstream in the Min River. The two spans have over 100 arches and a double parapet running along their length. The city itself has a relatively "new" feel to it because of recent redevelopment, and is rather open and sprawling. But a stroll around Dong Jiekou, Taijia, or some of the other busy sections can be quite interesting. Bayiqi Lu and Wuyi Lu are also busy shopping streets.

西湖公园
West Lake Park. This lovely park, dotted with peony bushes in brilliant shades of red, white, and violet, and with graceful willow trees, runs along Hubin Road. The park was first laid out as an imperial garden more than 1,000 years ago. Widely regarded as a scenic site since the Tang Dynasty, it was expanded several times over the years to its present 40 hectares (100 acres). East of the "flying rainbow" bridge is a Tang Dynasty temple, Kaihua

Si, last rebuilt during Emperor Kangxi's reign in 1705. A lovely garden is situated behind the temple. Northeast of the temple is the "Garden in the Hall," built in the Ming Dynasty and rebuilt in 1748. A chrysanthemum festival is held here every fall. West of the bridge is a recreation center for children and a pavilion that affords an overview of the entire park. Also within the park is the Fujian Provincial Museum, which exhibits a variety of ancient treasures, including the contents of a Song Dynasty tomb. Elsewhere in the park is the Fujian Province Exhibition Center (export products), a zoo (yes, pandas), and the West Lake Guest House.

于山

Yushan. A large hill in the center of town, Yushan was originally known as Nine Immortals Hill after a group of Daoists that came here during the Han Dynasty to practice alchemy and Daoist rites. At the time, the 58.6-m. (192-ft.) hill was in the middle of the river. Its summit, resembling a turtle, is called "Turtle-Top Peak." There are 24 traditionally demarcated scenic spots on the hill as well as a library, memorial hall, and exhibition hall, all added after 1949. A good view of all of Fuzhou can be had from the top. The famous White Pagoda (see below) stands at the foot of this hill along with a small White Pagoda Temple. On the east side is a memorial hall and shrine for a national hero, Qi Jiguang. In the hall with Qi's statue are paintings that depict his exploits in defending the coast from pirates. One hall houses an exhibit of the remains of a Qing tomb. The large, flat rock near the small pavilion is called "Drunk Rock," where Qi is said to have slept after getting drunk celebrating a victorious battle. Outside of the temple is the well that was used by the He brothers (the original Daoists) in performing their alchemy.

Set just above the temple is Dashi Dian, a small hall remaining from a temple built during the Kang Xi period. It was from here that the revolution of 1911 began in Fujian. The hall subsequently served as headquarters for the revolutionary army. Today it houses an exhibition of flowers. Higher still is the "Nine Immortals Temple" (Jiuxian Guan), a Daoist site and the largest edifice on the hill. Built in 1104 during the Northern Song Dynasty, it is now an art gallery with exhibitions of painting and other fine arts. This hill also has its share of rock-carved calligraphy: there are 113 different examples, valuable for both their historic and their artistic value and variously carved during the Song, Yuan, Ming, and Qing dynasties.

Yushan is three stops south of the Overseas Chinese Hotel on bus #2 (though you'll have to walk back a little way).

双塔

The Twin Pagodas. Two pagodas—the White Pagoda at the foot of Yushan, and the Ebony Pagoda at the foot of Wushan—have come to serve as symbols of Fuzhou. The White Pagoda was built in 904, destroyed by fire in 1534, and then rebuilt in 1548. It is 41 m. (134 ft.) high and has eight corners and seven levels. It's well worth a try to climb up and enjoy the view. The Ebony Pagoda was built in 941 during the Five Dynasties period and was twice renovated during the Ming and Qing. It is 33.9 m.

(111 ft.) high and is similar to the White Pagoda, with eight corners and seven stories. This one is also climbable.

鼓山

Drum Hill. About 10 km. (6.2 mi.) outside of Fuzhou stands Drum Hill, named after a large rock (now inaccessible) perched on its summit. The "hill" actually comprises three peaks, the tallest of which is 925 m. (3,034 ft.) high. Drum Hill encompasses 32 historic or scenic sites, including pavilions, halls, caves, hillside streams, and a popular hot-springs spa.

Most prominent is the Bubbling Spring Temple (Yongquan Si), which houses an important relic—a tooth of Buddha. First built in 908 during the Later Liang era of the Five Dynasties period, it has been expanded upon and rebuilt several times through the centuries. The architecture here is notably different from other parts of China, marked by acutely upswept white roofs with no *dougong* (the stacked, crisscrossed beams that usually support the eaves of a traditional Chinese house). The windows and ornamentation are also distinctive to Fuzhou. The signboard at the entrance was inscribed by the Kang Xi emperor in 1699. Two clay pagodas in front of the main hall, known as the "Thousand-Buddha Earthenware Pagodas," were fashioned in 1082 during the Northern Song Dynasty. Each is 7 m. (23 ft.) tall, with eight sides and nine levels. Most of the existing buildings in the temple date from the Ming and Qing dynasties. The temple archives house over 30,000 volumes of Buddhist texts, including some very rare Ming and Qing editions and a noteworthy set of 657 volumes transcribed by a monk in his own blood.

The grounds also contain a large orchid garden with several hundred varieties and an area called "Source of Wonder (Spirit) Cave" (Ling Yuan Dong) with over 300 carvings of calligraphy that span 1,000 years. Other interesting sites include "Shouting at the Water Rock," the Dragon Head Spring (and teahouse), and an "18-scenes" path that descends to the right of the temple.

Bubbling Spring Temple is an 8-km. (5-mi.) climb from the base of Drum Hill. But there is a road open to vehicles, including a public bus that charges 10 *fen*. Visitors should try to set aside a full day for a visit to Drum Hill. Lunch is available at the Songtao Restaurant near the summit.

乌山

Wushan. Also originally established as a Daoist mountain retreat with several temples, Wushan is now a secular scenic spot with a few pavilions and some Tang, Song, Yuan, Ming, and Qing dynasty calligraphy carved into its rock face. Notable is a relief of Buddha in late Tang Dynasty style on the southeast hillside. Wushan is 60 m. (197 ft.) high.

平山

Pingshan. The capital of Ye, set up by the Minyue king, was established at the foot of this 45-m. (148-ft.) hill. Nothing is left now but the Song Dynasty wooden hall of Hualin Temple, built in 965. It was rebuilt during the Qing Dynasty and renovated since 1953.

洪塘金山寺

Hongtang Golden Mountain Temple. This temple was originally built in the Song Dynasty on an island in the middle of the Wulong River, west of town. The temple was rebuilt in the Ming Dynasty, and most lately in 1934. Because of space limitations on the small island, Hongtang is different from most Chinese temples in layout and design. Front to back there is the Goddess of Mercy Hall, a 35-ft. pagoda (Jinshan Ta), the Great Compassion Hall, and two small side rooms.

Other highlights within Fuzhou include the Min King Temple and the Lin Zexu Memorial Hall—a Confucian temple that is now the Municipal Children's Palace, just off Bayiqi Lu. Also recommended are tours of the No. 1 Bodiless Lacquerware Factory at 16 Xinping Road, or the Fujian Province Arts and Crafts Research Institute at 22 Hexie Road, where lacquerware artists receive training in their complicated craft. Cultural performances are offered at the People's Theater (Wuyi Rd. at Dongjiekou; tel: 33858) and at the Fujian Provincial Gymnasium (Wuyi Sq.; tel: 34132).

马尾

Mawei. The last stop on the Nanping-Fuzhou railroad, Mawei (literal translation: horse's tail) is a bustling shipbuilding and ship-repair center downstream from Fuzhou. Its population is now 40,000 and it has become an important cog in the expansion of Fujian's export trade.

East of the port area is Luoxing Pagoda, on the north shore of the Minjiang. Set on top of Luoxing Hill, the 30-m. (98-ft.) pagoda was built during the Song Dynasty when the hill was in the middle of the river. It is said to have been built by a woman whose husband had been falsely accused of a crime and banished. A climb to the top will provide a good view of the port.

Mawei has recently been provided with a guest house, Friendship Store, and other facilities for foreign guests.

HOTEL ACCOMMODATIONS
温泉大厦

Hot Spring Hotel (May Fourth Road, Central; tel: 551818; telex: 92180 HSHFZ CN; cable: 8426; fax: 535150). This 311-room hotel is near the Fuzhou Foreign Trade Center, in central Fuzhou. A joint venture with Pearl International Hotels, the hotel is only five minutes from the railway station and 20 minutes from the airport. Room amenities include bath water from a natural hot spring, minibar, air-conditioning and direct-dial telephones. For dining, there are two Chinese and one Western restaurant, as well as a lobby lounge. Other facilities are a Business Center and meeting rooms for up to 1,200. Guests can relax at the swimming pool, tennis courts, health club, billiard room, bowling center, and disco. *Rates:* Y120–140 (singles/doubles); Y200–1,200 (suites).

The Foreign Trade Center has its own hotel, also on May Fourth (Wusi) Road (tel: 550154; telex: 92158 FTC CN; fax: 550358).

闽江饭店

Minjiang Hotel (Wusi Road; tel: 557895; telex: 92146 MJHT CN; cable: 8117). Fuzhou's "grand hotel," the Minjiang opened in November 1984, but is already said to be getting worn and is no longer recommended. The 17-story structure offers a total of 500 rooms (doubles: Y100; triples: Y80). The Minjiang's first-class facilities include piped-in hot-springs water and a massage room, as well as reservation booking services. The hotel is 4 km. from the railway station, 13 km. from the airport, and 6 km. from the pier.

华侨大厦

Overseas Chinese Mansion (Wusi Rd.; tel: 557603; telex: 92123 FJKTS CN; cable: 8008). This was the main hotel in Fuzhou for all foreign tourists until the Minjiang Hotel opened. Its 189 rooms have air-conditioning, TVs, telephones, and carpets. Showers and baths in the rooms are supplied with natural hot-springs water. Most services are located on the first floor, with some offices (including travel services) and shops in the adjoining building to the right of the lobby. There are two dining rooms: the one on the first floor is for individual ordering (menu in Chinese); the second-floor dining room is for house dinners (Y10/day). A coffee shop is on the first floor, and there is a medical clinic on the second floor near the dining room.

The hotel is 13 km. from the airport, 4 km. from the train station (connect via public bus #2).

福州侨联大厦

Fuzhou Qiao Lian Mansion (88 North Wuyi Road; tel: 57858; cable: 8499). Located in the center of town, this hotel has 106 rooms and reasonable rates. All rooms have air-conditioning and color TV, most have private bath. Offered, too, are a Chinese and Western restaurant and a tea room with music.

西湖宾馆

Xihu (West Lake) Guest House (150 Northern Qianjin Rd.; tel: 557008; cable: 8903). Located by the lake, this enormous new hotel has more than 1,000 rooms with first-class facilities, including direct-dial phone, color TV, private bath, and air-conditioning. The Chinese restaurant serves Western food on request and there are the usual amenities, including post office, barbershop, foreign exchange, and taxi service.

The Xihu is 5 km. from the railway station and 10 km. from the airport.

Smaller hotels in Fuzhou include the **Hualian Mansions** (Wuyi Rd.; tel: 34944). Overseas Chinese are lodged at the **Wuyi Hotel** (Wuyi Zhong Rd.; tel: 32646); the **Fuzhou Hotel** (36 Dongda Rd.; tel: 33057); or the **Overseas Chinese Hotel** (Wusi Rd.; tel: 33492).

FUJIAN CUISINE

Seafood is the local specialty. Popular dishes in Fuzhou include fishball soup, fried conch slices, pickled chicken, sea scallops, and, probably the most famous (and irreverent) dish of all, "Buddha Jumping Over a Wall"—

so named because it is so irresistible that even the Buddha (who was a vegetarian, which this dish is not) would jump over a wall to get it. Visitors may sample Fuzhou's special cuisine at the Juchunyuan Restaurant (130 Bayiqi Bei Rd.; tel: 32338) and the Huafulou Restaurant (795 Bayiqi Zhong Rd.; tel: 2976). The Juchunyuan is the oldest restaurant in the city (in continuous operation for over 100 years) and is highly recommended. Its special dishes include eight-piece chicken *(bakuai ji)*, arhat's money *(luohanqian)*, dragon and phoenix leg *(longfengtui)*, and jade hatchet dumplings *(yufujiao)*. Muslim and vegetarian dishes are served at the Qingzhen Restaurant (342 Bayiqi Bei Rd.; tel: 33517). Finally, with supreme reluctance, we must advise of the existence of the Shanzhen Guan, a "wild game" restaurant in West Lake Park. It turns out that this restaurant's placement next to the city zoo was not without purpose—the chef proudly admits that many of its "exotic" dishes are culled from among the zoo's residents.

SHOPPING

Possibly one of the most remarkable stores in China is the Fuzhou branch of the Fujian Tourist Souvenirs Production and Supply Corporation. Located on Wusi Rd. (tel: 33491), just across from the new Minjiang Hotel, this emporium features a huge supply of all the different special products of Fujian at the lowest prices imaginable. The store can ship for you or you can take your purchases to the main post office for shipment (small wooden shipping boxes are sold at the post office). Bargain prices are also to be found at local lacquerware and stone-carving factories. Lacquerware, silks, and attractive paper crafts are available at the Friendship Store (103 Bayiqi Bei Rd.; tel: 555406), as well as at the Fuzhou Arts and Crafts Service Store and the Bailing Department Store, both on Bayiqi Nan Rd.

On the street, the busiest shopping areas are around Dongjiekou, Bayiqi Rd., and Wuyi Rd., a short walk south and a bit west of the Overseas Chinese Mansion. Fuzhou's "bodiless lacquerware" is considered one of the "three treasures" of China, as it is light, strong, and brilliantly colored. It is notably inexpensive here as well. The local factory carries a beautiful assortment of over 1,000 pieces. If you visit the Fuzhou Carving Factory you can see the fine Shoushan stone and Longan wood carvings being done. These products are also remarkably cheap when purchased at the source.

A note on film: color slide film is not sold anywhere in Fujian so visitors should stock up before coming here.

中国国际旅行社
CITS (Luxingshe) Office in Fuzhou ◼ 44 Dongda Rd. Tel: 55506/56293
Telex: 92201 FCITS CN.

广州

Guangzhou

broad region   *traditional spelling/Kwangchow*

GUANGZHOU (long known in the West as Canton) is the capital of Guangdong Province and the most important industrial and foreign trade center in south China. This steamy, subtropical metropolis, with its gray-green hues, lush parks, boisterous atmosphere, and world-famous cuisine, has an aura that is unique among China's large cities. Whether deserved or not, Guangzhou has acquired a negative reputation among foreign visitors. The muggy climate, congestion, and poor air quality are certainly distractions. But more than that, the lack of deference shown to foreigners—who are less of a novelty in Guangzhou than in most other Chinese cities—may be the greatest contributor to the city's image problem. Moreover, whether for reasons of its citizens' independent character or Guangzhou's geopolitical circumstance, ambition is very much alive in Guangzhou. Its hearty, practical people seem tense, driven, and single-minded in ways that go against the expectations of China visitors.

Guangzhou and its six surrounding counties support a population of about 5.3 million, densely packed into an area of 4,300 sq. km. (1,678 sq. mi.) on the northern bank of the Pearl River (Zhu Jiang) Delta.

After 1949, when the PRC was largely inaccessible to foreign visitors, Guangzhou continued to receive overseas Chinese from neighboring Hong

Climate		Jan	Feb	Mar	Apr	May	Jun	Jul	Aug	Sep	Oct	Nov	Dec
Temp.	°C	13.1	13.8	17.5	21.9	25.8	27.1	28.3	28.2	27.0	23.8	19.8	15.2
	°F	55	56.8	63.5	71.4	78.4	80.7	82.9	82.7	80.6	74.8	67.6	59.3
Precip.	mm.	152	203	254	279	381	508	457	406	330	203	152	127
	in.	6	8	10	11	15	20	18	16	13	8	6	5

Guangzhou and the Pearl River

Kong and Macao, many of whom had originally emigrated from Guangdong Province. With the establishment of the semiannual Chinese Export Commodities Fair (Guangzhou Trade Fair) in 1957, the city has been drawing an average of 25,000 foreign business representatives twice a year (see section on "Doing Business with China").

In recent years, the commerce and lifestyle of Guangzhou have become increasingly integrated with those of Hong Kong (182 km. [113 mi.] to the southwest). Official PRC encouragement of joint business ventures between Chinese and foreign firms and the creation of three Special Economic Zones in Guangdong Province since 1979 have led to substantial investment in Guangzhou by Hong Kong Chinese. Guangzhou's own status as one of the four "priority" zones among China's 14 Coastal Open Cities (the others being Dalian, Shanghai, and Tianjin) allows city authorities to approve contracts worth up to $30 million. Through mid-1985, foreign businesses had invested more than $850 million in thousands of projects and ventures in Guangzhou, ranging from processing and finishing, to large-scale industrial projects, to joint ventures such as the White Swan and Garden hotels. Moreover, foreign management and technical personnel are directly involved in many of these projects, some of which (such as the above-mentioned hotels) are regarded by Chinese economists as models of Sino-foreign cooperation. Expansion of Guangzhou's Economic and Technology Development ment Zone, located in Huangpu, 35 km. (22 mi.) from the city center, should encourage acceleration of this investment trend. With foreign trade hitting a record high Y9 billion in 1984 and growing at a booming 15% per year, Guangzhou appears destined to become one of new China's wealthiest cities. Furthermore, Chinese from Hong Kong who stream across the border to conduct business, to visit relatives, or to sightsee have acquainted the citizens of Guangzhou not only with various types of consumer goods that are not yet produced in China, but also with fashions and hairstyles that are quickly emulated by Guangzhou's youth.

GUANGZHOU IN HISTORY

Legend has it that Guangzhou was founded by five celestial beings who descended from heaven astride five goats, each animal bearing a stalk of rice in its mouth. The rice was the symbol of a promise by the gods that the region would never suffer from famine. Although the promise was not always kept, the legend stuck and Guangzhou is still referred to as Yangcheng (Goat City). Indeed, many products manufactured in Guangzhou today carry the "Goat Brand" and the statue of five goats which stands in Yuexiu Park has virtually become the logo of the city.

ON YOUR OWN IN GUANGZHOU

Arrival. If you arrive in Guangzhou via the Hong Kong–Guangzhou Railway, you'll have to line up (just follow the crowd) to pass through customs and immigration. Inside the hall, the line divides into categories: foreigners, overseas Chinese, and Chinese citizens. Just past customs is the money changer, with the station exit to the right (where you'll be asked to show your ticket). If you are planning to stay at the White Swan Hotel, your life is made easier by the fact that the hotel has a reception desk in the station (on your way out) and free minibus service to the hotel. If you are staying anywhere else you'll have to find a taxi in the parking area outside the station. The Dongfang Hotel is just five minutes from the station (bus #7 two stops south), as is the Liuhua Hotel. These two hotels enjoy the best locations in the city.

Getting Around Town. The White Swan is the preferred location in Guangzhou and is closest to the downtown commercial area. From the Dongfang you can walk to both Yuexiu and Liuhua parks, with convenient bus connections (bus #3) to the Liurong and Guangxiao temples (two stops), Huaisheng Mosque (four stops), Renmin South Road (six stops), or Cultural Park (eight stops). From the White Swan it is possible to walk out to Renmin Road (one block after leaving the island that the hotel is on) and get the #3 bus (its second stop going north) to go up into town and the park (last stop). To get to the Peasant Movement Institute or the Memorial Garden to the Martyrs of the Guangzhou Uprising you can take the #1 trolley (six and seven stops respectively).

The Baiyun Hotel is a bit out of the way, although bus #30 connects directly to the train station (five stops). If you take the #6 bus, which proceeds up Renmin Road South and passes by the Baiyun, you can get to the zoo (all the way to the end) and the Huagang Mausoleum of the 72 Martyrs just down the street.

To get to Foshan, Seven Star Crags, Conghua Hot Springs, or other sites outside the city, it is best to join one of the excursions set up by the CTS or CITS. Local transport outside of the city can be agonizingly slow as well as overcrowded.

Guangzhou lacks a simple system for purchasing train tickets to other points in China. You must go to the main train station if you want to leave that day; to CITS (near the station) if you want to go north of Zhengzhou; and to the east station (Baiyun Lu) for other tickets. In the vicinity of most tourist areas, taxis can be hailed with relative ease, although there are rarely cabs outside the East Station Ticket Office; so if you take a cab there, keep it, even though it may take a while to purchase your tickets.

The region was originally the home of tribal peoples over 2,000 years ago. During the Qin Dynasty (221–206 BC), numbers of Han Chinese were

New pedestrian footbridge, central Guangzhou

rounded up and sent to settle the area around Guangzhou, which became an active trading post known as Panyu. Although the region was nominally incorporated into the Chinese empire, it was considered for several centuries thereafter as a remote place of banishment. In 714, the Tang Dynasty officially sanctioned Guangzhou as a foreign trade center. The town already contained a sizable Muslim population, and as a result of its commerce with India, Persia, and Southeast Asia, Guangzhou became subject to a number of positive and negative foreign influences. From the 10th to the 17th centuries, it developed into a major port and shipbuilding town.

The earliest European influence in Guangzhou was Portuguese. Portugal established an embassy here before proceeding to colonize Macao, 105 km. (65 mi.) to the south, in 1557. Soon afterward, the Spanish and Dutch arrived, followed by the British, the French, and the Americans in the 18th century. Conflict between China and the West did not erupt until the 19th century when Commissioner Lin Zexu destroyed 20,000 chests of opium dumped into Guangzhou by the British. This event triggered the first Opium War of 1839–42. Guangzhou subsequently became one of five Chinese ports opened to foreign trade by the unequal Treaty of Nanjing. Following the second Opium War (1856–60), sections of Guangzhou were parceled out to foreign nations.

The decay of China's dynastic system and concomitant loss of national economic independence profoundly transformed Guangzhou. Western settlements in the city (remnants of which are visible today on Shamian Island) contained large compounds and spacious buildings, contrasting sharply with the squalid slums and cluttered canal boats inhabited by the local populace. As a result of pervasive poverty and overcrowding, large numbers of Chinese migrated during this period to other Asian countries, North America, and Europe, the vast majority exiting via the port of Guangzhou.

Guangzhou's Role in the Chinese Revolution. Although Guangzhou's culture was enriched by periodic migrations from northern China as well as by foreign influences, the local population remained fiercely independent. From 1839 to 1927, the Cantonese played a leading role in China's numerous reform movements and revolutionary struggles. A popular saying current in Guangzhou during this period was, "The people fear the officials, the officials fear the foreign devils, and the foreign devils fear the people." Hong Xiuquan, the original leader of the Taiping Rebellion in the 1850s, was a peasant from Huaxian, near Guangzhou.

Dr. Sun Yatsen, the father of the 1911 Revolution that overthrew the imperial system, was also a native of Guangzhou. He founded the Guomindang (Nationalist) Party here in 1923. The Whampoa (Huangpu) Military Academy, where many Nationalist and Communist leaders (including Chiang Kaishek and Zhou Enlai) were trained, was set up in Guangzhou in 1924. After 1926, Mao Zedong directed and taught at the city's National Peasant Movement Institute (still a staple on the Guangzhou sightseeing circuit). In 1927, following Dr. Sun's death, Chiang Kaishek, the new Guomindang leader, launched a bloody campaign to exterminate the Communists, resulting in the popular opposition rebellion known as the "Guangzhou Uprising." Although the insurgents succeeded in occupying government offices and leading a general strike, the revolt was quelled within three days. During its savage aftermath, the Guomindang is said to have slaughtered 5,700 protesters.

Communist activity did not flare up again in Guangzhou until the advent of the Sino-Japanese War (1937–45), when guerrilla forces fought the city's Japanese occupiers. In the subsequent Chinese civil war, Guangzhou remained in Nationalist hands from 1945 to October 14, 1949, when it finally went over to the Communists.

ECONOMY AND CULTURE

Prior to 1949, Guangzhou was a city of sprawling slums and dilapidated houseboats. Since 1949, a tremendous amount of urban renewal has occurred. Much of the new housing built along the shores of the Pearl River accommodates the 60,000 previously wretched boat people.

The rich alluvial soil of the Pearl River Delta provides the Guangzhou region with its highly productive agricultural base. Some 92,000 hectares

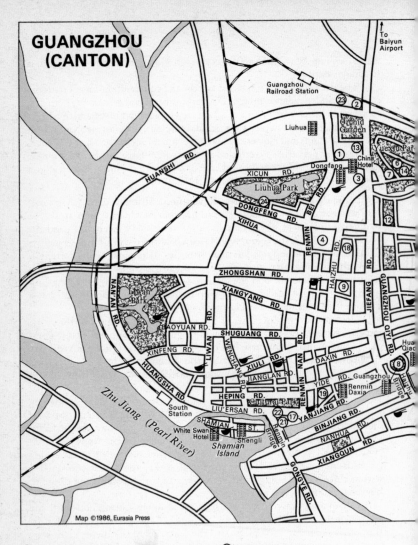

GUANGZHOU (CANTON)

To Baiyun Airport

Guangzhou Railroad Station

Liuhua

Orchid Garden

Yuexiu Park

China Hotel

Dongfang

HUANSHI RD.

XICUN RD.

Liuhua Park

RENMIN BEI RD.

HAIZHU RD.

DONGFENG RD.

XIHUA

ZHONGSHAN RD.

XIANGYANG RD.

JIEFANG

GUANGZHOU QIYI RD.

Liwan Park

NAN'AN RD.

AOYUAN RD.

SHUGUANG RD.

LIWAN RD.

WENCHANG RD.

XIULI RD.

DAXIN RD.

RENMIN NAN RD.

XINFENG RD.

HUANGSHA RD.

JIANGLAN RD.

YIDE RD. Guangzhou,

Renmin Daxia

Hua Qiao

HEPING RD.

Central Park

LIU'ERSAN RD.

BINJIANG RD.

South Station

SHAMIAN

SHAMIAN ST.

YANJIANG RD.

White Swan Hotel

Shengli

NANHUA RD.

Shamian Island

XIANGQUN RD.

GONGYE RD.

Zhu Jiang (Pearl River)

Map ©1986, Eurasia Press

① Chinese Export Commodities Fair

② Civil Aviation Administration (CAAC)

③ Public Security Bureau (Foreign Affairs Section)

④ Guangzhou No. 1 People's Hospital

⑤ Guangzhou Zoo

⑥ Zhenhai Tower and Guangdong Historical Museum

⑦ Statue of Five Goats

⑧ Haizhu Square

⑨ Huaisheng Mosque

⑩ Guangzhou Uprising Memorial

⑪ National Peasant Movement Institute

⑫ Sun Yatsen Memorial Hall

⑬ Guangzhou Gymnasium

⑭ People's Stadium

⑮ Antique Shop

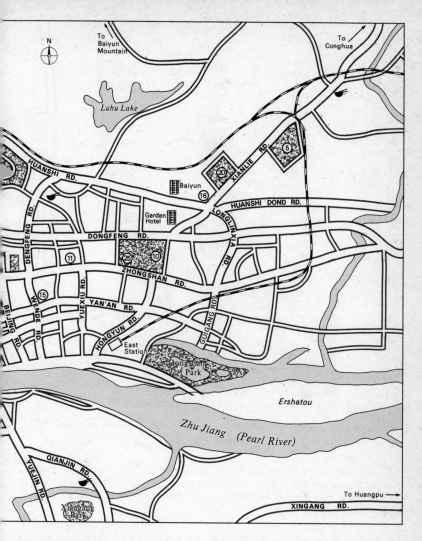

⑯ Friendship Store	㉒ Guangdong Cable Bureau
⑰ Nanfang Department Store	㉓ China International Travel Service (CITS)
⑱ Temple of the Six Banyan Trees (Liurong Temple)	㉔ Children's Palace
⑲ Roman Catholic Church	㉕ Guangdong Provincial Museum
⑳ Mausoleum of the 72 Martyrs (at Huanghuagang)	Restaurants
㉑ Guangdong Post Office	Hotels

*The goat monument in Yuexiu Park commemorates
Guangzhou's mythical origins*

(227,000 acres) are under cultivation. In addition to three rice crops a year, the area produces wheat, fruit, vegetables, sugarcane, and oil-bearing plants. Guangzhou municipality itself includes 33 townships (former communes) and 16 state farms.

The city also has over 3,200 factories producing newsprint, refined sugar, ships, cement, steel, chemicals, automobiles, machinery, textiles, rubber goods, canned goods, and fertilizer. Clothing (about one-third of which is exported), bamboo and rattan products, pottery, ivory, jade, and jewelry are also manufactured or processed here.

Guangzhou has over a dozen colleges and research institutes, including the renowned Zhongshan (Sun Yatsen) University, famous for its medical school. It is also the home of the Guangdong Province Historical Museum and several children's cultural palaces.

Guangzhou has staunchly maintained its unique cultural traditions, including its distinctive earthy dialect, vernacular literature, lively music, colorful opera, and splendidly varied cuisine.

HIGHLIGHTS
FOR TRAVELERS

越秀公园

Yuexiu Park. This public park was created in the 1950s in the northern part of the city in a formerly desolate area called Guanyin Hill. The park contains an exhibition hall, stadiums, swimming pools, and lakes for boating, as well as the Guangdong Historical Museum.

镇海楼和广州博物馆

Tower Overlooking the Sea (Zhenhailou) and the Guangdong Historical Museum. Atop the highest hill in Yuexiu Park stands the five-story red pagoda called Zhenhailou. Originally a temple built in 1380, it was restored after a fire in 1686 to serve as a watchtower. During the Opium War, it was seized by British and French troops. As a memento of that period, two Krupp cannons are displayed at the entrance. Zhenhailou functioned again as a lookout tower during the 1911 Revolution. In 1950, the handsome structure underwent extensive renovations, and in 1953 it was converted into the home of the Guangdong Historical Museum. Visitors who climb the five stories to the top of the tower are rewarded with a cup of green tea and a breathtaking view of verdant Yuexiu Park and the city.

While in the tower, visitors will find it worthwhile to examine the collection of the Guangdong Historical Museum. The displays are arranged chronologically, from the ground floor up, beginning with examples of archeological finds from the prehistoric and early dynastic periods. The second floor contains an eclectic display of artifacts from the Western Han era (206 BC–AD 23) through the 12th century. The third floor is devoted to materials from the Ming Dynasty (1368–1644), while the fourth floor covers the Qing Dynasty to the modern era.

五羊石塑

Five Goats Statue. A hundred yards past the entrance to Yuexiu Park, on top of a hill just north of Zhenhailou, stands the statue of five goats commemorating Guangzhou's mythical origins.

中山纪念堂

Sun Yatsen Memorial Hall. On the east side of Jiefang Road, heading south, are a monument and a memorial theater dedicated to Dr. Sun Yatsen. The memorial theater with its blue-tiled roof seats 5,000 people and is used for rallies and cultural performances. It was built in 1931 with funds donated by patriotic overseas Chinese. Inside the beautiful and dignified hall no pillars obstruct the view of the stage.

广州农民运动讲习所旧址

National Peasant Movement Institute. Founded in 1924 on the site of a 16th-century Confucian temple, this school was used by the fledgling

Communist Party to train cadres from all over the country for the revolution. Many leaders of the Communist movement, such as Zhou Enlai and Guo Moruo, taught at the institute. Mao Zedong served as director of the institute in 1926. Visitors are shown a replica of his room, various memorabilia, and a historical museum.

广州起义烈士陵园

Martyrs Memorial Park. This garden officially opened in 1957 on the 30th anniversary of the December 1927 Guangzhou Uprising, which led to 5,700 deaths at the hands of the Guomindang. Within its 25.4 hectares (64 acres) are pavilions, exhibits, and a striking fresco just inside the main gate. A stele dedicated to the friendship between the Chinese and Korean peoples commemorates the participation of many Korean students in the uprising.

黄花岗七十二烈士墓

Mausoleum of the 72 Martyrs. The revolution that overthrew the Qing Dynasty was actually a series of uprisings, 10 of which failed. Originally constructed in 1918 with funds donated by overseas Chinese, this mausoleum in the northeastern section of Guangzhou commemorates one abortive attempt, the uprising of March 29, which resulted in the loss of 72 lives. Yellow Flower Hill (Huanghuagang) is one of the loveliest segments of the mausoleum grounds.

广州动物园

Guangzhou Zoo. Further east is one of China's four major zoos, opened in 1958. Of the more than 200 species displayed here, most popular—predictably—are the pandas, although the monkeys, giraffes, hippopotami, camels, tigers, and aviary are also worth seeing. On the grounds are a restaurant, snack bar, and small retail shop. The zoo is open from 8 AM to 6 PM daily. Admission is 10 *fen*.

流花公园

Liuhua Park. Liuhua Park flanks the Dongfang Hotel on the northwestern side. Its artificial lake, palm-lined walkways, arched bridges, and pavilions make it an appealing setting for a casual stroll. Sporting activities here include boating, badminton, and table tennis. The park is popular in the early morning with joggers (mainly Westerners) and shadowboxers (mainly Chinese).

六榕寺

Temple of the Six Banyan Trees (Liurong Si). Constructed in AD 479, the temple received its present name from the famous 12th-century poet-statesman Su Dongpo, who was struck by the presence of six banyan trees (which have since disappeared) on the temple grounds. The temple was rebuilt after a fire in the 11th century and was renovated most recently in 1979. The temple's Flower Pagoda (Huata), built in 537, was partially destroyed by fire and restored in 1098. Today, the temple serves as headquarters of the Guangzhou Buddhist Association.

怀圣寺（光塔寺）

Huaisheng Mosque. Constructed in AD 627, this is generally considered to be the oldest mosque in China. It was said to have been built by the first person to bring the Koran to China—an uncle of the Prophet Muhammed. Attached to the mosque is a recently built minaret containing an immaculately maintained prayer hall. Closed during the Cultural Revolution, the Huaisheng Mosque is now used regularly by Guangzhou's Muslim community (said to number about 4,000).

天主教堂

Roman Catholic Cathedral. Built in 1860 by the French architect Guillemin, this Gothic-style cathedral was turned into a warehouse during the Cultural Revolution. The building was restored and consecrated in 1979 and is now open for services on Sundays. Visitors should inquire about seasonal schedules.

广州文化公园

Cultural Park. Just a block from the Pearl River, Guangzhou's Cultural Park is the site of most of the city's cultural events. Within its eight hectares (20 acres) are an aquarium, seven exhibition halls, flower gardens, an opera house, a concert hall, three huge television screens for public viewing, and two open-air theaters (one of which has an enormous stage) where classical dramas, traditional Guangdong opera, and revolutionary plays are performed. There is also a roller-skating rink, a teahouse, and a table-tennis area.

The park features some 30 exhibitions annually, including a permanent display called "Labor Created Man." Educational exhibits from other countries, such as "Artifacts from the Paris Commune" or "Wildlife of Australia," invariably draw large audiences. Storytelling and chess matches are also popular pastimes in the park. Admission is five *fen* during the day and 10 *fen* at night, but indoor cultural events and concerts require separate tickets available only from the host organization.

陈氏书院（陈家祠）

Chen Clan Academy. Known locally as the Chen Family Temple, this 19th-century compound is a well-preserved example of late imperial southern Chinese architecture. Nearly every door, window, roof beam, and column is intricately carved, while terra cotta sculptures and friezes grace the roof ridges and walls.

In the Confucian social scheme, ancestors and descendents were inextricably connected: the superior virtue of previous generations provided the example and good reputation for later generations to live up to; conversely, achieving fame and success, particularly in the political arena, for which high marks on the civil service examinations were a prerequisite, exalted one's ancestors. Thus, family-run schools of Confucian studies, such as the Chen Clan Academy, were often built around an ancestor temple where the memorial tablets and "spirit seats" of the clan's forebears were preserved. Called the "central hall," this inner sanctum is located at the back of the complex, where the altar and shrine can still be seen (although the memorial tablets themselves have long since disappeared).

华南植物园

South China Botanical Gardens. Located just north east of the city (about 15 minutes by taxi), this 300-hectare (750-acre) garden is the largest in China, and has one of the best botanical collections in the world. For the travel-weary, a visit to these lush and expansive gardens can be quite refreshing, a delightful respite from the noise and grit of urban Guangzhou.

沙面

Shamian Island. Also known as the "Island of the Former Concessions," this tiny piece of land less than 1 km. (0.6 mi.) long was once an exclusive British- and French-controlled enclave, guarded by gates posted with the infamous notice "No Chinese or dogs allowed." It is connected to the mainland by two bridges. Its streets, shaded by tall trees, are lined by French- and Victorian-style buildings. The former banks, churches, and foreign legations now seem rather forlorn. Laundry hangs from the windows of one church and political slogans garland its steeples. Some of these buildings have been converted into schools, municipal offices, and military barracks. One houses the Polish shipping office, another the seaman's club. Most of the structures are apartment blocks today, while many were torn down to make way for the new White Swan Hotel.

SPECIAL-INTEREST SITES

Guangzhou and its suburbs hold numerous attractions for special-interest groups, such as agricultural experts, botanists, and public health specialists, as well as for business travelers and other visitors seeking relief from the hectic pace and close confines of the city.

China Travel Service (CTS) organizes a number of tours to one of the six agricultural townships in Guangzhou's suburbs. A typical visit may last a day, starting with a short lecture on arrival, a tour of the facilities such as the medical clinics and primary schools, followed by lunch on the premises and a question- and answer-session to round out the day. Daili and Luogang townships are among those that receive foreign tour groups.

Other special-interest sights include the Chinese Trade Union Museum, the School for the Deaf and Dumb (famous for its acupuncture treatment), and the exhibition halls at the Guangzhou Foreign Trade Center.

SITES AROUND GUANGZHOU

从化温泉

Conghua Hot Springs. The mineral waters at the Conghua Hot Springs, located 81 km. (50 mi.) north of Guangzhou, are said to have a curative effect on certain chronic ailments. A total of eight springs supply water with an average temperature of 40°C (104°F). The region where the springs are located is mountainous and scenic, with lichee orchards, bamboo groves, plum trees, and flowering bushes.

During the Guangzhou Trade Fair, excursions for business travelers regularly leave the city at 2 PM on Saturdays and return on Sunday afternoon. The trip takes two hours each way. Overnight guests usually stay at one of the pleasant villas scattered around the grounds. Many are equipped with small bathing pools fed by the local springs.

从化温泉宾馆

Conghua Hot Springs Guest House. (Conghua; tel: through exchange line of the county). All 280 rooms have private bath, air-conditioning, and telephone. Rates are Y50 for double room, Y70 for a suite, and Y80–Y100 for a deluxe suite. The hotel has a restaurant, tea house, dance hall, and a conference hall that seats 500, as well as the usual amenities.

CITS can also arrange a stay at one of the pleasant villas at the Hot Springs, many of which are equipped with small bathing pools fed by local springs. Rates range from Y50 to Y70. All rooms have air-conditioning, private bath, and color TV. (Cable: 2464. Through the exchange line of Conghua Hot Springs.)

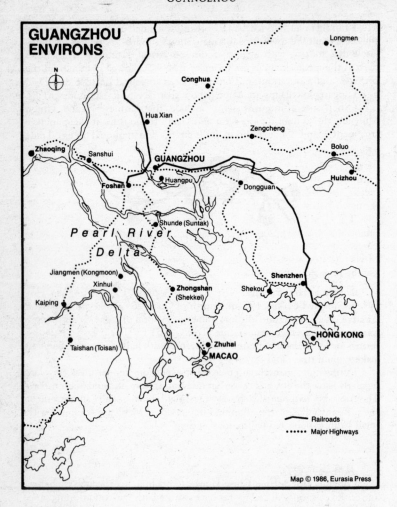

GUANGZHOU ENVIRONS

N

Longmen

Conghua

Hua Xian

Zengcheng

Boluo

Zhaoqing
Sanshui
GUANGZHOU
Huizhou

Foshan
Huangpu
Dongguan

Shunde (Suntak)

Pearl River

Delta

Jiangmen (Kongmoon)
Shenzhen

Xinhui
Shekou

Kaiping
Zhongshan
(Shekkei)

Taishan (Toisan)
Zhuhai
MACAO

HONG KONG

———— Railroads
••••••••• Major Highways

Map © 1986, Eurasia Press

白云山

White Cloud (Baiyun) Mountain. This 427-m. (1,400-ft.) mountain
is 14.5 km. (9 mi.) from Guangzhou and is the highest point in the region,
affording a panoramic view of the city, the Pearl River, and the surrounding
delta area. Pavilions and teahouses at the summit encourage a lingering
view. Further down the mountain are the Shanzhuang and Shuangxi hotels,
perhaps the most extravagant found in China — they comprise large, luxurious villas appointed with sitting rooms and sunken baths and surrounded
by private gardens, ponds, and bamboo groves. These hotels are used by
both high-ranking foreigners and Chinese officials.

Since the hill also bristles with defense installations, hikers are advised to follow the obvious path markers. A hike to the mountaintop takes about six hours.

七星岩

Seven Star Crags (Qixingyan). Local tour guides boast that the beauty of this region combines the best features of the lakes of Hangzhou and the mountains of Guilin. Although this description is arguable, the scenery at Seven Star Crags is remarkable, with special appeal to photographers.

The crags consist of a dramatic grouping of karst "towers"—a geological phenomenon typical of South China—which form a pattern similar to that of the Big Dipper. They are connected by arched bridges and winding pathways adorned with traditional-style pavilions. At their base are five small lakes and numerous caves containing underground streams and grotesquely shaped stalactites and stalagmites.

The region became famous during the Tang Dynasty, when many famous painters and poets were attracted by its beauty and left their verses carved in the stony hillsides. Today, Seven Star Crags attracts thousands of visitors annually. The distance from Guangzhou—104 km. (65 mi.)—can be covered in three hours by bus or taxi.

江门

Jiangmen (Kongmoon). This picturesque river port is situated about 112 km. (70 mi.) south of Guangzhou, not far from Macao. Jiangmen is the ancestral home of vast numbers of overseas Chinese, many of whom return here to visit relatives and to sightsee. Two hotels located near East Lake Park on the outskirts of town provide adequate lodging.

HOTEL ACCOMMODATIONS

Guangzhou's 56 hotels and guest houses contain some 12,000 guest rooms. Six cater especially to foreigners. Many overseas Chinese stay at the Huaqiao Daxia off Haizhu Square, just by the Pearl River. Japanese are generally booked into the Guangzhou Hotel, also off Haizhu Square, while Americans and Europeans usually stay at the Dongfang, Baiyun, White Swan, Garden, or China hotels.

DELUXE HOTELS

东方宾馆

Dongfang Hotel. Located directly across the street from the Trade Fair complex, the Dongfang is Guangzhou's main hotel for business travelers. The Dongfang is two minutes by car from the railway station and is within walking distance of some of the city's most beautiful parks. Although the Dongfang is not centrally situated with respect to Guangzhou's central commercial area, the city's main department store is only one stop away (on No. 3 trolleybus).

The original Soviet-style wing of the Dongfang, built in 1954, was augmented during the 1970s by three other wings. The four connected structures form a square which encloses a courtyard. In the courtyard are a small, traditional-style Chinese garden crisscrossed by streams and dotted with pavilions, ponds, and benches, and two badminton courts. An arcade with a battery of electronic games was added in 1980.

The old wing of the Dongfang has 400 rooms connected by vast stretches of broad corridors and grand, carpeted stairways. Some rooms have balconies, and each has a desk, two easy chairs, an old-style dresser with a mirror attached, a nightstand, and a telephone. The entire section was completely renovated in 1979. Now it is air-conditioned and newly carpeted, and rooms are equipped with color TV sets, refrigerators, and pushbutton telephones featuring direct-dialing to Hong Kong.

The three newer 11-story wings contain a total of 700 rooms. Some guests find their appearance a bit antiseptic, preferring the red carpets and spaciousness of the old wing to the impersonal metallic and plain wood trim of the new. In 1982, the US Consulate General in Guangshou was relocated in the southern courtyard of the new wing.

The Dongfang has some of the best service facilities of any hotel in China, including a new "Dongfang International Club" complex on the mezzanine floor of the old wing that includes a late-night café, a Western-style seafood restaurant (dimly lit, with large aquaria set into the walls), and a bouncy, Hong Kong-style disco. Much of the old wing's lobby has been converted to a gaudy shopping mall, while the new wing lobby accommodates spacious new banking, telex, and postal facilities. The new and old wings each have their own Chinese and Western restaurants, all redone to suit the imagined tastes of foreign and Hong Kong traders.

Service counters on each floor stock beer, soft drinks, mineral water, ice, and cigarettes. The staff takes care of laundry, dry-cleaning, and long-distance telephone bookings.

At the main service desk, located on the ground floor of each wing, one can make restaurant reservations, arrange to have business cards printed, and send out film for developing (including Kodacolor printing). Recreation facilities at the hotel include badminton, Ping-Pong, and billiards.

Credit cards are now accepted for most transactions at the Dongfang.

Address: 120 Liu Hua Rd. *Rates:* Single: Y102
Telephone: 669900 Double: Y138
Telex: 44439 GZDFH CN Suite: Y258
Cable: 4221

白天鹅饭店

White Swan Hotel. Rising some 100 m. (330 ft.) above the Pearl River on Shamian Island, the White Swan is being touted as China's first genuinely international-class, five-star tourist hotel. Indeed, few other hotels in China come close in terms of comfort, service, and modernity. Moreover, its rates are surprisingly reasonable. Its atrium lobby must rank as one of the most beautiful in the world.

Opened in February 1983, the White Swan is a joint venture of the Guangdong Tourism Bureau and Goodyear Investments Co. Ltd. of Hong Kong. It is reported to have cost HK$200 million to build. The 28 floors house 1,000 rooms of four basic types, but all done in luxury style and all suitably equipped with refrigerator, closed-circuit TV, direct-dial telephone service to Hong Kong, carpeting, air-conditioning, modern bath, balcony, and night-table radio/control console. There is 24-hour room and laundry service (although laundry is two or three times the price at other hotels). Daily newspapers in Chinese or English are delivered to each room. The staff of 2,000 (possibly the best in all of China) has been carefully selected for language ability and manner, and trained for months in special schools. All are conversant in at least three languages, and all seem genuinely interested in seeing that guests are happy and that service is efficient.

The White Swan has more than 30 dining areas, arrayed on the first, second, and third floors. These include a Japanese restaurant, an elegant European grill room, three types of Chinese restaurants, a Western coffee shop (offering milk shakes and mango ice cream), and a tea lounge. There are also three bars, including a Chinese nightclub, and a room that operates as a disco in the evening (Y15 weekends, Y12 weeknights) and serves a businessman's buffet for lunch. Other services include professionally trained hair stylists, sauna and massage, Jacuzzi, swimming pool, and weight room. The hotel also sells tickets to a rifle range near Guangzhou and offers its guests lessons in tennis, kite-flying, swimming, Ping-Pong, and even sky-diving.

There are two business centers, one with telex and telecommunications services, and the other with typists and translators. The 600-seat international conference hall is equipped for simultaneous translation. On the first floor is a large shopping arcade, along with postal sevices and an office that sells tickets for the train to Hong Kong. For guests arriving by train from Hong Kong, the White Swan maintains a special reception desk at the train station and a free bus to the hotel. The hotel is about 20 minutes from the train and about 25 minutes from the airport.

The spot on Shamian Island where the hotel was built was known as the White Swan Pool, where a legendary hero was carried away by a white swan. The exterior of the hotel is designed to resemble a swan with its wings folded back. Although it is a very modern place, the White Swan retains many touches of old Chinese culture, including a mountaintop pavilion over the waterfall in the lobby and a charming garden in the back.

The 887 rooms in the original tower have been refurbished, and a new adjoining wing of Garden Apartments was completed in February 1988. This wing consists of a five-story tower with 17 two- and three-bedroom units, which all have a view of the Pearl River. Most of the units have been rented by foreign companies with staff in Guangzhou.

Address: 1 South Street, Shamian Island, Guangzhou.
Telephone: 886968   *Telex:* 44688 WSH CN
Cable: 8888   *Rates:* Double: Y334–520

Rates for deluxe and presidential suites and office space are available on request.

广州文化假日酒店
Holiday Inn City Centre Guangzhou (Huansi Donglu). New in 1989, this latest member of the Holiday Inn chain is located in the business district of Guangzhou, only 12 km. from Baiyun International Airport. It has 431 rooms, each of which is supplied with air-conditioning, color TV, refrigerator and minibar. Facilities include convention and banquet rooms up to 500 and an exhibition center adjoining the hotel. Dining in the hotel is at their two Chinese restaurants, the Grill Room serving continental cuisine, and the coffee shop. Guests can enjoy movies on the premises in the 800-seat cinema, swim in the pool, work out at the health club, or stroll in their shopping arcade. A second Holiday Inn is planned in Guangzhou in 1990, the **Holiday Inn Garden Court Guangzhou,** part of their new chain of "modified-facility" hotels (rates are projected to be about $47), which offer similar quality but fewer services.

中国大酒店
China Hotel. A massive complex with 1,200 guest rooms, the China Hotel entered full service in early 1984. The China Hotel is ideally situated: Guangzhou's trade fair complex is just across the road, while the train station, airport, and central commercial district are each minutes away by car. The China Hotel complex also includes eight floors of residential apartments and a 15-story office tower—Guangzhou's first such facility for foreign businesses.

From the outset, the China Hotel has been a popular mecca for China traders ("for the merchant prince of today," as their ads have it), many of whom may have been put off by the insouciant atmosphere at the rival Dongfang. The giant lobby, done in Italian granite and brass, itself has the atmosphere of an East Asian bazaar. At times, the milling hotel staff seem to outnumber the guests. But numbers are not necessarily an expression of efficiency, especially at newly opened Chinese hotels. One China Hotel guest noted that it took 30 minutes to get a three-minute telex sent in an office staffed by six people.

The hotel's litany of facilities is impressive: 18 food and beverage outlets, tennis courts, a health club and gymnasium, a nine-lane bowling alley, a crystal ballroom with a capacity for 1,200 people and facilities for simultaneous interpreting, an outdoor swimming pool, and a fleet of

Mercedes-Benz limousines. Its business center offers secretarial services, photocopying, and telecommunication links. Rooms are comfortable and most have superb views. Food preparation is, by and large, excellent.

The China Hotel is managed by New World Hotels International and accepts direct bookings. Most major credit cards are accepted.

Address: Liu Hua Lu
Telephone: 666888
Telex: 44888 CHLGZ CN

Cable: 6888 GUANGZHOU
Rates: Doubles: Y130–190
Suites: Y250–350

花园酒店

Garden Hotel. Set amidst acres of sumptuous formal gardens, the Garden Hotel marks a stunning addition to Guangzhou's growing number of high-caliber hotels. The newest hotel in town, the Garden entered service in October 1984, following several years of planning and construction. The hotel is only a five minutes' drive from the railway station and is within walking distance of Guangzhou's Pearl River ferry terminals.

The Garden has 1,000 rooms, including 35 suites. It is among the first hotels in China to offer guests a choice of bedding: two twin beds or one queen-size. Facilities thoughtfully include a well-stocked lending library, children's pool (in addition to a full-sized rooftop pool), and videocassette rentals that include good international films and sporting events. Otherwise, there are tennis and squash courts, a health club, Jacuzzis, a theater, and a huge conference/banquet hall—its seating capacity of 1,400 makes it one of the largest in Asia.

The Garden's business services are the most extensive of any hotel in China: private offices, a business library, multilingual secretarial services, computers and word processors, and document facsimiles, along with telex and cable.

Certainly, the Garden will benefit from its affiliation with Hong Kong's Peninsula Group, whose first foothold in China was the eminently successful Jianguo Hotel in Beijing. Direct bookings can be made through Peninsula, Cathay Pacific, or Steigenberger Reservation Service (SRS).

Address: 368 Huanshi Dong Lu
Telephone: 773388
Telex: 44788 GDHTL CN
Cable: 4735 GUANGZHOU

Rates: Doubles (standard): Y279
Doubles (superior): Y297
Doubles (deluxe): Y334
Suites: Y440–1040

FIRST-CLASS AND STANDARD ACCOMMODATIONS

白云宾馆

Baiyun (White Cloud) Hotel. Opened in 1977, the Baiyun was built to ease the pressure on the Dongfang. With the Dongfang mainly set aside for foreign traders, many tourist groups are assigned to the 33-story, 718-

room Baiyun, which is next door to Guangzhou's new Friendship Store. The Baiyun's suburban location (in the northeast section of town, halfway between Yuexiu Park and the Guangzhou Zoo) affords a view of neighboring farms and the Baiyun hills.

The Baiyun's restaurant overlooks a pleasant inner courtyard. The cuisine is mediocre at best. The hotel has complete service facilities, including a beauty shop and bank. Rooms are plainly furnished with only the barest essentials. An indifferent service staff and poor maintenance were hallmarks of the Baiyun during its first years. Management has taken pains to make improvements in these areas, but certain problems—such as slow elevator service and poor air-conditioning—may be endemic.

The Baiyun accepts Visa and American Express credit cards.

Address: 367 East Huanshi Road   *Rates:* Single: Y90
Telephone: 333998   Double: Y138
Cable: 0682

人民大厦
Renmin Dasha (People's Mansion). This old, 14-story "mansion" dates back to 1936, but was enlarged in 1965. It is located downtown, near Shamian Island. Magnificent views of the city can be had from its two restaurants. Its 413 rooms are spacious, simply furnished, comfortable, and equipped with private baths.

Address: 207 Changdi Road   *Rates:* Single: Y85
Telephone: 661445   Double: Y120
Cable: 1947 CANTON   Suite: Y160

广州宾馆
Guangzhou Hotel. Located in the city center, the Guangzhou has 480 rooms offering closed-circuit color TV, direct-dial phone, and a paging system, as well as useful amenities such as a reservations booking service and sightseeing tour desk. The Guangzhou is 5 km. from the railway station and 9 km. from the airport.

Address: Haizhu Square   *Cable:* 0520
Telephone: 338668   *Telex:* 44336 KCHTL CN

东山宾馆
Dong Shan Hotel. Opened in 1986, this 500-room facility has three restaurants, a coffee shop, shopping center, bank, hairdresser, and disco.

Address: 44 Shanyu Road   *Rates:* Deluxe: US$50–60
Telephone: 773722

远洋宾馆
Ocean Hotel. The Ocean Hotel, which opened in 1985, has 300 rooms. Facilities include two restaurants, a coffee shop, lounge, disco, hairdresser, and bank.

Address: 390 Huan Shi Road East   *Rates:* Single: Y98
Telephone: 765988   Double: Y172
Telex: 44638 GOHOL   Suite: Y310

南湖宾馆

Nanhu (South Lake) Hotel. Located on Nanhu Lake, this 310-room hotel is 18 km. from Guangzhou Railway Station and Baiyun International Airport. All rooms offer private bath, air-conditioning, television, refrigerator, telephone, and taped music. The Nanhu Hotel has Chinese and Western restaurants, teahouse, bar, swimming pool, tennis courts, disco, barber shop, postal and telegram services, souvenir shop, and bank.

Address: Sha He, Tong He   *Telex:* 44511 NANHU CN
Telephone: 776367/706706   *Cable:* 0945

Guangzhou's other major hotels are the **Overseas Chinese Mansion** (Huaqiao Dasha, 2 Qiaoguang Rd.; tel: 336888); the **Cathay Hotel** (376 Huanshi Dong Road; tel: 765787; telex: 44765 CATHL CN); the **Liuhua (Floating Flowers) Hotel** (Renmin Road North; tel: 668800; telex: 44298 GZLHH CN); and the **Guangdong Guest House** (603 Jiefang Rd.; tel: 332950). Other choices for accommodations in the suburbs include the **Luhu (Green Lake) Hotel** (Baiyun Shan, Lu Rd.; tel: 334516). By the lake is the **Meihua (Plum Flowers) Hotel** (Shahemeihuayuan; tel: 775600). Visitors may also find accommodations on Shamian Island at the **Shamian Guest House** (52 S. Shamian St.; tel: 88124), and the **Shengli (Victory) Guest House** (54 Shamian Avenue; tel: 889822).

CANTONESE CUISINE

If there is one activity in Guangzhou that threatens the preoccupation with business and sightseeing, it is eating. Local statisticians avow that there are some 22,000 seats available for dining in the city, and it seems there are at least that many dishes and variations in how they are prepared.

Cantonese chefs have fanned out across the world over the years and have had to substitute local varieties of vegetables, meats, and spices for Guangzhou ingredients. Not surprisingly, their dishes sometimes bear little resemblance to the Guangzhou originals. In addition, Cantonese food has gained an undeserved reputation as "second-rate" ever since Hunan, Sichuan, and Beijing cuisines have become part of the international gourmet's vocabulary. But even people from other parts of China admit that Cantonese cooking, so appealing to the eye and subtle in its flavors, is one of the gastronomic wonders of the world.

In Guangzhou, the dishes vary noticeably with the seasons. Casseroles and potages prevail in the damp winters, while light soups and less oily dishes are preferred during the hot summer months. In general, Cantonese cuisine is characterized by its variety, the freshness of its ingredients, and its delicate sauces and seasonings. Because of Guangzhou's location in the heart of a fertile delta near the sea, fruit, vegetables, and seafood, such as crabs, prawns, abalone, and squid, are popular cooking ingredients.

Typical Cantonese methods of cooking include lacquer-roasting, in which meat, usually pork, is marinated, hung in the oven, then basted and roasted until it shines like lacquer; "explosive" stir-frying, a method of preparing seafood which calls for adding seasoned seafood to very hot oil; and steaming, in which whole fish are rubbed with ginger and salt, marinated in a mixture of wine, sugar, and soy sauce, and then covered with vegetables and steamed for about 20 minutes.

Compared to the meals at local restaurants, food at the hotels is adequate at best. Perhaps the most enjoyable way to spend an evening in Guangzhou is to muster a group and head off together to make a new culinary find or revisit an old favorite. To simplify the procedure, fill out a "restaurant booking form" at the hotel service desk. The staff will arrange reservations and also order specialties in advance. At the restaurants, guests are escorted to private dining rooms where tea is served and moist washcloths are provided. Additional dishes and beverages (beer and wine are *de rigueur*) are provided. Additional dishes and beverages (beer and wine are de rigueur) 9 PM, and lingering is frowned upon.

According to local guides, there are some 34 restaurants with special sections for foreigners, but opinions vary about which are the best. We have listed a few of our favorites.

泮溪酒家

Banxi (Friendship) Restaurant. The Banxi is one of Guangzhou's loveliest, as well as largest, restaurants employing a staff of 400. Up to 1,000 people can be accommodated in its many pavilions, which overlook a lake and surrounding gardens. The newer section, though not attractive, is air-conditioned.

The Banxi is noted for its *dim sum* (dumplings), which are richly varied in size, taste, and fillings, and elegantly presented in the shape of little animals and birds. Other specialties include chicken in tea leaves, stewed turtle, roast pork, and a heavenly crabmeat-shark's fin consommé. The winter melon soup (in season) and the squash soup with tiny shrimp are recommended for their subtle flavor.

Address: 151 Xiangyang Yi Road   *Telephone:* 885655

北园酒家

Beiyuan (North Garden) Restaurant. Unpretentious from the outside, the Beiyuan surprises the visitor with its inner courtyard, small brook, bamboo trees, leaded-glass windows, private dining rooms, and elegant, court-style furnishings. Specialties here include goose with sweet-and-sour sauce, fish with pine nuts, and fried duck web with oyster sauce.

Address: 439 Dengfeng Road   *Telephone:* 333365

南园酒家

Nanyuan (South Garden) Restaurant. The Nanyuan Restaurant comprises 10 small teahouses situated in a magnificent bamboo glade within a beautifully landscaped garden. Specialties here include pigeon in plum sauce, fish balls, chicken in honey and oyster sauce, rockfish, and chicken rolls.

Address: 120 Qianjin Road   *Telephone:* 448380

大同酒家

Datong Restaurant. The Datong is one of the more expensive restaurants, but is a favorite of foreign traders attending the Fair. The top floors, reserved for foreigners, overlook the Pearl River, whose sounds, lights, and water traffic provide a unique setting. Specialties of the house include roast pig (the skin is the delicacy; roasted to crisp perfection, it is dipped in bean sauce, salt, and sugar and served with a scallion in a steamed roll).

Address: 63 Yanjiang Road   *Telephone:* 888988

广州酒家

Guangzhou Restaurant. This restaurant, famous for its banquets, stays open a bit later than most (until about 9:30 PM). Its specialties include shark's fin soup with shredded chicken, chopped crabmeat balls, and braised dove.

Address: 2 S. Wenchang Road   *Telephone:* 887136

经济餐馆

Jingji (Economical) Restaurant. The Jingji on Shamian Island will suit visitors craving Western food. Chicken is prepared in various European styles. A seasonal specialty is rice birds stuffed with liver sausage. A number of excellent fish dishes are listed on the Chinese menu.

Address: 8 Shamian Street, 2nd section   *Telephone:* 888784

太平馆

Taipingguan (Peace) Restaurant. Western and Chinese dishes are served in this restaurant, which is frequented by a largely local clientele. The roast pigeon here is said to have been a favorite of Zhou Enlai.

Address: 344 Beijing Road   *Telephone:* 332938

蛇餐馆

Snake Restaurant. This unique restaurant is for those with strong stomachs and an adventuresome spirit. Snakes are skinned alive in front of the diners to demonstrate their freshness.

Address: 43 Jianglan Road   *Telephone:* 883811

Some other restaurants are worth noting: the Yeweixiang (Delicious Wild Game) Restaurant (249 Beijing Rd.; tel: 330997) serves every kind of game imaginable. Turtle, a Cantonese specialty, may be tasted at the Sanru Restaurant (423 E. Nanhua Rd.; tel: 448841). Noodles—plain, sweet, spicy, crispy, and so on—are served at the Shahe Restaurant (318 E. Xianlie Rd.; tel: 777239) out in the northeastern suburb near the zoo. The Muslim Restaurant (326 Zhongshan Liu Rd.; tel: 888414) serves excellent vegetarian dishes. In the southwest part of the city, there is the Yuyuan (Happy Garden) Restaurant (90 S. Liwan Rd.; tel: 886838) and the Taotaoju Teahouse (288 Xiuli Er Rd.; tel: 887501).

442
GUANGZHOU

SHOPPING

Antiques. Guangzhou attracts antique shoppers from the world over. Unfortunately, there are few bargains to be had, owing to China's efforts to keep prices level with those prevalent on international markets. The Chinese government stipulates that antiques over 120 years old may not leave the country.

☞*Guangzhou Antiques Shop.* The Antiques Shop on Wende Road is actually an amalgamation of several small shops catering exclusively to foreigners. A spacious center gallery contains glass cases displaying jade, seals, and ink stones; its walls are decorated with scrolls. Two other rooms feature wooden carvings, screens, vases, and porcelains. The helpful staff here is knowledgeable about their wares.

☞*Antiques Warehouse.* The Antiques Warehouse on Hongshu Road provides a somewhat less pleasant atmosphere for shopping. Although its four back rooms house hundreds of items, some have yet to be cleaned and prepared for sale (i.e., sealed with the obligatory red wax certifying them for export).

☞*Guangzhou Antiques Export Company.* Also located on Hongshu Road, the Export Company is a wholesale outlet for foreign antique dealers. The minimum permissible purchase here is US$2,000—a bit steep for the average tourist. For the professional buyer, however, it carries an excellent array of antique porcelains.

Business people visiting the grounds of the Guangzhou Trade Exhibition can shop for antiques in the arts and crafts section of the Light Industry Products exhibition hall. The hall also has six full-time retail shops: a curios and food shop, a bookshop, two textiles shops (one for garments, the other for piece goods), a fur goods shop, a down and feathers shop, and a newly opened arts and crafts shop that features such things as a Mona Lisa needlepoint.

工艺美术轻工产品大楼

Arts and Handicrafts. The vast exhibition space known as the **Hall of Arts and Crafts and Light Industrial Products** is located at Haizhu Square near the Pearl River. The upper floors are devoted to displays, while the crowded ground floor sells sandalwood fans, handbags, chops, bolts of cloth, bamboo carvings, and many other arts and crafts.

友谊商店

Friendship Store. The three-story Friendship Store, adjacent to the Baiyun Hotel, is a standard stop on the tourist itinerary. Despite the variety, many of its mass-produced offerings lack the artistry and charm of the goods available at the Friendship Stores in Beijing or Shanghai. The ground floor features canned goods, beverages, tobacco products, stationery, toiletries, appliances, bicycles, and sewing machines. The second level sells clothing and textiles, including a good selection of silks. On the top floor are handicraft items ranging from ashtrays decorated with pandas to double embroideries. A separate section sells scrolls and artists' supplies. Ivory and linen at the Friendship Store are perhaps the only items not found elsewhere in the city. The store is usually open from 9 AM to 9 PM and has a banking office to facilitate currency exchange.

SHOPPING DISTRICTS

In addition to the above-mentioned specialty stores, the city's two main shopping districts on Beijing Road and Renmin Road carry a wide variety of practical and ornamental items.

北京路

Beijing Road. This area can be reached in a 30-minute walk from either the Baiyun or Dongfang Hotel. The following excursion begins at the intersection of Beijing Road and Zhongshan Road.

On the northwest corner of the intersection, at No. 4 Zhongshan Wu Road, is the Guangzhou Department Store (tel: 334152). This store, renovated in 1978, has a selection rivaling that of Guangzhou's largest department store, the Nanfang Daxia. East of the intersection, at No. 10, is the largest music shop in Guangzhou. A big drum costs approximately Y30 here, and a traditional Chinese lute, Y35. Also available is a large selection of flutes (the membranes give Chinese flutes their distinctive "reedy" sound). *Wushu* (martial arts) paraphernalia are also sold here.

At No. 11 Zhongshan Road is a traditional medicine store, easy to find because of the aromas wafting into the street. West of the herbalist, at No. 7, is a store selling dresses, shirts, and a wide selection of sewing patterns.

Continuing east on Zhongshan Road, past the Beijing Road intersection, the shopper will come upon an aquarium store (No. 415) and a Cantonese sausage shop (No. 189). Further east is an interesting basketware and hardware shop. The Decorative Ornaments and Housewares Store at No. 393 has signs in English advertising cloisonné and jade. The narrow shop has counters flanking each side. Walking toward the back, up the stairs, past the bamboo furniture and through the swinging doors, visitors enter a small room "for foreigners only." The staff here serves tea while showing their wares.

Back at the intersection of Beijing and Zhongshan roads, turn up North Beijing Road. The Sporting Goods Store at No. 335 carries a good selection, from Ping-Pong balls to warm-up outfits. At No. 344 is the Taipingguan Restaurant (see "Cuisine" section). The dining area catering to foreigners is a few flights up at the back of the restaurant; portions are large. A few doors up at No. 363 is a general merchandise store which sells everything from door hinges to toilet paper. This is a good place to look for handmade items such as brooms, baskets, crockery, and leather bags.

Heading south on Beijing Road, one comes to the Foreign Languages Bookstore (Waiwen Shudian) at No. 326 (tel: 334584), a well-stocked general interest bookstore. At No. 322 is an art supply store, formally called the First Cultural and Antique Supplies Stores. The store has a "back room" frequented by Japanese buyers and other calligraphy buffs looking for ink stones and Chinese brushes. It also sells scrolls.

Another hardware store at No. 319 carries everything from bicycle-wheel rims (stacked high in the center of the floor) to television sets and radio parts. The poster shop at No. 314 is one of the two places (the other is on Renmin Road) to buy political posters, still an important mass art in China. Subjects range from Mao's calligraphy to diagrams teaching children how to brush their teeth to traditional art.

The most chic beauty salon in Guangzhou is located at No. 303. The maximum charge here is Y6; no tipping. Next door, at No. 301, is a store selling stationery and school supplies.

Chinese cookware, available in sets or random pieces, can be quite attractive. The crockery store at No. 291 carries a good selection as well as straw items, including hats (although peasant hats are ubiquitous in China, they are rarely sold in stores; in cities they are nearly impossible to find).

Several doors down at No. 276 is another bookstore specializing in high-school texts and literature. The produce store at No. 273 is the most popular shop in th area for fresh fruit (all fruit should be peeled before eating) or a thirst-quenching soft drink. Winding up this excursion is the general store at No. 246, an "odd-lot" shop with merchandise ranging from second-hand items to new clothes, plastic flashlights, and pen knives.

人民路

Renmin Road. This major commercial strip stretches from Zhongshan Road all the way south to the Pearl River, but the heaviest concentration of shops is closer to the river. South Renmin Road is a good 50-minute walk from the Dongfang Hotel and is therefore best reached by taxi or the #3 bus. For the return trip, a taxi can be hired at the stand in front of No. 10–12 South Renmin Road; the more adventurous can try the three-wheeled vehicles (covered scooters) available across the street. Scooters charge about half the rate of regular taxis, but they are not permitted to enter the gate of the hotel.

The tour starts at the Nanfang Department Store, which is located at No. 49 Yanjiang Road (tel: 886022), just west of Renmin Road. This multilevel store is the largest retail outlet in Guangzhou, an ideal place to mingle with the local people and to gauge the range of commodities available in the local economy. The store was renovated and greatly expanded in 1979. There are some bargain counters both inside and outside the store.

Situated across the street from the Nanfang, at No. 35, is the most popular dumpling house in town. The system here is to pay in advance for your order, collect a receipt, and hand it to the person scooping the dumplings out of a huge wok.

East of the intersection of Yanjing and Renmin roads, there is a "gathering place" where "big-character posters" and slogans have been known to appear during political campaigns. The best way to explore Renmin Road itself is to go up one side of the street and back down the other. Thus, starting on the west side and proceeding north, one finds a bookstore at No. 9, a good place to buy a map of Guangzhou (eight *fen*). Although the map legend is in Chinese, the street plan is clear and correlates easily with the map in this book. A clearly numbered system shows the city's bus routes. All along the street in this vicinity, young girls and boys often sell small items on the pavements; wares range from hairpins to seasonal nuts and spices.

At No. 23 is an aquarium store which sells not only fish, but also plants, flowers, vases, and lanterns. The film shop at No. 27 sometimes sells Kodak film (minus the canisters) in addition to the Chinese Seagull brand. Further north, at No. 47, is a bookstore specializing in academic journals. At No. 65 is a lantern shop where you will find Chinese lanterns ranging from 6 in. to 6 ft. across; all are collapsible for easy packing.

Crossing to the east side of Renmin Road and heading south toward the river, you will come upon a barbershop at No. 60. This shop, with its swinging wooden doors, old-style chairs, and striped barber pole, somewhat resembles the set for a Western cowboy film. At No. 44 is a shop selling dried fruits, a popular commodity in China. The stationery and school supplies store at No. 40 stocks an item of old "Americana"—hand-held school bells (Y3.50).

The housewares shop at No. 20 is a good place to buy crockery. Restraint is advised, however; some items are heavy and their lead content exceeds the US recommended levels. At No. 14 is a store carrying a wide variety of Chinese teas, and the poster shop at No. 8 stocks the largest variety of posters in Guangzhou, both political and artistic.

GUANGZHOU DIRECTORY

HEALTH AND EMERGENCY SERVICES	Telephone
Guangzhou First People's Hospital, N. Renmin Rd.	333090
Zhongshan Hospital	778223

TELEPHONE AND TELEGRAPH SERVICES	Telephone
Information (local calls)	114
Information (international calls)	115
Long-distance (domestic)	116
Guangdong Cable Bureau, 96 N. Renmin Rd.	4205
Guangdong Post Office, Yanjiang Rd.	886615

FOREIGN CONSULATES	Telephone
US Consulate General, Dongfang Hotel	669900 x100
Japanese Consulate General, Dongfang Hotel	661195

TRAVEL	Telephone
China International Travel Service (CITS)	
Main Office, 179 Huanshi Rd.	662447
Branch Office, Dongfang Hotel, Rm. 2366	669900 x2366

China Travel Service (CTS), 2 Qiaoguang Rd.
  Tickets — 336888
Public Security Bureau (Foreign Affairs Section) — 331862
  863 N. Jiefang Rd. — 331326

AIR

Civil Aviation Administration of China (CAAC)
  Ticketing, 181 Huanshi Rd. (International Flights) — 661803
  Domestic Flights — 678901 x2955
  Baiyun Airport Inquiry Desk — 678901

RAIL

Guangzhou Railroad Station
  Information — 661900
  Tickets — 662868
  Luggage — 661949

LOCAL TRANSPORTATION

Guangzhou Taxi Company
  Head Office, N. Renmin Rd. — 661251
  Municipal Taxi Company — 662014

POINTS OF INTEREST	Telephone
Chinese Export Commodities Fair, 117 Liuhua Rd.	
(Guangzhou Foreign Trade Center and Exhibition Hall)	677000
Children's Palace, 169 Dongfeng Xi Rd.	886560
Cultural Park, Ermalu, Xidi	887232
Friendship Store, 369 E. Huanshi Rd. (adjacent to Baiyun Hotel)	776296
Guangzhou Antiques Shop, 146 Wende Rd.	334229
Guangzhou Gymnasium, 119 Liuhua Rd.	661747
Guangzhou Provincial Museum, 215 Wenming Rd.	332194
Guangzhou Uprising Memorial, Zhongshan Er Rd.	778521
Guangzhou Zoo, Xianlie Rd.	775574
Huaisheng Mosque, 56 Guangta Rd.	331878
Liuhua Park, Xicun Highway	664095
Liwan Park, Longjin Rd.	887880
National Peasant Movement Institute, 42 S. Zhongshan Rd.	330743
People's Stadium, Dongjiaochang	775132
Sun Yatsen Memorial Hall, Dongfeng Zhong Rd.	332430
Temple of the Six Banyan Trees, Liurong Rd.	887563
Yuexiu Park, Dabei Rd.	335676
Zhenhai Tower and Guangdong Historical Museum, Yuexiu Park	330627

Guilin

cassia woods

traditional spelling/Kweilin

THE landscape of China—at least the image that most Westerners have of it—is actually the landscape of Guilin. Guilin's scenery is unique—both to China and to the rest of the world. From a lush green plain laced with rivers and lakes suddenly spring steep, rounded towers of stone which loom singly like battlements or fade in ranks toward the horizon. This bizarre range of peaks has caused Guilin to be immortalized in Chinese painting and poetry. The celebrated Tang Dynasty poet Han Yu (768–824) described the region this way: "The river forms a green silk belt, the mountains are like blue jade hairpins." The karst formations were thrust up from the limestone sea bed which covered the region some 300 million years ago. Eroded over centuries by the area's unique wind and water conditions, this "stone forest," with its many subterranean caves and rivers, creates a haunting atmosphere.

The ancient town of Guilin is located on the west bank of the Li River in the northeastern part of the Guangxi Zhuang Autonomous Region. Many of its 300,000 inhabitants are Zhuang, a Muslim people who comprise China's largest national minority (12 million in all, 90% of them living in Guangxi). Although renowned mainly for its beauty, Guilin is also a regional manufacturing center and an important link in the transportation network of southern China. Since 1973, the area has received a large influx of foreign tourists to complement the steady, perennial flow of Chinese visitors.

Climate		Jan	Feb	Mar	Apr	May	Jun	Jul	Aug	Sep	Oct	Nov	Dec
Temp.	°C	9.2	9.7	13.4	19.0	23.7	23.7	28.4	27.9	26.5	22.0	15.6	11.1
	°F	48.5	49.4	56.1	66.2	74.6	74.6	83.1	82.2	79.7	71.6	60	51.9
Precip.	mm.	33	56	97	160	206	193	160	178	84	43	38	38
	in.	1.3	2.2	3.8	6.3	8.1	7.6	6.3	7	3.3	1.7	1.5	1.5

During the spring and fall especially, tourist buses line the streets and long skeins of sightseeing boats make their way through the mountains along the Li River. Because of the enormous influx of tourists, some people feel that the area has been spoiled, but nothing can diminish the spectacular scenery. Moreover, the fact that the local people have become accustomed to the foreign presence has made Guilin one of the few cities in China where it is possible to wander through the stores and parks, looking at things and talking to people, and not become the center of everyone's attention.

Since 1960, Guilin has been the site of much new construction, partly because of economic expansion and partly because the city, severely damaged by bombing during World War II, had yet to be rebuilt. Wide boulevards and avenues have appeared, and streets throughout the city are lined with cassia trees, most of which were planted after 1949.

Guilin's climate is subtropical, with an average annual temperature of 19°C. Forty percent of the average annual precipitation occurs in May and June, when it can pour for days on end. Summers are hot and steamy. September and October are the best months of the year to visit the area.

GUILIN IN HISTORY

Until the Qin Dynasty (221–205 BC), the town of Guilin was a minor way station along the Li River. It gained in importance with the construction of the Lin Canal in 214 BC. This canal, by linking the Yangtse and Pearl rivers via the Li River, enabled the emperor's supply trains to bypass hazardous mountain trails when provisioning his conquering troops in the south. Today the Lin Canal is used as an irrigation aqueduct.

The first Westerners ever to see Guilin were Portuguese sailors taken prisoner by the Ming government in 1550. In 1644, when the Manchus came to power, the retreating Ming made Guilin their capital. It remained a provincial capital until 1912 and briefly became the national capital again in 1936. In the wake of the Japanese invasion of the 1930s, the exodus of Chinese nationals from northeastern China caused Guilin's population to expand from 100,000 to over one million. Hundreds of Western missionaries also sought refuge here. During the anti-Japanese war (1937–45), Guilin was a stronghold of resistance and the site of a US Air Force base. Printing plants, newspapers, hospitals, and even theatrical companies took refuge in the karst caves (the location of some of these caves was not rediscovered until the late 1950s).

The missionaries are gone, along with the other refugees of war. Today, Guilin is a neatly laid-out city, with two- and three-story stucco buildings in place of the huts that formerly lined the riverbanks. Every autumn, the air is redolent with the fragrance of yellow, red, and white cassia blossoms.

ECONOMY AND CULTURE

In 1949, Guilin had only a printing press, a few small factories, and some cottage handicrafts. Since then, over 250 factories have been built, now employing a total work force of about 100,000. Guilin today produces nitrogen fertilizers, spun silk, cotton cloth, tires, medicines, rubber, machinery, and a wide range of other items. Machine-tool manufacturing gained prominence here during the Cultural Revolution, and today the city also supplies the country with electronic components, semiconductors, and transistor radios. Since the government decided to develop Guilin as a major tourist attraction in the late 1970s, many of the heavy industries have been moved into outlying regions. Traditional commodities still produced here include wine, bean products, candy, pepper sauce, bamboo chopsticks, and umbrellas.

The agricultural sector has also expanded as a result of the addition of over 2,000 water-control and irrigation projects. Land in this region is naturally arid, because much of the groundwater sinks into the deep, underground river system. The Guilin area produces an abundance of grain, rice, bamboo, pomelos, and cassia by-products (tea, herbal medicines, fragrant oil, and a flavorful local wine). Fishing and river commerce are also important to the local economy.

HIGHLIGHTS
FOR TRAVELERS

Any sojourn in Guilin invariably seems too short. The scenery is magnetic: the crags and rivers seem to take on a new appearance with every change in light; clouds, sunlight, mist, and rain all create their own visual drama. Equally distinctive are the region's caves. The unearthly beauty of their stalagmite and stalactite formations rivals that of the scenes aboveground. Many visitors coming to Guilin at the end of a grueling China tour have noted the remarkably uplifting and invigorating effect of Guilin on their spirits.

One of the easiest and most pleasant ways to get around Guilin is by bicycle. Near the Li River Hotel, a small shop called Charlie's Cousin's Coop (11 Shahu Bei Road) rents bikes for five *yuan* a day. Bicycles are also available at several stores located in the central section of Zhongshan Street. All have signs in English.

两湖区

District of the Two Lakes. This park in southern Guilin is landscaped with gardens, walkways, and stylized pagodas. At the time of the Tang Dynasty (618–907), a single lake in the district formed part of the moat protecting the town walls. Later, when the officials of the Song Dynasty (960–1279) constructed the Green Belt Bridge here, two lakes were created—Banyan Lake (*Rong Hu*) and Fir Lake (*Sha Hu*). Two hotels and a new city auditorium flank the lakeshores. South of the park is Elephant Trunk Hill (*Xiangbi Shan*), with a pagoda at its summit.

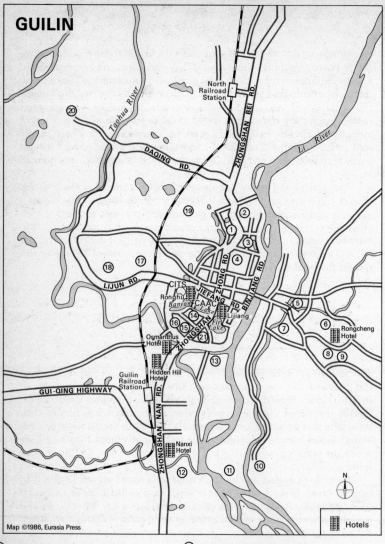

GUILIN

North Railroad Station

Taohua River

Li River

ZHONGSHAN BEI RD.

DAQING RD.

LIJUN RD.

CITS

Ronghu
Banyan Lake

JIEFANG RD.

ZHONG RD.

CAAC

Lijiang

Fir Lake

ZHONGSHAN RD.

BINJIANG RD.

Osmanthus Hotel

ZHONGSHAN NAN RD.

Hidden Hill Hotel

Guilin Railroad Station

GUI-QING HIGHWAY

Nanxi Hotel

Rongcheng Hotel

N

Map ©1986, Eurasia Press

 Hotels

① Treasure Hoard Hill (Baoji Shan)
② Folded Brocade Hill (Diecai Shan)
③ Fubo Hill
④ Duxiu Peak
⑤ Flower Bridge
⑥ Seven Star (Qixing) Park
⑦ Crescent Moon Hill (Yueya Shan)
⑧ Zoo
⑨ Potted Landscape Area
⑩ Tunnelled Hill (Chuan Shan)
⑪ Pagoda Hill (Baota Shan)

⑫ South Creek Hill (Nanxi Shan)
⑬ Elephant Trunk Hill (Xiangbi Shan)
⑭ Friendship Store
⑮ Department Store
⑯ Antiques Store
⑰ Hidden Hill (Yin Shan)
⑱ West Hill (Xi Shan)
⑲ Old Man Mountain (Laoren Shan)
⑳ Reed Flute Cave (Ludi Yan)

 Hotels

伏波山

Fubo Hill. Located within a park in the northern part of the city, Fubo is a hill rich in ancient legends. Along the steps leading to its summit sit an enormous cooking pot and a cast-iron bell weighing 2.5 tons. Both objects were formerly located inside the Fubo Temple, which is dedicated to the Han general of that name, a local hero. The temple, facing south, contains a number of pavilions that afford magnificent views of the region. Within the southern slope of Fubo Hill is Pearl Returning Cave, whose name derives from a local legend about a dragon's cave lit by a single gleaming pearl. A fisherman stole the pearl, but was so filled with shame that he returned it. Inside the cave is a pillar known as the Stone Where Swords Are Tried. On the Thousand Buddha Cliff, which is reached from the cave, stand over 300 statues dating from the Tang and Song dynasties.

Another legend tells that the region was once inhabited by fierce beasts and demons. One day, a giant demon clutching poisonous snakes threatened the townfolk. A huge man named Jie Di suddenly appeared, bow in hand, on the top of Fubo Hill and slew the demon with a single arrow, freeing the town of demons forever.

七星公园（七星岩）

Seven Star Park. This lovely park in the eastern section of the city is reached via a covered bridge across the Li River. The park is named after Seven Star Hill, whose peaks form a pattern similar to that of the stars in the Big Dipper. The hill contains six caves, the most famous of which is the Dragon Refuge Cave (*Longyindong*). Also known as the "Forest of the Tablets," the cave contains hundreds of stelae and carved inscriptions on its walls and ceilings, some dating from the Tang and Ming dynasties. The park also has a small zoo, which features a very tired 24-year-old panda, and a bonsai garden.

芦笛岩

Reed Flute Cave. Of the many caves in the Guilin area, Reed Flute in the northwestern suburbs is the most famous. Its name derives from the reeds at its entrance which were once used to make flutes. First discovered during the Tang Dynasty (618–907), the cave was a frequent refuge for the local population to escape bandits and the ravages of war. Since 1959, it has been transformed into a tourist attraction. A 500-m. (1,640-ft.) trail winds past unusual stalactite and stalagmite formations which colored lights cause to resemble coral, agate, amber, and jade. With prompting from tour guides, their shapes will conjure up images of old trees, dense shrubs, ferocious beasts, and human forms. Inside the cave is a vast grotto, known as the Crystal Palace (*Shuijinggong*), capable of holding up to 1,000 people. According to legend, the stone pillar in the grotto is the Dragon King's magic needle, used as a weapon by the Monkey King in the immensely popular Chinese fable and novel *Journey to the West*. The underground path opens onto a terrace which affords a panoramic view of the surrounding mountains, farmland, and river courses. (A safety note: the footing inside these caves can be extremely slippery, so the use of walking shoes with a deep tread is recommended.)

GUILIN

The town of Guilin

甑皮岩洞
Zengpiyan Cave. Some 10,000 years ago, this cave was actually the site of a Stone Age village. Excavations began here in 1973, and the cave was opened to tourists in 1979. Archeologists believe that this was originally the site of a matriarchal community. Later it was a burial ground. Of the human remains unearthed here, 14 skeletons were preserved intact. Most had been buried in a flexed or squatting position. The skeletons of a large number of wild animals were also uncovered, including boar, deer, Asian elephants, palm civets, and Tibetan goat antelopes (serows).

敬国寺
Venerate the Country Temple. A small museum containing artifacts from the great Taiping Rebellion and memorabilia of Dr. Sun Yatsen is located underneath Elephant Trunk Hill. The collection is limited (and labeled almost exclusively in Chinese), but there is some interesting material which provides a glimpse of history from a Chinese perspective.

中国国际旅行社
CITS (Luxingshe) Office in Guilin ■ 14 Ronghu Bei Road. Tel: 2475/2936
Cable: 0948. Telex: 48460 GLITS CN.

漓江畅游
LI RIVER CRUISE

***

Visitors board a one- or two-deck pleasure boat at 8:30 AM for a spectacular five-hour cruise along the winding Li River. The boats travel approximately 25 km. down the river, then turn back to dock at the small village of Yangdi. Every boat load of tourists is met by hundreds of local peasants, all eager to profit by selling whatever they can to the foreigners. In late autumn, when the low water level makes navigation difficult, visitors are driven to Yangdi, where they then board a boat for the trip downstream to Yangshuo.

Legend tells us that every sailor drowned in the Li is transformed into a demon, clutching at the boats which navigate the rapids. As the launch floats past valleys, bamboo groves, and mist-shrouded crags, one has the sensation of being carried backwards in time through a traditional Chinese painting. Local river craft are still physically towed upstream in convoys.

Along the way, famous rock formations come into view: **Elephant Trunk Hill**, just outside Guilin, suggests an elephant drinking from the river; **Old Man Mountain** resembles the head and neck of a man in profile; and the varicolored veins on the rock face of **Mural Hill**, also known as Nine Horse Hill, resemble horses in different poses.

The boat passes through the Luogu Rapids. Further along looms **Folded Brocade Hill,** with its multicolored vegetation, and **Crescent Moon Hill,** whose summit contains a cave shaped like a half moon. The two-hour bus ride back to Guilin from Yangdi (or Yangshuo) provides a fleeting glimpse of typical Guangxi countryside.

HOTEL ACCOMMODATIONS

漓江饭店
Lijiang Hotel (1 Shanhu Bei Road; tel: 2881 or 5991; cable: 0044; telex: 48470 GLLIR CN). The Lijiang (Li River) Hotel is the most conveniently located and most stately hotel in Guilin, though the service tends to be haphazard. The 14-story, 360-room hotel is within easy walking distance of the main shopping district and has an unrivaled view of the city and surrounding mountains. Facilities include a gift shop, carpet store, bank, and post office. There are two restaurants, one for groups on the first floor and another for individuals on the second, and the food is usually very good in both. The coffee shop and bar, located on the 13th floor, are open from 7 PM–11 PM. A disco, replete with flashing lights and raucous music, is on the 14th floor. Admission is Y3.

喜来登 — 桂林文华大饭店
Sheraton Guilin Hotel (Bingjiang Nan Road; tel: 223855/225588; telex: 48439 GLMAN CN). Opened in March 1988, the Sheraton Guilin

Hotel is situated on the banks of the Lijiang River, within walking distance of Elephant Trunk Hill. Formerly called the Mandarin, it is about 20 minutes from the airport and two blocks from downtown. The 493 rooms, including 18 suites, offer air-conditioning, color television, minibar, and in-house music. Hotel features include Chinese and Western restaurants, three lounges, and Guilin's first scenic "bullet" elevators. For recreation, there is an Olympic-size swimming pool, fully-equipped health club with sauna, Jacuzzi, billiard and table-tennis rooms. Business center and conference and meeting rooms, with capacity to 250 are also available. *Rates:* Single: $75–85; double: $85–90, $110–180.

假日桂林宾馆

Holiday Inn Guilin (14 South Ronghu Road; tel: 3950; telex: 48456 GLHCL CN). Set on the Li River beyond the din of city traffic, the modern Holiday Inn promises to emerge quickly as Guilin's hotel-of-choice. Opened in early 1987, the 259-room hotel offers all major facilities and services of an international-class hotel.

The Holiday Inn accepts direct booking (telex: 48456 GLHCL or cable: 6333 or reservations may be placed through the world-wide Holiday Inn system). *Rates:* Single: US$112; double: US$164.

丹桂饭店

Guilin Osmanthus Hotel (451 Zhongshan South Road; tel: 2261/ 5316; cable: 0030). Guilin's largest hotel consists mainly of a modern new high-rise attached to an older facility. The new Osmanthus boasts 400 guest rooms, equipped with closed-circuit TV, air-conditioning, refrigerators, and radios. Hotel amenities include a swimming pool (rare for Guilin) and disco. The hotel's dining rooms specialize in Cantonese and Western cuisine.

Reservations can be made by contacting the hotel direct (telex: 48455 GLOSH) or through the Vista International system.

榕城饭店

Rongcheng Hotel (San Li Dian, Eastern Suburb; tel: 2311/4881; cable: 1004; telex: 48447 GLRCH CN). Located in peaceful surroundings near Seven Star Hill, the Rongcheng is among Guilin's newest hotels. All rooms are air-conditioned. Amenities include restaurants, a bank, a post office, and a gift shop.

榕湖饭店

Banyan Lake Hotel (17 Ronghu Bei Road; tel: 3811/2647; telex: 48461 GLRHU CN). The Banyan Lake (Ronghu) Hotel qualifies as the preferred place to stay in Guilin. It is located within a walled compound adjacent to Banyan Lake, about a 10-minute walk from the center of Guilin. The hotel has eight buildings, four of which are generally reserved for visiting heads of state and other dignitaries. All the rooms are air-conditioned and comfortable, though occasionally mouse infested. Facilities include a gift shop, money exchange, and hairdresser.

甲山饭店
Jiashan Hotel (near the Reed Flute Cave; tel: 2986/4712; telex: 48459 GLJSH CN). Opened in 1981, the 300-room hotel was built as a joint venture between China and Australia. It consists of three identical (and rapidly deteriorating) prefabricated steel compounds. The quality is reminiscent of a cheap motel in the rural Southwest—peeling veneer furniture, paper-thin walls, and warped door and window jams. Rooms are small, but have TVs and refrigerators. Facilities include a gift shop, bank, post office, late-night snack bar, and hairdresser. The hotel is located at about a 20-minute drive from the center of Guilin and is pleasantly surrounded by hills and fields.

漓苑宾馆
Guilin Riverside Resort (Anjiazhou; tel: 4633/3586; cable: 5031; telex: 48457 GLRSR CN). All 236 rooms and suites at Guilin Riverside Resort have air-conditioning, private bath, television, and mini-bar and overlook either the river or nearby farmland. The hotel offers Chinese and Western restaurants, café and bar, a tennis court, outdoor swimming pool and whirlpool, shopping arcade, and leisure river rafting.

桂林花园酒店
The Ramada Renaissance Hotel (Yuanjiang Road; tel: 2611/3611; telex: 48468), opened in 1987, has 354 rooms, while an additional 450 rooms will be added by 1990. All rooms have air-conditioning, television, videos, refrigerators, and a mini-bar. The property has a garden atrium with a waterfall, an outdoor swimming pool overlooking the Li River, two tennis courts, and a full-service health club with sauna and massage.

隐山饭店
Hidden Hill Hotel (97 South Zhongshan Rd.; tel: 333540; cable: 7148). Conveniently located next to the railroad station, the Hidden Hill has 79 double (Y45–Y55) and five single (Y40) rooms, all with air-conditioning and private bath.

桂山饭店
Guishan Hotel (Chuanshan Road; tel: 44378; telex: 48443 GSHTL CN). New in 1988, the Guishan overlooks the Li River. The 610 rooms in this first-class hotel are complemented by eight restaurants and lounges, a swimming pool, billiard room, bowling alley, business center, tennis courts, and ballroom facilities. Direct reservations through New World Hotels of Hong Kong or China Express in San Francisco. Rates range from $70 for a standard to $400 for a suite.

桂林悦华饭店
Guilin Mandarin. This joint venture of Tai Hing Promotion of Hong Kong and the Qigong Hotel Organization of Guilin opened in 1988. The 500-room hotel is deluxe standard, with Cantonese and Western restaurants, Olympic-sized swimming pool, and a health center.

香港桂林饭店
Hong Kong Hotel Guilin. Managed by Pearl Hotels International of Hong Kong, the Hong Kong Hotel Guilin has 300 rooms. Open since May

1988, its facilities include tennis courts, bowling alleys, health club and jacuzzi, snooker tables, a disco, and a revolving restaurant.

Two lower-priced, but adequate hotels are located on Zhongshan Zhong Road, the main street of the city. These are the South Brook Hotel (Nanxi Fandian) and the Guilin Hotel (tel: 2249). The Taihe Hotel (427 Zhongshan Nan Road; tel: 5720) and the Mandarin Hotel (Binjiang Road; tel: 5713; telex: 48339 GLMAN CN) also receive foreigners.

Budget-minded travelers may be tempted to stay in Yangshuo, just outside Guilin, in the mountains. The same Li River cruises are accessible and for a lower price than in tourist-laden Guilin. A bus trip from Guilin takes 90 minutes, costing Y2. Yangshuo has many pleasant hotels for a fraction of the cost to stay in Guilin proper. Among the best is Qingnian Fandian, which offers hot showers all day, for only Y8 per night, and reportedly makes the best omelettes in town.

Shopping. Downtown Guilin offers one of the best opportunities in China to wander through ordinary hardware stores, pharmacies, and other shops along with local people. The residents are accustomed enough to foreigners that you will not draw a crowd, and almost all shopkeepers now speak a smattering of English and Japanese. The main street of the city is Zhongshan Road, which crosses the Li River and is divided into three sections: south, north, and central. On the corner of Zhongshan Zhong (Central) Road and Shahu Nan (South) Road, near the Li River Bridge, is the department store, open daily from 9 AM to 9 PM, where you can buy a wide range of toiletries and other necessities. Next door is the Friendship Store, which is not worth visiting.

On the other side of Zhongshan Zhong Road, take the first right after the Guilin Restaurant and you will find a large "free market." Here the shops are lined with wooden stalls where vendors sell clothing, children's toys, and household goods. Further down the main street is the Guilin Bookstore, which has a large selection of books in Chinese.

If you go to the left of the bridge at the intersection of Zhongshan Zhong Road and Shahu Bei Road, there is an arts and crafts store. Continuing along, there are several excellent bakeries and a large pharmacy. On Shahu Bei Road, near the Li River Hotel, there are an ever increasing number of stores designed specifically for tourists.

Cuisine. Guilin is famous for the variety of peculiar foods consumed there. The most innocuous local offerings are the thick chili sauce and fermented bean curd. Among the most well known are pangolin (also called scaly anteater); bamboo rat, which only looks like a rat and eats bamboo; lynx, and tortoise stew with duck eggs. The above fare is regularly available at the Tonglai Guan Restaurant (Zhongshan Zhong Road; tel: 3449).

Guiyang

prize the sun　　　　　　　　　　　　　*traditional spelling: Kuei-yang*

GUIYANG, the capital of Guizhou, one of China's poorest provinces, was fully opened to foreign tourists only in 1985. In this city of 1.3 million, broad post-1949 thoroughfares and apartment blocks are interspersed with ramshackle wooden and stone dwellings (the latter found mainly outside of town). Like nearby Guilin, Guiyang sits in a basin nestled among imposing karst formations. The nearby countryside is quite hilly and rock-strewn, and the wheat, rice, and tea grown here are planted in terraced fields that extend to the hilltops. Several minorities inhabit the area, with the Miao and Buyi peoples most in evidence. The women don their traditional costumes even when laboring in the fields; but the men generally do not wear distinctive clothing. Buyi women wear several wraparound aprons of various colors and patterns. They have elaborate hairdos pulled off to the sides of their heads, and usually don caps. Miao women wear long, dark dresses and pointed hats.

Not unlike Kunming, Guiyang enjoys a mild climate, with a range of −2° to 32°C. It lies on major railway lines and is easily accessible from Kunming, Guilin, Chongqing, and Changsha. Air service is available but flights are infrequent and difficult to book.

► HIGHLIGHTS
► FOR TRAVELERS

黔灵公园

Qianling Park (Soul of Guizhou) is located in the northwest part of the city, on the #1 and #2 bus lines. "Qian" is an abbreviation for Guizhou Province. The park has a zoo, some caves, and a martyr's monument. There is a long tunnel, originally built against air raids, that ends up at Qianling Lake, at which point boats can be rented.

弘福寺

Hongfusi (Great Happiness Temple) is situated halfway up the Qianling Hill in Qianling Park. This is an undistinguished Zen Buddhist Temple built in the early Qing. Continue walking up the hill behind

Climate		Jan	Feb	Mar	Apr	May	Jun	Jul	Aug	Sep	Oct	Nov	Dec
Temp.	°C	9.6	11.0	14.4	17.8	19.3	19.5	20.1	19.8	18.3	15.7	12.7	10.2
	°F	49.2	51.8	57.9	64	66.7	67.1	68.1	67.6	64.9	60.2	54.8	50.3
Precip.	mm.	8	18	28	41	127	132	196	198	97	51	56	15
	in.	.3	.7	1.1	1.6	5	5.2	7.7	7.8	3.8	2	2.2	.6

the main hall to the Kanzhu Pavilion. "Zhu" is the abbreviated name for Guiyang, and this spot affords an excellent view of the entire city and the karst formations surrounding it.

花溪公园

Huaxi Park lies 17 km. southwest of the city proper. At the Hebin Park, catch an unnumbered bus with the character 郊 (suburbs) on the front. It's a ride of 40 minutes to the main entrance of the park. Dating to the 10th century, this is a lovely park in a Guilin-like setting of karst hills, streams, and greenery. You can row boats, hike, and have lunch here. Be sure to climb Linshan for a magnificent view of the area. Many minorities live near the park and frequent it. The Huaxi Guesthouse (Biyunwo) is on the grounds.

南郊公园

Nanjiao Park is on the same road as Huaxi Park. Catch the bus returning to Guiyang from Huaxi and get off at the Taiciqiao stop. There is a highly irregular shuttle bus that takes visitors to the park entrance. But the 20-minute walk along a stream (that gets progressively cleaner as one nears the reservoir at its source) is pleasant, and the reservoir is open for swimming. You pay 20 *fen* to enter the Bailong (White Dragon) Cave. Forty-minute tours through the 600-m.-long cave start every 20 minutes. Opened in 1965, it is characterized by fanciful formations and pools. Visitors exit into Nanjiao Park from where they walk back to the main entrance.

甲秀楼

Jiaxiu Lou (Number One Scholar Pavilion). This graceful building was built in the Ming to encourage scholars. It sits astride the brackish Nanming River, near the Post and Telecommunications Building. There is a small exhibit inside.

河滨公园

Hebin (Riverside) Park. This inner-city park lies on major bus lines. Undistinguished except for the Azalea Hall, which is located by the river, it is the scene of nightly dance parties. Tickets for the dance may be purchased at the main entrance to the park.

黄果树和龙宫

Huangguoshu Waterfall and Longgong (Dragon Cave) are located in Zhenning Buyi-Miao Autonomous County. Although public transportation from Guiyang or the large city of Anshun is available, groups of 10 or more would do better to contact CITS for day trips to both places. From Guiyang, the waterfall is 150 km. away and the cave, 130 km. The opportunity to see the striking countryside and small towns along the way alone makes the excursion worthwhile. There is a batik factory in Anshun which can be visited on request. A tasty lunch is available at the waterfall.

Huangguoshu is China's largest waterfall, reaching a height of 74 meters and falling into Rhinoceros Pool. For 50 *fen*, you can traverse the Cascade Veiled Cave behind the waterfall for a thrilling perspective.

Dragon Cave is toured in a boat rowed by a guide who points out interesting rock formations. One can either return to the entrance by the same boat, for a fee, or take a strenuous hike up and down hills.

HOTEL ACCOMMODATIONS

There are three hotels open to foreigners, all badly in need of remodelling.

金桥饭店
Jinqiao Hotel (26 Ruijin Road; tel: 24872/23867). This is a typical Soviet-style hotel. The Jinqiao is Guiyang's most central hotel, right on bus lines #1 and #2. There is a small shop and a decent restaurant. CITS has its main office here.

云岩饭店
Yunyan Hotel (36 Beijing Road; tel: 23564/23324). In a more tranquil setting, replete with pond, the Yunyan is near the provincial government's offices, and the city's most famous restaurant, the Qianyang.

花溪宾馆
Huaxi Guesthouse (also called the Biyunwo—at Huaxi Park; tel: 25973/32969). Remote, but quiet and in a beautiful setting. Rooms cost about twice as much as at the other hotels.

CUISINE

Guiyang cuisine is basically the same as Sichuan cuisine. The best restaurant outside the hotels is the **Qianyang Canting**, at the corner of Beijing Road and Zhonghua Road, near the Yunyan Hotel; tel: 22451.

贵阳饭店
The **Guiyang Fandian** serves local specialties at 170 Zhonghua Road; tel: 25512.

小上海餐厅
The **Xiao Shanghai** (Little Shanghai) serves reasonable Shanghainese fare, and is on one of the main shopping streets (the other is Zhonghua Road), 105 Zhongshan Road; tel: 24698.

中国国际旅行社
CITS (Luxingshe) Office in Guiyang ■ 7 Yan'an Zhong Rd. Tel: 29693/25121

海南島 Hainan Island

south-of-the-sea island   *traditional spelling/Hainantao*

HAINAN Island, an island with palm-fringed beaches, luxuriant forests, and exotic tribal communities, is China's closest approximation of a tropical paradise. It lies 48 km. (30 mi.) off the Leizhou Peninsula in southern Guangdong Province, about one hour by plane from Guangzhou and four hours by bus and ferry from Jiangmen. With an area of 34,000 sq. km. (13,000 sq. mi.) and a population of 5.8 million, Hainan ranks as China's second-largest offshore island.

The Limu Ling Mountains running down the center of Hainan from the northeast to the southeast are covered with dense tropical forests on their higher reaches—one of the major remaining timber stands in China, and a source of rare woods such as ebony and rosewood. Bamboo, fruit trees, and a variety of flowering bushes also grow on the island. In addition to timber, Hainan's natural resources include some 50 kinds of minerals (principally titanium, iron, rock crystal) and considerable hydroelectric power from harnessing the Sun and Nandu rivers on the western side of the island. Offshore oil deposits recently discovered at Yinggehai, off the southwestern coast of Hainan, may also prove important.

On the fertile coastal plains, rice, sugarcane, tobacco, cotton, coffee, rubber, and various tropical fruits are intensively cultivated. Fishing has always been an important means of livelihood. And since 1949, machine building, sugar refining, and food processing industries have been developed.

At present, large stretches of Hainan's southern shore are barren and deforested. In the last few years, however, the Chinese have been actively seeking foreign investment, especially from Hong Kong, with a view to developing the tourist industry, as well as dairy farms, fish hatcheries, and fruit plantations in the area. To expedite this development, Hainan was accorded status similar to that of the 14 Coastal Open Cities (in 1984). The new economic policies came under a shadow, however, with the unfolding, in August 1985, of a corruption scandal involving millions of dollars worth of smuggled Japanese cars and trucks.

HAINAN IN HISTORY

The original inhabitants of Hainan were the Li and Miao minorities who settled the island's northern coast, an area called Zhuya (Shore of Pearls). Beginning in the Song and Tang dynasties, Han Chinese officials and others

Climate		Jan	Feb	Mar	Apr	May	Jun	Jul	Aug	Sep	Oct	Nov	Dec
Temp.	°C	13.1	13.8	17.5	21.9	25.8	27.1	28.3	28.2	27.0	23.8	19.8	15.2
	°F	55	56.8	63.5	71.4	78.4	80.7	82.9	82.7	80.6	74.8	67.6	59.3
Precip.	mm.	152	203	254	279	381	508	457	406	330	203	152	127
	in.	6	8	10	11	15	20	18	16	13	8	6	5

who incurred displeasure at the imperial court were sent into exile on Hainan.

With the discovery of rose quartz deposits on the island, Hainan became commonly known as Qiongzhou (Rose-jeweled Kingdom). The name still survives in the name of a number of towns and counties on Hainan's eastern shore: Qiongshan, Qionghai, and Qiongzhong.

During China's civil war, Communist forces took refuge in the mountains of Hainan, where they were helped by the Li and Miao peoples who, by then, had moved to the higher reaches of the island. After 1949, overseas Chinese from Malaysia and Indonesia settled in Hainan; in recent years, they have been joined by thousands of refugees from Vietnam who now work on the vast state farms reserved for overseas Chinese.

HIGHLIGHTS FOR TRAVELERS

Hainan is divided into several large counties, each with its distinctive population mix and geographic characteristics. On the island's north shore is Haikou, the largest town and the economic and cultural center of Hainan. Located at the estuary of the Nandu River, Haikou handles the bulk of Hainan's commerce with the mainland. Five Lord Temple in Haikou is a memorial to some of the most famous exiles the island has known: Su Dongpo, the great Song Dynasty poet; his son, Su Guo; Li Deyu, who served as prime minister under the Tang; Lu Tosun, a Northern Song poet; and Ding Wei, a poet of the mid-11th century.

West of Haikou is the huge Songtao Reservoir, completed in 1969. It has a catchment area of 1,440 sq. km. (555 sq. mi.). To Haikou's east, in the area originally named the "Shore of Pearls," is Xincun Commune. Populated almost exclusively by the Danjia (Tanha) minority, Xincun thrives on fishing and the cultured pearl industry.

In Yaxian county, on Hainan's southern shore, is the port of Sanya. The harbor at Sanya can accommodate coastal craft of up to 800 tons and handles shipping coming from Hong Kong. Near Sanya is the popular holiday resort of Luhuitou (Deer Turns Around), a wide stretch of beach set off by pine groves. A number of guest houses in the area consist of detached bungalows set in palm-studded compounds facing the sea—a setting reminiscent of the South Pacific.

Inland from Sanya is Tongzha, the county seat of the Li and Miao Autonomous Area created by the Chinese government after 1949, partly with a view to encouraging minority cultural traditions. About 40 km. (25 mi.) west of Sanya is Yazhen, a farming commune with a population of 27,000 people. When the 8th-century Buddhist monk Jian Zhen set sail from Yangzhou for Japan to propagate the faith, he was driven south by storms at sea on his fifth voyage and took refuge in the harbor of what is now Yazhen for two months before continuing on his travels.

A heap of gigantic granite boulders on the road between Sanya and Yazhen is inscribed with the names "Heaven's Limit" and "The Sea's Margin." The legend attached to these rocks says that the fisher folk who lived in the area in ancient times were persecuted by marauding pirates until, one day, a heavenly eagle appeared and dropped a shower of rocks on the pirates' boats, thus saving the local populace.

HOTEL ACCOMMODATIONS

During the late 1980s, several new hotel/resort complexes were under development on Hainan mainly to support an influx of regional tourism from Hong Kong, Macau, and Japan. A string of older Chinese-style hotels and guest houses exist throughout the island. Among the new hotels in Haikou, whose rooms are expected to double the tourist capacity in Hainan, are: the Overseas Chinese Guesthouse, Haikou Guesthouse, Qiongzhou Hotel, Haikou International Financial Hotel, and Wanghai International Hotel. The following are newer establishments commonly frequented by touring foreigners:

泰华酒店
Haikou Tower Hotel (Binhai Road, Haikou; tel: 86750, 23990; telex: 45050 TOWER CN). This new 240-room complex is situated on the sea, 10 minutes from the airport and central Haikou. Rooms have telephones, closed-circuit TVs, mini bars, refrigerators, and central air-conditioning. Facilities include two swimming pools, tennis courts, and a delightful jogging trail. The ballroom seats up to 500 for banquets or conferences.

Rates: Twins: superior, HK$270; seaview, HK$300.

叶庄宾馆
Yezhuang Guest House (Dadong Beach, Luhuitou—2 km. southeast of Sanya). See description preceding page.

通扎渡假村
Tongzha Villa Resort (Li and Miao Autonomous District, Tongzha). Located in a mountain valley on the central route traversing the island, the Tongzha Villa is an ultramodern resort designed to take advantage of surrounding mountain air and scenery. Guestrooms are large, bright, and comfortable. The restaurant specializes in local game. The Tongzha may be booked through its Hong Kong office (tel: 3-659003; telex: 57869 STT HX).

兴隆渡假中心
Xinglong Resort Center (Xinglong Hot Spring, Xinglong). Situated in a secluded area on the southeast coast, the Xinglong offers private villas in the midst of tropical forests and plantations. Bookings are available through Hong Kong (tel: 3-659003; telex: 57869 STT HX).

Hangzhou

city across the river   *traditional spelling/Hangchow*

INTRODUCING Hangzhou to visitors, Chinese guides inevitably quote the popular expression, "Above there is heaven, below there are Hangzhou and Suzhou." Hangzhou's "heavenly" beauty attracts hundreds of thousands of tourists—Chinese as well as foreign—to its exquisite Xi Hu (West Lake) vicinity each year, to enjoy the placid lake, beautiful gardens, reflecting pools, lavish temples, and friendly lakeside teahouses. Although West Lake is the main attraction, the graceful city of Hangzhou itself is also well worth a visit.

The capital of Zhenjiang Province and a prosperous industrial and agricultural center, Hangzhou is situated on the Qiantang River at the southern end of the Grand Canal. It occupies an area of 429 sq. km. (166 sq. mi.) with a population of about one million.

In recent years, increasing numbers of Westerners have visited Hangzhou—only 5,000 in all of 1977, but more than 2,000 per day by 1981. This is in part due to the excellent flight connections from Beijing, Guangzhou, Nanjing, and Hong Kong. The city is only a three-hour train ride from Shanghai. It is possible, therefore, for those with limited time to take an early train down and a late one back and thus absorb some of Hangzhou's sights in one day.

HANGZHOU IN HISTORY

According to legend, the great King Yu, who harnessed China's river systems and thereby succeeded in controlling floods, came here in 2198 BC—hence Hangzhou's original name, Yuhang, which means "Yu's boat crossing." But it was the extension of the Grand Canal southward from the Yangtse River late in the 6th century AD that transformed Hangzhou from a sleepy fishing village into a bustling commercial center. The first city walls were built in 606 by Yang Suo, who also gave the city its present name.

Hangzhou's continued growth was assured as the fertile lower Yangtse Valley supplanted the North China Plain as the country's prime agricultural region. Between the 8th and 12th centuries, it was the capital of several kingdoms and dynasties. Although the city was devastated by the Mongol invasion in the late 13th century, its importance did not diminish. Its role as a trade center and the splendor of its religious monuments continued to attract merchants and visitors from all over the world (including Marco Polo).

Climate

		Jan	Feb	Mar	Apr	May	Jun	Jul	Aug	Sep	Oct	Nov	Dec
Temp.	°C	3.5	4.7	9.2	15.2	20.6	23.9	28.7	28.4	23.8	17.6	12.2	5.9
	°F	38.3	40.4	48.5	59.3	69	75	83.6	83.1	74.8	63.6	53.9	42.6
Precip.	mm.	254	254	330	330	305	356	279	279	305	254	203	178
	in.	10	10	13	13	12	14	11	11	12	10	8	7

① Solitary Hill (Gu Shan)

② Precious Stone Hill
   (Baoshi Shan)

③ Great Buddha Temple (Dafo Si)

④ Zhejiang Province Exhibition Hall

⑤ Hangzhou Friendship Store

⑥ Antiques Store

⑦ Zhejiang Province Library

⑧ China Liberation Monument

⑨ Department Store

⑩ Branch of Xinhua (New China) Bookstore

⑪ Wu Mountain

⑫ Fenghuang Mountain

⑬ Yuhuang Mountain

⑭ Qiantang Bridge

⑮ Six Harmonies Pagoda (Liuhe Ta)

⑯ Running Tiger Cave
   (Hupaodong)

⑰ Nanping Hill

⑱ Rosy Cloud Mountain (Yanxia Shan)

⑲ Rosy Cloud Cave (Yanxiadong)

⑳ Water Pleasure Cave (Shuiledong)

㉑ Stone House Cave (Shihudong)

㉒ Viewing Fish at the Flower Stream
   (Huagang Guanyu)

㉓ Dragon Well (Longjing) Temple

㉔ Tianzhu Mountain

㉕ Shangtianzhu Mountain

㉖ Zhongtianzhu Mountain

㉗ Xiatianzhu Mountain

㉘ Peak that Flew from Afar (Feilai Feng)

㉙ Northern High Peak (Beigao Feng)

㉚ Monastery of the Spirits' Retreat (Lingyin Si)

㉛ Botanical Garden

㉜ Zhejiang Hospital

㉝ Jade Spring (Yuquan)•

㉞ Hangzhou University

㉟ Geling Hill and Tomb of Yue Fei

㊱ Yellow Dragon Cave (Huanglongdong)

㊲ Purple Cloud Cave (Ziyundong)

㊳ Autumn Moon and the Calm Lake

㊴ Mid-Lake Pavilion (Huxinting)

㊵ Three Pools Mirroring the Moon (Santanyinyue)

 Restaurants

 Hotels

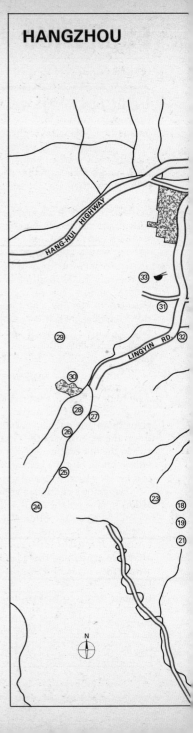

HANGZHOU

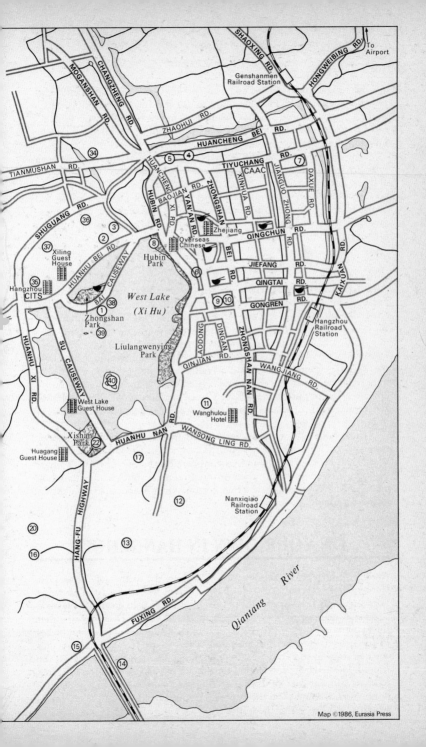

To Airport

SHAOXING RD.

HONGWEIBING RD.

Genshanmen
Railroad Station

MOGANSHAN RD.

CHANGZHENG RD.

ZHAOHUI RD.

HUANCHENG BEI RD.

RD.

③④

TIANMUSHAN RD.

⑤ ④

TIYUCHANG

CAAC

⑦

DAXUE RD.

HUANCHENG XI RD.

HUBIN RD.

BAOJIAN RD.

YAN'AN RD.

ZHONGSHAN RD.

XINHUA RD.

JIANGUO ZHONG RD.

SHUGUANG RD.

③⑥

③

②

Xiling
Guest
House ③⑦

HUANHU BEI RD.

⑧

Hubin
Park

Overseas
Chinese

Zhejiang

BEI

QINGCHUN RD.

JIEFANG RD.

KAIXUAN RD.

Hangzhou
CITS ③⑤

①

Zhongshan
Park

③⑧

BAI CAUSEWAY

⑥

RD.

QINGTAI RD.

⑨⑩

GONGREN RD.

Hangzhou
Railroad
Station

③⑨

West Lake
(Xi Hu)

Liulangwenying
Park

AODONG RD.

DINGAN RD.

QINJIAN RD.

ZHONGSHAN NAN RD.

HUANHU XI RD.

SU CAUSEWAY

④⓪

West Lake
Guest House

WANGJIANG RD.

⑪

Wanghulou
Hotel

Xishan
Park ②②

HUANHU NAN RD.

WANSONG LING RD.

Huagang
Guest House

⑰

HANG-FU HIGHWAY

⑫

Nanxiqiao
Railroad
Station

②⓪

⑬

①⑥

Qiantang River

FUXING RD.

①⑤

①④

Map ©1986, Eurasia Press

Hangzhou's political and commercial significance was dramatically curtailed in the mid-19th century as a result of the Taiping Rebellion. Much of the city was reduced to ashes, many of its most venerable religious structures were damaged or destroyed, and thousands of its inhabitants were killed in the course of the ensuing turmoil.

The local guides take pride in pointing out that the city has been virtually rebuilt since 1949. Until then, it had only a few small factories and one cotton textile mill. After the Great Leap Forward (1958), capital construction began on a massive scale. Today, old, crowded houses are overshadowed by newly constructed apartment buildings. As the Chinese say, the city has taken on "a new look," but the downtown shopping area retains its traditional charm.

ECONOMY AND CULTURE

Although industry came relatively late to Hangzhou, the pace of progress has been rapid. Before 1949, the estimated size of the work force for the 33 small-scale factories and one large silk mill was 5,000. Today, industrial workers comprise nearly one-third of the population. The value of the city's industrial output has doubled since 1965 and is reported to have increased 24-fold since 1949. The city now boasts an iron and steel mill, machine tool factories, petrochemical and oil refining facilities, and an electronics industry. The Xinan River Hydroelectric Power Station, situated on the upper reaches of the Qiantang River, has a capacity of 650,000 kw. Power generators, light trucks, and small tractors are also manufactured in Hangzhou.

Hangzhou's silk industry, established in the 7th century, is famous throughout China. Green Longjing (Dragon Well) tea, produced at the West Lake People's Commune, is considered to be one of China's finest varieties. Important crops raised in the rural areas surrounding Hangzhou include bamboo, wheat, barley, rice, cotton, and sweet potatoes, in addition to silkworms and tea leaves.

ON YOUR OWN IN HANGZHOU

Arrival. If arriving by train, proceed to the right to the soft berth exit. Here you can call for a cab, and have a cup of the famous local Longjing (Dragon Well) tea while you wait. An alternative is to go straight outside and begin negotiating with the pedicab drivers. It's not very far to either the Hangzhou Hotel or the Overseas Chinese Hotel (two of the best places to stay), so it shouldn't be more than a few yuan. You can also take bus #7 five stops to the Overseas Chinese Hotel. The #7 also stops down the street from the Hangzhou Hotel (but not directly in front). It is a good line to know, since it goes all the way to Lingyin Temple and passes other sites on the way. Coming from the airport you can take bus #5 to the end, then switch to #27 to get to the hotels.

Getting Around Hangzhou. Bus #27 also goes all the way out to the Longjing Temple and Longjing Commune (where the tea is grown), both interesting places to see. Most of the sites around West Lake can be seen on foot or by renting a boat. For others, you can hire a motorized three-wheeler, a cab, or a pedicab (if you took one from the train, the driver probably tried to talk you into hiring him for the day to do all your sightseeing). A special tourist shuttle bus operates between Longjing Temple and the zoo, stopping at some of the famous caves along the way. CTS (in the Overseas Chinese Hotel) has one- and two-day packages. CITS (in the Hangzhou Hotel) sells train tickets to other cities.

HIGHLIGHTS
FOR TRAVELERS

丝厂

Silk Factories. Zhejiang Province's extensive tracts of mulberry trees supply the filatures of Hangzhou with China's finest quality silkworm cocoons. In order to watch the process of manufacturing silk and its products, visitors are invited to one of Hangzhou's two major silk complexes. By far the largest such establishment in the city is the Hangzhou Silk Dyeing and Printing Mill, established in 1958, where 4,700 workers engage in the various stages of production, from reeling silk fiber off the cocoons to printing designs on the finished fabric. Silk is produced here both for export throughout the world and for domestic consumption.

At the smaller Hangzhou Brocade Factory, established in 1922, 1,700 workers design and weave brocade tablecloths, bedspreads, sofa covers, and wall hangings—favorite gift and souvenir items purchased by foreigners in Friendship Stores across the country.

西湖人民公社

West Lake People's Commune. Plum Family Village and Double Peak Tea Production are the brigades most frequently visited by foreigners at West Lake. The commune's major product is its exclusive, renowned Longjing (Dragon Well) tea. Three crops are harvested annually—spring, summer, and autumn—but the spring leaves are considered to be the most delicate. Depending on the season, visitors are occasionally invited to try their hand at tea-leaf picking. Drying, formerly done over burning firewood, has been modernized with the introduction of drying machines. The highest quality Longjing tea leaves are still processed by hand, however. In the brigade workshops one can watch the unprocessed leaves being transformed into the finished product.

Longjing tea brigade, West Lake People's Commune

杭州动物园

Hangzhou Zoo. Hangzhou's new zoo was completed in 1975 and features skillful re-creations of natural environments that house more than 100 kinds of animals and birds. Among them are giant pandas, gold-striped and black-leaf monkeys, and Manchurian tigers.

西湖

WEST LAKE

The focal point of a visit to Hangzhou is West Lake, an area of striking beauty. Originally a shallow bay adjoining the Qiantang River, it was gradually transformed into an inland lake by the silting-up of the outlet.

The first dike was built in AD 821 by the poet Bai Juyi. About AD 1090, another famous poet, Su Dongpo (1037–1101), who served as the prefect of Hangzhou during the Northern Song Dynasty (960–1127), had the lake bottom dredged and created some formal gardens along the shore.

He also had a second dike built along the western margin. These two dikes—the Bai and the Su—still stand today, and serve to divide the lake into three parts.

After AD 1130, West Lake became the residence of the Southern Song emperors. The great Qing Dynasty (1644–1911) emperors Kang Xi and Qian Long expanded the lake to its present proportions. They loved the area so much that they built "Hangzhou-style" pavilions and temples all over northern China (Beijing and Chengde both have good examples of this architectural influence).

There are four islands on West Lake, the largest of which is Gu Shan (Solitary Hill), in the northwest.

NORTH SHORE

孤山

Solitary Hill Island. Linked to the north shore by a bridge and to the east shore by the willow- and peach-tree-lined Bai Juyi Causeway, the island was originally landscaped during the Tang Dynasty (618–907), when its first pavilion was built. Its name is misleading, for the island has become a favorite spot for visitors. The famous Autumn Moon and Calm Lake Pavilion, used as a study retreat by Qing emperor Kang Xi (r. 1662–1722), derives its name from its striking appearance in the clear and silvery moonlight of autumn. Other places of interest on Gu Shan include the Crane Pavilion, the Zhenjiang Provincial Museum (consisting of a small botanical garden and exhibits on physical geography, popular arts, and history), the Seal Engravers Club, and the Zhejiang Library. Additions since 1949 include the Octagonal and Quadrangular pavilions.

弯院风荷

Lotus in the Breeze at the Crooked Courtyard. This poetic name refers to a modern pavilion and small park directly facing the Hangzhou Hotel. At night the benches at this romantic spot fill up with lovers.

岳飞墓

Tomb of Yue Fei. Yue Fei was a famous Song Dynasty (960–1279) general who defended China against northern invaders. His tomb, built at the spot where he was executed, was badly damaged during the Cultural Revolution, but restoration began in 1978. The first phase of the restoration project included the tomb itself, the memorial hall, the pavilion sheltering the pine stump where Yue Fei was beheaded, and a gallery of stone carvings.

宝石山

Precious Stone Hill. This is the most prominent hill on the north side of the lake, with an altitude of 200 m. (656 ft.). The hill is famous for its oddly shaped boulders, the inspiration for an assortment of legends. A prehistoric cave, Chuanqing, contains stone furniture and a seven-story pagoda originally erected in the 10th century and rebuilt in 1933.

Tai Ji Quan *in the morning mist, West Lake*

葛岭

Geling Hill. At the summit of this hill, which rises just behind the Hangzhou Hotel, is the Daybreak Terrace, where one can enjoy not only the sunrise but the best panorama of the lake and the city of Hangzhou.

紫云洞

Purple Cloud Cave (Ziyundong). Of the five caves on the "Mountain on Which Clouds Stay" (Qixia Shan), this one is a favorite place for picnics. The site is surrounded by peach trees and provides a splendid view.

WEST SHORE

苏堤

Su Dongpo Causeway. This north-south causeway, the lake's largest, has six curved bridges (Crossing the Rainbows, Dongpo, Suppressing Dike, Viewing Hills, Locking Waves, and Reflecting Waves).

花港观鱼

Viewing Fish at Flower Harbor. This site is located on the southwestern shore where a small creek formerly emptied into the lake. During the Qing Dynasty, a pavilion was built on the south side and fish were stocked in an artificial pond. The area has since been enlarged to 23 hectares (55 acres) and several lotus ponds have been added.

SOUTH SHORE

三潭印月

Three Pools Mirroring the Moon. This second largest island in the lake is really a series of circular embankments, creating the impression of a "lake within lakes." It is landscaped in typical Chinese style with the Nine-Bend Bridge (actually bent in a series of right angles) linking the islets. There are many small pavilions, terraces, display rocks, and flower beds. Its covered walkways are punctuated by circular windows, each providing a different perspective on the surrounding landscape.

When the poet Su Dongpo was commissioned to dredge and landscape the lake, there were three deep pits here, thought to be occupied by evil spirits. He had a pagoda built over each pit to lock in the spirits so that boats could pass without fear. Each pagoda has four parts: the base, the body, the cap, and a gourd-shaped top with five openings. On moonlit nights the openings are sealed with thin paper and candles are burnt inside the top. The reflection on the lake gives the illusion that many moons are dancing upon the water—hence the island's name.

南平山

Nanping Hill. Built during the Qing Dynasty, the Jingci Temple on Nanping Hill overlooks the south shore of West Lake. Its ceiling contains elaborate painting of cranes and the rooftop is adorned with flying dragons. Just opposite the temple's main entrance are the remains of the Lei Feng Pagoda—the scene of a fairy-tale romance of a scholar and a white snake.

烟霞山

Yanxia Mountain. A number of caves are located on the sides of this hill, including the Yanxia, the Shuile, and the Shi Hu.

EAST SHORE

The eastern shore of the lake boasts a number of parks (Qingbo, Children's, Liulangwenying, and Hubin), with the China Liberation Memorial as the centerpiece. At the hotel for overseas Chinese located on this side of the lake, excursion boats depart and rowboats may be rented.

THE WEST LAKE VICINITY

靈隱寺

Lingyin Temple. This Buddhist temple, founded by the monk Wei Li in AD 326, is the best-known monastery in Hangzhou. It contains two main halls—the Hall of the Four Major Protectors and the Great Buddha Hall.

Inside the first hall is a 200-year-old Maitreya Buddha. At the back, facing out toward the main hall, is a statue of Weituo, chief guardian of the Buddha, carved from the trunk of a camphor tree. It was completed during the Southern Song Dynasty (AD 1127–1279). In the main hall itself stands a 19-m. (62.3-ft.) camphorwood statue of Sakyamuni, the historical Buddha. The same room contains a group sculpture called "Fairy Island," composed of about 150 images. The stone towers flanking the entrance of the main hall contain 10th-century copies of the Buddhist sutras.

Facing the Lingyin Temple monastery is the 219-m. (719-ft.) hill known as "The Peak Flown from Afar." Its slopes and caves are covered with 330 stone carvings from the Five Dynasties period, the Song Dynasty, and the Yuan Dynasty (907–1368). They are the most famous ancient stone carvings south of the Yangtse River.

六和塔

Six Harmonies Pagoda. This pagoda is located at the top of Yuelu Hill, on the north bank of the Qiantang River. Originally built in 970 AD, it was thought that its cosmic force would deflect the huge waves of the powerful tidal bore brought on by the full moon. It also served as a lighthouse for river traffic. Its name refers to the six codes of Buddhism: to observe the harmony of body, of speech, and of thoughts, to abstain from temptation, from uttering opinions, and from accumulating wealth.

The octagonal structure, 60 m. (196 ft.) high, appears from the outside to have 13 stories and from the inside only seven. It is uniquely constructed of a combination of brick and wood. The exterior, which had deteriorated badly since the 17th century, was rebuilt during 1893–1901. The pagoda was repaired and renovated in 1953 and again in 1970.

HOTEL ACCOMMODATIONS

黄龙饭店

Dragon (Huanglong) Hotel (Shuguang Road; tel: 54488; telex: 351048 DRAGN CN; cable: 8083 HANGZHOU; fax: 58090). Opened in September 1987, this new joint-venture luxury hotel is managed by New World Hotels International of Hong Kong. The hotel is near West Lake, below the Yellow Dragon Cave hill. Its 570 rooms and suites are equipped with color television, minibar, and direct-dial telephones. There are three restaurants offering Chinese cuisine, a Western coffee shop, lobby lounge and poolside snack bar. Tennis courts, swimming pool, health club, massage, bicycle and boat rentals, and the Flash Dance Disco are just some of the recreational offerings. The Crystal Palace Ballroom can be used for conferences of up to 500 people. The Business Center provides access to facsimile machines and word processing equipment. Special winter rates available. *Rates:* $70–85 (single or double). Direct bookings or through New World Hotels in Hong Kong and China Express in San Francisco.

杭州大厦

Hangzhou Mansion (1 Wulin Square; tel: 51795; cable: 0280; telex: 351034 HIB CN). Jointly managed with Shoulun Ltd. of Hong Kong, this new hotel is due to open in July 1988. The 29-story building, which overlooks the West Lake, has 139 rooms. All rooms are air-conditioned. Four restaurants and a business center are on the premises. Room rates are Y110–120 (singles/doubles); Y190–280 (suites).

望湖楼

Wanghu (Overlooking the Lake) Hotel (2 W. Huanchen Road; tel: 71024/73027; telex: 351029 OLWH CN; cable: 9980 HZWH). Completed in 1983, this eight-story building is Hangzhou's largest hotel, offering 340 double rooms (Y55–Y80) and 10 suites. The hotel boasts a full array of services, including massage, dancing, and while-you-wait film developing. The Wanghulou stands near Wu Mountain, and, as its name suggests, towers over West Lake.

杭州香格里拉饭店

Shangri-la Hangzhou (78 Beishan Street; tel: 22921; telex: 35005/6 HOTCH CN). Formerly the Hangzhou Hotel, the Shangri-la Hangzhou has been extensively remodeled. This six-story building is located on the bottom of a hill facing West Lake. Its facilities are expansive by PRC standards, with old-fashioned, high-ceilinged rooms, terraces around the dining room, and gardens and its suites and doubles are serviced with air-conditioning, private bath, and closed-circuit television. The third-floor dining room serves both Chinese and Western food. For entertainment, the hotel café offers dancing accompanied by live music.

西冷宾馆

Xiling Guest House (78 Beishan Rd.; tel: 22921). The Xiling is a more modernized version of the Shangri-la Hangzhou, offering more spacious rooms with generally better views of West Lake. The Xiling is a three-minute walk from the Shangri-la Hangzhou. Services for both accommodations are similar and often interchange. Rates for doubles at the Xiling are Y185, and deluxe suites go for as much as Y1100.

花港饭店

Huagang Guest House (4 Huanhu Xi Rd.; tel: 71324; telex: 35007 HUAJG CN; cable: 3263). Located next to the Huagang (Flower Pond) Park, Hangzhou's biggest park, the Huagang Guest House is composed of two buildings, one old and one new. Both provide comfortable and adequately furnished rooms. The two buildings share a common dining area that serves Chinese and Western food.

西湖宾馆

West Lake Guest House (7 Xishan Rd.; tel: 26867; telex: 35004 BTHXN CN). The West Lake Guest House is sandwiched between West Lake in front and a hill at the back, thus creating the illusion of a peaceful hideaway. To further enhance the idea of retreat, the guest house is surrounded by quaint pavilions and tiny winding bridges. The four villa-type buildings offer comfortably furnished rooms. The Hangzhou cuisine served in its dining room is genuinely impressive.

花家山宾馆

Huajiashan Hotel (12 Faxiang Alley, West Huanhu Rd.; tel: 71224; telex: 35063 HISGH CN). Located in a very scenic part of town, the Huajiashan has 187 double rooms and nine suites. Accommodations are more modest than some of the other hotels, but rates are more reasonable. All rooms have private bath, air-conditioning and color TV, and the hotel offers the usual amenities.

杭州华侨饭店

Overseas Chinese Hotel (15 Hubin Rd.; tel: 26911). Located on the northeast shore of West Lake, the Overseas Chinese Hotel offers 306 rooms at reasonable rates. All rooms have private bath, color TV, and air-conditioning. Dormitory rooms are available to students for Y10. The hotel is 4 km. from the railroad station.

浙江宾馆

Zhejiang Guest House (68 Santaishan Road, Xihuqu; tel: 25601; telex: 351044 ZJGH). In addition to the usual amenities, the Zhejiang features a tea house and a swimming pool. Like the Overseas Chinese Hotel, accommodations are modest, but the Zhejiang is closer to town.

Foreign tourists can also stay at the Friendship Hotel (53 Pinghai Rd.; tel: 20639; telex: 35068 FRISH CN).

CUISINE

Given West Lake's prominence as a resort, the chefs of the area have succeeded in elevating the level of the local cuisine to a high standard. A nutritious local vegetable, *xuancai*, is one of the noted products of Hangzhou. Combined in a soup with lake perch, it becomes a delicacy. It is said that the ancient emperors received this dish as a special tribute from the local populace. West Lake vinegar fish, snow-white shrimps cooked with Longjing tea, and stewed duck tongues are also specialties of the region, as is the honeyed ham. Plain noodles are served with fried shrimp and eel, and there is an exotic noodle dish called "cat's ears." Other local dishes include steamed rice with lotus leaves, cassia and maize soups, and assorted pastries.

For delicate fish, fried eel, and other local seafood dishes, the scenic Louwailou Restaurant located at the southeast corner of Gu Shan on the Bai Juyi Causeway (tel: 21654) is recommended. The restaurant is divided into six dining areas, which together can serve a maximum of 1,000 people. Each hall is set out to provide diners with views of the lake. Su Dongpo Pork (after the poet) and the giant West Lake shrimp are specialties of the Tianxianglou Restaurant (676 Jiefang Rd.; tel: 22038). Sweet dumplings and tiny noodles are recommended breakfast fare at the Kuiyuan Restaurant (124 Jiefang Rd.; tel: 25921), near the lake. On the way to the Botanical Garden and Jade Spring are the Shanwaishan Restaurant (tel: 26621), which features a wide selection of hors d'oeuvres as well as caramelized pineapple and pork with melon, and the Tianwaitian Restaurant (2 Tianzhi Rd.; tel: 22429), where the specialties include Longjing Tea Shrimp and Reed Flute Shrimp (*pipa xiaren*). For those who would like to try authentic Beggar's Chicken (another local specialty), the Hangzhou Restaurant (52 Yan'an Rd.; tel: 26414) is the place to go. The dish is so-named because a tale has it that a beggar uniquely prepared a chicken by covering the bird with clay and then baking it over a slow fire. Today, the chefs at Hangzhou prepare it with filet stuffing, lard, lotus leaf wrapping, and a variety of spices; the chicken is then cooked until it's golden and succulent.

SHOPPING

Hangzhou's arts and crafts are famous for their high quality. Most visitors favor the silk weavings of local scenes and the delicate, brightly colored embroidery. Chinese visitors like the local silk umbrellas and parasols which resemble stalks of bamboo when closed, but reveal painted scenes when unfurled. Hangzhou fans are also renowned. Most have slats made of sandalwood with an overlay of paper or silk. But other materials used include ivory, tortoise shell, mahogany, bamboo, coral, and even chicken feathers. Even common household items produced in Hangzhou, such as scissors and chopsticks, are of high standard, befitting the reputation of the region.

Tea lovers will appreciate the green Longjing tea as well as the famous chrysanthemum tea which is prized as a digestive aid. Cooked hams, sold at the Jinhua railroad station, also make excellent purchases, but because of import regulations back home, these are best consumed while in China.

Places to shop include the Friendship Store at 158 Tiyuchang Road (tel: 26480; the antiques store at 92 Dongpo Road; the Paintings and Calligraphy Shop, 198 Jiefang Road (tel: 24540); and the main department store on Jiefang Road.

中国国际旅行社
CITS (Luxingshe) Office in Hangzhou ■ 1 Shihan Rd. Tel: 56576/27160
Telex: 35031 HZT CN.

Harbin

fish-drying place   *traditional spelling/Harbin*

HARBIN is the capital of Heilongjiang Province in China's northeast region. It is one of China's most important railway junctions and a major industrial center with a population of two million.

Harbin sits in the heart of the famous Manchurian Plain—China's largest wheat- and corn-producing area and one of the most extensive plains in the world. The city is known as the gateway to China's "Great North Waste," named for its virgin lands set among scenic, rolling plains which stretch out to distant mountain ranges.

Located 1,110 km. (695 mi.) north of Beijing, the city is 19 hours by rail (or 2½ hours by air) from the capital. In summer Harbin can warm up to a temperature of 30°C (86°F), but in winter it is bitterly cold, with temperatures falling as low as −38°C (−36°F).

Harbin's entire length fronts the banks of one of China's great rivers, the Songhua (Sungari). The urban core is composed of two main sections: a relatively new industrial area with modern three-story, yellow-block apartment buildings in the Beijing-style, and an older residential district, dotted with Russian-style, onion-domed churches.

HARBIN IN HISTORY

For about 800 years, Harbin was little more than a fishing village (its name literally means "fish-drying place"). Its location on the Songhua River near Heilongjiang's southern border eventually made it strategically important. Only after the Manchus concluded a treaty with Russia for the construction of the Chinese Eastern Railroad (a branch of the Trans-Siberian Railway) in 1894, did Harbin become a major east-west/north-south railroad junction. This change marked the beginning of modern Harbin's development.

Following the 1917 Russian Revolution, about half a million "White" Russians fled south to Harbin. Together with the earlier Russian settlers, they came to dominate the city, which explains Harbin's architectural resemblance to Leningrad.

China and the Soviet Union jointly operated the Trans-Siberian Railway until Japan invaded Manchuria and occupied Harbin in 1932. In 1945, the Soviet army defeated the Japanese and occupied the city under authority of the Allied forces. A year later the Soviet army withdrew, taking with it most of Manchuria's industrial plant and equipment. Both Nationalist and

Climate		Jan	Feb	Mar	Apr	May	Jun	Jul	Aug	Sep	Oct	Nov	Dec
Temp.	°C	−19.7	−15.8	−4.8	6.5	14.7	20.2	22.5	21.2	14.2	5.8	−6.2	−16.0
	°F	−3.4	3.6	23.4	43.7	58.4	68.3	72.5	70.1	57.5	42.4	20.9	3.2
Precip.	mm.	8	8	18	28	69	84	183	170	64	36	28	15
	in.	.3	.3	.7	1.1	2.7	3.3	7.2	6.7	2.5	1.4	1.1	1.6

Harbin's central square

Communist troops rushed northward in an attempt to fill the vacuum in this valuable industrial area. Communist contingents were the first to arrive, and Harbin came under their control on April 28, 1946.

Before 1949, the city was already the major food-processing center for China's entire northeast. Since then, economic activity has diversified substantially, and Harbin is today an industrial center of national significance. Harbin is noted for its machine industry, linen mills, beet-sugar refineries, paper manufacturing, and "Songhua River" tractors. The more than 1,000 factories in Harbin today employ about 50,000 workers.

The city is situated in a fertile area which grows wheat, corn, and soybeans, among other crops, and the plentiful fish from the Songhua River provide for about half the province's needs. Forests to the east and north of Harbin supply timber, pulp, and paper.

HIGHLIGHTS
FOR TRAVELERS

Although Harbin has few sites of historical significance, the atmosphere and architecture of the city are unique to China. The city's design is similar to that of Washington, DC: broad avenues radiate off circles like the spokes of a wheel. Harbin's distinctly Russian-style buildings are constructed of cream-colored stucco. Russian-type interior stoves provide homes in Harbin with central heating, a comfort as yet enjoyed by no other Chinese city.

A tall monument, dedicated to the many Russians who sacrificed their lives in the World War II battle to defeat Japan, stands prominently in the public square.

Harbin has a number of notable universities and institutes, such as Harbin Polytechnic. The handicrafts factory, with a small retail shop for travelers, specializes in stone, jade, and ivory carvings, as well as reed and straw paintings and collages of oxhorn and other natural materials.

斯大林公园

Stalin Park. The city-long riverfront, where beaches and greenery stretch for several kilometers on the south bank of the Songhua, is the site of the metropolis's major recreational area, Stalin Park. During the warm summer months, Harbin's population congregates here for swimming, sunbathing, and sailing in both large and small craft. Tourists can arrange boat excursions on the Songhua for Y4 per person, a fee that includes refreshing cold sodas and watermelon. In winter, the frozen river is used for skating.

太阳岛公园

Sun Island Park. This is one of the most beautiful of Harbin's parks, occupying an entire island on the Songhua River. It used to house the villas of the rich, but today contains public facilities for volleyball, Ping-Pong, and basketball, as well as several convalescent homes. Pine, clove, and peach trees grace the walking paths. In winter, the whole town takes part in making attractive ice lanterns and huge, intricate ice sculptures. Spring Festival, which falls in late January or early February, is the most festive period for viewing this unusual handiwork.

儿童公园

Children's Park. Located on a tributary of the Songhua River, this park has a miniature railway run by and for children.

动物园

Harbin Zoo. Open in 1954 in a spacious, pleasant park, the zoo has more than 100 different animal species, including wolverines, red-crowned cranes, sika deer, and reindeer. The Harbin Zoo is noted for successfully breeding the rare and protected Northeast China Tiger, on view year-round. During the summer, two pandas are displayed.

Harbin Summer Music Festival. Suspended in 1967 as a result of the Cultural Revolution, this annual music festival was reinstituted in July 1979. Performances that summer were held in Harbin's eight major theatres for 12 days running.

HOTEL
ACCOMMODATIONS

黑龙江省招待所

Heilongjiang Province Guest House (52 Hongjun St.; tel: 32950). Set on one of the largest public squares, directly across the street from the Heilongjiang Museum, this fine, old-style guest house was formerly a railroad hotel. Many rooms are very spacious. A new wing with 290 beds was built in late 1979.

The hotel dining room serves some regional specialties. (There are extra charges here for a second cup of coffee and for butter patties.) The lobby is excellent for people-watching, since both Chinese and foreign visitors use the hotel.

北方大厦

Beifang Mansion (Zhongshan Rd.; tel: 31485). Also known as the Northern Mansion, this Soviet-style building has 160 beds. Parts of the hotel were renovated in 1979.

天鹅饭店

Swan Hotel (73 Zhongshan Rd.; tel: 220201; telex: 87080 TIANE CN). The Swan Hotel has 250 rooms, including 18 suites. Rates range from Y50 for a single to Y80 for a suite. Located 7 km. from the railway station, the Swan Hotel has a restaurant, bar, and tea house, as well as all the usual services.

Other possibilities include the **International Hotel** (124 Dazhi Jie; tel: 31441; telex: 87081 GUOLU CN) and the **Harbin Guest House** (56 Dazhi Jie; tel: 30846).

CUISINE

As might be expected, this region has some specialties not found elsewhere in China: bear paw, grouse, salmon, and nose of camel deer. Regular dishes are often garlic-flavored. The white fish from the Songhua River is bony but tasty. The special local fiery spirit is Chen Liang Bai Jiu, a white liquor.

Unique for China, white potatoes form a major part of the diet in Harbin. Ice cream is consumed year-round by the entire population, an addiction introduced by the Russians.

中国国际旅行社
CITS (Luxingshe) Office in Harbin ■ 73 Zhongshan Rd. Tel: 221088/52496
Telex: 80080 TIANE CN.

Hefei

harmonious and fertile   *traditional spelling/Hofei*

HEFEI, the provincial capital of Anhui, was little more than a market town of 50,000 persons until 1949. Today, it is a rapidly growing industrial city and mining center of over a million inhabitants, producing steel, iron, electricity, chemicals, and textiles.

By train, Hefei is 18½ hours from Beijing and 12 hours from Shanghai. The train passes miles of flat wheat fields and rice paddies, reminiscent in some ways of a trip across the Canadian prairies or the American midwest. At the end of this rather taxing journey, the visitor will be rewarded with the open enthusiasm (and curious stares) of the local population, since Hefei has only recently been opened to Western tourists. Hefei can be reached by air from Beijing, Guangzhou, Shanghai, and Wuhan.

HIGHLIGHTS FOR TRAVELERS

Hefei is a new industrial city, not noted for its scenery, and it has few tourist attractions as such. The Hefei Museum has some 100,000 artifacts, dating back 7,000 years. The prize here is a 2,000-year-old jade burial suit stitched with silver thread. Visitors may be taken to see Anhui University, where they will be bombarded with questions about their native land, their lifestyle, their views on international politics. The enthusiasm and openness of these young students' questions is possibly one of the best testimonies to China's "bright future."

At the East is Red Commune, home of almost 19,000 people, it will be the visitor's turn to ask questions—about rice and grain production, work incentives, and care of the elderly. The tour of the commune will also include a visit to the factory and hospital facilities.

Hotel Accommodations. The number of hotels in Hefei has multiplied in recent years. Visitors will find spacious rooms and excellent meals at the **Daxianglou Guest House** (intersection of Dazhai Road and Yan'an Road; tel: 74791) and at the **Jianghuai Hotel** (68 Changjiang Rd.; tel: 52221). This is wheat country, so gear up for delicious fried dumplings at breakfast.

中国国际旅行社
CITS (Luxingshe) Office in Hefei ■ 43 Tunxi Rd. Tel: 61890-206.
Telex: 90024 AHPBD CN.

Climate		Jan	Feb	Mar	Apr	May	Jun	Jul	Aug	Sep	Oct	Nov	Dec
Temp.	°C	2.3	4.0	9.3	15.3	21.1	25.0	28.5	28.5	23.1	17.2	10.7	4.6
	°F	36.1	39.2	48.7	59.5	69.9	77	83.3	83.3	73.5	62.9	51.2	40.2
Precip.	mm.	254	254	330	330	305	356	279	279	305	254	203	178
	in.	10	10	13	13	12	14	11	11	12	10	8	7

Huang Shan

yellow mountains   *traditional spelling/Hwang Shan*

HUANG SHAN is the collective name of a famous range of granite mountains found in southern Anhui Province and known throughout China for its extraordinary aesthetic features. Located 1,045 km. (650 mi.) south of Beijing and 402 km. (250 mi.) southwest of Shanghai, the name of the range was changed in the Tang (AD 747) from Bei Yi Shan (Northern Black Mountains). The mountain range covers an area of 150 sq. km. (57.9 sq. mi.) and comprises over 72 distinct peaks of varying heights. The three highest are Lotus Flower Peak (Lianhua Feng) at 1,873 m. (6,147 ft.) above sea level; Bright Summit (Guangming Ding), 1,840 m. (6,039 ft.); and Heavenly Capital Peak (Tiandu Feng), 1,829 m. (6,000 ft.)

Over the centuries, Chinese poets and painters have immortalized the four great attractions or "four ultimate beauties" of Huang Shan—fantastically shaped rocks, the "sea of clouds" swirling around the peaks, ancient pines clinging to the rockface, and hot springs. Huang Shan was, and is, a favorite vacation retreat for Chinese officials and important state guests. (Ho Chi Minh was said to have vacationed here during a lull in the Vietnam War.) Closed during the Cultural Revolution, the area was only opened to foreigners beginning in 1979.

Huang Shan is not easily accessible. To reach the foot of the range, one must first go by train or plane from Shanghai to Wuhu (seven hours, or 80 minutes respectively), then drive six hours through the countryside. Although the better part of a day will be consumed in getting there, the rail trip through some of China's most rural areas affords the visitor a vision of emerald-green rice paddies, tea bushes, and mud-walled villages.

Upon arrival at Huang Shan, the visitor is confronted with thousands of stone steps set into an 80-degree cliff. The very hardy may want to climb all the way to the top, but they should be warned that the ascent will be roughly as exhausting as climbing the stairs of the Empire State Building— with no recourse to elevators. For most visitors, tour buses provide transport along a winding dirt road to a point halfway up the mountain. From there, it is a leisurely three-hour climb to the top, with frequent rest stops at the many pavilions and terraces which overlook the proverbial limpid pools and thundering waterfalls. The reward for all who arrive at the top is a truly unforgettable experience—walking into a living Chinese ink-wash landscape painting.

The weather on top of the mountain range is generally moist and cold. Winter temperatures can fall as low as −1.8°C (28°F), and even summer temperatures average no more than 8°C (46°F). The best times to visit Huang Shan are early spring or fall, when the peaks are jade-green with new growth or purplish-red with autumn foliage.

HIGHLIGHTS FOR TRAVELERS

Most visitors observe the ritual of waking up at 5 AM to catch the sunrise, but the occasions on which one can actually see the sun appear above the jagged peaks, which float like islands amid a sea of clouds, are relatively rare.

Huang Shan's famous hot springs are hidden between Purple Cloud Peak (Ziyun Feng) and Peach Blossom Peak (Taohua Feng) at 630 m. (2,067 ft.) above sea level. The waters maintain a constant temperature of 42°C (107°F). A bathhouse and swimming pool were built next to the springs after 1949. Nearby are the Pavilion for Watching Waterfalls and the Peach Spring Pavilion.

HOTEL ACCOMMODATIONS

Visitors may stay at the **Huang Shan Guest House** situated next to the hot springs, or the **Peach Brook Guest House** (tel: 2295), which is perched on a steep slope amid ancient pine trees and churning mountain streams. The main building at the Peach Brook Guest House has five stories with comfortable rooms and small bathrooms with primitive showers. The **Jade Screen Hotel** (Yuping Lou), formerly the Temple of the Bodhisattva of Wisdom, commands the most beautiful view: from its windows, one can take in three of Huang Shan's most famous peaks at a single glance.

The **Beihai (North Sea) Hotel** (tel: 2225) — named for the "sea of clouds" — is located at Huang Shan's summit. Despite its Western-style furnishings, and televisions in the bedrooms, this hotel is rather austere. Bathrooms are found at the ends of corridors. Under the press of growing numbers of tourists, the Beihai has pushed its guest capacity to 2,000 by putting two or even three beds to a room.

Meals at all the hotels are excellent despite the enormous difficulties of transporting provisions up the mountain. A veritable army of porters makes the arduous climb on foot several times a day, carrying food and even water in buckets slung on bamboo poles.

The **West Sea Hotel** (tel: 2223), Huang Shan's first luxury-class joint venture hotel, is expected to open in August 1988.

中国国际旅行社
CITS (Luxingshe) Office in Huang Shan ■ Hot Spring Area. Tel: 2200.

内蒙古 Inner Mongolia

WITH the vast beauty of its grasslands and endless, powder-blue, pollution-free skies, the outer reaches of Inner Mongolia are no longer beyond the ken of the traveler to China. During the mid-1980s, this remote region on China's northern frontier was expanding steadily as a tourist attraction. Still off the beaten path, Inner Mongolia hosts only about 10,000 tourists each year. More than half of this number seem to be young people from Hong Kong. Yet, for those seeking something different from the usual China fare, Mongolia offers an exciting diversion. Apart from conventional modes of tourism, overland excursions can be arranged by bicycle, camel, or horseback, venturing through the grasslands and even into the Gobi Desert. Travelers sleep in traditional Mongolian yurts—circular tents made of felt.

Occupying 1,180,000 sq. km. (456,000 sq. mi.) on the vast Mongolian Plateau, the Inner Mongolia Autonomous Region makes up a major portion of China's north-central region. It was the first area of China to be designated as an autonomous region, having been established on May 1, 1947—well before the founding of the People's Republic itself in 1949.

Inner Mongolia has a population of about 20 million, of whom only

483

about 2.6 million (or 13%) are ethnic Mongolians. The remainder of the population consists mainly of Han Chinese, many of whom have been brought to the region as settlers since 1949. There is also a smattering of several minority communities, including Hui, Manchu, Dahur, Oronchon, Ewenki, Korean, Zhuang, and Tibetan. The region is divided into nine leagues (equivalent to prefectures), three municipalities, 86 counties (referred to as "banners" in the pastoral areas), and hundreds of *sumu* (equivalent to townships).

Climate. Situated on a plateau ranging from 1,000 to 2,000 m. above sea level, the area's climate is predominantly cool and dry, although there are wide swings in temperature in the course of the year. There are often major fluctuations even within a single day. During winter, temperatures may fall below −30°C (−22°F), with bitter northern winds. As protection against the prevailing wind, traditional dwellings in the countryside are built with very thick northern walls. The entranceways, often adorned with colored homemade papercuts, invariably face south. There are only 110 to 150 frost-free days each year. During this "summer" period, the weather is quite pleasant, averaging 20°C (68°F). Hot conditions occur only during direct exposure to the midday sun. Summer mornings and evenings remain quite cool. Precipitation amounts to only 150–400 mm. per year and falls mainly during the transition from summer to autumn. Thus, the sun shines in Mongolia's incredibly clear blue skies virtually every day of the year. The color of the sky in itself almost makes the trip worthwhile.

ECONOMY AND CULTURE

One of the five major bases for animal husbandry in China, Inner Mongolia has an estimated animal population of 6.5 million, consisting of sheep, goats, cattle, horses, and camels. No longer as nomadic as they once were, most Mongolian herdsmen now live in heated homes and have permanent sheds for their animals. They have become more scientific in their agricultural methods, and the level of mechanization of production has been rising steadily.

Although the growing season only permits one crop per year, agriculture has seen a great increase in production. Most crops are raised on the Hetao Plain of the Yellow River, just west of Baotou—the "breadbasket" of Inner Mongolia. However, there are over 13 million acres of cultivated land and over 214 million acres of pasture beyond the central agricultural belt. The major crops are wheat, oats, sorghum, rice, maize, potatoes, flax seed, and sugar beets.

Inner Mongolia's industry is also coming into its own. The area has abundant mineral deposits, including coal, iron, chromium, manganese, copper, aluminum, zinc, gold, silver, mica, sulfur, asbestos, and what are thought to be the largest rare-earth deposits in the world. Before 1949, there was almost no industry here at all, and the most common necessities had to be brought in from other areas. But now there are booming metallurgical enterprises, as well as power, machine-building, coal, chemical, and textile industries. The animal by-products industry, in particular, has advanced to the stage where it can handle the processing of all materials produced within the region itself. During the three decades from 1949 to 1979, the value of heavy industry overall multiplied 423 times, and that of light industry, 48 times. Along with this growth has come the development of transportation and communications, with the result that Mongolia is now not nearly as remote or isolated as it once was, a circumstance reflected in the growth of the tourist industry.

Education. Before 1949, 90% of Inner Mongolia's population was illiterate. At that time there were only 2,156 primary schools and 200 high schools. Now there are some 27,000 primary schools and 5,194 middle schools, plus 170 research institutes, 84 technical schools, and 15 centers of higher learning, with a combined enrollment of over 15,000. Of the total school-age population, 95.2% are receiving formal education. Minority students have priority over Han students in terms of admission to college, and there are special Hui and Mongolian primary and middle schools. Tourists are welcome to visit these special schools.

草原
THE GRASSLANDS

The singular highlight of any trip to Mongolia is a visit to the grasslands, which stretch northward across the Daqing Mountains from the regional capital of Hohhot. The best way to sample Inner Mongolian culture in its most natural setting is on an overnight outing to this region. Organized excursions into the grasslands invariably offer horseback riding, camel riding, a combined show and tea party (where according to tradition, the guests are also expected to perform), a visit with a Mongolian family, archery and riflery displays, and a trip to an *aobao*. These are mounds made of stones (*aobao* means "to pile up" in Mongolian) set up on high points throughout the grasslands. They were originally used as directional markers, but later developed into focal points for religious services and festivals.

Three grassland settlements commonly receive foreign visitors: Xilamulun Sumu, Huitengxile, and Baiyunhushao. Independent travelers can join daily bus excursions from Hohhot to any of these sites. The price of the outing depends on the distance traveled from Hohhot and on the number of people traveling together (overseas Chinese pay about 9% less than other foreigners; children under 5 may travel free of charge, while those aged 6–11 go for half price). Costs cited below include transportation, guides, a night in a yurt, three meals, and some sightseeing in Hohhot upon return.

希拉牧仑苏木（乌兰图格）

Xilamulun Sumu. The oldest tourist site on the grasslands, Xilamulun is also the closest to Hohhot, reachable in two hours (87 km.) by bus. Xilamulun is, in fact, the only grassland community that can be visited on a day trip from Hohhot. It consists of an area of 1,000 sq. km., lying at 1,700 m. above sea level. It has a population of 2,200 people, 70% of whom are Mongolian, who tend some 40,000 animals. Set up near the 230-year-old summer temple of the Xilitu Zhao Living Buddha, there are 33 yurts for tourists, 20 of which have attached toilet and shower facilities. Accommodations are clean and well maintained. Meals are taken in the nearby temple compound. Prices range from Y41 to Y220 for a day trip (1–21 persons) and from Y61 to Y297 for two days.

灰腾锡勒

Huitengxile. About 40 km. beyond Xilamulun, and considerably more rustic, is Huitengxile. Unlike Xilamulun, there is nothing nearly resembling a "Yurt Motel" in the vicinity. The yurts here do not have private bathrooms yet, but the public toilet/shower facilities are tolerable. The settlement consists of 150 sq. km. of almost unbroken grasslands at an altitude of 2,000 m. Aside from the activities mentioned above, visitors are taken to one of the 99 small lakes and ponds that dot the area. It is also possible here to rent (for Y1) Mongolian robes to wear while you're on the grasslands. Excursion prices range from Y68 to Y333.

白音忽少

Baiyunhushao. The farthest and most primitive of the three grassland sites, Baiyunhushao, is 178 km. from Hohhot, at an altitude of 1,500 meters. It covers an area of 250 sq. km. and has a population of 360 souls, 80% of whom are Mongolian. Being the farthest away from Hohhot, Baiyun-hushao is the most untouched, in terms of both its natural environment and the indigenous culture. Costs for an excursion range from Y78 to Y402.

呼和浩特
HOHHOT

Although the name Hohhot (alternatively spelled Huhehot) means "green city" in Mongolian, it cannot be ranked among China's more colorful or impressive cities. It is visited mainly as a required starting point for trips to the Mongolian interior. The capital of Inner Mongolia, Hohhot is located on the Tumet Plain bordering on the Yellow River at the southern foot of the Daqing Mountains. It covers an area of 6,079 sq. km. (2,347 sq. mi.), divided into four urban districts and two counties. It has a population of 1.2 million, less than 3% of whom are Mongolian. The urban area is 69 sq. km., with a population of about 500,000.

Several trains per day travel between Beijing and Hohhot. The scenic journey takes about 13 hours. The city's small airport is now being expanded, but the overnight train is still the recommended means of access.

History. The town was founded in 1581 by a group of nomads known as the Tumet. In 1735, the Qing Dynasty began construction of another town adjacent to that of the Tumet to function as a garrison for defending the frontier. The two towns were joined together during the Republican period, but it wasn't until after 1949 that the original Mongolian name, Hohhot, was used to denote the entire area.

Economy and Culture. Before 1949, there wasn't much in the way of industry except for a few small handicrafts workshops. Today, however, there are large metallurgical, machine-building, and textile industries. The economy also includes electronics, chemicals, building materials, coal mining, and food processing. The townspeople are now also looking toward tourism as a means of further developing the area.

Within the city are a dozen cinemas, a few theaters, a dozen or more cultural centers, eight public libraries, two museums, four stadiums, three gymnasiums, a horse-racing area, three public swimming pools, a shooting range, a film studio, and a TV station. There are also some scenic and cultural sites worth visiting.

HIGHLIGHTS FOR TRAVELERS

昭君墓
The Tomb of Wang Zhaojun. About 20 minutes south of the Xin-cheng Guest House by car is the tomb of Wang Zhaojun, a Han Dynasty

Five-Pagoda Temple, Hohhot

princess who was wed at age 16 to the chief of the Xiongnu, the "northern barbarians" of that era. The Xiongnu had often fought with the Chinese, but this marriage, conducted in 33 BC, kept peace between the two peoples for over 60 years. Thus, Wang is regarded as a great heroine. The tumulus is 33 m. high, and is relatively easy to climb for a good view of the surroundings. There is also a teahouse and a shop to the right (through a corridor of shops) and a small historical exhibit on the left. The inscription in front of the tomb is a poem written in 1963 by Dong Biwu, then China's acting head of state.

内蒙古自治区博物馆

The Museum of Inner Mongolia. Divided into four sections, the museum has a large collection covering paleontology, historical relics from the Xia to the Yuan dynasties, relics of local minority peoples (including the Orochon, Dahur, and Erwenk), and Mongolian revolutionary history of the 20th century. This last category covers much about Ulanhu, a Mongolian freedom fighter who became Inner Mongolia's first governor and was until recently vice president of the PRC. There is an antique shop just north of the museum (on the same street). (Museum telephone: 24924.)

大召

Da Zhao Lamasery. Da Zhao, a 410-year-old temple of the Yellow Lamaism sect, was turned into a clothing factory during the Cultural Revolution. It is now in the process of being restored. As of 1985, only the Main Hall and Scripture Hall had been restored, but these alone are definitely worth the visit. The Main Hall divides into the Chanting Hall and the Buddha Hall. In the chanting section, the highest lama of the temple is seated to the left during prayers; the center seat is reserved for the Dalai Lama, the Panchen Lama, or, traditionally, the emperor. The large flag-umbrellas that hang in the hall symbolize a yearning for peace. The books displayed on both sides of the hall are the entire 108 volumes of the Tibetan canon, a national treasure. Only three such sets exist in China. Also be sure to note the intriguing murals. In the Buddha Hall, Sakyamuni sits in the center; to the left is Zongkaba, the founder of Lamaism. Buddha's 18 warriors line the walls. The Scripture Hall also functions as the headquarters of the Hohhot Buddhist Association. Visits to this temple must be arranged through CITS or CTS.

To the east of the temple is a small neighborhood that is being rebuilt according to traditional architecture. There is also a large free market, selling clothing and other goods.

席力图召

Xilitu Zhao. Just across from Da Zhao is another Lamaist temple which is also being restored. Although not yet open as of mid-1984, its exterior is already adorned quite beautifully, and there is a "two-ear" dagoba in the courtyard. The Xilitu temple was originally opened by the Third Dalai Lama to spread Lamaism into Mongolia. He died here, and his successor, the Fourth Dalai Lama, was a Mongolian. The Living Buddha of this temple, who was appointed by the Third Dalai Lama, is now in his 15th incarnation.

清真大寺

The Great Mosque. The largest of the four mosques in Hohhot, the Great Mosque is located in the center of the Hui nationality quarter. Built in 1693, it was expanded to its present size in 1789. The minaret (called Wangyue Lou), which was finished in 1940, took 20 years to construct. The main hall holds 500–600 people, but sometimes as many as 1,000 of Hohhot's 26,000 Muslims will gather here for prayer, filling the courtyard. Five daily services are held: before dawn, just after noon, before sunset, after sunset, and after dark. Visitors are welcome to participate.

五塔寺

The Five-Pagoda Temple. All that is left of the original 18th-century temple is the Vajira Sharil Suburga (a stupa for housing Buddhist relics) and an 8.8-m.-high "sutra" base with five pagodas on top. The base is carved with the four heavenly kings; an astonishing 1,563 small buddhas; the "seven treasures and eight precious things" of Lamaism; and the Diamond Sutra in three languages—Mongolian, Tibetan, and Sanskrit. If you climb to the top of the base, you can see a bit of the old town. Behind the stupa are three rare carvings representing the six worlds of

Hohhot's Great Mosque

Lamaism, Sumeru Mountain (analogous to the universe), and an ancient planisphere (chart of the constellations). The planisphere is the only one in China containing Mongolian inscriptions. The temple has a small souvenir counter at the back.

民族用品厂

National Minority Handicrafts Factory. This factory of 220 workers was formally set up in 1974. Before that it was a small cooperative workshop. Its four units currently produce Mongolian-style knives, boots, saddles, robes, and other items. A tour of the factory of course includes a stop at their retail outlet (tel: 25379). There is also a Mongolian carpet factory that can be visited in Hohhot (tel: 25262).

Shopping. The large department store on Zhongshan Lu is the closest thing to a Friendship Store in Hohhot. This two-story emporium attracts local shoppers from both the city and the grasslands, making the crowd at least as interesting as the merchandise. Recommended local crafts include blankets, native costumes, millinery goods (adorned with colorful lace), knives, and artifacts such as reindeer statues made of freshwater shells. Even Mongolian traditional wooden saddles are offered for sale.

Climate		Jan	Feb	Mar	Apr	May	Jun	Jul	Aug	Sep	Oct	Nov	Dec
Temp.	°C	−4.7	−1.9	4.8	13.7	20.1	24.8	26.1	24.8	19.9	12.8	3.8	2.8
	°F	23.5	28.6	40.6	56.6	68.1	76.6	78.9	76.6	67.8	55	38.8	37
Precip.	mm.	76	76	76	102	152	203	305	254	178	152	102	76
	in.	3	3	3	4	6	8	12	10	7	6	4	3

HOTEL ACCOMMODATIONS

新城宾馆

Xincheng (New City) Guest House (23 Hulun Nan Lu; tel: 24513).
Until the opening of the Inner Mongolia Hotel (see below), the Xincheng
was the foremost hotel in Inner Mongolia, but it had grown rather shabby.
Accommodations ranged from very inexpensive, dormitory-style rooms
(two beds per room) for Y10 (Y6 for students) to somewhat nicer rooms
(with TV and private bath) for Y40. Meals are served in an adjoining
building. There is a CITS office in the hotel for onward bookings. Just outside the gate, to the right, is a bicycle rental office; fees are 50 *fen* per hour.

内蒙古饭店

The **Inner Mongolia Hotel** (Hulun Nan Rd.; tel: 25754) nearby
opened in 1986 with 500 beds and highly modern facilities, including
computerized reservations and furnishings imported from Hong Kong.

中国国际旅行社

CITS (Luxingshe) Office in Hohhot ■ North Building of Hohhot Guesthouse,
7 Yingbin Rd. Tel: 24494.

包头

BAOTOU

Baotou is known as the "steel city of the grasslands." It is Inner
Mongolia's largest city and sits between the Daqing Mountains
to the north and the Yellow River to the south. Occupying an
area of 9,991 sq. km. (3,858 sq. mi.), it can be reached via a three-hour
train ride due west from Hohhot. The city has three very separate urban
sections, three mining districts, one banner, one county, and one suburban district.

Three hundred years ago, this area was called by the Mongolians
Baoketu ("land with deer"). In the 17th century, the Qing government
moved people from other parts of China to create a loyal Han bastion
here, called Baotou. Later, improved roads, the river, and a rail line
linked Baotou with north and northwest China and western Mongolia,
helping it develop into an important trade city. After 1949, during a
period of close cooperation with the Soviet Union, there was a plan to
expand Baotou to the size of Shanghai. Originally, the East River section
of the city was to be joined with the other two major districts, forming
one large unit. But shortly after construction started, Soviet/Chinese
relations broke down. The Soviets left, taking all the plans with them.
Baotou to this day still seems more like three cities than one.

Baotou now has 966 industrial enterprises, compared to a mere six
in 1949. Much of today's economy centers around iron, steel, coal, and
nonferrous metals production. Light industry includes sugar refining,
textiles, carpets, leather, and furs. The city is also nearly self-sufficient
agriculturally, specializing in vegetables.

HIGHLIGHTS FOR TRAVELERS

Although an open city for foreigners, Baotou has little to offer in the way of tourism. Except for visits to factories, there is only one genuine tourist site, the Wudang Zhao, and one rather peculiar attraction—the "talking sands" of the Kubuki Desert. Both sites are reachable from the

city only after very long, arduous jeep rides along terrible roads and rough riverbeds. Only those with the most diffident bottoms might consider the effort (and expense) worthwhile.

五当召

Wudang Zhao. Nestled high in the Daqing Mountains, past Baotou's mining districts and about 75 km. from town, is a Lamaist temple said to have been first built to resemble the Potala Palace in Lhasa. Whatever its original aspect, the temple today retains a Tibetan cast, although it is in no way like the Potala. Built in 1749, it is the largest lamasery in western Mongolia. It has six halls, five rooms for Living Buddhas, a crypt, and several residences for monks. The murals in the main halls, though 200 years old, retain their rich coloration, and the former residences of the Living Buddhas are filled with treasures.

There is a restaurant for tourists next to the temple. A jeep hired for the trip to the temple costs about Y105.

响沙湾

Xiangshawan. About 45 km. south of Baotou, across the Yellow River, is a small desert region that forms part of the Ordos Plateau in Dalatechi. This is the Kubuki Desert, site of the "noisemaking sand." In one part of the sand dune, about 40 m. high and 30 m. wide, a low rumbling noise will be heard if you slide down the slope and push the sand (when it's very dry) forcefully in front of you. The folk explanation is that this was once the site of a monastery. While the 1,000 or so monks were chanting for seven days and nights, an avalanche of sand covered the temple. The sounds now heard are the monks still chanting. Scientists say that the sand has a high metallic content: the rubbing of the fine sand particles causes static electricity—and the noise.

A trip to the desert often includes a stop at a fishery for lunch. The entire excursion covers 140 km. and costs Y120.

HOTEL ACCOMMODATIONS

Baotou has three hotels—one in each district—with a combined total of about 1,000 beds. The best of the three is the **Qingshan Guest House** (Yingbin Lu; tel: 33355). Rooms range from Y30 to Y70. The **Baotou Guest House** (Gangtie Boulevard; tel: 26612) has 617 beds arranged in 180 rooms. Here there are eight grades of rooms, with prices ranging from Y5 for a bed in a dormitory to Y140 for a private suite (prices are somewhat cheaper for overseas Chinese). There is a taxi stand, and the CITS office is located in the hotel compound (tel: 24615). The third establishment, the **Donghe (East River) Guest House,** is infrequently used by foreign visitors.

锡林浩特
XILINHOT

An ancient caravan town located some 500 km. northeast of Hohhot, Xilinhot (also known by its Mongolian name, Abagnar Qi) is the preferred destination in all of Inner Mongolia for encountering an authentic Mongolian lifestyle. Reaching Xilinhot by overland routes remains problematic, even by means of four-wheeled vehicles, but permission can be acquired for flight connections—five times weekly from Hohhot. Visitors stay in yurts near the airstrip, a few kilometers from town. The region's grasslands are Mongolia's most beautiful and unspoiled and the people most naturally Mongolian.

MONGOLIAN CUISINE

Mutton is the staple of the Mongolian table. It is often served in large chunks meant to be carved and eaten with a Mongolian-style knife, the only utensil on the table besides chopsticks. The mutton may be barbecued, spit-roasted, or grilled. Mongolian Hot Pot has become a popular dish throughout China. A pot of bubbling broth is simmered at the table in Swiss fondue fashion, and diners watch as their slivers of lamb and vegetables quickly cook. Then the lamb is dipped into spicy sauces and condiments, and eaten together with round sesame buns. Mongolian-style, hotly peppered shish kebob has also become a favorite national dish of China. The traditional tea is also worth a try, especially since it is a breakfast staple on the grasslands. It consists of rich, warm broth made from boiled brick tea (using the roots of the tea, not the leaves) and either cow's or goat's milk. The brew is served with millet (to be put in the tea), crackers, or fried dough. Hard cheese is a frequent accompaniment (the cheese can also be dipped in the tea to soften it up a bit).

Jiayuguan

impregnable defile under the sun   *traditional spelling/Chia yukuan*

For an overnight stop at Jiayuguan, a large industrial town about 525 km. (315 mi.) northwest of Lanzhou, the primary reason is proximity to the unforgettably impressive Ming fortress at the western end of the Great Wall. Two other reasons have to do with itinerary-making: it may be convenient to break at Jiayuguan the long train journey between Lanzhou and Ürümqi, and it is possible to arrange travel by CITS car from Jiayuguan to Dunhuang.

The great fortress, which stands only about 15 minutes from the town by car or bus, was originally built in 1372 to guard the pass between the Qilian Shan to the south and the Black Mountain to the north. Inside the battlemented outer wall, which is nearly 11 m. (35 ft.) high and just over 733 m. (802 yds.) in circumference, the visitor comes first to the Wenchang Pavilion, the Guandi Temple, and an open-air theatre; then to the eastern gate, the Guanghua Men (Gate of Enlightenment), matched on the western side by the Rouyuan Men (Gate of Conciliation). Over these gates, richly decorated towers rise to a height of 17 m. (56 ft.). From the walls, turreted at the four corners, one can see the mountains, the desert, and a few remnants of the Great Wall. At one time, the Wall extended at least 85 km. (51 mi.) westward, as far as Yumen; indeed, some vestiges have been uncovered near Dunhuang. Since the Ming dynasty, however, Jiayuguan, "Impregnable Defile Under the Sun," has been considered the terminus—the western outpost dividing civilization from the land of barbarians.

Jiuquan, about 30 km. (18 mi.) southeast of Jiayuguan, has a noteworthy Drum Tower, a pleasingly laid-out People's Park, and an airport.

To travel westward by car from Jiayuguan to Dunhuang, with leisurely halts at Yumen and Anxi, takes about seven hours. The Yumen Number Two Hostel provides a very good midday meal, and it has admirably clean washrooms as well as a shop.

嘉峪关饭店

The **Jiayuguan Hotel** (1 Xinhua North Rd.; tel: 5931/5084) is adequate for moderately seasoned travelers who will climb stairs and not expect hot water to run at all hours. Meals are quite edible but not distinguished. At the height of the season, the "Small Shop," the "Barber Shop," and the CITS "Sub-Branch" (tel: 5231) may be open for business; in the off-season, they are not.

Climate		Jan	Feb	Mar	Apr	May	Jun	Jul	Aug	Sep	Oct	Nov	Dec
Temp.	°C	−15.2	−12.2	0.7	10.8	18.9	23.4	25.7	23.8	17.4	8.2	−2.6	−12.0
	°F	4.6	10	33.2	51.4	66	74.1	78.2	74.8	63.3	46.7	27.3	10.4
Precip.	mm.	15	8	13	38	28	38	18	25	15	43	41	10
	in.	.6	.3	.5	1.5	1.1	1.5	.7	1.0	.6	1.7	1.6	.4

Jinan

south of the River Ji

traditional spelling/Tsinan

JINAN, the capital of Shandong Province, is known as the "City of Springs," because of its 102 bubbling natural springs. Lying in a valley between the Yellow River and the Taishan Mountains, Jinan is an industrial city and a junction on the Beijing–Shanghai railway line, some 350 km. (217 mi.) south of Beijing. It has a population of nearly two million.

The major industries in Jinan include metallurgy, machine building, chemicals, and textiles, as well as flour milling and high-quality paper production. Agricultural products include wheat, corn, cotton, tobacco, peanuts, and a variety of fruits (peaches, pears, grapes, and dates). It is a major provincial center of higher learning; Shandong University, the provincial teachers' college, and a polytechnic institute are all located here, as are the provincial museum, library, and several medical training facilities.

The best time of year to visit Jinan is in autumn or early spring. During the dry, hot summers, most of the springs for which Jinan is famous are reduced to little more than muddy trickles.

JINAN IN HISTORY

Jinan was settled in Neolithic times, as evidenced by discoveries of black pottery from that period. In the northeastern part of town, a number of artifacts from the ancient Shang Dynasty (c. 1523–1066 BC) have been discovered. Under the Zhou (1066–221 BC), it was a fortified walled town called Luo. Under the Han (206 BC–AD 220), it acquired its present name, Jinan, meaning "south of the River Ji." Although this river no longer exists, the lower reaches of the Yellow River mark its approximate course. Because of Jinan's river link to the sea and to the area that now constitutes the port of Qingdao, the town emerged some 13 centuries ago as a major commercial center, especially under the Tang (618–907) and Song (960–1279). From the 12th to the early 20th centuries, as the capital of Shandong Province, Jinan also developed into an important political center.

In 1898, China granted certain concessions to Germany, including the right to build a railway from Qingdao to Jinan. The opening of this railway in 1904, together with other rail links to different parts of China in subsequent years, made Jinan a major communications center. In the early 1900s, other Western countries began setting up commercial and textile operations in the area, as well as Christian missions. A Western guidebook

Climate		Jan	Feb	Mar	Apr	May	Jun	Jul	Aug	Sep	Oct	Nov	Dec
Temp.	°C	−1.4	0.9	7.6	14.7	22.3	26.6	27.6	26.6	21.4	15.7	7.9	0.9
	°F	29.4	33.6	45.6	58.4	72.1	79.8	81.6	79.8	70.5	60.2	46.2	33.6
Precip.	mm.	76	102	76	102	127	203	279	254	152	152	102	76
	in.	3	4	3	4	5	8	11	10	6	6	4	3

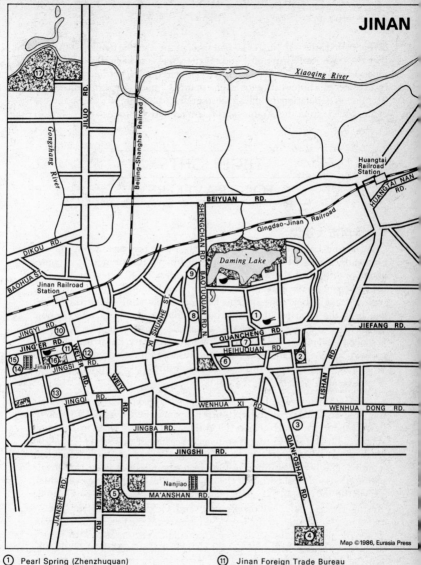

JINAN

Xiaoqing River

Huangtai
Railroad
Station

HUANGTAI NAN RD.

Gongshang River

JILUO RD.

Bejing-Shanghai Railroad

BEIYUAN RD.

Qingdao-Jinan Railroad

DIKOU RD.

SHENGCHAN RD.

BAOTUQUAN RD. N.

Daming Lake

BAOHUA ST.

Jinan Railroad
Station

XI SHUNHE ST.

⑨

⑧

①

JIEFANG RD.

JINGYI RD.

⑩

QUANCHENG RD.

⑦

LISHAN RD.

JING'ER RD.

⑪

HEIHUQUAN RD.

⑥

②

⑮ ⑯

⑫

WEIER RD.

⑭ Jinan JINGSI RD.

WEIYI RD.

⑬ JINGQI RD.

WENHUA XI RD.

WENHUA DONG RD.

JINGBA RD.

③

QIANFOSHAN RD.

JINGSHI RD.

JIANSHE RD.

WEIER RD.

⑤

Nanjiao

MA'ANSHAN RD.

④

Map ©1986, Eurasia Press

① Pearl Spring (Zhenzhuquan)
② Black Tiger Spring (Heihuquan)
③ Shandong Provincial Stadium
④ Thousand Buddha Hill (Qianfoshan)
⑤ Martyrs' Cemetery
⑥ Gushing from the Ground Spring (Baotuquan)
⑦ Department Store
⑧ Five Dragon Spring (Wulongquan)
⑨ Children's Palace
⑩ Worker's Club

⑪ Jinan Foreign Trade Bureau
⑫ New China (Xinhua) Bookstore
⑬ Shandong Province People's Hospital
⑭ China International Travel Service (CITS)
⑮ Civil Aviation Administration of China (CAAC)
⑯ People's (Renmin) Park
⑰ Golden Ox (Jinniu) Park

🏢 Hotels
🍴 Restaurants

of that period attests to Jinan's favorable reputation among foreigners, noting that the town was "salubrious, and, as the streets are kept clean under the supervision of the Police Office, the city has rarely suffered from epidemics." In all respects, a noteworthy achievement for a Chinese city at that time.

Jinan's population includes a substantial Muslim minority whose antecedents, traders from the Arabic world, settled here centuries ago.

HIGHLIGHTS
FOR TRAVELERS

济南市大明湖

Daming Lake. Located in the northeastern part of town by the old city walls, Daming Lake is the source of Jinan's 102 springs. It occupies about one-third of the old city (460 hectares; 1,140 acres) and has an idyllic setting, with water lilies, gardens, and teahouses. The visitor may wish to take a boat ride on the lake or simply stroll along the shore, watching the local population gather to chat or play *weiqi*, the Chinese version of Go. There are a number of temples around the lake, as well as a small museum with some interesting Han pottery unearthed in local excavations. At the entrance gate is an inscription that translates: "Lotus on four sides, willows on three; encircling hills, a lake within."

济南温泉

Jinan Springs. The four main springs which comprise Jinan's greatest tourist asset all have colorfully descriptive names: Five Dragon (Wu Long); Pearl (Zhenzhu); Black Tiger (Heihu); and Gushing from the Ground (Baotu). Black Tiger Spring is so named because of three tigers carved in black stone. They appear to be roaring as water spouts forth from their mouths. The largest spring, Gushing from the Ground, is set in a lovely park in the southwest corner of the city. It consists of three crevices which spew water into the air as high as ten feet. Other springs in the park include Racing Horses, Jade, Willow Branch, and Golden Thread, the last so-called because the rays of the setting sun transform the water's color to gold. The park also contains pavilions and a temple. Visitors may wish to stop at the Li Qingzhao Museum, named after the famous female poet who was born in Jinan in 1084.

千佛山

Thousand Buddha Mountain. Recently, a guide remarked that this should be called "No Buddha Mountain," since so many of its original statues were demolished in the late 1960s through the excesses of the Cultural Revolution. However, the mountain is still worth a visit since the two temples halfway up afford a stunning view of Jinan and the surrounding countryside.

千佛岩
Thousand Buddha Cliff. Also located in the southern part of the city, this area does have some Buddhas, albeit only 210 (a "thousand" is a Chinese figure of speech denoting "many"). While the view is not as good as from Thousand Buddha Mountain, the famous Four Gate Pagoda is located here, as is a lovely bamboo grove where a spring bubbles year-round.

黄河河堤
Yellow River Dikes. Jinan's dikes are nothing short of remarkable, and a visit here (only a half-hour from downtown) is a must. Standing on top of the massive stone embankment, one can only wonder at the mercurial, impetuous nature of this anemic-looking stream. For it was here that the Yellow River earned the sobriquet "China's Sorrow" by periodically flooding Jinan and the surrounding area. The embankment, together with a number of pumping stations, now harnesses the river for irrigation. Upkeep stations line the vast length of dikes, while horses, carts, and building materials testify to the continuous all-out effort necessary to hold off the ever-present threat of devastation.

金牛公园
Golden Ox Park. This park is located on the mountain slopes just outside of Jinan. Its highest point affords a panoramic view of the city. The park also houses a zoo.

HOTEL
ACCOMMODATIONS

济南饭店
Jinan Hotel (240 Jingsan Rd.; tel: 38981; telex: 39106 TSHJIV CN). The address of this hotel reflects Jinan's preoccupation with textiles: it sits at the junction of Jingsan (Warp 3) and Weiliu (Woof 6) roads. Part of the hotel was formerly a Japanese consulate. Its 65 rooms are rather small and the dining room is distinguished neither for its cuisine nor its cleanliness. (It should be noted, however, that as tourism spreads in China, hotels in smaller towns such as Jinan are beginning to learn to change tablecloths after each sitting, to provide shower curtains in bathrooms, and so on.) The hotel's garden is a pleasant place to stroll in the evening or early morning.

南郊宾馆
Nanjiao Hotel (2 Ma'anshan Rd.; tel: 23931; telex: 39104 NJBJN CN). On the southern edge of the city stands the Nanjiao ("Southern Suburbs") Hotel. Although the Jinan has the advantage of being close to downtown, the Nanjiao is far from the urban clamor and offers the mountains as scenic backdrop. Food, service, and rooms are at about the same level as at the Jinan Hotel.

SHANDONG CUISINE

Shandong cuisine, of which Jinan cooking is a branch, ranks among the most accomplished of China's regional cuisines. The distinctive ingredient here is *qingtang* (also called *gaotang*), a condiment prepared as a broth and used in preparing a variety of dishes. Visitors can sample the best of Jinan dishes at the following restaurants:

燕喜堂饭店
Yanxi Tang Restaurant (292 Quancheng Rd., Old City District; tel: 23451). The specialty here is soup, particularly the Pucai in Cream Soup, a prototypical example of Jinan fare.

聚丰德饭店
Jufengde Restaurant (100 Jingshan Rd.; tel: 33905). From 30 to 40 varieties of fish and seafood dishes are prepared in this restaurant.

汇泉饭店
Huiquan Restaurant (22 Baotuquan Bei Rd.; tel: 20391). This restaurant is housed on the first floor of a five-story building (floors 2–5 serve as a hotel). The famous specialty is "Sweet and Sour Carp of the Yellow River," said to have been originated by an imperial chef of the Qing Dynasty.

大明湖饭店
Daming Lake Restaurant (opposite the South Gate of the Daming Lake Park; tel: 20584). Famous for its crispy "Bapi Guozi" (mainly eaten for breakfast), the restaurant also serves delicacies such as "Pork in Lotus Leaf," "Squirrel Fish," and "Chicken in the Bag."

SHOPPING

The most interesting stores of Jinan are located within a few blocks of the Jinan Hotel. Especially noteworthy is the Shandong Provincial Antiques Shop (321 Quancheng Rd.; tel: 23446), with its marvelous selection of straw and bamboo products, including lovely hexagonal and cylindrical hats which, at about US$.50, rank among China's great souvenir bargains. The store stocks over 300,000 antique items, including jade, emerald, bronze and porcelain items, and hardwood furniture. Other stores that merit a visit include the Shandong Display-and-Sale Service Department for Tourists (junction of Jingsi and Wei'er roads, opposite the Daguanyuan Bazaar), which mostly features local arts and crafts, and the Jinan Arts and Crafts Service Department, a two-story building at 3 Nanmen Street that carries a wide spectrum of mosaics and mahogany carvings.

中国国际旅行社
CITS (Luxingshe) Office in Jinan ▣ 26 Jingshi Road. Tel: 45945 x74.
Telex: 39144 SDTJN CN.

开封

to open the seals

Kaifeng

traditional spelling/Kaifeng

KAIFENG is located in eastern Henan Province, a few kilometers south of the Yellow River and east of the provincial capital, Zhengzhou. Unlike most other Chinese cities, its population has increased little in recent decades (from 280,000 in 1923 to about 340,000 today). Kaifeng is known for its fine silks and embroidery work. It is also a commercial center serving the Huabei Plains region to the east. New industry has been developed here since 1949, including electrical, chemical, and agricultural machinery plants, and flour and edible oil processing mills. Winters in Kaifeng are cold and dry, while summers are hot and wet. Spring and autumn are the best times to visit.

KAIFENG IN HISTORY

Kaifeng served as the capital of the State of Wei (220–265) and later as the capital of China during the Five Dynasties period (907–960). It achieved its greatest fame, however, under the Northern Song (960–1127), when it became an elegant and prosperous city. It was laid out in three concentric circles—an Imperial City, Inner City, and Outer City—a pattern later replicated in rectangular form by the Yuan Emperors in Beijing. Canals were built alongside its merchant arcades and filled with lotus blossoms.

Kaifeng was pillaged by the invading Jin in 1127 and was never restored. Today all that remains of its former magnificence is a scroll painted by Zhang Zeduan (now in the Imperial Palace in Beijing) depicting the busy town center.

During the Jin Dynasty (1115–1234), a sizable Jewish population of Mediterranean origin, who migrated to China in about the 7th century, moved to Kaifeng from Hangzhou. Jewish merchants and bankers wielded significant influence in the city during the 14th and 15th centuries, when they numbered over 1,000. Three important stelae in the town, dated 1489, 1512, and 1619, memorialize the presence of this community. By the late 19th century, the Jewish presence in Kaifeng all but ceased to exist. In the 1980s, only a handful of elderly survivors—with only tenuous recollections of their Jewish roots—could be found in the city.

In 1644, attempting to defend Kaifeng against the invading Manchus, the city elders opened the dikes of the Yellow River. A disastrous flood resulted, killing over 300,000 people. Indeed, the constant flooding of the Yellow River has always been a problem here, and may explain why Kaifeng never became a major industrial center.

Climate		Jan	Feb	Mar	Apr	May	Jun	Jul	Aug	Sep	Oct	Nov	Dec
Temp.	°C	−0.3	2.1	7.7	14.8	21.1	26.3	27.5	25.9	21	15.1	7.8	1.6
	°F	31.5	35.8	45.9	59.7	70	79.4	81.5	78.6	69.8	59.2	46	34.9
Precip.	mm.	76	76	76	102	152	203	305	254	178	152	102	76
	in.	3	3	3	4	6	8	12	10	7	6	4	3

A commune wedding, central China

HIGHLIGHTS
FOR TRAVELERS

Most of Kaifeng's historic sites are within the city walls (which still stand) and in walking distance of one another. For those so inclined, bicycles can be rented at the small private shop near the railway station.

东大寺

Dong Da Mosque. One of Henan province's most active Muslim religious centers, Dong Da Mosque was rebuilt in 1922 after a disastrous flood destroyed most of the city. Some of the materials used to restore the mosque are said to have come from the old Jewish synagogue, most of which was washed away in an earlier flood.

龙亭

Dragon Pavilion. Dragon Pavilion is located in the northwest section of the city near the old town walls, marking the site of the former Song imperial stronghold. The pavilion is a pyramid-shaped building composed of several massive terraces. At one time it served as the hall where national candidates sat for the imperial civil service examinations. Its name derives from the huge stone at its center, which is carved with dragons. The stone may once have served as a pedestal for the throne.

铁塔

Iron Pagoda. This beautiful 13-story pagoda, built in 1049 under the Song, stands 53.4 m. (175 ft.) high. Although badly damaged by Japanese bombings in 1938, it has been fully restored. It is entirely covered with brown glazed tiles and decorated with mythical animals and Bodhisattvas.

相国寺
Xiangguo Si Monastery. The original monastery was founded in AD 555; rebuilt several times under the Tang, Northern Song, and Ming dynasties; and completely destroyed in the flood of 1644. The current buildings, dating from 1766, used to house one of China's foremost Buddhist monasteries. The structures, completely restored, now contain a nursery school, a youth palace, a library, and other cultural facilities.

古吹台（禹王台）
Old Music Terrace (King Yu's Terrace). This structure is located in a beautiful park in the southeastern section of Kaifeng. Great Tang poets such as Du Fu and Li Bai came here to drink wine and recite poetry. Even today, the park retains its peaceful, evocative atmosphere.

HOTEL ACCOMMODATIONS

开封宾馆
Kaifeng Guesthouse (102 Ziyou Road; tel: 23901) receives most of the foreign travelers to Kaifeng. *Rates:* Y130 (double); Y250 (suite).

东京宾馆
Eastern Capital Hotel (Yingbin Avenue; tel: 31075), opened in 1987, has doubles for Y110 and suites for Y200.

中国国际旅行社
CITS (Luxingshe) Office in Kaifeng ■ 64 Ziyou Road. Tel: 23737.

Retired workers play a match of Chinese chess

Kashgar

喀什

alternate spelling / Kashi

KASHGAR is the westernmost city in China and, certainly, one of the most remote urban settlements on earth. More than 2,000 miles west of Beijing, some 665 miles west of Ürümqi, and less than 100 miles from the USSR, Kashgar was effectively closed to foreign visits until 1985. It lies at an elevation of 1,289 m. (4,229 ft.) in the broad strip of arable land bounded on the north by the Tian Shan ("Celestial Mountains"), on the west by the Pamirs ("Roof of the World"), and on the east by the formidable Taklamakan Desert. With less than four inches of rain a year, the city and its surroundings are watered by streams from the snow-clad mountains. For centuries, the economy had depended primarily on agriculture and somewhat less heavily on handicrafts; in recent years, it has made room for some light industry. Kashgar, however, is one of China's least Sinicized cities and retains a distinctly medieval, central Asian cast.

The population of the city and the suburbs now approaches 200,000. It is made up mostly (about 90%) of so-called "minorities," and it is predominantly Muslim. Uighurs constitute the largest segment, far outnumbering the Kirghiz and the Kazakhs as well as the Han Chinese. Particularly since the Cultural Revolution, the People's Republic has tried to conciliate the Muslim "minorities" and to encourage preservation of their cultures. For example, Uighurs have held important offices, may worship freely in their mosques, and do not have to restrict the number of their offspring. They have built a reputation throughout China for their fruit-growing, their elegant craftsmanship, and their spirited singing and dancing. The signs on shops and other buildings are rendered in the Uighur language as well as in Chinese.

Two roads that cross near the center of Kashgar divide the city into four sectors. Liberation Road leads northeastward, in the direction of Ürümqi, and southward to Yarkant; Tluze Road runs westward to the Karakoram Highway, which continues southward to Taxkorgan and into Pakistan. The Tuman River bounds the northwestern sector of the city on the north and then flows down through the two eastern sectors, past the East Lake.

The rail line does not extend to Kashgar. Normally, tourists come from Ürümqi by air. The flight to the Kashgar airport, 13 km. (8 mi.) northeast of the city, takes four hours, with a 20-minute stop at Aksu. Some travelers, moved by curiosity or impecuniousness, ride from Ürümqi to Kashgar on the bus, which takes nearly four days.

Climate		Jan	Feb	Mar	Apr	May	Jun	Jul	Aug	Sep	Oct	Nov	Dec
Temp.	°C	−4.1	−0.5	7.5	15.2	20.8	24.7	26.6	25.5	21.1	13.8	5.2	−2.5
	°F	24.5	31	45.5	59.5	69.5	76.5	80	78	70	57	41.5	27.5
Precip.	mm.	15	3	13	5	8	5	10	8	3	3	5	8
	in.	.6	.1	.5	.2	.3	.2	.4	.3	.1	.1	.2	.3

The Karakoram Connection. Alternatively, since May 1986, foreigners may be permitted to approach Kashgar from the south on the Karakoram Highway. The journey from Islamabad in Pakistan via Gilgit and the Khunjerab Pass (4,899 m. = 16,072 ft.)—1,280 km. (795 mi.)—entails approximately 36 hours of arduous travel by four-wheel-drive vehicles in extraordinarily mountainous country.

KASHGAR IN HISTORY

Kashgar has existed for more than 2,000 years. The old city, called Shule, was taken by the Chinese in 76 BC. As an important station on the Silk Road linking China with Persia and the Mediterranean world, and as the northern terminus of a trading route that connected Eastern Turkestan with India, Kashgar became a meeting place of cultures. In 640, under the Tang Dynasty, it was established as one of the "Four Garrisons" of western China; but it lay at such a distance from Chinese governmental and military headquarters that it was difficult to defend against roving Turkic tribesmen, Tibetans, and Arabs. Moreover, after a period of adherence to Buddhism, the people turned in the 10th century to Islam and, for a millennium thereafter, responded sporadically to separatist agitation. In short, the history of Kashgar before 1955, although often obscure, was complex and often tumultuous.

The earliest known dwellers at Kashgar appear to have been blue-eyed Indo-Europeans who derived their culture from India and Persia. By the 4th century the city was a recognized center of Buddhist learning. The first Uighurs reached the area in the 9th century; their successors founded a separatist régime, adopted Islam, and made Kashgar their capital for a time. This kingdom fell in 1120, and the next was swept away 100 years later by Genghis Khan, whose second son, Jagatai, held Kashgar as a dependency. In about 1275, Marco Polo noted both the activity of Kashgari traders and the presence in the city of several Nestorian Christians. Ravaged by the Mongol emperor Timur (Tamerlane) in 1389–90, the fortifications were leveled and then reconstructed in the early 16th century.

Islam. During the 17th century, conflict erupted in Kashgaria between two factions of *khojas*, or Muslim holy men. As leader of the White Mountain People, the venerated Hazrat Apak defeated the Black Mountain People, displaced the last Jagatai khan of Kashgar, and briefly reunited the country as a protectorate of the Dzungars to the north. In 1755 a later White Mountain chief put down a Black Mountain rebellion and declared independence both from the Dzungars and from the Chinese; but in 1759, Qing generals annexed the "New March" (Xinjiang), and in 1779 they quelled a further revolt. In the winter of 1864–65, the Muslim adventurer Yakub Beg took Kashgar and set up an independent kingdom; he died in 1877, and the Chinese recaptured the entire region.

Western Contacts. Muslim restiveness not only complicated developments in China but also attracted the attention of foreign powers. In 1882 a Russian consul arrived at Kashgar; in 1890 a British consul took up residence at Chini Bagh and commenced endeavors to counteract Russian influence. For years, the consulates were familiar ground to Western travelers and explorers, from Sven Hedin and Aurel Stein to the Roosevelt brothers and Peter Fleming. During the 1930s the Japanese, as well as the Russians and the British, showed interest in manifestations of anti-Chinese sentiment. For several months in 1934, a Muslim rebel based his army at Kashgar, and in 1945 two dissident groups proclaimed the short-lived Eastern Turkestan Republic.

Ultimately, in 1955, the People's Republic established the Xinjiang Uighur Autonomous Region, with Kashgar as the principal city in the southwest.

HIGHLIGHTS
FOR TRAVELERS

With the assistance of a CITS guide, tourists without a heightened sense of verisimilitude might arrange to visit a Uighur family and to see a song-and-dance performance by adult Uighurs at a local theater (in season) or by six-year-olds at the Kashgar Minority Kindergarten.

艾提尕尔清真寺
Id Kah Mosque. The Great Mosque, one of the largest in the country, faces a broad square near the heart of the city. Said to have a history of 500 years, it continues to attract worshipers at prayer times and on festival days. The strength of Islam in Kashgar is further borne out by the existence of nearly 100 small neighborhood mosques.

集市
Open Markets. To browse or buy in the market just east of the Id Kah Mosque is fascinating enough on any day. On a Sunday, the Great Market in the northeast sector of the city makes a quite unforgettable spectacle, not to be missed. Thousands come from miles around to buy, sell, or inspect sheep and camels, pelts and hides, hats and boots, dazzling fabrics and rugs, doors and metal piping for their houses, spices and delicious Hami melons, goats' heads and desiccated amphibians. Innumerable Central Asian faces—bearded Uighur elders with fur-trimmed hats, and Muslim women with colorful kerchiefs or brown veils covering their heads—remind the visitor that this region was once called Turkestan. The crowd is immense, and the drivers of donkey carts press through with a cry that sounds like "Push, push"; and yet one turns away from the scene with the greatest reluctance.

阿巴和加麻扎（墓）
Tomb of Abakh Hoja. This domed mausoleum in the northeast corner of Kashgar is so named in pamphlets for travelers and, alternatively, transposed on postcards as the Tomb of Huja Abbak; it figures in the reports by earlier 20th-century travelers as the tomb of the khoja Hazrat Apak. Though much redone and still in need of attention, it deserves a visit. Here five generations of a respected family lie entombed. A girl of the family, the beautiful Xiangfei, taken away in the 18th century to the court of the Emperor Qian Long, wept for her native place and was

brought back after her death. Locally, on her account, the mausoleum has still another name: Tomb of the Fragrant Concubine. There is an extensive graveyard behind the main building. It is said that the body of Yakub Beg was buried in the grounds but removed after the city was recaptured.

Ancient Sites. Kashgaria has been devastated so often that the ancient remains are few. Of the old city of Shule hardly a trace is left. Hanoi, a town 29 km. (18 mi.) to the east, was prosperous under the Tang Dynasty but was seemingly abandoned after the 11th century. The conspicuous feature today is a ruined temple. On a cliff north of Kashgar, in the San Xian (Three Immortals) Caves, which are not easy to reach, there are discernible Buddhist frescoes.

帕米尔高原

Pamir Plateau. Distance and haze work against the tourist's hopes to see high peaks from Kashgar. Anyone who can manage to travel 185 km. (115 mi.) to the southwest, by car or bus on the Karakoram Highway, will come to the Kalakuli (or Karakol) Lake on the Pamir Plateau, close to the USSR frontier. To the north looms Kongur Shan (7,719 m. = 25,325 ft.); to the south, Mustagh Ata (7,546 m. = 24,757 ft.). A Sino-Soviet expedition made the first ascent of Mustagh Ata in 1956, and three US skiers reached the summit in 1980; a British party climbed Kongur Shan in 1981.

► ◄

HOTEL

ACCOMMODATIONS

喀什噶尔宾馆

Kashgar Hotel (Tawohoze Road; tel: 2367, 2368). This comfortable hotel in the northeast sector of the city is now clearly the first choice for tourists. It offers double rooms with private baths, and it provides good and plentiful meals; it stands in a spacious compound, away (indeed, far away) from the town's bustle and dust.

色满宾馆

Seman Hotel (Seman Rd.; tel: 2129, 2060). During the busy summer season, tour groups are often accommodated here, just west of the city proper. The hotel is the old Russian consulate, which has been renovated. Like the Kashgar Hotel, it has double rooms with private baths, but no dormitory facilities.

齐尼巴克宾馆

Qinibake Hotel (tel: 2291, 2103). Formerly Chini Bagh, the British consulate, this hotel has been described in recent years as a resting place for transport workers. Each of the rooms inspected has three or four beds, a stove, and a portable washbowl or two.

中国国际旅行社
CITS (Luxingshe) Office in Kashgar ■ Liberation Road. Tel: 3156/2217.

Kunming

KUNMING, the capital of Yunnan Province, is distinguished both by its delightful year-round climate and by its ethnically rich population. The city is also a regionally important manufacturing center and a major transportation crossroads for southwest China. Although traditionally regarded as one of China's more isolated and backward provincial capitals, the growing economic and strategic importance of China's southwestern provinces since the late 1930s has spurred rapid growth. Kunming municipality (including rural areas and satellite towns) now boasts a population of 1,930,000, many of whom are members of China's ethnic minority groups, including the Yi, Hui, Bai, Miao, and Hani.

Kunming lies on a flat, fertile plain at an elevation of 1,894 m. (6,200 ft.) in the center of the Yunnan Plateau. The city is encircled by mountains to the north, west, and east; a large lake, Dianchi, adjoins the southwestern edge of the city. Subtropical Kunming is often termed the "city of eternal spring" because of its temperate weather and perpetually blooming flowers. Its short winters are sunny and dry. Late afternoon thunderstorms occur during July and August. The mean annual temperature is the most pleasant of any city in China: 15°C (59°F).

KUNMING IN HISTORY

Kunming's history goes back over 2,000 years to 279 BC, when a general of the Chu Kingdom settled with his troops near Lake Dianchi. In AD 109, during the reign of Emperor Wudi of the Han Dynasty, the city of "Kunzhou" was established to the southeast of present-day Kunming. Towards the end of the Yuan Dynasty, the area became known as Kunming County. In 1832, a traditional walled city was erected, which became Kunming municipality in 1928. From its founding through the 19th century, this isolated provincial capital was the region's major market and transport center. Until this century, Kunming was an archetypal Chinese city—characterized by congestion, dirt, and a maze of winding cul-de-sac crooked lanes lined with one- and two-story wood and mud-brick buildings. The residents were considered "provincial" and Kunming was considered a hardship post by Chinese administrators sent there to govern the province. Until 1949, many of Beijing's political "undesirables" were banished here.

Climate		Jan	Feb	Mar	Apr	May	Jun	Jul	Aug	Sep	Oct	Nov	Dec
Temp.	°C	9.6	11.0	14.4	17.8	19.3	19.5	20.1	19.8	18.3	15.7	12.7	10.2
	°F	49.2	51.8	57.9	64	66.7	67.1	68.1	67.6	64.9	60.2	54.8	50.3
Precip.	mm.	8	18	28	41	127	132	196	198	97	51	56	15
	in.	.3	.7	1.1	1.6	5	5.2	7.7	7.8	3.8	2	2.2	.6

Kunming in the Revolution. Although the completion of the French Indochina Rail Line into Kunming in 1910 stimulated the city's commercial development, major changes and sizable growth did not occur until the Japanese invasion of China and the onset of World War II. When the Nationalists moved their capital to Chongqing, refugees from East China poured westward, with many reaching Kunming. Moreover, thousands of Yunnanese peasants from the countryside migrated to work in the numerous factories that were established. During the Second World War, the US Air Force's "Flying Tigers" were based in Kunming. In fact, the foundation and basic design of Kunming's present airport is a legacy of US military forces. Inevitably the impact of the 1937–45 period eroded the city's parochialism and brought a gradual turn toward more progressive and more modern attitudes.

Today, urban Kunming resembles other major Chinese cities. Industrial and commercial districts have been established, new, wide streets and modern office buildings have been built, and roads and railroads now connect the city with the surrounding region and other parts of China.

ECONOMY AND CULTURE

Kunming, as the center of transportation routes and communications in Yunnan, is served by both the "Burma Road" of World War II fame and the former French Indochina Rail Line, which was originally constructed to facilitate copper extraction. Built between 1910 and 1913, the railroad once stretched 975 km. from Kunming to Haiphong in Vietnam. Service now terminates at the Vietnamese border. Industrialization has been aided by a mineral-rich hinterland (including important deposits of coal, iron ore, and copper), and the city's factories produce a wide range of industrial and consumer goods. Kunming also serves as Yunnan's military center. Today there are over 900 major industrial enterprises in the city which manufacture a wide assortment of steel and other metal products, machinery, mining equipment, chemicals, motor vehicles, textiles, and several consumer items such as bicycles, watches, and sewing machines.

There are 11 colleges and universities in Kunming, including the tree-lined campuses of Yunnan University, Kunming Normal College, Yunnan Agricultural University, and the Institute for Nationalities.

HIGHLIGHTS
FOR TRAVELERS

Kunming is famous for its comfortable climate, its beautiful scenery, and the diversity of its inhabitants. Twenty-two of China's minority ethnic groups live in Yunnan Province and visitors here would be remiss if they did not take advantage of the opportunities afforded here to learn more

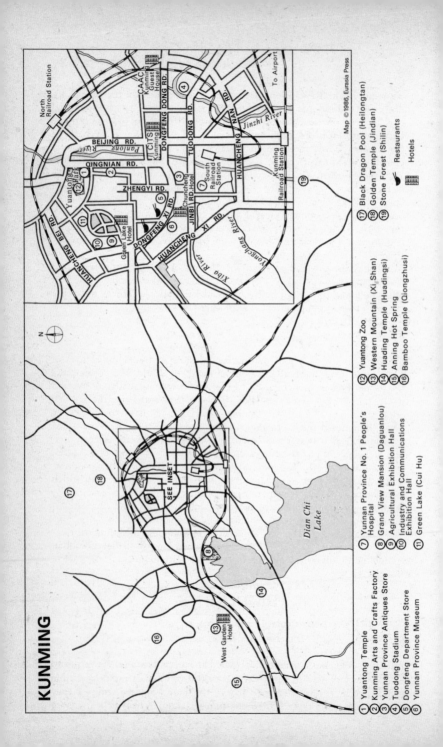

KUNMING

N

① Yuantong Temple
② Kunming Arts and Crafts Factory
③ Yunnan Province Antiques Store
④ Tuodong Stadium
⑤ Dongfeng Department Store
⑥ Yunnan Province Museum
⑦ Yunnan Province No. 1 People's Hospital
⑧ Grand View Mansion (Daguanlou)
⑨ Agricultural Exhibition Hall
⑩ Industry and Communications Exhibition Hall
⑪ Green Lake (Cui Hu)
⑫ Yuantong Zoo
⑬ Western Mountain (Xi Shan)
⑭ Huading Temple (Huadingsi)
⑮ Anning Hot Spring
⑯ Bamboo Temple (Qiongzhusi)
⑰ Black Dragon Pool (Heilongtan)
⑱ Golden Temple (Jindian)
⑲ Stone Forest (Shilin)

 Restaurants
 Hotels

Dian Chi Lake

West Garden Hotel

SEE INSET

North Railroad Station

CAAC Kunming Guest House

BEIJING RD.

QINGNIAN RD.

Yuantong Park

DONGFENG DONG RD.

CTS/CITS Kunming

Chunchang

ZHENGYI RD.

Green Lake Hotel

DONGFENG XI RD.

HUANCHENG BEI RD.

HUANCHENG XI RD.

JINBI RD.

Chunchang Hotel

South Railroad Station

TUODONG RD.

HUANCHENG NAN RD.

To Airport

Jinzhi River

Kunming Railroad Station

Xiba River

Yongchang River

Panlong River

Map © 1986, Eurasia Press

National minority women inspecting "Shan bags," Kunming

about China's non-Han peoples. It is possible to see some of the most beautiful folk dances in the world at the National Minority Institute or in the Stone Forest area.

The southern half of Kunming has new office and commercial buildings, although old residential structures remain along the alleyways leading from the main thoroughfares. The northern part of the city, devoted primarily to institutional and recreational use, is Kunming's most beautiful section. An excellent view of the area can be had from the remaining section of the old city wall in the northeast, where an elevated, tree-lined promenade passes over a small hill.

翠湖

Green Lake. Located on the northeast edge of Kunming, to the west of Wuhua Hill, Green Lake (Cui Hu) is a large, willow-lined lake with walkways, a temple, and pleasant fields and flower gardens. During the early morning, hundreds of local Chinese come here to exercise and practice martial arts.

园通公园

Yuantong Park. Yuantong Park has been a famous site in Kunming since a Buddhist temple was built here in the middle of the Yuan Dynasty. Located to the northeast of the city at the base of Yuantong Hill (often called "Chignon Hill" because its shape resembles the hairstyle), the park is famous for its zoo. Among the animals on display are pandas, lions, tigers, leopards, elephants, bison, and crocodiles.

筇竹寺

Bamboo Temple. Hidden in a wooded area 11 km. (7 mi.) west of the city, the 700-year-old temple (Qiongzhu Si) is known for its 500 lifelike statues of Buddha's Chinese disciples. These were made between 1883 and 1890 by a sculptor from Sichuan Province and three apprentices. Within the temple is a 14th-century tablet bearing an edict of a Yuan Dynasty emperor. This is of particular historical interest because it is written in the vernacular style, in both Chinese and Mongolian. The temple is called the "Bamboo Temple" because, according to legend, two young princes were chasing a rhinoceros in the hills when it suddenly turned into a monk leaning on a bamboo stick. By the time they reached the spot, all that remained was a bamboo stick which immediately sprouted forth leaves. The temple was built to commemorate this encounter.

金殿

Golden Temple. The Golden Temple (Jindian) is a cast copper structure weighing over 300 tons standing on a carved marble base. An earlier version of the same construction was built in 1602, but was moved elsewhere. The building now standing here was cast in 1670. In front is a large, water-filled urn containing a stone fish with an open mouth. Legend guarantees good luck to visitors who succeed in throwing a coin into the fish's mouth. The temple is 6.5 km. (4 mi.) northeast of the city on Mingfeng Hill.

黑龙潭

Black Dragon Pool. Located in the Wulao Hills, on the northern outskirts of Kunming, the Black Dragon Pool is known for its "four sources of beauty"—the Han Temple, the Tang Plum Tree, the Song Cypress, and the Ming Tomb. Legend has it that ten dragons once lived here, wreaking havoc with the local people. A sympathetic deity killed nine of the dragons and buried them in the pool. A small black dragon was spared and ordered to help local residents by guarding the pool, thus giving the area its name.

滇池

Dianchi Lake. Covering an area of 340 sq. km., Dianchi is the sixth-largest freshwater lake in China. Surrounded by mountains and dotted with multicolored sails, it is one of the loveliest spots in Yunnan. Pleasure boats often stop at a small island where a rest home for retired workers and soldiers is located. Daguang Park, with its many pavilions and flower gardens, is on the northern bank.

西山

Western Hills. Also known as "Sleeping Beauties" because their form is said to resemble a sleeping woman, the Western Hills overlook Dianchi Lake. Several famous temples and pagodas are located here. The San Qing Pavilions and Dragon Gate stand atop Buddha Hill, the high point of the range. The San Qing Pavilions, which jut out from the steep cliff wall, were built in the Yuan Dynasty as part of a summer resort for the royal family. They were extended and renovated during the Qing Dynasty. Dragon Gate, a group of caves and statues carved from the mountain rock, is on the summit. This work was begun in 1781 and completed after 72 years of constant labor by over 70 masons from a nearby village. The Huating Temple, the largest Buddhist temple in Kunming, is also in the Western Hills. Although the temple dates back to the 14th century, most of the buildings now standing were erected during a major expansion in 1920.

云南民族学院

The Institute for Minority Studies. The Institute for Minority Studies is a university focusing on studies related to the more than 20 minority ethnic groups that live in Yunnan Province. Most of the 20,000 students attending the institute are either themselves minority members or the children of Han parents who have worked in the border areas. It is occasionally possible for tourists to visit demonstrations or exhibitions at the university.

石林
THE STONE FOREST

Located 126 km. to the southeast of Kunming in Lunan County, the Stone Forest ranks with Guilin and the Yangtse River Gorges as one of China's remarkable natural phenomena. Towering peaks of bizarre-shaped limestone, some as high as a six-story building, cover an area of over 80 hectares (200 acres). The Stone Forest is a typical karst structure formed by the erosive effect of streams of water when the area was submerged some 270 million years ago. A 2-km.-long path winds through the densest portion of the "forest"; within this area are a number of pavilions, caves, and ponds, each with its own legend. Each year during June 23–25 the local Yi nationality people hold their Torch Festival—three days of singing, dancing, and game playing—in the Stone Forest.

Adjacent to the Stone Forest is the village of Wulouke, inhabited by the Sanyi, a subgroup of the Yi. From the early morning until dusk, elderly women and girls, dressed in traditional blue and black hats and tunics, sell embroidered clothing on the banks of the Stone Forest Lake.

The area is certainly engaging enough to warrant an overnight stay, and the **Stone Forest Guest House** is now available for that purpose. The six-building complex has 80 rooms. Sanyi music and dance troupes visit the hotel each evening to provide entertainment for visitors.

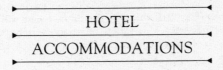

HOTEL
ACCOMMODATIONS

Foreign travelers in Kunming generally stay at either the Green Lake or Kunming hotels. Rates at each are Y36 for a double room.

翠湖饭店
Green Lake Hotel (6 Cuihu Nan Lu; tel: 22192/23514; telex: 64027 KMITS CN). The Green Lake Hotel is a comfortable, modern facility located in the western part of the city, opposite Green Lake Park. Built in 1956 and completely renovated in 1981, the hotel now contains 172 twin-bedded rooms and suites. Facilities include a bank, a post office, and hairdresser on the first floor, a large gift shop and antiques store on the second, a coffee shop on the third.

昆明饭店
Kunming Hotel (145 Dongfeng Dong Road; tel: 22063; telex: 64058 KMHTL). The Kunming Hotel has two buildings, one built in 1950, the other in 1979. Both are well maintained and comfortable. Facilities include a gift shop, antiques store, bank, hairdresser, coffee shop, and auditorium.

西园饭店

West Garden Hotel (at the foot of the Western Hills; tel: 9969). This small hotel faces Dianchi Lake and has the Western Hills as its backdrop. Composed of two villas, the hotel has only 30 rooms. Those in the inner-court villa are furnished with private baths, while outer-court rooms offer only shared facilities. A definite attraction is the hotel's swimming pool, which is set in the midst of a peaceful garden.

昆湖饭店

Kunhu Fandian (tel: 7732). This noisy but clean hotel provides budget accommodations at Y15 for doubles and grim dorms full of spunky backpackers who pay just Y3 a bed. It is located 1 km. north of the railroad station.

SHOPPING

Batiks (surprisingly uncommon in China) and delightful handwoven products are produced in profusion in Yunnan. The gift shops in the Green Lake and Kunming hotels both offer a good selection of items. The Friendship Store, located on the second floor of the department store in downtown Kunming, must certainly rank among the worst in China for its limited and unimaginative array of offerings. The Provincial Minority Municipal Store on Zhengyi Road specializes in products made by local minority people. Travelers who visit the Stone Forest will find that the peasants in the area sell a wide variety of attractive embroidered clothing and bags, though often at high prices.

YUNNAN CUISINE

Yunnan ham and Yunnan duck are justly famous local dishes. Yunnan chicken is steamed with only minimal spices in an earthernware crock until it is tender and flavorful, and is served with a delicious broth. The food in both hotels is excellent. Visitors should also try eating at the Beijing Restaurant (Xin Xiangyun St.; tel: 3214), the Shanghai Restaurant (Dongfeng Xi Rd.; tel: 2987), and the Chuncheng Restaurant (Dongfeng Xi Rd.; tel: 4154).

中国国际旅行社
CITS (Luxingshe) Office in Kunming ■ 145 Dongfeng Dong Road. Tel: 25922/24992.
Telex: 64027 KMITS CN.

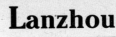

Lanzhou

the fragrant city   *traditional spelling/Lanchow*

LANZHOU, situated on the upper reaches of the Yellow River, is the capital of Gansu Province, which forms a narrow desert corridor between northeast China and Xinjiang. Lanzhou occupies one of the oases dotted along the old Silk Road extending westward across Central Asia to the Middle East and Europe. The "fragrant city" functioned for more than two millennia as a vital stopping-place for caravans and as a garrison town. During World War II, Lanzhou was a crucial supply depot for China's struggle against Japanese occupation.

Since 1949, Lanzhou has become one of the principal industrial bases in northwestern China, with oil refineries, petrochemical complexes, copper and aluminum plants, machine-making factories, and textile mills. It has emerged since the 1960s as the center of China's atomic energy industry, with a number of scientific institutes. The population has swelled to more than 2,000,000. The National Minorities Institute at Lanzhou serves the large numbers of minority peoples who live in the region, including Mongols, Tibetans, Uighurs, and Hui people.

Location and industrial development have enhanced the importance of the city as a junction for northwest China. Lanzhou is linked by rail to Beijing and Shanghai via Xi'an, to Beijing via Baotou and Hohhot, and to Urümqi via the Gansu Corridor. Generally, travelers either break the very long train journeys here or arrive at Lanzhou by air. The airport is 72 km. (43 mi.) from the city. In 1979, a four-lane bridge of reinforced concrete was built across the Yellow River.

Another consequence of industrial development has been pollution. One well-traveled Westerner thinks of the smog over Lanzhou as suggestive of nuclear winter; another, ignoring the fact that the sky not far from town may well be clear blue, explains the pall as mainly dust from the Gobi. The old city, however, retains picturesqueness, with a number of quaint streets set off by interesting, though dilapidated, oriental arches. Visitors will notice the squat towers distributed about town. These are for garbage collection and disposal: accumulated rubbish is let out through a trap door onto the back of a waiting cart or truck.

Climate. Winters are harsh and dry, with temperatures in January as low as −20°C (−12°F). There are strong winds in the spring, but summers

Climate		Jan	Feb	Mar	Apr	May	Jun	Jul	Aug	Sep	Oct	Nov	Dec
Temp.	°C	−7.3	−2.8	5.0	11.5	17.0	20.1	22.0	21.0	15.5	9.6	1.3	−5.6
	°F	18.9	27	41	52.7	62.6	68.1	71.6	69.8	59.9	49.2	34.3	22
Precip.	mm.	76	76	76	102	152	203	305	254	178	152	102	76
	in.	3	3	3	4	6	8	12	10	7	6	4	3

are dry and comfortably warm. Wheat, millet, tobacco, and sorghum are grown in fertile areas within the municipality. The region's honeydew melons are prized throughout China, as are such locally grown exotica as angelica, asiabel root, and black watermelon seed. Traditional handicrafts available in Lanzhou include Dao ink slabs, Jiuquan jade cups, and carved bottle gourds.

HIGHLIGHTS

FOR TRAVELERS

甘肃省博物馆

Gansu Province Museum. Just across the street from the Friendship Hotel, the museum houses the "Flying Horse of Gansu," one of China's most reproduced sculptures. It has also the complete skeleton of a mammoth, a good selection of Neolithic Yangshao pottery, Western Zhou sacrificial tripods, and a reconstruction of a Han tomb with some lovely primitive wall paintings. The exhibition has three sections: Primitive Society, Slave Society, and Feudal Society.

白塔山

White Pagoda Mountain (Baita Shan). On terraces of this hill on the north bank of the Yellow River, there is a park with pavilions and towers of the Qing Dynasty. The White Pagoda, a Buddhist shrine, has stood atop the hill for more than 500 years. On a clear day, the view of the city and the river is extensive.

五泉公园

Five Springs Park (Wuquan Gongyuan). The springs in this park, which lies in the southeastern part of the city, at the foot of the Kaolan Mountain, are said to have been uncovered by a Han general. A temple stands in the grounds. Among the relics to be seen are a 13th-century bell and a 14th-century Buddha. Nearby are a small restaurant and a zoo.

炳灵寺石窟

Bilingsi. Currently, the finest available excursion from Lanzhou leads to the Buddhist caves of Bilingsi, near Yongjing. To get there takes an interesting hour-and-a-half by road to the dam at the Liujiaxia Hydroelectric Power Station and then about two enjoyable hours by boat on the Yellow River. The first conspicuous feature on arrival is a seated Buddha 27 m. (88½ ft.) in height. Statues and murals in the caves date from the Western Qin and Tang dynasties. Inscriptions in Cave 169, the oldest, date from AD 420.

HOTEL ACCOMMODATIONS

友谊饭店

Friendship Hotel (14 Xijin Xi Rd.; tel: 33051; telex: 72143 LFSHL CN). Though an uninviting gray building in the Soviet style, this hotel is reasonably comfortable, with functional if old-fashioned bathrooms. The dining room serves Western and Chinese food, but neither with much flair. The center of town is a 15-minute ride to the east.

金城宾馆

Jincheng Hotel (209 Tianshui Rd.; tel: 27931). Closer to the city center, in a fairly new seven-story building, the Jincheng Hotel provides decent accommodations, serves food that is at least middling, and has shops and services on the ground floor.

兰州饭店

Lanzhou Hotel (204 West Donggang Rd.; tel: 2832029; telex: 72131 FANDN CN). Located 72 km. from the airport and 10 km. from the railway station, the Lanzhou Hotel, with 254 rooms (Y30–Y50), has both private and shared bath accommodations. There are TVs, telephones, and carpeting in the rooms. A Chinese restaurant and a garden are on the premises.

CUISINE

The **Lanzhou Canting**, a three-story restaurant on Jiuquan Road in the center of town, caters to foreigners. Many of the offerings are splendid. Any dish starting with the words *bai he* includes white lily petals, a local specialty. The crisp *mantou*, a kind of fried bread, makes a change from rice. There are also mutton dishes, favorites of the local Hui (Muslim) people.

中国国际旅行社
CITS (Luxingshe) Office in Lanzhou ■ 209 Tianshui Road. Tel: 26798/26181.
Telex: 72103 CTSLB CN.

Lianyungang 连云港

reaching the clouds harbor   *traditional spelling/Lienyunkang*

EASTERN terminus of the Longhai Railway, China's main east-west trunk line, Lianyungang is the least developed, but potentially one of the most important, of the 14 Coastal Open Cities. Situated in northeast Jiangsu province 400 km. (250 mi.) north of Shanghai and about 300 km. (185 mi.) south of Qingdao, Lianyungang, with its fine rail connections and deep-water harbor, is a natural gateway to China's heartland.

With a population of 2,950,000 (430,000 in the urban districts), Lianyungang is set among low, green hills. Vast salt flats extend south along the coast all the way to the mouth of the Yangtse, nearly 350 km. to the south. The region enjoys a mild, maritime-temperate climate, with the annual mean temperature a pleasant 14°C (57°F); rainfall averages around 1,000 mm. (39 in.) per year.

Construction of Lianyungang's port began only in 1936, when the Dutch built a breakwater and two small docks. The harbor has since been expanded manyfold, and it now ranks as China's eighth largest.

The area around Lianyungang has been one of China's most important salt-producing centers for nearly 2,000 years. In imperial times, salt production and distribution was a state monopoly and provided an important source of revenue for the government. The salt makers themselves, however, were among the poorest people in the country. Today, salt processing still accounts for more than 20% of Lianyungang's total industrial output.

There are several historical sites and scenic spots of note in the vicinity, including a group of Neolithic rock carvings depicting various primitive deities and religious symbols, and a series of small Buddhist sculptures cut into a cliff side just south of the city. These are said to be nearly 2,000 years old, making them among the oldest examples of Buddhist art in China. Within the city limits is a hill topped by a Tang Dynasty temple. Local people claim this hill was the model for Huaguo Mountain, home of the Monkey King, in the classic novel *Journey to the West*.

连云饭店

Lianyun Hotel (75 Zhongshan Rd.; tel: 23776/23479/23541). Located by the sea, the Lianyun has nearly 100 rooms, with most of them triples (Y55). Singles are Y45; doubles Y45–50; and suites, Y70. All rooms are air-conditioned, have private bath, color TV, refrigerator, telephone, and carpeting. The Lianyun has a coffee room, a Chinese restaurant, a 250-seat auditorium, and three meeting rooms.

Climate		Jan	Feb	Mar	Apr	May	Jun	Jul	Aug	Sep	Oct	Nov	Dec
Temp.	°C	−1.1	0.1	4.4	10.3	15.7	20.0	23.7	25.1	21.4	15.9	8.6	1.6
	°F	30	32.1	39.9	50.5	60.2	68	74.6	77.1	70.5	60.6	47.4	34.8
Precip.	mm.	254	254	330	330	305	356	279	279	305	254	203	178
	in.	10	10	13	13	12	14	11	11	12	10	8	7

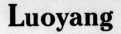

Luoyang

north of the River Luo   *traditional spelling/Loyang*

NOW chiefly an industrial and agricultural city, Luoyang was once the cultural heart—and for centuries, the capital—of ancient China. At its height under the Sui Dynasty (581–618), it was said to have had one million inhabitants. Today the population numbers about 700,000. Luoyang is situated in Henan Province, along the railway line linking Xi'an, 109 km. (68 mi.) to the west, and Zhengzhou, 112 km. (70 mi.) to the east.

In the past, the Luoyang region suffered periodic flooding from the silty Yellow River to the south of the city. The floods are now under control due to the construction of dams and irrigation canals, and the rich soil around Luoyang produces a variety of crops, such as wheat, sorghum, corn, sesame, peanuts, and cotton.

Industrial products of Luoyang include mining equipment, glass, construction machinery, pumps, ball bearings, and tractors. The model East Is Red Tractor Plant is famous throughout China for its modern equipment and the comprehensive social services provided for its workers. In operation since 1959, it was the first such factory to be designed in China, boasting its own hospital, club, technical school, 17 day-care centers, and five primary schools.

The best season to visit Luoyang is autumn. The winters are cold and the summers are hot and humid. Frequent dust storms swirl in March and April, although the weather in late spring can be quite pleasant. Luoyang now has its own recently opened airport to accommodate visitors.

LUOYANG IN HISTORY

Luoyang's history dates back to the Neolithic era (6000–5000 BC), at which time the area was already densely populated. During China's Bronze Age, it served as the capital of the Shang Dynasty (c. 1523–1066 BC) and later as seat of the Zhou Dynasty (c. 1066–221 BC). Excavations at Luoyang, then known as Luoyi, have revealed traces of palaces, temples, marketplaces, and altars from this period.

Luoyang's importance continued under the Qin (221–206 BC) and the Han (206 BC–AD 220), particularly the Eastern Han (AD 25–220). During this latter period, which saw the invention of paper and the introduction of Buddhism to China (AD 68), the city expanded significantly. Historical records speak of the huge imperial college and library, and of the city's illustrious community of writers, historians, astronomers, and scientists.

Climate		Jan	Feb	Mar	Apr	May	Jun	Jul	Aug	Sep	Oct	Nov	Dec
Temp.	°C	−0.2	1.8	8.0	14.6	21.4	26.4	27.8	26.3	20.5	15.0	7.9	1.7
	°F	31.6	35.2	46.4	58.2	70.5	79.5	82	79.3	68.9	59	46.2	35
Precip.	mm.	13	18	18	23	51	102	178	76	25	18	15	13
	in.	.4	.7	.7	.9	2	4	7.0	3.0	1	.7	.6	.4

During the reign of the Northern Wei (386–534), the south-pointing Chinese compass was invented and rock-engraving work on the first of the Longmen Caves was begun. No less than 1,367 Buddhist temples were reported as functioning in Luoyang at the time.

The Sui (581–618) completely destroyed the flourishing town when they conquered the Wei. A new city was constructed, with streets laid out in a grid pattern and two major canals flowing through it, one leading to Beijing and the other to Hangzhou. These canals were capable of handling 500–800-ton barges—all this at a time when Western civilization was deeply mired in the Dark Ages. Under the Sui, Luoyang became a major marketing and commercial center, and 400 inns were established to accommodate the large number of foreign merchants. The emperor, who was also a composer and music lover, brought 3,000 musicians and their families to Luoyang.

Under the Tang (618–907), the city remained prosperous but functioned only as a secondary capital. Wu Zetian (684–710), the famous Tang empress, built magnificent palaces and gardens here. Foreigners from Central Asia introduced Nestorian Christianity to Luoyang in this period, and the city was renowned for its imperial library, its treatises on astronomy and pharmacology, and its beautiful Buddhist frescoes. Its fame as a library center brought important Tang-era poets flocking to Luoyang—among them Du Fu, Bai Juyi, and Li Bai.

The city began to decline after 937 when the Jin moved their capital to Kaifeng. Although it temporarily remained a center for literature, the population steadily dwindled and the town all but disappeared. The Song retreat to the lower Yangtse at the end of the 10th century brought to an end Luoyang's place in national politics. From the 13th century until 1949, Luoyang served as the capital of Henan Province. In recent decades its significance has become that of an industrial town serving the region.

► HIGHLIGHTS
► FOR TRAVELERS

The Longmen Caves are the most famous historical relics in the area, but there are some interesting sights within Luoyang itself.

皇城公园

Royal Town (Huangcheng) Park. The park is noteworthy for its two Han Dynasty tombs, which are located in subterranean caves. Although the coffins have been removed, the artwork in the tombs, including wall paintings and bas-relief carvings on the stone doors, remains.

During the Chinese New Year, the park houses an exhibition of lanterns, which are among Luoyang's traditional crafts.

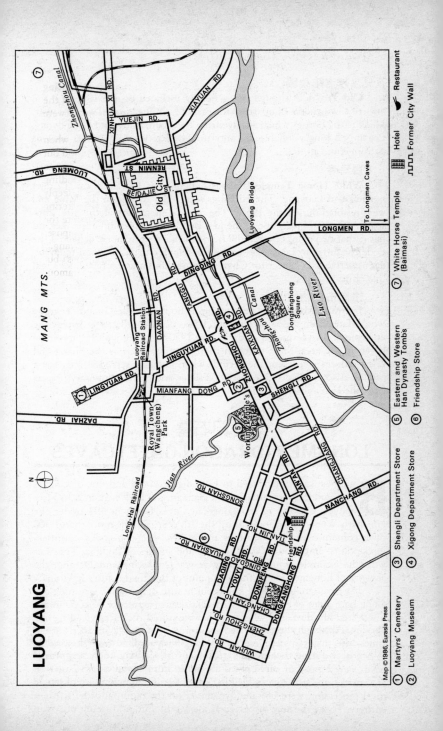

LUOYANG

Map © 1986, Eurasia Press

MANG MTS.

Long-Hai Railroad

Luoyang Railroad Station

DAZHAI RD.

LINGYUAN RD.

Royal Town (Wangcheng) Park

Jian River

MIANFANG DONG

Working People's

ZHENGZHOU RD.
WUHAN RD.
HUASHAN RD.
DAQING RD.
TOUYI RD.
DONGFENG RD.
CHANG'AN RD.
QINGDAO RD.
DONGFANGHONG RD.
SONGSHAN RD.
YAN'AN RD.
CHANGJIANG RD.
TIANJIN RD.
NANCHANG RD.

Friendship

JINGUYUAN RD.

DAONAN RD.

TANGGU RD.

DINGDING RD.

ZHONGZHOU RD.

KAIYUAN RD.

Canal

SHENGLI RD.

Dongfanghong Square

Luo River

Zhongzhou Canal

XINHUA XI RD.

YUEJIN RD.

REMIN ST.

BEIDAJIE ST.

Old City

LUOMENG RD.

XIAYUAN RD.

Luoyang Bridge

LONGMEN RD.

To Longmen Caves

① Martyrs' Cemetery
② Luoyang Museum
③ Shengli Department Store
④ Xigong Department Store
⑤ Eastern and Western Han Dynasty Tombs
⑥ Friendship Store
⑦ White Horse Temple (Baimasi)

🏨 Hotel   🍴 Restaurant   ᴖᴖᴖ Former City Wall

汉魏洛阳故城

Old Town. Although not generally included on the itinerary, the ancient town and its ramparts to the east of Luoyang are well worth a visit. Many of the houses which survive from the Yuan, Ming, and Qing dynasties are no longer inhabited. Lantern and pottery shops line its ancient pathways and streets.

白马寺

White Horse Temple (Baimasi). Baimasi is located 8 km. (5 mi.) northeast of Luoyang. The buildings seen today date from the Ming and were restored during the 1950s. The original monastery at this site, constructed in AD 75, was one of the first Buddhist temples in China. Legend has it that two monks from India riding astride a white horse delivered the Buddhist sutras to Luoyang—hence the temple's name. Baimasi today remains active as a center for Chan (Zen) Buddhism and a few monks still live on its grounds.

洛阳市博物馆

Luoyang Museum. The museum is housed in the Guandi Temple, which dates from the Ming Dynasty. It was opened in 1958 to display the archeological finds unearthed during the 1950s when agricultural terracing began in the area. Most items in the collection—such as the Shang and Zhou bronzes—represent the periods when Luoyang served as a dynastic capital. Also on display are inscribed stelae and ceramic funerary objects from the Han and Tang periods.

龙门石窟
LONGMEN (DRAGON GATE) CAVES

Buddhism was introduced to Luoyang in AD 68 and one of China's first Buddhist monasteries, the Baimasi, was built here in AD 75 (see above). Carving in the Longmen Caves began in 494 under the Northern Wei and continued until the 7th century. The more than 1,300 caves contain over 2,100 grottoes and niches, several pagodas, countless inscriptions, and about 100,000 images and statues of Buddha. Together with the examples found in the caves at Dunhuang and Datong, the artwork of Longmen marks the high point of Buddhist culture in China.

The caves are located 14 km. (9 mi.) south of Luoyang, spanning out along both sides of the Yi River. Here artisans (reputedly 800,000 in all) discovered an ideal site, where the hard-textured rock took well to fine carving. Although there has been some erosion at Longmen since ancient times, the major losses here are said to have resulted from looting by Westerners during the 19th and 20th centuries. Many finely sculptured heads were lopped off and carried abroad to Europe and North America. Saw marks are still clearly visible. Two magnificent murals depicting a royal procession were literally dynamited off the mountainsides in their entirety. Today they are displayed at the Metropolitan Museum of Art in

New York and in the Nelson Gallery of the Atkinson Museum in Kansas City.

From north to south, the main caves on the west bank of the Yi are the Qianqisi; Northern, Central, and Southern Pingyang; Jingshansi; Ten Thousand Buddhas; Lotus Flower; Wei and Tang Character; Juxiansi; Medical Prescription; Guyang; Burned by Fire; Shikusi; and Ludong. On the east bank are three main caves dating from the Tang period: Kanjingsi; Three Caves on the Terrace Where the Drum Is Beaten; and another Cave of Ten Thousand Buddhas.

The visitor will note a distinct progression in styles, first under the Northern Wei (386–534) and, to a lesser extent, under the Sui (581–618), and reaching the apogee during the first half of the Tang (618–907). The grandest example of Northern Wei style can be seen in the Central Pingyang Cave, which contains 11 large statues of Buddha as well as a number of smaller sculptures of Buddha and his disciples. The figures have elongated features, reminiscent of early Gothic art. The style is two-dimensional and highly energetic, characterized by rhythmic, flowing lines. The robes are draped in a splayed or "fish-tail" form. The Guyang Cave, the oldest in the Longmen complex—it was begun in 495—has some magnificent Northern Wei rock paintings and bas-relief wall carvings which depict wonderfully elegant flying apsaras. (Apsaras are celestial beings, similar to Christian angels, who carry newborn babies into paradise. They are frequently portrayed as musicians, or bearers of flowers and incense.) The Shikusi (Shiku Temple) Cave, also Northern Wei, contains the best processional and adoration scenes at Longmen, second only to those which were removed from the Pingyang Caves and sent to the US.

Tang art is best exemplified in the Fengxian Temple Cave, which contains a striking 17-m. (55-ft.)-high Buddha, as well as crowned bodhisattvas, a celestial guardian, and a defender of Buddha. Tang sculpture can also be seen in the Qianqi Temple (Qianqisi) Cave, the Cave of Ten Thousand Buddhas, and the three large caves on the eastern riverbank. The Tang figures are more voluptuous and three-dimensional than those of the Northern Wei, standing out in high relief as if freed from their stone backdrop. They appear in natural poses, and nuances of mood and expression have been carefully portrayed in their faces.

The Buddha is frequently displayed in a basic triad, with a bodhisattva on either side. The latter are Buddhist "saints" who, having arrived at the gateway to Nirvana, vow to stay in the material world until all sentient beings achieve salvation. Their faces express joy, serenity, and compassion. Sometimes the basic triad is supplemented by representatives of Buddha's first two disciples, the youthful Ananda and the older Kasyapa.

The lotus flower, a common symbol in Buddhist art, represents purity and serenity—its blossoms rise out of black waters of rivers and lakes, just as Buddha rose above earthly desire. Fine examples of lotus carving can be seen on the ceilings of the Central Pingyang and Lotus Flower caves.

The Medical Prescription Cave has more than artistic interest: at its entrance are numerous stelae inscribed with over 120 remedies for diseases which afflicted the local population in the 6th century. The dated inscriptions are a veritable gold mine for medical historians, as well as for practitioners of traditional medicine.

The art of Buddhist carving was abruptly halted in AD 845, when thousands of sculptures and temples were destroyed during a persecution of Buddhism sanctioned by Emperor Wu. Although Buddhist art and religion continued in China, they never again reached the heights achieved under the Tang.

HOTEL
ACCOMMODATIONS

友谊宾馆

Friendship Hotel (6 Xiyuan Rd.; tel: 22159/22995). Renovated in 1980, the Friendship Hotel in the southwest part of Luoyang has been long noted for its excellent service and cuisine. With over 300 rooms and suites (Y18 for triples, Y50 for doubles, Y60 for suites), the Friendship also features private baths (except in triples), air-conditioning, color TVs, wall-to-wall carpeting, and refrigerators (in service counters outside the rooms).

In addition, the hotel has a coffee shop, Chinese and Western restaurants, a swimming pool, and some unusual souvenir choices: guests can dress up in Chinese period costumes and have their pictures taken. They can also have signature seals custom carved or order calligraphy done to their own specifications. The Friendship is also the site of the CITS office in Luoyang.

Visitors are also accommodated at the **Yingbinguan** (Renmin Rd.; tel: 7155).

SHOPPING

The Shengli and Xigong Department Stores on Zhongzhou Road carry a wide selection of daily necessities. Visitors staying at the Friendship Hotel will find the Friendship Store located conveniently nearby on Huashan Road.

中国国际旅行社
CITS (Luxingshe) Office in Luoyang ■ Friendship Hotel. Tel: 22200

Nanchang

NANCHANG, the capital of Jiangxi Province, is a city of 2.4 million people located in a rich agricultural region 520 km. (325 mi.) southwest of Shanghai.

Founded during the Eastern Han Dynasty (AD 25–220), Nanchang became a major distribution center for the famous "kaolin" pottery and fine porcelain produced in the nearby town of Jingdezhen. It was also a rich rice-growing area from the 8th century on.

Since 1949, the town has become an important industrial and commercial center, with railway links to Changsha, Shanghai, and the port of Jiujiang on the Yangtse River. Industries here include chemicals, porcelain, paper, and food processing.

Nanchang is also well-known for its revolutionary history. On August 1, 1927, a peasant army of 30,000 led by Zhou Enlai and Zhu De defeated Chiang Kaishek's Nationalist forces at Nanchang and held the town for several days. The so-called Nanchang Uprising was a cardinal event in that it marked the first occasion that an organized military force fought under the direct control of the Communist Party.

The climate in Nanchang is subtropical: summers are unbearably hot and humid; autumn is pleasantly warm and dry.

HIGHLIGHTS FOR TRAVELERS

江西省历史博物馆

Jiangxi Provincial Museum. Built in 1952, this museum on Bayi Road features informative geographic and historical exhibitions. Nearby is the Exhibition Hall of Provincial Revolutionary History.

南昌起义纪念馆

Former Headquarters of the Nanchang Uprising. This building on Zhongshan Road has been converted into a museum.

南昌市八大山人书画陈列馆（青云谱）

Bada Shanren Exhibition Hall. Located a few miles south of Nanchang, this former monastery was the home of Zhu Da, one of the Eight Great Hermit (Bada Shanren) artists who lived and worked in the area during the 17th century. Today the building houses a display of the paintings and calligraphy of these ancient artists.

Climate		Jan	Feb	Mar	Apr	May	Jun	Jul	Aug	Sep	Oct	Nov	Dec
Temp.	°C	5.1	6.3	11.0	17.0	22.6	25.3	29.7	29.7	25.4	19.3	13.2	7.3
	°F	41.1	43.3	51.8	62.6	72.6	77.5	85.4	85.4	77.7	66.7	55.7	45.1
Precip.	mm.	152	152	203	279	304	381	254	203	178	178	152	127
	in.	6	6	8	11	12	15	10	8	7	7	6	5

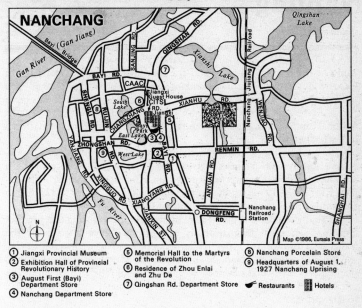

NANCHANG

① Jiangxi Provincial Museum
② Exhibition Hall of Provincial Revolutionary History
③ August First (Bayi) Department Store
④ Nanchang Department Store
⑤ Memorial Hall to the Martyrs of the Revolution
⑥ Residence of Zhou Enlai and Zhu De
⑦ Qingshan Rd. Department Store
⑧ Nanchang Porcelain Store
⑨ Headquarters of August 1, 1927 Nanchang Uprising
⚓ Restaurants   ▥ Hotels

Map ©1986, Eurasia Press

HOTEL ACCOMMODATIONS

江西宾馆

Jiangxi Guest House (64 Bayi Rd.; tel: 67891; telex: 95005 JXH CN). The Jiangxi is centrally air-conditioned. All of its rooms have private bath, telephones and wall-to-wall carpeting. Its suites also have color TVs. The guest house's other amenities include a Chinese and a Western restaurant, and barber and souvenir shops. Rates are Y45 for doubles and triples; Y90 for suites; and Y250 for a deluxe suite.

青山湖宾馆

Qingshanhu Guest House (11 Wujiao Rd.; tel: 64901). The Qingshanhu has single rooms (Y65), doubles (Y60), triples (Y60), a few suites (Y80), and two deluxe suites (Y100). All accommodations are air-conditioned and have private bath and telephone.

Other accommodations include the **Nanchang Hotel** (2 Zhanqian Rd.; tel: 63595).

SHOPPING

The city's major department stores are the Bayi at 318 Zhongshan Road; the Nanchang, at the intersection of Bayi and Zhongshan roads; and the Qingshan, at the intersection of Qingshan and Bayi roads. Fine examples of local pottery, including porcelain from the renowned kilns of Jingdezhen, may be found at the Nanchang Porcelain Store, 12 Shengli Road.

中国国际旅行社
CITS (Luxingshe) Office in Nanchang ▥ Jiangxi Hotel. Tel: 65180

Nanjing

南京

southern capital

traditional spelling / Nanking

NANJING is set in beautiful natural surroundings along the southern banks of the Yangtse River and at the foothills of the Zijin (Purple and Gold) Mountains. With its abundant greenery, broad boulevards, and unharried pace, Nanjing ranks among the most pleasant of China's great cities. At several points in China's history, Nanjing has served as the national capital. Today it is the capital of Jiangsu Province and a national industrial and cultural center.

In modern times, Nanjing's significance has been enhanced by the completion in 1968 of the Yangtse River Bridge. The bridge provides a vital link in China's transportation system, connecting Nanjing with Beijing, 1,157 km. (719 mi.) to the north; Guangzhou, 2,127 km. (1,322 mi.) to the south; and Shanghai, 300 km. (186 mi.) to the southeast.

Nanjing's climate is marked by intense dry heat during the summer months—hence its designation as one of the "three furnaces of the Yangtse." However, few cities in China can be rated as comfortable during the summer season and Nanjing at least has the advantage of splendid, well-planted park areas that can provide a modicum of relief. Throughout the remainder of the year, the city has a temperate climate, with a rainy season in late spring.

Nanjing covers an area of 778.6 sq. km. (300 sq. mi.) and has a population of over three million.

NANJING IN HISTORY

Although archeological relics indicate that the area was first settled some 6,000 years ago, the town itself dates from the 8th century BC. It first served as China's capital from AD 220 to 589, spanning the period of the Three Kingdoms through the fall of the Southern Dynasties. The surrounding area was able to sustain a rich variety of crops due to an extensive irrigation system developed under various rulers. During this period, Nanjing's importance as a river port and trade center grew considerably. China's first iron foundries were established here, while Nanjing's pottery and weaving became famous throughout Asia.

Nanjing's intellectual, cultural, and artistic achievements continued to grow under the Tang Dynasty (618–907). One of China's greatest classical poets, Li Bai (Li Po. *c.* 700–762), lived here during his later years. Throughout most of the Five Dynasties and Ten Kingdoms (907–79) period, Nanjing served as the national capital.

Climate		Jan	Feb	Mar	Apr	May	Jun	Jul	Aug	Sep	Oct	Nov	Dec
Temp.	°C	1.9	3.7	8.6	14.6	20.3	24.4	28.2	28.2	23.0	16.8	10.6	4.2
	°F	35.4	38.6	47.4	58.2	68.5	75.9	82.7	82.7	73.4	62.2	51	39.5
Precip.	mm.	254	254	330	330	305	356	279	279	305	254	203	178
	in.	10	10	13	13	12	14	11	11	12	10	8	7

Nanjing owes its present character and dimensions to the founders of the Ming Dynasty, who established their first capital here in 1368. To ensure the city's growth, the emperor ordered 20,000 wealthy families to move to Nanjing and bestowed honors on those who underwrote new construction and economic expansion. This policy, however, lasted for only one generation, as the succeeding Ming emperor, Yong Le, moved the capital north to Beijing.

As an "adjunct capital," Nanjing continued to grow in size and importance under both the Ming and the succeeding Qing Dynasty. It became a national center for astronomy and other sciences and its silk and cotton industries achieved wide repute. Wu Jingzi's famous novel, *The Scholars,* widely read in China today, is set in 18th-century Nanjing. *The Scholars* provides a vivid portrait of the corruption and pretensions of the aristocracy in that period.

Nanjing was bombarded by the British during the Opium War (1840–42). In 1842, the Treaty of Nanjing was signed aboard a British gunboat anchored in the city's harbor. The treaty dealt a profound blow to China's independence, forcibly opening five sea and inland ports, including Nanjing, to foreign trade. Two years later, similar concessions were "granted" to the US and France.

The Taiping Rebellion. As a result of the inequitable treaty of Nanjing, additional tax levies were imposed on the already impoverished Chinese peasantry. In response, peasant revolts, endemic in China, increased in both frequency and intensity. The participants in the grassroots Taiping Rebellion, begun in 1851, had by 1853 succeeded in establishing a government centered in Nanjing. The city was renamed Tianjing ("heavenly capital"). Palaces were built for the Taiping leader, Hong Xiuquan, who declared himself the Heavenly King. Similar edifices were constructed for his lieutenants.

For the next 11 years the Taipings ruled over most of southern China. In 1864, after a seven-month siege, loyalist Qing forces led by Cheng Guofeng captured Nanjing and slaughtered 100,000 Taipings in three days. Many committed suicide but, as Chinese historians record it, not one person surrendered.

Nanjing's Role in the Chinese Revolution. The Chinese imperial armies left Nanjing a devastated city, having destroyed most of the Taiping buildings and artwork. The city did not begin to recover until the early 20th century. In 1911, Nanjing played a key role in the revolution that overthrew the imperial Qing Dynasty and established the Republic of China. Delegates from 17 provinces met in the city to elect Dr. Sun Yatsen president of the Republic and to ratify the new constitution. A few months later, Dr. Sun ceded power to General Yuan Shikai, who moved China's capital to Beijing.

Nanjing returned to national prominence only in 1927, when Chiang Kaishek set up the Republican Guomindang government in Nanjing. He established his headquarters in the former Taiping palace of Hong Xiuquan. Threatened by a Japanese invasion, Chiang moved his administration to Chongqing in 1938. Japanese forces then took the former Nationalist capital by storm, wantonly killing and looting in an episode remembered as the "rape of Nanjing." Within a four-day period, approximately 44,000 women were raped and 100,000 Nanjing residents were murdered.

Modern-day visitors to Nanjing are told that during the period of Nationalist rule in the city, nearly one-third of the city's population of 700,000 was occupied in the service of high bureaucrats and politicians. Industry waned as more and more people were drawn off by that society's demands for domestic servants, prostitutes, and the like. During that period, the industrial work force is said to have dwindled to less than 10,000.

The Japanese occupied Nanjing until their surrender in September 1945. In April 1949, during the civil war between the Communists and Chiang Kaishek's Nationalists that followed the victory over Japan, the People's Liberation Army crossed the Yangtse and captured the city. The campaign was personally directed by Mao Zedong and led by Liu Bocheng and Deng Xiaoping. In a commemorative poem, Mao wrote:

Over Zhongshan swept a storm, headlong,
Our mighty army, a million strong, has crossed the
    Great River.
The City, a tiger crouching, a dragon curling, outshines
    its ancient glories;
In heroic triumph heaven and earth have been overturned.

ECONOMY AND CULTURE

Since 1950, Nanjing's industrial sector has been greatly enlarged. Today, about 1,600 industrial and mining enterprises employ 300,000 workers (compared to only 10,000 before the Revolution). Nanjing industry includes coal mining, metallurgy, petroleum refining, machine tool manufacturing, food processing, and auto and shipbuilding enterprises.

The 63 agricultural communes administered by Nanjing total 110,000 hectares (271,810 acres) of land that yield grain, tea, vegetables, apples, cherries, and watermelons. Nanjing is proud of its afforestation programs—over 28 million trees have been planted since 1949.

The city's cultural, educational, and medical facilities have expanded rapidly since 1949. Today Nanjing has 14 institutions of higher learning, including the famous Nanjing University, founded in 1902 and known as Central University prior to 1949. Following the educational reforms of 1977, Nanjing University emerged as one of the most prestigious institutions of learning in China. Among its 14 departments in the liberal arts and natural sciences, its Department of Chinese History is rated as one of the best in the nation. Nanjing is also known for its institute of technology and for its teachers' college, which has trained some 20,000 high school teachers for Jiangsu Province since its founding in 1952. Its Provincial Hospital for Traditional Chinese Medicine is among the most eminent institutions of its kind in China.

HIGHLIGHTS
FOR TRAVELERS

南京长江大桥

Yangtse River Bridge. It is hard to overstate the symbolic importance of the Yangtse River Bridge and the pride which all Chinese take in it. Until its completion in 1968, there was no direct overland link between the important lower Yangtse River Valley (encompassing Nanjing and Shanghai) and Beijing. But even more significant, perhaps, is that the Chinese people accomplished this engineering feat by their own labor and ingenuity. The 21.3-m. (70-ft.) depths of swirling, silt-laden waters — covering a bedrock floor — had proved too much of a challenge to Western engineers. Relying completely on their own efforts after the Soviets withdrew with their blueprints in 1960, the Chinese succeeded in constructing a 1,577-m. (5,171-ft.), two-tiered bridge for rail and vehicular traffic. It required almost 10 years of labor by 7,000 workers.

A splendid overview of Nanjing can be had from the top of the building which houses the Yangtse River Bridge Administration.

In April 1979, on the 30th anniversary of the capture of Nanjing by the Communist army, a 23-m. (75-ft.) monument was unveiled commemorating that crossing of the Yangtse River. The monument bears an inscription in the handwriting of Deng Xiaoping, one of the campaign's commanders. It is the only inscription by Deng known to be publicly displayed in China.

江苏省博物馆

Nanjing Museum (321 E. Zhongshan Rd.; tel: 41554). On the eastern outskirts of the city, just inside the Sun Yatsen Gate (Zhongshan Men), is the Nanjing Museum (Banshanyuan), containing a collection of artifacts spanning 5,000 years of Chinese history. Six exhibition rooms display prehistoric and Shang Dynasty pottery, bronzes, jewelry, and tortoise-shell ware; iron agricultural tools; printed works; handicrafts from the Ming and Qing dynasties; and furniture. Items not to be missed include a 2,000-year-old jade burial garment of the Eastern Han Dynasty, constructed from 2,600 pieces of green jade; an example of what may be the world's first seismograph, invented by Zhang Heng in AD 132; and the Ming porcelain collection. A separate exhibit portrays the events of the Taiping Rebellion and aspects of the "Heavenly Kingdom."

Other museums in Nanjing include the Museum of the Kingdom of Heavenly Peace (128 Zhanyuan Road; tel: 23024) and the Municipal

Sun Yatsen's former residence, Nanjing

Museum of Nanjing (6 Chaotiangong; tel: 48683). For those interested in
art history, there is the Jiangsu Provincial Art Gallery at 266 Changjiang
Road (tel: 642884).

中山陵

Sun Yatsen Mausoleum (tel: 43973). Although a native of
Guangdong, Sun Yatsen requested to be buried in Nanjing and, upon his
death in 1925, construction of this imposing monument was begun. The
mausoleum is situated on the southern slopes of the Zijin Mountains in
the city's eastern suburbs. The grounds cover 80,000 sq. m. (20 acres),
and the memorial hall itself is approached by climbing 392 granite steps.

Within the domed circular hall stands a white statue of Sun. On
exhibit are replicas of his will and an inscription of his Three People's
Principles for leading China into a new age: "nationalism, democracy, and
livelihood." The vault itself contains his coffin (his remains were moved
here from Beijing in 1929 when the monument was completed) and is
surmounted by a reclining statue of Sun.

灵谷寺公园

Linggu Temple Park. This park, regarded by local residents as one of
the "40 famous scenic spots" of Nanjing, is located just south of the Sun
Yatsen Mausoleum, at the foothills of the Zijin Mountains. The park has
several well-kept gardens and is particularly favored in summer for its

dense and shady pine forest. Its main feature is the Wuliang Temple, originally built in 1381 but reconstructed several times since. The park also contains a 61-m. (200-ft.) pagoda, built under the Nationalist regime.

明孝陵

Ming Emperor's Tomb. Hong Wu (1327–98), the first Ming emperor, is buried here. Unlike the founders of most dynasties, Hong Wu was an orphan raised by Buddhist monks because his relatives were too poor to support him. He abandoned the priesthood, joined a group of bandits, and became their leader. Eventually he declared himself emperor and seized nationwide power. His "rags to riches" history explains why he is called the "Beggar King."

His tomb, constructed in 1381, was laid waste during the Taiping Rebellion. All that remains is a stone gate and a courtyard. The main feature of the tomb today is a narrow sacred path leading up to the site, lined with 12 pairs of stone animals in standing and reclining positions.

紫金山天文台

Zijin (Purple) Mountain Observatory (tel: 633921/631096). Atop a mountain northeast of Nanjing stands the Zijin Mountain Observatory, China's third largest (after Beijing and Shanghai). Construction was begun in 1934. A staff of 250 is engaged in research under the auspices of the Chinese Academy of Sciences. A highlight for visitors is the observatory's museum. The observatory houses centries-old star charts still useful today. Also exhibited are a replica of the original armillary sphere (a set of circles and rings showing the relative positions of heavenly bodies), invented over 1,800 years ago; an ancient celestial globe; and a device used to detect the movement of the the stars.

玄武湖

Xuanwu Lake. Also known as Yuanwu Lake (tel: 32286), it is located in People's Park just outside the city's Xuanwu Gate. The park was formerly a private imperial preserve. It was opened to the public in 1911 but was not restored until the early 1950s.

The lake contains five islets, linked by embankments and classic arched bridges and surrounded by thousands of weeping willows. Lotus blossoms appear in summer. Xuanwu Lake's enchanting setting makes boating a popular pastime.

In the 1950s and 1960s, the concentration of factories around the shores of Xuanwu Lake created severe pollution. Today, however, chemical wastes are recycled and the lake is once again able to support an abundance of marine life.

A zoo, a children's playground, a skating rink, an open-air theater, a bonsai exhibition, and a goldfish aquarium are also situated in the park.

莫愁湖

Mochou Lake. Near Nanjing's western wall is Mochou Lake and park. In the 5th century AD, a woman of the royal household named Mochou ("free of sorrow") used to retreat here. "Sorrow-free" Mochou was eulogized

1. Yangtse-River Bridge
2. Nanjing City General First Aid Station
3. Drum Tower (Gu Lou) Department Store
4. Friendship Store
5. Drum Tower (Gu Lou)
6. Nanjing University
7. Wutaishan Stadium
8. Pavilion of Victory at Chess
9. Nanjing City Antiques Store
10. People's Market
11. Nanjing City Post Office
12. Nanjing Foreign Languages Bookstore
13. Jiangsu Province Art Gallery
14. Memorial to Communist Party Delegation at Plum Tree Village (Meiyuan Xincun)
15. Historical Museum of the Taiping Heavenly Kingdom
16. Rain of Flowers Terrace (Yuhuatai)
17. Nanjing and Jiangsu Province Museum
18. Zijin Shan Observatory
19. Ming Emperor's Tomb (Ming Ling)
20. Dr. Sun Yatsen's Mausoleum
21. Linggu Pagoda
22. Nanjing Zoo

Hotels
Restaurants
Former City Wall

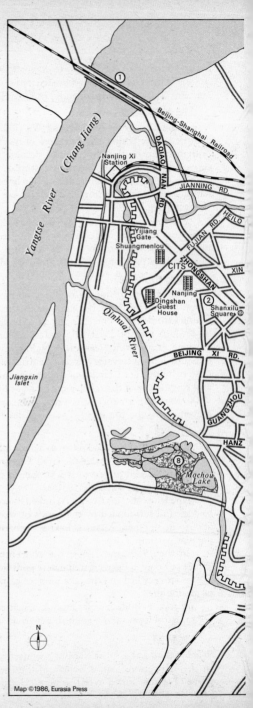

Map ©1986, Eurasia Press

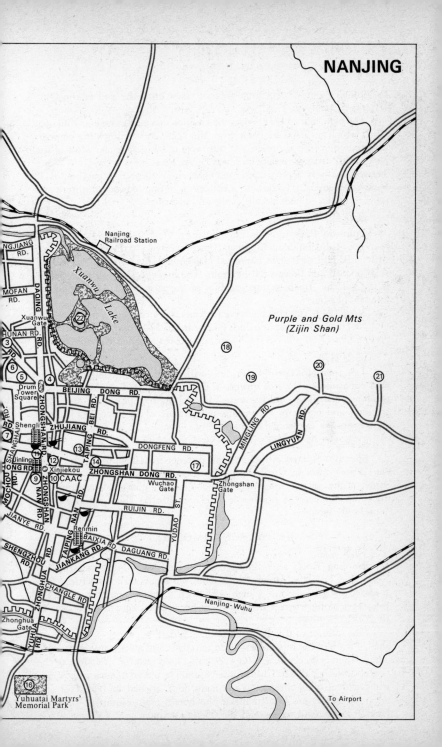

NANJING

Nanjing
Railroad Station

Xuanwu Lake

NGJIANG RD.

MOFAN RD.

DAQING RD.

Xuanwu Gate

22

HUNAN RD.

3

RD.

6

5

4

Drum Tower Square

ZHONGSHAN BEI RD.

Shengli

Zhujiang

BEI RD.

TAIPING RD.

7

Jinling

11

12

13

14

Xinjiekou

10

CAAC

9

ZHONGSHAN NAN RD.

MOCHOU RD.

SHANGHAI RD.

ONG RD.

Renmin

BAIXIA RD.

TAIPING NAN RD.

JIANKANG RD.

ZHONGHUA RD.

CHANGLE RD.

SHENGZHOU RD.

JIANYE RD.

NAN RD.

BEIJING DONG RD.

DONGFENG RD.

ZHONGSHAN DONG RD.

Wuchao Gate

RUIJIN RD.

DAGUANG RD.

YUDAO ST.

Zhongshan Gate

17

MINGLING RD.

LINGYUAN RD.

Purple and Gold Mts
(Zijin Shan)

18

19

20

21

Zhonghua Gate

YUHUA RD.

16

Yuhuatai Martyrs'
Memorial Park

Nanjing–Wuhu

To Airport

by China's famous poets from ancient times until the end of the Qing Dynasty (1911).

The park (tel: 25412) houses the Pavilion of Victory at Chess (Shengqi Lou), which received its name from the occasion when a Ming emperor defeated one of his counselors at this favorite Chinese game. Most of the park's other attractions date from the 1950s. These include the Lotus Water Terrace, a cherry-apple garden, and an open-air theater. A pavilion overlooking Mochou Lake contains a collection of fine redwood furniture and some examples of famous calligraphy and painting.

雨花台

Yuhuatai Park (outside Zhonghuamen Gate; tel: 41893). Formerly known as Yuhuatai Gardens, legend dates its origins to the 6th century AD when a Buddhist priest so impressed heaven with his sermonizing that the skies opened and flowers fell like rain. The more prosaic will note that it is the colorful, finely grained pebbles of the area that lend the park its rainbow-like hues.

Since 1949, Yuhuatai has served as a memorial to the more than 100,000 victims executed in Nanjing during 22 years (1927–49) of Nationalist rule under Chiang Kaishek. For this reason, the site is also called Martyr's Park.

汤山温泉

Tangshan Hot Springs. For those with ample time, the 40-km. (24.8-mi.) excursion to the hot springs in the neighboring Tang Mountains is recommended. The curative waters here contain potassium, sulfur, and calcium, and maintain a constant temperature of 40 °C (104°F). Long immersions are said to aid skin ailments.

山西路广场

Shanxilu Square. Although some distance from downtown, this local market area is usually bustling. A department store stands on the southeast corner of the square, and a neighborhood medical clinic is located just to the southwest (on the north side of Hunan Road). There are also some "storefront" factories.

HOTEL ACCOMMODATIONS

南京饭店

Nanjing Hotel (259 Zhongshan Bei Rd.; tel: 634121; telex: 34102 NKHNK CN). The Nanjing Hotel is known for its tranquil setting. Surrounded by gardens and a high wall (with a soldier standing guard), it is located along a street lined with plane trees brought from France in the 1930s.

The interior of this Soviet-style hotel is dark but spacious. Rooms are shaded—a blessing in summer—and have fans and air-conditioning units. The kitchen is excellent, serving everything from regional specialties to the best chocolate soufflé in China (orders should be placed in advance). A new wing, with a small theater on the main floor, opened in 1981. Post and telegraph offices are located inside the hotel's main entrance. Rates are US$20–35 for twin rooms and US$55–75 for suites.

金陵饭店

The Jinling Hotel (Xinjiekou Square; tel: 644141/641121; telex: 34008 JLHNJ; cable: 6855). Opened in the spring of 1983, the Jinling Hotel is the tallest hotel in China, towering 37 stories over this historic city. All of the 760 rooms and suites are equipped with color television, bathroom, two telephones, refrigerator, and individually controlled air-conditioning. In addition to six restaurants and bars, the Jinling Hotel houses the largest pillarless hotel ballroom in China. The Purple Mountain Ballroom has a seating capacity of 1,125 and can be divided into four self-contained units. The hotel's proudest feature is the Sky Lounge, China's first revolving restaurant/lounge. Turning 360° every hour, the Sky Lounge offers spectacular views of the legendary "Curling Dragon" of the Purple Mountain and the "Crouching Tiger" of the old Stone City on the banks of the Yangtse.

The Jinling Hotel offers a wide range of services and facilities, including 24-hour room service, a health club with sauna and massage, and even its own shopping center which overlooks a re-creation of a classic Suzhou formal garden. Rates are US$20–35 for twin rooms and US$55–75 for suites.

丁山宾馆

Dingshan Hotel (90 Chahaer Rd.; tel: 685931; cable: 6333; telex: 34103 DSHNJ CN). The fully air-conditioned Dingshan has 341 double rooms (Y50–60), 13 suites (Y50–92), and two deluxe suites (Y240, Y300), all with private bath, closed-circuit color TV, telephone, piped-in music, and wall-to-wall carpeting. Most rooms also have refrigerators. The hotel boasts a ballroom, coffee shop, and Chinese and Western restaurants. The array of services includes post and telegram offices, foreign exchange, and taxis. Barber and souvenir shops are also on the premises.

胜利饭店

Shengli Hotel (75 Zhongshan Rd.; tel: 648181; telex: 34083 VHNJ CN). Rates for the centrally located Shengli Hotel range from Y30–45 for singles and doubles; Y52–180 for suites and deluxe suites. All the Shengli's rooms are air-conditioned, and have private bath, color TV, telephone, and wall-to-wall carpeting.

Other hotels in Nanjing include the Shuangmenlou Hotel (38 Shuangmenlou; tel: 685965); the Renmin Hotel (591 Taiping Nan Rd.; tel: 623779); and the Shuangmenlou Guest House (185 N. Huju Rd.; tel: 685961/685965; telex: 34118 SMLNJ).

CUISINE

Each region of China boasts its local delicacies, and Nanjing is no exception. Autumn is the season for plump lake crabs. Other specialties are pickled vegetables, Nanjing "flat duck," duck kidneys, and fish. Cherries, watermelons, and other fresh fruits are abundant in season. The tea from the nearby hills has its particular aroma and flavor.

Some of Nanjing's more well-known restaurants and their specialties are Jiangsu Restaurant (126 Jiankang Road; tel: 23698), specializing in eggwhite and minced chicken, and eel braised with rib pork; Liuhuachun Restaurant (248 Shaoshan Road; tel: 52318) which serves braised vegetable heart and smoked pork with pine nuts, among other Shanghai-style cuisine; and Ma Xiangxing (5 North Zhongshan Road; tel: 635807), which features "squirrel fish" (a dish of mandarin fish garnished with winter bamboo shoots and fresh mushrooms; the texture is sweet and delicate) and phoenix-tail prawn.

Most restaurants fall into the "masses" category. Local dishes can be sampled at the Luliuju (Green Willow House) Restaurant, 248 Taiping Nan Road, tel: 43644. Zhongshan Road, in the center of the city, boasts a variety of restaurants specializing in several regional Chinese cuisines: Lao Guangdong (Old Canton) Restaurant, 45 Zhongshan Bei Road (tel: 42482); Dasanyuan Restaurant, 40 Zhongshan Bei Road (tel: 649027); and Beijing Yangrou (Beijing Mutton) Restaurant, 94 Zhongshan Dong Road (tel: 42585). The Sichuan Restaurant, 171 Taiping Nan Road (tel: 642243), is also recommended for its hot, spicy dishes.

SHOPPING

The shopper will find Nanjing's craftsmen skilled at making reproductions of old relics such as tomb figurines. Chinese tourists often collect pebbles from the Yuhua Terrace at Martyrs' Park; they reveal an array of colors when immersed in water. Nanjing's major antiques outlet is at 9 Hanzhong Road (tel: 644550).

Two of Nanjing's largest department stores are the Drum Tower (Gu Lou) Department Store and the Xinjiekou Department Store, located, respectively, on Zhongshan Bei Road (off Shanxilu Square) and Zhongshan Nan Road. Visitors will also find a wide array of everyday items at the People's Market, just south of the busy Xinjiekou intersection (79 South Zhongshan Rd.; tel: 642766), as well as at the Yong'an, a bazaar located in the busy Fuzimiao District (also called Confucius Temple).

中国国际旅行社
CITS (Luxingshe) Office in Nanjing ■ 202-1 North Zhongshan Road. Tel: 33412.
Telex: 34024 ITSNJ CN.

Nanning

NANNING is China's southernmost city. It lies some 500 km. (310 mi.) due west of Guangzhou and has a population of 350,000. Closed to visitors until 1977, it is now being included in many itineraries, especially South China circuits that originate in Hong Kong and include Guangzhou, Kunming, and Guilin.

Nanning is the capital of the Guangxi Zhuang Autonomous Region, which is the home of China's largest minority nationality, the Zhuang, a Muslim people who now number over 12 million. Since 11 other nationalities also live in the region, a Minorities Institute was set up at Nanning in 1952. Visitors may have an opportunity to encounter Zhuang, Miao, Yao, Shi, and other minority peoples. Some are still distinguishable by their national costumes, although most urban dwellers have begun to adopt contemporary styles. The Zhuang maintain particularly distinguished traditions in theater, puppetry, and handicrafts—notably their colorful style of weaving known as *Zhuang Jing.*

NANNING IN HISTORY

The town of Nanning was founded during the Yuan Dynasty (1279–1368), when it first served as a market center on the trade routes that extended west to the Himalayan Plateau and south to Annam (Vietnam) and elsewhere in Southeast Asia. Nanning did not begin to develop industrially until the 20th century. It now has food-processing factories, flour mills, sugar refineries, tanneries, printing works, chemical fertilizer plants, and bauxite and coal mines. The predominant crops are rice and sugarcane. The region is also China's leading producer of tung oil.

Among the popular cultural attractions in Nanning is the annual Dragon Boat Regatta, a 2,000-year-old Han festival traditionally held on the fifth day of the fifth moon (usually falling in late May or early June). Prizes are awarded for both the fastest and the best-designed boats. Both men's and women's teams compete. About a quarter of a million onlookers now turn out each year for the regatta and accompanying festivities.

Because of its proximity to China's borders, Nanning has been an important military supply and staging area, both during the Vietnam conflict in the 1960s and again in 1979 during the Sino-Vietnamese confrontation.

Climate		Jan	Feb	Mar	Apr	May	Jun	Jul	Aug	Sep	Oct	Nov	Dec
Temp.	°C	13.1	13.8	17.5	21.9	25.8	27.1	28.3	28.2	27.0	23.8	19.8	15.2
	°F	55	56.8	63.5	71.4	78.4	80.7	82.9	82.7	80.6	74.8	67.6	59.3
Precip.	mm.	152	203	254	279	381	508	457	406	330	203	152	127
	in.	6	8	10	11	15	20	18	16	13	8	6	5

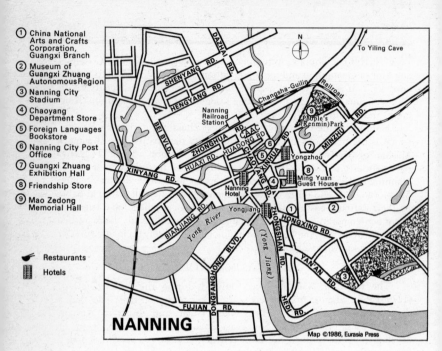

① China National Arts and Crafts Corporation, Guangxi Branch
② Museum of Guangxi Zhuang Autonomous Region
③ Nanning City Stadium
④ Chaoyang Department Store
⑤ Foreign Languages Bookstore
⑥ Nanning City Post Office
⑦ Guangxi Zhuang Exhibition Hall
⑧ Friendship Store
⑨ Mao Zedong Memorial Hall

🍴 Restaurants
🏢 Hotels

NANNING

Map ©1986, Eurasia Press

HIGHLIGHTS FOR
TRAVELERS

Tourist groups are often taken to the Baisha Production Brigade, affording an opportunity to see a productive commune in the tropics.

A trip to the Yiling Stalactite Cave is also of interest. Located a pleasant hour's ride north of the city, this huge cave boasts artificially lighted formations bearing the sobriquets "bumper harvest," "fruit bowl," and "city skyline." Nan Hu (South Lake) Gardens are also on the itinerary, as is a visit to the Nanning Arts Institute, which exhibits some of China's most colorful minority arts and crafts. Examples of local crafts include bambooware, lacquerware, and wood and stone carvings.

HOTEL ACCOMMODATIONS

西园饭店

Xiyuan Hotel (38 Jiangnan Rd.; tel: 29923/22075; telex: 48137 XIYUH CN). The Xiyuan has a 400-seat conference hall, a swimming pool, barber shop, Chinese and Western restaurants, and a souvenir shop. Its rooms (Y36–55; Y60–70 for suites; Y100–500 for deluxe suites) are air-conditioned, with private bath, color TV, telephone, and wall-to-wall carpeting.

邕州饭店
Yongzhou Hotel (59 Xinmin Rd.; tel: 28323/23120; telex: 48145 YZT CN; cable: 1558). The Yongzhou has over 350 rooms (Y35–70), all air-conditioned and with private bath, color TV, and telephone.

邕江饭店
Yongjiang Hotel (41 Quannan Nan Rd.; tel: 28123). This hotel flanks the river which bears the same name. Catering to overseas Chinese, the Yongjiang is the most centrally located of Nanning's larger hotels. The South Building (with nearly 100 rooms; Y36 to Y56) is the one in which most foreign guests are lodged.

Other hotels in Nanning include the Ming Yuan Guest House (38 Xinmin Rd.; tel: 28923). A three-story L-shaped structure with private terraces, it overlooks a pond and a park and is a 15-minute walk from downtown Nanning. The good news at Nanning's hotels is their notably friendly and attentive staffs; the bad news is a preponderance of straw mattresses.

CUISINE

Similar to Cantonese cuisine, Guangxi cooking features exotic items such as suckling pig, turtle, lizard, and snake. For the less intrepid, there are simpler yet elegantly prepared vegetable dishes. The Nanhu Park Restaurant and Bailong Dining Hall in People's Park are two local restaurants popular for their wild game specialties (e.g., anteater stew and a kind of ragout of fox) as well as for their pleasant settings.

中国国际旅行社
CITS (Luxingshe) Office in Nanning ◼ 40 Xinmin Road. Tel: 22042.
Telex: 48142 CITSN CN. Cable; 1954.

Nantong

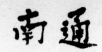

southern passage   *traditional spelling/Nantung*

NANTONG, on the north bank of the Yangtse, 100 km. (62 mi.) northwest of Shanghai, is one of the river's chief transfer ports. Though lacking rail or road connections with the interior, this municipality of 7.4 million (220,000 in the city proper) has been able to build up a strong industrial and trade base founded on its deep water harbor (oceangoing) ships up to 50,000 tons can be berthed here) and proximity to one of China's most important cotton-producing areas. The city, opened to tourism in 1983, was designated as one of the 14 Coastal Open Cities in 1984, and port expansion, factory upgrading, and hotel construction have been proceeding apace ever since. Nearly 120 contracts have been signed with foreign business interests, with about $80 million invested through 1985. Textiles are Nantong's most important export item. The port was handling over 10 million tons of cargo annually in the mid-1980s. Plans call for upgrading of cargo handling facilities to accommodate 25 million tons annually by 1990.

While little of historical or scenic interest is to be found in Nantong itself, the trip upriver from Shanghai, or downstream from Nanjing, provides a fascinating glimpse of life on the lower reaches of the Yangtse. The boat ride from Shanghai takes about six hours, although hovercraft service has been available since mid-1986 (for more details, inquire at CITS in Shanghai or Nanjing.

Climate		Jan	Feb	Mar	Apr	May	Jun	Jul	Aug	Sep	Oct	Nov	Dec
Temp.	°C	3.1	4.3	8.4	13.9	19.1	23.0	27.8	28.1	24.1	18.1	12.5	5.9
	°F	37.5	39.7	47.1	57	66.3	73.4	82	82.5	75.3	64.5	54.5	42.6
Precip.	mm.	254	254	330	330	305	356	279	279	305	254	203	178
	in.	10	10	13	13	12	14	11	11	12	10	8	7

Ningbo

calmed waves   *traditional spelling / Ningpo*

NINGBO is an ancient port city situated in eastern Zhenjiang Province at the mid-point of China's coastal sea lanes, 70 nautical miles south of Shanghai. For more than 800 years, it served as a key trade outlet for Chinese silk and export porcelain. It sits at the confluence of three rivers: the Fenghua, flowing towards the north; the Yuyao, flowing east; and the Yong, where the Fenghua and Yuyao meet and empty into the East China Sea. Like Wuhan, Ningbo is split into three sections by its rivers. It is linked to Hangzhou in the east by rail, and to Wenzhou in the south by road. Fishing and ship-building, which were already well-developed here by the Song Dynasty, are Ningbo's traditional activities, with a range of high-technology enterprises related to shipping and oil refining added in recent decades. A former "treaty port," the city is endowed with an excellent silt-free and ice-free deepwater harbor. Ningbo is one of the 14 Coastal Open Cities.

Ningbo comprises four districts and seven counties, with a total area of 9,345 sq. km. (3,607 sq. mi.) and a population of 4,783,300; the urban center has an area of 234.5 sq. km. (90.5 sq. mi.), with 600,000 residents. The city's subtropical climate yields an average annual temperature of 16.1°C (61°F), ranging from an average low of 4.2°C (40°F) in January to an average high of 28.8°C (84°F) in July. Heavy rain falls between mid-June and late July. July to September is the typhoon season.

NINGBO IN HISTORY

Ningbo is thought to have been inhabited as early as 7,000 years ago. Just south of the site of present-day Ningbo, a town named Yin was established during the Warring States Period (403–221 BC), but owing to the high salinity of both the Yuyao and Yong rivers, the location of present-day Ningbo remained uninhabitable until about the 6th century. At that time, artificial freshwater lakes were created at the base of the surrounding hills to collect water from mountain streams. Toward the end of the Tang Dynasty (618–907), a network of irrigation canals and locks was constructed. During the Tang, production of a local variety of porcelain known as Yueyao Qingci reached its zenith, with large quantities exported throughout Asia and even as far as East Africa. After a breakwater was installed in the natural harbor in the 12th century, trade with Japan began to flourish. In 1381, under the Ming, the town's name was changed to Ningbo Fu.

Climate		Jan	Feb	Mar	Apr	May	Jun	Jul	Aug	Sep	Oct	Nov	Dec
Temp.	°C	3.5	4.7	9.2	15.2	20.6	23.9	28.7	28.4	23.8	17.6	12.2	5.9
	°F	38.3	40.4	48.5	59.3	69	75	83.6	83.1	74.8	63.6	53.9	42.6
Precip.	mm.	254	254	330	330	305	356	279	279	305	254	203	178
	in.	10	10	13	13	12	14	11	11	12	10	8	7

Japan paid for the fine ceramics and silk of Ningbo with precious gold, silver, and copper. Portugal managed to gain a virtual monopoly as "middleman" in the lucrative silk trade during the 16th century, when it established a commercial base in Ningbo (along with a settlement at Macao further south). The British East India Company also gained a short-lived foothold here during the 17th century. In 1841, Ningbo was attacked by British forces during the first Opium War. By the terms of the resulting Treaty of Nanjing, Ningbo was opened to British commerce. A British consulate was established there in 1843. The Taiping rebels occupied the city briefly in 1861.

Ningbo entered the 20th century as a relatively poor, undeveloped area, long since overshadowed by the commercial pre-eminence of nearby Hangzhou and Shanghai. Large-scale construction and industrialization projects undertaken since 1949 have revitalized the town: the new dock area at Beilun (also the site of Ningbo's Economic and Technology Development Zone) includes a computerized cargo wharf of 100,000 ton capacity, the largest in China. Further port expansion is planned, including a major dredging project which will connect Ningbo to the Grand Canal and its vast inland waterway network.

In addition to modern shipbuilding, new industries now include metallurgy, machine building, electronics, and oil refining. By the early 1980s, Ningbo's industrial output had expanded more than 32-fold over 1949 levels: Two power stations, with a total output of 2.45 million kw, are being built to facilitate the further development of both light and heavy industries. The agricultural sector has achieved a high level of mechanization, with major products including grain, food oils, tea, cotton, fruits and vegetables, and, of course, fish.

HIGHLIGHTS

FOR TRAVELERS

天一阁

Tianyi Ge Library. Built in 1561, Tianyi Ge is the oldest existing "library" (literally, "place for storing books") in China. Constructed with a view to preventing fires, the structure included a water trough in front. In 1665, one of Fan Qian's descendants added the "false mountains" at the front and rear entrances, making the place even more striking. In the middle of the Qing Dynasty, the Qian Long emperor used the design of Tianyi Ge as a basis for constructing seven imperial libraries to house the "Complete Books of the Four Storehouses" (Siku Quanshu). The site fell into disrepair during the early part of this century, but in 1933 a group of private patrons restored the building and added a collection of stone calligraphy tablets from a nearby Confucian temple. There were originally more than 70,000 volumes in Tianyi Ge, but by 1949 only about a fifth of these were left. Since 1949, efforts have been made to reassemble the original collection, which by 1983 stood at about 300,000 volumes, of which at least 80,000 were rare volumes. The majority of these books are only available to scholars, but some can be seen on display in the main hall. The hall also includes an exhibition on the history of Tianyi Ge. Visitors should also note the interesting lions inside and outside of Tianyi Ge: the balls in their mouths can still be spun.

天封塔
Tianfeng Ta. Although the present structure dates from the 14th century (1330), the pagoda was first built 800 years earlier during the Liang Dynasty. The tower is still the highest structure in Ningbo (and thus also affords the best view). It has seven "obvious" stories and seven "hidden" stories, with four more reportedly buried underground.

月湖
Moon Lake. Widely regarded as a scenic spot for over 1,300 years, Moon Lake has been immortalized in poetry by such famous Chinese statesmen/literati as Wang Anshi and Sima Guang. Dykes designed to resemble those of Hangzhou's West Lake now form the site of Moon Lake Park. There is also a children's park and playground in the northeast corner. The lake is situated just east of Ningbo's hotels.

Other Highlights. Ningbo has two pleasant urban parks, Zhongshan Park and Riverside Park, both in the main area of the city. Zhongshan Park was formerly the seat of the region's imperial administration. It now includes a small zoo. Riverside Park is newer, and is favored for its path along the river. Other sites worth a visit are the arts and crafts factory on Jiefang Nan Lu; an embroidery factory on Dongfeng Lu; an active Buddhist temple (Seven Pagoda Temple — Qita Si); the Guangji Jie Primary School; the Jiefang Bei Lu Residence; the No. 1 Nursery School; and the No. 2 Hospital (opened in the 1920s by a US missionary) — all accessible with prior appointments or by arrangement with CITS. Ningbo also boasts a special school for the deaf, 15 research institutes, and five local Chinese opera troupes.

Walking Tour. A visit to the Tianyi Ge Library can be incorporated into a pleasant walking tour of the town. Make a right outside of the Overseas Chinese Hotel (or a left outside of the Ningbo Guest House), then right (or left) over the bridge so that you are walking north along the east bank of the river. Just past the second bridge (about four blocks), the first right leads to the entrance to Tianyi Ge. When exiting Tianyi Ge, walk around to the right and east down the alley to Moon Lake. At the lake, you can walk to the right (south) until you get to Ding Jie and then right again to the hotel. A more interesting route would be to go left at the lake and through the alleys heading north until you reach Zhongshan Lu, the main street of Ningbo. Here you can go left to the river and then walk south (left) until you reach your starting point. For those with ample time and energy, there is also the possibility of going right at Zhongshan Lu, a route that passes directly through the main part of town. The Drum tower is up one street on the left a few blocks from where you first come upon Zhongshan Lu. Behind it (to the north) is Zhongshan Park. You can continue down Zhongshan Lu to the river (along the river there are free markets), or turn off at Jiefang Lu (the first large intersection along the way) to head back towards the hotels. You need to walk a fair distance (crossing four large intersections) before taking another left that will lead to the hotels.

A better approach may be to hail one of the three-wheeled pedicabs on the street or at a station for the return to the hotel. These cabs can also be used to explore the rest of the city. You can cover virtually every worthwhile point in town for Y2, while the ride from Zhongshan Lu to the hotel should cost about 50 *fen*. There are no bike rentals in the city, and few taxis; private bikes and pedicabs are the main means of transportation.

SITES NEAR NINGBO

保国寺
Baoguo Si. One of the oldest wooden structures south of the Yangtse River, this complex was built during the Northern Song Dynasty (1013). About 45 minutes (20 km.) north of town, the site has special appeal for travelers interested in Chinese architecture. Included is an exhibition on Chinese architecture through the centuries as well as an exhibit of photos, maps, and artifacts on Ningbo's history. Another section has a display of treasures from each period of history: inlaid wood, porcelain, bronze, pottery, and cloisonné. Unfortunately, all descriptive information at the site is in Chinese.

The complex can be reached via a branch of bus #11 from New River Bridge (just north of the bridge where the three rivers meet), but a taxi is much simpler. You can make a day-trip to Baoguo Si as well as to the two other main attractions in the areas (in Ning County) by taxi for about Y70.

宁县
Ning County. Two of the main attractions in Ningbo are actually not in Ningbo proper, but in Ning County, southeast of the city. Since they are not in the city, visitors must first acquire a travel pass from the Public Security Bureau. But the passes can be gotten en route, and the procedure only takes about five minutes. The two sites worth visiting are:

阿育王庙
Ayuwang Temple. About 20 km. east of town, the Sheli ("Buddhist relic") Pagoda is the main attraction at this temple. The relic is said to have been first discovered in 281 (Jin Dynasty). Legend has it that the monk who found it was looking for one of the many Sheli pagodas that the Indian ruler Ayuwang had established throughout the world. The monk was walking in the area and heard a bell ringing from underground. He sat down and prayed for three days and three nights, at which point the pagoda came surging up from beneath the ground. A temple was eventually completed

on the site in 522 and named Ayuwang Temple. It has been famous ever since. The famous Tang Dynasty traveling monk, Jian Zhen, once came here to view the Sheli, which is said to contain an actual bone of Sakyamuni, the founder of Buddhism. An exhibition features artistic and Buddhist artifacts, paintings, and calligraphy, some personally executed by Chinese emperors. The temple remains quite active and, as of the mid-1980s, housed over 50 monks. Originally considered a Zen temple, it is now associated with the Pure Land Sect. There is a nice vegetarian noodle and cold dish shop in the temple as well as a small kiosk that sells Buddhist publications and souvenirs.

天童寺

Tiantong Temple. Located about 120 km. to the east past Ayuwang Temple, the Tiantong Temple was founded in the Western Jin Dynasty (c. 300) as an assemblage of ascetic grass huts. It was later destroyed and then rebuilt during the Tang Dynasty, growing to become one of the largest Buddhist complexes in China. At its apex, it had 990 rooms and several thousand monks. About 730 chambers remain to the present day, covering an area of 44,600 sq. m. The temple now has about 60 monks, about half of whom, notably, are young.

The temple is one of the five sacred mountains of Zen, as it is where the famous Japanese monks Dogen and Yonsai came to study Buddhism during the Song Dynasty. Upon their return to Japan, they founded the Soto and Rinzai sects of Japanese Zen, respectively. There is a story that the monk Yixing, who first built the grass huts, so moved the Jade Emperor with his piousness that the emperor sent a star (known in Chinese as the Taibai star) that turned into a youth, to act as Yixing's servant. Thus derived the name Tiantong (Heavenly Youth) for the temple and Taibai for the mountain on which it rests. As with Ayuwang Temple, there are no organized activities for lay Buddhists, but many come to burn incense.

The ride up to these two temples is quite pleasant, leaving the Ningbo plain and rising into the mountains after passing fields of rice, watermelon, and rape seed. The road through the hills winds sharply and is flanked with pipes. An abandoned nunnery, known as Sweet Dew or Peaceful Nunnery, is passed along the way.

In addition to the overland route, it is also possible to get to Ayuwang and Tiantong temples by boat. You can board the boat at Dahe Lu (Xinhetou) on the east side of the river (tel: 2915). To Ayuwang, take the boat that goes to Dongwu; to Tiantong, take the boat to Baodong.

普陀山

Putuoshan. Putuoshan is an island off the coast of Ningbo. It is considered a sacred Buddhist site associated with the Goddess of Mercy. The island features an array of temples and scenic spots. It was first developed in the late Tang Dynasty (9th century).

天台山

Tiantai. This is the site where the Tiantai (in Japanese, Tendai) School of Buddhism was founded. It is still quite active. Located 140 km. south of town, it can be reached in about four hours by car (or 5–6 hours by bus). A travel pass is also required for Tiantai. Several temples have been built on the mountain, the largest of which is Guoqing Temple, built in 598 during the Sui Dynasty. The pagoda in front also dates from the Sui. It has nine halls, several pavilions, and an exhibition hall. Small pagodas around the temple mark the graves of famous monks. The Zhizhe Pagoda (northwest of the temple) is where Dharmamaster Zhi-yi, the founder of the Tiantai School, is buried. There is also a spectacular waterfall near the temple. Another temple, Gaoming Temple, is to the northeast. It is possible to stay overnight at these temples for a small fee.

Tiantai can be reached by car or bus from Hangzhou, Wenzhou, Shaoxing, or Ningbo.

HOTEL

ACCOMMODATIONS

宁波饭店

Ningbo Hotel (65 Mayuan Rd.; tel: 66334; telex: 37019 NBHOT CN; cable: 2451). Officially opened in October 1983, the Ningbo is a six-story structure with 100 rooms, including five two-room suites. All rooms are air-conditioned and well appointed. The hotel has two dining rooms, one Chinese, one Western. Facilities also include a coffee shop and antiques shop. An enclosed deck on the roof affords a splendid view of the city. Newly renovated in 1988.

华侨饭店

Overseas Chinese Hotel (130 Liaoding St.; tel: 63175; cable: 3579). Built in 1962, this unprepossessing hotel has 300 beds, 200 of which are designated for use by foreigners. Air-conditioning is provided in about 40–50 of these rooms. Rooms are simple, but comfortable. The hotel dining room is open 7–8 AM, 11:15–noon, and from 5–6 PM. Only Chinese food is served. Hot water for bathing begins in the morning at 6:30, and is turned on at night from 7–10 PM. The post office (downstairs) can send packages and is open from 7:30 AM to 5 PM.

花园宾馆

The **Huayuan Guesthouse** (Mayuan Rd.; tel: 66888), a new joint venture hotel, also receives foreigners. *Rates:* Single: Y100; double: Y140; suites: Y200–500.

NINGBO CUISINE

Ningbo is known for its seafood and for a local method of combining fresh and pickled (salted) foods. Another regional specialty, "soup dumplings," is available at the **Ningbo Soup Dumpling Shop** on Zhongshan Lu. Other popular restaurants include the **Chunlai Beiwei Guan,** at the corner of Zhongshan Lu and Kaiming Jie (tel: 2959); the **Dongfuyuan Caiguan,** at Dongmenkou (tel: 2669); and the **Changzheng Fandian** on Zhongshan Lu (tel: 2022). There is also a vegetarian restaurant next to the Chunlai Beiwei Guan.

SHOPPING

Ningbo's Friendship Store (70 Mayuan Rd.; tel: 61345) is located on the second floor of the Port Station in the northeast section of town. It consists of only two rooms, but offers a good selection of imported items such as liquors, soft drinks, and cigarettes (but no film; indeed, foreign film is nowhere available in Ningbo). Zhongshan Lu is the city's main shopping area. There are free markets along the river and near the main bus stations (the South Station market is the largest).

中国国际旅行社
CITS (Luxingshe) Office in Ningbo ■ 106 Liuding St. Tel: 53175/52181.

Qingdao

青島

green island   *traditional spelling/Tsingtao*

QINGDAO is one of China's most popular coastal resorts. The city is situated on the southern coast of the Shandong Peninsula overlooking the Yellow Sea. Located about 400 km. (250 mi.) southeast of Beijing, with a population of 1.4 million, Qingdao is also a major seaport as well as the most important industrial center in Shangdong Province, a fact underscored by its designation, in 1984, as one of China's 14 Coastal Open Cities.

The city is surrounded on three sides by the sea, with Mt. Lao (Laoshan) as a backdrop. Qingdao's red-tiled roofs and verdant foliage complement its picturesque setting. When one also considers its fine beaches, pleasant climate, and brewery—which produces the most famous beer in China—one can readily understand the appeal of this city to tourists.

There is twice-a-week air service to Qingdao from Beijing, as well as a 15-hour overnight train. Both Chinese coastal steamers and foreign cruise ships dock in Qingdao's harbor.

Cool currents from the north keep summer temperatures pleasantly mild, although it can be foggy and wet from mid-June to August, and the winds in winter are fierce. The best seasons to visit Qingdao are spring and fall.

QINGDAO IN HISTORY

Prior to 1891, when the Chinese government constructed a fort and a naval station here, Qingdao was little more than a small fishing village. In 1898, the Germans "selected" Qingdao as a port concession and forced a treaty upon the Chinese imperial government. It was on the occasion of dispatching Prince Henry of Prussia to assume the administration of Qingdao that Kaiser Wilhelm made his famous "mailed fist" statement: "fahre darein mit gepanzerter Faust."

Within a decade, the Germans had built a European-like city, complete with deep-water harbor, business district, and—like most areas then under foreign control—a segregated section for Chinese residents. Japan took over the city during World War I. China was not able to regain control of Qingdao until 1922.

Before 1949, the city's economy was stagnant, relying mainly on trade, silk weaving, essential oils, and Qingdao (Tsingtao) beer. Today, Qingdao is a major manufacturing center for both heavy industry (steel, diesel locomotives, tractors, automobiles, and generators) and light industry (television

Climate		Jan	Feb	Mar	Apr	May	Jun	Jul	Aug	Sep	Oct	Nov	Dec
Temp.	°C	−1.1	0.1	4.4	10.3	15.7	20.0	23.7	25.1	21.4	15.9	8.6	1.6
	°F	30	32.1	39.9	50.5	60.2	68	74.6	77.1	70.5	60.6	47.4	34.8
Precip.	mm.	254	254	330	330	305	356	279	279	305	254	203	178
	in.	10	10	13	13	12	14	11	11	12	10	8	7

sets, textiles, watches, cameras, and precision equipment). It is also well known for its workers' sanatoriums.

HIGHLIGHTS
FOR TRAVELERS

Railroad buffs may seek to visit Qingdao's locomotive factory—a source of pride to local residents, but also a major contributor to the city's pollution. Visitors may also be taken to a nearly housing development to see a day-care center or workers' dormitories. But most travelers will want to linger at Qingdao's beaches and museums.

青岛海滩
Qingdao Beaches. East of the Qinghai Pier are six large bays with smooth sand beaches and clear, calm waters. In addition to snack bars, restaurants, stores, photo studios, and medical stations, all beaches have facilities for swimmers to change their clothes and shower. Swimming areas are marked off by buoys, and lifeboats patrol the area. All the beaches are protected by shark nets.

For a lovely view of the city and coastline, take the cable car to the top of the hill which overlooks the main beach.

花东醸酒厂
Huadong Winery (tel: 495875). Opened in 1986, the winery is a newly-built château set on the northern slopes of Laoshan, surrounded by vineyards that, in this wood-starved area, use granite posts to train the vines. The winery produces the only varietal vintage wine in China, and the only Chinese wine which has ever taken prizes in international competition, winning the 1986 Silver Medal in Bordeaux. Tours include wine tasting; the winery will send a car to Qingdao to pick up groups.

小青岛
Little Qingdao. This small island, first developed as a lighthouse by the Germans in 1900, was a military area until 1987. It is now open for tourism, and tours include the lighthouse and the gardens. The gardens have a variety of rare flowers, including the rare "Qingdao White Lily," which blooms only in Southern Shandong.

黄岛
Yellow Island. This peninsula southeast of Qingdao is the newest of China's Special Economic and Development Zones. A small fishing village until 1987, the island now houses joint ventures approaching Y30 million in value. In the center of Huangdao are the remains of the tip of an approximately 311-mi.-long wall built in around 600 BC, when Shandong Province was the Ducal state of Qi. From Huangdao a ferry connects to Xuejia Island, the "Hawaii of the East," whose beaches are among the most spectacular in North China.

青岛啤酒厂

Qingdao Brewery. Perhaps one of the few positive legacies of Western colonialism in China is Qingdao's brewery, established by the Germans at the turn of the century. Some of the old wooden machinery is still in use, although it is being supplanted by glistening new bottling machines recently imported from the Federal Republic of Germany. Instead of the usual "briefing with tea," visitors to the brewery will get a "briefing with beer," served ice-cold in the traditional green bottles.

Although there are other well-known beers in China (Wuxing in Beijing, Baiyun in Guangzhou, and the somewhat watery Shanghai brand), Qingdao beer is the most popular export brand (it is now being marketed under the old name, Tsingtao, throughout the world). Its fine flavor is attributable to the water from Mt. Lao (Laoshan), which also produces the best-known mineral water in China.

前海栈桥亭

Zhanqiao Pavilion. This pavilion is located at the end of Qinghai Pier. Its two floors of exhibition space contain paintings and other examples of fine craftsmanship, much of its destined for the export market.

青岛市博物馆

Qingdao Art Museum. Originally built in 1931 by some of the city's wealthy citizens as a welfare institution for the local poor, this fine building now houses extensive collections of Yuan, Ming, and Qing paintings. The exhibits are changed four times a year. In the building adjacent to the painting gallery is a somewhat less impressive archeological exhibit.

鲁迅公园

Lu Xun Park. Named after one of China's most famous modern authors, this park has lovely winding pathways. It also houses an aquarium where visitors may see a number of rare and protected species.

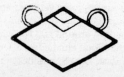

崂山
LAOSHAN

Dotted by temples and waterfalls and surrounded by the sea, the 1,133-meter Laoshan and her sister peaks star among Qingdao's top attractions. Laoshan is famed for her granite, quarried for the Shanghai Museum and Mao's Tomb; and for her top-selling mineral water, as well as for the contributions her temples have made to the history of Daoism. Formed by volcanoes and plate shifts that hoisted her from the sea some 1.4 billion years ago, leaving behind Jiaozhou Bay, Laoshan bears traces of her origins still. The highest slopes bear marine fossils, and granite cracked and jumbled by the mountain's growth has formed snowmen, needles, and towers of stone, each with its local legend. The house-sized boulder forming "Split-Rock Pass" was "slashed by the sword of the hero Wu Cong," and the chip-shaped stones atop White Cloud peak are "chess pieces of the Gods."

Tourists at Laoshan generally must choose either the North or the South route. A new road connects the two, and is great for hardy bikers and sturdy cars, but few tour buses dare make the trip.

The more popular South Route road winds along the coast, past villages and pear orchards to the lower peaks, never reaching Laoshan itself. Most tours stop by a rock called the "Old Stone Man," and a white-sand beach called Liuqing He. First stop by Laoshan is Bashuihe (Eight Water-River) village. From there, stone steps rise to Longtan Pu (Dragon Pool Waterfall), with its statue commemorating a PLA man killed while rescuing stranded tourists. Most tours turn back here for a drive to Taiqinggong, but for those with time, the path above is gorgeous, rising past altars and bamboo groves to the lovely, if only partly restored, Upper Purity Temple (Shangqinggong), and then to the Cave of Bright Mists (Mingxia Dong). There, according to legend, the partly natural, partly man-made cave and monastery complex once turned dawn mists to a rainbow. An earthquake cracked the roof and spoiled the effect, but the view remains stunning. Mingxia Dong now houses a government project researching Chinese medicine.

From Mingxia Dong, a curving path down ends at Extreme Purity Temple (Taiqinggong), home to all 35 of Laoshan's active monks. Laoshan's monks follow Quanzhen, an orthodox Daoist sect which split from the Zhengyi mainstream in 1167 under Zheng Zong, a local monk striving to unify Daoism with Buddhism and Confucianism. Zhengyi wags claim the Quanzhen sect has the worst of all worlds: Buddhist diets, Confucian obedience, and Daoist hairstyles. But Laoshan's monks seem proud of their traditional clothes, and study hard. Curious tourists willing to rise at 5 AM are welcome to watch morning prayers and martial arts; courtesy demands registering with the monastery office a day before. The busy 86-year-old Head Monk Kuang Yaming also occasionally receives visitors. He's a nationally reknowned expert at qigong, Chinese medicine, and five types of martial arts.

The North Route passes the Huadong Winery, the Qingdao Reservoir, the all-stone village of Licun carved from the mountain, and the nature reserve at Hualou Mountain, arriving at the health resort of Beijiushui (Nine Northern Waters). From there, paths lead North and Southeast to cold but refreshing mineral pools, and South straight up Laoshan. Most North Route tours end at Yangkuo (Slack Mouth) beach, named for an off-shore rock shaped like the head of a slumped back man.

The East Route connecting the two features two partly restored temples, and the least peopled and most spectacular path up Laoshan.

Getting There. Laoshan lies 13 km. northeast of Qingdao. The cheapest way there is by city bus, #15 for the North route to Licun, #4 for the South route to Liuqing He, and a Y1 shuttle from there. But this takes hours. Dozens of one-day van tours to both routes start at or near the railway station, for from Y5 to Y15 each. If you stay overnight, you forfeit the return. Cars can be hired starting at around Y80 roundtrip. And a one-day boat tour leaving from the Laiyang Pier (tel: 385639) gives a spectacular view, but is crowded and not for the faint of stomach.

Food and Accommodations. Food stands and restaurants cover the lower slopes of both routes. The best at Laoshan is the Taiqinggong Restaurant (Taiqinggong Fanzhuang), which features several Daoist dishes and a hotel. Tourists may also stay at the White Cloud Hotel (Baiyun Lou), some 20 minutes up the slope from Taiqinggong. Both have beds from Y6 to Y30 a night. The White Cloud has a better view, but the Taiqinggong is nearer to both the temple and the beach.

◄━━━◆

HOTEL

◄━━━◆

ACCOMMODATIONS

◆━━━►

汇泉宾馆
Huiquan Guest House (9 Nanhai Rd.; tel: 285215; telex: 32178 HQDTY CN; cable: 0565). Opened in 1979, the Huiquan is situated conveniently near both Zhongshan and Lu Xun parks, and overlooks No. 1 Beach—the largest of Qingdao's bathing areas. Rates range from Y45–55 for doubles, and Y80–90 for suites. All rooms are air-conditioned and have private bath and telephone; most also have color TV.

栈桥宾馆
Zhanqiao Guest House (31 Taiping Rd.; tel: 83402; telex: 32184 ZQHTL CN; cable: 1384). Although older than the Huiquan, the Zhanqiao is far-and-away the most charming place to stay in the city. It is located just across the road from No. 6 Beach. Rooms facing the waterfront have enclosed verandas with rattan furniture. The splendid scenery is matched only by the fine cuisine (another vestige of colonial days is the good German sausage which now and again appears at breakfast). Room rates range from Y50 to Y80.

华侨大厦

Overseas Chinese Hotel (72 Hunan Rd.; tel: 86738; cable: 8236). This small hotel (two single rooms, 14 doubles, four suites; Y40–80). has rooms with private bath and air-conditioning, a Chinese restaurant, and a souvenir shop.

黄海饭店

Yellow Sea (Huang Hai) Hotel (75 Yanyi Rd.; tel: 270215). The Yellow Sea is one of the largest hotels in Qingdao, boasting 450 rooms and some 875 beds, ranging from Y150 to Y300 per bed. The hotel front is on beach #1, and is convenient to most tourist areas. One disadvantage is the hotel's distance from any good restaurants; the one in the hotel is primitive.

八大关宾馆

Badaguan Guesthouse (15 Shanhaiguan Rd.; tel: 62800). The Badaguan consists of about 30 small villas, as well as the Old Stone House and German Governor's Mansion. The rooms, considered the most interesting in Qingdao, are also the most expensive in town, costing Y200–800 per night.

For budget travelers, the **Beihai Hotel** (23A Zhanliu Road; tel: 363500) offers rooms to foreigners. The **Qingdao University Guesthouse** is another possibility. It is open to foreigners without the usual letter of introduction necessary at other university guesthouses. The University Foreign Affairs Office (tel: 363772) arranges housing.

Other hotels for the budget-minded include the Friendship Hotel (12 Xingiang Rd.; tel: 228865); Haibin Hotel (Guangxi Rd.; tel: 24447); Ying-binguan Hotel (26 Longshan Rd.; tel: 826120); and Qingdao Hotel (53 Zhongshan Rd.; tel: 86069).

CUISINE

Relatively unknown and therefore underrated, Shandong cooking is among the most elegantly presented and richly flavorful in China (several of the best restaurants in Beijing serve Shandong-style food). The most famous of Qingdao's restaurants is the Chunhelou Restaurant on Zhong-shan Road (tel: 227371).

SHOPPING

The best area for shopping in Qingdao is along Zhongshan Road, just off Qingdao Road and not too far from the Zhanqiao Guest House. There are two fine department stores; an antiques store; a dry-goods store, where you will find the elegant but inexpensive hexagonal hats of the Shandong region; and a handicrafts shop which features locally produced shellware. This is the old German quarter, certainly among the most colorful and scenic sections of modern Qingdao.

中国国际旅行社
CITS (Luxingshe) Office in Qingdao ■ 9 Nanhai Road. Tel: 284830.
Telex: 32202 QCITS CN.

Qinhuangdao

island of the Qin Emperor   *traditional spelling/Chinhuangtao*

TRACE your finger east from Beijing and you run into the famous port of Qinhuangdao on the Bohai Gulf. Qinhuangdao was chosen as one of the 14 Coastal Open Cities, due chiefly to its ice-free harbor, China's third largest: the port handles about 40 million tons annually. Coal (from Shanxi) and oil (from Daqing) are the primary cargos. The town was best known in the past as a coal depot supplying the factories of Shanghai.

Coal would come in from British-controlled mines in the northwest and be transferred quickly south by boat to the Shanghai Power Company. The port was also used to land foreign troops during the Boxer Rebellion in 1900 and to ship out whole boatloads of Chinese for work in the South African gold mines for several decades thereafter.

Today the Qinhuangdao harbor is linked by rail to Beijing and other major cities and plays an important role in the industrial output of Hebei Province. It also has a few industries of its own, including a metals plant and a modern glass-fibers factory. The latter is open to visitors and probably worth a peek if you've never watched the process of glass being woven and spun. Huge bags of glass marbles go through what looks like a washing machine and on to the melting furnace. From there, they emerge in long silken threads which are wound on reels for the spinning and weaving shops. The end results are ingenious substitutes for steel piping and plastic materials.

The countryside around Qinhuangdao is open and rolling. Fields of corn and grassy meadows are only a short walk from the town and may provide a welcome relief to the clamor of the busy port and the chemical fumes of glass spinning.

Hotel accommodations include the **Zhonghaitan Guest House**, at 30 Xijing Rd., Haibinqu (tel: 2398); **Gold Mountain Guesthouse** (Harbin qu; tel: 41338); **Xinyi Hotel** (Yingbin Rd.; tel: 32243); and the **Sea Mountain Guesthouse.**

Climate		Jan	Feb	Mar	Apr	May	Jun	Jul	Aug	Sep	Oct	Nov	Dec
Temp.	°C	−4.7	−1.9	4.8	13.7	20.1	24.8	26.1	24.8	19.9	12.8	3.8	2.8
	°F	23.5	28.6	40.6	56.6	68.1	76.6	78.9	76.6	67.8	55	38.8	37
Precip.	mm.	76	76	76	102	152	203	305	254	178	152	102	76
	in.	3	3	3	4	6	8	12	10	7	6	4	3

Quanzhou

perfecture of springs   *traditional spelling/Ch'uan Chou*

ONCE a world-renowned port, Quanzhou is a city of 400,000 on a silted-up bay in the heart of the Minnan ("south of the Min River") region of Fujian Province, 106 km. (66 mi.) northeast of Xiamen, and 196 km. (122 mi.) southwest of Fuzhou. The hilly southern Fujian countryside is lush and fertile, with abundant water and extensive irrigation networks. Rice, sugarcane, and fruits are the chief crops; the region's prized lychees ripen in June and July. An economic backwater since the late Ming (16th century), there has been very little industrial or infrastructural investment in the Quanzhou region until quite recently. However, as part of a proposed Coastal Open Area (see section on Doing Business in China, above) centered in Xiamen, Quanzhou has begun preparations for an economic renaissance. Projects include a recently completed airport—offering scheduled service to Fuzhou, Guangzhou, and Shanghai. A railway link to Xiamen is under construction.

Quanzhou's climate is subtropical, with summer temperatures often reaching 32°C (90°F), and dropping only rarely below 4°C (40°F) in January and February. Humidity is high throughout the year. July to September is typhoon season.

Quanzhou can be reached by bus from both Xiamen and Fuzhou.

► QUANZHOU IN HISTORY ◄

Founded as Wurongzhou in the Tang Dynasty, Quanzhou was once one of Asia's busiest ports. At its peak, in the Song and Yuan dynasties (11th–14th centuries), the town had close commercial and cultural ties with the Arab world and was the site of a thriving Islamic community. Marco Polo visited Quanzhou, calling it "Zayton" (possibly a corruption of its Song Dynasty name, Qingyuanjun), and marvelled at its wealth and bustle. During the Ming Dynasty, the harbor began to silt up, and Quanzhou gradually gave way to Xiamen (Amoy) as the region's economic center. Economic decline, overcrowded living conditions, and the local populace's strong allegiance to the fallen Ming Dynasty, sparked massive migrations to Taiwan and Southeast Asia during the early Qing Dynasty. Much of the new housing and other construction in Quanzhou and the surrounding countryside was paid for by funds remitted home by overseas Chinese with ancestral origins in the region.

Climate		Jan	Feb	Mar	Apr	May	Jun	Jul	Aug	Sep	Oct	Nov	Dec
Temp.	°C	10.3	10.3	13.2	18.3	22.7	25.0	28.8	28.3	26.3	21.7	17.9	12.9
	°F	50.5	50.5	55.7	64.9	72.8	77	83.8	82.9	79.3	71	64.2	55.2
Precip.	mm.	152	152	203	279	304	381	254	203	178	178	152	127
	in.	6	6	8	11	12	15	10	8	7	7	6	5

HIGHLIGHTS FOR
TRAVELERS

Quanzhou is a delightful place to explore on foot. Many of the houses and shops lining the narrow side streets and alleys date from the Ming and Qing dynasties. Temples in various states of disrepair can be found throughout the city. Some of these structures (such as the pagoda next to Baiyuanquan Pond, across from the Overseas Chinese Mansion) are being restored. Quanzhou's lively "free market," located near the hotel, is also a good place to get a feel for local lifestyles.

There are no public buses or taxis in Quanzhou. The best way to get around the city is on foot, or by pedicab. As pedicabs have no meters, a price should be agreed on before setting off. These vehicles are also available for hire on a full- or half-day basis. Most of the temples and other sites are within walking distance of each other, but many of the more distant sites are accessible only by hired car or minibus, available at the Overseas Chinese Mansion. Tickets for a minibus tour of Qingyuan Mountain, Luoyang Bridge, and other sites can be purchased at the travel service office just south of the park.

开元寺

Kaiyuan Temple (Xijie, between Zhongshan Road and Xinhua Road). This extraordinarily beautiful temple was initially built in the Tang Dynasty (AD 686). At first called the "Lotus Temple," it took its present name in 738, during the reign of Emperor Xuan Zong. Most of the present structure dates from the Ming and Qing. Bombed by the Japanese and later occupied by Guomindang troops, the temple has since been fully restored. Passing through the first courtyard, full of carved stone pillars and statues, one reaches the main hall, which dates from the 14th century. Inside are five golden Buddhas, representing the center and four cardinal directions of the manifest world, and the five analogous Buddha-realms. Above the central Buddha (Vairocana, the Buddha of the highest eternal reality) is a plaque inscribed in 1642, just before the fall of the Ming Dynasty, which reads, "Hall of the Great Hero's (i.e. the Buddha's) Treasure." Along the beams are 24 carved "flying" musicians (apsaras), an Indian Buddhist motif unique in Chinese temple statuary. Distributed among the hall's 100 or so columns are statues of the 18 Arhats and numerous Bodhisattvas. Several Brahmanic-style columns and stone carvings are found inside and outside the hall as well, hinting at Quanzhou's historical connections with the Hindu and Buddhist nations of Southeast Asia. Behind and to the west of the main hall, through a gate, is a 1,300-year-old mulberry tree which, legend has it, once produced lotus blossoms.

A large sandalwood statue of Vairocana dominates the altar of the second hall, a wooden structure dating from the Ming Dynasty. The statue's pedestal is a thousand-petal lotus, each petal itself supporting a small Buddha. Other statues in this hall include four pairs of fierce guardians, and another series of "flying" musicians, each playing an instrument peculiar to the Quanzhou area. The last building in the temple complex is a scripture repository, which is not generally open to the public.

东西塔
Twin Pagodas. Situated on the grounds of the Kaiyuan Temple are two very ancient hexagonal pagodas. The present granite structures were built during the Southern Song Dynasty (ca. AD 1250) to replace the earlier wooden pagodas. It is sometimes possible to climb the East pagoda which, at 48 m. (157 ft.) is the taller of the two. On the base are carved scenes from 39 tales of the life of Sakyamuni, the historical Buddha.

泉州海外交通史博物馆
Quanzhou Foreign Trade History Museum. Located in a building at the eastern end of the Kaiyuan Temple, the museum's main exhibit is a Song Dynasty ocean-going junk, discovered in 1974 in the shallows of Quanzhou Bay. Measuring 9 by 24 meters, the boat displaced upwards of 200 tons. Upstairs is an exhibit of everyday and artistic objects found in the boat, while steles and stone carvings from various periods are displayed in the downstairs gallery.

清净寺
Qingjing Mosque. In its heyday, Quanzhou had several active mosques to serve its large Moslem community. Qingjing (Purity) Mosque, also called Al-Ashab Mosque, is the oldest extant mosque in China, and the only one in Quanzhou to survive into the 20th century. The middle-eastern-style gate and worship hall were both part of the original Song Dynasty building, erected in 1009. There is a small exhibit inside, where steles, gravestones and other Islamic inscriptions, in Chinese and Arabic, are displayed. The mosque is near the Overseas Chinese Mansion, on Tumen Street.

文庙
Confucian Temple (Wen Miao). Also near the Overseas Chinese Mansion, the buildings in this temple complex are currently serving a variety of non-religious functions. The hall directly behind the hotel is now Quanzhou's municipal library, while a Youth Palace and a grain warehouse occupy structures on the main temple grounds beyond.

清源山
Qingyuan Mountains. Just north of the city proper, this group of scenic hills boasts numerous caves and springs, in addition to the many stone temples and shrines, as well as many fine examples of rock-carved calligraphy. Most of these cultural relics date from the Song Dynasty. There is a good view of the surrounding countryside from the summit.

老君岩
Laojunyan. West of Qingyuan Mountain is a large statue of an old Daoist sage, carved out of a rock outcropping in the 11th century.

灵山圣墓

Lingshan Tomb. On a hillside east of town is the graceful Chinese-style tomb of two Moslem missionaries who died at Quanzhou near the end of the Southern Song Dynasty. There is a display of steles and stone carvings from various periods at the site.

洛阳桥

Luoyang Bridge. Spanning the Luoyang River 10 km. (6 mi.) north east of the city, this stone bridge was completed in AD 1058. The bridge links Quanzhou with Hui-an County, the source of Quanzhou's granite and a district famous since the 10th century for its stonecarvers and masons. All along the bridge's 834-m. length, and at either end, are wonderful examples of their handiwork.

HOTEL

ACCOMMODATIONS

The only hotel currently accommodating foreign visitors is the **Overseas Chinese Mansion** (Beiyanqingci Rd.; tel: 22192), although a new joint venture hotel is under construction. All rooms in the Overseas Chinese Mansion are air-conditioned and have mosquito nets. Amenities include a bar, on the top floor, and a lobby gift shop, where local handicrafts such as lacquerware, embroidery, wood carving, and wooden puppets can be purchased. Food at the hotel's restaurant is adequate. For foreign exchange, the local branch of the Bank of China is located just up the street, at the corner of Baiyuan and Jiuyi roads. Other hotels receiving foreigners include the **Qiaolian Mansions** (Dong Dalu; tel: 25601), and the **Jinquan Guesthouse** (Beiyanqingci Rd.; tel: 25078).

CUISINE

Quanzhou cuisine is similar to Xiamen's, with the emphasis on seafood. Rice threads (*mifen*), either fried or in soup, are a local specialty. Local fare may be sampled at the Mantang Restaurant (Zhongshan Zhong Rd. at Tushan St.; tel: 2887), and at Furenyi Restaurant (Zhongshan Nan Road at Shuimen Lane; tel: 2759).

中国国际旅行社
CITS (Luxingshe) Office in Quanzhou ◾ 9 Jinyi Road. Tel: 2039/5643.

曲阜

song of abundance   *traditional spelling / Chü-foo*

QUFU, birthplace of Confucius, fits a tourist's image of what North China should be. It's an 8,000-year-old small town, where mule carts and bicycles outnumber cars, and grandparents gossip on their stoops. Set in Southwest Shandong Province, 175 km. from Jinan, amid China's vast Northern plains, yet ringed by mountains that until recently have blocked trade, Qufu has preserved architecture and customs that have all but disappeared in larger cities. With neither airport nor train station, Qufu can be a strain to reach. But for the extra effort, the tourist can glimpse the lives of that great part of China's people who know more about farming than foreign trade. As one visitor put it, "I've been to Beijing and Xi'an, but *this* is China."

Biweekly flights to Jiaxiang, 83 km. to the north, connect with taxis that charge around Y80 into town. Cars can be prearranged through the city Foreign Affairs Office (tel: 411843), or the Touring Car Company (tel: 411673). But most tourists take the train to Yanzhou Station, about 20 km. south of Qufu, a small stop on many big lines from Beijing, Shanghai, and Qingdao. Yanzhou is just two hours from Jinan, or one hour from Tai'an and Mt. Tai, so time-conscious tourists can see some of Qufu's attractions and then move on in one day. From Yanzhou buses connect to Qufu, but stop running at 6 PM. Tourists on later trains must choose a night taxi (about Y20) or a night in Yanzhou. The **Yanzhou Guest House** (Yanzhou Bingguan; tel: 3905), just out of the station, has spartan but clean beds for from Y5 to Y15 a night. Around the corner, the **Yanzhou Hostel** (Yanzhou Lushe; tel: 2518) is the same price, but rooms are dank and noisy, and lack televisions. In the morning, Yanzhou is worth a glance before moving on to Qufu; there's a pleasant park, and a Sui Dynasty Buddhist tower set in a magnificent rose garden.

Once in Qufu the best way around is by bike; unfortunately, at present bikeshops are not allowed to rent to foreigners. This law may change, but for now the best options are the many three-wheeled pedicabs and decorative horsecarts that fill the streets. Only two sites — Ni Mountain and the Forest of Mencius's Mother — are so far away as to require renting one of the Touring Car Company's cars.

Climate		Jan	Feb	Mar	Apr	May	Jun	Jul	Aug	Sep	Oct	Nov	Dec
Temp.	°C	−1.4	0.9	7.6	14.7	22.3	26.6	27.6	26.6	21.4	15.7	7.9	0.9
	°F	29.4	33.6	45.6	58.4	72.1	79.8	81.6	79.8	70.5	60.2	46.2	33.6
Precip.	mm.	76	102	76	102	127	203	279	254	152	152	102	76
	in.	3	4	3	4	5	8	11	10	6	6	4	3

CLIMATE, ECONOMY, AND CULTURE

Qufu's climate is temperate, snowing only lightly in winter and rarely getting below −9°C, or above 32°C in summer. The population of 560,000 is 98% Han, with a smattering of Islamic Hui people, descendents of Western traders who washed up in this quiet area when the Silk Road went bust and never left. Their legacy remains; though few in number, the Hui own a great many local restaurants and shops. Some 70% of Qufu's people are farmers. The remaining 30% work in light industry (textiles, fertilizers, and liquor), and in service trades, increasingly centering on tourism. Working under the Confucian motto "when friends come from afar, is it not delightful?" the city has launched an all-out campaign to attract tourists. Two major hotels have gone up in the last five years, and more are planned. The old canal around the city is being rebuilt, and a park has been planted beside it. Temples and tombs are being renovated at a fast pace, and strict zoning laws ensure that all future architecture will match the city's white-walled, tile-roofed style. And a "greening of Qufu" campaign is planting trees and bushes trying to combat the area's one major atmospheric flaw — dust.

In the surrounding countryside, most houses are still made of thick-walled mud and thatch, centered around a village well where families gather for news and gossip. The days of "big bitterness," when Qufu's farmers ate millet-and-yam flour gruel (when they could get it, and little else) have ended, and the average income approaches the city average of Y100 per month. But traditional customs continue, and while biking or walking around the villages it is not uncommon to see a red-veiled bride being delivered by sedan chair to her husband's home, a funeral with bright paper houses and furniture to burn with the corpse, or a birth festival, with grandmothers on carts delivering presents and baskets of red-dyed eggs.

The central figure of local cultural history is Confucius, and there's an awareness of his philosophy here unequalled elsewhere in China. Most everyone seems to enjoy quoting snatches from the *Analects* and *Odes*. As tourism plays a larger role in the local economy, and naturally centers on Confucius, the sage's role is likely to grow larger still.

QUFU IN HISTORY

Qufu has history so long it fills the earth, and local farmers find relics in their fields after every hard rain. Legend claims the great Emperor Shaohao ruled here in 6000 BC, parting the mountains to form a rich, black plain. By 2000 BC the Yi people had a kingdom here, making bronze vessels and filling them with wine, and by Confucius's time Qufu's craftspeople made glass decorations, boneware chopsticks, and incense. Confucius (a westernization of Kong Fuzi—"master Kong") was born around 551 BC. At that time Qufu was capital of the State of Lu, and even today much in Qufu is named after Lu. Confucius was made a sage in his lifetime, and worshipped by two years after his death. In 205 BC Confucianism became China's official religion under the Han emperor Wudi, who built a temple to Confucius that was expanded in every dynasty. Meantime, the ever-growing clan of Confucius's descendents came to greater and greater power, becoming by the Yuan Dynasty among the highest advisors of the emperor. The Qufu area, of neither strategic nor mineral importance, was left pretty much to their control, and the emperors gave them "living allowances," while they sacrificed to the imperial health. With the 1911 revolution, imperial gifts ended and rent collection became difficult—especially after the 1919 campaigns against the "Confucian Curiosity Shop." The clan cut the wages of their servants in hard times and hid in the mansion from the warlord battles outside. But with the Japanese invasion, the clan became increasingly involved with national politics, some joining the Nationalists and others the Communist Party. Occupying Japanese generals worshipped Confucius assiduously, but put increasing pressure on his descendents. Most of the clan fled the mansion in 1948, leaving much of what was not destroyed by the warlords to be stripped by the Nationalists on retreat to Taiwan. Since 1949 both the local economy and the historical buildings in Qufu have been steadily renovated, aided by a Confucius Foundation formed in 1961. Even during the Cultural Revolution, the anti-Confucius campaigns were lightly felt here. By 1973, with the Gang of Four still in power, the Confucius Foundation had applied for and received federal funding to repair damage done.

HIGHLIGHTS FOR

TRAVELERS

孔庙

Confucius Temple. Located in the center of town, this tremendous series of interlocking courtyards was begun in the Han Dynasty, burnt down, rebuilt, and has been growing ever since. It's a labyrinth of red walls and gold roofs very much like a miniature Forbidden City. The centerpiece is a tremendous hall, restored with replicas of its original statues, and supported by eight fantastically carved "dragon pillars." Local legend claims that when the Empress Dowager Ci Xi, known for having provincial treasures removed to Beijing, came to visit, Confucian priests had the pillars covered with silk, apologizing for the "ugly pine posts" which were "unworthy" of Ci Xi's view. The Temple is the site, in the mid-seventh month of every lunar year (August–September) of the Confucian Festival, a five-day re-creation of traditional dances and ceremonies that forms the greatest tourist attraction of the year.

孔府

Kong Family Mansion. Begun in 1068, the mansion, set by the temple, is another maze of courtyards and pavilions, storehouses, and rooms, many with original furnishings. At the center are two rooms and an "Apricot Altar," purportedly on the site of Confucius's original school in Qufu. The front courtyard, with its elaborate Records Offices and Archives, is a tribute to the complexity of the seigneurial rule the Kong family maintained for nine centuries from this house.

孔林

Confucius Forest. This peaceful, pine-scented forest set some 6 km. north of the city is the family cemetery for some 78 generations of Confucius's descendents. Paths wind under trees, past graves and sculptures whose styles reflect a thousand years of Chinese art. The earliest graves are for Confucius and his wife, constructed during the Song Dynasty a thousand years after the sage's death. The newest are recent indeed; there are some 100,000 members of the Kong family still in the area, now living in rather ordinary conditions. A number of them are Party members.

周公庙

Temple of the Duke of Zhou. This small temple in the east of the city, reached by picturesque, winding lanes, commemorates Duke Wen of Zhou, the one leader whom Confucius admired as a model of proper rule. Most of the courtyards are empty, but the temple is peaceful, and beyond it are some mouldering stones said to be from the original city wall from when Qufu was the capital of Lu.

颜庙

Yanhui Temple. This temple to Confucius's most famous disciple sits just north of the Confucius Temple, a group of four courtyards shaded by cyprus trees. Most of the original statuary is gone, but there are several fine steles and a well whose water, now black and greasy, was said to once bring immortality. Five of the halls have been converted into display rooms for local archaeological finds. The very earliest relics have been taken to Beijing, but there are some fine Han vases, and a few stone tools from about 6000 BC.

邵号陵

Tomb of Shaohao. Some 5 km. east of Qufu, this tomb to a semilegendary 6th millenia BC ruler is said to have originally been a pyramid equal in beauty, if not in size, with those in Egypt. That pyramid, if there ever was one, disappeared long ago. The current one was built in the 1100s and resurfaced in the 1970s with fresh-cut granite, leaving a structure that looks more like a cyclotron with a temple on top than an ancient tomb. The road out to it, however, is spectacular, winding through fields and small villages of great beauty.

泥山

Ni Mountain. The legendary birthplace of Confucius, Nishan is now home to a lovely, if barren, Yuan Dynasty temple, and a Confucian academy which was emptied in the late Qing and now houses a family and their pigs. Below is an ersatz cave constructed in the 1950s as the "Cave of the Sage," and dotting the hill are several real caves used as homes by peasants in the years of "big bitterness," but whose origins are obscure. Nishan is scheduled for restoration and regular bus service by 1996, but for now a car must be rented, and the key to the temple borrowed from the family with the pigs. The drive out is lovely and the view from Nishan's crown spectacular, but beware: local boys earn money catching scorpions in these hills.

HOTEL

ACCOMMODATIONS

Three hotels in Qufu accept foreigners. By quality and price, high to low, they are:

阙里饭店
Queli Guest House (tel: 411300; telex: 39105 BTHQF CN). Located near both the Confucius Temple and the Kong Family mansion, the Queli is a two-star joint venture built as a traditional Chinese courtyard. Considered the best hotel in Qufu, it has 164 rooms and 380 beds, ranging from Y20 (rarely available) to Y300 a night. All rooms are modern and air-conditioned, and decorated with a Confucian motif. Banquet and conference facilities available.

孔府饭店
Kong Family Hotel (tel: 412374/412686). The Kongfu is the renovated guest quarters of the family mansion itself. Built around 1550, the hotel is a one-story labyrinth of courtyards and bungalows subdivided into several classes of rooms. Prices start at Y40 per night and go up to Y160 for a mammoth room appointed with its original late-Qing furnishings. The hotel has 60 rooms and 145 beds. The restaurant has banquet facilities.

鲁都饭店
Lu Capital Hotel (tel: 411157). Set south of the downtown area, the Ludu is a noisy, utilitarian brick building with hard beds and poor showers in all but the priciest rooms. Charges, ranging Y8–34 a night, are the cheapest in Qufu, but service is poor and foreigners have been charged for beds they didn't ask to have left empty in their rooms. The restaurant is best avoided.

RESTAURANTS AND SHOPPING

The hotel restaurants of the Queli and the Kongfu hotels are among the best in Qufu and, together with the Queli Kongshan (tel: 412794), are the best sources of traditional Confucian feast dishes. The intricate pastries sold at the Kongfu are a special treat. The other area specialty is Hui cooking. While this type of Islamic fare may surprise those familiar with the Middle Eastern variety, its light sauces and many fish dishes make a nice change from standard Han cooking. The best of Qufu's many Hui restaurants is the Qufu Islamic Restaurant (Gulou Rd. East; tel: 411457). If you are puzzled about the menu, the cook, Ma Shangbin, will happily show you the kitchen, and then sit down with tea to talk with you as you eat.

Qufu's best shopping centers on the traditional. Good local buys include stone rubbings from the many steles and carvings around town, cedarwood carvings, and small woven decorations made by local women. There are also several outlets selling the newest and least valuable of the relics the government buys from farmers. Little in those stores would tempt an antique dealer, but there is much that is lovely if bought for its own sake, and not for investment. The best stores are those in the Kong Family Mansions; the Lu Treasure House (corner of Dongmen Dajie and Gulou Road East); the Fanzhen Shutan (kittycorner from the bus station); and the Queli Street Bazaar.

中国国际旅行社
CITS (Luxingshe) Office in Qufu ■ Qufu Luyou Hotel. Tel: 412491.

Shanghai 上海

SHANGHAI, the fifth largest city in the world, is one of China's most cosmopolitan areas — virtually the only one which strikes an immediately familiar chord with most Western visitors. The decaying elegance of once expansive and luxurious town houses, now divided into dozens of cramped apartments, and the broad tree-lined avenues all bring back memories of London or Paris in the 1920s. For 50 years the physical structure of Shanghai stood frozen in time while extraordinary political and social upheavals took place within it.

Beginning in 1986, modern change has come suddenly to Shanghai. Contemporary metal and glass hotels and office towers have sprung up throughout the city, replacing the solid grey granite buildings and transforming the familiar waterfront skyline. Coffee shops and even discotheques have opened where, for a steep admission price, customers can dance to alternating selections of big band music and pop hits from Hong Kong.

Shanghai is changing in other ways too. Still the commercial center of the country, its position as a leader in economic reform is being challenged as neighboring provinces leap ahead in response to the greater economic freedoms available during the past few years. The city is also struggling to find a means to deal with an infrastructure designed for an urban area with one tenth of the present population.

Shanghai has traditionally been the center of China's trade and industry, and is now one of China's 14 open coastal cities and the center of the Shanghai Economic Zone (which also includes regions of Jiangsu, Jiangxi, and Zhejiang provinces). Almost half of the country's internal and external commerce passes through the city, conveyed by ocean vessels, river craft, planes, and trains. Situated on the Huangpu River, the city lies 28 km. (17 mi.) upstream from the Yangtse River. The Yangtse in turn links Shanghai to the Pacific Ocean on the east and to the interior cities of Nanjing, Wuhan, and Chongqing. The city is also linked to the Grand Canal via the east-west Wusong River, more commonly known as Suzhou Creek.

Shanghai has an area of 6,100 sq. km. (2,355 sq. mi.) and a population of over 12 million people, of whom more than half live in the urban core. The city is divided into 14 urban districts and 7 rural districts. Shanghai is one of three cities in the PRC (Beijing and Tianjin are the others) which

Climate

		Jan	Feb	Mar	Apr	May	Jun	Jul	Aug	Sep	Oct	Nov	Dec
Temp.	°C	3.1	4.3	8.4	13.9	19.1	23.0	27.8	28.1	24.1	18.1	12.5	5.9
	°F	37.5	39.7	47.1	57	66.3	73.4	82	82.5	75.3	64.5	54.5	42.6
Precip.	mm.	254	254	330	330	305	356	279	279	305	254	203	178
	in.	10	10	13	13	12	14	11	11	12	10	8	7

The Bund, Shanghai

reports directly to the central government instead of to a provincial administration.

Shanghai is served by four airports, two of which are civil. Hongqiao Airport is the principal link for international and domestic travel. Recently rebuilt, the terminal is the most modern and efficient in China. The main railway station, with its huge freight yards, is in the north-central section of the city. Shanghai is about two hours by air from both Beijing and Guangzhou and has excellent links to many other Chinese cities and international destinations.

Geography. The city is divided physically and in atmosphere by the Wusong River. The area to the north still bears evidence of the former Japanese concession, while the section just south of the Wusong is the site of the former international concessions and Shanghai's famous Bund — a wide boulevard of 1930s-era high-rise buildings along the Huangpu River. Formerly hotels, clubs, banks, and offices for foreigners, they now house municipal offices, branches of PRC Foreign Trade Corporations, a customs house, and banks owned by the state. Just south of the French Concession is the Old Town — the formerly notorious "Chinese Quarter" — now demarcated by Renmin Road and Zhonghua Road. Its architecture is typically Chinese, with low, closely packed buildings, small shops, busy markets, and narrow winding alleyways. The Old Town offers sharp contrast to China's new trends in construction as evidenced by the new high-rise apartment blocks and modern structures such as the Shanghai Indoor Stadium in the southwest sector of the city. In the outlying areas and along much of the waterfront are vast industrial districts, looking dreary but functional.

PASSENGER SHIP SERVICES FROM SHANGHAI

For visitors who would welcome the addition of a ship voyage to their China itinerary, Shanghai is an ideal point of departure. Advance tickets for most sailings may be purchased at the General Navigation Passenger Ticket Office, at 222 Renmin Rd. (tel: 261261); same-day bookings are sold at the Shiliu Pu Station (tel: 282070); tickets for Wenzhou, Qingdao, and Dalian are also available at the Gongping Lu Station. Yangtse River sailings are handled at 6 Huangli Rd. Primary services include the following (note—fares quoted are subject to increase and do not include meals):

HONG KONG ▣ (56 hours; 850 miles). Weekly sailings on the M. V. *Shanghai* or M. V. *Haixing*. Board at the Waihong International Station Dock; tickets at 255 Jiangxi Zhong Rd.; (tel: 216327). Fares: Special Class—"A": Y234 (lower bunks), "B": Y216; First—"A" (single room): Y198, "B" (2 or 3 people): Y180; Second—"A": (2 or 3 people): Y170, "B" (2 or 4): Y156. All of the above accommodations have private bathrooms. Third class (public bathroom, 4 or more to a room)—"A": Y143, "B": Y130. Common (80 people)—Y111. Groups of 16 or more can apply for a 10% discount; 25 or more receive a 20% discount.

YANGTSE RIVER SERVICES. ▣ Board at Shiliu Pu Dock. Two daily sailings to Wuhan. The slow boat takes 66½ hours (1,125 km.), making 12 stops on the way. The express sailing takes 51½ hours, making 6 stops. At Wuhan, passengers can change for a slow daily boat to Chongqing (100 hours, 1,370 km.) or take a direct boat that departs once a week. Express fares to Wuhan: second class, Y44.00; third class, Y19.20. Slow boat: Y41.40, Y16.60. Direct to Chongqing: Y142.10, Y60.50.

NINGBO ▣ (12 hours; 140 miles). Daily on *Gongnanbing* vessels #18 and 19. Fares: Y60 (Special) to Y5.70 (Third).

WENZHOU ▣ (21 hours; 300 miles). Daily on *Fanxin*, *Rongxin*, and *Changxin* vessels. Fares: Y91.20–8.70 (four classes).

QINGDAO ▣ (26 hours; 404 miles). Daily on *Changshen*, *Changzi*, and *Changgeng* vessels. Fares: Y103.20–9.80 (four classes).

FUZHOU ▣ Weekly sailings. Fares: Y54.70 (2 to a cabin) to Y27 (10 to a cabin).

DALIAN ▣ (36 hours; 563 miles). Daily on *Changhe*, *Changshan*, and *Changzheng* vessels. Fares: Y152.80–14.60 (four classes).

ON YOUR OWN IN SHANGHAI

Shanghai

Arrival. Upon disembarking from the train, follow the crowd to the end of the main platform. From there, bear right, until you see a sign (on the left) for the foreigners' exit. There are usually taxis outside. If you need to check with CITS about a hotel or other travel arrangements, the office is to the left of the exit just before the souvenir counter. Hotel space in Shanghai is in short supply (Shanghai may be the most overbooked city in China) and it is best to try to make arrangements for a place to stay before arrival, particularly during the spring and fall when the city is most crowded.

If you arrive by plane, directions are clearly marked in the airport, which was completely renovated in 1986. It can be a very long walk from the disembarkation gate to the exit, and it is wise to keep this in mind when packing carry-on bags. Luggage carts are available for international arrivals, but not in the domestic section. Taxi cabs are located outside the exits; drivers solicit business in a variety of vehicles. Major hotels run shuttle vans or will pick you up if you have made prior arrangements.

Getting Around. If you are staying at one of the downtown hotels, you can do much of your sightseeing on foot. Central Shanghai is surprisingly compact. Places within walking distance include Nanjing Road, the Bund, Old Town, the Friendship Store, and some of Shanghai's most interesting back-street neighborhoods and markets. For other sites, you can go by bus or taxi. Many hotels now offer full and half-day tours of the city and surrounding area. These can be booked the day before by the concierge or at most hotel reception desks. Visitors with only a few days in Shanghai will miss very little by focusing on the downtown area.

If you are not staying near the Bund, it is relatively easy (with the help of the hotel staff) to find a bus route that goes through the downtown area. Except at lunch time, taxis are almost always available at the Peace or Park hotels and at most of the new international hotels. It is also possible to hire taxis for a half or full day at reasonable rates.

CLIMATE

Shanghai's climate is temperate in spring and autumn — the best seasons for a visit. The winters are chilly and gray — much like London's — while summers are stifling and rainy. If you are in the city in October, your visit may coincide with the Mid-Autumn Festival (moon cakes are the traditional fare at this time). The annual Shanghai Music Festival takes place every spring and thousands of amateur and professional musicians, singers, and dancers perform throughout the city. The Shanghai Marathon Cup, China's premier running race and the occasion for city-wide festivities, resumed in 1980 and is held each March.

SHANGHAI IN HISTORY

Compared to most other major cities of China, Shanghai has a brief history. Under the Tang and Song, it was in undistinguished port and fishing village built atop mud flats. Japanese envoys landed here en route to the Tang court at Xi'an. Under the Yuan (1260–1378), it became a minor center for cotton spinning and weaving, partly as a result of innovative techniques introduced by a woman named Wang Daopo. To defend against Japanese pirates, the Ming fortified the ramparts around the Old Town.

During the 17th and 18th centuries, with the development of silk production in the surrounding areas, Shanghai became more of a trading center. By the early 1800s, it was a flourishing domestic port of some 50,000 people.

Significant growth did not occur until the arrival of Europeans in the mid-19th century. In 1842, near the end of the Opium War, Shanghai's garrison surrendered to the British fleet. From that point until 1949 the city developed largely as an enclave for Western commercial interests in China. Lying off the sea and just upstream from the Yangtse — a river that could be navigated several hundred miles into the interior on oceangoing vessels — Shanghai provided a gateway to a vast internal market. Each of the major foreign powers claimed a section of the city. Residents of these infamous "international concessions" were exempt from the laws of China, and Chinese were subjected to the added humiliation of being barred from free access to large portions of their own territory. Shanghai soon surpassed Guangzhou as China's most important foreign trade center. Numerous

Shanghai Mansions Hotel

traders and speculators—French, US, and Japanese—soon joined the British. By 1936, the Western population of Shanghai numbered 60,000.

Shanghai in the Revolution. While Western merchants prospered and Shanghai's export-oriented industry and commerce flourished, the city spawned vast urban slums. Gradually, these conditions prompted growing discontent, strikes, and revolts against foreign rule and influence. On July 1, 1921, the Chinese Communist Party held its first National Congress in Shanghai. In 1925, the Party helped carry out the demonstrations and strikes known as the May 30th Movement. Between October 1926 and March 1927, workers organized armed uprisings, but they were bloodily suppressed by Chiang Kaishek's Nationalist troops in 1927.

During the 1930s, Shanghai was relatively quiet politically as the revolutionary movement shifted its focus to the countryside. Entering the 1940s, the city had earned a reputation as an "adventurer's paradise." Under its glittering surface festered opium dens, brothels, crime syndicates, and rampant corruption. Day-to-day scenes in Shanghai's streets vividly and cruelly exhibited the extreme limits of the human condition—during winter, Shanghai's gutters were littered with the corpses of the poor who had died the previous night from exposure and starvation; nearby, the wealthy could be seen using sable rugs to cover the motors of their parked limousines.

During 1937–45, Shanghai was occupied by the Japanese. The city's International Settlement functioned intact, however, until the declaration of war by the Western powers in 1941, whereupon most members of Shanghai's foreign community were interned by the Japanese. With the defeat of Japan in 1945, the Allies agreed to relinquish their territorial claims in the city and all of Shanghai reverted to the rule of the Guomindang. During the ensuing period, the dire struggle for survival of Shanghai's millions was, if anything, exacerbated. For example, inflation rates reached tragic dimensions—to the extent that a lifetime's savings might not suffice to purchase a single kilo of rice. In April 1949, one US dollar could be exchanged for 3.75 million Chinese yuan; Chinese money was worth less than the cost of printing it. Financial chaos worked merely to fuel the corruption and greed of the politicians and entrepreneurs. When the first columns of the People's Liberation Army entered the city during May 26–28, 1949, the prevailing attitude of most of the population was said to be that of overwhelming relief.

Shanghai Post—1949. Perhaps no other city in the world changed so quickly and profoundly as did Shanghai in the years following 1949. It had been the "Paris of the East," notorious throughout the world for its *laissez-faire* vitality and vice. Within a few months of the Communist victory, the new government began nationalizing major businesses and redistributing housing, meanwhile undertaking extensive social reforms. Tens of thousands of prostitutes and drug addicts were rehabilitated and given new employment; drug dealers who did not cooperate were summarily shot. Gambling was outlawed. The race track and amusement halls were converted into centers for sports and other sanctioned activities.

Overall, the 1950s were a period of relative prosperity and stability in Shanghai, when considerable progress was made in eliminating the excesses of the past while maintaining the city's vigor. Development slowed throughout China in 1959 when the government began the ill-fated Great Leap Forward, a national movement which emphasized heavy industry at the expanse of agriculture. Although Shanghai suffered less than many other areas of the PRC, there were still serious food shortages in the city in 1959 and 1960.

The Cultural Revolution, which caused havoc in China for more than a decade, received major impetus from Shanghai in 1965. Jiang Qing, the wife of Mao Zedong, and her chief supporters (the "Gang of Four"—all of whom are currently imprisoned), were at that time major political figures in Shanghai. Shanghai was a bastion of extreme leftism, and this legacy continued to exert an influence on the city well into the 1980s.

The Cultural Revolution has affected Shanghai in other ways as well. Intellectuals and students from the city were among those sent to the farms earliest and for the longest periods of time, and many were never permitted to return. It is estimated that over half a million young people were sent out of Shanghai at that time. Over 100,000 students were sent to the remote western province of Xinjiang, and over half have had to remain there to the present day.

A Chinese freighter takes on grain at new dock facility, Shanghai

ECONOMY AND CULTURE

When the government of the PRC began to take a more pragmatic approach to industry and agriculture in 1979, Shanghai immediately began to demonstrate the traditional initiative and business acumen for which it had been know. The city's rich suburban farmland and the proximity of a major metropolitan market made it possible for peasants to sell their surplus crops at a profit and to diversify into light industry. Hundreds of new two-story white stucco houses on the edges of Shanghai attest to this new prosperity. In the city itself, millions of willing consumers provided opportunities for private entrepreneurs to venture into occupations such as tailoring, haircutting, and bicycle repairs, as well as providing other services that were either unavailable or of poor quality in state-run enterprises. Bonuses increased greatly for salaried workers in the early 1980s. At the same time, inflation hit Shanghai sharply, as it did other cities, for the first time in 30 years. Many workers, particularly young couples who were paying for child care and contributing to the support of other relatives, felt squeezed. They frequently expressed envy at the flexibility and economic opportunities were open to peasants and private entrepreneurs but closed to state employees.

In the mid-1980s Shanghai provided one-sixth of China's total exports, one-sixth of the total revenues, and one-eighth of the GNP. However, until 1984, Shanghai was required to remit 90% of all of the municipality's revenue to the central government in Beijing; it was permitted to keep only 10%, an amount insufficient to meet the city's needs. In 1984, Shanghai's proportion was increased to 25%.

Although Shanghai in many ways continues to be the driving force in China's economy, its growth has not continued at the same rate as neighboring areas. Until recently, foreign investment in Shanghai has been limited compared to Beijing or Guangzhou, a factor detrimental to the city's development. Foreign businesspeople cite residual leftism and unusually uncooperative attitudes on the part of local officials as some of the problems which confront them regularly. Still, many companies have begun to invest in Shanghai. McDonnell Douglas, Volkswagen, and Foxboro are among those which have been there longest and are doing well.

A self-evident problem is that Shanghai has outgrown its infrastructure. Water mains, sewage disposal, roads, and virtually all other municipal service systems were built in the 1920s and 1930s by the British and French, and nothing has been significantly expanded or updated since then. Housing is overcrowded — 20 million sq. ft. of new housing has been built, but newly married couples may still have to wait as long as seven years for a two-room flat.

Shanghai began to exert its financial importance again in 1986 with the re-opening of a stock exchange, which had flourished in the city from 1919 to 1949, together with the establishment of a bond market. The Bank of Communications opened in Shanghai at the end of 1986. This is the first post-revolutionary competition in China's state-run banking system.

In August 1986, the city issued 16 regulations on foreign trade. This marked the first attempt to direct foreign investment projects towards Shanghai's development needs and to assure potential investors that contracts would be honored. The current policy is to encourage foreign investment in industry rather than in the tourism sector (hotels and restaurants have attracted the most investment so far) and to develop tourism domestically.

Shanghai's products include heavy machinery, chemicals, electrical equipment, motor vehicles, ships, tires, paper, glassware, tires, and toys. With the possible exception of Guangzhou (and there are many who would disagree with that), Shanghai is the best source of consumer goods in China.

The surrounding countryside makes Shanghai self-sufficient in total food needs and provides one of the best fresh vegetable sources in China. Over 360,000 hectares (889,560 acres) are cultivated; local farms yield four times the annual output of the early 1950s. Shanghai's rural suburban districts are divided into over 200 towns. Formerly communes, they are now officially designated as townships and villages, although they are still generally referred to as communes by most people. Local crops include rice, wheat, barley, cotton, and all sorts of produce. The region now supports three grain crops each year, and is almost totally irrigated by electric pumps.

Shanghai also considers itself, with some justice, as the leading cultural and educational center of China. The city has six professional performing arts troupes, including several outstanding ballet and opera companies, symphonies, puppet troupes, acrobats, and a circus. Its reputation as a literary center has been enhanced by famous writers such as Lu Xun, whose powerful accounts of misery and corruption in Shanghai during the 1930s are now regarded as classics of modern Chinese fiction. In the 1980s, Shanghai has been at the forefront of China's cultural development, with considerable experimentation and innovation in music, theatre, and the plastic arts.

There are a total of 190 research institutes, colleges, and universities in Shanghai, employing nearly 30,000 people. Major scientific achievements have been made here in the fields of electronics, laser technology, infrared rays, vacuums, and atomic energy.

Fudan and Jiaotong universities are among Shanghai's leading educational institutions. The city has pioneered in the creation of part-time schools where workers are trained in technical skills. At the Shanghai Science and Technical Exchange, industrial workers from different sectors meet to exchange scientific and technical information.

Shanghai is also important in medical training and cancer research. The city now has 380 hospitals staffed by some 80,000 medical personnel.

HIGHLIGHTS
FOR TRAVELERS

Although Shanghai is not known for its scenic beauty, many Western tourists list Shanghai as their favorite Chinese city. Unlike Beijing, which emanates majesty and reserve, Shanghai has an air of intense vitality and sophistication. Today Shanghai offers visitors an opportunity to see how a rapidly modernizing Chinese city works. A number of excursions are possible—boat cruises through the harbor; visits to new residential areas, villages, and factories. There are also many other attractions, reflecting China's recent revolutionary history but many dating back to earlier times. A good place to begin is the heart of Shanghai—the Bund.

江边（外滩）

The Bund. Zhongshan Road is a wide, tree-lined avenue along the Huangpu River. The parklike promenade between the Wusong River and the Old Town is known as The Bund, the former "Wall Street" of the foreign powers. The name itself reflects those colonial days—"bund" is an Anglo-Indian word meaning embarkment or quay.

The tall buildings that line the west side of the Bund were once the exclusive domain of Western powers. Their exteriors have remained unchanged but they have been turned to new purposes. The green-towered Cathay Hotel has been renamed the Peace Hotel and now accommodates thousands of tourists each year. The four smaller buildings adjacent to the Bank of China once housed US and Japanese banks and now serve as branch offices for China's Foreign Trade Corporations. The former American Club is now a police station, and the Clock Tower atop the Customs house until recently chimed out the melody of "The East is Red," the anthem of the Cultural Revolution.

On the west side of the Bund, people hurry along, darting in and out of office buildings, while the side that fronts on the river is used for strolling and recreation. In the evening, the narrow park that traces the water line is dotted with young couples walking hand in hand and whispering quietly to each other. In the morning, young and old alike turn out *en masse* to perform *Tai Ji Quan* and other morning exercises (huge sessions take place in Huangpu Park, just opposite the Friendship Store). Westerners are welcome to join in. The park (formerly barred to Chinese) has lovely rock gardens, flower beds, and shade trees—perfect for relaxing and taking in the changing river scene.

人民公园

People's Park and People's Square. West of Xizang Road, between Nanjing and Yan'an roads, are People's Park and People's Square, covering a full square mile in the heart of the city. The area was originally laid out in 1861 by a foreigner who traced a large oval on horseback with a sword and then bought up everything within it (including farmland and buildings) to build a park and a race course. The racetrack has now been replaced by a pleasant park with lawns, ponds, and tree-shaded walkways. The large, 35-hectare (86-acre) square to the south is used for celebrations, processions, and political rallies. An interesting historical museum is located within the park grounds. It houses ceramic figures, bronzes, jade objects, and some tortoise plastrons (in ancient times, heat was applied to the shells, producing cracks that were used to divine the future). The Shanghai Municipal Library is adjacent to the park.

Also of interest is the area just west of the park, off Fuzhou Road. This was the heart of Shanghai's "red-light" district, the famous Blood Alley. In 1949, there were an estimated 1.2 million opium addicts in Shanghai (20% of the population), as well as thousands of prostitutes. In "Meet-With-Happiness" Lane alone, there were 34 "high-class" brothels and over 1,000 prostitutes. During 1949–50, the brothels and opium dens were closed and the prostitutes given new work (and, if they chose, new identities). By 1954, all addicts had been detoxified and rehabilitated. Local guides state that some 24 former prostitutes still live in this street, now known as Liberation Lane.

上海美术展览馆

Shanghai Museum of Art and History. Located on Henan Road, this recently renovated, three-story museum houses one of the finest art collections in China. The first floor is devoted to bronzes, mainly from the Shang (c. 1523–1027 BC) and Western Zhou (c. 1066–771 BC) dynasties. Objects on display include tools, weapons, instruments of torture, food and wine vessels, some magnificent cauldrons (*ding*), mirrors, and bronzes of the minority nationalities. The second floor focuses on ceramics from the Neolithic era to the present. It includes examples of "black pottery," and life-size terra cotta statues of a horse and two warriors—the first of an estimated 10,000 such figures excavated in 1974 near the Emperor Qin Shi Huangdi's (c. 221–206 BC) gigantic tomb in Xi'an. (This find indicated the end of the practice of burying slaves with their master, and the substitution of funerary objects—statues of warriors, servants, and officials). A variety of similar objects from the Han, Sui, and Tang dynasties is on display at the museum, together with oil lamps, intricate head rests, and vases. There are some excellent examples of "crackle glaze" ceramics, multicolored Tang pottery, and blue-and-white Ming vases, as well as contemporary ceramics. The third floor has a collection of tools used in the arts of painting and calligraphy, as well as some magnificent scrolls from the Tang, Song, Yuan, Ming, and Qing dynasties. The third floor also houses an excellent collection of Buddhist stone sculptures. Hours are 9:30–11:30 AM and 1:30–5 PM. There is a shop selling reproductions and cards on the third floor. Entrance fee is Y1.

上海旧市
The Old Town. The area south of Jinling Road, demarcated by the circular Renmin Road and Zhonghua Road, is Shanghai's former "Chinese city." Once a rabbit-warren of festering slums where few Westerners dared set foot, it is now one of the few remaining places in Shanghai where visitors can view traditional architecture and observe a disappearing style of Chinese urban life. The streets here are very narrow and circuitous and it is very easy to get lost. A good precaution is to bring a note with your next destination written in Chinese so that people can point you in the right direction.

You should plan to visit the Old Town at the same time as the Yu Garden (see below), which borders it. Near the garden's gate are Shanghai's most famous dumpling shops. You can either push your way through the crowds and sit within the restaurants or order your dumplings through a window and eat them in a calmer environment. The Wuxing Ting Teahouse, in the middle of an ornamental pond, is also well worth a stop. This is reached by crossing a zig-zagging bridge, built in this way because of the belief devils can only cross water in a straight line.

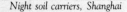

Night soil carriers, Shanghai

In the northeast part of the Old Town is a bazaar that sells traditional handicrafts such as Chinese lanterns and exquisitely carved walking stickes. A modern scissors store selling all conceivable varieties is also located here. A little further north is the Temple of the Town Gods and, behind it, the Garden of the Purple Clouds of Autumn.

豫园
Yu Garden (Yu Yuan). Near the Wuxing Ting Teahouse is a marvelous garden built is 1577 by a city official named Pan Yunduan who sought to create an idyllic spot for his father's old age. Hidden behind high, carved brick walls decorated with huge stone dragons is a small lake spanned by a magnificent zigzag bridge and surrounded by teahouses, pavilions, rockeries, goldfish ponds, and knolls. The garden may seem somewhat familiar — it served as the basis for the famous "willow pattern" chinaware. The Pavilion of Spring was headquarters in the 19th century for the Small Sword Society, which led a major uprising in 1853 against both the Qing Dynasty and the colonial powers. During festivals, the trees and pavilions are strung with lanterns and the gardens are filled with a sea of people.

Entrance hours are from 8 AM to 10:30 AM and from 2 to 5 PM. Visitors may stay on through lunch. There is an entrance fee of Y1 for foreigners.

玉佛寺
Jade Buddha Temple. This temple is located in the northwest part of the city and is famous for two rare statues of Buddha, each carved out of a single piece of white Burmese jade. One depicts Buddha at the moment of his enlightenment, and the other as he is passing into Nirvana. The two statues were brought from Burma by a Chinese monk in 1890, eight years after the temple's construction. There are a number of other statues of Buddha, his disciples, and other celestial beings to be seen in the other halls. Twenty-four monks live in the temple, and are supported by donations and a stipend from the state. The monks also run a gift shop and vegetarian restaurant. Services are held at dawn and around 4 PM.

上海工业展览会
Shanghai Exhibition Center. This large exhibition hall is almost always included on the visitor's itinerary and is well worth a stop for the serious shopper. Built by the Soviets in the early 1950s, it was formerly called the Palace of Sino-Soviet Friendship. It now sells thousands of high-quality export items ranging from silk blouses and jewelry to mahogany furniture and antique vases. An excellent Cantonese restaurant is located on the top floor of the center building.

复兴公园
Fuxing Park. This 9-hectare (22-acre) park, located in the south-central section of the city, was built in 1909. It is notable for its massive trees with foliage so dense that the hot summer sun hardly penetrates, and for a small zoo (Shanghai's main zoo is in Xijiao Park). The park offers a convenient airing for residents of the nearby Jinjiang Hotel. It is often filled with older people playing Chinese chess and minding the grandchildren. Nearby

1. Longhua Temple
2. Shanghai Municipal Children's Palace
3. Shanghai Industrial Exhibition
4. Jade Buddha Temple
5. Site of Founding of the Chinese Communist Party
6. People's Square
7. Workers' Cultural Palace
8. No.1 Department Store
9. Shanghai Museum of Art and History
10. Garden of the Mandarin Yu
11. Friendship Store
12. Shanghai No. 1 Hospital
13. Shenjiang Hotel
14. Chengqiao Guest House

Restaurants
Hotels
Consulates

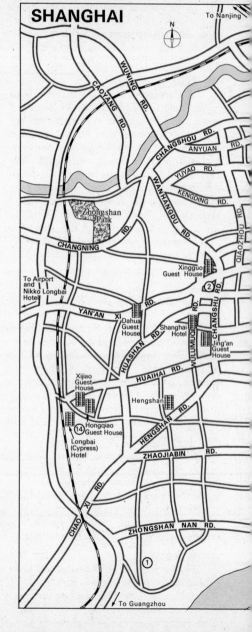

SHANGHAI

To Nanjing

N

Zhongshan Park

WUNING RD.

CAOYANG RD.

CHANGSHOU RD.

ANYUAN RD.

YUYAO RD.

KENGDING RD.

WANHANGDU RD.

QIAOZHOU RD.

CHANGNING

To Airport and Nikko Longbai Hotel

Xingguo Guest House

YAN'AN XI RD.

Dahua Guest House

Shanghai Hotel

Jing'an Guest House

CHANGSHU RD.

WULUMUQI RD.

HUASHAN RD.

HUAIHAI RD.

Xijiao Guest House

Hengshan

HENGSHAN RD.

Hongqiao Guest House

Longbai (Cypress) Hotel

ZHAOJIABIN RD.

CHAO XI RD.

ZHONGSHAN NAN RD.

To Guangzhou

ZHONGSHAN BEI RD.

Lu Xun Memorial Park

GONGHEXIN RD.

TIANMU RD.

Shanghai Railroad Station

HAINING RD.

Wusong River

(Suzhou Creek)

JIANGNING RD.

④

XINZHA RD.

ZHEJIANG RD.

SICHUAN RD.

Shanghai Daxia

CHANGZHI RD.

DAMING RD.

Shanghai Harbor

BEIJING RD.

Guoji Huaqiao

SHIMEN RD.

CHENGDU RD.

NANJING RD.

HENAN RD.

⑫ ⑪

③

WEIHAI

MAOMING RD.

People's Park

⑧

⑬

CITS

Peace

THE BUND

⑥

⑦

FUZHOU RD.

⑨

CHANGLE RD.

YAN'AN RD.

FUJIAN RD.

CAAC

Japan US

Jinjiang

⑤

HUAIHAI RD.

XIZANG RD.

RENMIN RD.

ZHONGSHAN RD.

RUIJIN RD.

Fuxing Park

CHONGQING RD. S.

FUXING RD.

HENAN RD.

FUYU RD.

⑩

FUMAN RD.

Ruijin Guest House

XUJIAHUI RD.

LUJIABIN RD.

ZHONGHUA

LUBAN RD.

Huangpu River

Map ©1986, Eurasia Press

is the former residence of Sun Yatsen. It is maintained as a small museum.

Further north, off Huaihai Road at 76 Xingye Road (formerly 106 Wangzhi Road), is an unprepossessing two-story house where the founding congress of the Chinese Communist Party was held on July 1, 1929. It is now maintained as a museum.

西郊公园
Xijiao (Western Suburbs) Park. Although it is rarely part of the tourist's itinerary, this park is delightful to explore on one's own (if there is a half-day's free time). As its name implies, it is located on the western edge of the city and is near Hongqiao Airport. The park contains a number of small lakes (e.g., Swan Lake), small pavilions, a children's playground, an open-air theater, and a skating rink. The Shanghai Zoo is also located here, boasting 400 species of animals kept in as natural an environment as possible.

鲁迅纪念公园
Lu Xun Memorial Park. Lu Xun (1881–1936), one of China's most famous modern writers, used to walk through this park, located in the northeastern section of the city. His grave is in the park, marked by a steel statue erected in 1961. In the garden surrounding the grave are two trees: one planted by Madame Lu, the other by Zhou Enlai. The calligraphy at the site is by Mao Zedong. A Lu Xun Museum contains photographs, letters, manuscripts, furniture, and other memorabilia.

宋庆龄墓
Tomb of Song Qingling. The widow of Dr. Sun Yatsen was highly revered in China during her later years for her international friendship activities. Prior to her death in 1981 she was proclaimed Honorary Chairman of the People's Republic of China. She is buried at the Wang Guo International Cemetery on Hongqiao Road.

上海自然博物馆
Museum of Natural History. Situated at the juncture of Yan'an Dong and Henan roads, the museum opened in 1963. Permanent exhibits focus mainly on local animals and birds, with rotating short-term exhibits. An exhibit of preserved ancient corpses from as early as 3,200 years ago occupies the ground floor. Hours are 8:30–10:30 AM and 1–3:30 PM (closed Tuesdays and Saturday mornings). There are film showings daily at 10 AM.

孙中山故居
Sun Yatsen's Former Residence (7 Xiangshan Road). Dr. Sun lived here from 1920 until 1924. Most objects are original and are arranged as they were actually used by China's first president.

天主堂
Xujiahui Catholic Church (Caoxi Bei Road). Shanghai's largest cathedral was built in 1906 in Romanesque style. Its two bell towers are 50 m. (164 ft.) high. The church has 19 altars and can hold 2,500 people — which it often does these days during Christian holidays and at Sunday mass.

上海杂技团

Shanghai Acrobatic Theater (400 Nanjing Xi Lu; tel: 564051 or 564704). China's first circular amphitheater built expressly for acrobatic performances opened in 1981. Although obviously tilted toward the foreign tourist trade, performances are consistently delightful—original, high-spirited, skillful, and unexpectedly beautiful to watch. Shows every day but Tuesday, 80 *fen* per ticket.

龙华塔和寺

Longhua Temple and Pagoda. In the southern suburbs, Longhua is the oldest and largest temple in Shanghai, possibly originating as early as the Three Kingdoms Period but no later than the Tang Dynasty (687). The seven-story pagoda was built in the Northern Song (977) of wood and stone, with the present base surviving from that time. The temple was last rebuilt at end of the Qing dynasty. It has four main halls plus drum and bell towers and an assortment of side buildings. The site served as headquarters for Shanghai's Guomindang garrison before World War II and many Communist martyrs were executed here. Longhua is also famous for its early spring peach blossoms (confined in an area now sectioned off as Longhua Park). There are several other parks and an aboretum nearby. An immense free market now operates just outside the temple grounds.

Bus routes to Longhua from the city include #41, 44, and 87, all of which terminate at the temple.

嘉定孔庙

Jiading Confucian Temple. Northwest of the city, Jiading was built in the Song Dynasty (1219). Now only two-thirds of its original size, its proportions are still immense.

松江兴圣教寺塔 (方塔) 松江明刻照壁

Songjiang Country Square Pagoda and Dragon Wall. Remarkably, most of the original wooden pagoda built here in the Song Dynasty (11th century) still stands. The structure is interesting for its square shape and for the Buddhist paintings on the third level. It is possible to climb to the top, although spaces become very narrow at the upper levels. The glazed tile wall in front dates from the Ming Dynasty. It depicts a greedy monster who tried to devour the sun. Beautifully crafted, the monster has treasures arrayed around his feet. The site is located in the southwest suburbs.

EXCURSIONS

The Harbor. Tourists may take an excursion on the *Pujiang*, a triple-deck tourist ship that makes daily trips down the Huangpu River to the mouth of the Yangtse. Where hundreds of coolies once sweltered, huge gantry cranes now load and unload containers. Oceangoing freighters and passenger ships from all over the world move slowly along the river, while junks and sampans in full sail dart among them. Tickets, costing Y10 and

Y15, are available at the ferry pier near the entrance to Huangpu Park, diagonally across from the Peace Hotel. There are morning and afternoon departures, both of which feature on-board magic shows and band performances.

工人新村

Workers' Residential Areas. Visitors are often taken to one of the new housing districts on the outskirts of Shanghai. Such visits seek to provide insights into the political, social, and economic changes that have taken place in the lives of ordinary people. These self-contained units are often built around large factory sites and operate at the neighborhood level of administration. A local committee exercises authority over the building of schools, shops, nurseries, recreational facilities, and medical services.

In 1986, a typical working couple employed by a state enterprise earned about Y300 per month. They had one child and probably also contributed to the support of their parents, who might share the same apartment. The couple paid out roughly 4% of their income for rent and electricity, but upwards of half of their income went towards food and clothing. Health care is provided at a nominal fee. If they live in a building constructed in the 1950s or 1960s, they would usually share a kitchen and toilet, and use public baths for washing. Some apartment houses built in the 1980s have private facilities.

少年官

Children's Palaces. Children between the ages of 7 and 17 who show particular skills in subjects such as dance, music, mechanics, and mathematics have an opportunity to receive part-time specialized training at "children's palaces." These schools have excellent facilities, with instruction often provided by leading professional artists. There are 11 such palaces in Shanghai. The largest, called the Shanghai Municipal Children's Palace, is on Yan'an Road near the Industrial Exhibition. It is also the city's first such institution, converted in 1949 from a mansion that belonged to the Sassoon family (since relocated in Hong Kong). The concept (with roots in the Soviet Union) was promoted in China by Song Qingling, Sun Yatsen's widow, who held high positions in the government until her death in 1981. Each visitor is assigned a star pupil and will be led by the hand to view an array of impressive skills mastered by the children. Although the friendliness borders on the saccharine, the energy, skill, and fierce dedication of the student body are awesome to behold.

CLUBS

国际俱乐部

International Club. Although the club's facilities include a small restaurant and banquet service, its primary assets are its swimming pool, two tennis courts, and playing areas for basketball and badminton. Tennis courts may be booked by the hour; a theater and auditorium are also available for hire. The club is located at 63 Yan'an Xi Road (tel: 538455). The complex is slated to be torn down and replaced by a Canadian hotel. The exact date has not yet been set.

锦江俱乐部

Jinjiang Club. The Jinjiang Club, one of Shanghai's most famous sites, no longer exists as a club. Formerly the French Colonial Club, located directly across the street from the main entrance of the Jinjiang Hotel, it had perhaps the most splendid Art Deco interior anywhere in Asia. The rear wing of the building, which contained an extraordinary, nearly Olympic-size swimming pool, was torn down in 1985. A Japanese hotel is being built on the site. The main part of the club, which includes the ballroom, billiard rooms, and restaurant, will be renovated and incorporated into the new hotel.

外商服务中心

Service Center for Overseas Traders. Opened in 1983, "SCOT" is the first facility of its kind in China—a comprehensive center for business travelers. A joint venture of the Jinjiang Club (to which it was attached), the Shanghai Import and Export Trade Corporation, and the Shanghai Investment and Trust Company, SCOT offers trade consultancy services; business introductions; and translation, secretarial and guide services. Telex, photocopying, and even desk space are available. Daily financial reports and newspapers are supplied direct to SCOT, which is open daily (except Sundays) from 8:30 AM to 6 PM. Office space for foreign firms will be available in the adjacent Foreign Trade Building, now under construction.

HOTEL
ACCOMMODATIONS

A new era began for visitors to Shanghai in September 1986 with the opening of the Hua Ting Sheraton Hotel, the first five-star hotel to open in the city. Other equally luxurious hotels, among them the Shanghai Hilton International and the Garden Hotel, are due to open by early 1988. Many others are scheduled to follow in late 1988 and 1989 including the Shanghai International Airport Hotel, Shanghai Asia Hotel, Meridien Hotel and Exhibition Center, Portman Hotel, and the Hyland Hotel. Although Shanghai still suffers from the most critical shortage of hotel rooms in China, plans are underway for the construction of over two dozen hotels in various categories by 1991.

With the exception of the new international hotels and a few recent Chinese projects such as the Shanghai Hotel, the majority of Shanghai's hotels were built in the 1920s and 1930s by the British and French. Although lacking in modern amenities, they are among the most well constructed and comfortable places to stay in China, and recall the elegance of that era with their parquet floors, hand-operated elevators, overstuffed couches, and velvet curtains.

Since Shanghai is the terminus for trans-Pacific telephone lines, international communication links are excellent. Unfortunately, the same cannot be said for telephone service within the city; it can often take hours to get a proper connection. All hotels have telephone, cable, and postal facilities on the premises. The Shanghai Municipality Hotels Services Center is located at 37 Tianmu East Road (tel: 242571).

DELUXE HOTELS

上海日航龙柏饭店

Hotel Nikko Longbai Shanghai (2451 Hongqiao Road; tel: 328888/ 328990). Opened in late 1987, the Hotel Nikko Longbai is set amidst lush cypress gardens and managed by Nikko Hotels International. It is five minutes from the airport by taxi and 25 minutes from the center of Shanghai. The hotel has 419 rooms (90 singles, 265 twins, 32 doubles, 32 suites). Features include banquet facilities, outdoor swimming pool, tennis courts, health center, business facilities, shopping arcade, beauty parlor, barbershop, and sauna. For dining and entertainment there are Continental and Japanese restaurants, a nightclub, a disco, and a cocktail lounge. Two small function rooms and ballroom/banquet facilities to 300 are also available. *Rates:* Single: US$95; twin: US$105. For reservations, call 1-800-NIKKO-US.

上海凯悦饭店

Hyatt Shanghai (Handan Road). Due to open in early 1989, the newest Hyatt is located near Peace Park and the tomb of the writer Lu Xun, four kilometers from the railroad station. A 40-minute drive from Hongqiao Airport, its 420 rooms, including 34 Junior Suites, two Executive Suites, and a Presidential Suite, will offer color TV, minibar, refrigerator, and individually-controlled air-conditioning. The Regency Club, which takes up two floors of the hotel, will offer deluxe accommodations. Among the several restaurants will be the Shanghai specialty restaurant, with eight private dining rooms. After dinner, guests can relax at the lounge or bar, which features live entertainment. Recreational facilities include a Health Spa, shopping arcade, rooftop swimming pool, sauna, whirlpool, massage, and jogging track. Their Hyatt Business Center will provide complete business services, notably, telex and facsimile transmission, business card printing, personal computers and word processors, interpreters, and an information library on local commerce, industry, banking, and finance. The Center will remain open for two hours beyond the normal office hours. Reservations can be made through the Hyatt International Reservations network, or through the Hyatt International Sales office in Hong Kong.

华亭宾馆

Hua Ting Sheraton Hotel. Opened in September 1986, the Hua Ting was Shanghai's first hotel with a major Western hotel chain affiliation. It also immediately became the city's largest hotel, with 1,008 rooms (including 40 suites). Situated about mid-way between the airport and the

Bund, the hotel is within a 15-minute drive of most points of interest. Facilities include a tennis court, swimming pool, and health club, as well as an excellent Business Center.

Bookings are available through the Sheraton Worldwide system.

Address: 1200 Cao Xi Bei Lu   *Telex:* 33589 SHHTN CN
Telephone: 38-6000

上海静安希尔顿酒店
Shanghai Hilton International. Hilton's first major facility in China opened in the spring of 1988. A 40-story tower with 800 rooms, the Hilton is located on Huashan Road, about 15 minutes from downtown and the waterfront. Active guests can enjoy swimming (indoors), tennis, and squash. The hotel also features three "executive" floors, a business center, and seven restaurants.

Address: 250 Huashan Road   *Cable:* HILTELS SHANGHAI
Telephone: 56-3343   *Telex:* 33612 HILTL CN

和平饭店
Peace Hotel. Despite a faded facade, worn carpets, and a rather gloomy lobby, the 14-story Peace Hotel (formerly the Cathay Hotel) remains one of the favorite hotels for many seasoned visitors to Shanghai. Before 1949, it was a bastion of old world niceties: personal valets or chambermaids were assigned to each suite, laying out the guest's clothing each morning and ironing the creases out of the newspaper before presenting it at breakfast. Noel Coward spent four days at the Peace finishing the play *Private Lives* while recovering from the flu.

Traces of the hotel's former glory are still evident in accoutrements such as the heavy velvet curtains which have hung untouched (and undusted) in the cloak rooms for the past 40 years. But the 180 rooms have become run-down and are poorly maintained. Food in the dining room can no longer be recommended and overall sanitary conditions in the hotel are bordering on the deplorable (these days Noel Coward wouldn't last 30 seconds at the Peace). There are rumors that Hong Kong's Peninsula Group plans to renovate the hotel, but no official announcement has been made.

Address: 20 Nanjing Dong Road   *Telegraph:* 3266
Telephone: 211244   *Rates:* Rooms: Y140–280
Telex: 33914 BTHPH CN   Suites: Y380

锦江饭店
Jinjiang Hotel. The Jinjiang is located in a tree-lined residential neighborhood near Fuzhou Park and Huaihai Road, in what was once the French Concession sector of the city. A wall surrounds the four buildings comprising the compound, as well as the grounds within, which are beautifully maintained. Because it was formerly an apartment complex, the Jinjiang boasts special features such as leaded glass windows and parquet floors. It has been completely renovated in the past few years and has a

variety of shops and airline offices in the lobby. A Western-style coffee shop serves light meals, snacks, and liquor until midnight, and the dining room on the 11th floor has excellent Chinese and Western food.

The ground floor bar, complete with live entertainment, has become a popular gathering spot for resident foreign business people and students. It is a curiosity here that practically all the foreigners speak to the staff in Chinese, who respond only in English, creating very odd conversations on both sides.

There are a variety of other specialty shops on the grounds of the hotel. These include a bookstore, an antique store, a women's clothing shop, a post office, and a grocery with goods imported from Hong Kong. There is also a coffee shop called the Café Reve. This joint venture with a Hong Kong restaurant shows videos, plays loud music, and arrays its guests in vinyl booths.

The Jinjiang Hotel is often used by foreign heads of state. The one-story modern building in the courtyard is the site where the Shanghai Communiqué was negotiated by President Nixon and Premier Zhou Enlai on February 28, 1972.

The Jinjiang is a 45-minute walk from the Bund, which may also be reached by a 10-minute ride via the No. 26 trolley along Huaihai Road.

Address: 59 Maoming Road   *Cable:* 7777 SHANGHAI
Telephone: 582582   *Rates:* Twins: Y55–110
Telex: 33380 GRJJH CN   Suites: Y100–360

龙柏饭店

Cypress Hotel (Longbai Fandian). The striking new Cypress Hotel, which opened in mid-1982, was China's first attempt at a Western-style resort hotel as well as the first new hotel to be built in Shanghai since 1949. This stunningly modern red brick and tile complex, a product of the Shanghai Industrial Design Institute, sits on the grounds of the former British-run Shanghai Golf Club, near Hongqiao Airport and about 25 minutes from the Bund by car.

The Bamboo Banquet Room features Sichuan cuisine, while the Silk Road Restaurant has a Western menu. Rates for the Cypress's 190 rooms range from Y95 for a standard double to Y240 for a suite. The Presidential Suite has a marble bath and purportedly the only king-size double bed in China (all at Y800 per day).

In 1986, the Cypress began accepting direct bookings. General Manager Huang advises that if you get no reply in 24 hours, the hotel is booked up.

Address: 2419 Hongqiao Road   *Cable:* 9921
Telephone: 32-9388   *Telex:* 33288 CYH CN

上海太平洋大饭店

Pacific Shanghai. Scheduled to open in late 1988, the Pacific is a deluxe joint Sino-Japanese hotel with 700 rooms and 91 suites. Located

Shanghai's Bund, viewed from the Huangpu River

within the new Hongqiao Open Zone, the Pacific is ideally situated for visitors with business interests in the zone (the hotel is 6.5 km. from the Bund and 5.5 km. from the airport).

Facilities include business and conference centers, indoor and outdoor pools, tennis courts, saunas, acupuncture and massage, and 24-hour room service. Restaurants feature Chinese, Japanese, French, and American cuisine. Direct international bookings will be possible.

长江饭店

Yangtse Hotel (Hongqiao, new area). Due to open in late 1988, the Yangtse will be located in the Foreign Trade Centre of the Shanghai Hongqiao Economic and Technical Development Zone. This four-star hotel will offer 577 rooms and suites, and convenient access to the airport. Facilities include eight restaurants and lounges, business center, swimming pool, shopping arcade, health club and sauna, and ballroom/meeting rooms. Managed by New World Hotels of Hong Kong.

假日银杏上海饭店

Holiday Inn Yinxing Shanghai. Scheduled to be completed in July 1990, this 500-room hotel will have a swimming pool, coffee shop, three restaurants, shops, health club, banquet room, and two bars.

FIRST CLASS HOTELS

上海宾馆

Shanghai Hotel. One of the city's newest hotels, this is the product of wholly Chinese design, construction, and management. The 23-story structure has 600 guest rooms designed to meet Western tastes, with carpeting, TV, refrigerators, and modern baths. Opened on May 1, 1983, the Shanghai Hotel is almost always chock full with tour groups. Unfortunately, within a short time of its opening, it was showing the wear and tear of 20 years. The rooms have not been maintained, and although staff members generally try to be helpful, the service leaves much to be desired.

The Shanghai Hotel offers Chinese, Japanese, and Western food, all of which is noted for its sub-par quality. The hotel does offer a fine array of shops and services, including telex, post office, film developing, railway bookings, and city tours.

Address: 505 Wulumuqi Bei Road   Cable: 0244
Telephone: 31-2312   Rates: Y90–Y230
Telex: 33295 SHP CN

国际饭店
International Hotel (Guoji Fandian). The International (formerly the Park) is an 18-story building overlooking People's Park. It is used by both Chinese and foreigners, and its most famous guest was probably Mao Zedong, who stayed here on his "business" trips to Shanghai. This hotel has an advantage in being located very near to the No. 1 Department Store.

Address: 170 Nanjing Xi Road   Cable: 1445
Telephone: 22-5225   Rates: Twins: Y140–160
Telex: 33269   Suites: Y300–350

上海大厦
Shanghai Mansions. The view from the rooftop terrace of the Shanghai Mansions (formerly the Broadway Mansions) is breathtaking, as it overlooks the river just at the point where the Wusong meets the Huangpu. Unfortunately, its location can become a drawback in the evening, as the sonorous horns of the river barges pose a constant challenge to sleep. In fact, one of the charges against the disgraced Jiang Qing was that she ordered all river traffic to cease when she slept in Shanghai.

The Mansions' ordinary but spacious guest rooms are more spartan than those of the Peace Hotel, but the suites are nothing short of spectacular. Some of the rooms still have grand pianos and private balconies (it was originally used as a British residential hotel). The restaurant is on the third floor, and the top floor is reserved for banquets and permanent residents, such as foreign experts. Some of the staff have been with the hotel since the 1940s and the kitchen is capable of turning out everything from bird's nest soup to lemon meringue pie.

Address: 20 Suzhou Bei Road   Cable: 1111
Telephone: 24-6260   Rates: Twins: Y65–110;
Telex: 33007 BTHSM CN   Suites: Y140–380

静安宾馆
Jing'an Guest House. Although not located on the Bund or in the heart of downtown Shanghai, the Jing'an is excellently situated right by upper Nanjing Road—Shanghai's major shopping artery—and within easy reach of the Bund by taxi. The Jing'an, reopened in 1979, was China's first hotel to honor a credit card—Diners Club.

Like the Jinjiang and Peace hotels, the Jing'an has an unmistakable elegance from the colonial era. It was originally built in the 1930s to serve as an apartment hotel for Germans then residing in Shanghai.

The hotel features a fine array of shops and services, including telex, post office, film developing, and railway bookings (but only at a minimum four days' notice). For diversion, a shop on the second floor will costume clients in ancient Chinese attire and photograph them against scenes of the Great Wall or mist-enshrouded peaks. The Shanghai is centrally located at walking distances to either Nanjing or Huaihai roads. Bus #48 stops just southwest of the entrance and connects to the Bund in less than ten minutes. Rates for the hotel's taxis are 60 *fen*/km.

Address: 370 Huashan Road   *Cable:* 3304
Telephone: 563050   *Rates:* Twins: Y40–90
Telex: 30022 BTHJA CN   Suites: Y120–400

衡山宾馆
Hengshan Guest House. The plain facade of this hotel, hidden behind a concrete wall, is at first sight utterly uninviting. The tiny, sparely furnished lobby does little to offset that impression. The Hengshan's 220 rooms and suites, however, more than compensate for the building's lack of distinction. Spacious and handsomely appointed, many rooms include bathrooms large enough to accommodate a small tour group (please note, this is not a suggestion). Formerly a European residential hotel, all guest quarters were renovated in 1980. The Hengshan is set in a quiet neighborhood and is about equidistant from the airport (12 km.) and the railway station (9 km.). A taxi ride to the Bund takes about 20 minutes.

Meals are of good quality, and the kitchen staff is often called on by local officials to turn out first-rate banquets. Sichuan and Cantonese cuisines are featured. A cafe, post office, barbershop, and retail shops are located on the premises.

Address: 534 Hengshan Road   *Cable:* 5295
Telephone: 37-7050   *Rates:* Twins: Y60–90
Telex: 33009 BTHHS CN   Suites: Y80–180

达华宾馆
Dahua Guest House. The Dahua's fine Art-Deco exterior is somewhat deceptive—owing to its poor interior upkeep. The original structure was built in 1934, with a section that includes the group dining room added in 1979. The Dahua's 93 guest rooms are large and all are air-conditioned. Service is excellent throughout.

The Dahua's third-floor restaurant deserves special mention, as it is the only place in Shanghai that offers replica cuisine from the Qing imperial household ("Fang Shan Tang"). Moreover, its everyday fare is remarkably good and reasonably priced.

Located near the main thoroughfare of Jiangsu Road, the Dahua's best bus connection to the city center is route #71.

Address: 914 Yan'an Road
Telephone: 523079   *Rates:* Doubles: Y180
Cable: 1028   Suites: Y250
Special student rates: Y12 per bed (subject to availablility).

东湖宾馆

Donghu Guest House. The Donghu has 128 rooms. It is fully air-conditioned and offers its guests a swimming pool, tennis court, and a Chinese restaurant. All rooms have private bath, color TV, refrigerator, and wall-to-wall carpeting. In 1988, the Donghu was no longer recommended for foreigners.

Address: 167 Xingle Road
Telephone: 570-050

Rates: Twins: Y70
Suites: Y100–2,400

Other hotels in Shanghai which welcome foreign tourists are the **Chengqiao Hotel** (2280 Hongqiao Road; tel: 329220; telex: 33277 SCITS CN); **Cherry Holiday Villa** (77 Nonggong Road; tel: 328350); and the **Jinsha Hotel** (155 Nujiang Road; tel: 547185; tel: 547185; telex: 33454 BTHJD CN).

DELUXE VILLAS

瑞金宾馆

Ruijin Guest House (118 Ruijin Er Lu; tel: 372653; cable: 2870; telex: 33003 BTHRJ CN). The Ruijin offers the best of all worlds to Shanghai visitors—a serene enclave with exquisite Chinese gardens set right in the heart of the metropolis. This colonial-style complex has five residential villas, each accommodating up to 28 persons in varying assortments of large rooms and suites. Rooms are appointed with hand-carved mahogany furniture and genuine antique accessories (many of which are available for purchase by guests). Added modern appointments include air conditioning, color television, and refrigerators. The large bathrooms are gradually being modernized. Rates range from Y80–120 for doubles; Y280–350 for deluxe doubles and suites; and Y700–2,000 for an entire building.

兴国宾馆

Xingguo Guest House (72 Xingguo Rd.; tel: 374503). Similar to the Ruijin but a trace less grand, the Xingguo has ten buildings of both Chinese and Western style. One of its gardens was the private retreat of a famous Qing minister, Li Hongzhang. Rates are Y80–100 for standard rooms; Y100–200 for deluxe rooms; and Y1,000–2,400 for an entire building. Both Western and Chinese food are available.

西郊宾馆

Xijiao Guest House (1921 Hongqiao Rd.; tel: 379643; cable: 9919; telex: 33004 BTHHQ CN). The largest garden villa hotel in Shanghai, the Xijiao (Western Suburbs) was built in the 1960s, but was not opened to foreigners until 1981. It is located near the airport, about 25 minutes from the city by car. In addition to its expansive gardens, the Xijiao also offers boating and fishing on the grounds. Its kitchen is supplied by its own vegetable gardens. The complex includes seven buildings of varied decor, with a total of 100 rooms: doubles, Y140; two-room suites, Y250–300; and five-room suites, Y2000–3000. All rooms are equipped with TV's and refrigerators. The main building has a bar, teahouse, ballroom, banquet hall, and an atrium garden. A full range of shops and services are on the premises. Chinese or Western cuisine is provided at a fixed rate of Y30 per day. Visa, MasterCard, and American Express cards are accepted.

虹桥宾馆

Hongqiao Guest House (attached to the Xijiao Guest House, 1591 Hongqiao Rd.; tel: 522847). The Hongqiao offers a step up in elegance and privacy from its neighbor the Xijiao. It consists of four large villas set amidst a large garden. Rates, available on request, run about 20% higher than those at the Xijiao.

BUDGET ACCOMMODATIONS

申江饭店

Shenjiang Hotel (740 Hankou Rd.; tel: 225115). Bordering on People's Park, the Shenjiang is a nine-story structure built in 1934 as the Yangste Hotel. Renovated in 1978, it now has 200 rooms. Rates are Y15–20 for singles, Y30 and up for doubles, and Y40 and up for triples. Rooms are supplied with hot water in the evening (some rooms have shared baths). Guest rooms are not air-conditioned (although equipment was said to be on order in 1983). The Shenjiang's dining room is known for its Cantonese, Sichuanese, and Yangzhou-style food. As of 1988, the Shenjiang is not recommended for foreigners.

华侨饭店

Huaqiao Hotel (104 Nanjing Rd.; tel: 226226; telex: 33909 BTHHF CN). The Huaqiao, used mainly by overseas Chinese, has inexpensive rates and it is superbly located in Shanghai's very center. Built in 1924, the exterior is quite striking. It also has the benefit of housing Shanghai's head office of the China Travel Service (CTS). The Huaqiao's restaurant is famous for its Fujian-style food but also serves Cantonese and Chaozhou dishes.

蒲江饭店

Pujiang Hotel (15 Huangpu Rd.; tel: 246388). Despite its exceptional location near the Bund (across the road from the Shanghai Mansions Hotel and the Seamen's Club), the Pujiang is recommended only to travelers well prepared for "roughing it." Dormitory-style sleeping accommodations begin at Y20–30 per night. The hotel has a small dining room and a gift shop.

海佳饭店

Haijia Fandian. The Haijia has double rooms for Y40 and 5-bed dorm rooms for Y12, now the cheapest in Shanghai.

SHANGHAI CUISINE

Shanghai boasts one of China's best and most distinctive cuisines. Influenced by its position just south of the Yangste and at the mouth of the Huangpu, the region abounds in a selection of freshwater fish and shellfish. Dishes from this area are lightly and delicately seasoned. Shanghai's people have a "sweet tooth" and more sugar is used in Shanghai than in any other part of China. Shanghai's neighbors also contribute to the diversity of the area's cuisine: Hangzhou, known for its West Lake carp; Zhenjiang to the west, for its vinegar; and Shaoxing, for its rice wine—warmed like sake before serving.

The most popular method of cooking in Shanghai is "red" cooking, a method of braising in which the food is cooked in a combination of soy sauce, wine, sugar, and stock. It is called red cooking because the effect is to darken the food. Cooking time is relatively long, during which the sauce becomes heavy (without the use of a thickening agent) and highly flavored.

The Shanghai area has always produced a multitude of vegetables and the practice of vegetarianism was a fad of the rich. (The toast of Shanghai society in the 1930s was the Buddhist "Abbot" Khi Veh-du, who lived in baronial splendor with his wife and seven concubines.) Vegetarian chefs vied with each other to see who could produce the most imaginative creations. Many were imitations of non-vegetable dishes such as mock Beijing (Peking) Duck, vegetarian stir-fried shrimp, and sweet-and-sour vegetarian whole fish. In Shanghai cuisine, a great deal of thought still goes into the physical appearance of each dish and it is not unusual to be served steaming soup in a bowl elaborately carved from a winter melon. Carrots, turnips, beancurd, and other foods are fastidiously shaped to resemble miniature animals and flowers. Among the most famous seafood dishes are steamed freshwater crab (in season from October through December) and shrimp served over sizzling rice. Other items include eel (prepared in a heavy garlic sauce) and sweet-and-sour river fish. "Beggar's chicken" (small chunks cooked slowly in caked mud, popular throughout China) is said to have originated in this area.

Shanghai has over 600 restaurants serving 14 different kinds of regional cooking, in addition to thousands of cold drink stands, food stalls, and cafés (an unmistakable foreign legacy) where you can stop for a quick snack of ice cream or *tangtuan* (dumplings made with rice flour, ground nuts, and sesame seeds). Unlike Beijing and Guangzhou, Shanghai has few large restaurants that cater to foreigners, although this situation is changing. A national chefs' school has been opened in Shanghai to train restaurant workers in cooking and serving, as well as in speaking English and Japanese. At present, however, the finest restaurats are still to be found in the hotels.

On Nanjing Dong Road are a number of restaurants serving excellent regional cuisine: the Yangzhou at No. 306 (tel: 22-2777); the Sichuan,

No. 457 (tel: 22-1965); and the Xinya (Cantonese cuisine), No. 719 (tel: 22-4393). Hot and spicy Sichuan fare is also available at the Chengdu Restaurant (129 Shunchang Rd.; tel: 28-3767). The Dahongyun Restaurant (556 Fuzhou Rd.; tel: 22-4459) and the Moslem Restaurant (710 Fuzhou Rd.; tel: 22-4273) are also recommended. French cuisine is the specialty of the Hong Fangzi (Red House) Restaurant, formerly known as "Chez-Louis" (37 Shaanxi Nan Rd.; tel: 56-5748). Although this restaurant is recommended by many, one tourist recently reported that he had his "one truly inedible meal" in China there.

There are no less than 60 candy and cake factories in Shanghai producing 90,000 tons of pastries and confectionery. A favorite spot for such indulgences is the Kaige Bakery and Coffee Shop on Nanjing Xi Road. Most Westerners find Chinese soda drinks much too sweet, but Shanghai beer (as compensation) is excellent and refreshing.

Perhaps the ultimate gastronomic experience in Shanghai is to rent the Yu Yuan (Garden of the Mandarin Yu) Restaurant for an evening. Up to 25 guests can be accommodated but only as a private party and at a minimum of about Y40 per person. Chefs who prefer not to work in hotels are hired, and a special feast is prepared. It is not possible to arrange such an affair on the general tourist itinerary; business people and others should be sure to make arrangements well in advance through their local hosts.

SHOPPING

If there is one place where China's new "consumerism" is evident, it is in Shanghai. The city has more than 17,000 shops (including many 24-hour stores), with 400,000 employees.

FRIENDSHIP STORE

The three-story Friendship Store is located on the Bund, just two blocks north of the Peace Hotel and across the Suzhou Creek bridge from the Shanghai Mansions. It has an excellent selection of high-quality silks and clothing on the second floor. In the antiques section, there are thousands of different curios, antiques, reproductions, and ancient artworks. Objects for sale include pearls and gems, ivory and jade carvings, imitation bronzes, redwood screens, traditional Chinese stationery, writing brushes, ink tablets, plates, boxes, and vases. There are also woodblock prints of famous calligraphy and painting. Some good examples are reproductions of the remarkable horses by the famous painter Li Longmian of the Song Dynasty; bamboos by Ni Yunlin of the Yuan Dynasty; mynahs and ladies by Tang Yin of the Ming Dynasty; bamboos and orchids by Zheng Banqiao; flowers, birds, and figurines of Ren Boni of the Qing Dynasty. Horses by Xu Beihong and shrimp, flowers, and birds by Qi Baishi—both famous contemporary artists—are also included. Other articles on sale include embroidery and stone, wood, and bamboo carvings. Shoppers should take care to note the many non-antique items on display next to the 100-year-old items (all antiques are marked with a red or brown wax seal). Prices are relatively high.

Tired and thirsty tourists can sit down for a soft drink on the first floor. Foreign students tend to congregate here for socializing with visitors.

SHOPPING DISTRICTS

Nanjing Road. The main shopping street has over 400 stores and qualifies as China's nearest equivalent of Fifth Avenue or Oxford Street. During the day, the area is so dense with people that it is virtually a pedestrian mall with buses and cars honking their way down the crowded streets.

The **No. 1 Department Store** is located at 830 Nanjing Dong Road, at the corner of Xizang Road. Although barely one-half the size of Macy's, it is the largest such emporium in all of China. It carries over 36,000 items and serves 100,000 customers a day (twice that many on holidays). It is open from 8 AM to 8 PM, and has a special 24-hour section. The store is currently undergoing a complete renovation under the direction of the Wing On Department Store of Hong Kong (which was itself one of the largest stores in Shanghai before 1949).

The top floor has radios, expensive handicrafts, and stationery. The middle two floors specialize in clothing, and the street floor features items ranging from hand luggage (the canvas bags with a picture of Shanghai stenciled on the side are a popular souvenir) to tea (prized Hangzhou chrysanthemum tea is available here in bulk). Increased consumerism in China accounts for the varieties of bicycles, sewing machines, wristwatches, cameras, TV sets, cosmetics, colorful textiles, musical instruments, and even Frisbees being sold in the No. 1 Department Store.

Walking west on Nanjing Road from the Peace Hotel toward the No. 1 Department Store, you will encounter a music store at No. 118, probably Shanghai's best, with a selection of Chinese and Western instruments; a sporting goods store at No. 156; and the **Guanlong Photo Materials Store** at No. 180. The **Signs and Banners Store** at No. 309 was renovated in 1980. This shop lacks its earlier "rummaging" spirit, but will still appeal to those interested in banners, Chinese flags, and Chinese home decorative arts.

The **Xinhua Bookstore** at No. 345 is Shanghai's largest bookstore and a beehive of activity. Here readers can rent books as well as buy them. Further down the street at No. 422 is the **Duoyunxuan Paintings and Calligraphy Store,** which features a wide selection of prints and scrolls by famous artists. There is greater variety in this store than in the Friendship Store or the No. 1 Department Store. Past the Sichuan Restaurant at No. 457, you will come to the Shanghai Fabric Store, No. 592, Nanjing Road's most fashionable place for silks in many colors and weights, cottons, and some ready-made garments.

The **Shanghai Overseas Chinese Store** at No. 627 is a few doors farther down the street, followed by the **No. 10 Department Store** at No. 635, noted for its eye-catching window displays. The **Shanghai Arts and Crafts Shop** at No. 751 offers papercuts as well as scrolls, wall mountings, and an opportunity to have your photograph transferred onto an enameled wall hanging.

The **Shanghai Arts and Crafts Service Department** is further along at 190 Nanjing Xi Road (next to the Park Hotel). Its third floor is exclusively set aside for foreign shoppers.

Huaihai Road. A half-block from the Jinjiang Hotel, Huaihai Road is another major shopping area where, among other things, a number of hair-dressing salons and lingerie stores are located. The **Chuanxin Shop** at No. 1297 carries a good selection of pewter, lacquerware, ceramics, and porcelain. At 557 Yan'an Road, in the **Shanxi Shop,** you will find a similar selection of goods, along with jewelry. Shops selling shoes (some fashionable even by Western standards) and children's wear abound in the area.

Shanghai Directory

HEALTH AND EMERGENCY SERVICES	Telephone
Huashan Hospital, 12 Wulumuqi Zhong Rd.	31-1600
Shanghai No. 1 Hospital, 190 North Suzhou Rd.	24-0100
Outpatient Department, 410 North Suzhou Rd.	24-0100

TELEPHONE AND TELEGRAPH SERVICES	Telephone
Information (domestic calls)	114
Information (international calls)	112
Shanghai Post Office	24-5025
Shanghai Telegraph Office	21-1130

FOREIGN CONSULATES	Telephone
Australian Consulate, 17 Fuxing Xi Rd.	37-4580
Belgian Consulate, Jing'an Guest House, Rm. 307	53-8882
British Consulate, 244 Yong Fu Rd.	37-4569
Republic of France Consulate, 1431 Huaihai Zhong Rd.	37-7414
Federal Republic of Germany Consulate, 181 Yong Fu Rd.	37-9953
Italian Consulate, 127 Wu Yi Rd.	52-4373
Japanese Consulate, 1517 Huaihai Zhong Rd.	37-2073
Polish Consulate, 618 Jianguo Xi Rd.	37-0952
US Consulate, 1469 Huaihai Zhong Rd.	37-9880

TRAVEL	Telephone
China International Travel Service (CITS), 33 Zhongshan Rd.	21-6129
Independent Travel Dept., Peace Hotel	21-1244
China Travel Service (CTS), 104 Nanjing Xi Rd.	22-6226
Shanghai Tourism Corporation, 14 Zhongshan Rd.	21-9341
Air	
Civil Aviation Administration of China (CAAC), 789 Yan'an Rd.	53-5953
Reservations (domestic)	53-5953
Reservations (international)	53-2255
Cargo (international)	53-1640

Japan Air Lines, 205 Maoming Nan Rd.	37-8467
United, Shanghai Hilton International, Huashan Rd.	55-3333
Singapore Airlines, Jinjiang Hotel, 59 Maoming Nan Rd., West Bldg., Rm. 1341	37-7602
Cathay Pacific, Jinjiang Hotel, Rm. 123	37-7899
Northwest Airlines, Jinjiang Hotel, North Bldg., Rm. 127	37-7387
Hongqiao Airport Flight Information Desk	53-7664

Rail

Shanghai Railroad Station	66-5281
Information	24-2299

Shipping

American Bureau of Shipping, Peace Hotel, Rm. 707-8	21-1244 ext. 707
Chinese-Polish Joint Stock Shipping Co., 18 Zhongshang Dong Yi Rd., 2/F	21-5400
Germanischer Lloyd, Shanghai Mansions, Rm. 902	24-6260 ext. 902

Local Transportation

Friendship Taxi Service (24 hours)	58-4584
Shanghai Taxi Co.	22-2999
Three-Wheeled Taxi Service	23-0230

POINTS OF INTEREST	Telephone
Friendship Store, 33 Zhongshan Rd.	21-9698
Fuxing Park, 105 Yandang Rd.	28-3296
Garden of Happiness (Yu Yuan), 132 Anren St.	28-3251
International Club, 63 West Yan'an Rd.	53-8513
Jade Buddha Temple, 170 Anyuan Rd.	58-0098
Longhua Temple, 2887 Longhua Xi Rd.	38-9997
Lu Xun Memorial Museum, 146 Dongjiang Wan Rd.	66-1181
People's Park, Nanjing Xi Rd.	58-2084
Shanghai Industrial Exhibition, Yan'an Rd.	56-3037
Shanghai Municipal Children's Palace, 64 West Yan'an Rd.	52-5537
Shanghai Museum of Art and History, 16 South Henan Rd.	26-2460
Shanghai Music Conservatory, 20 Fengyang Rd.	37-0137
Shanghai No. 1 Department Store, 830 East Nanjing Rd.	22-3344
Shanghai Zoo, Xijiao Park, 2381 Hongqiao Rd.	32-9775
Site of Founding of the Chinese Communist Party, 76 Xingye Rd.	28-1177
Workers' Cultural Palace, 120 Xizang Rd.	22-6155

BANKS	Telephone
Bank of America, 100 Yan'an Dong Rd., Union Bldg., Rm. 1802	26-2933
Bank of China, 23 Zhongshan Rd.	21-5666
Bank of East Asia, 299 Sichuan Zhong Rd.	21-6863
Bank of Tokyo, Ruijin Bldg., Rm. 2301, 205 Maoming Nan Rd.	37-4657
Banque de Paris et du Pays Bas, Jin Jiang F.T.B., Rm. 3-134	37-0115
Banque Indosuez, Jin Jiang F.T.B., Rm. 58547	31-1753
Banque Nationale de Paris, Jin Jiang F.T.B., Suite 58142 G/F	58-2582 ext. 58142
Banque Paribas, Bureau de Shanghai, Jin Jiang F.T.B., Rm. 58134	58-2582 ext. 58134
The Chartered Bank, 185 Yuan Ming Yuan Rd., 4/F	21-8253

Citibank, N.A., 100 Yan'an Dong Rd., Union Bldg., #1904	28-9661
Dai-Ichi Kangyo Bank, Ltd., Jin Jiang F.T.B., Rm. 58356	58-2582
	ext. 58356
Daiwa Bank, Ltd., 100 Yan'an Dong Rd., Union Bldg., Rm. 1401	26-4248
The Hong Kong and Shanghai Banking Corp., 185 Yuan Ming Yuan Rd., 5-6/F	21-8383
Industrial Bank of Japan, Jin Jiang F.T.B., Room 58236	37-5746
Mitsubishi Bank, Jin Jiang F.T.B., Rm. 58360	37-4086
Overseas-Chinese Banking Corp. Ltd., 120 Jiujiang Rd.	21-3176
Toyo Trust and Banking Co. Ltd., Jin Jiang F.T.B., Rm. 58535	37-6373

CHURCHES	Telephone
Community Church (Protestant), 53 Hengshan Rd.	37-6576
Muen Church (Protestant), 316 Xizang Zhong Rd.	22-5069
Shanghai Cathedral (Catholic), 158 Puxi Rd.	37-1328

CHINA NATIONAL FOREIGN TRADE ORGANIZATIONS	Telephone
China Council for the Promotion of International Trade (CCPIT) 33 East Zhongshan Rd.	23-3575

CHINA NATIONAL IMPORT AND EXPORT CORPORATIONS, Shanghai Branches

Animal By-products, 23 East Zhongshan Rd.	21-5630
Arts and Crafts, 16 East Zhongshan Rd.	21-2100
Cereals, Oils, and Foodstuffs	
Cereals and Oils, 11 Hankou Rd.	21-9760
Foodstuffs, 26 East Zhongshan Rd.	21-6233
Chemicals, 27 East Zhongshan Rd.	21-1540
Foreign Trade Transportation Corporation, 74 Dianchi Rd.	21-3103
Light Industrial Products, 209 Yuanmingyuan Rd.	21-6858
Machinery Imports and Exports, 27 East Zhongshan Rd.	21-1220
Metals and Minerals, 27 East Zhongshan Rd.	21-1220
Textiles (garments), 27 East Zhongshan Rd.	21-8400
Textiles (silk), 17 East Zhongshan Rd.	21-5770
Shanghai Investment and Trust Corporation, 100 Yan'an Dong Rd.	28-4120

The venerable Peace Hotel, Shanghai

Shanhaiguan

mountain-to-the-sea pass   *traditional spelling / Shanhaikuan*

SHANHAIGUAN is a small, walled city located at the eastern extremity of the Great Wall, about 310 km. (192 mi.) northeast of Beijing along the Beijing–Shenyang Railway. The town is over 3,000 years old and owes its historical importance to its strategic location. Three mountain ranges join together at the Shanhaiguan Pass and end in a bluff at the edge of the Bohai Sea.

Shanhaiguan is best known for the massive gate here which marks the point at which the Great Wall meets the sea. It was built in the Ming Dynasty (1368–1644) as part of a Great Wall extension stretching from the ocean to the Badaling Pass north of Beijing (a site which most tourists visit). The prominent characters on the gate exterior read *Tianxia Diyiguan*—The First Pass Under Heaven. From atop this gate the Great Wall can be seen snaking its way down from the Yanshan Mountains to the west; eastward its crumbling remains stretch 10 km. (6 mi.) to the coast.

SHANHAIGUAN
IN HISTORY

Records of settlement at the present-day site of Shanhaiguan date back to the 6th century BC. In AD 618, a barrier gate was first constructed and the city named Yuguan. During the Sui, Tang, and Song dynasties (7th–13th century), the area played a strategic role in battles waged by the Han people against northern tribes and Korean invaders.

After the Manchus established themselves in Beijing at the onset of the Qing Dynasty (1644–1911), Shanhaiguan became a stopping-off place for the emperors on their way to visit ancestral shrines in the north.

Shanhaiguan's modern development began in the last two years of the 19th century during the building of the Beijing–Shenyang Railway. During the Boxer Rebellion, the city was occupied by foreign troops. The British, French, Italians, and Japanese maintained garrisons there until the mid-1920s.

The city, about 20 km. (12.4 mi.) north of the port city of Qinhuangdao, is usually visited as part of a one-day excursion originating in Beidaihe.

Climate		Jan	Feb	Mar	Apr	May	Jun	Jul	Aug	Sep	Oct	Nov	Dec
Temp.	°C	-4.7	-1.9	4.8	13.7	20.1	24.8	26.1	24.8	19.9	12.8	3.8	2.8
	°F	23.5	28.6	40.6	56.6	68.1	76.6	78.9	76.6	67.8	55	38.8	37
Precip.	mm.	76	76	76	102	152	203	305	254	178	152	102	76
	in.	3	3	3	4	6	8	12	10	7	6	4	3

►━━━━━━━━━━━━◄
HIGHLIGHTS
►━━━━━━━━━━━━◄
FOR TRAVELERS
►━━━━━━━━━━━━◄

天下第一关

Tianxia Diyiguan. "The First Pass Under Heaven" is actually a gate dating back to 1639 (previous gates were destroyed by the ravages of war). The tower surmounting the gate is a two-story structure 10 m. (33 ft.) high. On the edge of the roof and the upturned eaves are lifelike animal figurines sculpted of stone. The most famous decoration, however, is the large sign proclaiming the gate's name in Chinese. Emblazoned with striking, bold calligraphy, it is 6 m. (19.7 ft.) long and 1.5 m. (4.9 ft.) high. Each character is 1 m. (3.3 ft.) high. The inscription, etched in beautiful characters by the scholar Xiao Xian, has become renowned throughout China for its aesthetic power.

The section of the Great Wall around Shanhaiguan is 10 m. (33 ft.) high and 5 m. (16.4 ft.) wide. Five horses could gallop abreast along its battlements. Around the gate itself, the ramparts have eight shooting slots for archers. Other towers along the wall stretching in the distance were used for sending signals. Wolf droppings were then the preferred fuel for the signal fires because the smoke produced is a fine grey color and rises straight up even in moderate winds.

Remnants of the wall extend eastward to the "Dragon's Head," so called because there was once a carving of a stone dragon at the end facing the sea.

The tower above the gate houses a small museum with illustrations that portray its construction, several military uniforms (which date from the Qing), cannons, rifles, and other military equipment. Its centerpiece is an 83-kg. (183-lb.), spearlike weapon of bronze which, it is said, can only be lifted by a true scholar. On the north side of the gate is a small park with a statue of a People's Liberation Army soldier who was designated an international martyr for saving the life of a Korean child.

贞女祠

Woman of Fidelity Temple (Zhennü Ci). About 10 km. (6 mi.) north of Shanhaiguan, along a dusty road leading through the cornfields and by an ancient beacon tower, is a small hill with some simple temples dating from 1594.

Legend has it that during the Qin Dynasty (221–206 BC) a young woman's fiancé was taken away by the authorities on their wedding day to do forced labor on the Great Wall. As winter approached, she remembered that he did not have proper clothing, so she came to this site to bring him warm things. After waiting for weeks for news of him at this spot (hence the "Waiting for Husband Rock"), she was finally told he had perished. When she began to cry, 60 miles of the wall crumbled. Thereupon, she climbed to the top of a large boulder jutting up from the ocean (visible from the hill) and threw herself in the sea.

Mud statues of the woman and her two attendants are housed in a temple here. Most notable are the Roman-like blue paint and facial features of the woman and the yellow cloth cape slung about her shoulders. On the doorway of the temple are two signboards with linguistic puns: the seven characters on each board have the same pronunciations, but actually mean different things. The right slogan refers to the ebbing and flowing tide, while the left one speaks of the coming and going of the clouds.

HOTEL ACCOMMODATIONS

In the past, visitors have only rarely stayed overnight in Shanhaiguan. They usually stayed in the hotel here reserved for Chinese visitors and a small guest house adjacent to the Beijie Restaurant accommodating about ten people. But a new resort hopes to change that.

喜来登老龙头避暑

Sheraton Old Dragon Head Resort. A joint venture of the First Brown Development Company in Minnesota and the Shanhaiguan Economical Development Corporation, this new resort will have 300 rooms and is scheduled to open in 1990. Recreational facilities will include tennis and squash courts, a health club and sauna, indoor swimming pool, and a bowling alley. The Great Wall is the major attraction near the hotel, and guests will have access to the first 12 kilometers of the Wall, only 100 meters away. Among the other features will be two lounges, two restaurants, a 400-seat ballroom, meeting rooms, and a business center. Sheraton Corporation will provide management services.

CUISINE

There are a number of pleasant cafés opposite the gate, all featuring the "best" *qishui* (orange soda) in China.

The main restaurant in Shanhaiguan is the Beijie (North Street), located on a back street within the old city walls. It often prepares lunches for foreign visitors. The Beijie was formerly a private home. It consists of a series of low buildings with trees and flower-filled courtyards. The rattan chairs under the arbors are a lovely place to relax before sitting down to a meal.

The restaurant has three classes of service: first, tourist, and local. First-class, for banquets, has to be reserved ahead of time and is most often used by officials and military men on an outing to Shanhaiguan. Foreign tourists generally dine together in a spacious room with six large round tables and simple table d'hôte fare in second-class, while locals dine in plainer surroundings.

The specialties of the house are *suanyangrou* (an excellent mutton dish) and *donglaishunfan* (a local variety of fried rice).

汕头

Shantou

fish trap promontory

traditional spelling/Swatow

SHANTOU, a quaint and colorful port city of 700,000, is situated at the confluence of the Han, Rong, and Lian rivers on the coast of the South China Sea. It is 361 km. (191 nautical mi.) northeast of Hong Kong. Thanks to its well-protected deep water harbor, it has become Guangdong Province's second largest city, next to Guangzhou. Shantou is at the center of a prefecture made up of 11 counties with a total population over 10 million. Shantou is also the site of the smallest of China's four Special Economic Zones.

The city can be reached by bus from Guangzhou (15 hours; Y25) and Shenzhen (Y35); or by air from Guangzhou (one hour; Y56; daily service). For the adventuresome, there is an overnight steamer, the *Dinghu,* which sails from Hong Kong to Shantou on alternate days (HK$150). The region enjoys a mild, subtropical climate with summer temperatures hovering around 28°C (82°F); in winter, the temperature seldom drops below 10°C (50°F). The spring monsoon (known throughout southern China as the "plum rain season") occurs during May and June and is the wettest time of year.

SHANTOU IN HISTORY

Although extensive Han Chinese settlement of the Shantou area began in the Six Dynasties period, Shantou itself was little more than a fishing village until the 19th century. In 1855, at the conclusion of the Second Opium War, concession rights in Shantou were granted to Britain under the Treaty of Tianjin. Shantou's importance as a commercial center, as well as much of its architecture, dates from this period of foreign domination.

While British and other foreign entrepreneurs traded in silk, porcelain, and tea, enriching themselves as well as the local merchants and mandarins, the people of the surrounding countryside enjoyed few windfalls. Like Macao and Guangzhou to the south, and Xiamen and Fuzhou to the north, Shantou became a major emigration point for poor peasants seeking to improve their families' fortunes overseas. The scale of this exodus can be reckoned from the widespread use of the local Min and Hakka dialects among millions of overseas Chinese throughout Southeast Asia, and from the fact that nearly 15% of the area's residents receive

Climate		Jan	Feb	Mar	Apr	May	Jun	Jul	Aug	Sep	Oct	Nov	Dec
Temp.	°C	13.1	13.8	17.5	21.9	25.8	27.1	28.3	28.2	27.0	23.8	19.8	15.2
	°F	55	56.8	63.5	71.4	78.4	80.7	82.9	82.7	80.6	74.8	67.6	59.3
Precip.	mm.	152	203	254	279	381	508	457	406	330	203	152	127
	in.	6	8	10	11	15	20	18	16	13	8	6	5

remittances from abroad. This overseas connection has been by far the single most important factor in Shantou's modern economic development.

ECONOMY

The upheavals of the early and middle 20th century forced foreign business out of Shantou and brought an end to the city's short-lived era of prosperity. Seemingly doomed to decline, Shantou was rescued from the fate of becoming a perennial economic backwater by the central government's choice of the city, in 1980, as site of one of China's four new Special Economic Zones. By the end of 1985, much of the preliminary infrastructure work had been completed, including 6 km. of roads, 15 km. of pipeline, a 1.1-megawatt power station, and several factory buildings. Through 1985, the Shantou SEZ had agreed to undertake 46 joint-venture projects—including textiles, light industrial products, consumer electronics, shipping, and agricultural and aquacultural products—with a total value of $51.2 million. As of 1985, nine of these projects were in production, with agriculture and aquaculture leading the way in total exports. In 1984, the Shantou SEZ exported over $1 million worth of seafood, flowers, fruits, and animal products.

The establishment in 1985 of an agricultural research and development center, along with the announcement of plans to expand food processing, packaging, and cold-storage facilities, indicates that for the time being the SEZ authorities intend to stress this area of development.

For further information on the Shantou SEZ, readers may contact the Special Economic Zone Administrative Committee, Foreign Trade Building, Fourth Floor, Yingchun Lu, Shantou, People's Republic of China (tel: 3456; cable: 3678 SHANTOU). (See also above, Doing Business in China: Special Economic Zones.)

HIGHLIGHTS FOR TRAVELERS

Having attained status as a city only within the last 100 years, there are few sites of historical or archeological value in Shantou itself. Much of the European colonial architecture from the late 19th and early 20th centuries has been preserved, however, and its distinct South China sea-coast flavor remains untainted.

SITES AROUND SHANTOU

妈屿

Mayu Island. This small island near Shantou was once part of the British concession. More recently, it has been developed as a beach resort.

灵山寺

Lingshan Temple. Located near Chaoyang, south of Shantou, this well-known Buddhist temple was established during the Tang dynasty. Most of the present buildings date from the Qing period.

潮州
CHAOZHOU

***

Some 50 km. northwest of Shantou (bus Y1, about one hour) is the ancient city of Chaozhou. Established in the Former Han dynasty, it first became a major urban center during the Sui (581–618). With a long and illustrious tradition of both Buddhist and secular art and literature, Chaozhou is famous today for its unique style of popular opera, and its crafts, especially porcelain and embroidery: Chaozhou's is one of the "famous four" among Chinese embroidery styles, joining those of Suzhou, Hunan, and Sichuan. The city also retains its links to the past through preservation of its temples and other historical sites.

西湖

West Lake. Although the name of Hangzhou's pleasure park has been wishfully bestowed upon at least a dozen more or less scenic spots throughout China, Chaozhou's West Lake is in fact as picturesque and even more ancient than the "original."

湘子桥

Xiangzi Bridge. Work on this bridge, named after Han Xiang, a Daoist adept and nephew of the Tang poet Han Yu, began in the Song dynasty. But the builders quickly came up against an apparently insurmountable obstacle—the Han River's swift and turbulent current. The river remained unspanned until an ingenious Ming dynasty engineer devised a unique solution: a flexible pontoon bridge, resting on 18 barges floating in midstream. Unfortunately for posterity, the pontoon bridge was replaced by a steel cantilever span in the late 1950s.

开元寺

Kaiyuan Temple. Originally built in the 8th century, it is one of the few Tang Dynasty temples in which some of the original architecture has been preserved. Currently undergoing repairs, this still-active Buddhist temple also houses an archeology exhibit.

韩愈庙

Han Yu Temple. Han Yu, one of the "Eight Great Masters of Literature" of the Tang and Song, was banished to Chaozhou after presenting a vehemently anti-Buddhist memorial to the emperor, who was a devout believer. It was his presence in Chaozhou that first gave the city its reputation as a center of learning and culture. The small Confucian temple which honors him was built during the Southern Song dynasty.

HOTEL ACCOMMODATIONS

汕头国际饭店

Shantou International. Managed by the Lee Gardens International Group of Hong Kong, this new 400-room hotel has a business center, meeting rooms, billiard room, and beauty salon. Rates are $40–60 (single) and $45–65 (double).

龙湖饭店
Longhu Hotel (Yingbin Rd.; tel: 60703/6; telex: 45458 LHHTL CN; cable: 2160). A 50-room hotel (nine suites are available at Y80 to Y90; the rest are doubles, at Y50 to Y60). All guest rooms feature air-conditioning, in all its rooms, which also all have private bath, closed-circuit color TV, telephone, and wall-to-wall carpeting. Public facilities include a coffee room, Chinese and Western restaurants, and a dance hall. There is an 80-seat hall for business functions.

国际海员俱乐部旅馆部
Guest Room Division, International Seamen's Club (40 Li'an Rd.; tel: 2578). Twenty-seven double rooms are available here at Y40 to Y45, and one triple room at Y30. Only some of the rooms have private bath, but there is a Chinese restaurant and a gift shop.

汕头大厦
Shantou Mansion (12 Yongping Rd.; tel: 5711). A small, inexpensive hotel near the city's center, the Shantou Mansion offers single rooms for as little as Y6, and doubles for Y12. It should be noted, however, that all the rooms here are without private bath.

Several other hotels have opened recently in Shantou to accommodate the anticipated influx of tourists and businessmen. Foremost among these are the Tuodao Guesthouse on Jinsha Road, the Friendship Hotel (Youyi Binguan) at 7 Wai Malu (tel: 74426) and the Overseas Chinese Hotel on Shanzhang Road.

CUISINE

The cuisine of the Shantou area has its source in Chaozhou cooking. It bears resemblance to the Cantonese style of cooking in its emphasis on fresh ingredients, and as in Guangzhou, the main theme of most banquets is seafood.

From elaborate banquet dishes to simpler but equally delicious home-style fare, Shantou and Chaozhou food can be enjoyed at a wide variety of restaurants. In Shantou, banquets can be arranged at both the Overseas Chinese Hotel and Toudao Guesthouse dining rooms. For more impromptu meals, the Xinxing, at 75 Xinxing Road, and the Chaozhou, gourmets should make a point of visiting Taiping Road, where they can choose from among innumerable food stalls and several very good restaurants. Of the latter, the best are probably the Hurongquan and the Chaoan.

中国国际旅行社
CITS (Luxingshe) Office in Shantou ■ 243 Wai Malu. Tel: 75226.

Shaoshan

vernal mountain   *traditional spelling/Shaoshan*

SHAOSHAN is located 131 km. (81 mi.) southwest of Changsha, accessible by motor coach (three hours) and train (two hours). The village is in Xiangtan County and is so small it does not appear on many large-scale maps of China. Its importance to the Communist movement, however, surpasses its physical dimensions, as it is the birthplace of Mao Zedong.

The road to Shaoshan is well paved and passes through some of the most verdant countryside in China. The distinctive styles of Hunan dress (the unique peasant hats, for example), carts, and architecture quickly become apparent.

Shaoshan itself is nestled in a narrow valley surrounded by hills, the highest of which is the site of a Daoist hermitage. If time permits, a walk through the surrounding countryside and the small village is recommended.

HIGHLIGHTS FOR TRAVELERS

毛泽东故居

Mao Zedong Birthplace. The house where Mao Zedong was born in 1893 will surprise many by its relatively large size (officially, Mao is said to have had "prosperous peasant roots"). It contains three bedrooms (the third for one of Mao's brothers, killed during the civil war), a spare guest room, rice granary, separate kitchen, adjoining bathroom, stable area, and sheds for cows, tools, and wood. Just in front of the house is a small pond with lotus flowers where Mao used to swim as a small boy.

毛泽东博物馆

Mao Zedong Museum. Opened in 1967, the museum focuses on Mao's early childhood and his revolutionary activities spanning the three decades between 1920 and 1950.

HOTEL ACCOMMODATIONS

韶山宾馆

Shaoshan Guest House (Shaoshan, Xiangtan County; tel: 2127). The Shaoshan, in the center of town, has about 100 rooms, most with private bath. Rates range from Y30 for triples to Y45 for a suite.

湘潭宾馆

Xiangtan Guest House (Western Shaoshan Rd.; tel: 23165). Located 3 km. from the railway station, the Xiangtan has 18 rooms (Y30–34) and three suites (Y56), all with private bath. Some rooms have air-conditioners and/or private bath. There are Chinese and Western restaurants, and a retail shop.

Climate		Jan	Feb.	Mar	Apr	May	Jun	Jul	Aug	Sep	Oct	Nov	Dec
Temp.	°C	4.6	6.2	10.9	16.7	21.7	26	29.5	28.9	24.5	18.2	12.5	7
	°F	40.3	43.2	51.7	62	71	78.8	85.1	84	76.1	64.7	54.5	44.6
Precip.	mm.	152	152	203	279	305	381	254	203	178	178	152	127
	in.	6	6	8	11	12	15	10	8	7	7	6	5

Shenyang

north of the Shen River   *traditional spelling/Mukden*

SHENYANG, the capital of Liaoning Province, is among China's largest and most important industrial cities. Previously known by its Manchurian name, Mukden, the city is also a major communication and transportation center for Dongbei, China's northeastern region.

Dongbei, comprising what was formerly Manchuria, consists of the three provinces of Liaoning, Jilin, and Heilongjiang. For centuries the region was little more than a barren steppe sparsely populated by nomadic tribes. During the 19th century, the Western powers began to exploit Manchuria's vast natural resources, and the region became a focal point of foreign contention.

Japan gained dominance over the area in the early part of the 20th century. In 1932, it set up the puppet state of Manchukuo and installed the deposed Manchu emperor, Henry Pu Yi, at its head. The area was rapidly industrialized under the Japanese, but its infrastructure was largely dismantled during the postwar Soviet occupation and withdrawal.

Since 1949, the region has been methodically redeveloped, particularly the cities of Shenyang (steel) and Harbin (oil). Liaoning Province is still relatively underpopulated, but Shenyang's growth is underscored by the fact that in 1910 it had a population of 100,000, whereas by 1980 the population had soared to over four million.

Located just north of the Hun River, Shenyang includes a number of urban and suburban districts and two rural counties, covering a total area of *c.* 8,000 sq. km. (*c.* 5,000 sq. mi.). The administrative center of the city is located in the older Chinese section. Much of Shenyang is "new," having been constructed in the last 50 years, and its wide, tree-lined streets, tall buildings, and spacious squares give the city a Central European appearance.

Shenyang is 841 km. (522 mi.) northeast of Beijing (the express train takes 12 hours; jet flights, about one and a half hours). The best time of year to visit Shenyang is in the summer. Winters are bitterly cold.

SHENYANG IN HISTORY

Although the origins of Shenyang can be traced back some 2,000 years, it did not emerge as a city of note until the 11th century when, under the Song Dynasty, it thrived as a trading center for nomads. Among the powerful tribes in the region were the Manchus, who began their rise to power by

Climate		Jan	Feb	Mar	Apr	May	Jun	Jul	Aug	Sep	Oct	Nov	Dec
Temp.	°C	−12.7	−8.8	0.1	9.5	17.5	21.5	24.5	23.8	17.2	9.5	0.1	−8.7
	°F	9.1	16.1	32.1	49.1	63.5	70.7	76.1	74.8	62.9	49.1	32.1	16.3
Precip.	mm.	8	8	18	28	69	84	183	170	64	36	28	15
	in.	.3	.3	.7	1.1	2.7	3.3	7.2	6.7	2.5	1.4	1.1	.6

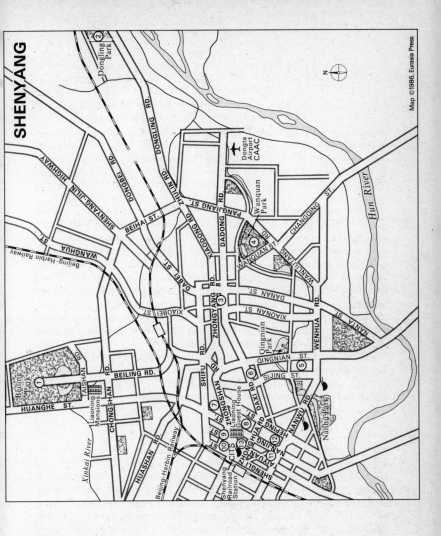

SHENYANG

① North Tomb (Beiling)
② East Tomb (Dongling)
③ Imperial Palace
④ Shenyang Zoo
⑤ Liaoning Exhibition Hall
⑥ Liaoning Province Museum
⑦ Shenyang Bureau of Foreign Trade
⑧ Zhonghua Theater
⑨ People's Store / Friendship Store
⑩ Central Post Office
⑪ City Cultural Palace
⑫ Provincial Foreign Trade Bureau

🍴 Restaurants

▦ Hotels

Map ©1986, Eurasia Press

conquering and politically consolidating the northern border lands in the early 17th century. Nurhachi (1559–1626), founder of the Manchu state, began his open war against China's Ming rulers in 1618. By 1625, he controlled enough of the northern region to be able to establish a capital at Shenyang. In 1636, his 14th son and successor, Abukai, proclaimed the founding of the Qing ("pure") Dynasty from Shenyang. Beijing was finally seized in 1644 after a Chinese commander literally invited the Manchus inside the Great Wall. Shenyang remained a secondary capital, however, in part because the rulers did not want to give up the lucrative ginseng trade—the Manchu equivalent of the salt monopolies established under the Ming.

Shenyang played a role in the Boxer Rebellion of 1900 and was the site of a 17-day battle during the Russo-Japanese War of 1904–05. After the Republic of China was established in 1912, the city served as headquarters for a number of northern warlords, notably Zhang Zuolin, who held sway over the entire region from 1916 to 1928. In June 1928, Zhang's train was blown up by a group of Japanese officers in retaliation for his lack of wholehearted enthusiasm for the Japanese occupation of Manchuria. In September 1931, the Japanese attacked Shenyang directly (the famous "Mukden Incident"), and in 1932, set up their puppet state of Manchukuo. They converted the entire region into an industrial base for Japan, siphoning off virtually all resources to the home country.

The Chinese Nationalists occupied the city after 1945. After a bitter ten-month siege, the city fell to the Communists on November 1, 1948. In 1949, the city was renamed Shenyang; the PRC government generally avoids the use of the former colonial names, Manchuria and Mukden.

ECONOMY AND CULTURE

Shenyang lies at the junction of both north-south and east-west rail routes. The largest industrial city in northeastern China, it manufactures electrical equipment (e.g., high-voltage transformers), machines, mining equipment, chemicals, and textiles, and engages in metal refining and food processing.

Efforts to make Shenyang agriculturally self-reliant have been stepped up, and the dry northern terrain now yields soybeans, cotton, tobacco, peanuts, apples, and pears. Afforestation is also a major undertaking, and there are two large nurseries in the area.

The city itself has a home for aged workers, a Workers' Cultural Palace, and 12 parks featuring numerous small lakes. Education facilities include the provincial university, several technical institutes, and a large medical institute.

Shenyang is famous for its acrobatic troupe. Such forms of entertainment have been popular in China for centuries (acrobats were depicted in tomb figures as early as the Tang Dynasty) and are today actively supported by the government. Although most of the major cities have their own troupes, the Shenyang group—which maintains its own school, dormitories, and training facilities—is better known in the West because of its tours to North America and Europe in the 1970s.

◆────────◆
HIGHLIGHTS
FOR TRAVELERS
◆────────◆

The principal incentive for a visit to Shenyang is the chance to tour the city's factories and see some of China's industrial development firsthand. Apart from the Manchu palace and tombs, Shenyang has few points of historical interest.

辽宁省展览中心

Liaoning Exhibition Center. This vast, Soviet-style building in the southern section of the city was constructed in 1959. The exhibit is continually updated with new industrial products turned out in the Shenyang area.

沈阳故宫

The Imperial Palace. When the Manchus established their capital in Shenyang in 1625, the first order of business was to build a proper palace. The result was a complex of some 70 buildings, occupying a space of 50,000 sq. m. (59,800 sq. yd.) and replete with lacquered roof tiles. The project was completed in 1636.

The Shenyang palace was kept up, serving as the second seat of power in the empire after the Manchus moved their capital to Beijing in 1644. The library (Wen Shu Gallery) once held 35,533 volumes, including a massive history of China completed in 1782.

Today, visitors still file past the stone tablets written in Chinese, Manchurian, Mongolian, Uighur, and Tibetan, informing those who enter that they must dismount from their horses before being admitted. The exhibits include the personal effects of the Emperor Qian Long (1736–96) and an assortment of bows, arrows, musical instruments, dresses, pottery, porcelain, carvings, and a bell weighing over four tons. The two 19th-century cannons on display were built for use against the British in the Opium War, but were never fired.

The east and west wings of the palace museum, closed during the Cultural Revolution and reopened only in 1979, contain an exhibition of archeological relics unearthed in the area. Among them are coins of the Warring States period (403–221 BC), bronze articles excavated from tombs of the Han Dynasty (206 BC–AD 220), Neolithic artifacts (from the "Xinyue Site"), and an array of ancient paintings.

北陵公园

North Tomb (Beiling). The tomb bears the remains of Abukai (1592–1643), Nurhachi's son and heir. Succeeding emperors came here to pay homage to their ancestors. By the 19th century, however, the tomb had fallen into disrepair. Since 1949, it has been restored and a large park built around it with lakes, pavilions, and a virtual forest of trees. In the style of the Ming emperors, animal statues line the walkway to the tomb and a stele is inscribed with Abukai's calligraphy. There is a hall of ancestors and an inner court, with the burial mound lying just beyond.

东陵公园

East Tomb (Dongling). Located about 8 km. (5 mi.) east of Shenyang on the banks of the Shen River, this site is the tomb of Nurhachi, the father of Abukai. Nurhachi (who was given the posthumous title of Taizu—"grand progenitor") was a gifted leader, military commander, and scholar.

Travelers who are interested in museums have a choice of two in Shenyang: the Liaoning Provincial Museum (No. 9, Lane 3, Section 2, Sijing Street; tel: 25064); and the Palace Museum (No. 10, Section 2, Shenyang Rd.; tel: 44192). The former was China's first museum erected after 1949. It has on display over 3,000 items, most of which are historical relics from the region.

HOTEL ACCOMMODATIONS

Visitors arriving in Shenyang without prior bookings can receive assistance at the city's Hotel Introduction Center (No. 30, Section 3, Shengli Jie; tel: 33744).

凤凰饭店

Phoenix Hotel (No. 3, Section 6, Huanghe St.; tel: 64854; cable: 6324; telex: 80045 FHFD CN). The Phoenix is Shenyang's newest and most modern hotel. It has 230 double rooms, 20 singles, and 10 suites, all air-conditioned and with private bath, closed-circuit color TV, telephone, and wall-to-wall carpeting. The Phoenix has three restaurants (Chinese, Western, and Japanese), a bar, coffee room, dance hall, and the usual array of services.

Rates for twins are Y50–60; for suites, Y120..

辽宁宾馆

Liaoning Guest House (27 Zhongshan Rd.; tel: 32641). The Liaoning is Shenyang's "grand" hotel, built during the 1930s. Its high ceilings, wide corridors, and marble lobby make it something of a landmark. During the 1940s, it served as a meeting place for representatives of contending political factions in China's civil war. Among the more tangible legacies of those days are some of the finest slate billiard tables found in China. The Liaoning's restaurant serves Beijing, Shandong, and Sichuan dishes.

辽宁大厦

Liaoning Mansion (1 Huanghe St.; tel: 62546). This older hotel is located near Beiling Park in the north of the city. With over 500 rooms, the Liaoning Mansions is the largest hotel in Shenyang. In addition to conference rooms of all sizes, the hotel has a banquet hall, several dining rooms on the ground floor, a club, and an antiques shop.

辽宁友谊宾馆

Liaoning Friendship Hotel (1 Huanghe St., Section 7; tel: 62822; telex: 8002). On the same street as the Liaoning Mansion is the Friendship Hotel. This villa-style hotel has 93 rooms and is set in the midst of a peaceful wooded area. Aside from the usual array of facilities, the Friendship features a heated indoor swimming pool.

Rates range from Y50 for single and double rooms to Y80–130 for suites, and Y180–220 for one of five deluxe suites.

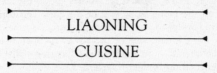

LIAONING

CUISINE

The cooking of northern China is not as elaborate as in other parts of China, but the region has a famous dish said to have originated with the Mongols: *huoguo* ("fire pot"). A charcoal brazier is placed on the table and water boiled. While the water is heating, the service workers will prepare a sauce from rice wine, vinegar, chili sauce, sesame oil, shrimp paste, and soy sauce. Plates of raw meat (beef, mutton, chicken, and perhaps a surprise or two), sliced razor thin, are placed around the table. Guests then cook their own meat.

For dumpling lovers, the Lao Bian Dumpling Restaurant (6 Zhongyang Lu; tel: 447941), located in the Northern Market area, has been serving this famous specialty for over 150 years. Dumplings are stuffed with meat or vegetable fillings.

Restaurants where *huoguo* and other regional specialties may be sampled include the Lumingchun and Shaoyuan on Zhonghua Road in downtown Shenyang, and the Yingbin and Nanhu located on Nanwu Road.

SHOPPING

Handicrafts from Shenyang are relatively undistinguished. Fur items are the favored local purchases. Many tours include a visit to a feather products factory. The city's biggest department store is the Joint Company, located on Zhonghua Street in Heping District. The Liaoning Provincial Antiques Shop, at 29 Taiyuan Street, has a limited selection of porcelain, bronze ware, and handicrafts. Overseas Chinese favor Shenyang's ginseng and antler powders. Shenyang's Friendship Store is located on the third floor of the People's Department Store on Zhongshan Road.

中国国际旅行社

CITS (Luxingshe) Office in Shenyang ■ 3 Huanghe Rd. Tel: 66037.
Telex: 30045 CITSS CN.

Shenzhen

深圳

deep channel   *traditional spelling/Shumchun*

ANYONE riding the Hong Kong–Guangzhou train into China in the 1970s of necessity visited Shenzhen, the sleepy Chinese border station whose main distinction came in providing the first footstep into the People's Republic of China. It used to be that all tourists got off the train at the Lowu customs point on the Hong Kong side of the New Territories and walked across the covered bridge to proceed through customs formalities and money exchanging on the Chinese side of the border at Shenzhen. Since 1978, direct trains, hovercraft, and flight routes have virtually eliminated the stopover at Shenzhen for foreign travelers.

In 1979, however, Shenzhen was snatched from apparent oblivion on the tourist map and earmarked for rapid development into a major tourist site, with added status as a special zone for manufacturing and processing PRC exports. By the mid-1980s, the town was beginning to resemble the satellite towns of Hong Kong's New Territories, replete with traffic jams, high-rise buildings, and youths sporting Walkman stereos and "Twisted Sister" T-shirts. The tremendous influx of new workers and their families has swelled the population more than ten-fold since 1979, reaching some 300,000 as of 1985.

Shenzhen is situated northeast of Hong Kong's Kowloon peninsula and southeast of Guangzhou, between Shenzhen Bay and Mirs Bay. To the west lies the Pearl River Delta. The natural attractions of Shenzhen include sandy beaches, hot springs, strings of lovely islands in the surrounding South China Sea, and a picturesque backdrop of cloud-shrouded mountains.

Its climate is humid and subtropical, like that of neighboring Hong Kong and Guangzhou.

ECONOMY

Early in 1979, Shenzhen city and surrounding Bao'an County were reorganized into a special district called the New Shenzhen Municipality. Local officials were empowered to conclude joint equity business ventures with firms in Hong Kong and Macao, and could do so without seeking the prior approval of Beijing. Shenzhen could also issue visas directly to foreign businesspeople. In May 1980, about one-sixth of the area of Shenzhen Municipality (328 sq. km.; 127 sq. mi.) was declared a "Special Economic Zone"—one of three in Guangdong Province. With respect to this new

Climate		Jan	Feb	Mar	Apr	May	Jun	Jul	Aug	Sep	Oct	Nov	Dec
Temp.	°C	13.1	13.8	17.5	21.9	25.8	27.1	28.3	28.2	27.0	23.8	19.8	15.2
	°F	55	56.8	63.5	71.4	78.4	80.7	82.9	82.7	80.6	74.8	67.6	59.3
Precip.	mm.	152	203	254	279	381	508	457	406	330	203	152	127
	in.	6	8	10	11	15	20	18	16	13	8	6	5

The new face of Shenzhen Special Economic Zone

status, Shenzhen's primary asset may be said to be its proximity to Hong Kong. By mid-1985, foreign investment in the Shenzhen SEZ amounted to over $600 million, about 60% of which was in property-related projects; the remainder was spent on export-oriented assembly and processing industries and agricultural production to increase the supply of foodstuffs to Hong Kong and Macao. The government has invested heavily in infrastructure, including the construction of 80 km. of new roads, a heliport at Nantou, a deepwater port at Shekou, numerous water and power projects, and an up-to-date (and still expanding) telecommunications network.

Since 1979, nearly 3,500 contracts have been signed, and about 1,000 new projects have been started. These include garment factories, knitting mills, radio and automobile assembly plants, and a printing press. In one example, a glove factory was established near the railway station. Its machinery, technicians, and foremen were brought up from Hong Kong while the factory manager was assigned by China. Agricultural development projects are focusing on increasing production of vegetables, lichees, citrus fruits, pineapples, and persimmons, and the expansion of hog, poultry, fish, oyster, and prawn breeding enterprises.

Prices in the SEZ are not linked to China's domestic pricing system but rather to local and international markets. Chinese Foreign Exchange Certificates as well as Hong Kong dollars are the preferred means of exchange; even most wages are paid in these currencies, rather than in renminbi.

HIGHLIGHTS FOR TRAVELERS

The focus of tourist development in Shenzhen is to provide a convenient taste of China for visitors to Hong Kong who might find other PRC tour options prohibitive in terms of time or expense. However, Shenzhen should offer Hong Kong residents a sought-after spot for a quiet respite.

China Travel Service tours feature visits to a factory, a commune, and a trip to the Shenzhen water reservoir, 3 km. (1.9 mi.) north of the city. The reservoir, which is situated amidst striking natural surroundings, provides a substantial proportion of Hong Kong's water supply.

Several old monuments in the area are being spruced up for visitors. These include the Hong Lou (Red Building), the Huzhongting (Pavilion in the Middle of the Lake), and the Changlang (Long Corridor). The Guangming Hot Springs will also be added to the tourist itinerary.

HOTEL ACCOMMODATIONS

The completion of the Bamboo Garden Hotel in February 1981 marked the beginning of a wave of hotel development in Shenzhen that local authorities claimed would produce nearly 200 hotels of various shapes and sizes by 1987. These rather optimistic statistics notwithstanding, the increase in Shenzhen's housing and hotel space since 1980 has been dramatic. As of mid-1985, the town had about 20 major hotels and resorts, most catering to foreign business travelers and weekend sojourners from Hong Kong. Local planners expect Shenzhen to become a popular destination for domestic tourists as well.

One such recent development is the Shenzhen Golf Club Co., Ltd., constructed in 1985. Facilities at this 18-hole course, located on Shen Nan Road, include a clubhouse with a large dining hall and Japanese-style baths. In the future, a 300-room hotel, tennis courts, swimming pool, bowling alley, and villas will be built.

海外讲坛深圳饭店
Overseas Forum Hotel Shenzhen. Due to open in 1989, the Overseas Forum Hotel, operated by Intercontinental Forum Hotels, is located near Lowu railway station. The hotel has 637 rooms. Three restaurants, a lounge, and a disco provide dining and entertainment. Amenities include central air-conditioning, a shopping arcade, Health Club, indoor and outdoor gardens, swimming pool, and closed-circuit television. The four meeting rooms and banquet facilities are available for up to 950. Call 800-327-0200 for reservations.

竹园宾馆
Bamboo Garden Hotel (Dongmen Rd.; tel: 222-934, ext. 500; telex: 420390 BGH CN). This five-story, 183-room hotel has a restaurant and recreation facilities. Rates are HK$310 for twins and singles, and HK$410 for suites.

广信酒店
Guangxin Hotel (East Wing, International Commercial Building, Renmin South Rd.; tel: 22-6471; cable: 2121). Located in the heart of the Special Economic Zone, the Guangxin is geared towards foreign business travelers. Amenities include restaurants and a shopping arcade.

东湖宾馆
Donghu Hotel (Shenzhen Reservoir; tel: 222-77; telex: 42236 ELHSC CN). Located on a hillside along the Shenzhen reservoir, the centrally air-conditioned Donghu features balconied rooms with private bath, color TV, and telephone. Rates are HK$370 for singles and doubles; HK$430 is charged for a suite.

A waterway in South China.

The Donghu has resort facilities, including swimming and wading pools, tennis courts, game and billiard rooms, a playground for children, a health club, and saunas. The Green Lake Restaurant, serving Chinese cuisine, is on the premises, as is a banquet hall which can accommodate groups as large as 250.

雅园宾馆
International Hotel (1 Dong Men Bei Rd.; tel: 222763; telex: 420299 SIHTL CN). In the city itself, the 100-room International (HK$330 for doubles, HK$550 for suites, HK$800 for deluxe suites) is also centrally air-conditioned. Its rooms all have private bath, TV, sound system, and telephone. In addition to a shopping arcade, guests will find a bar, coffee shop, Chinese restaurant, recreation room, and barbershop.

小梅沙海滨度假营
Xiaomeisha Seaside Holiday Camp (Yan Tian). Located in a Shenzhen suburb near a beach, Xiaomeisha Seaside Holiday Camp has 26 air-conditioned rooms with private bath (HK$250 for doubles, HK$330 for triples) as well as camping facilities (HK$20 per person per day). The youth resort features horseback riding and shooting, and also has a bar, coffee shop, and a Chinese restaurant.

香蜜湖渡假村

Honey Lake Country Club (tel: 22-3493). Meant primarily as a holiday resort for Hong Kong residents, the Honey Lake's grounds cover 2.66 sq. km. in Shenzhen's western suburbs. The hotel's chief attractions are its extensive outdoor facilities and a Disneyland-type amusement park, which boasts the world's longest suspended monorail and a 36-meter-high rollercoaster. *Rates:* HK$280 (double); HK$320 (deluxe); HK$450 (suite).

华中国际饭店

Huazhong International Hotel (40 Renmin Nan Rd.; tel: 23-8060). This new joint venture hotel features a rooftop revolving bar. Rates are HK$160 (single); HK$200 (double); HK$350 (suite).

Other hotels include the **Overseas Chinese Mansion** (16 Heping Road; tel: 22-811); the **Nanhai Hotel** (Shekou; tel: 22-2626; telex: 420879 NHHTL CN); and the **Century Plaza** (1 Jianshe Rd.; tel: 22-0888).

中国国际旅行社
CITS (Luxingshe) Office in Shenzhen ◼ 2 Chuanbu St., Heping Rd.
Tel: 38401/27956. Telex: 420250 CITS.

Shijiazhuang 石家庄

Shi family village   *traditional spelling/Shihchiachuang*

SHELTERED by the red-soiled Taihang Mountains to the west and bordered by the fertile Hebei plain which fans out on its other three sides, Shijiazhuang is a railway junction on the Beijing–Guangzhou line, 283 km. (176 mi.) south of Beijing, a four-hour train ride. The city owes its existence almost entirely to the railway; before its construction in 1905, Shijiazhuang was a village of only 500–600 people and had only "six roads, six temples, and four walls," according to county records. Now it has a population of almost 970,000, and serves as the capital of Hebei Province.

The largely residential city center is laid out along broad, tree-lined avenues built since 1949. To the west is a mining area where coal, iron ore, limestone, and marble are extracted. This is a major cotton-growing region. Industry is located mainly in the eastern part of the city and includes textile manufacturing, dyeing, and printing. Shijiazhuang is also the home of northern China's largest pharmaceutical plant, which specializes in antibiotics.

HIGHLIGHTS FOR TRAVELERS

Shijiazhuang is of special interest to Canadian visitors since one of its hospitals (the Norman Bethune International Peace Hospital of the People's Liberation Army) is dedicated to the memory of Dr. Bethune, a Canadian surgeon who came to China in the 1930s to assist the Communist cause.

There are a number of sites in Shijiazhuang which are of religious interest. The Longcang Temple stele was erected during the Sui Dynasty. Adorned with elegant examples of Chinese calligraphy, the stele is one of the oldest and most famous in China. Built during the same period, the Longcang Temple (Buddhist) houses a notable bronze bodhisattva and an exquisite glass screen. Finally, there is the Zhuanlunzang Pavilion. Dating back to the end of the 10th century, the pavilion was orginally used for reciting Buddhist scriptures. Located inside the structure is an octagonal, revolving scripture cabinet representing the Wheel of Life.

Other sites on the tourist's itinerary are likely to include the ancient An Ji Bridge, which dates back to AD 605; the Dongfanghong (East is Red) Exhibition hall, which features local crafts and artwork; a textile mill; and

Climate		Jan	Feb	Mar	Apr	May	Jun	Jul	Aug	Sep	Oct	Nov	Dec
Temp.	°C	−1.4	0.9	7.6	14.7	22.3	26.6	27.6	26.6	21.4	15.7	7.9	0.9
	°F	29.4	33.6	45.6	58.4	72.1	79.8	81.6	79.8	70.5	60.2	46.2	33.6
Precip.	mm.	76	102	76	102	127	203	279	254	152	152	102	76
	in.	3	4	3	4	5	8	11	10	6	6	4	3

Wheat threshing in Hebei Province.

the former Communist Party headquarters from which Mao Zedong, Zhou Enlai, and Zhu De directed the Northern Campaign in 1947–48.

HOTEL ACCOMMODATIONS

河北宾馆
Hebei Guest House (23 Yucai St.; tel: 48961; telex: 26240 PBLSJ CN). Most rooms at this new hotel are doubles (Y45–55), but some triples (Y30) and suites (Y70–90) are also available. All are air-conditioned and have private bath.

A new air-conditioned, eight-story annex has recently been added to the **Shijiazhuang Guest House** (Chang'an Xi Rd.; tel: 49986), which is located in the southeast section of the city.

中国国际旅行社
CITS (Luxingshe) Office in Shijiazhuang ◾ 22 Yucai Rd. Tel: 44766/45239.

The Silk Road

By Mary Israel

AN AURA OF MYSTERY and adventure has always surrounded the Silk Road—an ancient network of caravan trails across the snowcapped mountains and forbidding deserts of Central Asia. Travelers have left vivid accounts of their journeys through the heartland of this vast continent, describing sandstorms called "black hurricanes" (*kara buran*), cities buried under shifting dunes, and desert demons who lead the unwary to their deaths. For more than a millenium this East—West artery not only carried silk and other exotic goods to the Roman and Byzantine empires but also provided the conduit for the eastward expansion of Buddhism. From the 16th century, the development of maritime trade began to displace the arduous land route from commercial prominence and once prosperous regions became provincial backwaters.

The original Silk Road was a matrix of routes that led westward from the Chinese capital of Chang'an (present-day Xi'an) through the narrow

Tajik dance troupe, Xinjiang

Hexi ("West of the River") Corridor (now Gansu Province), passing Lan-zhou, Jiuquan, Jiayuguan, and Dunhuang. Beyond Dunhuang were the terrors of the dread Taklamakan ("No Return") Desert, which occupies most of the Tarim Basin. The caravans traveled by skirting the edge of the Taklamakan, following the string of oasis towns at the foot of the mountains which ring the desert. The northern route out of Dunhuang passed the salt crusts of Lop Nor to Loulan, Kucha, and Aksu—with a safer detour bypassing Lop Nor to Hami and Turpan—leading to Kashgar in the far west at the foot of the Pamirs, over which the road led to Samarkand, Syria, and the Mediterranean. The southern route out of Dunhuang led to Niya, Khotan, and Yarkand before either joining the northern road at Kashgar or heading south to India. A far northern road led through Ürümqi to Ili north of the Tian Shan mountains.

THE SILK ROAD IN HISTORY

The Silk Road first became important during the early Han Dynasty (206 BC–AD 8) when Zhang Qian was sent by Emperor Wu (141–86 BC) to seek allies against the marauding Xiongnu. Although his expedition to the far western regions as far as Bactria failed to produce any military alliances, it brought back detailed knowledge of Central Asia. It also introduced to China important commodities such as the grapevine and alfalfa, as well as the fine horses of Ferghana. The oasis kingdoms became vassals of the Chinese empire and garrisons were maintained along the frontier during subsequent periods of imperial strength. Here in the area variously known as Serindia, Chinese Turkestan, Kashgaria, and Xinjiang, the various cultures of Eurasia met and merged. During the height of the cosmopolitan Tang Dynasty (AD 618–907), the flourishing cities along the trade routes thronged with a polyglot population of Turks, Uighurs, Sogdians, Persians, and Hindus. The religions represented the main belief systems of Asia—Buddhists, Nestorian Christians, Hindus, Manicheans, Zoroastrians, Jews, and Muslims. Religions spread along the trade routes as monasteries and shrines became way stations for caravans in remote areas. Wealthy merchants, local gentry, and craftsmen contributed to the carving and decoration of cave temples, the most extensive of which still survive at Dunhuang's Mogao Grottoes.

The realms to the west took on a luster of romance and mystery for the Chinese as travelers' tales became a part of folklore and legend. Kunlun Mountain was the dwelling place of the Queen Mother of the West (Xi Wang Mu). For the Buddhists, there was the Western Paradise of Amitabha. The best known of Chinese travelers was the Buddhist monk Xuan Zang. He made a pilgrimage to India in search of scriptures, with which he returned to China in AD 445. His journey was fictionalized in the traditional Chinese epic narrative, Xi You Ji (Journey to the West). The supernatural exploits of his companion, the Monkey King, are still celebrated in opera and even animated film. The cultural influences which flowed into China along the Silk Road included the artistic traditions of

Kazak horsewomen

Gupta India, Sassanian Persia, and Indo-Scythia, as well as important motifs in dance and music. The Mongol conquest of China in the 13th century marked the last period of prominence for the Silk Road. Under the rule of Khublai Khan, the Venetian merchant-adventurer Marco Polo served as an official in China from 1275 to 1292. It was during this period that the Muslim influence predominated in the northwest frontier.

Little attention was paid to this remote area during the centuries of maritime exploration and discovery. In the 19th century, Britain and Russia became rivals in the geopolitical "Great Game" over control of Central Asia, sending spies and diplomats into Afghanistan, Turkestan, and Tibet. However, it was the archeological discoveries of the early 20th century that brought world attention to the region. A treasure trove of manuscripts and paintings was found in a sealed cave at Dunhuang; most of this collection eventually found its way to the British Museum and the National Library of Paris, brought there by Sir Aurel Stein and Paul Pelliot. Other relics from the cities and shrines along the Silk Road were carried off by waves of other museum expeditions.

THE CONTEMPORARY LEGACY

As regions just being opened to tourism, Xinjiang and Gansu present a challenge for the adventurous. Hotel facilities are spartan, travel connections are uncertain, and distances are long. The railroad now extends to Ürümqi from Lanzhou, with the following open towns along the route: Turpan, Liuyuan (nearest stop to Dunhuang), Jiayuguan, and Jiuquan. Kashgar,

Ürümqi, Dunhuang, Jiuquan, and Lanzhou are also accessible by air. Bus travel between Dunhuang and Jiuquan passes through the town of Anxi ("Pacify the West"), where roads also lead to Qinghai and Tibet. Roads and rail lines in this arid region are subject to flash flooding, resulting in very bumpy bus travel and train delays. Nevertheless, the intrepid traveler will find his efforts rewarded, not only in the wealth of relics and monuments of the past but also in the multicultural flavor of the region.

The provincial museums at Ürümqi and Lanzhou hold fine collections of cultural relics. The most extensive of the rock-cut temples which mark the millennial spread of Buddhism into China is the Mogao cave complex at Dunhuang. Other Buddhist caves are found at Binglingsi near Lanzhou and Bezeklik near Turpan. Important tombs have been excavated near Jiuquan and at Astana near Turpan, featuring well-preserved bodies and colorful brick tomb paintings. Ruins of the ancient cities of Gaochang and Jiaohe can be visited near Turpan. The western terminus of the Ming Dynasty segment of the Great Wall is located at Jiayuguan.

The heavily Muslim population of Xinjiang, despite the settlement of numerous Hans in the cities and on reclaimed land, gives a special flavor to contemporary life. The costumes are more colorful—embroidered caps on the men, bright scarves and patterned dresses on the women, who also wear jewelry. The bazaars sell everything from whole roast lamb to herbal medicines. Tourists are entertained with Uighur folktales, songs, and dances. Mosques are being refurbished after the destruction of the Cultural Revolution. Visits to encampments of the nomadic Khazakhs often include an exhibition of horsemanship and visits in yurts. The features of many of the minorities in Xinjiang appear more Middle Eastern than Oriental (bearded foreigners find it easier to pass unnoticed in a crowd). Kashgar, the most recently opened tourist city (1983), is probably the most colorful for ethnic population, and its proximity to the Soviet border adds piquancy.

The caravans of foreign tour groups bring a new commercial dimension to the old Silk Road. The vast mineral wealth of the region is being developed in mines and oil fields. Under the demand of tourism, other oasis towns may eventually be opened; Khotan (Hotan), which has an airfield, was once a center for silk, jade, and rugs, and is a likely candidate.

Suzhou

苏州

region of mint   traditional spelling/Soochow

SUZHOU is one of China's oldest continuously inhabited towns and is, by Chinese criteria, among the country's most beautiful cities. As is said in an ancient Chinese proverb, "In Heaven there is Paradise. On Earth, Hangzhou and Suzhou." Suzhou is reachable in no more than a few hours by train from Shanghai, Nanjing, and Wuxi (it has no airport). It sits astride the ancient Grand Canal, not far from the banks of Lake Tai. The city's extensive network of canals is still a vital link for local transportation, truly making Suzhou the "Venice of the East." (Alas, fetid canal water is another feature Suzhou shares with Venice.) Although factory chimneys now far outnumber Suzhou's seven pagodas, the old city has retained its traditional appearance as well as its economic focus on fine handicrafts.

SUZHOU IN HISTORY

Historical records indicate that Suzhou was settled over 3,000 years ago. In 518 BC it rose to prominence as the capital of the Kingdom of Wu. At that time the city was said to have "eight gates and eight water gates." It acquired its present name in AD 589, when work began on the Grand Canal. Marco Polo, who visited Suzhou in the 13th century, found a "noble city and great," with "quite six thousand bridges of stone."

More important, it was a busy merchant town, renowned in China for its fine textiles in gold and silk. The silk industry, still famous today, was developed as early as the Tang Dynasty (AD 618–906). From the 15th century on, there are repeated historical references to silkworkers' strikes, often violent. Yet the people of Suzhou are regarded as graceful and subtle, in part because of the mellifluous quality of the local Wu dialect. According to a popular saying, "Argument in Suzhou is more pleasing than flattery in Ningbo."

The city was held briefly by the Taipings in the 19th century. Treated as an adjunct to Shanghai by the Western powers, it came under the Japanese sphere of influence at the end of that century. Suzhou was occupied by the Japanese during World War II.

ECONOMY AND CULTURE

Until 1949, silk was the city's mainstay. There has been considerable industrial diversification in the last 30 years, including metallurgy, chemicals,

Climate		Jan	Feb	Mar	Apr	May	Jun	Jul	Aug	Sep	Oct	Nov	Dec
Temp.	°C	3.1	4.3	8.4	13.9	19.1	23.0	27.8	28.1	24.1	18.1	12.5	5.9
	°F	37.5	39.7	47.1	57	66.3	73.4	82	82.5	75.3	64.5	54.5	42.6
Precip.	mm.	254	254	330	330	305	356	279	279	305	254	203	178
	in.	10	10	13	13	12	14	11	11	12	10	8	7

machine tools, electronics, and precision instruments. The tradition of craftsmanship has been nurtured and advanced under the modern rubric of light industry, which includes jade and wood carving, sandalwood products, lacquerware, velvet, and tapestries.

The city has a number of educational institutes, among which the National Embroidery Institute is notable. The quality of Suzhou embroidery perhaps rivals that of any in the world today. Sukun opera and Pingtan drama both survive as reflections of the area's distinct cultural heritage.

HIGHLIGHTS
FOR TRAVELERS

GARDENS

It is difficult to dispute the local claim that Suzhou has the most beautiful gardens in all of China. Natural ponds and waterways have been enhanced by more than 150 exquisite gardens that combine traditional elements—pavilions, temples, and rock sculptures—with distinctive arrangements of trees and flowers. The aim has been to create as many perspectives as possible within a confined space and to replicate in miniature scenes from nature not found locally.

The Chinese Garden Society, suspended during the Cultural Revolution, resumed activities in 1978, and the Suzhou Garden Society, a local branch, was founded a year later. Activities of these clubs include academic exchanges with other countries, the fruit of which can be seen at the Metropolitan Museum of Art in New York, where a replica of a Ming Dynasty Suzhou garden went on view in 1981.

As further testimony to the craftsmanship of Suzhou landscape gardeners, an export company was established in late 1979 especially to design and construct large and small classical "Suzhou gardens," including pavilions, courtyards, and rockeries, for overseas clients.

沧浪亭

Surging Wave Pavilion (Canglangting). Laid out on a 10th-century estate, the garden was completed about 1044. Dotted with lookout points, such as the Fish-Watching Pavilion, the Pavilion for Viewing Waters, and the View-of-the-Mountain Pavilion, the garden is designed to evoke the feeling of rambling through thickly forested hills. The garden's poetic name is suggestive of the ebb and flow of the "waters of life." Canglangting has been destroyed and partially reconstructed several times, its most recent demise occurring in 1873 following the Taiping Rebellion. It was fully restored and opened to the public in 1954.

狮子林

Lion Grove (Shizilin). Described in a local brochure as a "veritable labyrinth of hollow caves of spectacular shapes," this garden was first

SUZHOU

Suzhou Railroad Station

Beijing-Shanghai Railroad

Grand Canal

Shantang River

SHANTANG ST.

YAN AN RD.

XIYUAN RD.

LIUYUAN RD.

FENGQIAO RD.

TAOHUAQIAO RD.

JINGGANGSHAN RD.

BEISITA

BAITA RD.

LINDUN RD.

PINGJIANG RD.

East Park
Dong Yuan

N. RENMIN RD.

ZUNYI

JINGDE RD.

GUANQIAN ST.

FENGHUANG RD.

YAN AN RD.

HONGQI RD.

DONGDAJIE RD.

S. RENMIN RD.

GANJIANG RD.

WUSA RD.

Nanlin CITS

SHIQUAN ST.

Suzhou

LAODONG RD.

Grand Canal

NANMEN RD.

SU-FU HIGHWAY

Map ©1986, Eurasia Press

① North Temple Pagoda (Beisita)
② Suzhou Historical Museum
③ The Humble Administrator's Garden (Zhuozhengyuan)
④ Lion Grove (Shizilin)
⑤ Zoo
⑥ Daoist Temple of Mystery (Xuanmiaoguan)
⑦ Friendship Store
⑧ Foreign Languages Bookstore
⑨ National Embroidery Institute
⑩ People's Bazaar
⑪ Garden of Harmony (Yiyuan)
⑫ Stadium
⑬ Twin Pagodas (Shuangta)
⑭ No. 1 People's Hospital
⑮ Garden of the Master of the Nets (Wangshiyuan)
⑯ Surging Wave Pavilion (Canglangting)
⑰ Pagoda of the Temple of the Good Omen Light (Ruiguangsita)
⑱ Han Shan Temple (Hanshansi)
⑲ West Garden (Xiyuan)
⑳ Tarrying Garden (Liuyuan)
㉑ Tiger Hill (Huqiu)

Restaurants

Hotels

landscaped in 1350, during the Yuan Dyansty. The grotesque stones come from nearby Lake Tai. There is also a large pond replete with a stone boat.

拙政园

Humble Administrator's Garden (Zhuozhengyuan). Also known as "Plain Man's Politics Garden," this site was built in 1513 by Wan Xianchen. A not-so-humble administrator, Wang retired to Suzhou to "cultivate his garden"—but only after he had extorted enough money from a court official to build it.

The garden itself reflects the simplicity of Ming Dynasty artistic style. Bridges zigzag at right angles across the many ponds, which cover three-fifths of the entire area. At the center are two connecting islands covered with bamboo. Points of interest include the Pavilion of Fragrant Snow and Azure Clouds, the Pavilion of Expecting Frost, and the Small Flying-Rainbow Bridge.

The Hall of Distant Fragrance, which overlooks the water to the south, is set amidst verandas, towers, and bridges. The garden was completely restored in 1953, but visitors can identify older portions by the more subtle lines and more detailed decorations of the buildings.

留园

Tarrying Garden (Liuyuan). Located about a half-mile northwest of town, the Liuyuan is one of China's four nationally protected gardens (the others are the Humble Administrator's Garden, the Summer Palace in Beijing, and the Imperial Mountain Resort in Chengde). Originally a large country villa, it was first laid out under the Ming Dynasty and rebuilt as a public garden in 1876. It was fully restored in 1953.

Commune workers commute to work via canal, near Suzhou

True to its name, the garden encourages the visitor to amble slowly through its many courtyards and covered walkways. These give way unexpectedly to panoramic views, forested areas, and flower gardens. The halls and corridors of the Eastern Yard are decorated with ancient calligraphy. The pride of the garden is the Cloud-Capped Peak (Guanyun Feng), a rather hyperbolic name for this 400-year-old, 6.5-m. (21-ft.)-high rock from Lake Tai.

怡园
Garden of Harmony (Yiyuan). The most natural and untrammeled of the many gardens in Suzhou, this site features pools with colored pebbles and innumerable flower beds. The garden is noted for four characteristics: stones from Lake Tai, tablets above the entrances, white pine trees, and animal figures.

网师园
Garden of the Master of the Nets (Wangshi Yuan). This is the smallest of the Suzhou gardens (.5 hectare; 1.2 acres) and quite typical of those built by minor officials. Originally laid out during the 12th century, it was abandoned until 1770, when another official decided to restore it. The residence has three courtyards and two floors of chambers and halls. Reflected in a nearby pool are pavilions and a covered corridor with flying eaves, towers, and verandas.

虎丘
Tiger Hill (Huqiu). A "must" on any Suzhou itinerary, this artificial hill is located 3.2 km. (2 mi.) northwest of the main city. It reaches a height of 36 m. (117 ft.) and includes all the traditional elements considered essential to an aesthetically perfect Chinese hill: stones, rocks, plants, trees, pagodas, waterfalls, and a multitude of legends.

The hill was built 2,500 years ago by the King of Wu as a tomb for his father. The name derives from the legendary tiger that guards the tomb. The Yunyan Pagoda at the summit was built in AD 961. Over the centuries it began to tilt, a process halted by recent reinforcement with concrete and steel.

Among the noted sights on the hill is the Hanhan Spring. Legend has it that the spring could be diverted to flood secret passages and thereby trap intruders. There is also a Sword Testing Stone (the Chinese, like so many other cultures, have their own version of the King Arthur Excalibur legend), and a huge flat stone known as the Stone of One Thousand Men, so named because the stains on its surface were believed to be the blood of the workers who built the tomb.

SILK

东方红丝织厂
"East is Red" Silk Weaving Mill. Originally a small backyard workshop, the mill is now a major facility employing 730 pieces of equipment and 2,000 workers and producing more than 250 varieties of fabric.

苏州丝绸印花厂
Suzhou Silk Printing Mill. The factory was founded in 1958 and is almost completely mechanized. It produces nearly a thousand patterns of pure silk, rayon, and other fibers. Many of its products are made specifically for export.

东山洞庭人民公社
Dongshan Dongting Commune. This commune has a diversified economy of grain, fruit, fish, and silk, and is especially known for its tangerines and Lake Tai shrimp.

中国刺绣研究所
National Embroidery Institute. Embroidery is acknowledged as an art form in China and the Institute's display is unparalleled.

GRAND CANAL

The Grand Canal, located immediately west of the city, is the longest man-made waterway in the world. Originally constructed to bear tribute rice from the Yangtse Plain to the imperial government in Luoyang, portions of the canal have remained economically vital through the present day. The segment adjacent to Suzhou is heavily traversed by long lines of cargo barges carrying agricultural products and raw materials from commune fields to urban processing plants or warehouses. The canal's embankments have masonry towpaths which are still in use. The width of the canal averages 30.5 m. (100 ft.) but narrows to about 9 m. (30 ft.) at the numerous picturesque stone bridges that arch gracefully above it. Depths average 2–3 m. (7–10 ft.), adequate for small river craft.

HOTEL
ACCOMMODATIONS

亚士都饭店
Aster Hotel (Fenghuo Road and Sanxiang Road). Due to open in early 1989, this first-class hotel will offer 409 rooms and suites. Facilities at the hotel include six restaurants and lounges, swimming pool, bowling alley, billiard room, shopping arcade, function rooms, and sauna. New World Hotels of Hong Kong will provide management services.

祝回饭店
Zhu Hui Hotel. The first international-class hotel in Suzhou, the Zhu Hui will be managed by the Lee Gardens International Group of Hong Kong. Scheduled for completion in early 1989, this 400-room hotel will be located on a riverbank in one of Suzhou's famous gardens. Facilities will in-

clude Chinese and Western restaurants, a coffee shop, piano bar, health center, disco, tennis courts, and shops.

Visitors to Suzhou will find comfortable lodgings at the **Suzhou Hotel** (115 Shi Quan Rd.; tel: 24646; cable: 6333; telex: 36302 SZTLX CN). Near Canglangting, the hotel is set among farmhouses in a charming old section of the city and has a walled garden. The hotel comprises two buildings: a new, nine-story East Wing, opened in 1979, and the three-story West Wing, built in 1964. The new section's 147 rooms (including two- and three-room suites) are carpeted and air-conditioned. Rooms in the old wing are air-conditioned with comfortable furnishings, although the bathroom facilities are a bit outmoded. Dining rooms in both buildings are located on the ground and first floors. The hotel houses a Friendship Store and a theater that features acrobatics, films, and plays.

The 110-room **Gusu Hotel** (115 Shi Quan Rd.; tel: 25126; telex: 36302 GSH CN; cable: 1196) is located within the same complex as the Suzhou. All of its rooms are equipped with air-conditioning, TVs, and refrigerators. Facilities include a nightclub, dance hall, and coffee shop. Recent reports from the Gusu indicate that management needs to clean up its act before it can be recommended.

The new nine-story **Nanlin (South Forest) Hotel** (20 Gunxiu Lane; tel: 24641; telex: 34094 SZCC CN) in the same part of town offers visitors pleasant rooms and the usual tourist amenities.

Lower priced accommodations are available at the **Lexiang (Paradise) Hotel** (18 Dajing Lane, off Renmin Rd.; tel: 22-890).

CUISINE

Suzhou has a well-earned reputation for dining. The city's restaurants—usually small and simply furnished—have traditionally attracted patrons from as far away as Nanjing and Shanghai. Regional seafood specialties, including eel, fish, shrimp, and crabs, Suzhou-style almond duck, and sugar-braised pork are served at the Xinjufeng Restaurant (615 Renmin Rd.; tel: 23794); the Songhelou Restaurant (141 Guanqian St.; tel: 22066); the Yichangfu Restaurant (1 Shi Rd.; tel: 22832); and the Suzhou Hotel and Nanlin Hotel dining rooms. No Suzhou repast is complete without a pot of jasmine tea.

Restaurants do an especially brisk business during the city's numerous food festivals, the most popular ones coinciding with changes in season. One of the most esteemed is the crab feast, which takes place in early autumn. Local fishermen congregate at a small, shallow lake 8 km. (5 mi.) northeast of Suzhou. There, armed with bamboo traps, they snare crabs as they emerge from the crevices where they have just laid eggs. The resulting dish is called *dazhaxie*.

Suzhou is also known for its sweets. The renowned Daoxiangcun Candy and Cake Store and Huangtianyuan Stuffed Dumpling Shop on Guanqian Street feature saltwater pumpkinseed candy, pine nut and sesame cakes, and dried and roasted nuts. Indeed, weight-watchers are advised to miss Guanqian Street altogether—or to visit it only at a dead run.

SHOPPING

Handicraft fanciers will also enjoy Suzhou, which is known for its embroidery, sandalwood fans, jade carvings, wrought gems, and, of course, silks. Selections are available at the Friendship Store, across from the "Wonderful Lookout" (92 Guanqian Street; tel: 4824), or at the department store, located on Ziyuanchang just across the street from the Pleasure Garden. Both are within 4 km. (2.5 mi.) of the above-mentioned hotels.

Other shops of interest include the Antiques Store (central section of Renmin Rd.; tel: 4972); the Renmin Market (Beiju; tel: 2508); and the Arts and Crafts Shop (entrance of Jingde Rd.; tel: 5513). Traditional Chinese musical instruments can be bought "for a song" at the crafts shop in the rear of the Temple of Mystery, just off Guanqian Road.

中国国际旅行社
CITS (Luxingshe) Office in Suzhou ▣ 115 Shiquan Rd. Tel: 22593.
Telex: 36302 SZTLX CN.

泰山

Tai Shan

exalted mountain

traditional spelling / Taishan

ANCIENT Chinese cosmology theorized that the earth was square and, likewise, that China—bounded by four cardinal mountains—had a square shape. Emperors periodically toured the four peaks in order to take stock of their realm. Tai Shan, the most easterly of the four sacred mountains, commanded the emperor's greatest attention since it was believed that from here the sun began its westward journey across the sky.

No longer do Chinese "sons of heaven" ascend Mount Tai to investigate their dominion, but contemporary pilgrims, ordinary Chinese, and foreigners alike make the arduous climb up rugged Mount Tai (the emperor used to be carried by slaves on a sedan chair), most in hope of catching a spectacular sunrise.

Alas, at an altitude of 1,545 m. (5,069 ft.) above sea level, the peak of Tai Shan is frequently enveloped in mist. It is therefore strictly a matter of good fortune to be able to enjoy the fabled view of the surrounding countryside of Shandong Province. Clear skies are usually encountered about halfway down the mountain.

THE ASCENT OF MOUNT TAI

Central Route. The central of the three available routes (eastern, central, and western) is the most popular. This trail passes a number of ornamented gateways, arches, temples, and caves, many bearing inscriptions and each having its own history and legends based in Chinese folklore. Besides these historical monuments, scattered peasant huts and tiny plots of cultivated land are seen along the route. Conveniently, a number of teahouses beckon weary climbers.

A popular resting spot is the ground under the Wutaifu pines, about halfway up the mountain. Qin Shi Huangdi (221–210 BC), the first emperor of China, named these trees "Wutaifu" after an official of his court who sheltered the emperor from a torrential downpour under the pines at this spot. Today's pines were planted in 1730. Other landmarks include the Taicong archway at the southern foot of the mountain; the Wangmuchi (Pool of Wangmu), named after the most prominent Daoist goddess, the Queen of the Immortals; and a former Buddhist convent called the Doumugong (Temple of the Goddess of the Great Bear), situated near the Wutaifu pines. Nearby is the Baidong (Tunnel of Cypresses), a shady walkway formed by the intertwining branches of ancient cypresses. Approaching

Climate		Jan	Feb	Mar	Apr	May	Jun	Jul	Aug	Sep	Oct	Nov	Dec
Temp.	°C	−7.7	−6.6	4.4	15.5	21.1	26.6	26.6	26.6	21.1	15.5	4.4	−7.7
	°F	18	20	40	60	70	80	80	80	70	60	40	18
Precip.	mm.	76	102	76	102	127	203	279	254	152	152	102	76
	in.	3	4	3	4	5	8	11	10	6	6	4	3

the summit, one reaches the Nantianmen (South Gate to Heaven), a stone archway which leads to the iron-tiled roof of the Bixia Si (Azure Cloud Temple). At the summit of the peak itself is the Yuhuang Ting (Emperor of Heaven Pavilion).

Western Route. For variation, some pilgrims descend via the western trail. Although it contains no historic monuments comparable to those of the central path, it does offer some splendid natural scenery, including a lovely waterfall. It is worth stopping at Feng Yuxiang's tomb, where a large stone monument was erected in 1952 in memory of the "Christian General," a powerful warlord of northeast China in the 1940s. The tomb bears an inscription by Guo Moruo, the famous PRC poet-intellectual who died in 1978.

A road has been constructed along the western trail to take tourists by motorbus from the foot of Mount Tai to the Zhongtianmen (Central Gate to Heaven). By 1982, an aerial tramway began operation to complete the ascent to the Yuhuang Ting. Some pilgrims complain that the asphalt and gondolas will defile the sacred mountain and eliminate the experience of climbing by foot. But modern transportation will make it possible for the lame, the old, and the lazy to reach the top of Mount Tai. Devotees of Buddhism (and fitness) will still be able to trek up the central trail, with views unobstructed by modern improvements.

The ascent can be completed by speedy climbers within three hours. At a leisurely pace—including rest stops and pagoda-gazing—the journey should require seven or eight hours. From Zhongtianmen—midway up the mountain—the rather steep grade coupled with unpredictable weather may slow the walk. Although about 6,000 steps are carved into the side of Tai Shan, and rest stops such as teahouses and pavilions dot the central route up, it is still recommended that only the physically fit, shod in the sturdiest footwear, attempt the climb.

泰山寺
Tai Shan Temple. At the foot of the mountains stands the Tai Shan Temple, a group of ancient buildings containing many cultural relics. Tai

Shan Temple is one of China's three great, ancient, palace-style buildings, the other two being the Hall of Supreme Harmony in Beijing's Forbidden City and the Confucian Temple in Qufu, Shandong Province. The original temple was built during the Han Dynasty (206 BC–AD 220), with pavilions constructed during the Tang (618–907) and Song (960–1279). Inside the temple, an enormous Song mural depicts the god of Tai Shan setting off on an inspection tour and later returning to his palace here.

HOTEL

ACCOMMODATIONS

Tourists whose schedules permit an overnight stay and who hope to catch the sunrise from atop Mount Tai can stay at a simple hostel at the peak of Tai Shan. Although utterly lacking in luxuries, the Mount Tai Guest House does provide warm bedding—a welcome and necessary comfort during the cold nights that enshroud Mount Tai year-round.

At the foot of Tai Shan there is another hostel which can accommodate about 100 overnight visitors. A new hotel contains about 250 beds.

Day trips to the mountain by train or car from Jinan, the capital of Shandong Province, or from Qufu, the birthplace of Confucius, can also be arranged.

Taiyuan

great plain

TAIYUAN, the capital of Shanxi Province, is situated at the north end of the fertile Taiyuan Basin. As late as 3000 BC, this vast plain was covered by a huge lake. Thousands of stone artifacts dating from the end of this region's Neolithic era, about 2,500 years ago, have been discovered near the town.

Taiyuan's long and dramatic history stems in part from its proximity to rich natural resources—the Taiyuan Basin contains some of the largest coal and iron ore deposits in the world. Strategically located at the gateway to southeast China, Taiyuan was repeatedly invaded by northern armies determined to conquer the Chinese empire.

Between 1889 and 1909, Western powers promoted Taiyuan's development. They built a railway line from Taiyuan east to Hebei Province, introduced electricity, installed telephone and telegraph lines, and established a military academy and a university. Since the founding of the PRC in 1949, Taiyuan's industrial base has been further expanded, particularly in coal mining, steel production, chemicals, and textiles. The city's population, continuously on the increase from the end of the 19th century, today totals two million and is rapidly growing.

Taiyuan's climate is temperate. In January, the coldest month, temperatures drop to about −12°C (6°F). In July, the hottest month, temperatures average 26°C (78°F), and rains are frequent in summer.

TAIYUAN IN HISTORY

Taiyuan has been the site of constant armed conflict from its earliest beginnings. The city and its environs have 27 temples originally dedicated to the God of War. Jinyang, the forerunner of Taiyuan, was founded under the Western Zhou Dynasty (c. 1066–771 BC). During the Han Dynasty (206 BC–AD 220), the Xiongnu tried but failed to break through the Great Wall to invade the Taiyuan area to the south. In AD 312, they succeeded in capturing Jinyang, which they retained until the Central Asian Toba people established the Wei Dynasty in AD 396. When the Toba were defeated in 532, Jinyang was declared the capital of the Northern Qi (550-77). Numerous palaces, gardens, Buddhist temples, and shrines were built at this time. In 576, the Northern Qi Dynasty was conquered by the Northern Zhou (577–81), whose armies briefly occupied the town until the Sui

Climate		Jan	Feb	Mar	Apr	May	Jun	Jul	Aug	Sep	Oct	Nov	Dec
Temp.	°C	−4.7	−1.9	4.8	13.7	20.1	24.8	26.1	24.8	19.9	12.8	3.8	2.8
	°F	23.5	28.6	40.6	56.6	68.1	76.6	78.9	76.6	67.8	55	38.8	37
Precip.	mm.	76	76	76	102	152	203	305	254	178	152	102	76
	in.	3	3	3	4	6	8	12	10	7	6	4	3

Dynasty was established in 581. The Sui fortified Jinyang with palaces, towering walls, and military roadways leading east to Hebei. A successful revolt in Jinyang overthrew the Sui and led to the establishment of the Tang Dynasty in 618. The Tang (618–907) introduced great wealth and splendor to Jinyang, transforming it into a cultural as well as a political center. However, the city was continually harrassed by northern Turkic armies, who finally deposed the Tang in 906.

Between 906 and 960, Jinyang changed hands several times, as a succession of rulers attempted to assert dynastic control over the area. When China finally reunited under the Song (960–1279), the inhabitants of Taiyuan resisted integration into the new empire. After a prolonged siege in 969, Emperor Tai Zu resorted to flooding the city by diverting the waters of the Fen River. In 976, his imperial army was nevertheless forced to retreat. In 976, he attempted a second siege, this time forcibly resettling tens of thousands of peasants in Henan Province to the east, but to no avail. In 979, Tai Zu attacked with five armies, finally forcing the city to surrender. He burned Jinyang to the ground and diverted the waters of the Fen and Jin rivers to wash away the ashes. Today no trace of this fiercely independent city remains.

Taiyuan, the city which subsequently grew up on the site of the former Jinyang, emerged with a wholly different character. It was a busy commercial center, with narrow streets, bustling markets, and an urbane populace. It also became a center for handicrafts and culture. The first state pottery

Iron tapping at a foundry

kilns were established here under the Song. Taiyuan opera and theater developed. Taiyuan remained an enticing military target, however. It was attacked by the Jin in 1126 and again by the Mongols in 1218. The Ming Dynasty (1368–1644) strengthened its walls and fortifications, but internal revolt remained a problem. In 1644, when the famous peasant leader Li Zicheng attempted to establish a new dynasty here, he was welcomed by the Taiyuanese, but the town fell under the cannonades of the just-founded Qing Dynasty (1644–1911). (The story of Li's popular uprising is currently being made into a film and several novels have already been written about it. The Taiyuanese annually commemorate Li Zicheng at the time of the Lunar New Year.)

Secret societies, established in Taiyuan as far back as the 11th century, participated in the Boxer Rebellion of 1900. After the Revolution of 1911, the northern warlord Yan Xishan seized the city and ruled it as an absolute dictator from 1912 until the Communist victory of 1949.

HIGHLIGHTS
FOR TRAVELERS

The temples in the suburbs and area surrounding Taiyuan include the Jindaifu Si (Temple of the Jin Minister), whose buildings date from 1343; the Guguandi Miao (Ancient Temple to the God of War), which dates from the Song and contains a rare 10-ft.-high bronze statue of the god of war; and the Yongzuo Si (Monastery of Endless Happiness), whose two pagodas also appear on the Taiyuan municipal banner. Visitors may also want to see the valuable collection of sutras at the Chongshan Si (Temple Where Goodness is Esteemed) in the southeastern part of town. Other highlights include:

山西省博物馆
Shanxi Museum. This provincial museum is well worth a visit. It displays many Neolithic artifacts discovered in recent years, as well as examples of the area's famous handicrafts, including bronze coins from the Warring States period (403–221 BC) and glazed tiles from the Tang and Song eras. Stone carvings from the Western Han (206 BC–AD 23) and numerous artifacts from Han, Tang, and Song burial sites are also exhibited.

晋祠文物保管所
Jinci Temple. Some 25 km. (15 mi.) southeast of Taiyuan, near bubbling springs in a grove of cypress trees, stands a group of temples built by the Jin family during the Northern Wei Dynasty (386–534) in memory of Shu Yu, the son of the famous King of Wu.

The largest and most important of these temples is the Shengmudian (Sacred Mother Hall), a beautiful example of Song architecture, which contains 44 statues of Song ladies-in-waiting. Realistically depicted in natural poses, these figures provide an example of the sophisticated art of an urbane society. Unfortunately, they have been repainted in somewhat garish colors. The Shengmudian area, replete with bridges, pools, pavilions, and caves, is well worth a visit.

五台山

Wutai Shan (Mt. Wutai). Situated about 175 km. (110 mi.) northeast of Taiyuan (midway between Taiyuan and Datong) is 3,058-m. (10,033-ft.)-high Mt. Wutai. It is one of the Chinese Buddhist "Four Great Peaks" (the others are Emei Shan, in Sichuan; Putuo Shan, near Ningbo; and Jiuhua Shan, in Anhui Province), each of which is associated with a particular bodhisattva. Mt. Wutai is traditionally the spot where the Bodhisattva of Wisdom—Manjusri—appeared in China. Remote and cold, even in summer (it is also known as Cold Clear Mountain), Mt. Wutai will nevertheless prove to be a worthwhile stop for Buddhists, temple enthusiasts, and those who enjoy getting off the beaten path. Of the many monasteries and lamaseries that once dotted the mountainside, only two remain intact: the Foguang (Light of Buddha) Temple and the Nanchan (Southern Zen) Temple. A travel permit is required.

SHANXI CUISINE

Perhaps the most famous local cuisine is *tounao*, a thick soup made of mutton, lotus root, yam, herbs, and rice wine. The dish is said to have been concocted by Fu Shan, a noted philosopher and a scientist of the Qing Dynasty. Originally named "eight-treasure soup," *tounao* was created as a tonic for his ailing mother, who thereupon recovered to live a very long life. The best *tounao* in town is served at the Qingheyuan Restaurant (Qiatou Jie; tel: 29160). Taiyuan is also noted for dishes made with wheat, such as *shaomei* dumplings. Visitors can sample these and other local dishes at the Jinyang Restaurant (located on May 1st Square; tel: 25702) and the Jinyuanchun Restaurant (Mao'er Lane).

HOTEL
ACCOMMODATIONS

Taiyuan's newest hotel is the **Sanjin Hotel**. Located on the southeast corner of May 1st Square, the 14-story hotel has 300 rooms (suites, doubles, and singles), a souvenir shop, restaurants, and conference rooms. Directly across the square from the Sanjin is the **Bingzhou Hotel** (32 Yingze St.; tel: 25924; telex: 28125 TYBZH CN; cable: 1629). The hotel's south and west buildings contain 10 first-class suites as well as singles and doubles. Both hotels are in the downtown area, close to the bus terminal and the Taiyuan Railway Station.

The biggest hotel in Taiyuan is the **Yingze Guest House** (51 Yingze Jie; tel: 23211). The hotel's east and west wings contain a total of 596 beds. In addition to the usual array of services, the Yingze Hotel offers a choice of 26 lounges and conference rooms and 10 dining halls.

The hotel with the most scenic surroundings is the **Jinci Guest House** (Nanjiao; tel: 29941), located 25 km. from Taiyuan and directly behind the Jinci Temple. Each of the eight villas which make up the Jinci has its own dining area.

中国国际旅行社
CITS (Luxingshe) Office in Taiyuan ◼ Yingze Guest House. Tel: 441155.
Telex: 28009 ITSTY CN.

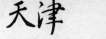 # Tianjin

entrance to the heavenly capital   *traditional spelling/Tientsin*

TIANJIN, China's third largest city, is located some 50 km. (31 mi.) from the Bohai Gulf and is easily reached from Beijing by a two-hour train ride. It sits astride China's largest artificial harbor and is a key transportation hub serving the populous North China Plain. The city is also one of China's leading industrial centers. Tianjin has a population of 7.9 million spread over an area of 11,000 sq. km. (4,200 sq. mi.), and is the smallest of China's three centrally administered municipalities (the others are Beijing and Shanghai). The city extends for almost 16 km. (10 mi.) along the banks of the Hai River, a factor which in the past made the city (with an average elevation of 4.8 m. [16 ft.]) constantly vulnerable to flooding. In recent years, water-control projects have all but eliminated this threat.

Designated in 1984 as one of China's 14 Coastal Open Cities, Tianjin was one of the four urban centers (including Dalian, Guangzhou, and Shanghai) chosen for accelerated economic development in 1986. Through mid-1985, nearly 40 joint-venture contracts had been signed. In that year, construction began on a new industrial park in Tanggu, site of Tianjin's Economic and Technical Development Zone.

TIANJIN IN HISTORY

Recently unearthed records indicate that Tianjin's original site dates back to the Warring States period (403–221 BC). However, continuous settlement apparently did not begin until about 800 years ago, when the city was known as Zhigu ("buying and selling").

The origin of the city itself can be traced back to AD 1368 when a frontier garrison was established there. From this point, Tianjin began to assume its characteristic role as a transshipment point for grain from the southern provinces to Beijing (then called Beiping). The city walls were built in 1404 but were destroyed during the Boxer Rebellion of 1900.

In 1858, Western powers seeking a foothold for the China trade pressed for Tianjin's designation as a treaty port. When the Chinese refused to ratify the treaty within the stipulated one-year period, the British and French governments took matters into their own hands. In 1860, they bombarded the city, landed troops here, and marched on to the capital, Beijing. Tianjin was subsequently parceled out among British, French, and other Western concessions. Western-style buildings were constructed, an electric tram installed, port facilities improved, and light

Climate		Jan	Feb	Mar	Apr	May	Jun	Jul	Aug	Sep	Oct	Nov	Dec
Temp.	°C	−4.2	−1.7	4.7	13.2	19.7	24.4	26.6	25.8	20.9	14.0	4.6	−2.2
	°F	24.5	28.9	40.4	55.7	67.4	75.9	79.8	78.4	69.6	57.2	40.2	28
Precip.	mm.	76	76	76	102	152	229	330	279	178	152	102	76
	in.	3	3	3	4	6	9	13	11	7	6	4	3

industry (mainly textiles) expanded. By 1915, nine foreign powers maintained territorial concessions in the city: Britain, France, Japan, Germany, Belgium, Russia, Italy, Austria-Hungary, and the US.

Early in the 20th century, heavy silting of the Hai River forced the rebuilding of the port 50 km. (31 mi.) downstream at the town of Tanggu. During the Japanese occupation (1937–45), a major construction program was begun to develop an artificial harbor and deep-water berthing facilities. These were completed under the PRC in 1952. A second major expansion, including facilities to handle containerized cargo, was carried out in 1976.

The city suffered heavy damage during the Tangshan earthquake (1976). A massive housing construction effort was completed in 1982 providing new homes for persons displaced by the earthquake. Tianjin remains notable for its European-style public buildings and Victorian mansions. One such house—on Racecourse Road—was the home of Herbert Hoover during the Boxer Rebellion of 1904.

ECONOMY AND CULTURE

Tianjin's economy is dominated by its port and heavy industry. Ships displacing up to 10,000 tons can berth in the new artificial port, with vessels up to 3,000 tons serving Tianjin itself. Heavy industry includes iron and steel, motor vehicles and parts, and heavy machinery. Chemicals, electronics, watches, sewing machines, and cameras comprise some of the city's light industry. Tianjin-made elevators are used throughout China.

The city's most famous products are Tianjin carpets. Eight major factories produce some 125,400 sq. m. (150,000 sq. yd.) of carpets yearly. Other notable handicrafts items produced are "Zhang family" colored clay sculpture and fancifully designed Tianjin kites. Tianjin also takes pride in producing two of China's most prestigious brands of bicycles, Flying Pigeon and Red Flag. They are considered the "Cadillacs" of Chinese bicycles.

The area is also rich in natural resources. Some of the China's largest coal mines are in nearby Tangshan. The major Dagang oil field is now supplemented by extensive new offshore discoveries. In agriculture, the Tianjin area produces wheat, corn, and rice, and has a thriving dairy industry. Fruit is also grown, and the local pears are notable for their size and juiciness.

HIGHLIGHTS
FOR TRAVELERS

While Tianjin is becoming an important stop on the itineraries of business travelers, it still remains off the beaten track for most foreign visitors to China. Foreign tourist volume in 1985 was 38,156, about 8% of Beijing's total. Tourists, however, will find that the city holds a number of attractions, including two major new projects: a Science and Technology Exchange Center, which entered service in early 1987; and a new Trade Exhibition Center, completed in 1987. Both are located near the Tianjin Guest House.

地毯二，三，五厂

Nos. 2, 3, 5, Carpet Factories. Visitors are frequently taken to one of these factories. They are large enterprises with over 1,000 workers, mostly women. Carpet weaving has a 2,100-year-old history in China. Most Tianjin carpets are still woven entirely by hand. Designs are then etched with scissors to impart an embossed effect.

天津杨柳青画社

Yanglin Art Society. The Yanglin is a commercial workshop for artists and artisans who "mass produce" their materials—a typical Chinese commercial art enterprise. Yanglinqing New Year Pictures originated in the small town of the same name in the Western suburbs of Tianjin during the early 17th century. These pictures have developed into a local art form, characterized by combining woodblock printing with handpainting. A familiar motif of Yanglinqing prints are groupings of cherubic children. A typical New Year picture depicts a chubby child holding a large fish (which in Chinese has the same sound as the word for "abundance") and a lotus flower (assonant with the word for "continuous"). Prints are offered for sale at a shop on the premises. The Yangling Art Society is located at III Sanhelin, Tonglou, in the Hexi District.

古文化街

Ancient Culture Street. Ancient Culture Street spans about 600 m. along the Hai River in downtown Tianjin. This area was the earliest residential area of Tianjin, originally inhabited by fishermen, and has been restored with period buildings from the Ming and Qing dynasties.

Culture Street is entered through an archway proclaiming it to be "The Cradle of the City." It was here that local fishermen later entered the business of shipping grain via the Grand Canal to Beijing. Today's Culture Street is home to numerous shops selling old and new books, stationery, porcelain, carpets, and local arts and crafts. There are also a number of small snack shops offering *baozi* and *jiaozi*, as well as a pleasant restaurant called Tian Fei Lou, offering Cantonese cuisine.

In the midst of Culture Street one comes across the Temple of Lin Mo Niang, a goddess who was said to protect fishermen going out to sea. The temple was built in 1326, and currently houses a Folk Museum, which displays various artifacts descriptive of Tianjin lifestyle during the Ming and Qing periods.

In front of Lin Mo Niang Temple is a small square with stage. Here on some evenings amateur performances take place. It is also the site of a major celebration at the time of Lin Mo Niang's birthday, usually falling in late March (by the Chinese calendar).

Weaving Tianjin's world-famous carpets

商业街

Commercial Street. Called "Heping Lu" in Chinese, this street is touted locally as the busiest shopping center in China. Some 3 km. in length with more than 500 shops and commercial outlets, the street is said to attract upwards of 700,000 shoppers daily.

财政街

Financial Street. Located in the old British and French concessions, this was once called Tianjin's "Wall Street." Buildings on both sides of the street still maintain a distinct Western architectural style. Financial Street is currently the seat of Tianjin's banking and investment institutions as well as its municipal government.

水上公园

Park on the Water (Shuishang Gongyuan). One of the many large parks in Tianjin, Park on the Water contains a museum (with Ming and Qing dynasty paintings), a restaurant, and a lake for boating.

Other sites of interest include the Tianjin Art Museum at 77 Jiefang Bei Road, the Industrial Exhibition Hall on Machang Road, and the Zhou Enlai Memorial Hall in the city's western sector (commemorating Zhou's student days at Nankai University and his early revolutionary activities in Tianjin). Tianjin is an interesting city for casual strolling. Visitors will find the old city with its maze of narrow streets, bazaars, and traditional houses a delightful contrast to the pink marble villas and Victorian mansions in the former concession areas. The Friendship Hotel, located near the center of town, is a good departure point for walking tours.

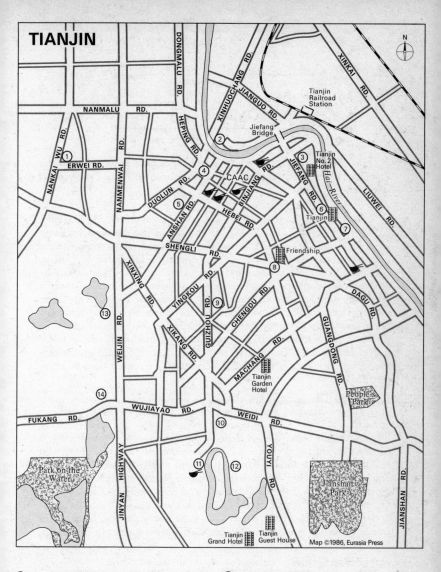

TIANJIN

N

- NANKAI WU RD.
- ERWEI RD.
- NANMALU RD.
- DONGMALU RD.
- HEPING RD.
- NANMENWAI RD.
- XINHUOCHANG RD.
- JIANGUO RD.
- XINKAI RD.
- Tianjin Railroad Station
- Jiefang Bridge
- Jiefang Bridge
- JIEFANG RD.
- Tianjin No. 2 Hotel
- Hai River
- LIUWEI RD.
- CAAC
- BINJIANG
- DUOLUN RD.
- ANSHAN RD.
- HEBEI RD.
- Tianjin
- SHENGLI RD.
- XINXING RD.
- YINGKOU RD.
- GUIZHOU RD.
- CHENGDU RD.
- Friendship
- DAGU RD.
- WEIJIN RD.
- XIKANG RD.
- MACHANG RD.
- GUANGDONG RD.
- People's Park
- Tianjin Garden Hotel
- FUKANG RD.
- WUJIAYAO RD.
- WEIDI RD.
- YOUYI RD.
- JINYAN HIGHWAY
- JIANSHAN RD.
- Jianshan Park
- Park on the Water
- Tianjin Grand Hotel
- Tianjin Guest House

Map ©1986, Eurasia Press

① Zhou Enlai Memorial Hall
② First Workers' Cultural Palace
③ Art Museum
④ Department Store
⑤ Tianjin Medical College Hospital
⑥ Post and Telecommunications Office
⑦ Friendship Store
⑧ Foreign Trade Bureau
⑨ People's Gymnasium
⑩ Yangliuqing (Green Willow) Paintings Store
⑪ Tianjin Friendship Club
⑫ Industrial Exhibition Hall
⑬ Tianjin University
⑭ Nankai University

⏖ Restaurants

🏢 Hotels

HOTEL

ACCOMMODATIONS

A brace of new hotels added in the mid-1980s have begun to transform Tianjin's rather uninviting image and have substantially raised the comfort level of a stay in the city.

天津喜来登大酒店

Sheraton Tianjin (Zi Jin Shan Road, Hexi District; tel: 33-3388; telex: 23353/4 SHTJH CN; fax: 318740). Surrounded by the Yan Gardens, waterways, and a lake, this newest Sheraton is located only 10 minutes from the downtown business district. The hotel, opened in December 1987, offers 282 rooms, including 15 suites and 17 alcove studio suites. Such amenities as direct-dial telephone, electric coffeepot, refrigerator, minibar, and color television are available in all rooms. Among the facilities are three restaurants and a bar, Tianjin's only indoor swimming pool, gymnasium, sauna and steam room, jogging path, business center, banquet hall for up to 325, function rooms, and gift shop. The hotel also has bicycles available free of charge for guests and its own fleet of taxis. Special winter rates available. *Rates:* Singles/doubles: $55–65; executive suite: $95; presidential suite: $200.

胜利宾馆

Victory Hotel (11 Jintang Road, Tanggu District; tel: 984984/985833; telex: 23375 TJVH CN; cable: 5833). New in 1988, the Victory Hotel, managed by the Nendels hotel chain, is the product of a joint venture with Sinden Co., Ltd., of Hong Kong. It is situated near the Bohai seashore, next to Xingang harbor and the Tianjin Economic and Technical Development Zone. The hotel has 350 rooms, including standard rooms and suites. Features include a coffee shop, athletic and recreational facilities, a disco, and two restaurants, the Emerald Fragrance Palace, serving Chinese cuisine, and Columbus' Restaurant, which offers American-style food. Reservations can be booked in the U.S. at (800) 547-0106. *Rates:* Single: $45–57; double: $55–67.

天津凯悦饭店

Hyatt Tianjin. The 450-room Hyatt Tianjin officially opened for business on August 15, 1986, becoming Tianjin's first entry in the deluxe hotel category. It is a joint venture between a Hong Kong company and the Tianjin No. 1 Hotel, which it has supplanted. The Hyatt is located on the banks of the Hai River, about four minutes' walk from both the central train station and the city's commercial district.

Rooms at the Hyatt are large and inviting, decorated in tones of salmon-peach. All rooms have air-conditioning, color TV, radio, in-house movies, piped-in music, executive bar and refrigerator, and international direct-dial telephones. The top two floors house Hyatt's well-established Regency Club system, with concierge service and a Regency Club lounge offering complimentary continental breakfasts, all day tea/coffee service, and complimentary evening cocktails and canapés.

Among the services to be introduced through 1987 will be a Hyatt Business Center—offering secretarial services, interpreters, and information on local commerce, industry, and finance. Also available will be an airport limousine service, beauty salon (with Hong Kong hairdressers), shopping arcade, photo service, in-house medical clinic, and 24-hour room service. Restaurants include the Pines Café restaurant—a bright, airy room with a river view—serving an imaginative selection of Western food; a Cantonese restaurant; Nimaguchi—a Japanese restaurant with tempura bar and teppanyaki; and a Tianjin Dumpling Snack Bar. On the culinary side, the Hyatt claims a strict policy of using only fresh fruits and vegetables. To this end the hotel has purchased ten hothouses on the outskirts of Tianjin, where they grow their own lettuce, tomatoes, mushrooms, etc. Soon, Hyatt plans to begin raising its own pigs and chickens (also presumably off the premises). The Hyatt Tianjin also has a health spa, with sauna, steam rooms, Jacuzzi, and massage. But due to some unfathomable Tianjin city ruling, the spa is restricted to men only.

The Hyatt offers its facilities at rates averaging about $20 less than those at the luxury hotels in Beijing. They are therefore hoping to attract commuter clientèle who will transact their business in Beijing and return to Tianjin for the evening, using the one-hour, 40-minute express train service.

Bookings at the Hyatt Tianjin may be made through Hyatt's worldwide reservations system.

Address: Jiefang Road North
Telephone: 31-8888
Telex: 23270 HYTJN CN
Rates: Standard: $80; superior: $90; deluxe: $90; Regency Club: $100; junior suite: $180; parlor suite: $300; presidential suite: $550

天津水晶宫饭店

Crystal Palace Hotel. With its rather unlikely sounding name (for China), the Crystal Palace opened in 1987. The deluxe, 348-room hotel is a joint venture with a US architectural firm (Wu International) and is managed by Swissôtel, the hotel management division of Swissair. The hotel graces the edge of a small lake, approximately 12 minutes from downtown Tianjin and 20 minutes from the railroad station. Its design consists of two wings which radiate from a central core containing the lobby and major facilities. The left wing (with more than 200 rooms) opened in October 1986.

The hotel's facilities will include a health club, swimming pool, tennis courts, beauty parlor, drugstore, boutique, and business center with its own lounge and bar. There is a banquet hall for up to 250 guests, and six fully equipped function rooms for conferences and private parties. The hotel also plans to provide a shuttle bus service between Tianjin and Beijing. Restaurants include a Chinese restaurant serving local specialties; a Japanese restaurant; a French gourmet restaurant: and Café Swisse — a Western restaurant for breakfasts, meals, and snacks. There will also be a seventh-floor Club Bar, cocktail lounge, and summer terrace.

Rooms at the Crystal Palace will be fully modern, with marble baths and a choice of king-size or twin beds. Reservations can be made through any Swissair office.

Address: Youyi and Binshui roads
Telephone: 31-0567
Telex: 23277 TCPH CN
Rates: Single: $70–80; double: $85–95; superior suite: $130;
      deluxe suite: $170; presidential suite: $250

利顺德大饭店

Astor Hotel. Originally put up by the British in 1900, the Astor went through the post-1949 era as the Tianjin Hotel. In July 1985, a major renovation was completed and the Tianjin once again became the Astor — a somewhat controversial decision in a country where imperialist-era names are eschewed. By late 1986, a new seven-story annex (a joint-venture with a Hong Kong company) added 130 rooms to the Astor's existing 86. The current renovation has maintained the original wood paneling along the length of the hallways. The lobby and public areas are attractive, with marble-tiled floors, crystal chandeliers, and a reasonably priced combined Chinese and Western restaurant.

When the new building is completed, a cocktail lounge will feature live music. Other facilities include a banquet hall that may be converted to a meeting room or ballroom; a bakery; business center; barber and beauty salon; and shopping arcade.

Rooms at the Astor are comfortably furnished with cream-colored carpets and modern furniture. All rooms are air conditioned and have refrigerators and color TVs which receive closed-circuit movies. Bathrooms are spacious and fitted with American Standard fixtures.

Room rates are quite reasonable, the best buys being the economy rooms which are a bit smaller and have one single bed. There are only 4–5 such rooms in the hotel, however.

Address: 33 Tai'erzhuang Road
Telephone: 39-0013
Telex: 23266/8 ASHTL CN
Rates: Economy: Y100; standard: Y150; superior: Y200;
      deluxe: Y310; standard: Y310; deluxe suite: Y350

Other tourist hotels in Tianjin include **The Friendship Hotel** (94 Nanjing Rd.; tel: 310372; telex: 23264 FRHTL CN) located near the center of the city. The **Tianjin Guest House** (Youyi Road; tel: 287313) in the southern part of the city presents an aura of disintegrating luxury in a scenic setting. The **Tianjin Garden Hotel** (337 Machang Rd.; tel: 24010) in Hexi District is a four-villa complex located on a 73-hectare (180-acre) compound. Almost a third of the area is made up of lakes, thus providing an extremely tranquil environment for visitors. Also in Hexi District is the **Tianjin Grand Hotel** (Youyi Rd.; tel: 287613; telex: 23276 THJOT CN). Built in 1960, this hotel consists of two buildings with a total of over 1,000 beds, as well as a separate four-story building designed for conferences. The hotel's auditorium has a seating capacity of 1,057.

► ◄

CUISINE

► ◄

Tianjin cuisine lacks the distinction of both authentic Shandong and northern Chinese cooking, and there are few noteworthy local dishes. However, the steamed dumplings at the famous Tianjin Goubuli Baozi (Dumpling) Shop, on Shandong Street, and dishes of Ningbo origin are well worth trying. Quanye Chang, one of the main shopping districts of Tianjin, boasts a number of good restaurants, such as the Hongye Restaurant (Huazhong Rd.; tel: 22710), which serves Cantonese dishes. Local diners also recommend the Tianjin Roast Duck Restaurant (142 Liaoning Rd.; tel: 702600). Visitors yearning for a taste of European food should seek out the Ji Si Ling (formerly the German-owned Kiessling Restaurant) on Zhejiang Road, and its bakery outlet on Jiefang Bei Road, two blocks south of the Astor Hotel.

The Tianjin Friendship Club reopened in 1979 on the grounds of the former Country Club (268 Machang Rd.; tel: 30329). The club's restaurant is now the favored spot in town for banquets and posh dinners featuring fine examples of local cuisine. The main building offers bowling, billiards, and a pool fed by natural hot springs.

食品街
Chinese Food Street. Located in the south city area, Food Street is a three-story, arcade-style complex that houses more than 100 restaurants and snack bars. It is said to be the largest dining complex of its kind in China. Both local and Chinese as well as the cuisines of Italy, Russia, and other nations are represented. The spot has become so popular among Chinese tourists that a brace of new hotels for local Chinese is under construction at an adjacent site.

Street-level shops serve mostly snacks — *jiaozi* (dumplings), *baozi* (steamed stuffed buns), noodles, soft drinks, and sweets. Tianjin's famous "Goubuli" Baozi Shop has an outlet here. There are also several places to buy another Tianjin specialty — *mahua* or fried dough twists with sesame seeds. You can recognize these shops by the crowds of out-of-town Chinese buying boxes of *mahua* to carry home to their families and friends.

On the second level is a branch of the famous colonial carryover, Kiesslings, known in Chinese as Ji Si Ling. If you have a craving for Western food, this is the place to indulge it. Also of interest on Level Two is "San Mao" (Three Hairs) Restaurant. San Mao is a cartoon character beloved by Chinese childern—a baby with only three hairs on his head. This restaurant is for children (of all ages) and specializes in children's birthday parties. It is not unusual to see several parties going on simultaneously. The birthday child is recognized by the cardboard crown on his head. In addition to the birthday cone and other goodies, he also gets a certificate to have a color photo taken of himself with "San Mao."

Level Three houses mostly banquet facilities. Other restaurants on the outside perimeter of the complex are well worth investigating. Among them are two joint-venture restaurants—one Japanese and one Hong Kong (Xiang Gang Jin Lou). Both are rather expensive and more frequented by the foreign community than by Tianjin Chinese. A unique specialty restaurant is Lao Yan Le, which prepares soft foods for the elderly, young children, or for anyone whose teeth cannot handle regular meals.

Food Street is open daily until 9 PM.

► SHOPPING ◄

Visitors have several options in purchasing local products. One of Tianjin's largest stores is the Quanyechang Department Store (352 Heping Rd.; tel: 703771). The seven-story building serves more than 100,000 customers daily. In addition to carrying a wide variety of products, the Quanyechang houses two cinemas and other entertainment facilities.

The Yilinge (175 Liaoning Rd., tel: 700308) in Heping District is the city's most famous art gallery. It carries a wide selection of bronzes, cloisonné paintings, and jade and ivory carvings. The shop's services include currency exchange, packing, and insurance; the shop will even arrange for the commissioning of artists for the creation of custom works. Tianjin's Friendship Store is located on Jiefang Rd. (tel: 392513).

国际商场

The International Market. The International Market opened in May 1986 and consists of two modern five-story structures on opposite sides of Binjiang Road, adjacent to the Catholic Cathedral. They display vast quantities of both imported and domestic goods. One of these buildings, by far the more crowded of the two, displays goods for retail sale. The other is an exhibition hall, where the merchandise displayed is only available on a wholesale basis for quantity orders.

Both buildings offer an array of goods seldom if ever seen in one outlet anywhere in China. These range from such mundane items as cockroach traps, canned foods, and women's underwear to more exotic items such as X-ray and surgical equipment and theatre-size popcorn machines. In between are electrical appliances, sportswear, musical instruments, leather goods, furniture, carpets, and porcelain—to list but a few. Betty Crocker Cake Mix was on sale on the ground floor of the Sales Building.

Hours are from 10:30 AM to 7 PM.

中国国际旅行社
CITS (Luxingshe) Office in Tianjin ▣ 20 Youyi Road. Tel: 314889.
Telex: 23281 TJITS CN.

Tibet

contemporary spelling/Xizang

TEN YEARS ago, China was a tantalizing land, inaccessible to most Westerners and shrouded in mystery. Times change. China still bears the aura of an exotic, mysterious place and its hundreds of thousands of annual visitors show no signs of declining interest; nevertheless, Tibet has stolen the mantle as the most coveted, most extraordinary, most unobtainable, and most remote tourist spot in the world.

In spring of 1980, the first small tourist groups in some 30 years began to arrive in Lhasa. In 1984, the authorities in Beijing, recognizing the vast potential of Tibet's tourist industry, initiated a number of projects aimed at upgrading and expanding Tibet's hotel, food, and transportation facilities. Then, in an unexpected development in April 1985, the governments of China and Nepal jointly announced the reopening of the Tibet–Nepal border, closed since the early 1950s. With the opening up of this and, in the forseeable future, other land and air routes, the flow of tourists into Tibet is expected to increase dramatically: in 1987 alone, 43,500 foreign tourists visited Tibet. For now, however, the "Roof of the World" remains a place of mystery and adventure, far off the well-worn China trail.

During 1988, in the wake of the demonstrations in Lhasa, travel to Tibet was curtailed for individual travelers. Previously, most tourists were backpackers who entered Tibet through Nepal or Sichuan province. The new restrictions stipulated that only organized tour groups will now be permitted; individual tourists will be required to form groups—even if the "group" consists of only two or three people—in order to be admitted. Moreover, travelers are obliged to hire a tour guide from a government travel agency.

Tibet—Xizang is its Chinese name—is an autonomous region of the People's Republic of China, occupying a huge 1,007,000-sq.-km. (413,000-sq.-mi.) area in China's southwest corner. Nepal, Burma, India, and Bhutan cluster along its southern border. Most of Tibet consists of high-altitude plateaus and mountain wilderness. Wild grasses and endless reaches of snow blanket the higher elevations, which comprise a good three-quarters of its land area.

Overland Routes. Getting there by surface transport from China is still something of a problem. The trunk road from Qinghai to Tibet has been widened and re-graded, and the Chinese have recently resumed construction of a railroad begun in 1951. The highway link is effectively off-limits to foreigners, however, and the railroad will take decades to complete. Hardy travelers can now make the overland journey from Kathmandu, the capital of Nepal, but at present this route is still arduous and primitive; moreover, the number of visas issued for travel to Tibet via Nepal is limited, and arrangements must be made far in advance.

Flying is a much shorter two-to-three hours from Chengdu (daily flights except Sundays) or Xi'an (twice weekly) in Western China. The challenge to navigation is such that the mere hint of cloudy weather—en route, in the Lhasa Valley, or on the return run—is sufficient reason to delay take-off, often for a day or more. The landing strip at Lhasa is located 86 km. (53 mi.) from town, about one hour's drive on the newly widened and asphalted airport road.

Lhasa, the "City of Sun," is nestled high in the Gyi Qu Valley and is blessed with seasonally mild and humid weather from monsoons in India, 160 km. (100 mi.) to the south. Tibetan winters, as might be supposed, are fiercely cold. But for half the year, strong sunlight warms the thin air, making most days in Lhasa comfortably mild and, owing to protective mountains, relatively windless. Summer temperatures hover above 30°C (high 80s F) only to plummet to a searing –23°C (–10°F) in midwinter. The best times to visit are from late spring to early fall.

HEALTH CONSIDERATIONS FOR VISITORS

No matter when you visit, however, the 3,600-m. (12,000-ft.) altitude of the Lhasa Valley will be a factor to consider, even if you live year-round in the Rocky Mountains or Switzerland. For the first few days, at least, the ubiquitous green canvas oxygen bags will be constant—and most welcome—companions. At first, most sea-level sojourners must stop for a rest halfway up any given flight of stairs. Any form of overexertion (such as running or strenuous climbing) is patently dangerous, with even the fittest specimens courting dehydration and pulmonary strain.

Most visitors will feel some form of mild discomfort—usually some combination of headache, nausea, dizziness, chest pain, or insomnia. Lots of rest and aspirin are the best remedies, although extreme symptoms may signal the onset of more serious forms of altitude sickness. In these cases a physician should be consulted at once. The best cure in most cases may be an immediate return to level ground. Smoking and drinking will only exacerbate the discomfort.

Prior to 1980, the Chinese required rigorous physical exams of all passengers prior to boarding their flight to Lhasa. Since then, however, this requirement has been waived for many groups. But visitors with high blood pressure, or any respiratory or heart ailments, are advised to attend to the risks and reconsider their travel plans.

Whence the allure, you may ask. For one thing, Tibet is beautiful. Until 1950, no cars or trucks or carts were permitted to traverse the few

Lhasa's Potala, with the Red Palace at the center

dirt roads for fear their wheels would scar the earth and thereby release evil spirits. Few motorized vehicles exist even today. No pollution mars the magnificient, jagged mountain peaks or darkens the deep, clear lakes. An extraordinary remoteness and serenity still pervades James Hilton's inspiration for Shangri-la.

TIBET IN HISTORY

Tibet also has a mystical charm. The atmosphere of fatalistic serenity and powerful beliefs in evil spirits stemmed in part from Lamaism, an ancient strain of Tantric Indian Buddhism, coupled with Tibetan Shamanism, which held sway over every aspect of Tibetan life from the 7th century until the departure of the Dalai Lama and parallel political reforms begun in 1959. Remnants still remain. Rural families resist modern encroachments, including free schooling and medicine. And although most of the monasteries and temples are now officially designated as historical monuments, hundreds come to worship daily, with large throngs still appearing on religious holidays.

Tibet's entire history is marked by intense preoccupation with religion, and by sporadic political autonomy through the centuries. Briefly conquered by the Mongols when they ruled China (1279–1368), the region came under Manchu control in the 18th century. Chinese authority weakened in the last years of the Qing Dynasty (1644–1911) and almost vanished during the Republican period (1912–49).

Under the rule of the Dalai Lama, spiritual head of the Tibetan Buddhist religion, Tibet exercised full control over its internal affairs, although most of its people languished under a harsh feudal theocracy. In 1951, China's political sovereignty in Tibet was restored, partly through military action and partly by negotiation. A brief revolt broke out in 1959, during which the Dalai Lama fled to India. Six years later, Tibet was organized as an autonomous region of the People's Republic.

China's minority regions suffered greatly from the ravages of the Cultural Revolution, and Tibet was among the most severely affected. Thousands of monks and lay Buddhists were sent to labor camps or otherwise persecuted. Red Guards destroyed monasteries wholesale, sometimes using artillery to level thousand-year old temples. Arbitrary agricultural reforms, including the forced planting of winter wheat instead of the traditional barley, and the collectivization of yak and goat herds, caused severe economic dislocation. The economic and ideological reforms of the post-Mao era have partially reversed the damage, however, as freedom of religion, private enterprise, and traditional family-unit land-use patterns have been restored. A Buddhist college has been set up in Lhasa with state support. About 3,000 monks and 150 nuns now reside in Tibetan lamaseries, compared to fewer than 1,000 in 1978. Tibetan-language education is being encouraged, and a fledgling movie industry has sprung up. Rooftops all over Lhasa are sprouting TV antennas, lending credence to the claim of a 40% increase in per-capita annual income since 1983. Large-scale capital construction projects, aimed at modernizing Tibet's economic base (and, not incidentally, its tourist industry), have been underway since 1980, and the central government has taken an active role in helping to restore many of the temples and shrines damaged during the Cultural Revolution. Through 1985, 50 monasteries and temples have been restored and opened to tourists and pilgrims. An additional 43 were to be opened in the near future, and there are plans to restore another 80 or so over the next few years.

Some of the age-old intransigence still remains, however. Young Tibetans are not nearly as devout or tradition-bound as their parents, but full integration into the PRC's political and ideological fabric has been slow, despite substantial early gains in improving Tibet's economic base. During the early 1980s, talks were under way in both Beijing and Lhasa with special envoys of the Dalai Lama about his possible return to Tibet. The main issue driving these discussions was the precise role the Dalai Lama would then assume—ordinary citizen, figurehead, or quasi-independent ruler.

ECONOMY AND CULTURE

Since China reestablished its presence in Tibet in the early 1950s, economic reforms have focused on abolishing the feudal system which permitted only a handful of leading lamas and serf-owners to live in material splendor while their illiterate subjects, comprising over 90% of the population, eked out a meager, squalid existence.

Redistribution of land on a more equitable basis was the first reform. A concerted if not completely successful effort to eradicate the unequal Lamaist hierarchy was next. Establishing schools, including Tibet's first secondary school in 1956 as well as teacher's training college, was another

Rinzin Bajor, a contemporary Tibetan muralist, at work in a Lhasa monastery

top priority. Children are now taught both Tibetan and Chinese in the classroom. Hospital facilities are also expanding and basic health care is available to the entire population for the first time.

With the gradual introduction of farm machinery into the fertile valleys of Tibet, barley and wheat have yielded bumper crops in recent years. Nevertheless, livestock—the yaks and goats and sheep—are still the main agricultural resource. Hydroelectric stations and irrigation works have been set up along the mighty Nyanqu River, but the power potential still remains largely untapped. Similarly, with the exception of coal, the rich mineral resources of Tibet have yet to be exploited. For general information on travel to and in Tibet, inquiries may be made directly to the Xizang (Tibet) Bureau of Tourism, Lhasa (tel. 22980).

拉萨
LHASA

The political and economic center of Tibet for the last 350 years, Lhasa is Tibet's largest, most important, and most visited city. Lhasa is the former seat of the Dalai Lama, and temporal center of Tibetan Buddhism for hundreds of years. Lhasa's palaces and temples, set against the backdrop of towering, precipitous peaks, are among the most impressive in the world.

Climate		Jan	Feb	Mar	Apr	May	Jun	Jul	Aug	Sep	Oct	Nov	Dec
Temp.	°C	-1.6	1.1	4.7	8	12.2	16.1	16.3	15.5	14.1	8.8	3.8	0
	°F	29	34	40.5	46.5	54	61	61.5	60	57.5	48	39	32
Precip.	mm.	0	13	8	5	25	64	122	89	66	13	3	0
	in.	0	.5	.3	.2	1	2.5	4.8	3.5	2.6	.5	.1	0

INDISPENSABLE for the CHINA TRAVELER

CHINESE LANGUAGE LEARNING KIT

includes China Traveler's Phrase Book and 60-Minute Cassette

$12.95

PLUS free China Beginner's/Traveler's Dictionary
($6.95 retail value) with this order.

- Over 2000 useful words and phrases—in English, Chinese characters, pinyin (China's official romanization system), and phonetic transcriptions

- Learn to pronounce words and phrases with a native speaker on companion cassette tape

☐ Please send me _____ CHINESE LANGUAGE LEARNING KIT(S) and free China Beginner's/Traveler's Dictionary at $12.95 per kit, plus $1 shipping.

☐ Bill me
☐ Payment enclosed: $_____

NAME

ADDRESS

CITY   STATE   · ZIP

New Jersey residents add 6% sales tax.

We hope you enjoyed **THE CHINA GUIDEBOOK.** Please send your comments to help us improve future editions.

Comments: _____

BUSINESS REPLY CARD

FIRST CLASS   PERMIT NO. 619   TEANECK, N.J.

POSTAGE WILL BE PAID BY ADDRESSEE

EURASIA PRESS, INC.
168 State Street
Teaneck, NJ 07666-3516
U.S.A.

The town lies in a broad valley along the banks of the Lhasa River, a tributary of the Tsanpo (Brahmaputra), at an altitude of 3,600 m. (11,800 ft.). Prior to the departure of the Dalai Lama and his supporters in 1959, about half the population of Lhasa was made up of Buddhist monks.

Lhasa is divided into two sections: the older, Tibetan section which surrounds the Jokhang (Dazhao) Temple; and the newer, larger, predominantly Chinese section. The urban center, architecturally undistinguished except for its grand palaces and temples, underwent a facelift during 1984–85, ostensibly in preparation for the visit of the Panchen Lama and the celebration of Tibet's 20th year as an autonomous region. Roads were paved, new housing and public buildings were put up, and reconstruction work on temples and monasteries was intensified. Two new tourist hotels were also completed.

HIGHLIGHTS FOR TRAVELERS

布达拉宫

The Potala. If and when the Dalai Lama ever comes back, he certainly won't live in the splendor of the Red Palace, his former quarters within the Potala. The huge 17th-century edifice, built on the site of its 7th-century forerunner, dominates the entire city and valley.

The Red Palace in the center used to be the headquarters of Tibetan religious and political life. Now it's a museum and you can see for yourself the Dalai Lama's rather spartan private living quarters and not-so-spartan private treasury. The white buildings on either side of the palace were once secular apartments and offices of lay staff-members.

Underneath the 13-story, 1,000-room fortress lurks a more sinister past. Refusal to pay taxes, expressions of anger or passion, or an imagined slight to a Lamaist monk usually resulted in jail torture. The Cave of Scorpions, which ate people alive, is only part of a ghoulish labyrinth of dungeons. Upstairs, the gigantic bejewelled Buddhas—many surmounting solid gold crypts holding the remains of the preceding line of Dalai Lamas —and astonishing mural chronicles depicting Buddhist folklore and long-ago Tibetan life equally evoke the singularity of the Potala. After only a short time the visitor is struck by the certain sense that there never has been, nor will there ever be, another building like it.

The Chinese government has spent approximately $2.5 million since 1976 restoring the Potala and other Lhasa attractions. (Many were ransacked and defaced during the Cultural Revolution, despite Premier Zhou Enlai's direct orders to spare them.) The Potala was in particularly dire need, as the top four stories over the West Gate were on the verge of toppling. The floors have been jacked up and the upper stories replaced; no danger remains—you needn't miss a famous Buddhist scripture or a single one of the 10,000 chapels with their human skull and thighbone wall decorations. But you may have some trouble photographing them: a new policy in 1980 required payment of Y20 for each camera exposure made of art objects inside the Potala.

哲崩寺

Drepung Monastery. Lesser regents of the Tibetan church lived 5–6 km. (3–4 mi.) out of town in the Drepung Monastery, one of the ten active lamaseries remaining in Tibet today. Once the largest cloister in the world, the ancient stone buildings, which date back to 1416, still cling in tiers to the sharp face of a mountain. You can wander up and down cobbled stairways with your guide and peek inside parts of the temple, old granaries, and dark monastic cells.

Approximately 300 lamas still live and work in the Drepung Monastery (compared to some 10,000 in 1959). Before the assertion of Chinese authority, every Tibetan family gave at least one son to the priesthood and the 2,500 monasteries were brimming with close to 110,000 monks.

大昭寺

Jokhang Temple. The third wonder in the City of Sun is the Jokhang Temple. (The three are usually referred to as "The Three Sites of Lhasa.") Built 1,300 years ago to house a golden Buddha, the temple is still one of Tibet's holiest shrines. In the early morning or at evening, prostrate pilgrims fingering prayer beads and murmuring sutras are a common sight. Inside, a dazzling array of Buddhist inconography awes visitors of all faiths. The "first treasure" is the Sakyamuni Buddha, brought to Tibet by a Chinese princess named Wen Chang in 652. The figure is pure gold with encrusted jewels and long, blue-lidded eyes. The Buddha of the Future (Maitreya) is the next treasure. It, too, is golden, but larger and clothed in rich brocade. In a nearby chapel, you can see the embroidered images of the princess and her husband, King Songstang Kampo (later designated as the first Dalai Lama). Outside, in a dark stone niche, waters from an underground lake reflect visions of the future for the worshipful.

Visitors are forewarned of the Jokhang's dank, airless interior: the small, crowded chambers are saturated with fumes of fermented yak butter, which is burned as an esoteric ritual. The effect can be overwhelming in ways that are neither spiritual or aesthetic.

色拉寺

Sera Monastery. Located about 5 km. (3 mi.) north of the city proper, this temple complex is still one of the major active monasteries of Tibet. Although the number of lamas is only a fraction of what it used to be, monks are training and practicing here in increasing numbers. Those temples that are still active attract scores of pilgrims, many seeking blessings for their young and newborn children. At the other end of the temporal and spiritual scale, Sera is also a preferred site for the Tibetan sky burial—by Western standards a rather grisly ritual, wherein the corpse is hacked to bits and fed to vultures. Visitors must now obtain special permission to view the ritual, and picture taking is strictly prohibited. Those who do make their way to the burial site will be tolerated as long as they maintain a low and respectful profile. Groups are definitely not welcome, and may be asked to leave in less-than-polite terms (in one extreme case, a particularly noisy and obtrusive tour group was stoned by angry relatives of the deceased).

杆丹寺

Ganden Monastery. One of the five holiest monasteries in Tibet (the others are Sera, Johkang, and Drepung in Lhasa and Tashilhunpo in Xigaze), Ganden is a bumpy 60 km. (37 mi.) from Lhasa. Nearby, in addition to the still-active lamasery, there is a ruined fort built to defend against an invasion by the British around the turn of the century.

HOTEL
ACCOMMODATIONS

拉萨饭店

Lhasa Hotel. Tibet's first and only "first-class" hotel, the Lhasa opened its doors in September 1985. In Spring 1988, management was taken over by the Holiday Inn chain. The 486-room, 1,332-bed hotel complex is located just west of the city proper, next to Norbulingka (Summer Palace), at 1 Minzu Road (tel: 22221; telex: 68010 HILSA CN). All rooms are equipped with air-conditioners, telephones, closed-circuit TVs, and piped-in oxygen tanks. The hotel is centrally heated, and features two restaurants serving Chinese and Western cuisine.

Room rates begin at $75 per day plus 10% service. Tour members, who must pay up to a whopping $200 a day, not including airfare, for room, board, and guided tours, are admonished by travel authorities to bear in mind the inordinate transport costs that apply to virtually all tourist amenities now provided in Tibet. Most supplies come by truck convoys, with one truck in five carrying fuel for the other four. It is by this means that foreign guests get their mattresses, hot-water heaters, beer, pork chops, toilet paper, and canned mandarin oranges.

西藏宾馆

Tibet Guest House (tel: 23738/23729; telex: 68013 TGSTH CN). Located just to the west of the Lhasa Hotel, this four-story structure was built to resemble the Potala Palace. Local stone was quarried for the outer walls, and the red-and-white exterior matches the Potala's color scheme. Rates range from Y120–140, with all meals included.

中国国际旅行社宾馆

Lhasa CITS Guest House. Formerly the only hotel accommodating foreign tourists, the Lhasa Guest House is set in the middle of Qu San Suo (tel: 22225), a huge government compound (of which it used to be a part) that is mostly devoid of interest for walking or exploring. Situated an inconvenient 8 km. (5 mi.) from town, the complex fronts a broad meadow—formerly marsh—that separates it from the city of Lhasa and the Potala, which looms as a tiny jewel on the horizon. Visitors are condemned to travel en masse with their group or else walk to Lhasa (three hours roundtrip), as there are no taxis or public buses available. A walled-in compound comprising a dozen U-shaped stone villas, each with eight two-room suites, the premises include a gift shop, a dining hall, and a large auditorium for films and cultural performances. Rooms are adequately furnished, heated, and equipped with both Western-style bathrooms and appliances labeled as water heaters. As of 1988, this hotel was no longer recommended for foreign guests.

There are a number of hotels and guest houses in Lhasa offering, relatively speaking, budget accommodations. The Third Regional Reception Center and the Second City Reception Center are both low, functional buildings, each with around 100 guest rooms. Rates are Y35–45 per person, not including meals. Often booked up in advance by Chinese and overseas Chinese tourists, these two guest houses are, when available, the best bargain in town for independent travelers. Two dormitory-style hotels, the Snowlands and the Banak Shol, are located in the older section of Lhasa, near the Jokhang Temple. Rates range from Y5 for a dorm bed to Y10 per bed in doubles and triples. Neither has modern sanitary facilities.

SHOPPING

After the three sites of Lhasa, you might enjoy an afternoon exploring old Lhasa's thriving bazaar. Although the buildings and people are Tibetan, the mood suggests medieval Europe. Lovely rugs decorated with good-luck dragons, phoenixes, and cranes are on sale in *pulu*, a wool-like material indigenous to Tibet. Another authentic touch might be a pair of Tibetan boots with pointed, curled-up toes and heavy fringes, or a striped apron. Wooden bowls and beautiful ornamental knives are also available. Apart from the state store and the nearby Lhasa Department Store, prices in the bazaar are not fixed. Local Tibetans are also not shy about offering for sale to tourists personal items such as jewelry or religious artifacts. But buyers should be aware that unauthorized antique purchases are subject to confiscation under Chinese customs law. Indeed, most passengers holding Tibetan visas now undergo especially rigorous scrutiny at exit points in Guangzhou and Beijing. Purchases made through authorized channels and affixed with appropriate seals and/or documentation are of course exempt from seizure.

ALONG THE FRIENDSHIP ROAD

With more of Tibet open to tourism, and with the opening of the Nepal–Tibet frontier, many visitors will have the opportunity to venture out of Lhasa and into the Tibetan hinterland. Most will find themselves on the Friendship Road, which threads through southern and western Tibet for 850 km. (530 mi.) to the Nepalese border, about 100 km. (62 mi.) north of Kathmandu. The trip from Lhasa to Zhangmu, the border town, can be made in as little as two days, although most travelers will undoubtedly want to break up the journey by visiting the towns and monasteries along the way.

One of the most beautiful and spectacular stretches of this austere and magnificent highway lies between Lhasa and Tibet's second most important city, Xigaze. The road crosses two 5,000-m. (16,400-ft.) passes, skirts Yang Zhao (Yamzho) Lake, in the shadow of Mt. Kambala, and descends to the village of Gyangze, before finally reaching Xigaze, where the Gyangze Valley meets the Brahmaputra River. A day's drive beyond Xigaze, near the village of Dingri (Tingri), the north face of Mt. Everest (Qiumolangma) comes into view. This is an arid region, resembling—except for the altitude and sheer size of the mountains—the high plateaus of southern Utah or northern New Mexico. Near Mt. Xixabangma, 8,012 m. (26,286 ft.) high, the road crosses a high pass that marks the edge of the Tibetan Plateau. As the road descends the remaining 90 km. (56 mi.) to the Nepalese border, the harsh, arid chaparral gives way to the lush, green river valleys typical of the Himalayas' southern slope.

Although the road is not paved, owing to its strategic importance it is graded and well-maintained, so the travel is actually fairly easy, assuming one has already adjusted to the altitude.

江孜

GYANGZE

***

A bout 250 km. (155 mi.) west of Lhasa and 100 km. (62 mi.) east of Xigaze, Gyangze is a pretty market town lying in a fertile river valley dotted with small farming villages. Altitude is about 3,800 m. (about 12,500 ft.). Once the center of Tibetan trade in wool, Gyangze was an important link to the outside world. The town is now something of a backwater, although it still serves as a trucking stopover on the main overland route between Tibet and Nepal. Gyangze is split almost down the middle by a steep ridge with the ruins of a fortress running along the top. The old town, with some primitive handicraft workshops, is on the eastern side of the ridge. The main market area and a large monastery dominate the western section of town. There are a few small Chinese communities in the suburbs.

白居寺

The Kumbum. Recently restored and still active, the Kumbum (or "Place of Myriad Images") is the largest stupa in Tibet and arguably the most magnificent. A unique feature is its large, white dagoba—originally built in the 13th century—which contains 10,000 Buddha-figures. It was constructed by the Newar people of the Kathmandu region in Nepal, who were admired in Tibet as the greatest fresco artists of the period. The Kumbum is frequently crowded with Tibetan pilgrims.

Accommodations. There are two small, rather spartan hotels, one Chinese- and one Tibetan-style. The **Gyangze No. 1 Guesthouse** has some 50 beds placed in large chambers around a central courtyard. The hotel, located about 300 m. to the left of the main crossroad, mainly caters to Tibet-Nepal drivers, but foreigners are welcomed. A small kitchen serves Chinese-style meals. Beds range from Y3-5 per day. The **Gyangze County Guesthouse** is just beyond the same crossroad to the right. It also has about 50 beds evenly distributed among some 15 rooms. Rates are Y4 per bed at this spartan establishment.

Climate		Jan	Feb	Mar	Apr	May	Jun	Jul	Aug	Sep	Oct	Nov	Dec
Temp.	°C	−1.6	1.1	4.7	8	12.2	16.1	16.3	15.5	14.1	8.8	3.8	0
	°F	29	34	40.5	46.5	54	61	61.5	60	57.5	48	39	32
Precip.	mm.	0	13	8	5	25	64	122	89	66	13	3	0
	in.	0	.5	.3	.2	1	2.5	4.8	3.5	2.6	.5	.1	0

日喀则
XIGAZE

The former seat of the Panchen Lama, Xigaze is Tibet's second largest city. Of its population of around 49,000, about half are Tibetan. Second only to Lhasa in both religious and political importance— Xigaze is the administrative center for 18 counties in southern and western Tibet—the city lies 350 km. (220 mi.) southwest of the capital, at an elevation of 3,900 m. (12,795 ft.). Xigaze is now commonly included on many group itineraries in Tibet. It can be reached from Lhasa in about six hours via a semi-paved road that surmounts two high passes.

Within traditional Tibetan history, Xigaze has often emerged as a bitter political and religious rival to Lhasa. The urban center of Tibet's west-central region, Xigaze dominated the area once known as Tsang and noted for its productive agricultural lands. In the 15th century, a schism divided Tibetan Lamaism between the reformist "Yellow Hats" of Lhasa and the "Red Hats" of Xigaze. With the help of a powerful Mongolian army, the Fifth Dalai Lama (the builder of the Potala) finally put down the Tsang opposition and, in the late 17th century, appointed the first Panchen Lama as administrator of Tsang under the central authority of the Dalai Lama.

In recent decades, Xigaze has followed the urban development pattern exhibited by Lhasa (albeit more slowly), with a new, undistinguished Chinese town emerging astride the old market areas. Symbolic traces of the ill-fated Red Hats are still visible on some of the older structures, as are "swastika" symbols from Tibet's pre-Buddhist animist followers, the Bon.

扎什伦布寺

Tashilhunpo Monastery. The Tashilhunpo Monastery ("Mound of Glory") is Xigaze's main attraction. The gold-pinnacled temple was built in 1447, but sustained heavy damage during the Cultural Revolution. Reopened in 1980, the temple complex is now home to over 600 monks, including the Living Buddha Qiangzha Chilie. A number of monks also live at the lamasery's farm about 15 km. out of town. One of Tashilhunpo's most notable features is its monumental nine-story-high retaining wall, the Thanka Wall. The rose-colored monastery itself is one of the largest and most architecturally striking building complexes in Tibet.

Housed in a separate structure is a six-story-high bronze Buddha, the largest in Tibet. The Maitreya Buddha is 26 m. (86 ft.) high and contains 279 kg. (614 lbs.) of pure gold.

Climate		Jan	Feb	Mar	Apr	May	Jun	Jul	Aug	Sep	Oct	Nov	Dec
Temp.	°C	−1.6	1.1	4.7	8	12.2	16.1	16.3	15.5	14.1	8.8	3.8	0
	°F	29	34	40.5	46.5	54	61	61.5	60	57.5	48	39	32
Precip.	mm.	0	13	8	5	25	64	122	89	66	13	3	0
	in.	0	.5	.3	.2	1	2.5	4.8	3.5	2.6	.5	.1	0

Accommodations. Xigaze has four hotels that accept foreigners. Among these, none is ever likely to earn the comment "It's worth the trip." The best may be the worst. The **Xigaze Hotel** (Xinjie; tel: 414 x216/217) is the town's "new" hotel, having been completed in early 1985. But raised expectations are likely to be dashed brutally by the fact that while most things in the hotel only resemble what they are supposed to be, most hardly ever function that way. Service runs from indifferent to attrocious. Rooms rent at Y100 per day, including three meals that are entirely consistent with other standards. CITS offices are in the lobby.

日喀则第一招待所

The **Xigaze No. 1 Guesthouse** is adjacent to the entrance of Tashilhunpo. It has 20 rooms with beds that cost Y6 per night. There is hot tap water on the premises—a welcome luxury anywhere in Tibet.

日喀则第二招待所

Xigaze No. 2 Guesthouse consists of about six small buildings near the center of town. There is no plumbing, no heat, no gift shop, no disco. But there is a small Chinese restaurant; and beds that rent from Y6 per night and up. The **No. 8 Reception House of the Commodity Committee**, at Y3–5 per night, is a backpacker's delight.

萨嘎（加加）

Saga (Gyagya). About 350 km. (220 mi.) west of Xigaze, along the main east-west highway (the Friendship Road leaves the main east-west highway at Laze) is the village of Saga, which served as the capital of an independent kingdom in western Tibet during the Yuan Dynasty. Today Saga is a small, pleasant village with an active lamasery.

协嘎尔

Xegar (New Tingri). About 8 km. off the main highway, Xegar is little more than a way station halfway between Xigaze and the Nepalese border. The road to the Rongbuck Glacier and monastery, with spectacular views of Everest's northeast face, leaves the main highway about 15 km. up the road; some groups may spend two nights in the town for a chance to visit Rongbuck. In Xegar, there is a small monastery and a fort, but little else to see or do. The guest house charges Y20, or Y60 with three meals included.

定日

Old Tingri. Lying in a flat, swampy valley amidst towering peaks, Tingri is a small, very picturesque village 60 km. (37 mi.) due west of Xegar. The valley is frequented by nomadic herdsmen, who graze their yaks and goats in the flat, open meadows. The town's chief attraction is its views of Everest and other high peaks (weather permitting). A small guest house accepts foreign guests.

樟木
ZHANGMU

The descent from the high plateau to the border town of Zhangmu is one of the most spectacular stretches on the Friendship Road. Zhangmu (or Kasa) is 530 km. (330 mi.) southwest of Xigaze and 800 km. (498 mi.) from Lhasa. The excursion ("drive" is not really appropriate) usually takes two days, with an overnight stop at Shegar. Zhangmu itself is built into a steep hillside, with no discernable town center. Here, Tibetans, Nepalese, Chinese, and the occasional foreigner mingle in one of the world's most arcane frontier towns.

Lying at an altitude of only 2,700 m., Zhangmu sits in a humid, subtropical belt where temperatures never drop below freezing. With some 850 inhabitants (500 of whom are Sherpas and seven of whom, according to Chinese statistics, are college graduates), Zhangmu is a lively roadside market town, where barter is the chief medium of exchange. Nepalis carry in rice, bananas, pottery, jewelry, and peacock feathers, which are exchanged for Chinese manufactured commmodities (such as rubber shoes and thermos bottles) and live animals.

Accommodations. The **Friendship Hotel,** at three stories, is the town's 'skyscraper.' Built mainly for tourists in 1981, the Friendship now also serves as a reception center for overseas Tibetans returning (mainly from India and Nepal) to their homeland. The **Zhangmu Hotel** also receives foreign guests.

► TIBETAN CUISINE ◄

Eating out in Tibet has its limitations. For one thing, there are no restaurants. Roadside peddlers offer raw meat, butter, and several other staples derived from the yak, a silky-haired, long-horned distant cousin to the American bison. Local diets consist of at least one yak product daily. Other choices may include goat, barley, and a variety of cheeses. Commodities such as rice, tea, and most fruits and vegetables, mainly brought in from Sichuan, are gourmet foods in Tibet. The small new dining hall at the Lhasa Guest House, affectionately known as the "Yak in the Box," bravely struggles to create a varied cuisine from weekly shipments of four or five fresh ingredients—usually including at least one fresh meat product and one green vegetable. As relief, canned mandarin oranges, apparently available in infinite supply, are served at every available juncture. Beer (beware the health cautions above) is available, but expensive.

Increasing numbers of visitors are taking sojourns outside of Lhasa, and along the Friendship Road, where supplies of hygienic foods and beverages can be a problem. Local guides may not yet be sensitized to these problems, so travelers to these outlying areas should be sure to have on hand some backup food supplies (preferably from sources outside of Tibet).

Turpan

alternate spellings / Turfan, Tulufan

ONCE an important way-station on the ancient northern Silk Road, now a large town with nearly 200,000 inhabitants, Turpan is situated in an extensive oasis on the edge of the vast deserts of the Xinjiang Uighur Autonomous Region. By rail, it is approximately 3½ hours southeast of Ürümqi and 13½ northwest of Liuyuan (for Dunhuang). The town is 46 km. (27.6 mi.) south of the railway station (Daheyon), at an altitude of 30 m. (98.4 ft.) above sea level. The Turpan Depression, which drops to 155 m. (505 ft.) below sea level, lies just to the south.

Climate. Precipitation at Turpan is minimal: 16 mm. (.63 in.) a year. The oasis is irrigated by underground channels, called *karezes*, which bring melted snow from the eastern extremity of the Tien Shan, or Celestial Mountains, beyond the rail line to the north. In contrast to the barrenness of the surrounding desert, the abundance of trees and vines is all the more pleasing. Walkers will find roads leading to the fields and scattered settlements south of the town. Summers at Turpan get extremely hot, with temperatures rising to 40°C (104°F); winters are dry and very cold, though not quite so cold as at Ürümqi. The best time for a visit is early autumn.

The population is predominantly Muslim: Uighurs (60%) and Hui people (10%). Their faces, their garb, their adobe brick houses, their donkey carts, their busy market—all belong, entrancingly, to Central Asia. Within easy reach by hired car, there are several highly important archeological sites.

TURPAN IN HISTORY

Nineteen centuries ago, being far to the west, Turpan lay exposed to attack by the Hsiung-nu, or Huns. At the same time, as a station on the Silk Road, it began to absorb cultural influences not only from China but also from India and Persia; it became a center of Hinayana Buddhism and a haven for communities of Manicheans and Nestorian Christians. In the 9th century, however, Uighur domination of the Tarim Basin brought about a change: the Uighur ruler, with his capital at Karakhoja (Gaochang), near Turpan, adopted Islam, which has continued ever since to be the religion of Xinjiang's Turkic peoples. Four centuries later, the Mongols of Genghis Khan overran the region. The old cities near Turpan were ravaged and then abandoned.

Climate		Jan	Feb	Mar	Apr	May	Jun	Jul	Aug	Sep	Oct	Nov	Dec
Temp.	°C	-15.2	-12.2	0.7	10.8	18.9	23.4	25.7	23.8	17.4	8.2	-2.6	-12.0
	°F	4.6	10	33.2	51.4	66	74.1	78.2	74.8	63.3	46.7	27.3	10.4
Precip.	mm.	15	8	13	38	28	38	18	25	15	43	41	10
	in.	.6	.3	.5	1.5	1.1	1.5	.7	1.0	.6	1.7	1.6	.4

In dry conditions, artifacts and ruined buildings lasted remarkably well; they suffered as much at the hands of local vandals as from the elements. In 1879, a Russian botanist came upon the ruins of Karakhoja; in 1898, another Russian visited Karakhoja, Astana, and Yarkhoto (Diaohe). But it remained for German expeditions, between 1903 and 1907, to undertake systematic exploration, particularly at Karakhoja and in the Thousand-Buddha caves a Bezeklik, and for Sir Aurel Stein, in 1914–15, to dig in the cemetery at Astana. The "foreign devils" shipped many treasures to Europe. Still, in the museums at Turpan and Ürümqi, interested travelers may see artifacts, documents, and mummies that, for better or for worse, were not thus alienated. Since the Cultural Revolution, the government has assiduously sought to protect Buddhist sites and relics.

In recent periods, for other reasons, the Chinese have maintained an important military outpost near Turpan.

HIGHLIGHTS

FOR TRAVELERS

苏公塔

Suleiman's Minaret (Sugong Ta) stands 44 m. (144 ft.) high on the eastern outskirts of the town. Suleiman built it, 1776–79, in a simple Afghan style, to honor his father, Imin Khoja, who had supported the Qing rulers against rebellious aristocrats. The patterns of brickwork vary from the bottom to the top. Beside the minaret is a large mosque, used by both Uighurs and Hui people on festival days.

交河故城

Jiaohe (Yarkhoto), a ruined citadel, lies 13 km. (8 mi.) west of Turpan, on an eminence between two rivers. Chinese of the Hang Dynasty used it in defense of the borderlands; Mongols destroyed it in the 13th century. The extensive remains cover an area approximately 1,600 m. × 300 m. (5,249 ft. × 984 ft.). On close inspection, seemingly random shapes become recognizable as a city gate with a lookout post, a monastery, dungeons, houses with smoke-stained chimney flues—evocative vestiges of habitation centuries ago.

柏孜克里克

Bezeklik, half an hour east of Turpan by car, is the site of the Thousand-Buddha Caves (Qianfodong), hewn in a cliff above the Sengim gorge in the Flaming Mountains. The king came from Karakhoja, it is said, to worship in a grotto now designated as "Cave 20." Losses from the caves have been many—figures damaged by vandals, and frescoes cut out and sent to Europe. But no one interested in art of the Tang Dynasty would miss a chance to see as many of the caves as may be open and to look about in the extraordinary setting, with great dunes above and snowy mountains hovering to the north.

高昌

Gaochang (Karakhoja, Khocho), the ancient walled capital of the Uighurs, is not far south of Bezeklik and can be visited in the same half-day. The outer walls, 12 m. (39 ft.) thick and 6 km. (3.6 mi.) long, enclosed dwellings, a palace, and a temple. In these ruins, German excavators discovered traces of an 8th-century Manichean community; but travelers are likely to find the site less impressive than Jiaohe.

阿斯塔那

Astana, near Gaochang, was the burial ground for that city. Of the several hundred tombs, three are open to visitors: one with painted figures (Tang), the second with a fresco of birds, the third with two mummified bodies. The finds include silks, embroideries, and gauze "as thin as cicada's wings." Some of the funerary objects—shoes, hats, sashes—were made of recycled paper, using a method unique to Turpan. Since some of the paper had been used for records of everyday business transactions, it has provided historians with invaluable insights into daily life a thousand years ago.

►◄ HOTEL ACCOMMODATIONS ►◄

吐鲁番宾馆

The attractive if somewhat primitive **Turpan Guest House** (tel: 2907/2301) now has a 100-bed annex, opened in 1983. Rooms with private baths have air-conditioners for the summer and radiators for the winter, but temperatures may still become a bit extreme at times, and the plumbing is no more than adequate. In winter the hot water may run tepid at best. Dormitory accommodations are available, with access to a shower; and there is a small shop in the inner court.

Since Turpan lacks restaurants, travelers (and many local residents) take meals in a separate building of the guest house. The food is quite satisfactory—particularly the kabobs and the breads. Local grapes and Hami melons are prized throughout China.

A new 300-bed hotel was supposed to open nearby in 1986.

中国国际旅行社
CITS (Luxingshe) Office in Turpan ■ Turpan Guest House. Tel: 2907/2847.

乌鲁木齐

Ürümqi

traditional spelling/Urumchi

ÜRÜMQI is the capital of the Xinjiang Uighur Autonomous Region, China's most western province. The most "inland" city in the world—the furthest from any major body of water—Ürümqi is 3,270 km. (2,050 mi.) from Beijing (a five-hour flight). With a population of one million, the city lies as a green-blanketed oasis amidst Xinjiang's barren and uninhabited deserts, loess highlands, and the snowcapped peaks of the Tian Shan Mountains.

Xinjiang covers 16% of the total land area of China and is populated by 13 of China's 55 minority nationalities. Of the total population of 11 million, roughly half are Uighurs, a mostly Muslim Central Asian people who favor dressing in gay costumes and have distinct cultural traditions. Other prominent nationalities of this region are ethnic Chinese, Khazakhs, and Hui.

Although forbidding in winter, Ürümqi's climate is pleasant during the summer, with warm days and cool evenings. An extensive series of tree belts planted around the capital has helped to reduce wind, dust, and cold.

Those who travel to Ürümqi by rail from Lanzhou will pass Jiayuguan, the westernmost part of the Great Wall. It is also the oldest surviving segment, dating back to the Han Dynasty (206 BC–AD 220), with a few sections originating in the Qin Dynasty (221–206 BC), when China's northern defensive ramparts were first linked together.

ECONOMY AND CULTURE

Historically a poor region, Xinjiang has been developed both agriculturally and industrially in recent years. Because rainfall is scarce, many parts of Xinjiang are barren. The main source of irrigation water is the snow and ice at the higher reaches of the Tian Shan range. To harness this supply, rivers have been rechanneled and irrigation canals dug. Xinjiang now has over 400 reservoirs and 30,000 km. (18,800 mi.) of rechanneled waterways.

Referring to the period before 1949, a local inhabitant recounts that "at that time, one could get an ampule of penicillin only by exchanging it for a horse, a battery flashlight for a lamb, a meter of cloth for three catties of wheat, and a small box of matches for a kilogram of wool." Now Xinjiang produces steel, oil, chemicals, sugar, tractors, and various other

Climate		Jan	Feb	Mar	Apr	May	Jun	Jul	Aug	Sep	Oct	Nov	Dec
Temp.	°C	−15.2	−12.2	0.7	10.8	18.9	23.4	25.7	23.8	17.4	8.2	−2.6	−12.0
	°F	4.6	10	33.2	51.4	66	74.1	78.2	74.8	63.3	46.7	27.3	10.4
Precip.	mm.	15	8	13	38	28	38	18	25	15	43	41	10
	in.	.6	.3	.5	1.5	1.1	1.5	.7	1.0	.6	1.7	1.6	.4

kinds of farm machinery. Trucks are the main method of transportation and thousands of miles of roads have now been paved.

There are eight universities in Xinjiang, including two medical schools. One medical college specializes in cancer research (Uighur people have a high incidence of laryngeal cancer, attributed to drinking hot liquids).

Islam is the dominant religion in Xinjiang. In cities such as Ürümqi and Kashi, huge mosques are still in use. Religious festival days are still observed and it is even possible to encounter older women wearing veils.

HIGHLIGHTS
FOR TRAVELERS

Ürümqi's exotic features have been considerably obscured by industrialization and a haze worsened by pollution. Still, visitors will find unusual attractions, such as a camel ride or, in some cases, a night in a Uighur tent. They may also be taken to the People's Park on the west bank of the Ürümqi River, or the Hong Shan Baota (Precious Pagoda of the Red Mountain), reputedly built in the Tang Dynasty. A tour of one of the local carpet factories will interest those who cherish colorful Central Asian rugs. Other ethnic products, such as embroidered caps, leather boots, and horn-handled knives, can be purchased in the department stores at the city center. The Ürümqi Jade Carving Studio is supplied by Xinjiang's rich jade deposits which include famous "King of Kunlun" and "Sheep Fat" (white) varieties.

新疆博物馆
Ürümqi Museum. The building has been renovated (1985), and many of the objects on display—although short on labels in English—are fascinating. Clearly enough, the purpose of the exhibition is to illustrate, in Marxist fashion, stages in Xinjiang's development: slavery, feudalism, capitalism, and socialism.

八路军驻疆办事处纪念馆
Eighth Route Army Headquarters. Ürümqi was a headquarters for the Communist forces during the 1930s and 1940s, and a memorial hall to its martyrs is located here. Mao Zedong's brother, Mao Zemin, was a political activist in Ürümqi until he was executed by a local warlord in 1943.

天池
Heaven's Pool (Tian Chi). This beautiful lake is about halfway up the 5,000-m.-high Bogda Mountain (part of the Tian Shan range). It is about 50 km. (31 mi.) from Ürümqi and accessible only from late April to the end of September. In winter, both the roads and the lake are frozen.

哈萨克公社

Khazakh Nomads. Summer visitors to Ürümqi will probably have an opportunity to visit a Khazakh community at its summer pastures. The Khazakhs herd sheep and cattle on horseback and move camp four times a year in rhythm with the seasons. Guests are invariably treated to a display of Khazakh horsemanship, often including a sort of tug-of-war on horseback using a dead sheep. The grim contest resembles the "buskachi" game of Afghanistan, said to be the origin of polo, field hockey, and soccer.

HOTEL ACCOMMODATIONS

新疆友谊宾馆

Xinjiang Friendship Guesthouse (Yan'an Rd.; tel: 22940/23991) occupies three buildings with a total of 155 rooms; it is very comfortable, provides good food, and stands within ten minute's walk of a Friendship Store. The location is relatively quiet but somewhat inconvenient: 14 km. (8.4 mi.) east of the center of town, and 28 km. (17 mi.) from the airport. Double rooms rent at Y80 per night. Suites are Y150. When traffic is heaviest (9–10:30 AM and 6–7:30 PM), the ride from the airport takes almost an hour.

新疆昆仑宾馆

Kunlun Hotel (Youhao Rd.; tel: 42411/43801) has the advantage of being closer to town. The old section, built in the 1950s, has been downgraded as old-fashioned and spartan; the new section, opened in October 1985, accommodates tourist groups. The Kunlun has 404 rooms, including suites. Rates for a double are Y80; for a suite, Y150.

Accommodations can also be had at the **Ürümqi Guest House** (Southern Xinhua Rd.; tel: 24576); at the **Xinjiang Hotel** (Changjiang Rd.; tel: 54099); at the **Xinjiang Tanshan Mansion** (People's Square; tel: 22481); and the **Ying Binguan** (tel: 22233/4).

Uighur carpet weavers

中国国际旅行社
CITS (Luxingshe) Office in Ürümqi ■ 72 Heping Bei Rd. Tel: 25794.
Telex: 79108 CITSW CN.

Wenzhou

温 州

hot-springs district   *traditional spelling/Wenchow*

A very old port city in Southeastern Zhejiang, Wenzhou has attracted a great deal of attention lately as a possible model for China's reforms. Designated one of 14 Coastal Open Cities in 1984, it is more notable for its freewheeling market economy, where private businesses and subcontracted collective and state enterprises compete vigorously in a distinctively unpolitical environment. Foreign investment is actively solicited. Light industry and commerce predominate, and Wenzhou merchants can be found all over China in search of goods and markets.

Located 12 miles up the Ou River from the East China Sea, Wenzhou was seen as a front-line site in the ongoing Civil War, so little investment came from Beijing until very recently. As a result, Wenzhou is extremely rundown. It is also relatively inaccessible: there is no railroad, an airport won't open until early 1989, and the highway to Hangzhou and Jinhua (the nearest train station) is only now being widened. The daily boat to Shanghai (20-plus hours) and less frequent boats to Ningbo, Xiamen/ Guangzhou, and now Hong Kong are the main links to the outside. Wenzhou only opened to foreigners in 1985.

Wenzhou is situated in a fertile plain surrounded by mountains. The main crops are rice, vegetables, and tangerines. The climate is subtropical, with temperatures ranging from 7.6°C to 27.9°C, with an average of 17.9°C. Wenzhou city proper has 520,000 people; the greater area, including nine counties, has over six million.

HIGHLIGHTS FOR TRAVELERS

Quite compact, Wenzhou is best explored on foot. Streets are very narrow and crowded with unmetered pedicabs, motorcycle taxis, and Polski Fiat taxis as well as bicycles and pedestrians all moving with no discernible pattern. There is a great deal of commercial activity and the most action is in the free markets, especially in Mushao Alley, Canghou Alley, and Xicheng Street by day, and Huancheng East Road and the Chan Road/Wuma Road/Gongyuan Road strip by night. Plans call for the newly widened Renmin Road to hold the liveliest market. Shell-carvings and ceramics are the local specialties. The best food (seafood is tops) is found in numerous private restaurants, some quite large and multi-storied. To see the way in which Wenzhou is redirecting surplus rural labor, go to

Climate		Jan	Feb	Mar	Apr	May	Jun	Jul	Aug	Sep	Oct	Nov	Dec
Temp.	°C	10.3	10.3	13.2	18.3	22.7	25.0	28.8	28.3	26.3	21.7	17.9	12.9
	°F	50.5	50.5	55.7	64.9	72.8	77	83.8	82.9	79.3	71	64.2	55.2
Precip.	mm.	152	152	203	279	304	381	254	203	178	178	152	127
	in.	6	6	8	11	12	15	10	8	7	7	6	5

Qiaotou Village in Yongjia County to see the mindboggling button market which supplies users nationwide with locally-manufactured buttons.

江心寺
Jiangxin Temple. There were originally two islands in the Ou River, each with a Buddhist Temple and pagoda. The Western one (now a martyr's shrine) dates from the Song; the Eastern one (now housing the Wenzhou Museum, which displays local archaeological relics and artworks) is from the Tang. The two islands were joined and a new temple built between them. It is under repair. Take the ferry (every half-hour) from Mahang Pier. Tickets are round-trip.

妙果寺
Miaoguo Temple. Located at the foot of Songtai Mountain behind the Overseas Chinese Hotel, this small Tang temple decayed and was reopened in 1988 after a French-Chinese contributed to its rebuilding.

雁荡山
Yandang Mountains. This imposing range is in Yueqing County. There are hotels at Lingfeng and Xianglingtou. In addition to striking natural scenery which centuries of Chinese have given fanciful names to, there are the ancient Lingyan and Lingfeng temples. Chinese prefer the nighttime scenery. Hire a car or take a bus from Anlan pier, for the 83-km. journey, which takes a little more than three hours.

HOTEL ACCOMMODATIONS

华侨饭店
Overseas Chinese Hotel (17 Xinhe Rd.; tel: 23911). The approximately 100 rooms here are air-conditioned (although heat is said to be a problem in winter). The hotel, currently undergoing renovation, also houses the local branch of the CITS. Rates are from Y24 to Y120.

温州饭店
Wenzhou Hotel (Chaiqiao Alley; tel: 4981). In the recently redecorated new wing for foreign guests, rates are Y33 to Y150.

景山宾馆
Jingshan Hotel (35 Xueshan Rd.; tel: 5901). This 100-room luxury hotel is scenically located, outside the city. Room rates are from Y33 to Y480.

东瓯大厦
Dong'ou Mansion (Wangjiang East Rd.; tel: 7900-07). This hotel occupies the tallest building in town, at the pier.

中国国际旅行社
CITS (Luxingshe) Office in Wenzhou ■ 17 Xinhe Rd. Tel: 22404. Telex: 27481.
Cable: 4000 WENZHOU.

武汉   Wuhan

Wuhan is a contraction of three city names—"Wu"
from Wuchang, and "han" from Hankou and Hanyang   traditional name / Han-kow

WUHAN, the capital of Hubei Province, is the collective name given to three closely linked municipalities—Wuchang, Hankou, and Hanyang. The three cities were physically connected in 1957 upon completion of the Changjiang Bridge, the first and only span to cross the Yangtse between Chongqing to the west and Nanjing to the east. (Prior to the construction of this bridge, all of China's north-south railway traffic had to be ferried across the river.) Located in central China, in the middle of the Yangtse Plain, Wuhan is roughly equidistant (1,600 km.; 1,000 mi.) from four of China's largest cities: Beijing and Guangzhou (on a north-south axis) and Shanghai and Chongqing (on an east-west axis).

In appearance, Wuhan reminds many visitors of Shanghai. Modern red-brick houses and apartment buildings intermingle with gray Victorian structures. Wuhan residents, like those of Shanghai, enjoy a faster pace of life than do most other city-dwellers in central and northern China.

The city is situated at the confluence of the Han and Yangtse rivers. Its three urban sections have a combined population of 3,070,000 living in an area of 168 sq. km. (64.8 sq. mi.), with an additional 1.2 million residing in the suburbs. It is the foremost city in a region noted for its population density and heavy industry. Wuhan is also a major transportation center. As an inland port, it can handle 8,000-ton vessels coming upriver from Shanghai. It is also a key rail center.

Wuhan's three urban components have similar geographical features: all situated on low, flat land interspersed with numerous ponds, canals, and natural waterways. Formerly vulnerable to flooding, Wuhan is today well protected by a newly reinforced series of dikes.

Wuhan's strategic location has also made it the third most important military center in China, a role that has considerable historical precedence. Battles fought here at the turn of the century accompanied the fall of the Qing Dynasty. In 1949, Communist forces in this sector won key victories over the last pockets of Guomindang resistance, paving the way to their final victory.

The extremely hot and humid summers here have won Wuhan a reputation as one of the "furnaces" of the Yangtse. Winters are mild and humid. Most rainfall occurs between April and July.

Climate		Jan	Feb	Mar	Apr	May	Jun	Jul	Aug	Sep	Oct	Nov	Dec
Temp.	°C	2.7	5.2	10.0	16.2	21.1	26.1	29.1	28.4	23.9	17.6	11.4	5.5
	°F	36.8	41.3	50	61.1	69.9	79.8	84.3	83.1	75	63.6	52.5	41.9
Precip.	mm.	152	152	203	279	305	381	254	203	178	178	152	127
	in.	6	6	8	11	12	15	10	8	7	7	6	5

WUHAN IN HISTORY

汉口

Hankou. Hankou occupies the northwest section of Wuhan, bordered by the Yangtse River on the east and the Han River to the south. Hankou began as a fishing village (with origins as early as the 3rd century BC) and it remained one until the mid-19th century. Under terms of the Treaty of Nanjing (1861), which ended the Opium Wars, it was designated a treaty port and its status gradually began to change as foreign firms started opening branches in the city. However, it was not until the building of the railway in the first decade of the 20th century that Hankou really began to expand. In the course of its rapid industrial build-up, Hankou was one of the focal points of the bloody "February 7th" strike of 1923, the first large-scale industrial strike in modern Chinese history. Today, Hankou is the most modern section of Wuhan and the site of an important military installation.

汉阳

Hanyang. Located south of the Han River and west of the Yangtse, Hanyang is the smallest of Wuhan's three municipalities. The area was first settled in about AD 600. The city gained prominence in the late 19th century as a center for political reform. Hanyang's political leaders were part of a movement that sought to revitalize China through "self-strengthening"—it was felt that by learning from the West rather than ignoring it, China could become strong enough to oust the foreign powers. Within the industrial sector, this policy led directly to the construction in Hanyang of China's first modern iron and steel complex in 1891. By the early 1900s, an arsenal and several other factories had been added along Hanyang's riverfront. The city's industrialization program collapsed during the depression of the 1930s. During the Sino-Japanese War (1937–45), much of the industry that remained was destroyed. Since 1949, however, the area has been developed as a center for light industry.

武昌

Wuchang. Wuchang, located on the eastern side of the Yangtse, is the oldest of the three municipalities and has long functioned as an administrative center for the region. In the 14th century (during the Yuan Dynasty), Wuchang served as the capital of a large administrative region (encompassing what are now four central provinces). Today, it serves as the administrative seat of Hubei Province.

On October 10, 1911, the first victorious battle of the 1911 Revolution took place in Wuchang (Sun Yatsen himself was absent—he was in Hawaii raising funds for the revolution). The site of the battle is commemorated by a bronze statue of Dr. Sun on Shouyi Roud. The National Peasant Movement Institute, an important political training ground during the early years of the Chinese Communist movement, was set up in Wuchang. It was headed by Mao himself in 1927.

ECONOMY AND CULTURE

The name Wuhan is synonymous with iron and steel production in China: the city is the site of some of the nation's most important foundries, surpassed only by the Anshan complex. With the assistance of West German and Japanese engineers, the Wuhan Iron and Steel Complex has been expanded to include a three-million-metric-ton steel rolling mill. A modern chemical fertilizer plant is being erected in the suburbs with the aid of American technicians. About 65 km. (40 mi.) southeast of the city is the open-pit Taiye Iron Mine, which provides almost all of Wuhan's iron ore and limestone. Wuhan also boasts China's largest heavy machine tool plant.

The area produces a substantial array of chemicals, fertilizers, construction materials, and rolling stock, as well as cotton fabrics and a number of other light industrial manufactures. Transportation also plays an important role in the local economy: the Yangtse River Bridge and the city's port facilities are the key links in this sector.

Although Wuhan is not primarily an agricultural region, rice and cotton output have substantially increased as the area has sought to attain self-sufficiency. A growing season of 300 days permits two yearly crops of both wheat and tea. Freshwater fisheries also contribute to local food production.

Wuhan is above all a working city. Nevertheless, its long history of intensive settlement and commercial activity have also made it a major cultural and political center in China since at least the Tang Dynasty. Among its 21 institutions of higher education are the prestigious Wuhan University, the Central China Engineering Institute, and the Central China Teachers' College.

HIGHLIGHTS FOR TRAVELERS

Tourism clearly takes second place to industrial development in Wuhan. Visitors will nevertheless discover several points of interest.

HANKOU

The most modern and commercial of the Wuhan municipalities, Hankou serves as a model for Chinese urban planning. Its broad, tree-lined boulevards are flanked by modern apartment houses, offices, and landscaped parks.

The city's legacy from the days of Western occupation is still visible along Yanjiang Road, which runs parallel to the Yangtse in the northeast section. Government offices now occupy what formerly were foreign banks, department stores, and palatial homes. Tourist sites include the Handicrafts Display Center, Sun Yatsen (Zhongshan) Park (formerly a private garden), the Institute of Medicine, and the Wuhan Zoo.

Wuhan's CAAC booking office is in Hankou, at 17 Liji N. Road (tel: 356780).

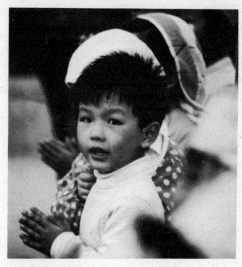

Welcoming foreign friends

HANYANG

Hanyang, a densely populated district made up primarily of a jumble of one-story, slate-roofed houses, is typical of old Chinese cities. The low-lying area just south of the Han River is now Hanyang's industrial district, connected to Hankou by the Yangtse River Bridge. Since Hanyang was formerly a popular residential retreat for the area's gentry, it includes numerous architectural reminders of the pre-1949 era.

中山公园

Sun Yatsen (Zhongshan) Park. This lovely park is studded with small lakes and pavilions as well as public swimming pools. Its small zoo houses more than 60 rare species, including giant pandas. Park hours are 5 AM–7:30 PM.

归元寺

Guiyuan Buddhist Temple (6 Cuiwei Rd.; tel: 441367). Behind a high stone fence in the central part of Hanyang is a Buddhist temple dating from the late Ming and early Qing dynasties, its entrance guarded by two green stone lions. As of 1984, the Guiyuan was the only such site in Wuhan open to the public. The pavilions flanking the main hall now house a museum. In the main hall itself is a 105-ton Buddha sculpted of white stone, a gift from Burma in 1935.

Another building displays gilded statues of additional Buddhist figures, including Sakyamuni and the goddess of mercy, as well as a series representing government officials gathered to welcome the Buddha. The goddess perches on the eye of a fish, symbolizing her ability to prevent earthquakes.

The main worship hall is filled with Buddhas—500 of them, seated in rows as if listening to a sermon. Standing upon a lotus flower is another statue of Sakyamuni, here shown with 1,000 hands and 1,000 eyes. The entire assemblage of extraordinary wood-carving was created by only two craftsmen, a peasant father and son from a county near Wuhan. It took nine years to complete.

The temple, open most days until late afternoon, also houses a vegetarian restaurant. Blind fortune-tellers still ply their trade along the street in front of the complex.

古琴台

Ancient Music Pavilion. This pavilion, also known as the Terrace of the Ancient Lute, has been extensively restored. It sits at the edge of Moon Lake near the Cultural Palace and Tortoise Hill. Legend has it that a musician used to come to the pavilion over a thousand years ago to compose melodies and perform on a 15-string instrument.

龟山

Tortoise Hill (Gui Shan). So named because of its resemblance to a tortoise, this is the only hill of any size in Wuhan and forms a promontory overlooking the Yangtse River. The area includes a park, some caverns, and an old monastery. A hotel has been built on the grounds.

WUCHANG

The old part of Wuchang clings to a low ridge (She Shan—Serpent Hill), along which runs the railway spur that bisects the municipality. On the hill are some old Daoist temples, and the newly restored Huanghe (Yellow Crane) Tower, first built in AD 223 as a sentry post. Wuchang is the cultural and political center of Wuhan. Although some of its ancient charm has been preserved in the area north of She Shan, most of Wuchang has large, drab buildings set on wide, tree-lined avenues.

长江大桥

Yangtse River (Changjiang) Bridge. This bridge, like its counterpart in Nanjing, was built under "impossible" geological conditions and is regarded as a symbol of China's modern industrial progress and self-reliance. The first modern bridge to span the Yangtse, it was completed on September 25, 1957, two years ahead of schedule. Both levels of the structure are flanked by broad sidewalks for pedestrians and cyclists. The lower deck supports the railway, and the upper, six lanes of vehicular traffic. The bridge is 1,156 m. (3,792 ft.) long, and rises 80 m. (263 ft.) above the water.

红山公园

Red Hill Park. This park encloses a seven-story pagoda built in 1307–1315 (during the Yuan Dynasty). Other sites in the park include a temple first erected in 552–554; a four-story "shadowless" pagoda built in 1270; and Iron Buddha Hall, with its main statue said to be cast during the Tang Dynasty. The park can be reached on bus routes #12 or 15 from the Wuchang bridge. The surrounding grounds are littered with old gravestones, some of which now serve as steps along the mountainside.

东湖公园
East Lake (Dong Hu). Several times the size of Hangzhou's West Lake, picturesque East Lake, with its surrounding park, occupies an area of 94 sq. km. (36.3 sq. mi.). Its relaxing atmosphere attracts painters and boaters. Among the park's numerous attractions are the Endless Sky (Changtian) Pavilion; Sparkling Lake (Huguang) Pavilion; Reciting (Xingyin) Pavilion, commemorating the ancient poet Qu Yuan who lived some 2,000 years ago; and the Nine Heroines Monument (Jiunüdun).

湖北省博物馆
Hubei Provincial Museum. Near East Lake is the Hubei Provincial Museum. Relics dating from feudal times to the present, including a magnificent set of musical bells, are exhibited on the ground floor. The second floor displays artifacts from primitive society. The museum also contains some of the objects excavated from the tomb of Jin Zhou; local residents maintain they rival the discoveries unearthed at the Han Tomb No. 1 at Mawangdui, Changsha. The museum is open from 8 AM–noon and 2–5 PM (closed Mondays). Bus #14 from the Wuchang bridge stops near the entrance.

武汉大学
Wuhan University. The campus consists of traditional-style pagoda structures, which overlook the Yangtse River and the city of Wuhan. Most of these buildings date from about 1913, when the university was established. Today, Wuhan University is a center for historical studies, library science, and paleontology. A Chinese-language study program for foreign students is conducted here during the summer.

江陵（荆州）
Jiangling. About 235 km. (146 mi.) upriver from Wuhan is the ancient city of Jiangling, better known by its former name, Jingzhou. Often visited by passengers on Yangtse River cruises (see also Yangtse River Gorges, below), the city entered Chinese recorded history as the capital of the State of Chu, during the Spring and Autumn Period (722–481 BC). The name "Jiangling" actually dates from the Han Dynasty (206 BC–AD 220), but "Jingzhou," first used during the Three Kingdoms period (AD 220–280), remained the city's official name for almost 1,700 years, until the early part of this century. Jiangling's chief attractions are its well-preserved Ming Dynasty walls, replete with Forbidden City-style watch towers and gates, as well as a number of other Ming Dynasty imperial-style buildings, notably the Daoist Kaiyuanguan and Yuanmiaoguan temples. Jiangling was opened to unrestricted foreign visits in 1985.

1. Monument to the Martyrs of the February 7th Strike
2. Monument to Combat Against the 1954 Flood
3. Wuhan Theater
4. Zoo
5. People's Stadium
6. Wuhan Exhibition Hall
7. Department Store
8. Gymnasium
9. Hanyang Worker's Cultural Palace
10. Guiyuan Buddhist Temple (Guiyuansi)
11. Ancient Lute Terrace (Qin Tai or Boya Tai)
12. Tortoise Hill (Gui Shan)
13. Arts and Crafts Building
14. Yangtse River Bridge
15. Site of the Central Peasant Movement Institute
16. Wuchang Workers' Cultural Palace
17. Site of Military Government of the 1911 Revolution
18. Serpent Hill (She Shan)
19. Red Hill (Hong Shan)
20. Luojia Hill
21. Wuhan University
22. Central China Teachers' College
23. Moshan Botanical Garden
24. Moshan Hill
25. Reciting (Xingyin) Pavilion
26. Hubei Provincial Museum
27. Endless Sky (Changtian) Pavilion
28. Sparkling Lake (Huguang) Pavilion
29. Monument to the Nine Heroines (Jiunüdun)
30. Passenger Wharf (boats from Chongqing)

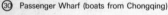 Restaurants

 Hotels

WUHAN

N

JIEFANG
XI RD.
XINHUA RD.
Hankou Airport
HANGKONGGE RD.
Zhongshan Park
Youth Palace
HANKOU
Hankou Hotel
YOU CST.
ZIZHI RD.
Xuangong
CITS
JIANGHAN
BLVD.
JIEFANG
QIAOKOU RD.
Qiaokou Park
ZHONGSHAN
HANZHONG RD.
WUSHENG RD.
DAJIA ST.
Jianghan Park
MINQUAN
Han Shui River
YANHE RD.
HANNAN RD.
Qingchuan Hotel
Yuehu Lake
Hanyang Railroad Station
Hanyang Park
HANYANG RD.
LANJIANG RD.
HANYANG
Moshui Lake
YINGWU RD.
GUADI RD.

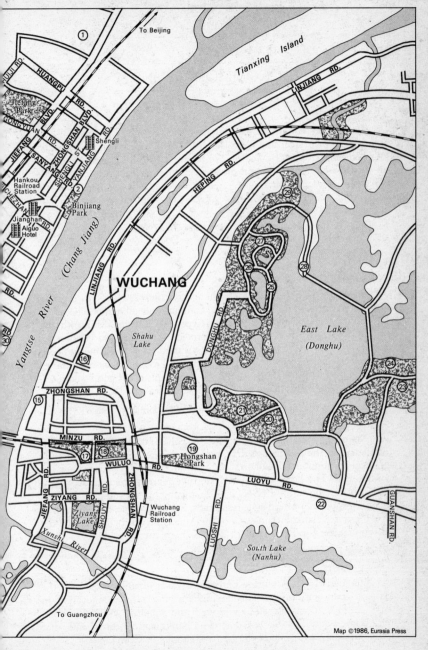

To Beijing

Tianxing Island

LINJIANG RD.

HEPING RD.

Jiefang Park

GONGYUAN RD.

JIEFANG RD.

SANYANG RD.

SHENGLI S. RD.

YANJIANG RD.

ZHONGSHAN BLVD.

HUANGPU RD.

JINGLIN RD.

Shengli

Hankou Railroad Station

CHEHAN RD.

Binjiang Park

Jianghan RD.

Aiguo Hotel

LINJIANG RD.

WUCHANG

Yangtse River (Chang Jiang)

Shahu Lake

DONGHU RD.

East Lake (Donghu)

ZHONGSHAN RD.

MINZU RD.

WULUO RD.

ZHONGSHAN RD.

ZIYANG RD.

JIEFANG RD.

Hongshan Park

LUOYU RD.

Ziyang Lake

SHOUYI RD.

Wuchang Railroad Station

LUOSHI RD.

GUANSHAN RD.

Xunshi River

South Lake (Nanhu)

To Guangzhou

Map ©1986, Eurasia Press

HOTEL
ACCOMMODATIONS

晴川饭店

Qingchuan Hotel. Wuhan's newest and largest hotel occupies an area between the river and Tortoise Hill. This 24-story structure has 298 air-conditioned rooms (including 274 doubles, 10 suites, and 14 singles), all with closed-circuit TV and other modern amenities. Services include three dining rooms (offering Western and local Chinese specialties), a coffee shop (20th floor), and roof garden. The Qingchuan was officially opened in late 1983.

Address: 1 Xima Rd.
Telephone: 44-1141
Telex: 40134 QCH CN
Cable: 8550

Rates: Single: Y30
Double: Y60
Suite: Y100

胜利饭店

Shengli (Victory) Hotel (222 Shengli Rd.; tel: 21241). This six-story hotel, built in the 1930s by the British, contains only 50 rooms. The rooms are spacious, and some overlook the river. Two features distinsuish this hotel from many others in China: it provides a sponge and cleanser for guests to use in the bathroom, and the standard glass desk lamp has been replaced by one featuring frolicsome pandas. All rooms are air-conditioned and equipped with telephones and TVs. Food is plain but good, and a section of the dining room is cordoned off as a "bar."

Rates: Single: Y40; double: Y60–80; suite: Y180; dormitory bed: Y10

璇宫饭店

Xuangong Hotel (45 Jianghan Rd.; tel: 21023; cable: 2543). Built during the 1920s, the Xuangong's drab, grey appearance is more than offset by its ideal location near Wuhan's commercial center. All rooms are air-conditioned. The hotel underwent extensive renovations in 1986, and is again under renovation in 1988. The Xuangong has all standard services, including a bank, Western-style restaurant, bar, post office, and taxi stand.

From the Hankou train station, the Xuangong can be reached by the #2 tram (three stops) or the #1 or 24 bus (both two stops).

Rates: Double: Y45; suite: Y80/100

江汉饭店

Jianghan Hotel. A vintage European-style structure located near the Hankou train station, the Jianghan underwent extensive renovation in 1985. All 100 rooms are air-conditioned and supplied with telephones, refrigerators, and TVs. Services include a bank, laundry, taxis, and what locals proclaim to be one of the best restaurants in China.

Address: 245 Shengli Street
Telephone: 21253
Telex: 40150 HBJAH CN
Cable: 2429

Rates: Double: Y90
Suite: Y110–200
Extra bed: Y15

The **Holiday Inn Wuhan,** with 350 rooms, is expected to open in the summer of 1990.

Budget accommodations are available at the **Aiguo Hotel,** on Zhongshan Road near the train station (tel: 21231); the **Hankou Hotel** (541 Jiefang Rd.; tel: 356941); and the **Wuhan Hotel** (332 Jiefang Rd.; tel: 356661).

CUISINE

Wuchang fish is the most famous dish of the region—it was even mentioned in a poem by Mao Zedong. Another local specialty is the "Triple Delicious," a combination of rice, egg whites, and prawns. Street hawkers all over town feature "malodorous bean curd"—if you can get past the aroma, the taste is surprisingly pleasant. Wuhan's Yeweixiang (Wild Game) Restaurant (128 Yingwu Rd., Hanyang; tel: 443198) features steamed wild goose. The Laotongcheng Restaurant (juncture of Zhongshan and Dazhi roads; tel: 511843) has been featuring bean curd "skin" and other local specialties for over 60 years (service is best on the third floor). The Sijimei ("masses") Restaurant (corner of Zhongshan and Jianghan roads; tel: 22842) specializes in the region's justly famous steamed dumplings. The restaurants at the Jianghan and Shengli hotels are both said to serve some of the best food in China.

SHOPPING

The best shops in Wuhan are along the streets near the railroad station in Hankou, including Zhongshan Road and Jiefang Road; Hanyang's main shopping street is Zhongjia Cun. Street peddlers also sell a variety of wares, from rolling pins (for making dumplings) to wicker baskets. Wuhan's Friendship Store is at Jiefang Road near Sanyang Road, Hankou (tel: 25794).

Regular stores are open from 9 AM to 7 PM, with the exception of the antiques store, which is open only until 6 PM. The handicrafts store and the antiques store on Zhongshan Boulevard are recommended. Local items include traditional-style paintings, bambooware, plastic flowers, paper-cuts, and stone and wood carvings. The Wuhan Department Store at 358 Jiefang Boulevard in Hankou carries these as well as everyday items.

中国国际旅行社
CITS (Luxingshe) Office in Wuhan ■ 48 Jianghan Blvd. Tel: 25649. Telex: 40211 CITWH CN.

WUXI, in Jiangsu Province, is an industrial and resort city on the north bank of Lake Tai (Tai Hu), one of China's five largest lakes. Important as a transportation junction, Wuxi is situated astride the Grand Canal linking Beijing with Hangzhou and along the Nanjing–Shanghai railway line, 145 km. (87 mi.) west of Shanghai. Wuxi has an area of 204 sq. km. (78.7 sq. mi.) and a population of about 800,000. Largely unrenovated, the town has retained a gritty, bustling atmosphere reminiscent of pre-modern Chinese industrial centers. The original name of the city, Youxi ("with tin"), referred to local tin mines first worked in the Zhou Dynasty (c. 1066–221 BC). When the tin was depleted during the Han Dynasty (206 BC–AD 220), the name was changed to Wuxi ("without tin").

WUXI IN HISTORY

Wuxi's long history dates back some 3,000 years to the Shang and Zhou periods, when scattered settlements existed in the area. The city was formally founded during the Han Dynasty, as the capital of a feudal state in the region. Yet few details appear in later dynastic histories and Wuxi remained for the most part a small country town. This image did not begin to change until the 1930s, when Wuxi began rapidly to expand its industry, the keystone of which was 45 silk filatures. The town also gained some importance as a transport center, transshipping manufactured goods and silks by water to Shanghai. Its period of greatest expansion, however, occurred after 1949.

ECONOMY AND CULTURE

Wuxi has long been associated with silk production, an activity that had its origins in the area some 1,500 years ago. Silk-reeling and weaving workshops were set up in the mid-19th century, but the industry remained relatively stagnant during the first decades of this century. After the founding of the PRC in 1949, the silk filatures (which separate silk fibers from the cocoons and wind them onto spools) were rebuilt and expanded, and related activities such as silk weaving, dyeing, and printing were started up.

Today, the city is also known for high-technology products such as

Climate		Jan	Feb	Mar	Apr	May	Jun	Jul	Aug	Sep	Oct	Nov	Dec
Temp.	°C	3.1	4.3	8.4	13.9	19.1	23.0	27.8	28.1	24.1	18.1	12.5	5.9
	°F	37.5	39.7	47.1	57	66.3	73.4	82	82.5	75.3	64.5	54.5	42.6
Precip.	mm.	254	254	330	330	305	356	279	279	305	254	203	178
	in.	10	10	13	13	12	14	11	11	12	10	8	7

diesel engines, air compressors, electric cables, boilers, precision instruments, machine tools, and electronics parts. In total Wuxi has 470 factories employing some 249,000 skilled workers. Light industry includes the production of bicycles, enamelware, glassware, and the famous Huishan Clay Figure Workshop. The city also produces concrete boats for use on the region's numerous small canals (surprisingly, these boats are lighter than wooden craft and have greater maneuverability and speed; moreover, they require less upkeep).

Wuxi is surrounded by rich agricultural land capable of yielding three rice crops a year. Hog breeding and fishing are also important sources of income in the Lake Tai area.

The city has 150 primary and middle schools and one university. Some of the factories have part-time technical schools on their premises. Wuxi also has 12 hospitals and a prominent historical library.

HIGHLIGHTS
FOR TRAVELERS

Wuxi now figures on several group itineraries. It is also possible to arrange a day-excursion here from Shanghai via train by contacting the Shanghai Branch of CITS.

锡惠公园
Xihui Park. Located on the western outskirts of Wuxi, this park encompasses the neighboring Hui Hills, including "Tin Hill." Two famous sites are its temple and Jichang Garden ("Garden for Ease of Mind"), all dating back to the Ming Dynasty (1368–1644). The garden at the foot of the hill was rebuilt recently as an exact replica of the 16th-century original. The temple on top of Hui Hill was built in AD 420 and affords a broad view of the surrounding region. Several pavilions and teahouses are scattered throughout the park. On hot summer days, the exquisitely decorated stone-slab chairs are always cool to the touch.

惠山泥人厂
Huishan Clay Figure Workshop. Local artisans of the Ming era

Sculpting clay figurines at Huishan Clay Figure Workshop, Wuxi

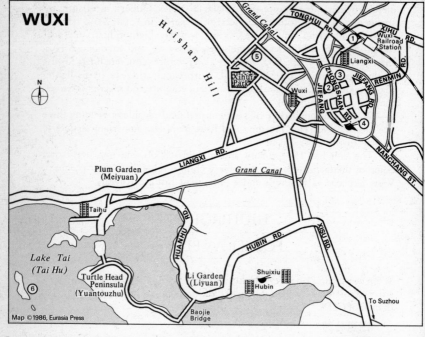

WUXI

Huishan Hill

Grand Canal

TONGHUI RD.

XIHU Wuxi Railroad Station

Liangxi

Xihui Park

Wuxi

ZHONGSHAN RD.

JIEFANG RD.

RENMIN RD.

JIEFANG

NANCHANG ST.

LIANGXI RD.

Plum Garden (Meiyuan)

Grand Canal

Taihu

HUANHU RD.

HUBIN RD.

XISU RD.

Lake Tai (Tai Hu)

Turtle Head Peninsula (Yuantouzhu)

Li Garden (Liyuan)

Shuixiu

Hubin

To Suzhou

Baojie Bridge

Map ©1986, Eurasia Press

① China International Travel Service (CITS)
② Dongfanghong Bazaar
③ No. 1 Department Store
④ Friendship Store
⑤ Huishan Clay Figure Workshop
⑥ Three Hills on Lake Tai

Restaurants
Hotels

were the first to discover the qualities of Hui Mountain clay. Excellent for molding, it also dries to a remarkable hardness and is thus suitable for firing. The local pottery factory underwent a modern revival in 1954 and today employs some 600 persons, about 60% female. Many of the figures produced here reflect contemporary literary and political themes. More than one-third of the output is exported. The factory has a small retail outlet for visitors.

无锡第一缫丝厂

Wuxi No. 1 Silk Filature. Another common spot on the visitor's itinerary is the No. 1 Silk Filature, which employs mainly women. This silk-reeling mill dates from 1933. Today's newly installed semi-automatic machines enable each worker to tend 60 threads of silk at a time.

大运河

Grand Canal. The Grand Canal cuts through the center of Wuxi as it meanders from Beijing to Hangzhou. The canal is excluded from most itineraries, possibly because it still reflects aspects of "old" China—much canal traffic is still manually propelled. The main canal dates from AD 605, when it connected the Yellow River in the north (at Luoyang) with the Yangtse in the south. By 610, the entire canal route between Beijing and Hangzhou was opened. Later, during the Yuan Dynasty (1279–1368), the waterway's northern segment was redredged. Over the centuries, the canal has remained a basic means of supplying the capital city with food from the south. The main canal bridge in Wuxi is a short distance from the central square of the city.

太湖
LAKE TAI

Lake Tai (Tai Hu) has an area of some 2,240 sq. km. (864 sq. mi.) and includes about 100 islands. Many of its sights may be visited by boat in the course of a morning or afternoon excursion.

工人疗养院
Workers' Sanitarium. Although there are several sanitariums located around the lake, most visitors tour the facility on Zhongdu Island, which provides treatment for noninfectious chronic diseases. It comprises three compounds with over 300 beds and commands a superb view of the lake and surrounding area. Both traditional Chinese medicine (e.g., acupuncture and moxibustion) and Western medicine are used to help patients, as well as physiotherapy and physical training programs.

鼋头渚
Turtle Head Island (Yuantouzhu). This small, pleasant island is situated off the lake's south shore. The island appears to form the head of a turtle, hence its name. There are several arched bridges, pavilions, and walkways, but the scenery itself is the main attraction, especially the lake, with its barges and fleets of sailing vessels. On the "head" of the turtle stands a small lighthouse, near which is a stone inscribed with the island's name.

太湖三山
Three Hills on Lake Tai. A restaurant on the main peak overlooks the lake and Turtle Head Island. Pears and apples, the source of considerable local pride, are served in season.

蠡园
Li Garden. One of three famous gardens in Wuxi, this pleasant spot lies south of the city on Lake Li, which feeds into Lake Tai. Li Garden reflects classic Chinese design, with grotesque rockeries, arched bridges, pavilions, walkways built on dikes that cross the lake, and a variety of flora. There is a miniature five-story pagoda at the mid-lake pavilion. It is reached via a covered promenade whose wooden walls are perforated by 89 flower-shaped windows. Legend has it that the garden was founded by a local king who courted a princess there.

HOTEL
ACCOMMODATIONS

太湖饭店

Taihu Hotel (Meiyuan; tel: 667901; telex: 36212 WXTUH CN). The Taihu is a modern two-story building with spacious, high-ceilinged rooms and small, screened windows which look out upon the tranquil expanse of Lake Tai. Ducks swim on a small pond in front of the hotel, and a lakeside garden invites an early morning or evening stroll. Services include a restaurant, post and telephone facilities, and a retail shop which will exchange foreign currency. The shop is well stocked with local crafts inlaid with semiprecious stones, silk merchandise, and hand-carved pipes.

湖滨饭店

Hubin Hotel (Liyuan Rd.; tel: 668812; telex: 36202 WXHB CN). The modern, multi-storied Hubin overlooks charming Lake Li and its bridges, pavilions, and surrounding greenery (the Hubin, regrettably, is also green and makes a rather unpleasant visual intrusion on the lake shore). It has 360 air-conditioned rooms and four dining rooms which specialize in regional seafood and fish dishes. The hotel's internal decor—mostly concrete, tile, and neon—is somewhat jarring amidst the subtle, quiet setting of the lake.

水秀饭店

Shuixiu Hotel (Liyuan Rd.; tel: 26591/668591). This recently built hotel stands alongside the Hubin and also affords a spectacular view of Lake Li.

All three of the above hotels are well out of walking range of Wuxi. Conveniently located in town, but far less commodious, are the Wuxi Hotel (Liangxi Daqiao; tel: 24553) and the Liangxi Hotel (intersection of Zhongshan Rd. and Shixin Lane; tel: 2951).

CUISINE

Visitors who do not speak Chinese may find it difficult to try a meal outside their hotel because Wuxi's restaurants do not have special sections catering to foreigners. The hotel dining rooms generally serve the standard fare. Fish dishes, of course, are quite popular, with shrimp, crab, and crisp-fried eel heading the specialties list. Spareribs in bean-curd sauce is a tasty local dish.

SHOPPING

Shoppers will be attracted by the fine regional handicrafts, which include pottery figurines, briar pipes, and linen embroideries. Silk products, the local specialty, range from finely woven wall hangings to dress fabrics. The best selections are found at the Dongfanghong Bazaar, a two-story emporium on Renmin Road, and the No. 1 Department Store on Zhongshan Road. Wuxi's small Friendship Store is located at 8 Chaoyang Road. There is also an antiques store that sometimes features items long since bought up in the larger cities.

中国国际旅行社
CITS (Luxingshe) Office in Wuxi ■ 7 Xinsheng Rd. Tel: 226812.

厦门

mansion gate

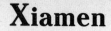

Xiamen

traditional spelling/Amoy

XIAMEN, a bustling and remarkably colorful enclave of 480,000 (a total of 965,000 live on the island), is located on the South China coast on an island of the same name. The island, with an area of 123.9 sq. km. (47.8 sq. mi.), is situated at the mouth of Jiulong (Nine Dragon) River in southern Fujian Province. The island is also known as Egret Island, some say because of its shape, others because it was once a nesting area for that elegant bird. Xiamen's climate is subtropical, with summer temperatures averaging 28°C (85°F) and winter temperatures no lower than 10°C (50°F).

In 1949, the island was connected to the mainland by a 5-km. causeway. The town is now connected by bus to all major points in Fujian as well as to Shantou and Guangzhou (bus information, tel: 3115). There is also indirect train service to Fuzhou and Shanghai (31 hours). (For train information, tel: 2812.) In addition, there is now twice-weekly passenger ship service to Hong Kong (22 hours; first-class bookings, US$45 per passenger).

XIAMEN IN HISTORY

First settled during the Southern Song Dynasty (1127–1279), the town was originally called Jiahe Yu (Good Grain Island) because of the abundant harvest afforded by its fertile soil and subtropical climate. At the beginning of the Ming, Zhou Dexin built what is now the city proper and called it Xiamen (Amoy in the local dialect). In the 17th century, Xiamen became one of the strongholds of the loyalist Ming general Zheng Chenggong (Koxinga), who launched an expedition against the Dutch who then occupied the island of Taiwan across the Formosa Straits. He renamed the town Siming, or "Remember the Ming."

By the Treaty of Nanjing in 1842, Xiamen was declared an open port. Europeans soon settled on Gulang Yu, an islet in Xiamen's harbor.

Many overseas Chinese in Southeast Asia come from Fujian Province and maintain close ties with relatives in China, often returning to live out their retirement in Xiamen. Their remittances and contributions, encouraged by special tax exemptions, have visibly enhanced Xiamen's prosperity and industrial development. An estimated 60% of the current population is said to have relations living abroad.

At the beginning of the 20th century, Xiamen exported tea (called

Climate		Jan	Feb	Mar	Apr	May	Jun	Jul	Aug	Sep	Oct	Nov	Dec
Temp.	°C	10.3	10.3	13.2	18.3	22.7	25.0	28.8	28.3	26.3	21.7	17.9	12.9
	°F	50.5	50.5	55.7	64.9	72.8	77	83.8	82.9	79.3	71	64.2	55.2
Precip.	mm.	152	152	203	279	304	381	254	203	178	178	152	127
	in.	6	6	8	11	12	15	10	8	7	7	6	5

cha in Mandarin, but *tê* in the local *Minnan* dialect, from which comes the English "tea"), sugar, dried fish, tobacco, fruit, and paper products. Today, as the most northerly of the four Special Economic Zones, it is an important center for foreign trade, with rail links to the hinterland and passenger cargo boats from Hong Kong crowding the harbor. Completion of the new airport, four new 10,000-ton docks, and a photographic film plant, built as a joint venture with Eastman Kodak, have combined to give a significant boost to the local economy. The entire city now functions as a Special Economic Zone.

HIGHLIGHTS
FOR TRAVELERS

Xiamen was opened to foreign tourism in 1980. Numerous natural and historic attractions await visitors to the island, not least of which are the gleaming white-sand beaches and parks scattered around the island.

万石公园

Wanshi Park. Nestled between Lion Hill (Shi Shan) and Jade Screen Hill (Yuping Shan) in the northwestern part of the city, Wanshi Park is known for its collection of tropical and subtropical flora. A reservoir and vegetarian restaurant are located on the grounds.

中山公园

Zhongshan Park. Also in the northwestern sector, Zhongshan Park is planted with pines and contains several monasteries and historical sites. At the park's eastern end is a massive marble stele erected to the memory of Dr. Sun Yatsen and to Xiamen's revolutionary heroes.

南普陀寺

Nanputuo Temple. This 1,000-year-old Buddhist temple is three miles east of the town on the slopes of Wulao Mountain. The temple compound faces the sea and commands a bird's-eye view of nearby Xiamen University on Daxue Rd. The present structure dates from the Kangxi period of the Qing Dynasty and has been renovated several times since the 1920s. The original temple is the tiny one-room structure in back, nestled under a rock ledge. In the main hall are the three Buddhas of the past, present, and future. The one in the center is Sakyamuni (the historical Buddha). On the base of these Buddhas are carved the stories of Xuanzang's journey to the West to retrieve the scriptures and of Sakyamuni's life. The Hall of Great Compassion is devoted to Guanyin, the Goddess of Mercy. The ceiling is 8 m. high, with a three-faced Guanyin statue inside. It has an ornate, three-tiered roof with flying dragons on top. The two sago cycad trees in the huge urns are over 1,000 years old. The first floor of the Scripture Hall is a study room for monks. This is also the site of a Buddhism School where the monks (there are more than 60 of them in the temple, two-thirds of them relatively young) pursue studies to aid in their work or to prepare them to take the test to enter one of the Buddhist academies. The second floor houses an interesting exhibition of Buddhist treasures.

厦门大学

Xiamen University. Just a short walk from Nanputuo Temple lies the campus of Xiamen University. It is at the southern tip of Xiamen Island, flanked by Wulaoshan and the sea. Founded in 1921 by overseas Chinese philanthropist Tan Kah Kee, it is still largely supported by overseas Chinese. It is a "key" school, with 11 departments, 37 degree concentrations, and 18 research institutes. It is best known for marine biology. There are 5,400 students and 1,200 teaching staff. The Overseas Correspondence College, which conducts short-term courses for foreigners on campus, is also quite advanced. Its library has 1.3 million volumes.

Aside from the interesting architecture of its old buildings, the campus boasts the Lu Xun Museum/Memorial Hall, the Anthropology Museum, and the nearby Overseas Chinese Museum. Lu Xun, the famous Chinese writer and revolutionary, taught at Xiamen University for one semester in 1926–27. The museum consists of his old room and five others, with an exhibition of objects, materials, and photos about Lu's life and activities in Xiamen, Beijing, Guangzhou, and Shanghai. The Museum of Anthropology is two floors of small rooms, each showing a different period in the development of mankind, especially in China. The Overseas Chinese Museum, located just northwest of the campus near the temple, features a compelling display devoted to the history and conditions of overseas Chinese around the world. The stress is on the suffering and oppression endured by these emigrants, along with the contributions they made to their host countries and to China. Also on exhibit are many artifacts brought back to China from these communities.

集美

Jimei. On the mainland north of Xiamen, and connected to it by the embankment, is Jimei, hometown of the well-known overseas Chinese patriot, Tan Kah Kee. Tan's mausoleum and the monument to commemorate his return to Xiamen are located in the southern part of the town, together with a number of schools that Tan had helped to establish. The Overseas Chinese Museum (Huaqiao Bowuguan) on Ciming Nan Rd. in Jimei was founded in 1959 with funds donated by overseas Chinese; it contains bronzes and pottery from the Ming and Qing dynasties.

鼓浪屿

Gulang Island (Gulangyu). This heavily forested island lies off the shore of Xiamen and can be reached by a 15-minute ferry from the foot of Zhongshan Rd. The island has flourished as a resort area since the arrival of Europeans in the 19th century. Its beauty and tranquility have earned it the nickname of "Garden on the Sea." The highest point on Gulang Yu, Sunlight Cliff (Riguang Yan), is 90 m. (297 ft.) above sea level and is the spot where Koxinga oversaw the nautical training of his

693

troops while they prepared to liberate Taiwan from the Dutch. A memorial hall to Koxinga is at 73 Yongchun Rd.

HOTEL ACCOMMODATIONS

华侨大厦

Overseas Chinese Mansion (70-74 Xinhua Rd.; tel: 25699/25606; telex: 93029 CTSXM CN). A 14-story building, the mansion opened in November 1982. As of mid-1983, many services and facilities at the hotel left much to be desired. It has already become the main hotel for foreigners visiting the city. There are 237 rooms and 472 beds, with rates ranging from Y30-75 per night. The adjoining building has large and small dining rooms, a bar, dance room, banquet hall, and nightclub.

厦门宾馆

The Xiamen Guest House (16 Huyuan Rd.; tel: 22265/22267; telex: 93065 GUEST CN; cable: 6333) is also a possibility for foreign tourists, but it is not nearly up to the standard of the Overseas Mansion. An alternative for budget travelers is the **Gulangyu Guest House** on Gulangyu Island (25 Huangyan Rd.; tel: 22052). It is situated in a lovely park filled with large banyan trees.

The Jinbao Hotel (on Xingang Rd.; tel: 46888; cable: 2888; telex: 93034 JINBO CN) features restaurants serving both Chinese and Western cuisine, a bar, nightclub, shops, and taxi service.

Other hotels in Xiamen include the **Lujiang Hotel** (3 Haihou Rd.; tel: 23235); **Xiamen Mansion** (tel: 2560); **Yanhua Hotel** (Huli Gongyuan; tel: 43333); **Xiamen Binguan** (South Guanyuan Rd.; tel: 24941); and the **Xiamen Mandarin** (Foreigners Residential Area, Huli; tel: 43333; telex: 93028 MANDA CN; cable: 0385), where President Nixon is rumored to have stayed once. The **Holiday Inn Xiamen** is scheduled to open in 1990.

CUISINE AND SHOPPING

There are said to be between 200–300 famous dishes emanating from Xiamen, combining the best of Cantonese and southern Fujian cooking, especially seafood and snacks (*dian xin*). The hotel dining rooms can prepare many of these, or you could try one of the many restaurants on Zhongshan and Siming roads. There is also a Western-style bar not far from the hotel.

Xiamen is also famous for its handicrafts, especially lacquer-thread sculpting, glass-bead embroidery, silk figurines (*caiza*), and painted clay and porcelain figurines. In lacquer-thread sculpting, a lacquer paste is rubbed or twisted into thin threads or small grains to form pictures and decorate wooden articles and porcelain. An array of these items can be found at the Friendship/Overseas Chinese Store just behind the Lujiang Hotel (near the ferry to Gulangyu), or at the Arts and Crafts Service Department at 143 Zhongshan Rd. Xiamen has two antiques stores: on Gulangyu Island at 71 Yongchun Rd. and in Xiamen town at 221 Zhongshan Rd.

中国国际旅行社
CITS (Luxingshe) Office in Xiamen ■ 7 Haihou Road. Tel: 25557/20846.
Telex: 93063 XMITS CN.

western peace

traditional spelling/Sian

OF ALL CITIES on the China itinerary, Xi'an and its history most vividly exemplify the extraordinary continuity of Chinese civilization. Once the largest city in the world and a paradigm of imperial splendor, Xi'an served as the capital of 11 dynasties. Only in recent years, however, has Xi'an become well-known outside of China, owing to the discovery there in 1974 of the astonishing burial site of Emperor Qin Shi Huangdi (3rd century BC). On the strength of the Qin tomb excavations, Xi'an has emerged almost overnight as one of the most popular tourist destinations in China, with a visit here becoming nearly as de riguer as a stop in Beijing.

Xi'an was also an active link in the major trade routes between China and the commercial enclaves of Central Asia and Europe during the 7th and 8th centuries. Today, Xi'an is the capital of Shaanxi Province and a model example of the PRC government's concerted efforts to create new inland centers of industry to counterbalance the traditional dominance of the large east-coast cities.

To the north of this city of 2.5 million people lie the rugged Western Hills, dotted with ancient tombs, and the Wei River, which forms a natural boundary. The entire region south of the river is fertile, suitable for growing cotton and coarse grains. The city's ancient walls and wide avenues, laid out in orderly grid patterns, are impressive, but the modern urban housing developments are undistinguished.

The climate in Xi'an is relatively harsh, with great seasonal variation. The average winter temperature is approximately 1°C (34°F), while in the summer it often rises to 28°C (82°F) and is sometimes even hotter. Early spring and fall are cool and comfortable. The rainy season begins in July and lasts until October. Dust storms and thunderstorms are not uncommon throughout the rest of the year.

Climate		Jan	Feb	Mar	Apr	May	Jun	Jul	Aug	Sep	Oct	Nov	Dec
Temp.	°C	−0.8	1.8	8.1	13.6	19.3	25.2	26.8	25.8	19.1	13.6	6.6	0.6
	°F	30.5	35.2	46.5	56.4	66.7	77.3	80.2	78.4	66.3	56.4	43.8	33
Precip.	mm.	76	76	76	102	152	203	305	254	178	152	102	76
	in.	3	3	3	4	6	8	12	10	7	6	4	3

XI'AN IN HISTORY

Remains of a Neolithic village in nearby Banpo indicate that the area was inhabited at least 8,000 years ago. Xi'an was effectively the captial of China as far back as the Western Zhou Dynasty (c. 1066–221 BC). When Emperor Qin Shi Huangdi unified China in 221 BC, he established his capital at Xiangyang (to the east of present-day Xi'an) and began construction of a magnificent palace (never finished) where the city of Xi'an now stands. Then known as Chang'an, the city flourished politically, culturally, and commercially. In 129 BC, it was linked to other regions of China by means of a canal that fed into the Wei River.

During the Sui (581–618) and Tang (618–907) dynasties, the city was considerably enlarged. The population then numbered about a million. Xi'an's strategic location along Asian trade routes brought frequent contacts with foreigners (evidence of these contacts is provided by tomb figurines of bearded horsemen, anomalous in China up to that time).

Following the demise of the Tang Dynasty at the start of the 10th century, Xi'an entered a decline and, despite periods of revival, never regained its prior eminence. By the 19th century, Xi'an was only one-sixth the size of the Tang Dynasty capital that existed eight centuries earlier.

Before the advent of modern communication links, Xi'an remained rather isolated. This condition began to change after 1930 with the completion of a rail spur that linked Xi'an to Zhengzhou as well as to cities to the west and north.

The "Xi'an Incident." In 1936, Chiang Kaishek visited the nearby hot springs to rest from his military campaign against the Communists and provincial warlords. In an event later known as the "Xi'an Incident," Chiang was captured and held prisoner by one of his own generals—a local warlord named Zhang Xueliang. Zhang sought to compel him to sue for peace with the Communists and join them in a united front against the Japanese. Zhou Enlai was dispatched to Xi'an to negotiate on behalf of the Communists and, despite Chiang's attempt to escape, a temporary agreement was effected.

ECONOMY AND CULTURE

When briefing visitors, local officials often point out that Xi'an is a city that "walks on two legs." That is, the industrial and agricultural sectors are mutually supportive and contribute almost equally to the economy. Traditionally, agriculture has predominated. The area surrounding Xi'an is flat, ideal for growing wheat and cotton, crops which have particularly benefited from mass programs to extend irrigation systems in the area. Corn is also produced, as are various fruits and vegetables. Xi'an's pomegranates and persimmons are particularly well flavored.

Dramatic changes in Xi'an have come about since 1949. The city has developed into the textile center of the northwest. Many other new industries such as fertilizers, chemicals, and electrical components have been introduced. Its wide streets have been paved. New buildings, department stores, sports arenas, universities, and a modern transportation system have contributed to its transformation.

Xi'an is the site of 11 of Shaanxi's 15 universities and research institutions, including Jiaotong University, one of China's largest polytechnical institutes. The region has its own theatrical, operatic, music, and dance traditions which continue to thrive. Huxian, a county west of Xi'an, has become world-famous for its peasant painters who began working in the late 1950s. Exhibitions of their work have toured the UK, France, Canada, Australia, and the US. Xi'an artisans produce shell and feather paintings and carved lacquerware items. An enamelware factory turns out everything from ashtrays to washbasins.

HIGHLIGHTS
FOR TRAVELERS

Xi'an's chief attraction is its rich archeological legacy. Visitors generally have time to see but a few of the myriad temples, tombs, and ruins in the area.

大雁塔

The Big Wild Goose Pagoda. The Big Wild Goose Pagoda was originally built in 652 as part of the Ci'en Temple, which was constructed in 648 by Crown Prince Li Zhi (later Emperor Gao Zong) in memory of his mother. When the monk Xuan Zang returned from India after an 18-year pilgrimage, he proposed that a building be constructed to store the manuscripts which he had brought back with him. Between 701 and 704, the original five-story pagoda was reconstructed into a seven-story, 64-m. (210-ft.)-high Buddhist temple. A large monastery with 897 rooms

Big Wild Goose Pagoda

was added to the site. The temple is believed to have been named after a Big Wild Goose Pagoda in India, which was called that because it was built on the site where a wild goose fell from the sky in answer to the prayers of a group of starving Buddhist monks. To express their gratitude, they buried the goose instead of eating it, and later built the temple. Xi'an's Big Wild Goose Pagoda was restored in the early 1950s and offers an excellent view of the city and surrounding area.

小雁塔

The Small Goose Pagoda. The 43-m. (141-ft.)-high Small Wild Goose Pagoda was built between 707 and 709, and was soon thereafter almost totally destroyed by the ravages of war. The temple was rebuilt but was again damaged seriously during a major 16th-century earthquake. Still bearing its scars, the frail structure was repaired and reopened to visitors in 1977. A pleasant garden with a stunning selection of poppies surrounds the pagoda.

钟楼

Bell Tower. The Bell Tower was built in 1384 in what was then the center of the city. It was moved to its present location in 1582. Major renovations were carried out in 1739. The two-story, 36-m. (118-ft.)-high structure has three layers of gracefully arched eaves. The first floor is now used as a briefing room (it held prisoners during the civil war). The second floor provides an excellent view of the city.

鼓楼

Drum Tower. Similar in construction to the Bell Tower, the Drum Tower was built under the Ming in 1375. It was reconstructed in the 17th and 18th centuries and again after 1949. The rectangular base is surmounted by a wooden superstructure topped by three glazed-tile roofs.

明代城墙

Ming Dynasty City Wall. Built between 1374 and 1378 during the reign of the Emperor Hongwu of the Ming Dynasty, the Xi'an city wall is a typical example of China's ancient city battlements. It is 12 m. (39 ft.) high, 12–14 m. (39–46 ft.) wide at the top, and 5–18 m. (49–59 ft.) wide at the base; its length is 14 km. (8.7 mi.). The city moat, which abuts much of the wall, is currently under reconstruction.

兴庆公园

Xingqing Park. Located in the eastern outskirts of the city, the park stands on the site of the Xingqing Palace, the official residence of the Tang Dynasty Emperor Xuan Zong. The park covers an area of 50 hectares (123 acres), and today contains an art gallery, reading room, teahouse, photo studio, and children's playground.

清真寺

The Great Mosque. The Great Mosque is located on Hua Ju Lane near the Drum Tower, in a primarily Muslim neighborhood. Originally founded in 742, Xi'an's principal mosque is one of the largest and best preserved Muslim sanctuaries in China. Renovations were first begun during the Song Dynasty, but most buildings date from 1527 and 1606 (Ming Dynasty), when major enlargements were made. It now has four courtyards and covers an area of 12,000 sq. m. (14,340 sq. yd.). This is one of four mosques in Xi'an that serve the city's 60,000 Muslim residents. The Great Mosque is open daily to visitors (except during religious services).

陕西省博物馆

Shaanxi Provincial Museum. Housed in a former Confucian temple in the southern district of the city, the museum boasts one of the richest collections of ancient artifacts in all of China. Three main buildings and three annexes have been remodeled twice in the last five years and can accommodate as many as 4,000 separate exhibitions. Notable objects include sandstone and granite animal figures, Tang Dynasty stone friezes, bronzes, Neolithic pottery, and jewelry. Detailed captions in English (still unusual in China) provide helpful descriptions.

The museum's centerpiece is its "forest of stelae," a collection of 1,095 stone tablets on which ancient texts—including the Confucian classics—were etched (some carved by emperors), resulting in a magnificent display of classical calligraphy.

咸阳博物馆

Xiangyang Museum. Opened in 1962, the museum is housed in a former Confucian temple built in 1371. It contains over 3,000 objects from the Warring states period and the Qin and Han dynasties. Particularly impressive is the collection of hundreds of Han Dynasty horses and riders unearthed at a tomb in Yangjiawan.

华清温泉

Hua Qing Hot Springs. The Hua Qing Hot Springs, an oasis of greenery and red-roofed pavilions set amidst the stark scenery of Xi'an, are located about 30 km. (19 mi.) east of the city at the foot of Lishan Hill. Discovered 2,800 years ago during the Western Zhou Dynasty, the springs for centuries served as a resort area for China's emperors and ruling families. In 644, the Tang emperor Tai Zong built a palace here. This was enlarged in 747 by Emperor Gao Zong, who lived here with his concubine, a fabled beauty named Lady Yang Yuhuan (Yang Guifei). She came to an unfortunate end—the emperor spent so much time with her that his ministers insisted she be put to death so he could concentrate on affairs of state. Today the bathtub and dressing room of the Lady Yang are still pointed out to tourists. In 936, a Daoist monastery was built on the ruins of the Tang Dynasty palace. More recently, the hot springs were the site of the so-called Xi'an incident (see Xi'an in History, above). The event is now commemorated by the "Catching Chiang Pavilion."

秦陵

Tumulus of Qin Shi Huangdi. Qin Shi Huangdi (personal name Ying Zheng, 259–210 BC) founded the Qin Dynasty in 221 BC when he succeeded in unifying China politically for the first time in history. A harsh but practical ruler, Qin was responsible for instituting a series of economic reforms as well as for standardizing weights and measures and initiating construction of both the Great Wall and Grand Canal. His tomb is located on the southen bank of the Wei River, 5 km. east of the town of Lintong. Work began on the tomb in 247 BC, the year in which he assumed the throne of the feudal state of Qin at the age of 13. The massive project required over 700,000 workers, many of whom had been sentenced to forced labor for disobeying the emperors' new laws. It took 36 years to complete the huge underground palace and surrounding structures. Although the tomb has not yet been opened, it is believed to contain great treasures, as well as the remains of many of the emperor's officials, eunuchs, and craftsmen who were buried alive when the tomb was sealed. Local peasants now sell their wares on the path through the wheat fields that leads to the tumulus. (See also, China's Archeological Treasures, above.)

1. Shaanxi Provincial Museum
2. Bell Tower
3. Drum Tower
4. Post Office Building
5. Department Store
6. People's Theater
7. Telephone and Telegraph Building
8. Xi'an People's Stadium
9. Memorial Museum of the Eighth Route Army, Xi'an Office
10. Great Mosque (Qingzhensi)
11. Five Western Terraces (Xiwutai)
12. Temple of the Eight Immortals (Baxian'an)
13. Small Wild Goose Pagoda
14. Shaanxi Provincial People's Stadium
15. Big Wild Goose Pagoda

▦ Hotels
ᴨᴨ Former City Wall

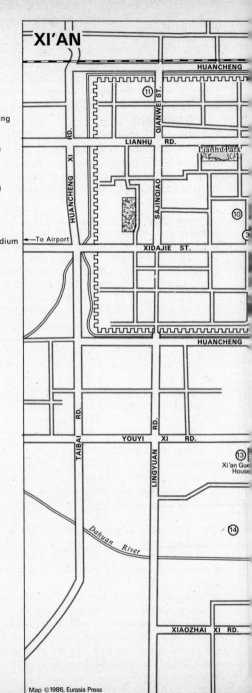

XI'AN

HUANCHENG

⑪

QIANWEI ST.

LIANHU RD.

HUANCHENG XI

Lianhu Park

SAJINQIAO

⑩

←To Airport

XIDAJIE ST.

HUANCHENG

TAIBAI RD.

YOUYI XI RD.

LINGYUAN RD.

⑬ Xi'an Gue House

⑭

Dahuan River

XIAOZHAI XI RD.

Map ©1986, Eurasia Press

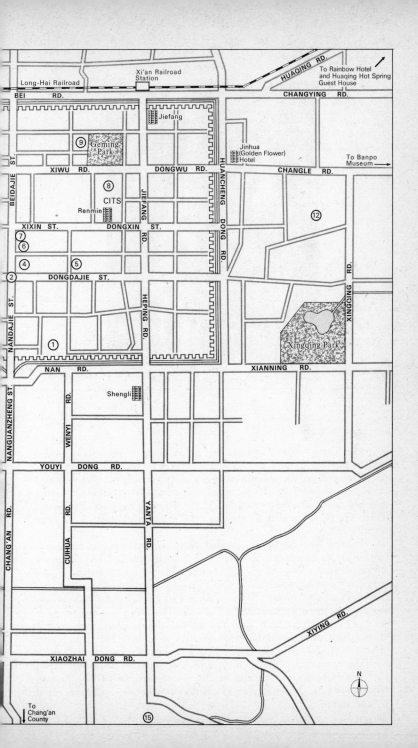

Terra cotta cavalry group from Qin Tomb

秦始皇兵俑

The Terra Cotta Warriors. In 1974, a group of peasants digging a well in Lintong County, about 30 km. east of Xi'an, accidentally made one of the century's greatest archeological discoveries. What they stumbled upon were thousands of life-size terra cotta warriors who had been standing guard by the tomb of the emperor Qin Shi Huangdi for over 2,000 years. Three vaults, containing an estimated 8,000 figures, have thus far been identified.

The first vault has been excavated. Now enclosed beneath a protective hangar-like construction, the site is open to the public. The cavern is 230 m. (754 ft.) long, 62 m. (203 ft.) wide, and 5 m. (16 ft.) deep, and contains the infantry section of Qin's massive clay army. Ranging in size from 1.78 m. to 1.87 m. (70 in. to 73 in.) in height, the 6,000 warriors are clad in armor or short, belted gowns. The torsos are hollow, with solid arms and legs. Each face was individually sculpted, with models chosen from throughout the military ranks of China. The figures were originally brightly painted. (Photography is not permitted on the site.)

The second and third vaults, which contain an additional 2,000 figures of men, horses, and chariots, were discovered in 1976. Following test excavations, the vaults were resealed until full-scale exploration could be undertaken.

昭陵

Zhaoling. The tomb of the second emperor of the Tang Dynasty, Tai Zong (personal name Li Shimin, 618–907), was opened to the public in 1978. Tai Zong, who ruled from 627 to 649, launched China into one of its greatest eras of political and cultural achievement. Under his patronage, both Daoist and Confucian traditions flourished, while the growth of Buddhism in China was given its greatest impetus: Tai Zong himself came out to receive the scholar Xuan Zang upon his return from India bearing the texts of the Mahayana.

Zhaoling is the first imperial tomb to employ the technique of burial on a mountainside rather than in a tumulus raised on flat land. It covers an area of 20,000 hectares (49,400 acres) near Liquan, some 60 km. (37 mi.) northwest of Xi'an. The tomb has been refashioned into an underground museum. It contains a historically precious set of stone tablets that provides a wealth of data on peasant uprisings that occurred at the end of the Sui Dynasty (AD 581–618) and on the unifying wars during the early Tang. Also on display are an exquisite collection of painted pottery figurines, murals, and utensils from subsidiary tombs at the site. Early Tang craftsmen achieved realistic characterizations by meticulously capturing gestures, movement, facial expressions, and costumes. Even eyebrows and moustaches are traced out stroke by stroke. Many minority people are represented in the pottery figurines. Pottery camels give evidence of extensive exchanges with other regions during the Tang Dynasty.

乾陵

Qianling. Qianling, the joint tomb of the Emperor Gaozong (AD 628–690) and his consort, the Empress Wu Zitian (AD 624–705), is located on Liangshan Hill, approximately 85 km. (53 mi.) from Xi'an. The tomb was originally surrounded by two walls (since destroyed), and buildings containing 375 rooms. The tomb has not been excavated, but is worth visiting to see the exquisite stone animal carvings which line the road to the tomb and the group of 61 statues depicting the foreign envoys (from countries as far away as Afghanistan) who attended the funeral of the Emperor Gaozong. Most of these figures have lost their heads. Legend has it that during the Song Dynasty local peasants believed that crop failures were due to the evil influence of the foreign spirits, and therefore knocked off the heads of the statues. Further damage was done during the Cultural Revolution. At the top of the hill there are two tablets, one bearing the "Records of the Holy Deeds of the Emperor Gaozong." The other is the "Tablet with No Inscription," left blank by the empress in the belief that future generations would fill it in with praise of her accomplishments.

There are 17 satellite tombs in the vicinity, of which six have been excavated since 1960. The tombs of Princess Yong Tai and Prince Chang Huai are located at about a 10-minute drive from Qianling.

茂陵

Maoling. The Mao mausoleum is the tomb of Liu Che, the great emperor Wu of the Han Dynasty. It took more than 50 years to complete, by far the longest period for a Han tomb. It is believed that many treasures are still buried in the tomb, including a jade trunk and stick which were gifts from a foreign emissary to China.

半坡博物馆

Banpo Museum. About 10 km. (6 mi.) east of Xi'an, on a bluff over-looking the Chan River, is the site of a Neolithic community which practiced the Yangshao culture (c. 6000 BC). It was discovered accidentally in 1953 when the foundations for a factory were being laid. Subsequent digging revealed the traces of a village of 100 houses, with remarkably preserved examples of Stone Age pottery, tools, and human and animal bones. The objects are on display in two exhibition halls.

The excavated village has been protected by the construction of a free-standing building that covers the entire site. Visitors view the original foundations, along with a reconstructed replica of a house, from a wooden walkway.

西五台

Five Western Terraces. Four of the original five Song Dynasty pavilions are still standing in the northwest corner of the city. They are also known today as the Anqing Temple.

青龙寺

Qing Long Temple. Recently restored, this Tang Dynasty Buddhist temple was reopened to the public late in 1984. Bus #5 stops near the temple site.

长安县

Chang'an County. Often visited by Japanese tour groups, but not generally found on other tour itineraries, the ancient Buddhist temples, pagodas, and monuments south of the city proper in Chang'an County are a worthwhile detour for those travelers not yet jaded from too much temple gazing. Of particular interest to Buddhists and historians is the Xingjiao Temple, which features three well-preserved stone pagodas. Nearby are the twin pagodas of Huayan Temple. This ediface was once the central temple of the philosophical Huayan sect, which survives in Japan today as Kegon Buddhism.

Set amidst the loess hills and plains of central Shaanxi Province, these and other sites are best reached by taxi, if only to avoid the crowds. But buyer beware: although most Xi'an taxi drivers are scrupulous and honest, some have been known to charge outrageous prices, and even cheat unwary tourists.

HOTEL ACCOMMODATIONS
DELUXE

金花饭店
Golden Flower Hotel (8 Chang An Rd. West; tel: 32981; telex: 70145 GFH). Xi'an's new "grand hotel," the Golden Flower opened its doors on April 15, 1985. Managed by the international Sara Hotels group, the hotel is exceptionally clean and well managed. Many supplies (such as American beef) are flown in, and prices reflect this, but so far the consensus has been that the Golden Flower is a cut above Beijing's highly touted joint-venture hotels. Rooms are well-appointed, and the Chinese and Western restaurants both serve good food (a rare find in Xi'an), including a sumptuous Scandinavian smorgasbord. There is also a piano bar and a disco. American Express cards are accepted, and direct booking is possible.

Scheduled for completion in April 1989, a second wing is being developed at the Golden Flower which will include 306 rooms and apartments. Among the new facilities added will be a banquet room, health club with sauna, heated swimming pool and jacuzzi, and a cocktail lounge.

Rates: Single: US$124; double US$144; suite: US$250

喜来登丝绸之路饭店
Sheraton Xi'an Hotel. Formerly called the Guo'an Hotel, the Sheraton Xi'an Hotel is located adjacent to the existing Xi'an Airport (which is due to be closed in 1988) just outside the city wall, on Fenggao Street. The new airport, now under construction, is 38 km. away. This 16-story hotel, 4.5 km. west of the Bell Tower, will have 476 rooms, including 15 suites. Amenities offered will include air-conditioning, minibar, refrigerator, direct-dial telephone, radio, color television, and closed-circuit movies. For dining, the hotel will have five restaurants (including two Chinese and one Western) and bars; among the recreational facilities are an indoor pool and Health Club. Business services such as a banquet hall for up to 300, function rooms, and a Business Center will be available. The hotel is scheduled to open in late 1989.

建国饭店
Jianguo Hotel (corner of Golden Flower Road and Huzuo Road). Currently under construction, the Jianguo Hotel is a member of the Steigenburger Reservation Service. 400 rooms are open in 1988, with the final opening slated for spring of 1989. It is situated on the edge of the Imperial City, close to Xingqing Park, the Banpo Museum, and the zoo. The airport is 15 km. away. All rooms are equipped with air-conditioning, color televisions, minibar, and direct-dial telephones. Facilities include business center, health club, beauty parlor, barbershop, Continental and Chinese restaurants, cocktail lounge, and 24-hour coffee shop. When completed, the hotel will offer 700 rooms.

Rates: Singles: US$46–60; twin: US$60–120; suites: US$120.

假日西安饭店

Holiday Inn Xi'an (8 Huangcheng East Road, South Section). This 350-room hotel is scheduled to open in July 1988. It is located at the East Gate, 10 km. from the airport. Rooms are equipped with individually-controlled air-conditioning, color television, refrigerator, and minibar. Facilities will include a health club and sauna, indoor swimming pool, business center, Games Room, barbershop and beauty parlor, bakery, two restaurants, and conference rooms.

Other joint-venture hotels due to open in Xi'an are the **Xi'an Grand,** a 700-room Sino-HK hotel to be managed by Accor of France, which is expected to open in August 1988; and the **Hawaii Hotel,** managed by Pearl Hotels International, which promises to offer a Polynesian/Hawaiian restaurant (56 Youji Dong Rd.; tel: 51888).

FIRST-CLASS AND STANDARD

唐华宾馆

Xi'an Garden Hotel (Tanghua Binguan; tel: 715111; telex: 8570027 GAHTL CN). Within sight of the Big Wild Goose Pagoda, the new Xi'an Garden Hotel is scheduled to open in April 1988. The Xi'an Garden is an ambitious Sino-Japanese (Mitsui) venture designed to meet international standards. Part of a 100,000-sq.-m. tourism development project being built just beyond the Old Capitol's South Gate, the 301-room Xi'an Garden is set amidst park-like grounds and is managed by Japan Travel Bureau International.

Adjacent is the new Tang Theater Restaurant, a 250-seat establishment which serves food and drink in the course of performances of traditional "Shanzisheng Gewu" (local acrobatic) spectacles; also within the complex is the Tang Culture and Arts Museum, devoted to the artistic and cultural achievements of the Tang Dynasty.

The hotel buildings themselves are in the grand Tang style, albeit with up-to-date amenities: a marble lobby; lounge and bar; banquet room; disco; Chinese, Japanese, and Western restaurants; a shopping arcade; sauna; barbershop and beauty parlor.

Rates: Twins: US$105–150; suites: US$250

朝代饭店

Hotel Dynasty (Lianhua Road and Sajin Bridge). Due to open in October 1988, this hotel will form part of the new Xi'an Art and Cultural Center. A first-class hotel, the Dynasty will have 550 rooms and suites, as well as four restaurants and lounges, ballroom and meeting facilities, a swimming pool, tennis courts, and a 1,200-seat theatre. The **Xi'an Cultural and Art Center,** a $37-million complex with a 14-story tower and adjacent buildings, will house the 490-room hotel, a multi-purpose hall, and exhibition hall. The hotel will be managed by Hong Kong's New World Hotels, represented in the US by China Express.

解放饭店

Liberation Hotel (Railway Station Square; tel: 28946). Recently remodeled, the 30-year-old Liberation Hotel is located only five minutes from the railway station on foot and only five minutes from the airport by car. All 363 rooms now have central air-conditioning, in-house cable television, and touchtone telephones. The hotel offers ticket-booking and tourist services.

Rates: Double: Y80; triple: Y99; four-person suite: Y110; double suite: Y120. Winter discount rates available.

西安宾馆

Xi'an Guest House (26 Chang'an Lu; tel: 71-1351; telex: 70135 XAHTL; cable: 6333). The Xi'an is a modern 14-story hotel opened in March 1982. The rooms are pleasant and well-maintained, with views of the Small Wild Goose Pagoda and other surroundings. Hotel facilities include a bank, post office, clinic, hairdresser, coffee shop, bar, and a variety of small shops. During the summer, a bar and disco are open on the roof. Special dance and acrobatic performances are often held there for guests. The food in the hotel's four dining rooms is reasonably good.

Rates: Double: Y58; renovated doubles: Y100/120

朱雀饭店

Scarlet Peacock Hotel (26 Xiao Zhai, West Rd.; tel: 53311; telex: 70186 TSDHL CN). Opened in March 1985, this 110-room hotel is mainly set aside for foreign tour groups. Indeed, the rates discourage individual travelers, who must pay nearly twice the group rate for accommodations. The hotel has been under construction for several years, and some of the rooms are already in need of renovation. All rooms have air-conditioning, TV, and telephone. The three dining rooms serve both Chinese and Western cuisine. Other amenities include a coffee shop, bar/disco, and small shops.

Rates: Double (group): Y43; (individual): Y75; "modern": Y100

钟楼饭店

Bell Tower Hotel (opposite Bell Tower; tel: 718760/718767; cable: 6988; telex: 70124 XABTH CN). Reopened in February 1988 after extensive renovation, the Bell Tower Hotel is now managed by Holiday Inn. It is located at East Gate, at the southwest corner of the Bell Tower. From the hotel it is only a 15-minute walk to the Bell Tower in the city center. The airport is 10 km. away. The 358 rooms are provided with air-conditioning, color TV, video, refrigerator, and minibar. For dining there is a coffee shop, Western restaurant, and Sichuan restaurant, as well as a bar and a bakery. Meeting and conference facilities are available for up to 200, in addition to two smaller meeting rooms. Recreational facilities include a health club and sauna, indoor swimming pool, and games room. Their Business center offers fax and telex services. *Rates,* including airport transfer and breakfast (3-night minimum): Single: $200; double: $280.

唐城饭店

Tangcheng Hotel (Jixiangcun; tel: 54171/55921; telex: 70013 TCH; cable: 3266). Opened in mid-1986, the Tangcheng had been planned as Xi'an's first-choice hotel for tour groups. Guest rooms, however, are small and even at opening appeared shabby and run-down. Baths feature slanted floors, leaking fixtures, and six-foot-high towel racks. All rooms are thinly carpeted and equipped with air-conditioning, telephone, and TV. The Tangcheng offers computerized, direct-dial long-distance and overseas telephone service. It has ten restaurants, featuring Japanese, French, and assorted Chinese regional cuisines; a coffee shop; a disco; and a banquet hall/ballroom. Food is above average and overall service at the Tangcheng is friendly.

Rates: Double: Y80–100

西安协和酒店

Concord Hotel (12 Fenggao Street; tel: 44828; telex: 70024 CONHL; cable: 4460). The deluxe rooms and suites at the modern Concord Hotel are equipped with private bath, air-conditioning, color television and in-house movies, telephone, and refrigerator/mini-bar. Facilities include Chinese and Western restaurants, coffee shop, bar, medical facilities, exchange, and air and rail bookings.

Rates: Single: $65; double: $75; suite: $130; single/double (group): $56

体育宾馆

Sportsman's Lodge (Chang'an Rd., inside Shaanxi Sports Center; tel: 53341/2/5). Located in peaceful surroundings amidst the fields and buildings of an expansive sports park, the Sportsman's Lodge is a pleasant hotel offering modest accommodations at reasonable rates. All rooms have private bath, air-conditioning, TV, telephone, and refrigerator. Direct booking by letter or phone is possible.

Rates: Double: Y55; suite: Y110

人民大厦

Renmin Hotel (319 Dongxin Jie; tel: 71-5111; cable: 0633; telex: 70176 RMHTA CN). Built in 1952 by Soviet technicians, the Renmin is a dark and uninviting place. Rooms vary in size from closets to comfortable suites. Hotel facilities include a bank, post office, and gift shop. Despite the lack of luxury, it is located within a few minutes' walk of downtown.

There are also three municipal hostels in Xi'an, located on Youyi Dong Lu, Qingnian Lu, and Xi Dajie near Da Xuexi Xiang.

SUBURBAN GUEST HOUSES

长安宾馆

Chang'an Guest House (Chang'an County; tel: 913-25031) is a Chinese-style hotel with small but comfortable rooms located at about a 15-minute drive south of Xi'an. Facilities include a coffee shop, gift shop, bank, and post office.

陕西宾馆

Shaanxi Provincial Guest House (Zhangbagou; tel: 41813; telex: 70181) is a state guest house located approximately 25 minutes by car outside of Xi'an. It may be one of the most depressing hotels in China. Once the estate of a regional warlord, the grounds are beautiful, dotted with 46 small lakes. All rooms are air-conditioned, with TV, telephone and private bath. Buildings 7, 8, and 9 are used most often; each has about 40 rooms which vary in size if not in quality. The hotel has a bank and gift shop, but these are rarely open.

长安饭店

Chang'an Hotel (7 Youyi Street; tel: 51592). Located less than 10 miles south of Xi'an, the Chang'an's architecture is in the style of the Tang Dynasty. There are 48 rooms, all with air-conditioning, private bath, color TV, and telephone. There is a bar and a Chinese restaurant that prepares Western-style cuisine upon request. Room rates are reasonable.

华清池宾馆

Huaqing Hot Spring Guest House (Lintong County). Built in 1977, the Huaqing is a small inn done in the style of the Tang Dynasty. There are rooms with hot spring baths for 40 people.

CUISINE

Put politely, the cuisine in Xi'an is not among the most sought-after in China. Dishes are frequently greasy and there is often a shortage of fresh fruits and vegetables. Local specialties include steamed fish, spicy noodles, and "Empress Dowager Cakes," a dry bun made from expensive ingredients to resemble a coarse grain roll which the Empress Cixi had enjoyed.

By arrangement with CITS, the following restaurants feed almost all the tourists in Xi'an, and can be relied on to serve reasonable, and sometimes excellent, meals: **Dongya Restaurant** (recommended), 46 Luoma Shi (tel: 28410); **Heping Restaurant,** 88 Heping Lu (tel: 24726); **Minsheng Restaurant,** 75 Jiefang Lu (tel: 23031); **Sichuan Restaurant,** 151 Jiefang Lu (tel: 24736); **Wuyi Restaurant,** 351 Dong Dajie (tel: 23824); **Xi'an Restaurant,** 298 Dong Dajie (tel: 22047).

For the more adventurous, there are a number of small restaurants along Dong Dajie. One of the most interesting of these is the **Qingya** (tel: 28268), which is run by the local Muslim community.

SHOPPING

The Xi'an Friendship Store, located on Nanxin Jie in the center of the city, has a good selection of standard merchandise (cloisonné, silk, jewelry, etc.), as well as some locally produced handicrafts. Contrary to trends elsewhere in China, prices here tend to be somewhat lower than in many of the small tourist shops. Next door, on the corner of Dong Dajie, is the Xi'an Department Store, where it is possible to obtain a wide variety of practical items. A block to the left of the Friendship Store is the Xi'an Jade Carving Workshop (173 Xi 1-Lu; tel: 22570). If you have never watched this intricate process, it is worth a quick visit. Directly across Nanxin Jie, there are a number of other small shops also catering to tourists. Ordinary shops are located on Dong Dajie. One of China's four cloisonné factories is in Xi'an (138 Huangcheng Xilu, tel: 28891). The working areas are open to the public, and there is a small shop and exhibition room.

Among the best purchases available in Xi'an are the hand embroidered animals and clothing made by local peasants. The biggest selection is available at the tombs and excavation sites, where women line the entrances to sell their handiwork.

There are three antiques stores in Xi'an. These are located on the second floor of the Drum Tower; inside the Shaanxi Provincial Museum; and at 375 Dong Dajie, near the Bell Tower.

XI'AN DIRECTORY

HEALTH AND EMERGENCY SERVICES	Telephone
Shaanxi Provincial People's Hospital, Youyi West Rd.	51331
Xi'an Red Cross Hospital, Nanshaomen	28926

TELEPHONE AND TELEGRAPH SERVICES	Telephone
Long-Distance Telecommunications Office, North Ave.	24007
Xi'an City Telephone Exchange, Yandian St.	24152
Post Office, Clock Tower	21182

TRAVEL	Telephone
China International Travel Service (CITS), Chang'an Rd.	51419
China Travel Service (CTS); Overseas Chinese Travel Service, 272 Jiefang Rd.	21191

AIR	
Civil Aviation Administration of China (CAAC) Administrative Office, Laodong Rd.	41989
Ticket Office, Laodong Rd.	42861

RAIL	
Xi'an Railway Inquiry Office, East Station	26076
Telephone Inquiry Office, Guibinlou	26976
Lianhu Lu Ticket Office, West Shangchang, Beidajie	25361

LOCAL TRANSPORTATION	
Xi'an Taxi Corp.	721863
Xi'an No. 2 Motorcar Co., West Ave.	26624

BANKING AND TRADE	Telephone
Bank of China, Xi'an Branch, 233 Jiefang Rd.	26817
Shaanxi Province Foreign Economic Relations and Trade Commission, West Xincheng	27043
Xi'an Foreign Economic Relations and Trade Commission, 159 Beiyuanmen	719186

CULTURAL ACTIVITIES	Telephone
Chinese Academy of Sciences, 3 Xiaozhai Rd.	51782
Shaanxi Provincial Museum, Sanxue St.	26857
Museum of Qin Shihuang Tomb Figures, West Ave.	28639
Banpo Museum, Banpocun, Eastern Suburbs	39691
Shaanxi Provincial Library, West Ave.	22420
New China Bookstore, 99 Lianhu Rd.	24609
Renmin Theater, North Ave.	21515
Wuyi (May Day) Theater, Duanlumen, East Ave.	27298
Wusi (May 4th) Theater, North Ave.	24973
People's Stadium, West-5 Rd.	22992

Xishuangbanna 西双版納

twelve districts   *traditional spelling/Hsishuangpanna*

THE Xishuangbanna Dai Autonomous Prefecture is one of China's most exquisite natural areas, with mountains rising out of forest canopies, graceful women in colorful printed skirts, and young boys in the golden robes of Buddhist monks. Located in the southwest corner of Yunnan Province, it was long one of the most inaccessible regions of China. In the mid-19th century, it took travelers over a year to reach the area from Beijing. The region, which encompasses the districts of Jinhong, Menghai, and Mengla, is covered with a dense forest inhabited by elephants, wild boar, golden-haired monkeys, deer, leopards, peacocks, and other tropical fauna. Between the mountains are 34 valleys, where most of the villages are clustered. Twelve ethnic minority nationalities—the Dai, Aini, Bulang, Jinou, Lahu, Awa, Yao, Hui, Zhuang, Yi, Bai, and Kucong—live here along with a substantial Han Chinese population.

Xishuangbanna covers an area of 20,000 sq. km., of which 96% is mountainous. Bordered on the southwest by Burma and on the southeast by Laos, it is divided by the Lancang (Mekong) River, which links it to Vietnam. The climate is subtropical, with an average yearly temperature of 21°C. The temperature varies greatly during the day, and afternoons can be very hot. There are two seasons: the monsoon, from May to October, and the dry season, which lasts from November to April. During the winter months, heavy fog descends upon the area, preventing drought.

Xishuangbanna's population is 650,000, of which approximately one third is Dai (Tai), one third is Han, and one third is made up of the other 11 ethnic groups. The largest town is Jinhong, the region's administrative center, with a population of 40,000.

GETTING THERE

Visitors to Xishuangbanna generally first go to Kunming. Upon arrival in the city, you must apply for a travel permit from the Public Security office. For group tourists whose trip has been arranged by CITS, this is largely a formality which can usually be completed in less than 24 hours. Individual travelers should expect to wait 3–5 days for their application to be approved, although in most cases it does not take this long.

There are biweekly flights from Kunming to Simao. These do not leave on a fixed schedule, so CAAC should be contacted upon arrival in Kunming. Flight times may also change suddenly and planes may depart earlier than the announced time without warning. From Simao, it is a five-hour bus ride over twisting mountain roads to Jinghong. Although few foreigners have the stomach for it, it is also possible to reach Jinghong by a four-day bus trip from Kunming.

XISHUANGBANNA IN HISTORY

According to a Dai legend, Xishuangbanna was discovered several thousand years ago by hunters chasing a golden deer. In Chinese historical records, the Dai people are mentioned as long ago as the Western Han Dynasty (second century BC). During the first and second centuries AD, Dai chieftains sent tribute missions to the Chinese capital at Luoyang, but the area's remoteness limited further ties. In the eighth century, Dali, in north central Yunnan (see section on Dali, above) became the capital of Nanzhao, an independent state ruled by the Bai minority people. Xishuangbanna was under the administrative rule of Nanzhao until its absorption into the Chinese empire in the 13th century. During the Yuan Dynasty (1279–1368), Xishuangbanna came under the nominal control of the central government. The Cheli Military and Civil Administration was formed in Jinhong at that time, and since then there has always been a representative of the ruling Chinese government there.

During the Nationalist period the central government strengthened its hold on Xishuangbanna, but did little to improve conditions in the area. In 1942 there was a major, but unsuccessful, uprising.

The Chinese Communist government asserted control over Xishuangbanna in February 1950 and began the reform of the administration. Most current leaders in the autonomous region are of the Dai, Aini, or Han nationalities. The Dai language and Chinese are used in all official transactions.

ECONOMY AND CULTURE

It is believed that the ancestors of the Dai cleared the valleys of dense jungle over 2,000 years ago, ploughed the land with elephants, and planted rice. Rice is still the primary crop. Wheat, maize, sugarcane, cashews, cocoa, rubber, camphor, coffee, tea, and tropical fruits are among the other important crops.

The main impediment to developing Xishuangbanna's economy has been the difficulty of transporting supplies into or out of the region. In 1950, the trip from Kunming to Jinghong took a minimum of 25 days. Today, however, the journey takes only four days. Rubber plantations and tropical plant research centers were developed during the 1950s, and many state-run light industry factories were opened. Electricity was introduced to Jinghong in 1955, and now most homes have at least one electric light. A hydroelectric power plant was completed in 1973.

The cultural traditions of the Dai people are closely linked with those of the Burmese. Even now, the people are free to cross the border at will, and until recently marriages between Chinese and Burmese Dai were not uncommon. The Dai are strongly religious and, like most South East Asian Buddhists, belong to Hinayana (Lesser Vehicle) School of Buddhism. It is customary here, as in Burma and Laos, for young boys to be educated by monks in the temples and to spend several years as "junior" monks before going on to other occupations. This tradition continues, and little boys in flowing saffron robes fill the streets on their way to school.

The Dai have had a written language since ancient times. Dai art works and handicrafts can be dated back to the 8th century and include worked gold, silver, and iron objects, bamboo products, porcelain, textiles, and paper. Gifts sent to Beijing as tribute during the Ming Dynasty show the high quality of silk and velvet that was produced in the area at that time. The performing arts tradition of the Dai is no less impressive. Their ballads, many of which have been preserved in written form for centuries, are known for their melodious quality. The most famous of the Dai dances, the peacock dance, is performed by dance troupes throughout China.

HIGHLIGHTS FOR TRAVELERS

Temples and other sites of interest are plentiful in Xishuangbanna, but it is the people—the diversity of the ethnic groups with their own traditions and ways of life—which distinguish the area and make it such a fascinating place to visit. The Dai people are famous in China for their hospitality and friendliness, and their reception of foreigners reinforces this reputation. Travelers in Jinhong who walk through the Dai section of the town, where houses are built on stilts, are often invited into neighborhood homes. In the evenings, the young people continue the practice of courting by singing to one another. A modern touch has been added with the arrival of flashlights. A boy now indicates his interest in a girl by shining the light in her face. On the outskirts of Jinhong, and in Menghai and Mengla, are villages of other minority nationalities. The Mengla district is known for its virgin forests and wildlife.

There are several well-known temples easily reached from Jinghong. The Man Ge Monastery, one of the most famous in Xishuangbanna, is in Jinghong. The Manfeilong Temple, said to be over 700 years old, is in Mengla. Three pagodas, each with three towers, were built as tombs for the hair, bones, and feet of Shixuenani, a Buddhist abbot. The Mengzhe Temple, near Menghai, has a pointed octagonal roof and is one of the best examples of Buddhist architecture in the area. The 60-ft.-high Menghan Temple, located six miles southeast of Menghai, is also worth visiting.

西双版纳植物研究所

Xishuangbanna Botanical Research Institute. Located in Jinghong, the research institute specializes in developing and improving strains of rubber trees and other tropical plants. Visits can be arranged through CITS or the hotel.

澜沧江

Lancang (Mekong) River. It is often possible to arrange a boat ride, either on a CITS "charter" or on a local ferry. A typical two-hour boat ride will take you through the dense jungle. If time allows, you can stop for a picnic or to pick papayas and other tropical fruits.

Festivals. There are three main festivals every year in Xishuangbanna. The most exciting is the Water Splashing Festival, usually held in the early summer. During the three-day celebration, dragon boat races are held, firecrackers are set off, and everyone pours water on everyone else. This is also the wedding season of the Dai.

The Closing Door Festival takes place around July 15. The period between this date and the Opening Door Festival, which takes place around October 15, is a time of extensive Buddhist activity, during which people are not supposed to travel far or marry. Normal social activities can be carried on in the months after the mid-October celebration.

HOTEL ACCOMMODATIONS

西双版纳宾馆

Xishuangbanna Hotel (37 Jialan Rd., Jinghong; tel: 2969). Located in a tree-lined compound in Jinghong, the Xishuangbanna has comfortable, if spartan, accommodations. The rooms in most of the buildings have private baths (rooms with shared facilities are available at lower rates), hot water, and mosquito nets. There is no air-conditioning or laundry service.

云南省思茅宾馆

Simao Guesthouse of Yunnan Province (tel: 2801). Although not in Xishuangbanna, almost all tourists stop in Simao en route to or from Jinghong and this unexpected oasis of order and friendliness should not be missed. Rooms are spacious and airy, accommodations are comfortable, and a standard of cleanliness is maintained which is rarely seen in Chinese hotels. Meals are excellent.

For budget travellers, the **Guoji Daizuren Guesthouse** constists of three hotels in a village outside Jinghong. A traditional Dai house, one can find Y4-bed accommodations and a restaurant there.

LOCAL CUISINE

The local specialties in Xishuangbanna are among the best—and most exotic—that you are likely to encounter anywhere in China. Hotel fare is nondescript, but most tourists whose trips are arranged by CITS will be treated to a home-cooked meal prepared by a Dai family. Travelers on their own should try to get invited home. Specialties include sticky rice roasted inside bamboo stalks, dragon's claw, vegetables in peanut sauce, and pork and chicken in herbal dressings. At a really extravagant meal you may find yourself eating fried bumblebees and bear's paws. All food is eaten with the fingers.

SHOPPING

For the traveler weary of Friendship Stores, Xishuangbanna will be a welcome relief—since there aren't any. The town of Jinghong has a large

free market where every kind of local food product is sold. This should be visited just to see the range of products and the colorful clothing of the shoppers. In Simao, the store for minority goods and the department store, both on New Street, sell a variety of goods produced and used by the local ethnic groups.

Xishuangbanna Foreign Affairs Office ■ Jinghong. Tel: 2581.
Simao Foreign Affairs Office ■ Fu Dalou, Xin Dajie. Tel: 2930.

Yan'an

Traditional spelling / Yenan

Yu.. *River tranquility*

YAN'AN, a market town of 30,000 people, is located some 270 km. (168 mi.) north of Xi'an in Shaanxi Province. Having served as the headquarters of the Communist Party of China in 1936–47, it is symbolically and historically one of the most revered sites in the People's Republic. (Arthur Miller, the American playwright, during a visit in 1978, described Yan'an as "China's Valley Forge.")

The Yan River, on which the town abuts, cuts a deep path between the surrounding dry loess hills, repositories of the innumerable cave dwellings characteristic of the area. The hills have been extensively terraced to provide an agricultural base for the local economy.

Yan'an has several factories, a university, and an assortment of historical sites (Buddhist caves, a Daoist hermitage, and a Song Dynasty pagoda—the town's symbol). However, the main points of interest for the tourist are the Museum of the Revolution and the caves where Mao Zedong and other Chinese leaders directed the revolution during its "Yan'an period."

In the 1960s and early 1970s, pilgrimages to Yan'an were often made by foreign groups, particularly by politically-oriented delegations. Since 1978, however, Yan'an has less frequently appeared on tourist itineraries.

YAN'AN IN HISTORY

In 1936, the Communist Eighth Route Army reached this remote area at the end of one of the great epochs in military history—the 12,800-km. (8,000-mi.) Long March, a two-and-a-half-year trek through central and western China from which only a remnant survived the incessant ravages of climate, terrain, and numerous encounters with the Nationalist forces of Chiang Kaishek. (Of the 90,000 who set out, less than half that number finally reached Yan'an.) It was during the Long March that Mao Zedong consolidated his control of the Party, and it was in Yan'an that Mao, Zhou Enlai, Zhu De, and others reassessed the failures of the formerly urban-based revolution and forged the political and military strategies that led to victory in the civil war and the establishment of the People's Republic of China.

The ordeals of the Long March had compelled its leaders to place survival ahead of orthodox doctrine. Once in Yan'an, ideology was again tempered by circumstances. The concerns of class struggle paled before the need to mount a national war of resistance against Japan. Appealing to the

Climate		Jan	Feb	Mar	Apr	May	Jun	Jul	Aug	Sep	Oct	Nov	Dec
Temp.	°C	−0.8	1.8	8.1	13.6	19.3	25.2	26.8	25.8	19.1	13.6	6.6	0.6
	°F	30.5	35.2	46.5	56.4	66.7	77.3	80.2	78.4	66.3	56.4	43.8	33
Precip.	mm.	76	76	76	102	152	203	305	254	178	152	102	76
	in.	3	3	3	4	6	8	12	10	7	6	4	3

latent nationalism of the rural population, the Party began to rebuild itself on a peasant basis. The Red Army gained considerable support for its guerrilla campaigns. With its ranks swelled by peasant volunteers, the Army became a strong, cohesive force, both politically and militarily.

The Yan'an Legacy. The specific policies developed by the Communists at Yan'an in the 1930s succeeded in winning broad, enthusiastic support from the peasantry. Indeed, their contribution to the eventual success of the Revolution prompted the application of many of these policies (for example, land reform and mass mobilizations) after the founding of the People's Republic in 1949. (The Great Proletarian Cultural Revolution of 1966–76 began partly as an attempt to reinfuse the Yan'an mass spirit into the workings of the government.) Since 1977, the leadership's emphasis on modernization has led, in many instances, to a more circumspect approach to some of these policies.

Readers are referred to Mark Selden's *The Yenan Way in Revolutionary China* (1971) and to Fairbank, Reischauer, and Craig's *East Asia: The Modern Transformation* (1956) for a more detailed account of the Yan'an legacy.

HIGHLIGHTS

FOR TRAVELERS

延安塔
The Yan'an Pagoda. Because of Yan'an's historic role as the Communist headquarters from 1936 to 1947, the Yan'an Pagoda became a national symbol after the victorious Revolution of 1949. It was originally built during the Song Dynasty (960–1279) and restored in the 1950s. The pagoda sits isolated atop a mountain overlooking the city.

毛泽东之四个故居
The Four Residences of Mao Zedong. Owing to Japanese bombing raids, Chairman Mao frequently moved his residence between 1936 and 1945. Each of his cave dwellings has become a small museum, displaying the original sparse furnishings and portraits of Mao at the time.

HOTEL ACCOMMODATIONS

The **Yan'an Guest House** (56 Dajie; tel: 3122) is a one-story structure built in the side of Yan'an's major mountain. Its 149 rooms are simply furnished with only cots and night tables in a manner reminiscent of early revolutionary days.

中国国际旅行社
CITS (Luxingshe) Office in Yan'an ■ 56 Yan'an St. Tel: 2363/2589.

长江三峡
Yangtse River Gorges

CHONGQING and Wuhan are the main starting points for cruises along the Yangtse River gorges, a stunning riverine passage that certainly ranks among the natural wonders of the world. The famous gorges of the Yangtse lie in a 189-km. (118-mi.) stretch between Chongqing and Yichang: Qutang Gorge, Wu Gorge, and Xiling Gorge. Towering mountains drop almost perpendicularly into the river as if hewn by an axe. The spectacular grandeur of these walls and the turgid river that roars through them have long been the subjects of China's romantic poets and painters. To boatmen and navigators, however, they meant dangerous bends, shallows, rapids, and reefs. Adding to these difficulties are a fast current (prior to recent man-made changes in the "green shallows," the flow reached 7.9 m. per second) and a variation of as much as 53 m. (175 ft.) in the river level between dry and flooded seasons. Yet boats have plied this part of the Yangtse since the Western Zhou Dynasty (1066–771 BC).

Foreigners who traveled this fabled stretch in the early 1900s recount that it took anywhere from 20 to 60 days to traverse the 648-km. (405-mi.) stretch between Yichang at the mouth of the gorges and Chongqing.

The first trip by power boat up the Yangtse from Yichang to Chongqing took place in 1898. The following passages from a guidebook published in 1915 describe the danger and wild beauty of the river at that time:

> Leaving Ichang [Yichang] and going up for about 2 mi., we suddenly find the channel narrowing to about 60 yds. and the waters flowing in whirlpools and rapids, while on both banks rise lofty, precipitous, wall-sided mountains, almost shutting out the sunshine. . . . The navigation is extremely difficult, on account of sudden bends in the channel and many projecting rocks on both sides, which give rise to great irregularities in the course of whirlpools and eddies. A place called Hsi-ling-shia [Xiling Xia] is particularly famous on account of the wild grandeur of its scenery and the difficulty of navigation. Here, hundreds (400 sometimes) of trackers are often at work hauling a large junk (a dozen or more trackers are required even in the case of a small craft)—these men straggling over irregular boulders with their shoulder-hawsers 1,200 ft. long and as thick as one's arm, all the time yelling, shouting, or chanting, their movements directed by

the beating of a drum or gong—a veritable pandemonium in the midst of extreme danger.

Later, in the second gorge, the writer saw:

the celebrated "12 peaks of Wushan" which are all more than 1,000 ft. high, making huge walls on the north side of the gorge, which is 20 mi. long. The channel here is not only very narrow, making it one of the most difficult passages, but so closed in by high mountains that it is impossible to see the sun except at noontime, and the moon is visible only when it is at the highest meridian. And in the uppermost gorge, the riverbed was filled with many huge boulders, which produce dangerous whirlpools when submerged during the summer flood, but which block the way when the river is low in winter, giving rise to many narrow, foaming, and dangerous rapids.

Today, the terrifying hazards of the passage are gone, as workmen have struggled—by blasting, digging, and rechanneling—to eliminate more than 100 danger spots in the river course. The hauling tracks are still etched against the cliffs, although they are less frequently used, since most traffic today is powered by motorized tugs, river steamers, and ferries. But spectacular scenery and great legends of the river still abound, and the journey remains unforgettable.

YANGTSE CRUISE
VESSELS

Six passenger ships designated for foreign tourists, as well as a number of other vessels which carry both passengers and freight, now ply the Yangtse River. Five ships (the M. V. *Yangzi Jiang*, the M. S. *Emei*, the M. S. *Kunlun*, the M. S. *Goddess*, and the M. S. *Three Gorges*) are run by the Chongqing or Wuhan Shipping companies. Space on these is sold as part of complete China tour packages or to individual travelers who have arranged independent "FIT" tours through a travel agency or CITS. The M. S. *Bashan* is chartered by Lindblad Travel. Space is allocated as part of complete China tour itineraries or on an FIT basis directly by the company.

Foreigners traveling on their own can purchase third-class accommodations aboard Jianghan steamers departing from Chongqing or Wuhan. First-class bookings (designated as "second class" because of the shared bath facilities) are harder to come by, given the great demand for such space by both Chinese and foreign tour groups.

Jianghan (formerly The East is Red) Steamers. Until 1984, most Yangtse travelers, both Chinese and foreign, were accommodated on the

The Yangtse

East is Red (Dongfanghong) fleet that has been sailing the river since the late 1950s. The name of the line was changed to Jianghan in the fall of 1984, but the ships are still commonly referred to by their old appellation. These ships average 71 m. (220 ft.) in length and 15 m. (50 ft.) across the beam, with a draft of just over 2.5 m. (8 ft.), and are powered by 2,400-hp twin-diesel engines. Maximum speed is 28 km. (17.5 mi.) per hour. A fleet of more modern versions of these vessels was launched in 1981.

The Yangtse steamers offer five classes of service. Space is set aside for a maximum of 32 passengers in second class on the top deck, with a reserved lounge overlooking the bow. Facilities include 16 cabins, each with two bunks, washstand, desk, and chair. It is usually possible to buy third-class tickets two to three days in advance at dockside. Third-class passengers sleep in cabins with 16 bunks. Although most tour groups are now put on the other ships, travelers should be forewarned that even groups that have reserved second-class accommodations on the Jianghan boats long in advance are not infrequently put in third-class dormitories on arrival because of overbooking. On lower decks, passengers sleep on bunks in fourth-class dormitories that span the width of the steamer. "Fifth-class" (also called "dispersed seating") travelers camp on their own bedding in the hallways and on the lower decks. Strollers must tread with great caution.

Jianghan vessels sleep over 800 persons. For all classes, toilet and shower facilities are shared. Small shops on board sell stationery, snacks, and soap. Meals are not included but can be purchased very inexpensively on board. Small boats pull up alongside to hawk fruits and other produce.

M. V. Yangzi Jiang. The largest passenger ship on the Yangtse, (84.5 m. or 277 ft. long) the 140-passenger *Yangzi Jiang* was launched in mid-1983 as the fastest vessel of its kind on the river, with a maximum speed of 29 km. or 18 mi. per hr. Its 70 two-bed cabins are spacious and tastefully furnished. Each faces outside and is equipped with stereo and closed-circuit TV, carpeting, sofa, and private bath.

The *Yangzi Jiang* offers five-day sails out of both Wuhan and Chongqing. Since slightly different shore itineraries are made in each direction, the ship also offers bookings for 10-day return cruises. The ship is administered by the Wuhan Sub-Branch of the Changjiang (Yangtse River) CITS. Only charters and group or FIT bookings are available.

M. S. Three Gorges (San Xia). This 60-passenger vessel entered service in 1982. It is the sister ship of the M. S. *Goddess*. The boat offers first-class accommodations throughout, with features that include a bar and shop, as well as central air-conditioning and heat. All cabins face outwards, with full-size picture windows. The ship operates under the administration of the Chongqing Sub-Branch of the Changjiang Branch of CITS.

Of the three Chinese-operated ships, the *Three Gorges* is the best maintained and most comfortable. The staff includes a cruise director, and interpreters from CITS. The *Three Gorges* offers a five-day cruise in both directions between Wuhan and Chongqing.

M. S. Emei. Launched in the summer of 1984, the M. S. *Emei* is 79 m. (259 ft.) long and 15.6 m. (51 ft.) wide, with accommodations for 90 passengers. Each of the twin-bedded cabins is air-conditioned and furnished with carpeting and a private bath. Facilities include a large bar and dance floor, outdoor lounge and swimming pool (rarely cleaned), ice machines, and a 360-degree observation tower. The M. S. *Emei* offers a five-day itinerary up- and down-stream between Chongqing and Wuhan. The ship is administered by the Chongqing Sub-Branch of the Changjiang Branch of CITS, and has a Chinese cruise director and interpreters.

M. S. Kunlun. Although the *Kunlun* has the same exterior dimensions as the Jianghan ships, the resemblance ends there. Refitted during the 1950s as a luxury cruise ship for high-level Chinese officials (including Chairman Mao) and visiting heads of state, the *Kunlun* carries a maximum of 36 passengers (plus over 90 service staff and crew) in a manner suited to its original purpose. Cabins and suties (the largest is 650 sq. ft.) are all equipped with private bath, and all face outwards. The *Kunlun* is centrally air-conditioned and offers gourmet Chinese and Western cuisine, afternoon tea, and cocktail parties on the deck. There are three lounges, two decks, and a promenade. Facilities include a hairdresser, clinic, bar, and an excellent antique store. It offers 12-day cruises up- and downriver between Shanghai and Chongqing. Interpreters and a CITS representative are provided by the Wuhan Sub-Branch of the Changjiang CITS.

M. S. Goddess. The 225-ft.-long *Goddess* was completed in 1981 in the Chongqing shipyard, and was specifically designed to carry small tourist groups along the upper reaches of the Yangtse River. The boat was refurbished while under the management of Lindblad Travel in 1983 and now has 26 double cabins available to tourists.

All cabins have picture windows, which makes it possible for guests to watch the scenery without moving from their beds. Facilities include two lounges, bar, dance floor with live music, shop, individual cabin air-conditioning and heat, hairdresser, and bank. The ship offers one-week itineraries up- and downstream between Chongqing and Wuhan.

M. S. Bashan. The twin sister of the *M. S. Emei*, the *Bashan* is under exclusive contract to Lindblad Travel and has been completely refurbished with materials from Hong Kong and the US to accommodate 66 passengers in suites and double and single cabins. Facilities include two lounges, two observation decks, a bar, swimming pool, hairdresser, clinic, and shop. The ship is staffed by CITS personnel and interpreters. The ship travels between Yichang and Chongqing in five days.

▶ ◀
YANGTSE GORGE
▶ ◀
ITINERARIES
▶

Luxury and first-class cruise ships (group bookings or by previous arrangement with CITS or a foreign travel agency only) now use five to seven days to traverse the 1,370-km. (850-mi.) stretch of river in either direction between Chongqing and Wuhan. Some of these ships stop at different locations on their up- and downstream voyages. Although the spectacular beauty of the gorges is the natural focal pont of these cruises, the Yangtse's riverine villages and cities, most of which are inaccessible by rail or air, give tourists an opportunity to glimpse life in the heart of China where the 20th century has barely begun to penetrate.

Cruises downstream from Chongqing on the Jianghan line begin early in the morning, usually at 7 AM. Ships depart from the Chaotian Men Dock (the eastern terminus of bus route #1). Individual passengers may board the ships from 8 PM on the evening prior to departure. Tickets may be purchased at dockside or at the CITS office (Renmin Hotel, room 138). Passage may be booked to Wuhan (arriving about 3 PM on the third day), to stops en route (Zhongxian, Wanxian, Fengjie, Wushan, Yichang, Shashi, and Yueyang on most ships), or through to Shanghai (change boats at Wuhan; minimum five days' sail). Upstream departures from Wuhan via the Jianghan fleet take from three to four days, depending on whether service is "local" or "express." Foreigners may book passage through the Wuhan branch of CITS.

ON THE RIVER

石宝寨

Shibao Zhai. After passing the former American Club on the right bank, ships move out of Chongqing and into the broad reaches of the upper Yangtse. Pagodas, built in the belief that they would prevent the wealth of the towns from being swept away by the rapid current, dot the riverbank near almost every settlement. Many Daoist temples can also be seen. On the first night, most tourist ships dock at Shibao Zhai (literally, "Stone Treasure Stronghold"), a site marked by a massive 90-m. (295-ft.)-high rock upon which a Buddhist temple, built in 1750, is perched.

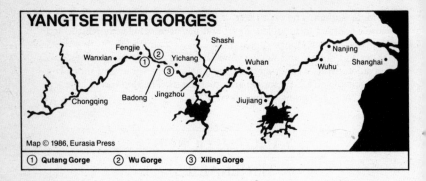

YANGTSE RIVER GORGES

Map © 1986, Eurasia Press

① Qutang Gorge　② Wu Gorge　③ Xiling Gorge

According to legend, rice for the monks flowed from a small hole in the stone floor of the temple until one day a greedy monk decided to enlarge the hole in the hope of obtaining more than his share. Instead, the rice stopped altogether and has never flowed again. An 11-story wooded pavilion was constructed in the early 19th century as a rest area along the ascent to the temple. Upon climbing the spiral staircase to the top, visitors gain a magnificent view of the river and surrounding countryside. A visit to the town of Shibao Zhai, which has no motor vehicles, makes it possible for tourists to take an imaginary step back in time. Tiny shops line the cobblestone streets, which lead to rice paddies and villages of thatched cottages.

万县

Wanxian. In the early evening of the first day, Jianghan steamers pull into the town of Wanxian and pause there until 2:30 AM so as to allow the ships to enter the gorges at sunrise. Tourist ships sail from Shibao Zhai before lunch and arrive at Wanxian in mid-afternoon. Situated amid rich and beautiful country, Wanxian is an old river city which once rivalled Chongqing and Chengdu in size and importance. Today, with a population of over 300,000, Wanxian is still Sichuan's fourth most important industrial and port facility. Wanxian's oranges, tangerines, and peaches are famous nationwide. Textiles are also an important industry, and most tourists are taken to see silk spinning and weaving factories. There is a free market not far from the dock, where local people sell their produce and handicrafts for extra income. It features a fine array of plaited bamboo ware, from baskets to wicker chairs.

As the ship continues down river, passengers will see the Zhangwang Temple on the right bank, across from the town of Yunyang. During the Three Kingdoms period (220–280 BC), many of the most famous battles in Chinese history were fought along this portion of the river by the rival kingdoms of Shu, Wu, and Wei. The Zhangwang Temple was built during the Song Dynasty as a memorial to General Zhang Fei of the Shu Kingdom, who was assassinated by two rebel officers. His head is supposedly buried at this spot. Stone carvings from the Northern and Southern Dynasties (420–589 AD) are housed within the temple.

奉节

Fengjie. The next spot of interest is Fengjie, a walled city which was once a major tax collection center for river traffic. To the east, a short ferry ride away at the mouth of Qutang Gorge, is Baidicheng (White King City), a small mountain where the Tang Dynasty poet Dufu lived. A temple on the peak commemorates heroes of the Three Kingdoms period. It can be reached by climbing a stone staircase (with 700–900 steps, depending on the water level).

长江三峡

The Yangtse River Gorges. The next day of the journey is devoted to the splendor of the gorges. According to an ancient legend, the three "great" gorges were created by the mythical emperor Yu the Great, who hacked apart a mountain range with a giant axe in order to drain an engorged lake which had submerged most of what is now Sichuan Province. The geological claim is that the gorges were created some 70 million years ago by massive water erosion. This occured after a major movement in the crust of the earth had squeezed two adjoining mountain ranges together.

The Qutang, Wu, and Xiling gorges each has its own distinctive ambiance and points of historical interest. The Qutang Gorge is only 8 km. (5 mi.) long and takes only a bit over 20 minutes to traverse. But it is by far the most spectacular, with its perpendicular cliff walls and dramatic vistas. The chief points of interest of Qutang Gorge include the Meng Liang Staircase, carved by the bodyguard of a murdered Song Dynasty official who was attempting to recover his master's body from the cliff; Bellow's Gorge, where coffins were buried in the cliffs over 2,000 years ago; and Wrongly Made Gorge (we'll allow our readers to venture their own explanations for this name).

Ships pass by the city of Wushan (named after a mountain once believed to be inhabited by witches) before entering the Wu Gorge, the most serene of the three. This gorge begins at the Daning River in Sichuan Province and runs 44 km. (27 mi.).

The Three "Little" Gorges, one of the most spectacular sights in China, were opened to foreigners in 1985. Similar to the great Three Gorges, but narrower and more impressive, they are the natural habitat of mandarin ducks and golden-haired monkeys. Ships now dock at Wushan, where passengers board 20-seat launches for a six-hour upstream voyage on the Daning River through the Longmen, Bawu, and Dizui gorges.

The Goddess Peak, the most important site on the entire river for Chinese tourists, is located in the Wu Gorge. This 12-m.-high stone pillar, which stands on the highest of all mountain peaks along the Yangtse, resembles a young girl from a distance. She is believed to be the youngest of 12 fairies who help to guide ships along the river. On days when the goddess emerges from the mist, she brings good luck to anyone who glimpses her. Other points of interest include the Kong Ming Tablet, upon which there is an inscription written by Zhuge Liang, the prime minister of the State of Shu; Bandong, an oppressive-looking industrial city that serves as a regional distribution center; and Zigui, the hometown of Quyuan, a statesman who drowned himself in 278 BC to protest the policies of the government. The Chinese "Dragon Boat Festival," held annually in many Chinese communities, commemorates this event.

The 75-km. (47-mi.) Xiling Gorge is the longest of the three, and is best known for its hidden rocks and dangerous shoals (which once made it the most dangerous part of the river). The gorge, whose banks are covered with orange orchards, is actually made up of four smaller gorges: the Gorge of the Sword and Book on the Art of War, the Horse-Lung and Ox-Liver Gorge, the Kong Ling Gorge, and the Gorge of Shadow Play. The Huangling Temple, first built during the Three Kingdoms period and reconstructed during the Tang Dynasty, lies between the Kong Ling and Shadow Play gorges.

Ships pass through one of the locks of the Gezhouba dam late in the afternoon. The 70-m. (230-ft.)-high dam is 2,561 m. (8,402 ft.) long and has 21 power generators with a total capacity of 2.715 million kw. per hour.

宜昌

Yichang. Tourist boats dock at the city of Yichang, which is the economic and cultural center of western Hubei and the major link between Hubei and Sichuan provinces. With a population of 360,000, the city's major industries are chemical and pharmaceutical production and textile manufacturing. The area is also famous for oranges and tangerines, porcelain, black tea, and mushrooms. Tourists are taken to the dam site and are shown an excellent film about its construction. Another place of interest is the Sanyoudong (Three Travelers Cave), situated in a beautiful spot in the hills overlooking the river near Yichang.

沙市和荆州

Shashi and Jingzhou. The next stop on most cruise itineraries is the city of Shashi, where Changkiang Thermos Bottles and Mandarin Duck Bed Sheets are produced. Jingzhou, located 7.5 km. away, has been a city of historical importance since 700 BC. It is noted for, among other things, the Jingzhou Prefectural Museum, which has a major collection of artifacts from the Eastern Zhou (770–221 BC), Qin (221–207 BC) and Western Han (206 BC–AD 8) dynasties. It also houses "Mr. Sui," an almost perfectly preserved corpse from the Western Han Dynasty that was unearthed from a nearby tomb (see also section on Wuhan, above).

城陵矶

Chenglingji. The last stop before Wuhan is Chenglingji, at the confluence of the Yangste River and Lake Dongting. The city of Yueyang is a short drive away and is best known for the Yueyang Tower, a wooden structure on the shore of Lake Dongting originally built in the Tang Dynasty, and for Jinshan Island, where Silver Needle tea is grown.

Jianghan boats dock at Hankou in Wuhan at about 3 PM of the third day. Depending on the itinerary, tourist cruise ships reach Wuhan in the morning of either the fifth or seventh day. The *Kunlun* continues downstream for another five days to Shanghai.

Yangzhou 扬州

traditional spelling / Yangchow   *kingdom of Yang*

SETTLED AS EARLY as 2,400 years ago, during the Spring and Autumn Period (770–476 BC), Yangzhou is an especially charming town lying at the juncture of the Yangtse and Hua rivers in Jiangsu Province.

YANGZHOU IN HISTORY

At the beginning of the Sui Dynasty (6th century AD), Emperor Yangdi ordered the recruitment of millions of workers in the area to dig the Grand Canal, a waterway linking Hangzhou in the south with Zhuojin, near Beijing, in the north. The canal, which became the major artery for the transport of grain from the rich agricultural southern provinces to population centers in the arid north, transformed Yangzhou into a major commercial and communications center by the Tang Dynasty (AD 618–907). At its zenith, Yangzhou had a population of 500,000—approximately double its present size.

Yangzhou was renamed Jiangdu (River Capital) for a brief period in the 10th centry, when the Southern Wu kingdom made the town its capital.

Many prominent figures have been associated with Yangzhou through the centuries. Jian Zhen, the Tang Dynasty Buddhist monk who made several attempts to reach Japan to spread the faith, and who is credited with introducing to Japan not only Buddhism, but also many aspects of China's art, culture, and medical science, was a native of Yangzhou. Owing to Jian Zhen's efforts, Yangzhou is still considered a holy site by Japanese Buddhists, who continue to donate treasures and gifts to Jian Zhen's shrine in Yangzhou.

The great Tang Dynasty poets Li Bai (Li Po), Bai Juyi, Gao Shi, and Du Fu, among others, visited Yangzhou often and wrote hundreds of poems praising its natural beauty. In the Song Dynasty, Bulhading, said to be a descendent of the Prophet Mohammed, traveled to China in the hope of spreading the Islamic faith. He made Yangzhou his home for 10 years and eventually died there. Ouyang Xiu and Su Dongpo, two famous Song Dynasty writers, also lived in Yangzhou and served as prefects of the city. When the legendary traveler Marco Polo visited Yangzhou during the Yuan Dynasty at the invitation of Kublai Khan, he served as mayor of the town for three years (1282–85).

Climate		Jan	Feb	Mar	Apr	May	Jun	Jul	Aug	Sep	Oct	Nov	Dec
Temp.	°C	1.9	3.7	8.6	14.6	20.3	24.4	28.2	28.2	23.0	16.8	10.6	4.2
	°F	35.4	38.6	47.4	58.2	68.5	75.9	82.7	82.7	73.4	62.2	51	39.5
Precip.	mm.	254	254	330	330	305	356	279	279	305	254	203	178
	in.	10	10	13	13	12	14	11	11	12	10	8	7

As the center of the salt trade in the Qing Dynasty (1644–1911), Yangzhou enjoyed great prosperity and dynamic economic growth. The burgeoning fortunes of salt merchants and other entrepreneurs created opportunities for conspicuous consumption and attracted important numbers of artists, scholars, craftsmen, and courtesans seeking wealthy patrons. It was during this "second golden age" that Yangzhou spawned the school of painters known as "the Eight Eccentrics." These artists sought to paint bold new pictures instead of imitating the old masters. Their favorite subjects were flowers and natural objects. Branded in their own day as heretics by more orthodox artists, the Eight Eccentrics developed a free, vigorous style that has reemerged to exert a strong influence on modern Chinese artists.

Today, Yangzhou remains an important center for artistic endeavor. It is famous for its carved lacquerware screens inlaid with mother-of-pearl, jade carvings, intricate papercuts, embroidery, miniature potted landscapes, and reproductions of ancient texts—printed from handcarved wooden blocks, with the pages stitched by hand in the traditional method.

HIGHLIGHTS FOR TRAVELERS

Among the many scenic and historic attractions for visitors to Yangzhou, perhaps the most notable are the local section of the Grand Canal, the many lovely gardens, and the buildings associated with the monk Jian Zhen.

法净寺
Fajing Temple (Fajing Si). Located on Shugang Hill, in the city's northwest, is Fajing Temple, formerly known as Daming Temple. The original temple was built by Jian Zhen some 1,500 years ago. In the latter years of the Southern Song Dynasty (1127–1279), a nine-story pagoda, the Qilingta, was built on the temple grounds. A recent addition to the temple complex is the Jian Zhen Memorial Hall, built according to Tang Dynasty methods and financed with contributions raised by Buddhist groups in Japan.

When the Qing emperor Qian Long visited Yangzhou in 1765, he was troubled by the temple's name—Daming (which literally means "Great Ming"), fearing that it might revive nostalgia for the Ming Dynasty, which was overthrown by his Manchu predecessors. He had it renamed Fajing Temple.

The temple was seriously damaged during the Taiping Rebellion in the middle of the 19th century. The present structure is a reconstruction dating from the 1930s.

平山堂
Flat Hills (Ping Shan) Hall. Built by the Song Dynasty writer Ouyang Xiu when he served as prefect of the city, this hall stands just west of Fajing Temple. As one looks out from this hall, the mountains to the south

of the Yangtse River appear as a line at the viewer's eye level—hence the name Flat Hills Hall. When Ouyang Xiu's student Su Dongpo moved to Yangzhou, he too served as prefect of the city. He had a hall built directly behind the one erected by his master, and called it Guling Hall.

文昌阁
Pavilion of Flourishing Culture (Wenchangge). This round, three-tiered pavilion in Yangzhou's eastern sector was built in 1585 and celebrates the city's rich cultural traditions.

石塔
Stone Pagoda (Shita). Standing west of the Pavilion of Flourishing Culture is a five-story Tang Dynasty pagoda. Built in AD 837, it is the oldest pagoda still standing in Yangzhou.

瘦西湖
Slender West Lake (Shouxi Hu). Named after Hangzhou's famous West Lake, this long, narrow stretch of water which meanders through Yangzhou's western limits is a well-known scenic spot. A long dike planted with weeping willows spans the lake; at its midpoint stands a square terrace with pavilions at each of the corners and one in the center. Around the lake is a park in which are found several attractions: Lotus Flower Pagoda (Lianhua Si), a white structure reminiscent of the White Dagoba (Baita) in Beijing's Beihai Park; Small Gold Mountain (Xiao Jin Shan); and the Fishing Platform (Diaoyutai), a favorite retreat of the Qing emperor Qian Long. The emperor was so gratified by his luck in fishing at this spot that he ordered additional stipends for the town. As it turns out, his success had been augmented by local swimmers who lurked in the reeds busily attaching fish to his hook.

普哈丁墓
Tomb of Bulhading. The tomb is in the eastern sector of the city and is adjacent to a mosque which houses a collection of valuable materials documenting China's relations with Muslim countries.

个园
Ge Garden (Ge Yuan). The entrance to this typical southern-style garden with its luxuriant bamboo groves, ponds, and rock grottoes is on Dongguan St. in the city's northeast section. Designed by the great Qing Dynasty landscape painter Shi Tao for Wang Yingtai, an officer of the Qing imperial court, this garden takes its name from the bamboo thickets which dot the grounds (the Chinese character *ge* means, and resembles, "a bamboo stalk.")

何园
He Garden (He Yuan). Built by He Zhidiao, a 19th-century Chinese envoy to France, this garden is famous for a 430-m. (1,410-ft.), two-storied winding corridor, the walls of which are lined with stone tablets carved with lines of classical poetry. In the garden is also an open-air theater set on an island in the middle of a fish pond.

冶春园

Yechun Garden (Yechun Yuan). In this garden, which lies on the banks of the Xiading River, the Qing Dynasty poet Wang Yuyang and a circle of friends used to gather to recite their works. The thatched roofs of the pavilions in this garden give it a quaint, rustic air.

扬州博物馆

Yangzhou Museum. Near the Yechun Garden is the Yangzhou Museum, which houses about 100 paintings and calligraphy scrolls by the Eight Eccentrics of Yangzhou and a research institute for the study of their work.

江都水利枢纽工程

Jiangdu Water Control Project. Construction of this multiple-purpose water control project—the biggest in China—started in 1961 and was completed in 1975. The project includes facilities for irrigation, drainage, navigation, and power generation. It consists of four large, modern electric pumping stations, six medium-sized check gates, three navigation locks, and two trunk waterways.

扬州宾馆 *HOTEL ACCOMMODATIONS*

Yangzhou Hotel (5 Fengleshang St.; tel: 22611 x452/453; telex: 34075 YZHTL CN). Located down the street from the Xiyuan, the Yangzhou is fully air-conditioned (public areas as well as guest rooms), and all of its accommodations have private bath, closed-circuit color TV, telephone, piped-in music, and in-room refrigerator. Amenities include a swimming pool, billiard room, table tennis room, a 300-seat auditorium, coffee shop, bar, tea house with musical entertainment, banquet hall, and both Chinese and Western restaurants. Most rooms are doubles (Y55), with six suites (Y85).

西园饭店

Xiyuan Hotel (1 Fengleshang St.; tel: 22611 x496). Most rooms here have private bath, air-conditioning, color TV, and wall-to-wall carpeting. Rates range from Y55–60 for a double room to Y75–95 for a suite, and to Y220–280 for a deluxe suite. Other features include coffee and gift shops, a meeting room, and a Chinese restaurant.

SHOPPING

A wide selection of Yangzhou's famed handicrafts can be found at the Friendship Store on Yanfu Road and at the People's Market on Dongfanghong Road. Reproductions of ancient Chinese classics, such as *The Romance of the West Chamber* and *The Peach Blossom Fan*, printed and handsewn in the traditional method, are available from the Yangzhou Guangling Ancient Books Block Printing Cooperative.

中国国际旅行社
CITS (Luxingshe) Office in Yangzhou ■ Xiyuan Hotel. Tel: 41925/42805.

Yantai

traditional name/Chefoo

smoke terrace

YANTAI is a little off the beaten track, but a worthwhile detour if you favor the combined activities of sitting in the sun and drinking wine. Indeed, Yantai is famous for two things: its magnificent beaches and its excellent brandies, rose-petal wines, and other grape by-products.

Once a small fishing hamlet on the northern coast of the Shandong Peninsula, Yantai overlooks the straits linking the Bohai Gulf with the Yellow Sea. Formerly known as Chefoo, the town became a summer resort for wealthy foreigners and a missionary headquarters during the 19th century. Its name changed to Yantai or "smoke terrace" during the Opium Wars when beacon fires were lit on its cliffs to warn Chinese fishing fleets of approaching British ships.

In 1949, the Yantai–Lancun railroad was built, linking the fishing port with the rest of Shandong Province. Yantai's harbor has been undergoing steady expansion since that time and, as of the mid 1980s, could handle between 6.5 and 7 million tons of cargo annually. This, combined with the region's abundant mineral deposits (Yantai produces 25% of China's gold), gives Yantai great potential for further economic development. This fact was recognized by the State Council, which named the municipality as one of China's 14 Coastal Open Cities in 1984.

Most Yantai residents still make their living from the sea or from tending the fertile orchards and vineyards. A lucrative export business has grown up around some of the region's red and white wines.

The town itself is divided into two parts. There is old Zhifu (Chefoo) with dark narrow streets and some classic examples of European-Chinese architecture at the turn of the century. Surrounding it on three sides is the new Yantai with busy boulevards and bright, modern buildings.

Yantai has three full-service hotels: the modern **Zhifu Guest House** (tel: 24381/9, 6989), located on the sea in the eastern suburbs, has 116 rooms, all with private bath and air-conditioning; rates are Y45 for twins and Y82 for suites. The **Yantai Hill Guest House** (Seashore St.; tel: 2936) is the town's largest hotel, with over 200 rooms, of which about half have private bath and air-conditioning; triple rooms rent at Y30, doubles at Y45, and suites at Y60–80. The **Overseas Chinese Hotel** (15 Huanshan Rd.; tel: 2231; cable: 0294) has 108 twins (Y45) and five suites (Y75); all rooms have private bath and some are air-conditioned.

For those on a budget, the **Yantai University (Yanda) Guesthouse** welcomes foreigners to clean guest rooms for Y15 a night.

Climate		Jan	Feb	Mar	Apr	May	Jun	Jul	Aug	Sep	Oct	Nov	Dec
Temp.	°C	-1.4	0.9	7.6	14.7	22.3	26.6	27.6	26.6	21.4	15.7	7.9	0.9
	°F	29.4	33.6	45.6	58.4	72.1	79.8	81.6	79.8	70.5	60.2	46.2	33.6
Precip.	mm.	76	102	76	102	127	203	279	254	152	152	102	76
	in.	3	4	3	4	5	8	11	10	6	6	4	3

Yixing

YIXING, an ancient and picturesque town in southeastern Jiangsu Province, is bounded by hills on three sides and by Lake Tai, nine miles to the east. According to legend, the town was founded by a Han Dynasty priest named Zhang Daoling who came here to seek seclusion.

Yixing is known mainly for a special kind of stoneware pottery, called *boccaro*, which is produced in the little village of Dingshu just south of the town. The local clay, dull brown in color, is used to manufacture flowerpots, casseroles, and, above all, teapots that are typically round or gourd-shaped. The clay assumes a purplish or vermilion hue after firing. No glaze is applied, but the stoneware is burnished and acquires a high natural gloss with long use. Serious tea drinkers the world over value Yixing teapots for both their decorative and their functional qualities.

HIGHLIGHTS FOR TRAVELERS

孔庙
Temple of Confucius. This temple, containing some exceptional statuary, stands behind a beautiful white marble archway dating from the 17th century.

善卷洞
Shan Juan Cave. Located at Luo Yan Hill, 24 km. (15 mi.) southwest of Yixing, Shan Juan Cave is in fact a series of four caves linked by underground streams. The caves are several stories high and cover an area of 5,000 sq. m. (54,000 sq. ft.). They contain spectacular stalactite and stalagmite formations that visitors can view by boat.

张公洞
Reverend Zhang (Zhang Gong) Grotto. Named for Zhang Daoling, the legendary founder of Yixing, this grotto in the Mengfeng Mountains is 20 km. (12.4 mi.) southwest of Yixing. The grotto consists of 72 smaller caves linked by over 1,000 hand-carved stone steps. Visitors enter the grotto through a spacious stone hall known as the Sea Mansions (patterns in the stone floor of the cave resemble a turbulent sea). From this cave, steps spiral upward to the Hall of the Ocean King, an eerily magnificent grotto overhung with jagged rocks and filled year-round with mist curling up from underground springs.

Overnight guests stay at the **Yixing Guest House,** (1 South Renmin.; tel: 2811/2179) a lovely pavilion-type structure surrounded by gardens. The 62-room hotel is air-conditioned and offers rooms for Y80–90 (double) and Y115–150 (suite).

Climate		Jan	Feb	Mar	Apr	May	Jun	Jul	Aug	Sep	Oct	Nov	Dec
Temp.	°C	1.9	3.7	8.6	14.6	20.3	24.4	28.2	28.2	23.0	16.8	10.6	4.2
	°F	35.4	38.6	47.4	58.2	68.5	75.9	82.7	82.7	73.4	62.2	51	39.5
Precip.	mm.	254	254	330	330	305	356	279	279	305	254	203	178
	in.	10	10	13	13	12	14	11	11	12	10	8	7

Zhanjiang

湛江

deep river   *traditional spelling/Tsamkung*

ZHANJIANG is set amidst vast sugarcane and peanut fields at the base of Guangdong's Leizhou Peninsula, some 500 km. (310 mi.) southwest of Guangzhou. It is the southernmost seaport on the China mainland, ranking eighth in total cargo handling capacity. With a population of 880,000 in the city proper, it is also one of the larger cities along the populous south China coast.

Zhanjiang is an ancient city, although its legacy is largely that of a sleepy backwater, where officials who had incurred the emperor's displeasure were exiled, and as a main embarkation point for travelers and banished officials going to Hainan Island. The only one of these officials to leave a lasting legacy in Zhanjiang was the famous Song Dynasty (960–1279) poet and scholar, Su Dongpo, who was exiled to southern Guangdong.

Primarily an agricultural and fishing zone, Zhanjiang's economy has traditionally revolved around sugarcane, rubber, and coffee. But port expansion and development have been accelerating since 1984, when the city was named as one of China's 14 Coastal Open Cities, due to its strategic location. Zhanjiang is close to both the South China Sea and the Gulf of Tonkin, making it an ideal support base for offshore oil exploration and recovery. It can be reached overland by road from Guangzhou or by train via Liuzhou. There is daily air service from Guangzhou.

HOTEL ACCOMMODATIONS

海滨宾馆
Haibin Hotel (Haibin Rd.; tel: 23555; cable: 8832; telex: 45233 BINTL CN). The commodious (430 rooms) and rather grandly appointed (swimming pool, sauna, tennis court) Haibin Hotel is fully air-conditioned. All its guest rooms have private bath, closed-circuit color TV, telephone, and piped-in music. In addition, the hotel boasts three restaurants (Chinese, Western, and Japanese), a coffee shop, bar, and dance hall. Rates range from Y66 (singles) to Y84 (doubles), Y165 (triples), and Y310 (suites).

Climate		Jan	Feb	Mar	Apr	May	Jun	Jul	Aug	Sep	Oct	Nov	Dec
Temp.	°C	13.1	13.8	17.5	21.9	25.8	27.1	28.3	28.2	27.0	23.8	19.8	15.2
	°F	55	56.8	63.5	71.4	78.4	80.7	82.9	82.7	80.6	74.8	67.6	59.3
Precip.	mm.	152	203	254	279	381	508	457	406	330	203	152	127
	in.	6	8	10	11	15	20	18	16	13	8	6	5

中国国际旅行社
CITS (Luxingshe) Office in Zhanjiang ■ 22 Xianshan Renmin Rd. Tel: 4960-667.

733

kingdom of Zheng

Zhengzhou

traditional spelling/Chengchow

ZHENGZHOU is the capital of Henan Province and a major city of north-central China. It is located a few miles south of the Yellow River and about 640 km. (400 mi.) south of Beijing. Geographically, it sits at the western edge of the agriculturally important North China Plain.

Since becoming a major railway junction linking Guangzhou and Beijing (on the north-south axis) and Xi'an and Shanghai (on the east-west axis), Zhengzhou has continued in its traditional role as a major market and transportation center. Although infrequently visited by tourists in the past, it recently became a common stop because of its central location and easy access, and because it exemplifies a well-planned municipality, balancing development of agriculture and industry. Zhengzhou provides a powerful visual symbol of the rebuilding that has taken place in new China.

The population of 1.2 million enjoys a pleasant climate in spring and autumn, but midsummer temperatures can soar above 32°C (90°F), with heavy rains occurring in July.

ZHENGZHOU IN HISTORY

Zhengzhou has a long history, the site having been continuously settled for more than 3,000 years. It ranked as one of the most populous regions in China during the Shang Dynasty (from the 16th century to 1066 BC), but for a period thereafter waned in importance in comparison to nearby Anyang, which emerged as the dynastic capital.

The modern development of the city began in 1898 when foreign interests were granted concessions for the construction of major north-south and east-west rail lines. These were completed by 1910. In the 1920s, the railway was the focus of several labor disputes, including a notorious incident on February 7, 1923, when a strike of the Beijing–Hankou railway workers' union was bloodily suppressed. Because of its importance as a major railway center, Zhengzhou was a primary objective of Japanese forces during their push through China in 1937. In an infamous incident now memorialized locally, the Guomindang (Nationalist) army breached the dike of the Yellow River less than 20 miles northeast of the city in order to deny Zhengzhou to the Japanese. The action resulted in devastating floods that cost thousands of lives through drowning or subsequent starvation. The diverted river continued to threaten the city until

Climate		Jan	Feb	Mar	Apr	May	Jun	Jul	Aug	Sep	Oct	Nov	Dec
Temp.	°C	−0.2	1.8	8.0	14.6	21.4	26.4	27.8	26.3	20.5	15.0	7.9	1.7
	°F	31.6	35.2	46.4	58.2	70.5	79.5	82	79.3	68.9	59	46.2	35
Precip.	mm.	13	18	18	23	51	102	178	76	25	18	15	13
	in.	.4	.7	.7	.9	2	4	7.0	3.0	1	.7	.6	.4

1947, when the break was repaired with US assistance. Zhengzhou was again severely damaged in fighting during the civil war in 1948–49. Labor troubles resurfaced in the 1970s, especially in the railway sector, and local officials complained about the "sabotage carried out by the 'gang of four' and their henchmen" in disrupting transportation and production. Today, all is apparently running smoothly again.

ECONOMY AND CULTURE

Zhengzhou was initially rebuilt during 1949–50, but significant urban expansion did not take place until after 1954, when the city was designated as a site for industrial development. Food processing and cotton textile industries were given priority. By the 1960s, Zhengzhou had become an important industrial center as well as a transportation hub.

The textile sector includes five mills that produce both yarn and finished cloth. Associated facilities include a textile printing and dyeing plant and several textile machinery plants. Food and agricultural industries include a meat-processing and by-products plant, flour mills, and a plant that processes cottonseed into edible oil and other products. Chemical fertilizer, insecticide, and tractor repair plants (the region's flat terrain makes it ideal for agricultural mechanization) are also located in Zhengzhou. Major agricultural products are rice, wheat, and cottonseed.

HIGHLIGHTS
FOR TRAVELERS

Zhengzhou is a verdant city. Visitors are left with an impression of a modern urban locality enveloped in multi-layered foliage. Although its tourist attractions do not rival those of Shanghai, Xi'an, or Beijing, Zhengzhou is nevertheless a city of considerable interest.

Most of Zhengzhou is modern in appearance, reflecting its tremendous growth since 1950 (when its population was only 100,000). In the new section of town, blocks of governmental, educational, and cultural buildings are intermingled with extensive residential areas. The old town core, with narrow, maze-like streets and traditional houses, serves as a reminder of another era. Some housing foundations and graves from the 3rd century BC have been discovered in this old section, and remnants of the ancient wall still stand.

To demonstrate the comprehensive development of modern China, factories, communes, and educational institutions are often included on the visitor's itinerary.

二七纪念碑

Cenotaph. In the heart of the shopping district of the old section stands a cenotaph built to commemorate the bloody general strike of railroad workers in February 1923.

河南省博物馆

Henan Provincial Museum. Located in the newer section of town, the museum contains exhibits on the Neolithic era, early dynasties, and the modern period. Artifacts from early dynasties include tools from Yang and Shang cultures, lacquerware, wooden figurines, bronzes, textiles discovered in tomb sites dating from the Zhou and Six Dynasties eras, bronzes from the Tang Dynasty, and samples of pottery from the Song. All these artifacts were discovered in Henan Province. In the 20th-century exhibit, photographs and articles relating to the railway strikes, the war of resistance against the Japanese, the civil war, and post-1949 developments are displayed.

人民公园

People's Park. Located just behind the Opera Theater, this park has pleasant walkways and a lake fed by the Jinshui River, connected by canal to the Yellow River to the north. The park serves as a rough dividing line between the old and new towns, with the city's major department store just one block south and workers' residential areas situated immediately to the north.

HOTEL

ACCOMMODATIONS

国际饭店

Guoji Hotel (114 Jinshui Ave., Eastern Section; tel: 23413; telex: 46061 HNZIH CN). All of Guoji's 252 rooms have private bath, air-conditioning, closed-circuit color TV, piped-in music, and carpeting. The hotel features a swimming pool, large and small meeting rooms, Chinese and Western restaurants, a coffee shop, and bar. Rates are Y50 for a double, Y54 for a triple, and Y85–140 for a suite.

河南省中州宾馆

Zhongzhou Guest House (115 Jinshui Ave., Eastern Section; tel: 24255, 24937; cable: 4255). All of the Zhongzhou's 171 rooms have private bath and are equipped with air-conditioning, closed-circuit color TV, telephone, taped music, and carpeting. Doubles here are Y50, triples Y58, suites Y84, and deluxe suites Y140–220.

In addition to a conference hall with a seating capacity of 400, the Zhongzhou features both Chinese and Western restaurants, a dance hall, and a coffee house.

河南饭店

Most foreign visitors are accommodated at the **Henan Hotel** (Huayuan Rd.; tel: 32227), a grand structure built in Soviet style, with a large fountain in front, a cavernous lobby, and a huge, red-carpeted marble staircase. The massive external scale telescopes into small but comfortable rooms. The hotel has the usual tourist amenities, including a retail shop (with relatively sparse selection), telegraph and post offices, and bank. The building is surrounded on three sides by wheat fields. During harvest times, many of the hotel employees leave to join in the agricultural work.

Closer to downtown are the **Henan Guest House** (tel: 22216) and the **Friendship Guest House** (tel: 25593), both on Jinshui Road.

SHOPPING

The lapidary shop is a common stop on most itineraries. Jade from several provinces is sold here. Linens and textiles are also a good buy. Handicrafts feature egg-shell painting, feather painting, and stuffed animals. Since the store in the hotel is not well stocked, a trip to the Hongqi Department Store on Jiefang Zhong Road (tel: 26925) or the Baihuolou (Emporium) on Erqi Road (tel: 25561) and local specialty shops is recommended. The Friendship Store (tel: 26110) and the Henan Province Antiques Store (tel: 26433) are both located on Erqi Road.

中国国际旅行社
CITS (Luxingshe) Office in Zhengzhou ▣ 16 Jinshui Road. Tel: 25396/32070.
Telex: 33335 FAOHN CN.

鎮江

guardian of the Yangtse

Zhenjiang

traditional spelling/Chenkong

ZHENJIANG is situated in the central part of Jiangsu Province at the confluence of the southern Yangtse River and the Grand Canal. It is an ancient city, founded under the Eastern Zhou Dynasty in 545 BC. Although there has been a considerable amount of new construction in recent years, most of the buildings are two- and three-story structures predating World War II. The streets are lined with hundreds of shade-giving sycamore trees, planted since 1949 to absorb the summer heat.

Zhenjiang's early importance can be ascribed to the opening of the Grand Canal under the Sui (AD 581–618). When Marco Polo visited the city at the end of the 13th century, he described its "great and rich merchants," its plentiful supply of game and other necessities, and its busy silk trade. In 1858, British and French concessions were granted at Zhenjiang under the Treaty of Tianjin.

Today, Zhenjiang is a medium-sized industrial city, containing a population of 270,000 and a total area of 90 sq. km. (55 sq. mi.). It is located on the Shanghai–Nanjing railroad and the Beijing–Hanzhou Grand Canal. It serves as a busy harbor on the Yangtse transportation route. Due to the convenience of both its land and water transportation, Zhenjiang's industrial production has developed rapidly. Its 300 factories employ about 140,000 workers. Industries here include metallurgy, machine building, automobile and ship construction, electronics, textiles, plastics, pharmaceuticals, and food processing. The city is situated in a major rice and cotton growing area.

Zhenjiang is surrounded on three sides by hills and mountains. In the southern suburbs, these vertical peaks are planted with countless old trees and bamboo groves. The natural beauty and peacefulness of this area have earned Zhenjiang the nickname of "City Forest Hill."

► HIGHLIGHTS

► FOR TRAVELERS

There are a number of scenic spots in the area, the most famous of which are Jinshan, Jiaoshan, and Beigushan, collectively known as "Three Hills of the Capital Gateway."

Climate		Jan	Feb	Mar	Apr	May	Jun	Jul	Aug	Sep	Oct	Nov	Dec
Temp.	°C	1.9	3.7	8.6	14.6	20.3	24.4	28.2	28.2	23.0	16.8	10.6	4.2
	°F	35.4	38.6	47.4	58.2	68.5	75.9	82.7	82.7	73.4	62.2	51	39.5
Precip.	mm.	254	254	330	330	305	356	279	279	305	254	203	178
	in.	10	10	13	13	12	14	11	11	12	10	8	7

金山
Jinshan. Jinshan is located a few miles northwest of the city. Two of its caves, the Fahaidong (Monk Cave) and the Bailongdong (White Dragon Cave) were immortalized in the beloved Chinese fairy tale, "The Story of the White Snake." The Jinshan Temple is one of the most ancient in the lower Yangtse area. At the peak of Jinshan stands the seven-story Cishou (Benevolence and Longevity) Pagoda, which provides a magnificent view of the surrounding region.

焦山
Jiaoshan. To the east of the city, Jiaoshan rears up like a giant in the midst of the Yangtse River. It is also known as Fuyushan (Floating Jade

Jinshan Temple, with origins in the 4th century

Hill) because of its verdant jasper-green growth. There are many temples and pavilions at its summit, notably the Tijianglou (Drawing River Pavilion) from which people enjoy watching the rising sun and the billowing Yangtse waters. There are hundreds of inscribed stone tablets in the hilly areas, including the famous Jingheming tablet (Swift Crane Inscription) which is said to be the "forerunner of big-character posters." Jiaoshan is still a working monastery. If visitors happen to arrive at the appropriate moment, it may be possible to observe ritual activities under way in the main temple.

北固山

Beigushan. Beigushan is located on the riverbank in the eastern part of Zhenjiang. At the top of Beigushan is the Ganlusi (Sweet Dew Temple), said to be the place where Liu Bei, king of Sichuan during the Three Kingdoms period (AD 220–280), was married to the sister of the king of Wu. Other points of interest include Dujinglou (Pavilion for Choosing Prospective Sons-in-Law), Henshi (Heartless Stone), Shijianshi (Testing Swords Stone), and Linyunting (Reaching Cloud Pavilion). There is also an iron pagoda on Beigushan which dates back to the Song Dynasty (AD 960–1279).

HOTEL ACCOMMODATIONS

一泉饭店

Yiquan Hotel (Yiquan Rd.; tel: 23422). All of the hotel's rooms but one (a triple) have a private bath. Some of the accommodations are also equipped with air-conditioning, color TV, and telephone. The charge for the one triple room with shared bath is Y28; the remaining triples are Y44; the doubles range from Y44–50. There is a Chinese restaurant at the hotel, which also has five meeting rooms with a total seating capacity of 260.

Travelers are also accommodated in three other hotels, two of which are older and quite small (larger groups may be divided among the three), but well maintained and nicely furnished. The **Jinshan Hotel** (tel: 24962) is located adjacent to the Jinshan Artificial Lake, a few miles out of town. The Jinshan is one of several undistinguished, prefabricated hotels built as joint ventures with an Australian firm in the early 1980s. The other hotels are the **Jinkou** (407 Zhongshan Rd.; tel: 23561) and the **Jingjiang** (111 Jiefang Rd.; tel: 22842). Both are similar in style and charm to the larger hotels of Shanghai's former French concession.

The dining rooms at all of these hotels are fine. Visitors might try the freshwater shrimp dipped in Zhenjiang vinegar, a local delicacy with an indescribable but quite palatable flavor.

中国国际旅行社
CITS (Luxingshe) Office in Zhenjiang ■ 25 Jiankang Road. Tel: 23281.

Zhuhai

珠 海

traditional spelling/Chuhai

pearl sea

IN the 1960s and 1970s, tourists could get a rare glimpse of China by looking across the narrow strait that separates Macao from Zhuhai on the mainland and search the nearby hills and fields for some sign of activity. But beginning in early 1980, anyone peering into China from the battlements of Monte Fortress would have seen a remarkable transformation taking place: What was once an area of sleepy fishing villages and farms bordering on a desolate "buffer zone" has, seemingly overnight, become a bustling tourist and industrial center.

Zhuhai, with a population of 138,000 (40,000 in the city proper), is located 156 km. (97 mi.) southwest of Guangzhou, to which it is connected by a newly completed trunk highway (about four hours by minibus, Y8), and 58 km. (36 nautical mi.) west of Hong Kong. Macao's Barrier Gate is located a few hundred yards south of the Chinese immigration and customs building at Gongbei. Most travelers get to Zhuhai via Macao, although there is direct Jet-Cat service four times daily from Hong Kong operated by the China-Hong Kong Hydrofoil Company. CAAC provides helicopter service from Guangzhou (40 minutes, Y69 one way).

Zhuhai's coastal, subtropical climate is similar to Hong Kong's, with summer temperatures reaching a high of 37°C (99°F) and dipping to around 3°C (38°F) on the chilliest January nights. Humidity is generally high, averaging around 79%. Late spring through late summer is the rainy season.

Rich in agricultural, aquatic, and mineral resources, the Zhuhai area, along with Zhongshan County to the north, has long been considered one of South China's most prosperous regions, thanks to its very fertile soil and abundant rainfall. After the Portuguese landed in 1557, it gained importance for its proximity to Macao. Aside from the profits realized by local merchants and government officials from the lucrative Macao–Guangzhou silk trade, the area benefitted in other, indirect, ways as well: having the earliest contact with foreigners, and an open door to the outside world in their backyard, the first Chinese to emigrate in large numbers were Zhongshan and Taishan peasants. Many of these emigrees— whether they became wealthy entrepreneurs in Penang or railroad workers in California—sent the lion's share of their earnings back to their ancestral villages, contributing in no small measure to the area's early economic development.

Climate		Jan	Feb	Mar	Apr	May	Jun	Jul	Aug	Sep	Oct	Nov	Dec
Temp.	°C	13.1	13.8	17.5	21.9	25.8	27.1	28.3	28.2	27.0	23.8	19.8	15.2
	°F	55	56.8	63.5	71.4	78.4	80.7	82.9	82.7	80.6	74.8	67.6	59.3
Precip.	mm.	152	203	254	279	381	508	457	406	330	203	152	127
	in.	6	8	10	11	15	20	18	16	13	8	6	5

However, during the early- and mid-20th century, with Macao's decline and the turmoil of world and civil wars, the area's fortunes took a turn for the worse. The ravages of the Cultural Revolution, when any foreign connection, no matter how tenuous, made one suspect and open to abuse, were felt most acutely here. The border with Macao was closed in 1967; the shoreline bristled with bunkers and machine-gun nests. But in the post-Mao era, the region has enjoyed an economic as well as a political rebirth, and the bunkers have been replaced by holiday resort villas, amusement parks, high-rise housing blocks, and factories.

ECONOMY

In August 1980, a 15-sq.-km. segment of Zhuhai, mostly lying along the waterfront facing Macao, was declared a Special Economic Zone. Since then, the construction of an all-purpose harbor at Jiuzhou and a heliport near Xiangzhou have made Zhuhai an important supply base for nearby South China Sea offshore oil platforms. But without a rail link to the interior, Zhuhai has been hard-pressed to compete with Shenzhen, and foreign investment and capital construction have lagged far behind Zhuhai's sister SEZ to the east.

Much of the necessary industrial infrastructure is already in place, however, with water and power in plentiful supply, and the recently completed highway to Guangzhou should do much to alleviate the transportation bottleneck. Zhuhai presently also boasts one of China's few modern telecommunications systems, with direct-dial telephone service available to Hong Kong, Macao, and Guangzhou.

Joint-venture investment has so far been concentrated in infrastructure projects and construction related to tourism. Garment and furniture factories, radio-assembly plants, a woolen mill, and a semi-conductor factory have already begun production. Through the mid-1980s, over $100 million in joint-venture capital has been invested, with another $1.5 billion committed for 16 planned industrial projects. The authorities have set a goal of $2.1 billion in total investments by the year 2000, with one-third of the total expected to come from foreign sources. Further economic development depends to a great extent on the success of the offshore oil industry, but will also focus on high technology and light industry. Construction is currently underway at two industrial parks.

Although tax rates, contractual, accounting, and other regulations are uniform for all of China's SEZs, Zhuhai authorities hope that the locality's relatively low land costs will act as an added incentive for investors otherwise interested in Shenzhen (see also section on the Special Economic Zones in Doing Business in China, above).

HIGHLIGHTS FOR TRAVELERS

For the independent traveler, entering or leaving China via Macao and Zhuhai is now a viable alternative to the popular Hong Kong–Guangzhou route. The four-hour ride to Guangzhou affords a fascinating glimpse of life in the towns and fields of the canal-laced Pearl River Delta. Especially interesting are the "tower houses" of Zhongshan County. These architectural oddities, unique to the villages in this area, were built by returned overseas Chinese in the late 19th and early 20th centuries as a way of displaying their wealth.

Cuiheng, 30 km. from Macao, is the birthplace of Sun Yatsen. The house he built for his parents (Zhongshan Guju) and the Sun Yatsen Memorial Hall (Zhongshan Jiniantang) are important pilgrimage sites for the thousands of Chinese tourists who make the trip to Cuiheng every year.

Halfway between Zhuhai and Guangzhou is the old market town of Shiqi (Shekkei), now officially called Zhongshan. Of interest are the Ming Dynasty pagoda, the Sun Yatsen Memorial Hall, and the twisting, crowded cobblestone streets of the town center.

HOTEL ACCOMMODATIONS

Hotels in the Zhuhai area are mostly of the resort variety, catering, as in Shenzhen, to the weekend recreational needs of Chinese tourists and Hong Kong and Macao residents. The most striking of these hotels is the **Zhuhai SEZ Gongbei Hotel** (36 Lianghua Rd., Gongbei; tel: 88-5260/88-6833), just a stone's throw from the Macao border. Its imperial-style main buildings are based, according to the architects, on the Qin Dynasty Afang Palace.

Other hotels include the **Zhuhai Resort** (tel: 22-221), the **Shijingshan Hotel** (1 Jingshan Rd.; tel: 33-2299/33-3518; telex: 45632 SCSHL CN), and the **Kiu Yuen Hotel** (tel: 22-391), all in the Xianglu Bay area. All of these hotels feature Chinese and Western restaurants, tennis, swimming, boating, shopping arcades, and similar tourist diversions. They can all be booked through travel agents and major hotels in Hong Kong or Macao. More conventional accommodations can be had at the **Fenghuang (Phoenix) Hotel** (135 Fenghuang Rd.; tel: 22-2421) in Xiangzhou.

中国国际旅行社
CITS (Luxingshe) Office in Zhuhai ■ Binhai Rd., Gongbei. Tel: 86851.
Telex: 88771 CHTLZ OM.

香港 # Hong Kong

ONE of the most common ways to enter the People's Republic is via Hong Kong. Several airlines now offer direct routes into China that bypass Hong Kong. Nevertheless, Hong Kong—offering a wide range of flexible and often inexpensive means of access to China—continues to function both as the world's primary gateway to China and as a major point of egress for China tours. (For details on Hong Kong's multifarious tourism and transportation links to China, see "The Hong Kong–China Connection," above.)

Beyond the convenience factor, it remains that a few days' stopover in Hong Kong at the beginning or end of a China trip can be worthwhile in its own right. Shoppers will enjoy the myriad array of items that the tax-free port has to offer. Although no longer the "bargain basement" of Asia, Hong Kong remains competitive with most parts of the region for watches, cameras, electronics, jewelry, and clothing. Business people will appreciate the host of PRC agencies and services situated here, many of them exclusive outlets for China trade and finance. The curious traveler will sample one of the world's most active, diverse, and colorful cities.

HONG KONG IN HISTORY

From the beginning, Hong Kong owed its existence to aggressive commercial ambitions, belonging either to the foreigners who established and ran this colonial enclave or to Chinese entrepreneurs who came here to profit under the foreigners' wing. Hong Kong's beginning was not auspicious. In 1842, the British government through force of arms (under the Treaty of Nanjing) compelled the Chinese government to accept Britain's opium trade and to agree to a variety of other concessions in support of the China trade, including the granting to Britain "in perpetuity" of Hong Kong island. In 1898, Hong Kong's territory was vastly extended through a 99-year lease of 350 sq. mi. comprising the New Territories in Kowloon and including 233 islands.

During the succeeding nine decades, the Colony's economic strength lurched forward, spurred especially by periods of war and instability in China. By the 1960s, the manufacturing sector, aided by a huge illegal influx of cheap labor from China, had supplanted trade as the cornerstone of the economy. In the 1980s, finance and related services had risen to share with

Climate		Jan	Feb	Mar	Apr	May	Jun	Jul	Aug	Sep	Oct	Nov	Dec
Temp.	°C	13.1	13.8	17.5	21.9	25.8	27.1	28.3	28.2	27.0	23.8	19.8	15.2
	°F	55	56.8	63.5	71.4	78.4	80.7	82.9	82.7	80.6	74.8	67.6	59.3
Precip.	mm.	152	203	254	279	381	508	457	406	330	203	152	127
	in.	6	8	10	11	15	20	18	16	13	8	6	5

manufacturing (where, incidentally, electronics had moved up to challenge textiles as Hong Kong's principal commodity export). Indeed, no period of change in Hong Kong's short history may have been more dramatic than the past three decades, when Hong Kong has progressed from one of the world's more squalid and congested urban environments to one of its most gleaming and well-organized high-density cities.

Today, Hong Kong boasts the most efficient tourism and transportation systems in Asia. It is the world's largest exporter of radios, watches, garments, and toys. It is the financial capital of Asia and ranks third (after London and New York) as an international banking and financial center. And, as a vestage of the circumstances that caused its founding, Hong Kong is today the world's third busiest container port and third largest air cargo center. However, these days computer chip toys are vastly more important than opium.

The 1997 Watershed. China's emergence in the post-1949 era as a powerful, assertive nation-state has had a broad impact on Asia and the world. Thus, it came as no surprise that Britain's anachronistic lease for the New Territories began to come under scrutiny. While anxious to reassert its sovereignty over Hong Kong, China was also quick to recognize the economic advantages of maintaining major aspects of Hong Kong's status quo. The Sino-British Joint Declaration, initialed on September 26, 1984, states that, following the creation on July 1, 1997, of a Hong Kong Special Administrative Region of the People's Republic of China, Hong Kong shall "retain the status of a free port and continue a free trade policy, including the free movement of goods and capital." While retaining absolute territorial control over the whole of Hong Kong, China allowed that a broad base of current economic and social regulations and practices could remain in effect during a 50-year transition period.

While a number of Hong Kong companies (including, most notably, the giant trading firm of Jardine Matheson) reacted to the Declaration by moving their headquarters out of Hong Kong, the population at large has thus far reacted to the prospective transition with equanimity. Entering the late 1980s, at any rate, Hong Kong seemed reasonably optimistic about the future in the short-term—an attitude not much different from the speculative postures of most previous epochs in Hong Kong's history.

HONG KONG

FOR TOURISTS

By the late 1980s, Hong Kong was receiving close to four million tourists annually (in 1985, Hong Kong received 3.4 million foreign visitors, compared with three million for all of China). Visitors are accommodated in some 18,000 hotel rooms, more than 90% of which are typically occupied during spring, summer, and fall peak seasons. The region most active in sending tourists is the one furthest away—North America, with 22% of total arrivals; it is followed by Southeast Asia with 21%; Japan with 19%; and Western Europe with 15%. Most tourists spend an average of 2–3 days in Hong Kong; the most casual observation will reveal that shopping and dining are the dominant time-fillers.

The primary source of information for visitors is the Hong Kong Tourist Association (HKTA) with its head office in Central at Connaught Center (tel: 5-244191); branch offices are at Kai Tak Airport, the Kowloon Star Ferry Terminus, and the Hong Kong Government Publications Centre (in the General Post Office Building, across from the Hong Kong-side Star Ferry Terminus).

Hotel Accommodations. Most group tours have little choice in hotel selection. But if you've been flying for 12 hours and don't know what day it is, you probably don't care much either. Fortunately, general standards of comfort, efficiency, and service in Hong Kong's hotel sector rank among the highest of any city in the world. Indeed, apart from a few slight advantages in terms of location, Hong Kong's first-class hotel offerings all fairly well adhere to a common, high measure of quality.

Some 80% of Hong Kong's large hotels—and almost all of its new ones—are concentrated in Tsimshatsui area, at the tip of Kowloon. Most package tours are consigned to hotels in this area, where the majority of shops, restaurants, and services catering to tourists are also located.

Of the 25–30 major hotels in Hong Kong, three have acquired reputations for maintaining standards at levels perceptively above the rest. In Kowloon, **The Peninsula** is Hong Kong's "grand dowager" hotel, with huge rooms and unsuppressed British-Colonial aura. Service is fastidious—ubiquitous fresh flowers and fruit baskets, Rolls-Royce pick-ups at the airport. The **Regent,** perched on the harbor across Salisbury Road, has the most stunning lobby (perhaps in the world), the best swimming pool (in Hong Kong), and the most chic and modern of veneers. In Hong Kong's financial district, the **Mandarin** is buttoned-down, efficient, and understated, with services skillfully designed to complement a harried schedule. At the other end of the price scale is the modern **YMCA International House.** A few miles up the Kowloon peninsula (near the Waterloo Road MTR station), this new addition to Hong Kong's YMCA family (there are four others) is clean, comfortable, and highly recommended to budget travelers.

Other good hotels on the Kowloon side include the **Ambassador** (somewhat elderly but very comfortable, right near some excellent shopping districts), the **Hyatt Regency** (wonderful restaurant—Hugo's—and a good location), and two **Holiday Inns.** A five-star hotel, the **Shangri-La** is about a half-mile up the Kowloon peninsula.

On the Hong Kong side, the **Furama Inter-Continental** has a pleasant Japanese flavor. **The Hilton** is just like most Hiltons everywhere—nothing exotic, always dependable. It is nicely situated at the foot of the Victoria

Peak funicular and next door to the major banks and central business district. Most rooms were renovated in the mid-1980s and its pool area is superb.

HONG KONG HOTEL DIRECTORY

KOWLOON	ADDRESS	TELEPHONE
Tsimshatsui		
Ambassador	4 Middle Road	3-666321
Grand Tower	627 Nathan Road	3-910468
Holiday Inn (Golden Mile)	50 Nathan Road	3-693111
Holiday Inn (Harbour View)	70 Mody Road	3-7215161
Hongkong Hotel	3 Canton Road	3-676011
Hyatt Regency	67 Nathan Road	3-111234
Kowloon Hotel	19–21 Nathan Road	3-698698
Marco Polo	Harbour City (Canton Rd.)	3-7215111
Miramar	130 Nathan Road	3-681111
New World	22 Salisbury Road	3-694111
Park	65 Chatham Road South	3-661371
Peninsula	Salisbury Road	3-666251
Prince	Harbour City (Canton Rd.)	3-7237788
Regal Meridien	71 Mody Road	3-7221818
Regent	Salisbury Road	3-7211211
Royal Garden	69 Mody Road	3-7215215
Shangri-La	64 Mody Road	3-7212111
Sheraton	20 Nathan Road	3-691111
YMCA	Salisbury Road	3-692211
Yaumatei, North Kowloon		
Airport Regal Meridien	Sa Po Road (at airport)	3-7180333
Fortuna	355 Nathan Road	3-851011
Riverside Plaza	Tai Chung Kiu Rd.	0-6497878
YMCA International House	23 Waterloo Road	3-319111
HONG KONG ISLAND		
Central		
China Merchants Hotel	160 Connaught Rd. W.	5-596888
Furama Inter-Continental	1 Connaught Road	5-255111
Hilton	2 Queens Road	5-233111
Mandarin	5 Connaught Road	5-220111
Victoria	200 Connaught Rd.	5-407228
Causeway Bay		
Excelsior	281 Gloucester Rd.	5-767365
Lee Gardens	Hysan Avenue	5-767211
Park Lane	310 Gloucester Road	5-8903355
Plaza	Gloucester Road	5-7901021

Restaurants. No matter where you're staying, a late evening ride up to the top of Victoria Peak for a drink and a view of all of Hong Kong is a breathtaking and inexpensive excursion. Exotic drinks and an excellent buffet meal can be had at the Victoria Peak Restaurant, right next to the Peak Tram's upper terminus. One specialty you shouldn't hesitate to try is an avocado sauce, served with several of the main courses.

Pinpointing Hong Kong's best restaurants is almost impossible, for the city offers an almost endless array of tastes and styles. Indonesian, Thai, Indian, every possible shading of Chinese cooking, Continental, Polynesian, and many other cuisines are all abundantly available.

Two tried-and-true old favorites are the City Hall Restaurant, opposite the Star Ferry Pier on the Hong Kong side, and the floating Jumbo in Aberdeen. Be brave and experiment on your own. Nearly everyone who works in business or tourist circles in Hong Kong speaks English and you will discover some wonderful little places with very little effort.

Shopping. Shopping may call for a more jaundiced eye. Hong Kong is a bargain hunter's paradise, but you have to know where to look. For silk and other fine materials, try the Chinese-owned Yue Hwa department store chain. Prices are cheaper and quality is often higher than in the better-known tourist outlets. The Chinese Arts and Crafts Building in Tsimshatsui (near the Kowloon Star Ferry terminal) stocks an extraordinary selection of Chinese jewelry, decorative furniture, and other fine crafts. For your watches, cameras, radios, cassettes, etc., the big, crowded department stores are usually more dependable than the tiny holes in the wall unless you have a specific recommendation from someone you trust. Textiles, bamboo, and porcelain are still good buys in Hong Kong. Electronic equipment and timepieces are becoming noticeably less so.

Even the most casual international shopper could not fail to notice the large proportion of designer-named clothing items now bearing Hong Kong labels. Many of these factories have opened outlet shops that may offer genuine bargains (along with unmarked damaged goods or rejects— beware!).

The traditional Hong Kong-to-US dollar ratio, which for years hovered at about $5 = 1$, soared to over $9 = 1$ in September 1983. In order to forestall any further such wild fluctuation and restore confidence in its currency, the Hong Kong government decided in October 1983 to peg the Hong Kong dollar to the US dollar. While the official exchange rate still varies slightly from day to day, it generally stays within the range of US\$1 = HK\$7.6–7.85.

The most reliable exchange venues are the banks; exchange counters at the hotels and airport usually take higher commissions on these transactions.

CHINA PRODUCT STORES

China Products Emporium	31 Yee Wo Street, Tung Luo Wan Hong Kong Island
Chungkiu China Products Emporium	Nathan Road (Shantung Street), Tsimshatsui, Kowloon
Ta Hwa China Products	92 Queen's Road, Central Hong Kong Island
Yue Hwa Chinese Products	301 Nathan Road, Kowloon

CHINA BUSINESS CONTACTS

The businessperson in Hong Kong en route elsewhere may also need the very latest in monetary exchange rates. If you want banking information on China, your first stop should be the Hong Kong Branch of the Bank of China (BOC), 2A Des Voeux Road, Central (tel: 5-234191). Besides the BOC, Hong Kong has 13 PRC-controlled banks. Eight are incorporated in China, the remainder in the colony.

If you're waiting to negotiate a deal in China or can't seem to get your foot in the door from New York or London, four Hong Kong firms acting as official agents of the PRC Foreign Trade Corporations (FTCs) can probably be quite helpful. In some cases, they are even authorized to enter into negotiations with foreigners for merchandise purchases or sales.

REPRESENTATIVES OF PRC TRADING CORPORATIONS

China Resources Holdings Company, Ltd.
(representing Chemicals, Machinery, Metals and Minerals, and Textiles FTCs, and China National Technical Import Corp.)
49/F China Resources Bldg.
26 Harbour Rd., Wanchai, H.K.
Telephone: 5-8317111

Hua Yuan Company
(representing Light Industrial Products FTC)
37 Connaught Road, Central, H.K.
Telephone: 5-445061

Ng Fung Hong, Ltd.
(representing Cereals, Oils and Foodstuffs FTC)
7/F China Resources Bldg.
26 Harbour Rd., Wanchai, H.K.
Telephone: 5-8318777

Teck Soon Hong Ltd.
(representing Native Produce, Animal By-Products, and Light Industrial Products FTCs)
9-10/F China Resources Bldg.
26 Harbour Rd., Wanchai, H.K.
Telephone: 5-8318222

Aberdeen harbor, Hong Kong island

OTHER USEFUL ADDRESSES AND NUMBERS

	ADDRESS	TELEPHONE
US Consulate General	26 Garden Road, H.K.	5-239011
American Chamber of Commerce	Rm. 1030, Swire House Chater Road, H.K.	5-260165
Canadian Government Trade Commission	P & O Building, 11th fl. 21 Des Voeux Road, Central, H.K.	5-282222

AIRLINES

Air France	5-223131	Korean	5-235177
Air India	5-221176	Lufthansa	5-225101
Air New Zealand	5-249041	Northwest	5-217477
Alitalia	5-237041	Philippine	3-662371
British Caledonian	5-260062	Qantas	5-242101
CAAC	5-216416	Singapore	5-201313
Canadian	5-227001	Swissair	5-293670
Cathay Pacific	5-252202	Thai International	5-295601
Japan	5-230081	United	5-261212
KLM Royal Dutch	5-220081		

Macao

CHINA travelers passing through Hong Kong and with a day or more to spare for unwinding might consider taking the 50-minute jetfoil ride to the Portuguese enclave of Macao. Macao lies 40 nautical miles to the west of Hong Kong and is connected to China via a narrow isthmus demarcated by the historic Barrier Gate.

The oldest extant European settlement in Asia, Macao was founded by the Portuguese in 1557 as their base for the lucrative China trade, and remains in Portuguese hands to this day. After Portugal's 1974 revolution, the Portuguese sought means to abolish the colony and return it to China. But because a change in Macao's status might touch on the more weighty issue of the neighboring colony of Hong Kong, China preferred to abide with the status quo for the present.

Macao offers some diverting contrasts to its burgeoning colonial cousin across the Pearl River Estuary. The pace is more relaxed, permitting leisurely bicycle rides or strolls along the narrow back streets. The scale of life and commerce is smaller and more intimate than Hong Kong, and a relatively Mediterranean flavor prevails. For travelers with only a few days to spare for seeing China, the Macao avenue offers a much more authentic glimpse of China than the day currently available out of Hong Kong (see section on Zhuhai, above).

Tourist visas for Macao, valid for up to 20 days, are issued upon entry for HK$25. Outside Macao, visas may cost even more. The local currency is called the pataca (M$) and is valued roughly at par with the Hong Kong dollar. Hong Kong dollars may be used freely in the territory, although about 5% is gained by exchanging them for patacas.

GETTING TO MACAO FROM HONG KONG

A variety of frequent and convenient links connect Hong Kong and Macao. Package tours may also be booked through tour desks at Hong Kong hotels. (Note, however, Macao is predictably booked up months in advance by Hong Kong residents for several holiday weekends throughout the year.)

All sea connections for Macao leave from the New Macao Ferry Pier, located about one mile west of the Star Ferry Terminal on Hong Kong island. Services include three types of craft:

Jetfoil. These glass and aluminum beasts, manufactured by Boeing Aircraft, offer the fastest service—about 50 minutes—with seven daily departures. The roundtrip fare is HK$65 (booking agent: Far East Hydrofoil Co.; HK tel: 5-455566; Macao tel: 3474).

Climate		Jan	Feb	Mar	Apr	May	Jun	Jul	Aug	Sep	Oct	Nov	Dec
Temp.	°C	13.1	13.8	17.5	21.9	25.8	27.1	28.3	28.2	27.0	23.8	19.8	15.2
	°F	55	56.8	63.5	71.4	78.4	80.7	82.9	82.7	80.6	74.8	67.6	59.3
Precip.	mm.	152	203	254	279	381	508	457	406	330	203	152	127
	in.	6	8	10	11	15	20	18	16	13	8	6	5

Hydrofoil. Smaller and slightly slower than the jetfoil, hydrofoils make the journey in about 70 minutes, with half-hourly departures during daylight hours. The roundtrip fare is HK$45 (booking agent: same as for jetfoil).

Ferry. Two modern ferries provide leisurely, scenic voyages to Macao, taking about 2½ hours. Roundtrip saloon seats cost HK$35, with private cabins available at higher rates (booking agent: Shun Tak Shipping Co.; HK tel: 5-457021; Macao tel: 3586).

HOTEL ACCOMMODATIONS

Macao's hotels fall into two categories: large and brassy, and small and sleepy. In the former category are the **Lisboa Hotel and Casino,** the **Hotel Sintra** (modern and a bit less noisy than the Lisboa), and the **Matsuya.** Two cheaper hotels that occupy old Portuguese buildings (with wooden floors and lovely verandas) are the **Bela Vista** and the equally pleasant **Caravela.**

HOTEL DIRECTORY

	ADDRESS	TELEPHONE
Bela Vista	Rua do Commendador Kou Ho Neng	3821
Caravela	Avenida da Republica	5151
Lisboa	Avenida da Amizade	7666
Matsuya	Estrade de São Francisco	5466
Sintra	Avenida de D. João IV	85111

Zhongshan Hot Springs Resorts (north of Yongmo village; tel: 22811; telex: 44828 CSHS; cable: 3306). Twenty-four kilometers from Macao, the Zhongshan Hot Springs Resort is, as its name suggests, more than a hotel. On the grounds are a swimming pool, swan boats, a superb 18-hole golf course, shooting range, and riding facilities. In addition, hot spring water is piped into all the hotel's baths. All rooms at the 407-room resort have private bath, air-conditioning, closed-circuit color TV, refrigerator, telephone, and piped-in music. Other amenities include a Chinese and a Western restaurant, a coffee shop, and a shopping center. Fourteen suites are available (Y410 to Y518); all the resort's remaining rooms are doubles (Y63 to Y69).

VISITING CHINA FROM MACAO

Travel connections between Macao and China have improved vastly since 1979; there is now even a taxi service into Guangdong Province from Macao's Barrier Gate. Short tours of 1–3 days are available for Macao's neighboring Zhongshan district, a scenic rural area that is famous as the birthplace of Dr. Sun Yatsen, Republican China's first president. Prices for day trips into China from Macao begin at HK$320.

A Macao branch of China Travel Service is located at 33-35 Rua do Visconde, Paco de Arcos; tel: 3770.

Mongolian People's Republic

Special Report by Nicholas J. Middleton

THE Mongolian People's Republic, sandwiched between the two Asian giants of China and the Soviet Union, is the world's second oldest Communist state, established in 1924 following a Soviet-aided revolution in 1921. For many years after the revolution, Mongolia's progress continued firmly under Soviet aegis and very largely out of sight of the West. As such, its effective independence remained in question. International recognition was boosted by Mongolia's admission to the United Nations in 1961. In 1987, Mongolia was recognized by about 100 countries, including the United States, but politically and economically it remains very closely linked to Moscow.

Every year about 10,000 foreign tourists visit Mongolia. With a land area about half the size of India's, Mongolia has a population of only 1.9 million. One-fourth of the people live in the capital, Ulan Bator ("Red Hero"), the political, economic, and industrial center of the country. Even within the city most people live in the round felt tents (*gers*) that have changed very little in the 750 years since Genghis Khan. These gers surround the city on all sides, while the center is occupied by government buildings and apartment blocks in the Eastern European style.

Mongolia's climate is extremely continental: predominantly dry, with low relative humidity (skin moisturizer is a must if you are staying for very long) and wide seasonal and diurnal temperature variations. In the winter the country is very cold: average January temperature in Ulan Bator is $-26.1°C$; in July, the average is $17.0°C$. Most precipitation occurs during the summer months; the annual average for Ulan Bator is 233 mm. During the spring, the Gobi Desert and, to a lesser extent, Ulan Bator, are characterized by strong winds and dust storms. Otherwise, Mongolia is blessed with some 250 sunny days a year. Hence in olden times the Blue Eternal Heaven was the Mongols' supreme deity.

GETTING THERE

Travel to Mongolia is either via Moscow or Beijing. From Moscow, Ulan Bator can be reached directly by air with stops at Novosibirsk, or Omsk and Irkutsk. These flights leave Moscow three times a week. Alternatively there are twice daily flights from Moscow to Irkutsk and from Irkutsk there are daily train departures and flights to Ulan Bator.

By train from Moscow there are 6 departures a week during the summer months (5 on the Russian train, 1 on the Chinese), which take 4 days and 6 hours to reach Ulan Bator; a reduced service operates from October to May.

From Beijing there is a daily train to Ulan Bator entering through Erlian, the customs post. This is usually a 28-hour trip depending on customs, which can take up to 6 hours. Mongol Air is soon to introduce a weekly flight between Ulan Bator and Beijing.

Visas for Mongolia (even if you are just transitting) must be obtained by all nationalities in advance, from embassies in Beijing, Moscow, London, Tokyo, New Delhi, or Jakarta. Application should be made at least 8 weeks in advance. No vaccinations are required.

Some US travel agencies arranging tours to the Mongolian People's Republic include General Tours, 49 West 57th Street, New York, NY 10019; and Travcoa, 875 North Michigan Avenue, Chicago, IL 60611; in the UK, Travel Promotions, 10 Glentworth Street, London NW1; and Thomas Cook, P.O. Box 36, Thrope Wood, Peterborough PE3 6SB.

ULAN BATOR

Glimpses of traditional Mongolian life can be gathered by wandering through the ger settlements around Ulan Bator city center. Many people still wear the *del*, a long coat-like garment often thickly padded against the cold. Be circumspect about taking photographs in the ger settlements, since gers are considered by officials to be an embarrassing remnant of the country's "feudal" past. The standard rules for photography in East European countries also hold for Mongolia, which means no military subjects or pictures of bridges, railway stations, or airports.

It is also possible to walk up the mountain slopes of the Tuul River Valley, in which Ulan Bator is situated. The hills afford good views of the city. But beware of penetrating too deeply into the forests that cover some of these slopes, since they are home to wild wolves and bears that have been known to show their irritation at being disturbed.

HIGHLIGHTS FOR TRAVELERS

Gandan Tegchinlen. In pre-revolutionary Mongolia, religion played a fundamental role in society and culture. The predominant religion was Tibetan Lamaism, a form of Buddhism introduced in the 14th century. One estimate suggests that Mongolia had 747 monasteries in 1921, with a total of 120,000 lamas, representing 40% of the country's male population. Today, Gandan Tegchinlen remains as the sole "working" monastery left in the whole country; it is 20 minutes' walk from Sukhe Bator Square in central Ulan Bator. You can wander around the compound of Gandan Tegchinlen (the name means "Great Vehicle of Complete Joy") and get a feel for what the country used to be like. The best times to visit the temples are at full moon and new moon, when the monks of the "Yellow Hat" order perform special ceremonies in an incense-laden atmosphere, yak butter lamps flickering before the golden Buddhas at the altars. But at almost any time you can see Mongolians prostrating themselves outside the temples or offering prayers at the many prayer wheels in the monastery compound.

Choijin-lama Temple. The large majority of the country's monasteries have been destroyed, but a few are preserved as museums. One such is the Choijin-lama Temple, situated midway between the hotels Ulan Bator and Bayangol. Entry is 2 Tugrik and the main temple is a veritable Aladin's Cave of silk wall hangings, incredibly intricate and brightly coloured paintings, appliqués and embroideries of Buddhist gods, golden statues, larger-than-life masks that were used in ritual dances, musical instruments, and other paraphernalia of Buddhist ritual.

The Bogd Khan's Summer Palace Museum. This museum displays more finery from times gone by. It is a half-hour walk straight down Lenin Street as it runs due south from the SW corner of Sukhe Bator Square and over a Chinese-built bridge with pagoda-like turrets that crosses the railway line and the Sdzlbdz River, a tributary of the Tuul. Before the bridge you will pass the State Library, in front of which is a large statue of Joseph Stalin, one of the few still standing in the world (most are in China).

The Bogd Khan was the last ruling Khan of Mongolia, and remained as ruling monarch after the revolution of 1921 until he died of syphilis in 1924. The clothes, thrones, and bedchamber of the Bogd Khan and his queen are on view with the Bogd Khan's own ger which is covered entirely in the skins of snow leopards. There is also the Bogd Khan's personal collection of stuffed animals, an extraordinary display of wildlife that he had brought to his palace from all over the world.

The State Museum. Situated just north of Sukhe Bator Square, the State Museum is worth a visit. There are three departments: natural history, which includes a palaeontological hall with several dinosaur skeletons and a very fine collection of dinosaur eggs, all of which were found in the Gobi; history, including a good ethnographic section; and art, both ancient and modern.

The Fine Arts Museum. Just around the corner from the State Museum, this museum houses some splendid examples of pre-revolutionary paintings, embroidery, appliqués, costumes, and very ornate household implements in the upstairs halls. Downstairs are the post-revolutionary offerings, mostly paintings and sculpture with a heavy European influence that are not in the same league artistically with their predecessors.

Other Museums on the northern side of the city are the **Museum of the Revolution,** with exhibits that trace the history of the Mongolian revolution and a **Lenin Museum. Ulan Bator Museum,** tracing the history of the city's development, is tucked away on the right-hand side of the road running east out of the city before the Indian and British embassies.

Sukhe Bator Square, the very heart of Ulan Bator, is twice the size of Moscow's Red Square. In the centre is a pink granite stature of Sukhe Bator, the hero of the Mongolian revolution, on horseback. On the northern side is the parliament building of the People's Great Hural, the highest legislative body of Mongolia. Situated immediately in front of this grey and forbidding structure is the Mausoleum that contains the bodies of Sukhe Bator and Choybalsan, another revolutionary leader who succeeded Sukhe Bator as premier after his death in 1923.

Entertainments in the evening are few in Ulan Bator. Opera and ballet can be seen in the National Opera House, an impressive neoclassical building in red and white on Sukhe Bator Square. There are resident troupes that perform classics such as Swan Lake and Tosca, as well as modern operatic versions of traditional Mongolian folk tales. Plays, folk dancing, and musical events are held at the National Theatre, and a permanent State Circus boasts acrobats, clowns, girl contortionists, performing bears, camels, and yaks.

Sports. The three national sports of horse racing, archery, and wrestling are common sights in and around Ulan Bator in the summer months. Wrestlers perform in traditional costume: thick leather boots and embroidered briefs and jackets. The winner performs a short ritual dance around a red flag, slowly flapping his arms like the wings of an eagle.

OUTSIDE ULAN BATOR

Travel in Mongolia is severely restricted both for Mongolians and, more especially, for tourists. There are essentially three destinations open to non-specialist Western tourists. Excursions are either by bus or by Mongol Air. All arrangements must be made through the national tourist agency, Zhuulchin, which has its headquarters in the Hotel Ulan Bator (Cable: ZHUULCHIN MONGOLIA; Telex: U-BT TLX 232). These trips are package deals that include an interpreter, and must be paid for in hard currency. There are many more areas of the country open to hunters who pay very high prices to shoot at Mongolia's extensive wildlife.

Terelj. About half an hour's drive from Ulan Bator, Terelj is a tourist camp, a small collection of gers in a majestic glaciated valley. You can stay overnight or for a few days in a ger and walk in the virgin countryside.

Karakorum. On the banks of the River Orhon, 300 km. west of Ulan Bator, is the town of Karakorum, the ancient capital of Mongolia. Construction of this important trading and cultural center of Central Asia was begun by Genghis Khan. The city was completed by his third son Ogatai in 1235 with the help of Chinese, Turkic, and Persian workers and craftsmen. Karakorum's preeminence was short-lived, however. Its importance declined gradually after Kublai Khan, Genghis' grandson, moved the capital to Beijing in 1267. About a century later the city was razed by invading Manchu forces, and today just a few remnants of the former ancient capital can be seen, among them one of the four original large stone tortoises that protected the city against floods.

Erdene Dzuu. Not far from the site of Karakorum is the oldest monastery in Mongolia, Erdene Dzuu, built at the end of the 16th century in part by taking columns, sculpture, and other materials from the ruins of the former capital. The monastery reflects Mongol, Chinese, and Tibetan styles, and the temples are surrounded by a stone wall with 108 white stupas. Each stupa honours an historic event or acts as a grave stone for a dignitary. Visitors to Karakorum and Erdene Dzuu are accommodated in gers at the nearby town of Hujirt, an hour's flight from Ulan Bator.

Gobi Desert. The word *gobi* means a stony pavement, and although one of the side trips from the South Gobi tourist camp is to see some large sand dunes, these features are in fact a rarity in this Central Asian desert. This part of the Gobi, just to the northwest of Dalanzadgad and less than two hours' flight from Ulan Bator, is surprisingly grassy. But there is a real sense here of the remoteness of Outer Mongolia, with frequent glimpses of wild Bactrian camels. Accommodation is in gers.

HOTEL ACCOMMODATIONS

There is a choice of two hotels open to foreigners in Ulan Bator: the Hotel Ulan Bator and the Bayangol. Both are rather faceless East European type buildings, each incorporating a dining room, bar, lounge areas, a small Mongolian shop, and a hard currency shop. The Hotel Ulan Bator is more up-market and rooms with a shower start from around US$60. Most rooms have telephones and some have a TV (two channels, one Mongolian, one Russian). A decanter of boiled drinking water is refilled every day, although the tap water gives no apparent ill effects. Within the Hotel Ulan Bator there is also a post office, a barbershop, and the Zhuulchin tour office where international railway bookings can be transacted.

CUISINE

Food in Mongolia is rather limited and not terribly exciting. Meat is the mainstay, augmented by rice (imported from Vietnam), bread, potatoes, and some canned vegetables. Fresh fruit and vegetables are rare; very little is grown in the country so most foodstuffs for visitors have to be imported. Hotel food is disappointingly "international": beefsteak, schnitzel, and fried chicken. The traditional Mongolian dish that is always available is "Hoitzer," a fatty mutton soup-cum-stew. Other Mongolian dishes can be ordered a day in advance; these include "Buudz," small steamed pastry parcels of mince; and "Banch," the same idea but boiled with a knob of butter in the water, often eaten in Mongolian tea that is very milky and salty. Occasionally venison and marmot may be available. It is advisable to take multi-vitamins if you plan to stay long in Mongolia.

Mongolian beer is an acquired taste; "Arkhi," the local vodka, is good, and "Oondha" is a local fizzy drink flavored with small apples or lemons. "Kumys," fermented mare's milk, is available in the summer months when the grazing has turned green after the winter. East German beer and Georgian mineral water are expensive since they have to be brought in across Siberia.

Restaurants outside the two hotels are difficult to find. They are not terribly hygienic and also offer a limited range of food.

SHOPPING

There is not a lot to buy in Mongolian shops. The hard currency shops, which accept all major Western currencies (US dollars are best), have a more interesting range of things available including items such as Teachers scotch, Cinzano, Coca-Cola, and Western cigarettes, all at duty-free prices. Knitwear is a bargain: Mongolian cashmere sweaters and cardigans from US$40, and soft camel-wool garments. Fur hats and the traditional Mongolian dress, the *"del,"* thick leather boots and silver Kumys bowls make good souvenirs, but be sure the bowls are in fact silver. An interesting collection of Mongolian folk tales, translated into English, can be bought from the hotel shops. The golden rule for buying things in any shop in Mongolia is to buy when you see something you want, since tomorrow it may not be there.

成田

Tokyo/Narita Airport

MOST travelers flying direct to China from the US or Canada stop en route at Japan's Narita Airport. Officially named New Tokyo International Airport, the terminus is located 60 km. (37 mi.) east of Tokyo near the historic city of Narita (1980 est. pop. 72,000). Second only to Hong Kong's Kai Tak Airport as a transfer point for East Asia and Southeast Asian destinations, the airport has been surrounded by controversy since the mid-1960s, when the Japanese government began buying up thousands of acres of precious farmland in Narita's eastern suburbs. The project angered local farmers, who were concerned about the airport's potential impact on the area's environment and traditional economy. Their demonstrations often turned into violent confrontations with the police, and the project was delayed for five years. The furor has died down somewhat, but Narita still maintains what may be the strictest airport security measures anywhere: armed soldiers man watchtowers around the airport's perimeter, while at outposts and roadblocks a mile from the terminal entrance, squads of riot police stand by in armored troop transports.

The terminal is an imposing V-shaped, four-level building radiating circular "satellite" boarding gates. Arriving passengers can change money as they leave Customs. There is also a bank on the fourth floor (open 24 hours). Shops selling souvenirs, gifts, and the latest in cameras and electronic gadgetry, as well as newsstands and restaurants, are located on the third level between the north and south wings.

If you are connecting with a morning flight to Beijing and are staying overnight at one of Narita's airport hotels, after clearing immigration, proceed downstairs to the Hotel Reservation Desk. Even those travelers whose overnight stays have been prearranged by the airline should stop here to pick up their vouchers. There are shuttle buses for all the airport hotels just outside the terminal building.

Travelers who have a day or less to spare on the way to or from China can get a taste of "old" Japan in nearby Narita City, with its busy markets, traditional Japanese houses, and the famous Shinsho-ji Temple. Established in AD 940, the temple was moved to its present site in 1705. Most of the buildings date from this period, although the main building is actually a concrete reconstruction, built in the 1960s. Dedicated to the fire god, Fudo, the shrine is one of the most popular in Japan, drawing more than 10 million visitors annually. The majority are Shingon Buddhists (a sect derived from esoteric Tibetan Buddhism) who come in January for the yearly shrine visit. Only true believers participate in the ritual, which is definitely not for the fainthearted: the pilgrims circle the temple for hours, chanting prayers and sutras, stopping only to douse themselves with icy water drawn from a nearby well. Less ascetic festivities accompany the Cherry Blossom Festival, in April; the Temple Procession, in early July; and the Chrysanthemum Show, which takes place during November. The temple, and the nearby Narita Historical Museum, are a ten- to twenty-minute walk from the Japan National Railway station, which can be reached by bus No. 5 from the airport (20 minutes, Y300), or by complimentary shuttle bus from any of the airport hotels.

GETTING TO TOKYO FROM NARITA

The simplest, and usually the fastest, way to get to Tokyo from the airport is by airport limousine. The 60-minute bus ride costs Y2500 (about $12.50) each way, and stops at the Tokyo City Air Terminal, on the eastern edge of the city proper. There are also buses to the major Tokyo hotels, to Tokyo JNR Rail Station, and to Haneda Airport (for domestic air connections). Buses depart Narita every 5 to 10 minutes during peak hours, and every 15 to 20 minutes in the early morning and late evening. The last bus back to Narita leaves the City Air Terminal at 8:40 PM. Trains to Tokyo leave from the Keisei-Ueno station, a six-minute bus ride from the airport (Y140), as well as from the Narita JNR station. The Keisei Line Skyliner Express makes the trip in about 60 minutes (Y1,300), while the cheaper regular express takes 15 minutes longer (Y650). From Narita JNR station, the limited express takes 65 minutes to downtown Tokyo Station (Y2,000). Helicopter service to Tokyo's Haneda Airport is available. Maps, schedules, and hotel and tour information for Tokyo and Narita can be obtained at the Tourist Information Counter, located in the main lobby of the terminal building (tel: 32-8711).

HOTEL ACCOMMODATIONS

Most travelers who overnight at Narita are put up at one or another of the modern, Western-style hotels near the airport. There are also a number of traditional Japanese inns (*ryokan*) in Narita City.

NARITA HOTEL DIRECTORY

Holiday Inn Narita	320-1 Tokko	32-1234
Narita Airport Rest House	Narita Airport	32-1212
Narita Prince	560 Tokko	33-3111
Narita View	700 Kosuge	32-1111
Nikko Narita	500 Tokko	32-0032

VII. APPENDIX

An Annotated
Reading List
For China Travelers

BACKGROUND

Andors, Phyllis. *The Unfinished Liberation of Chinese Women, 1949–1980.* Bloomington, IN: Indiana University Press, 1983.

Bai Shouyi, ed. *An Outline History of China.* Beijing: Foreign Languages Press, 1982. A new general history through 1911, from the Chinese viewpoint.

Beechy, Winifred Nelson. *The New China.* Scottdale, PA: Herald Press, 1982. A readable, firsthand account of daily life, health care, education, and Christianity.

Bennett, Gordon. *Huadong: Story of a Chinese People's Commune.* Boulder, CO: Westview Press, 1978. A study of a people's commune in Guangzhou over a 10-year period with factual information on organization and distribution of labor, farming methods, traditional festivals, and more.

Butterfield, Fox. *Alive in the Bitter Sea.* New York: Bantam Books, 1983. Some ascerbic observations from a former *New York Times* correspondent in Beijing.

Chen, Jo-hsi. *The Execution of Mayor Yin and Other Stories from the Great Proletarian Cultural Revolution.* Bloomington: Indiana University Press, 1978. Stories about life during this tumultuous period written by a Taiwan-born writer who spent the Cultural Revolution in the People's Republic.

Cheng, Nien. *Life and Death in Shanghai.* New York: Grove, 1987. Vivid, eloquent firsthand account of six-year imprisonment during the Cultural Revolution.

Chi Hsin. *The Case of the Gang of Four.* Hong Kong: Cosmos Books, 1977. The fall of Mao's widow, Jiang Qing, and the other members of the "gang of four" and the rise to power of Deng Xiaoping.

China Directory, 1988. Tokyo: Radiopress, Inc., 1988. A useful and important reference work on the organs and personalities of the Chinese Communist Party, the government, and mass organizations of the PRC.

China Handbook (1987–88). Hong Kong: Ta Kung Pao, 1988. Up-to-date information on the Chinese leadership, economic reforms, trade regulations, and the Special Economic Zones and 14 Coastal Open Cities.

Cleverley, John. *The Schooling of China*. Winchester: Allen and Unwin, 1985.

Coye, Molly Joel, and Jon Livingston, eds. *China Yesterday and Today*. Fourth edition. New York: Bantam, 1984. An inexpensive (US$4.95) compendium of readings, documents, and observations.

Creel, H. G. *Chinese Thought from Confucius to Mao Tsetung*. Chicago: University of Chicago Press, 1953. Confucianism, Buddhism, Daoism, and Neo-Confucianism.

Crook, Isabel, and David Crook. *Ten Mile Inn: Mass Movement in a Chinese Village*. New York: Pantheon Books, 1979. Firsthand account of a Liberated Area village southwest of Beijing in 1948.

Danforth, Kenneth C. *Journey Into China*. Washington: National Geographic Society, 1982. A magnificently produced photographic essay.

Dietrich, Craig. *People's China: A Brief History*. New York: Oxford, 1986.

Epstein, Israel. *From Opium War to Liberation*. Hong Kong: Joint Publishing, 1980. An interpretive history from 1840 to 1949 by the editor of Beijing's *China Reconstructs*.

Fairbank, John K. *The United States and China*. Fourth revised edition. Cambridge, MA: Harvard University Press, 1983. The standard history of US-China relations. Includes 100 pages of suggested readings.

———. *Chinabound: A Fifty Year Memoir*. New York: Harper & Row, 1981. America's most distinguished China scholar recalls his experience with the Far East after a lifetime of scholarship, teaching and writing.

Frolic, Michael B. *Mao's People*. Cambridge, MA: Harvard University Press, 1980. A selection of unusually insightful interviews.

Hinton, William. *Fanshen: A Documentary of Revolution in a Chinese Village*. New York: Vintage Books, 1966. An absorbing, intimate account of the revolutionary transformation of a farming village in Shanxi Province.

———. *Shenfan: The Continuing Revolution in a Chinese Village*. New York: Random House, 1983. *Fanshen's* Long Bow village revisited, including a mixed assessment of the Cultural Revolution.

Hook, Brian, ed. *The Cambridge Encyclopedia of China*. Cambridge, England: Cambridge University Press, 1982. An excellent single-volume compendium covering the gamut of Chinese civilization.

Hsu, Immanuel C.Y. *China Without Mao*. New York: Oxford University Press, 1982. The best concise account of the first five years after Mao's death, 1976–1981.

Hsu, Kai-yu, ed. *Literature of the People's Republic of China*. Bloomington: Indiana University Press, 1980. A broad survey which includes movie scripts, dialogues, operas, and essays, as well as poems, plays, and stories.

Johnson, Kay Ann. *Women, the Family and Peasant Revolution in China*. Chicago: University of Chicago Press, 1985.

Juliano, Annette. *Treasures of China*. New York: Richard Marek Publishers, 1981.

Kahn-Ackermann, Michael. *China: Within the Outer Gate*. London: Marco Polo Press, 1982. A strikingly lucid and intelligent explanation of Chinese politics.

Kaplan, Fredric M., and Julian M. Sobin. *Encyclopedia of China Today*, Fourth edition. New York: M.E. Sharpe/Eurasia Press, 1989. A one-volume encyclopedia offering an overview of contemporary China.

Lao She. *Camel Xiangzi*. Beijing: Foreign Languages Press, 1981. Shi Xiaoqing's new translation of the harrowing classic (originally titled *Rickshaw Boy*).

Leys, Simon. *Chinese Shadows*. New York: Penguin Books, 1978.

Link, Perry, ed. *Stubborn Weeds: Popular and Controversial Literature after the Cultural Revolution*. Bloomington: Indiana University Press, 1982. A collection of writings which reflect the consequences of the Cultural Revolution.

Myrdal, Jan, with photographs by Gun Kessle. *The Silk Road*. New York: Pantheon Books, 1979. The Myrdals retrace Marco Polo's footsteps.

Nathan, Andrew. *Chinese Democracy*. New York: Knopf, 1985.

Nathan, Robert Stuart. *The White Tiger*. New York: Simon and Schuster, 1987. A mystery novel set in contemporary China.

Needham, Joseph. *Science in Traditional China*. Cambridge, MA: Harvard University Press, 1981. A concise overview by the world's leading authority on Chinese science.

Orr, Robert G. *Religion in China*. New York: Friendship Press, 1980.

Qian Hao, Chen Heyi, and Ru Suichu. *Out of China's Earth*. New York: Abrams, 1982. A definitive account of the monumental Qin Dynasty excavation near Xi'an, profusely illustrated.

Saltzman, Mark. *Iron & Silk*. New York: Random House, 1987. Engaging observations from a young American China traveler.

Schell, Orville. *Discos and Democracy: China in the Throes of Reform*. New York: Pantheon Books, 1988. Personal view on the changing cultural atmosphere in China.

Schwartz, Benjamin I. *The World of Thought in Ancient China*. Cambridge: Harvard University Press, 1985.

Selden, Mark, ed. *The People's Republic of China: A Documentary History of Revolutionary Change*. New York: Monthly Review Press, 1979. Documents of China's history, 1946–79, including three constitutions.

Sidel, Ruth, and Victor W. Sidel. *The Health of China: Current Conflicts in Medical and Human Services for One Billion People*. Boston: Beacon Press, 1982.

Snow, Edgar. *Red Star Over China*. New York: Grove Press, 1971. Based on Snow's personal interviews with Mao and others in 1938, this is probably the most evocative firsthand account of the Chinese Communist movement in the period following the Long March.

Spence, Jonathan D. *The Gate of Heavenly Peace*. New York and London: Penguin, 1983. A masterful account of upheaval and revolution in China, 1895–1980.

Stalberg, Roberta H., and Ruth Nesi. *China's Crafts: The Story of How They're Made and What They Mean.* New York: Eurasia Press, 1980.

Sullivan, Michael. *The Arts of China.* Revised edition. Berkeley, CA: University of California Press, 1977. Perhaps the best concise survey available on traditional arts.

Terrill, Ross. *Mao: A Biography.* New York: Harper & Row, 1980. A reconstruction of Mao's life based on numerous accounts, conversations, and Mao's poems.

Topping, Audrey. *The Splendors of Tibet.* New York: Lee Publishers Group, 1980.

Unger, Jonathan, Anita Chan, and Richard Madsen. *Chen Village: The Recent History of a Peasant Community in Mao's China.* Berkeley: University of California, 1985.

BUSINESS AND ECONOMY

American Chamber of Commerce in Hong Kong. *Doing Business in Today's China.* Hong Kong: South China Morning Post, 1980.

Asia & Pacific. Essex, UK: World of Information, 1984. A business and trade annual.

Asia 1988 Yearbook. Hong Kong: Far Eastern Economic Review, 1988. Includes fresh, pointed analysis of PRC economic performance.

Baum, Richard, ed.: *China's Four Modernizations: The New Technological Revolution.* Boulder, CO: Westview Press, 1980.

MacDougall, Colina, ed. *Trading with China: A Practical Guide.* New York and London: McGraw-Hill, 1980. Wide-ranging essays by 14 experts.

Prybyla, Jan S. *The Chinese Economy: Problems and Policies.* Columbia, SC: University of South Carolina Press, 1980.

Sit, Victor F.S. *Commercial Laws and Business Regulations of the People's Republic of China, 1949–1983.* New York: Eurasia Press, 1983.

US Department of Commerce. *Doing Business with China.* Washington, DC: US Department of Commerce, 1979. Basic information for travelers as well as brief accounts of negotiations, arbitration, currency, payments, tariffs, etc.

Xue Muqiao, ed. *Almanac of China's Economy.* New York: Eurasia Press, 1982. The first official, comprehensive survey of China's economy, 1949–1981.

Xue Muqiao. *China's Socialist Economy.* Beijing: Foreign Languages Press, 1983.

TRAVEL GUIDES AND AIDS

China Bound: A Handbook for American Students, Researchers and Teachers. Washington, DC: US–China Education Clearinghouse, 1981.

China Phone Book and Business Directory. 1988 edition. Hong Kong: China Phone Book Company, GPO Box 11581, Hong Kong: 1988. A much expanded edition of the 1980 directory. Invaluable for frequent China travelers or long-term residents.

Earnshaw, Graham. *On Your Own in China*. London: Century Publishing, 1983. A fact-filled guide for the intrepid budget traveler.

Fodor's Guide to the People's Republic of China. New York: David McKay Company, 1986. An excellent compendium of detailed information; especially useful for PRC residents and long-term visitors.

Nagel's Encyclopedia Guide to China. Trans. Anne L. Destenay. Geneva, Switzerland: Nagel Publishers, 1979. Exhaustive descriptive information, especially on cultural aspects.

Schwartz, Brian. *China Off the Beaten Track*. New York: St. Martin's Press, 1983.

Stalberg, Roberta. *Shopping in China*. New York: China Books, 1988.

BOOKS FROM CHINA

Most foreign language titles from China are published by the Foreign Languages Press in Beijing. They are available from bookstores specializing in PRC materials, or may be ordered from China Publications Center, P.O. Box 399, Beijing, People's Republic of China; or from China Books and Periodicals, 2929 24th Street, San Francisco, California 94110. Most of the titles listed below are available in several languages.

Cao Yu. *Sunrise* (1935). Recently translated, this four-act play by one of China's foremost contemporary playwrights portrays the decadence of traditional Chinese society.

China: A General Survey. Second Revised Edition. 1979. This handy pocket-size book includes sections on China's geography, history, politics, economy, culture, commerce, and religion.

Chung Chih. *An Outline of Chinese Geography*. 1978. A guide to China's regions, climates, vegetation, mammals, and birds. Photos and maps.

Lu Xun. *Selected Stories of Lu Hsun*. 1972. A collection of 18 short stories by China's most prominent revolutionary writer.

Mao Dun. *Midnight* (1933). 1979. Story of a 1930s Shanghai industrialist.

Pa Chin. *The Family* (1931). Trans. Sidney Shapiro. Second edition. 1978. The emerging conflict between the old China and the new is shown through the struggles of a disintegrating feudal household.

Wu Jingzi. *The Scholars*. An 18th-century satirical novel still avidly read in China.

PERIODICALS

FROM CHINA

Beijing Review. Weekly. Authoritative political journal with documents and reports on domestic affairs and international relations.

China Daily. China's first and only English-language newspaper began publication from Beijing and Hong Kong in June 1981.

China Pictorial. Monthly. Good photographs accompanied by very brief articles on a wide range of subjects.

China Reconstructs. Monthly. Articles on many subjects, including daily life, the economy, and culture. Chinese-language lesson in every issue.

China's Foreign Trade. Bimonthly. Authoritative statements on trade policy, articles on China's trade and economics.

Women in China. Monthly. Highlights the important role of women and the issues concerning them in China today.

PUBLISHED OUTSIDE OF CHINA

Asian Wall Street Journal. Weekly. Dow Jones, 22 Cortlandt Street, New York, N.Y. 10007. A comprehensive, up-to-date chronicle of Asian economic news by Asia-based correspondents. (A daily edition is published in Hong Kong.)

Bulletin of Concerned Asian Scholars. Quarterly. P.O. Box 918, Berthoud, CO 80513. Originally an "alternative press" vehicle for US radical scholarship, it increasingly features academic research articles.

China Business Review. Bimonthly. US-China Business Council, Ste. 500, 1818 N Street NW, Washington, DC 20036. The Council also publishes special reports on China trade.

The China Quarterly. Quarterly. Contemporary China Institute, School of Oriental and African Studies, London University, Malet Street, London WC1E 7HP, United Kingdom. The foremost English-language journal on China.

Far Eastern Economic Review. Weekly. P.O. Box 160, Hong Kong. The best journalistic source on the Far East, covering both politics and economics. The quality of China coverage varies from middling to superb.

Journal of Asian Studies. Quarterly. Association for Asian Studies, 1 Lane Hall, University of Michigan, Ann Arbor, MI 48101. Scholarly essays.

Ta Kung Pao. Weekly. Joint Publishing Company, 9 Victoria Street, Hong Kong. English-language supplement to the Hong Kong Chinese-language daily. Informative articles, many digested from the PRC press.

Prominent Figures of
The PRC

NAME	POSITION
Chen Minzhang	Minister of Public Health
Chen Yun	Chairman, Central Advisory Commission, CCP
Chi Haotian	Chief of Staff, People's Liberation Army
Deng Xiaoping	Chairman, Central Military Commission of PRC (acknowledged to be China's most influential political figure and policy-maker; retired as a member of the CCP in 1987 at the age of 83)
Han Xu	Ambassador to the United States
Hu Qiaomu	President, Academy of Social Sciences
Hu Sheng	President, Chinese Academy of Social Sciences
Hua Guofeng	Former chairman of CCP
Li Guixian	President, People's Bank of China
Li Peng	Premier, State Council; Minister, State Commission for Restructuring the Economy
Li Tieying	Minister, State Education Commission
Liu Yi	Director-General, National Tourism Administration
Ma Hong	General Director, Economic Institute, State Planning Commission
Mao Zedong	*Deceased;* former chairman of CCP (1949-76)
Qian Qichen	Minister of Foreign Affairs
Qin Jiwei	Minister of National Defense
Song Jian	Minister of State Science and Technology Commission
Wan Li	Chairman, National People's Congress
Wang Bingqian	Minister of Finance
Wang Fang	Minister of Public Security
Wang Meng	Minister of Culture
Wang Renzhi	Director, Department of Propaganda
Wen Jiabo	General Director, Office of the CCP
Yang Shangkun	President of the People's Republic of China
Yao Yilin	Minister, State Planning Commission
Zhao Ziyang	General Secretary of the CCP
Zheng Tuobin	Minister of Foreign Economic Relations and Trade
Zhou Enlai	*Deceased;* former Premier, State Council
Zhou Guangzhao	President, Chinese Academy of Sciences

HOW THE CHINESE LANGUAGE WORKS

By the early 1980s, English-language fever was sweeping China. These days on buses, in classrooms, at home after dinner, Chinese people have their noses buried in English grammar and phrase books. There's even an immensely popular English-language instruction program, covering the fine points of pronunciation and colloquial usage, broadcast on TV every day from Beijing, and English lessons can be heard on the radio several times a day in some areas.

Although things are getting easier for the non-Chinese speaker, you're still going to need your tour guide as a translator and general adviser. (You'll probably have a hard time holding forth with the man on the street beyond a hearty "Hello, how are you?") Tour escorts and other representatives from host organizations speak excellent English (and usually several other languages as well). Older, more experienced personnel can tackle complex political and social issues with ease; the younger guides may have a little trouble with rapid-fire slang. If you make a point of speaking slowly and simply, especially in the beginning, you should have no problem being understood.

Unless you are already very comfortable in one or two Chinese dialects, you'd do well to abandon the idea of communicating with your guide in his or her native tongue (although a pleasant, "*Ni hao, ni hao ma*" is always warmly appreciated).

Chinese is the world's oldest continuously used language and more people claim it as a mother tongue than any other. However, you're going to have an almost impossible time learning it outside the classroom unless you're able to immerse yourself in a Chinese-speaking environment for a year or more.

Unlike most modern languages, Chinese doesn't have a phonetic alphabet. Instead, Chinese uses "ideographs," generally referred to as "characters." These denote objects, actions, and abstract ideas, and contain only scant indication as to how they are to be pronounced. Unless you can very quickly learn to distinguish between about 5,000 different squiggles, you're better off relying on the widespread English translations (or pinyin romanizations) on signs and menus.

SPOKEN CHINESE

The pitches or "tones" of spoken Chinese present another difficulty to the novice speaker. With its tens of thousands of characters, Mandarin Chinese has only slightly more than 400 syllables with which to pronounce them. As a result, a single sound can represent more than 100 different written characters. Tones and the use of compounds multiply the number of available word sounds. (*Putonghua*, the national language, has four separate tones and many compounds.) Some dialects, such as Cantonese, have more tones and syllable sounds, and fewer compounds.

Tones. The tone or pitch contour can completely change a syllable's denotation. For instance, the sound "mah" is represented by several different Chinese characters. Pronounced in *putonghua's* first tone, *mā (māh)*, it can mean "*mother*"; in the second tone, *má* (máh), it can mean "numb" or "hemp." In the third tone, *mǎ* (mǎh), it is "horse," and in the fourth, *mà* (màh), it means "to scold."

Unfortunately, you can't learn tones from a book. You have to hear and imitate them hundreds of times before you really grasp their subtle variations. Nevertheless, here's a very general guide for the sound "mah" in the four tones of *putonghua*. The first tone is pronounced at a level, fairly high pitch: *mā* (māh). The second tone rises from the middle register to the level of the first tone: *má* (máh). In the third tone, the voice dips and rises—the dip is low and rather elongated and the rise is somewhat quicker: *mǎ* (mǎh). The fourth tone begins high and falls to a low pitch, very abruptly and definitely: *mà* (màh).

Dialects. Written Chinese is uniform throughout China, but the spoken language varies from region to region, and sometimes from village to village. China has 10 major dialect groups. The Beijing dialect and closely related pronunciations are mainly found in the northeastern and southwestern regions of China. Since 1949, Beijing dialect has been the basis of the national language and is spoken today by 70% of China's Chinese-speaking population. As the official language of the People's Republic, it is used in government and commercial circles and on radio and TV broadcasts, and is taught in schools throughout the country. Outside the PRC, it's often referred to as "Mandarin."

Pinyin Romanization. As if Chinese weren't confusing enough already, you now also have two and sometimes three different spellings in English for the same word. The latest phonetic system of romanizing Chinese sounds is pinyin, meaning "phonetic transcription." Many of the Chinese place names familiar to Westerners, such as Peking (Beijing), Canton (Guangzhou), and Chungking (Chongqing) were originally used by the British colonial postal service, and bear little resemblance to the Chinese pronunciation. Other place names and words, such as Kuei-lin (Guilin), Tientsin (Tianjin), and Mao Tse-tung (Mao Zedong), are usually rendered into English using the Wade-Giles system. To make matters worse, many "traditional" English spellings of Chinese names and words are the legacy of 19th century merchants and missionaries who knew little or no Chinese, and may reflect local, rather than standard, pronunciation (e.g., Hong Kong and Amoy).

In some ways you're better off knowing absolutely nothing about Chinese and starting from scratch with the pinyin spelling. Your pronunciation will be more accurate and you won't be as bewildered as some of the old experts. Since 1958, pinyin has been the officially endorsed system in China, and the Western media are increasingly adopting pinyin.

PINYIN ALPHABET
PRONUNCIATION GUIDE

(Letters in parentheses are equivalents used in traditional Wade-Giles spellings)

a (a) Vowel as in *far*

b (p) Consonant as in *be*

c (ts') Consonant as in *chip*; strongly aspirated

d (t) Consonant as in *do*

e (e) Vowel as in *her*

f (f) Consonant as in *foot*

g (k') Consonant as in *go*

h (h) Consonant as in *her*; strongly aspirated

i (i) Vowel as in *eat* or as in *sir* (when in syllables beginning with c, ch, r, s, sh, z and zh.)

j (ch) Consonant as in *jeep*

k (k') Consonant as in *kind*, strongly aspirated

l (l) Consonant as in *land*

m (m) Consonant as in *me*

n (n) Consonant as in *now*

o (o) Vowel as in *law*

p (p') Consonant as in *par*; strongly aspirated

q (ch') Consonant as in *cheek*

r (j) Consonant as in *right* (not rolled) or pronounced as *z* in *azure*

s (s,ss, sz) Consonant as in *sister*

sh (sh) Consonant as in *shore*

t (t') Consonant as in *top*; strongly aspirated

u (u) Vowel as in *too*; also as in French *tu* or the German München

v (v) Consonant used only to produce foreign words, national minority words, and local dialects

w (w) Semi-vowel in syllables beginning with u when not preceded by consonants, as in *want*

x (hs) Consonant as in *she*

y Semi-vowel in syllables beginning with i or u when not preceded by consonants, as in *yet*

z (ts,tz) Consonant as in *adze*

zh (ch) Consonant as in *jump*

Tone marks: First tone ¯ Second tone ´ Third tone ˇ Fourth tone `

Chinese Phrases
for Travelers

GENERAL

ENGLISH	PINYIN (CHINESE PRONUNCIATION)	CHINESE CHARACTERS
I, me; mine	wǒ (*waw*); wǒde (*waw-duh*)	我 ；我的
You; your	nǐ (*nee*); nǐde (*nee-duh*)	你 ；你的
He, it/she	tā (*tah*) / tā (*tah*)	他 / 她
His, its/hers	tāde (*tah-duh*) / tāde (*tah-duh*)	他的 / 她的
We, us; our	wǒmen (*waw-mun*); wǒmen de	我们 ；我们的
You (pl.); your (pl.)	nǐmen (*nee-mun*); nǐmen de	你们 ；你们的
They, them (m./f.)	tāmen (*tah-mun*) / tāmen (*tah-mun*)	他们 / 她们
Their (m./f.)	tāmende (*tah-mun-duh*) / tāmende (*tah-mun-duh*)	他们的 / 她们的
Hello, how are you?	nǐ hǎo ;(*nee hao*); nǐ hǎo ma (*nee hao mah*)	你好 ；你好吗
Good morning!	zǎo (*dzao*); zǎo ān (*dzao an*)	早 ；早安
Good evening!	wǎn ān (*wahn an*)	晚安
Good-bye!	zài jiàn (*dzai jee-en*)	再见
I don't understand.	wǒ bù dǒng (*waw boo doong*)	我不懂
Yes, I agree; correct.	shì (*shir*); duì (*doo-ay*)	是 ；对
I don't agree.	bù tóngyì (*boo toong-yee*)	不同意
Please	qǐng (*ching*)	请
Thank you; many thanks.	xiè xie (*shee-eh shee-eh*); dūo xiè (*dwaw shee-eh*)	谢谢 ；多谢
It's nothing (don't mention it).	bú kèqì (*boo kuh-chee*)	不客气
I'm sorry.	duì bùqǐ (*doo-ay boo chee*)	对不起

English	Pinyin (pronunciation)	Chinese
O.K., you can	kěyǐ (*kuh-ee*)	可以
Not O.K., you can't	bú kěyǐ (*boo kuh-ee*)	不可以／不行
Not bad, so-so	hái kěyǐ (*hi kuh-ee*)	还可以
Good; very good	hǎo (*hao*); hěn hǎo (*hun hao*)	好；很好
No (not) good	bù hǎo (*boo hao*)	不好
Thank you, but I. . .	xiè xie, wǒ. . .(*she-eh, waw. . .*)	谢谢，我…
am unable to	bù néng (*boo nung*)	不能
don't want to	bú yào (*boo yao*)	不要
don't like	bù xǐhuān (*boo shee-hwahn*)	不喜欢
Pleased; happy	huānxǐ (*hwahn-shee*); kuàilè (*kwhy-luh*); gāoxìng (*gao-shing*)	欢喜；快乐，高兴
Very; extremely	hěn (*hun*); fēicháng (*fay-chahng*)	很；非常
Slow	màn (*man*)	慢
Fast	kuài (*kwhy*)	快
Hot	rè (*ruh*)	热
Cold	lěng (*lung*)	冷
Who?	shuí (*shway*)	谁
When is. . .?	shénma shíhòu (*shum-mah shir-hoe*)	什么时候…
Where. . .; . . . is where?	shénma dìfang. . . (*shum-mah dee fahng. . .*); . . .zài nǎlǐ (. . . *dzai nah-lee*)	什么地方…；…在哪里
Friend	péngyǒu (*pung-yo*)	朋友
Friendship	yǒuyì (*yo-yee*)	友谊
Friendly	yǒu hǎo (*yo-hao*)	友好
May I please ask your name?	qǐngwèn guìxìng (*ching-win gway-shing*)	请问贵姓
My name is. . .	wǒ jiào (*waw djeeow*)	我叫……

I am	wǒ shì (*waw shir*)	我是
American (i.e., US citizen)	měiguórén (*may-gwaw run*)	美国人
Australian	àudàlìyǎrén (*ow-dah-lee-ah run*)	澳大利亚人
British	yīnggúorén (*ying-gwaw run*)	英国人
Canadian	jiānádàrén (*jee-ah-nah-dah run*)	加拿大人
French	fǎguórén (*fah-gwaw run*)	法国人
German	déguórén (*duh-gwaw run*)	德国人
Italian	yìdàlìrén (*yee-dah-lee run*)	意大利人
Japanese	rìběnrén (*rih-bun run*)	日本人

TRAVEL

ENGLISH	PINYIN (CHINESE PRONUNCIATION)	CHINESE CHARACTERS
Right	yòu (*yo*)	右
Left	zuǒ (*dzwaw*)	左
Front	qián (*chee-en*)	前
Back	hòu (*hoe*)	后
Luggage	xínglǐ (*shing-lee*)	行李
Customs	hǎiguān (*hye-gwan*)	海关
Car	qìchē (*chee-chuh*)	汽车
Bus	gōnggòng qìchē (*gung-gung chee-chuh*)	公共汽车
Taxi	chūzū qìchē (*choo-dzoo chee-chuh*)	出租汽车
Airport	fēijīchǎng (*fay-jee-chahng*)	飞机场
Railroad station	huǒchēzhàn (*hwaw-chuh jan*)	火车站
Bicycle	zìxíngchē (*dze-sing-chuh*)	自行车
Bike rental	chūzū zìxíngchē (*choo-dzoo-dze-sing-chuh*)	出租自行车

AT THE HOTEL

ENGLISH	PINYIN (CHINESE PRONUNCIATION)	CHINESE CHARACTERS
Hotel	lǚguǎn (*lü-gwan*)	旅馆
Room	fángjiān (*fahng-jee-en*)	房间
Key	yàoshi (*yao shir*)	钥匙
Floor (story)	lóu (*lo*); céng (*tsung*)	楼；层
Elevator	diàntī (*dee-en tee*)	电梯
Stairs	lóutī (*low-tee*)	楼梯
Telephone	diànhuà (*dee-en hwa*)	电话
Light (electric)	diàndēng (*dee-en dung*)	电灯
Refrigerator	bīng xiāng (*bing-shee-ahng*)	冰箱
Television	diàn shì (*dee-en-shr*)	电视
Radio	shōuyīnjī (*show-yin-gee*)	收音机
Air-Conditioning	kōngtiáo / lěngqì (*kawng-tyaw / lung-chee*)	空调／冷气
Laundry	xǐyīdiàn (*shee yee dee-en*)	洗衣店
Toilet	cèsuǒ (*tse-swo*)	厕所
Men's	nán (*nahn*)	男
Women's	nǚ (*new*)	女
Bath	xǐzǎo (*shee-dzao*)	洗澡
Water	shǔi (*shway*)	水
Please come in!	qǐng jìnlái (*ching jeen-lye*)	请进来
(Please) wait a moment.	děngyīdeng (*dung-yee-dung*)	等一等
Sleep	shuìzháo (*shway-jao*)	睡觉
Bed	chuáng (*chew-ahng*)	床
Sheets	chuáng dān (*chew-ahng don*)	床单
Towel	máo jīn (*mao jeen*)	毛巾
Clean	gān jìng (*gahn jeeng*)	干净
Not clean	bù gān jìng (*boo gahn jeeng*)	不干净

Have	yǒu (yo)	有
Not have	méi yǒu (may yo)	没有
Hotel restaurant	cān tīng (kahn teeng)	餐厅
Hotel shop	xiǎomàibù (shao my boo)	小卖部
Post Office	yóujú (yo-joo)	邮局
Barber Shop	lǐfǎdiàn (lee-fah-dee-en)	理发店
Cable	diànbào (dee-en bao)	电报
Telex	diànchúan (dee-en choo-ahn)	电传

SIGHTSEEING

ENGLISH	PINYIN (CHINESE PRONUNCIATION)	CHINESE CHARACTERS
Welcome	huānyǐng (hwahn-ying)	欢迎
We would like to visit a...	wǒmen yào qù. . . (waw-mun yao chü)	我们要去…
See, watch	kàn (kahn)	看
commune	gōngshè (goong shuh)	公社
factory	gōngchǎng (goong chahng)	工厂
museum	bówùguǎn (baw-woo-gwan)	博物馆
park	gōngyuán (goong-yoo-ahn)	公园
school	xuéxiào (shoo-eh shee-ow)	学校
store	shāngdiàn (shahng-dee-en)	商店
university	dàxué (da shoo-eh)	大学
Temple	sìmiào (suh-myao)	寺庙
Buddhist temple	sì (see)	寺
Confucian temple	miào (mee-yao)	庙
Daoist temple	guàn (gwahn)	观
Take a picture	zhàoxiàng (jao shee-ahng)	照象

SHOPPING

ENGLISH	PINYIN (CHINESE PRONUNCIATION)	CHINESE CHARACTERS
Antique	gǔdǒng (*goo-doong*)	古董
Book	shū (*shoo*)	书
Bookstore	shūdiàn (*shoo dee-en*)	书店
Department store	bǎihuòshāngdiàn (*bye-hwaw shahng-dee-en*)	百货商店
Handicrafts	gōngyìpǐn (*goong yee-peen*)	工艺品
Stamps	yóupiaò (*yo-pee-ow*)	邮票
How much (money)?	duōshǎo qián (*dwaw-shao chee-en*)	多少钱
Expensive	gùi (*gway*)	贵
Cheap (inexpensive)	piányi (*pee-en yee*)	便宜
Dollar	kuài (*kwhy*); yuán (*yoo-en*)	块；元
Ten cents; cent	máo (*mao*); fēn (*fun*)	毛；分
Change	língqián (*leeng-chh-en*)	零钱
Where can I buy. . .?	zài nǎlǐ kěyǐ mǎi. . . (*dzai nah-lee kuh-yee my*)	在哪里可以买…
I would like that. . .	wǒ yào nèige. . . (*waw-yao nay-guh. . .*)	我要那个…
black one	hēide (*hay-duh*)	黑的
blue one	lánde (*lahn-duh*)	兰的
green one	lùde (*lee-yü-duh*)	绿的
red one	hóngde (*hoong-duh*)	红的
white one	báide (*bye-duh*)	白的
yellow one	huǎngde (*hoo-ahng-duh*)	黄的
gray one	hūide (*hoo-ay-duh*)	灰的
brown one	zōngde (*dzong-de*)	棕的

FOOD

ENGLISH	PINYIN (CHINESE PRONUNCIATION)	CHINESE CHARACTERS
I'm hungry.	wǒ èle (*waw uh-luh*)	我饿了
I'm thirsty.	wǒ kēle (*waw kuh-luh*)	我渴了
Eat	chī (*chir*)	吃
Drink	hē (*huh*)	喝
Restaurant	fànguǎn (*fahn gwan*)	饭馆
Breakfast	zǎocān (*dzao-tsahn*); zǎofàn (*dzao-fan*)	早餐；早饭
Lunch	wǔcān (*woo-tsahn*); wǔfàn (*woo-fan*)	午餐；午饭
Dinner	wǎncān (*wahn-tsahn*); wǎnfàn (*wahn-fan*)	晚餐；晚饭
Snack / dessert	diǎnxīn (*dee-en sheen*)	点心
Chopsticks	kuàizi (*kwhy-dzih*)	筷子
Knife	dāo (*dao*)	刀
Fork	chā (*chah*)	叉
Spoon	tāngchi (*tahng-chir*)	汤匙
What is your specialty?	yǒu shénma tèbiéde hǎochī (*yo shummah tuh-bee-eh-duh hao-chir*)	有什么特别的好吃
I've had enough to eat!	chībǎole (*chir bao-luh*)	吃饱了
The food was delicious!	hěn hǎochī (*hun hao-chir*)	很好吃
Bottoms up!	gānbēi (*gahn-bay*)	干杯
Water (cold)	liángkāishuǐ (*lee-ahng kai-shway*)	凉开水
Coffee	kāfēi (*kah-fay*)	咖啡
Tea	chá (*chah*)	茶
Beer	píjiǔ (*pee-jee-oh*)	啤酒
Beef	niúròu (*nee-oh row*)	牛肉
Chicken	jī (*jee*)	鸡
Duck	yāzi (*yah-dzih*)	鸭子

Pork	zhūròu (*jew-ro*)	猪肉
Fish	yú (*yü*)	鱼
Shrimp	xiā (*shee-yah*)	虾
Eggs (Chicken)	jīdàn (*jee-dan*)	鸡蛋
Rice	fàn (*fahn*)	饭
Vegetables	qīngcài (*ching-tsye*)	青菜
Soup	tāng (*tahng*)	汤
Fruit	shuǐguǒ (*shway-gwaw*)	水菓
Apple	píngguǒ (*ping-gwaw*)	苹果
Banana	xiāngjiāo (*shee-ahng-jee-ow*)	香蕉
Orange	júzi (*jü-dzih*)	桔子
Peach	táozi (*tao-dzih*)	桃子
Pear	lízi (*lee-dzih*)	李子
Watermelon	xīguā (*shee-gwa*)	西瓜
Ice cream	bīngqílín (*bing-chee-leen*)	冰淇淋
Western food	xīcān (*shee-tsahn*)	西餐
Vegetarian	chīsù (*chir soo*)	吃素
Sweet	tián (*tee-en*)	甜
Sour	suān (*swan*)	酸
Bitter	kǔ (*koo*)	苦
Spicy (hot)	là (*lah*)	辣

HEALTH CARE/MEDICINE

ENGLISH	PINYIN (CHINESE PRONUNCIATION)	CHINESE CHARACTERS
Medicine	yào (*yao*)	药
Pharmacy	yàodiàn (*yao deen-en*)	药店
Where can I find medicine?	nǎlǐ yǒu yào (*nah-lee yo yao*)	哪里有药
Aspirin	āsīpǐlín (*ah-suh-pee-leen*)	阿斯匹林

I have a cold.	wǒ gǎnmàole (*waw gone-mao-luh*)	我感冒了
I don't feel well.	wǒ bù shūfu (*waw boo shoo-foo*)	我不舒服
I am ill.	wǒ bìngle (*waw beeng-luh*)	我病了
Call a doctor.	qǐng yīshēng lái (*ching yee-shung lye*)	请医生来
Dentist	yáyī (*yah-yee*)	牙医
Hospital	yīyuàn (*yee yoo-en*)	医院
Headache	tóutòng (*toe-tuhng*)	头痛
Toothache	yátòng (*yah-tuhng*)	牙痛
Dizziness	tóuyùn (*toe yew-win*)	头晕
Diarrhea	lādùzi (*lah doo-dzi*)	拉肚子
Stomach sickness	wèibìng (*way-bing*)	胃病
Stomach pain	wèitòng (*way tuhng*)	胃痛
It hurts me here.	wǒ zhèli tòng (*waw juh-lee tuhng*)	我这里痛

TIME/NUMBERS

ENGLISH	PINYIN (CHINESE PRONUNCIATION)	CHINESE CHARACTERS
What time is it?	jǐdǐan zhōng (*jee dee-en joong*)	几点钟
[number] o'clock	. . .diǎn zhōng (. . .*dee-en joong*)	⋯点钟
Morning	zǎoshàng (*dzao-shahng*)	早上
Midday	zhōngwǔ (*joong-woo*)	中午
Evening	wǎnshàng (*wahn-shahng*)	晚上
Yesterday	zuótiān (*dzwaw-tee-en*)	昨天
Today	jīntiān (*jeen-tee-en*)	今天
Tomorrow	míngtiān (*ming tee-en*)	明天
Day	tiān (*tee-en*), rì (*rih*)	天，日
Month	yuè (*yweh*)	月
Year	nián (*nee-en*)	年

One	yī (*yee*)	一
Two	èr (*are*)	二
Three	sān (*san*)	三
Four	sì (*suh*)	四
Five	wǔ (*woo*)	五
Six	liù (*lee-oh*)	六
Seven	qī (*chee*)	七
Eight	bā (*bah*)	八
Nine	jiǔ (*jee-oh*)	九
Ten	shí (*shir*)	十
Eleven	shíyī (*shir-yee*)	十一
Twelve	shíèr (*shir-yee*)	十二
Thirteen	shísān (*shir-san*)	十三
Fourteen	shísì (*shir-suh*)	十四
Twenty	èrshí (*are-shir*)	二十
Thirty	sānshí (*san-shir*)	三十
One hundred	yībǎi (*yee-bye*)	一百
One thousand	yīqiān (*yee-chee-en*)	一千

PHOTOGRAPHIC CREDITS

Kathie Brown, 470, 685. **George Y. F. Chan,** 101, 106, 238, 349, 355, 382, 384, 419, 422, 477, 483, 486, 488, 490, 492, 494, 523, 570, 615, 623. **Gordon B. Clappison,** 66, 447. **Larry Cronin,** 73, 89, 95, 109, 112, 568, 572, 599. **Henry Forrest,** 261. **Great Wall Hotel,** 295. **Holiday Inn Hotel,** 57, 84. **John and Mary Israel,** 51. **Annette Juliano,** 224, 226. **Fredric M. Kaplan,** 278, 429. **Courtesy of Kodansha, Ltd. (Tokyo),** 654. **Media Tree,** 258, 281. **Tom Nebbia,** 452. **New China (Xinhua) News Agency,** 23, 41, 113, 147, 158, 190, 199, 218, 221, 243, 245, 246–47, 251, 262, 284, 321, 334, 335, 342, 353, 361, 368, 378, 386, 393, 403, 468, 502, 503, 511, 517, 532, 574, 617, 620, 621, 628, 634, 637, 644, 656, 671, 702, 711, 716, 721, 739, 758. **People's Art Publishers of China,** 269. **David Robertson,** 280, 668, 750. **Alvin Rosenblum,** 677. **Katherine Smalley,** 188, 580. **Steven C. Swett,** 21. **Theyssen-Missio,** 205. **US–China Business Council,** 426, 589.

Transliteration Glossary of Chinese Place Names

PROVINCES AND AUTONOMOUS REGIONS

TRADITIONAL SPELLING	PINYIN SPELLING	CHINESE
Anwei	Ānhūi	安徽
Chekiang	Zhèjiāng	浙江
Fukien	Fújiàn	福建
Heilungkiang	Hēilóngjiāng	黑龙江
Honan	Hénán	河南
Hopei (Hopeh)	Héběi	河北
Hupei (Hupeh)	Húběi	湖北
Hunan	Húnán	湖南
Inner Mongolia Auton. Region	Nèi Ménggǔ Zìzhìqū	内蒙古自治区
Kansu	Gānsū	甘肃
Kiangsi	Jiāngxī	江西
Kiangsu	Jiāngsū	江苏
Kirin	Jílín	吉林
Kwangsi Chuang Auton. Region	Guǎngxī Zhuāngzú Zìzhìqū	广西壮族自治区
Kwangtung	Guǎngdōng	广东
Kweichow	Guìzhōu	贵州
Liaoning	Liáoníng	辽宁
Ninghsia Hui Auton. Region	Níngxià Húizú Zìzhìqū	宁夏回族自治区

Shanhsi	Shānxī	山西
Shantung	Shāndōng	山东
Shenhsi	Shǎanxī	陕西
Sinkiang Uighur Auton. Region	Xīnjiāng Wéiwú-ér Zìzhìqū	新疆维吾尔 自治区
Szechwan	Sìchuān	四川
Taiwan	Táiwān	台湾
Tibet Auton. Region	Xīzàng Zìzhìqū	西藏自治区
Tsinghai	Qīnghǎi	青海
Yunnan	Yúnnán	云南

CITIES AND OTHER LOCALITIES

Anshan	Ānshān	鞍山
Ch'üfu	Qūfù	曲阜
Changchow	Chǎngzhōu	常州
Changchun	Chángchūn	长春
Changsha	Chángshā	长沙
Chaochow	Cháozhōu	潮州
Chefoo	Yāntái	烟台
Chengchow	Zhèngzhǒu	郑州
Chengteh (Jehol)	Chéngdé	承德
Chengtu	Chéngdū	成都
Chenkong	Zhènjiāng	镇江
Chiayukuan	Jiāyùguān	嘉峪关
Chinhuangtao	Qínhuángdǎo	秦皇岛
Ch'uanchow	Quanzhou	泉州

Chuhai	Zhūhǎi	珠海
Chungking	Chóngqìng	重庆
Foochow	Fúzhōu	福州
Foshan (Fatshan)	Fóshān	佛山
Gyangtse	Jiāngzī (Gyangze)	江孜
Hainantao	Hǎinán dǎo	海南岛
Hangchow	Hángzhōu	杭州
Harbin	Hā'érbīn	哈尔滨
Hofei	Héféi	合肥
Hohhot	Hūhéhàotè	呼和浩特
Hsiamen (Amoy)	Xiàmén	厦门
Hsilinhot	Xílínhàotè	锡林浩特
Hsishuangpanna	Xīshuāngbǎnnà	西双版纳
Hwang Shan	Huángshān	黄山
Ihsing	Yìxīng	宜兴
Kaifeng	Kāifēng	开封
Kasa	Zhāngmù	樟木
Kashgar	Kāshí	喀什
Kueiyang	Guìyáng	贵阳
Kunming	Kūnmíng	昆明
Kwangchow (Canton)	Guǎngzhōu	广州
Kweilin	Guìlín	桂林
Lanchow	Lánzhōu	兰州
Lhasa	Lhāsà	拉萨
Lienyunkang	Liányúngǎng	连云港
Loyang	Luòyáng	洛阳
Nanch'ang	Nánchāng	南昌
Nanking	Nánjīng	南京

PLACE NAME GLOSSARY

Nanning	Nánníng	南宁
Nantung	Nántōng	南通
Ningpo	Níngbō	宁波
Omei Shan	Eméi Shān	峨眉山
Pakhoi	Běihǎi	北海
Paoťou	Bāotóu	包头
Peitaiho	Běidàihé	北戴河
Peking	Běijīng	北京
Shanghai	Shànghǎi	上海
Shanghaikuan	Shānhǎiguān	山海关
Shaoshan	Shàoshān	韶山
Shenyang (Mukden)	Shènyáng	沈阳
Shihchiachuang	Shíjiāzhuāng	石家庄
Shikatse	Rìgézī (Xigaze)	日喀则
Shumuchun	Shēnzhèn	深圳
Sian	Xī'ān	西安
Soochow	Sūzhōu	苏州
Swatow	Shantóu	汕头
Taching	Dàqìng	大庆
Taishan	Táishān	泰山
Taiyuan	Tàiyuán	太原
Tali	Dàlí	大理
Talien	Dàlían	大连
Tatsu	Dàzú	大足
Tatung	Dàtóng	大同
Tientsin	Tiānjīn	天津
Tsamkung	Zhànjiáng	湛江

Tsinan	Jìnán	济南
Tsingtao	Qīngdǎo	青岛
Tunhuang	Dūnhuǎng	敦煌
Turfan	Tǔlǔfān (Turpan)	吐鲁番
Urumchi	Wūlǔmùqí (Ürümqi)	乌鲁木齐
Wenchow	Wénzhōu	温州
Wuhan (Hankow)	Wǔhàn	武汉
Wuhsi	Wúxí	无锡
Yangchow	Yángzhōu	扬州
Yenan	Yán'ān	延安

CONTRIBUTORS

John Israel, Professor of Chinese History at the University of Virginia, is the author of *Student Nationalism in China, 1927–1937* (1966) and co-author of *Rebels and Bureaucrats* (1976). Since 1978 he has served as Sinologist-escort for five China tours and has lived in China for a total of 16 months as an exchange scholar. **Mary Israel,** former Outreach Coordinator for the East Asian Center of the University of Virginia, has taught at the Beijing University School of Foreign Studies and has accompanied 16 groups to China since 1978. **Victor W. Sidel, M.D.,** and **Ruth Sidel, Ph.D.,** were among the first American health professionals to visit the People's Republic. Victor W. Sidel, is Distinguished University Professor of Social Medicine at Montefiore Medical Center/Albert Einstein College of Medicine, Bronx, New York. Ruth Sidel is Professor of Sociology, Hunter College, City University of New York. They are co-authors of *The Health of China: Current Conflicts in Medical and Human Services for One Billion People* (1982). **Mark Sidel** lived in Beijing during 1979–81, where he taught at the Beijing Foreign Languages Institute and currently works for the Ford Foundation in Beijing. **Annette Juliano** is an Associate Professor in the Art Department, Brooklyn College. Author of *Teng-hsien: An Important Six Dynasties Tomb* (1979), and *Treasures of China* (1981), she is also US correspondent for *Oriental Art* magazine. **Dr. Franklin J. Woo** is China Program Director for the National Council of the Churches of Christ in the US. **Roberta Helmer Stalberg** studied at the University of Pennsylvania and holds a Ph.D. in Chinese Language and Literature from Ohio State Unversity. She is co-author of *China's Crafts: The Story of How They're Made and What They Mean* (1980). **Barrie Chi** is a widely acclaimed expert on Chinese cooking and culinary arts. **Janet Yang,** a Chinese-American freelance writer, has twice visited the PRC with her family and spent a year working as an editor at Foreign Languages Press in Beijing. **Dr. Nicholas John Middleton** is lecturer at the School of Geography, University of Oxford. **Rebecca Weiner,** a freelance writer, taught at Qingdao University in Shandong province in 1987 and 1988.

INDEX

"As time goes on, will China pretty much
stick to chopsticks?"

Drawing by Eugene Theroux